THE MAKING OF MAN

THE
MAKING OF MAN
AN OUTLINE OF ANTHROPOLOGY

EDITED BY
V. F. CALVERTON

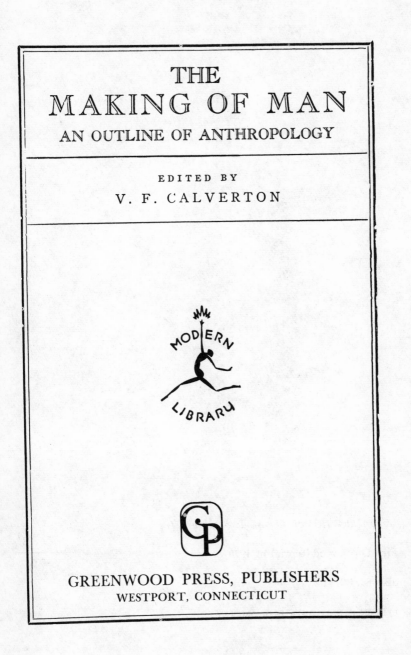

GREENWOOD PRESS, PUBLISHERS
WESTPORT, CONNECTICUT

To

ROBERT BRIFFAULT

warm friend,
and one of the most amazing and original
minds of our generation.

PREFACE

A WELL-KNOWN anthropologist described this volume, upon surveying its contents, as a "Golden Treasury of Anthropology." For my part, I should hesitate to call it that. Knowing the difficulties in its composition, I doubt whether it is even a bronze treasury. But some kind of treasury it aims to be, at least in the absence of any other book of this type.

The materials in this book have not been gathered together for the professional anthropologist or the professional research-worker. Any student of the subject already knows them. They have been collected, on the other hand, for social scientists in general, whose knowledge of anthropology on the whole is often very limited and is too seldom used for correct correlations, and for that vast army of readers who are interested in the development of the social sciences but are unable to pursue their interest through many of the ramifications of the materials.

With that end in mind this volume might have been edited in a number of ways. I chose the one that seemed to me at once the most economical and fruitful. As it is I have been forced to leave out much material that I originally planned to include. My particular regret in this respect is that I had to exclude, for lack of space, a whole section on primitive art. The only selection dealing with primitive art in this volume is that of Déchelette on the Art of the Reindeer Epoch. I had wanted especially to use a chapter from Boas' valuable work: *Primitive Art*, but that too had to be sacrificed along with the other articles in that section. Sacrifices of a different variety often had to be made in order to preserve something of the unity of the volume.

I have not aimed to use selections from anthropologists which are representative of their work as a whole—or which even stand forth as their best-known or their highest-valued contributions to their subject. My purpose was not of that character. I have thought of the book as a unit, and have selected those contributions which have helped preserve that unity. Wherever possible, of course, I have tried to use articles or chapters from an author's work which do represent his stand or position in the theoretical field. In many cases, to be sure, that was impossible. In a few cases I have had to use articles from various authors that are not representative of their work in general. Exigencies in the organization of the book made such choices in places unavoidable.[1] A chapter from Wissler's *American Indian* or *Man and Culture,* for example, would have been better, no doubt, than the chapter on Technology which I chose from his recent book, *An Introduction to Social Anthropology.* Chapters from the earlier books, however, did not fit as well into the plan of organization, or fulfill as specific a need, as the chapter on Technology. Similar considerations motivated a number of the other choices—especially those from Lowie and Kroeber. In the case of Boas in particular I should have liked to have had the selections more adequate and representative. Boas' main work, however, has appeared in monographic form. It covers a vast area of material, and in extensity of detail and excellence of analysis is unsurpassed by that of any other worker in the field. Unfortunately, though, most of these monographs are concerned with materials and problems that are too technical for use in this volume. I used Goldenweiser's monograph on Totemism only because it served a very definite purpose in the volume. Goldenweiser has contributed so many other important essays in the general field that I only wish it had been possible to have included more of his work—for sheer critical analysis Goldenweiser, in my opinion, is scarcely surpassed by any other American anthropologist. As a consequence of these necessities of choice and exclusion, the book undoubtedly has lost in individual representativeness, although it has gained in conceptual unity.

I am glad that the organization of the book made it possible for me to include representatives of four main schools
of anthropology: the French, the English, the German, and
the American. In a book of this kind, where theory is of
more interest and importance than the pure depiction of
fact, the divergent attitudes and positions of the various
schools should be represented, since, as Rivers says, "there
is so great a degree of divergence between the methods of
work of the leading schools of different countries, that any
common scheme is impossible, and the members of one
school wholly distrust the work of the others whose conclusions they believe to be founded on a radically unsound
basis." While the theoretic differences of the several schools
may not be fully elaborated in the respective essays—the
evolutionary and institutional emphasis of the English school
(Rivers, Perry, Briffault, etc.), the collectivistic emphasis of
the French (Lévy-Bruhl), the non-theoretical and somewhat
psychological emphasis of the American (Boas, Lowie,
Kroeber), and the environmental emphasis of the German
(Graebner)—the work of their several representatives that
are included here testify to their differences of approach.

A word of explanation is also needed to show why I have
included the work of various writers whose theories have
already been outmoded. In most cases such choices have
been made because the work of these writers was at one
time important, and because it exerted such a wide influence in its heyday, and in the history of the subject
cannot be neglected. The work of Bachofen, for example,
is a good illustration of this. No one to-day would take
Bachofen's arguments and evidence seriously, and yet no
one can deny that they were influential in their day. Yet no
one interested in the development of anthropological
thought, at least from a historical point of view, can neglect
Bachofen, however untenable they may view his conclusions.
The inclusion of this chapter from *Das Mutterrecht* marks
the first time, as far as I know, that Bachofen has been
translated into English. The same can be said to be true,

I believe, of Graebner. In addition to Bachofen and Graebner, I also have had a chapter from Déchelette's *Manuel d'archéologie préhistorique, celtique et gallo-romaine,* translated and included in this anthology. Although Tylor's work on animism has dated somewhat, no anthology of anthropological work would be complete without it.

Although I have not included any discussion of the theory of cultural origins, involving the whole problem of invention and diffusion or what has been called by Spinden the prosaic school versus the romantic, the general aspects of the controversy emerge from the essays of the various exponents of the different schools that are included. W. J. Perry and G. Elliot Smith are certainly typical enough of the romantics; and Malinowski, Goldenweiser and a number of others are representative enough of the prosaics. I included Freud and Roheim because I think the psychoanalytic approach—which, by the way, early influenced Rivers, Goldenweiser, and Malinowski, although Malinowski has lately repudiated much of its logic—should be represented, however far-fetched and unscientific may be its contentions and conclusions. The chapter from Carpenter was included, dubious though certain of its materials may be, because it represents a unique approach to the problem of homosexuality in primitive culture.

The only essay that was written especially for this volume is the one on Law and Anthropology which was done by Mr. Huntington Cairns. In the absence of any good material in this field, I asked Mr. Cairns, who has already done a great deal of work in the way of synthesizing law and the social sciences, to make a special study of the theme, and the happy result of my request is to be discovered in his essay in Part III.

I want to express here my particular thanks to Frida Ilmer for her translations of the selections from Bachofen, Graebner, and Déchelette. I owe a deep debt of gratitude also to Charles Smith who generously helped prepare the manuscript for the printer. In addition I want to thank Bernhard

J. Stern for several valuable suggestions which he made about the volume as a whole, and Ruth Benedict for her kind answers to my several letters about problems that concerned me in this book.

In conclusion let me add that if this book helps social scientists and the general reader get a better and more informed and various idea of the nature of primitive man and the theories concerning him, it will have served its purpose. We are in more need of syntheses in the social sciences to-day than ever before. Anthropology in general is neglected by the social sciences—or when it is utilized it is usually anthropological doctrine that is behind the times, or doctrine that is especially peculiar to a specific school. At least most of the prevailing schools are represented in these pages. Most of the doctrines represented here also are modern—with the exception of those of the classical school which have been included mainly for historical reference.

I also want to guard the reader against viewing my Introduction as representative of the spirit of the volume as a whole. I have expressed in the Introduction a point of view that is specifically my own, and which should be considered as such, and not looked upon as representing that of the other contributors to the book.

I want to thank the following publishers for permission to use certain of the chapters included in this book: George Allen & Unwin; American Anthropological Association; *American Journal of Sociology;* D. Appleton & Co.; *The Century Magazine;* Chapman & Hall; *Columbia Law Review;* Dodd, Mead & Co.; Harcourt, Brace & Co.; Harper & Brothers; Henry Holt & Co.; Alfred A. Knopf, Inc.; Horace Liveright, Inc.; The Macmillan Company; Macmillan & Company; Methuen & Co.; William Morrow & Co.; *The New Republic;* W. W. Norton & Co.; David Nutt; Oliver & Boyd; Kegan Paul; Alphonse Picard et Fils; *Psyche;* Carl Winter; *Scientia.*   V. F. CALVERTON.

NEW YORK,
September 10, 1930.

NOTES

[1] For those who wish to pursue the subject at greater length, however, the bibliography will provide material for further guidance. I have been particularly careful in the bibliography to avoid selections that would be of only technical interest to the reader. In certain cases I have noted technical articles, but only because I think the reader might find them of value. In general, however, I have confined the bibliography to materials of more theoretic character.

CONTENTS

xiii

CONTENTS

INTRODUCTION *

MODERN ANTHROPOLOGY AND THE THEORY OF CULTURAL COMPULSIVES

By V. F. CALVERTON

THE growth of the science of anthropology is closely bound up with the development of the doctrine of evolution. Neither could have advanced very far, however, without the aid of the other. Both were, and still are, part of a complete cycle of intellectual change. Curiously enough the rise of both illuminates a tendency in nineteenth century thought that we have no more than begun to escape to-day—a tendency to see the past in terms of the present, or, what is worse, in terms of what is thought to be the present. In different words, it is to view others, to interpret their ideas, to adjudge their institutions, in terms of ourselves, setting forth our own ideas and institutions as an absolute criterion. This whole tendency was an inevitable outgrowth of nineteenth century logic with its evolutionary emphasis.

Now the doctrine of evolution and the science of anthropology did not spring upon the nineteenth century mind full-blown, like a dazzling intuition, shattering all the previous fictions about man in a sudden intellectual sword-thrust. On the contrary, they were a result of a cumulative process which derived its momentum from the vast movements of men and materials that had been set agog in that century. While theories of evolution, as we know, arose first with the Greeks, it was not until the eighteenth century that they made any headway in the western world. Prior to

* This introduction had an English publication in *Psyche*, October, 1930, and an American publication in the *American Journal of Sociology*, March, 1931.

I

Charles Darwin, in the works of such men as Buffon, Erasmus Darwin, Goethe, Saint-Hilaire and Lamarck, evolutionary hypotheses had been advanced in rapid succession. The whole doctrine of evolution was the consuming topic of the day. The very simultaneity with which Darwin and Wallace struck upon the theory of natural selection and the survival of the fittest was magnificent proof of the intense activity of the idea at the time. Every force in the environment, economic and social, conspired to the success of the doctrine.

We should really wonder little at this when we realize that the outstanding characteristic of western Europe in the nineteenth century was *change*. Never before had man witnessed, in so brief a time, such vast revolutions in phenomena. The Industrial Revolution was the cause of these rapid transformations in western life. It was the dynamo that shot the age agog with new desires and fresh vision. Life became afire with activity and creation. Newness almost lost its novelty. New aspirations multiplied with every dawn. Invention succeeded invention until the genius of the age became a miracle in mechanics. Tiny wires became the conductors of great energy; inert metals became moving machines; water, air, and earth became the source of new discovery and power. Fantastic fictions became pragmatic achievements. Leonardo da Vinci's futile experimentations became realized science. Jules Verne became a clairvoyant prophet. New conceptions burst pellmell upon the old, burying them in the débris of discarded superstition. Men became interested not in the wherefore of existence, but in its mastery. The machine promised a new world at human command. Men came to look upon the earth with new eyes. Unknown sources of energy were tapped on every side. Nothing was left unexplored. New truths were derived from old materials. The search for one reality led to the unexpected discovery of ten more.

As a result of this vast release of energy, set thus in motion by the machinery of the new age, science became—at least for the new intellectuals—the new philosophy of life. Once an adventure into the strange and mysterious, it now became an open sesame to the control of the universe. Investigation succeeded analysis, and nothing was any longer safe from the invader's hands. Even the Bible, which had provided the mystic centerhood of western civilization, was no longer withheld from scientific scrutiny. The ancient æons of the earth's past soon disclosed themselves in geological formation and structure. The rapid mutations of the modern world revealed themselves in social science and historical theory. The idea of movement and change became an obsession. It was thus that the way was prepared for the acceptance of evolution not merely as a scientific formula but as a living addition to our culture.

If, before 1859, western civilization found its intellectual continuity in Biblical doctrine, after 1859 it found its new continuity in the doctrine of evolution. A doctrine is only seized upon in that fashion when it supplies some great need, emotional as well as intellectual, in the life of man. Darwin's theory of evolution supplied the need for a new philosophy of life. It not only afforded a new vista of human development, but it also provided a new justification of world-progress in terms of western civilization. The evolution of man was seen as a form of infinite progression, from lower forms to higher, with modern civilization as representative of the highest form in the evolutionary scale. But more than that, the Darwinian theory of natural selection made survival synonymous with advance. Since all life was a struggle for the *survival of the fittest,* that which survived was superior. And since western civilization had survived the most successfully in the struggle of civilizations, it must of necessity represent the highest point in human evolution. In keeping with this logic, the principles and institutions of western civilization were inevitably viewed as typical of the most advanced in the history of human mores. Private property, the monogamous family, the democratic political state, were all looked upon as exemplifying the great moral progress of man. Individualism was envisioned as marking the great advance of civilized man over the savage—the supremacy of the differentiated over the undifferentiated. In other words, the Darwinian doctrine of evolution and the consequences of its logic proffered the best justification of the *status quo* of nineteenth century Europe that had appeared in generations. It harmonized perfectly with the philosophy of the ruling class of that day. Modern commerce and industry had broken down the ideological defenses of the old order which had grown up with feudalism and the agrarian tradition; new defenses were necessary for the new ideological front. The Darwinian doctrine supplied that defense. It rooted *laissez-faire* economics with its competitive logic in the very scheme of nature itself. It sanctioned individualism and the division of classes on the basis of the necessary struggle for the survival of the fittest. It even served as a prop for nationalism and the expanding imperialisms of the time. Whatever was, was, because it had to be—because it ought to be.

It was in this cultural milieu that anthropology had its origins. The same economic and social factors that made the doctrine of evolution into a new intellectual force caused anthropology to spring up as an immediate adjunct of evolutionary cause. The doctrine of evolution became the basic structure of their whole approach. Beginning with E. B. Tylor's *Primitive Culture* in 1872, the main history of anthropological thought in the nineteenth century is concerned with the application of the doctrine of evolution to the interpretation of man's past. The application, however, was invariably made in relationship with nineteenth century values, values that are most often alluded to as Victorian. In other words, those early anthropologists studied primitive man not to find out what he was like, but what they thought he ought to be like. Blinded by the erroneous implications of the doctrine of evolution, namely that the values of nineteenth century civilization, having survived all other values, must exemplify the highest point in moral progress, these anthropologists sought to find in primitive life the traces of those forms of behavior that were the lowest in the evolutionary scale. They were determined, however unconsciously, to superimpose their own rationality upon that of the primitive. A whole state of mind was at work here—and not merely an error in scientific approach. A state of mind fostered by the enormous material advance of nineteenth century civilization and the new ideological armament which it had already begun to perfect! This state of mind made it impossible for the anthropologists of that day to use the facts as they really were, or to interpret them except in the caricatured forms of current prejudices. They studied primitive man as one would a puzzle, shifting facts in every which way, out of all sequence and context, in order to find solutions. They were too anxious to find universal evolutionary laws which would explain the rise of man from the crudities of primitivism to the refinements of nineteenth century civilization. Influenced particularly by Morgan, these anthropologists of the evolutionary school soon concluded that society had passed through certain definite stages, a constant progression from the lower to the higher, in which modern civilization stood as an apex toward which all the past had converged. Not content, for instance, with tracing the development of marriage through its various forms, these men were equally concerned with proving that monogamy was the ultimate stage in marital evolution. At first it was postulated that man had originally lived in a state of primitive promiscuity or sexual communism; then he had advanced to the stage of group marriage, a stage still found among lingering primitive groups to-day; and finally, after years of change and crisis, he had progressed to the stage of monogamy in which he is at the present time. More than that, Morgan in particular stressed the determining part that property played in the history of primitive relations, and it was not very long before Morgan's doctrine, tail, kite, and all, was seized upon by the radicals and adopted as proof of, if not part of, Marxian philosophy.

Almost every radical thinker in the nineteenth century cited Morgan as a final authority. Friedrich Engels built his whole book, *The Origin of the Family,* on Morgan's thesis. Kautsky used Morgan's evidence in his *Entstehung Der Ehe und Familie,* and Plechanov made frequent reference to Morgan in his various studies of primitive art and culture. Even today many radicals still continue to refer to Morgan's work as if it had never been outmoded.

Despite McLennan's attacks on Morgan's theory of nomenclature, and the assaults of many other thinkers upon Morgan's contentions, Morgan's doctrine made marked headway in nineteenth century anthropology. At first the hostility it aroused was mainly intellectual, for, when all is said, there was nothing in it to offend the Victorian conception of life. Rivers, I think, was strong when he claimed that the chief reason why Morgan's work was fought was that it pictured man's past in terms "bitterly repugnant to the sentiments of most civilized persons." After all, one should not expect savages to be elevated in morality, and if they practiced promiscuity that was all the more reason why civilized man should practice monogamy, for civilization must mark an evolutionary advance over primitivism. The progression, indeed, was perfect. Morgan's doctrine fitted in so precisely with evolution as an absolutistic concept. It was not the doctrine itself, then, but its widespread acceptance by the radicals, and the uses it was put to by divers revolutionary thinkers of the period, that made it suddenly become "bitterly repugnant" to the nineteenth century mind. It was not "bitterly repugnant" to the radical mind; it was only "bitterly repugnant" to the conservative, bourgeois mind which was concerned above all with the protection of the middle-class values that had been exalted by nineteenth century civilization. As long as Morgan's doctrine was concerned only with the past, and in its evolutionary emphases pointed to the present as something of an ultimate in the moral process—as in the case of monogamy—there was no terror in its proposition. The moment, however, that the radicals insisted upon interpreting *evolution as a relative instead of an absolutistic concept,* the danger began. No longer could the institutions of nineteenth century civilization be looked upon as a culmination in evolutionary advance. No longer could private property and the family, for example, which were inalienable parts of that civilization, be considered as indestructible. Private property and the family, therefore, were but part of a process and not a fulfillment of it. In fact, in accordance with the evolutionary progression postulated by the radicals, these institutions were destined to disappear with the next advance in the social process.

Once the doctrine of evolution was seen to carry in its wake the possibilities of destruction as well as construction, a new set of justifications was needed to defend the permanency of the prevailing values. Only in this way could the radical interpretations of the evolutionary process be answered. And thus began the search for absolutes—absolutes that would satisfy the nineteenth century mind. The existence of primitive communism was fought tooth and nail. Private property was declared an instinct, fundamental to all social life. Religion was defined as an impulse common to all men, savage as well as civilized, and not an outgrowth of environment. The family was defended as the corner stone of culture, the *sine qua non* of social existence. But more than that, monogamy, the specific form of the family dominant at the time, was declared the basic form of marriage of the human species. Even the animals were used to prove this thesis. No evidence, however dubious, was unexploited in this connection. Monogamy thus became not a form of marriage that had developed out of certain conditions of economic life, but a form of marriage that was fundamental to the human species, and those mammalian types that were closest to the human. In these ways, nineteenth century institutions were saved from the danger of change and decay. No matter in what direction evolution occurred, private property and the family were inviolable.

They were the absolutes, the invariables, as it were, in social organization, which no radical evolution—or revolution—could shake or shatter.

The class-logic at work here is obvious. Anthropology was thus made to serve as an excellent prop for the support of middle-class ethics. It defended the *status quo* by giving so-called final scientific sanction to its essential doctrines. The famous allusion in economic theory to the monkey with a stick as a capitalist—thereby proving to the satisfaction of every sophomore that whoever owns anything, however small, which can produce wealth is a capitalist—was not less absurd than the *rationalization* of monogamy as the natural form of human marriage which was foisted upon the nineteenth century world by anthropological dialectic.

The most amazing illustration of the truth of this contention is to be found in the history of the work and influence of Edward Westermarck. When his *History of Human Marriage* appeared in 1891 Westermarck was practically unknown to the scientific public. In fact, Alfred R. Wallace in his Introductory note to the original volume comments upon Westermarck as a "hitherto unknown student" and a "new comer." In less than ten years, however, this "new comer" becomes the leading authority on morality and marriage, sweeping aside the influence of his predecessors by virtue of his new logic. The appearance of his *Origin and Development of the Moral Ideas* only strengthened his influence. If his authority had been confined to his special science the achievement would have been significant enough; but the fact that it became extended to the other sciences as well and to the lay world in general makes its success even more of an event. Since the eighteen-nineties no other person in this field has exerted anything like the enormous influence of Westermarck. In almost every text, lecture, or article, verging on the theme of morality or marriage he was, and in many instances still is, the standard reference. The universities in particular adopted him at once as their guide. Few minds dared to defy his authority. The *History of Human Marriage,* indeed, became the new bible of the social sciences. And it remained so until the twenties of this century when its conclusions were assailed and annihilated by Robert Briffault in his work: *The Mothers.*

But Westermarck's former supremacy is of more importance than his present loss of it. In the light of Briffault's thoroughly valid and devastating criticisms of Westermarck's thesis, the sway that the latter exercised over the minds of his contemporaries for almost forty years becomes all the more revealing. The fact that his ascendancy went practically unchallenged during that entire period is even more of a revelation. Why should a man's doctrine become so widely accepted when his evidences were so flimsy and fallacious? Why should his conclusions be accepted so readily and completely when the problems involved were so controversial? Why should he suddenly become an authority when the evidence at hand was so unauthoritative? One answer might be that he argued his point with such adroitness that even the dubious became plausible. But granted that to be the case, the difficulty still remains of explaining why his evidence was seldom examined in a critical vein, and why such critical examinations as were undertaken were never able to win any considerable respect or authority.

The answer is to be found in another field of logic—or sociologic. Westermarck's doctrines did more than confute the doctrines of Morgan, McLennan, and Lubbock; they fulfilled a great socio-intellectual need of the day. In attacking the ideas of Morgan, for example, he was able to destroy the logic of the radicals who had based their anthropological conclusions upon Morgan's work. And in attempting to prove that in all likelihood "monogamy prevailed almost exclusively among our earliest human ancestors." that the family existed anterior to man, and that "human marriage, in all probability, is an inheritance from some apelike progenitor," he was able to provide nineteenth century civilization with an *absolute* that justified in perpetuity one of its main institutions. The family thus became an institution that radicals could no longer assail. No evolution in society could eradicate it. Nor could monogamy be attacked either, since it was rooted in man's primeval past, and was part of what Westermarck calls the "monogamous instinct."

It is no wonder, then, that Westermarck's doctrines were seized upon with such eagerness, and adhered to with such tenacity, by nineteenth century intellectuals of middle-class character and conviction. The only intellectuals who did not accept them were the radical minds of the time. College professors no longer had to rely upon Herbert Spencer's contention that "the monogamic form of the sexual relation is manifestly the ultimate form" in order to exalt nineteenth century institutions over those of other periods—and other civilizations. Anthropology now, through the work of Westermarck, had given scientific sanction to the conclusion of Spencer. "The laws of monogamy can never be changed," wrote Westermarck, "but must be followed much more strictly than they are now."

But all this discussion would be of little importance if it were not for the fact that Westermarck's conclusions to-day cannot be viewed as anything else than absurd. Let us take up certain of Westermarck's arguments in more careful and specific detail. Suppose we begin with his defense of monogamy. In order to root *the tendency to monogamy* deep in nature itself, in other words to give it something of an instinctive cast, he tries to trace its origins to the higher animals. If the higher animals are monogamous, then certainly man who is descended from them must carry within him the same instinct. Utilizing evidence often insufficient and untrustworthy, Westermarck, in his ardor to build up his case, claims that monogamy prevailed among the manlike apes. He cites the gorilla and chimpanzee as particular illustrations. Now let us see what kind of evidence he used to prove his thesis. Briffault's discussion of his evidence is very much to the point:

"Dr. Hartmann, relying exclusively on an article by Herr von Koppenfels in a German popular magazine, asserted that 'the gorilla is monogamous' (H. Hartmann, *The Anthropoid Apes*, p. 229), *and the statement was used by Dr. Westermarck as a foundation for his theory of 'human marriage.'* None of even the older information affords any ground for the supposition, and no other writer who has given attention to the subject makes such a statement. The oldest extant account of the gorilla, that of the sailor Andrew Bartell, who spent eighteen years in Angola, states that gorillas 'goe many together' ("The Strange Adventures of Andrew Bartell," etc., in *Hakluytus Posthumus, or Purchas His Pilgrimes*, vol. vi, p. 398). Darwin's conclusion was that 'the gorilla is polygamous' (C. Darwin, *The Descent of Man*, vol. i, p. 266; vol. ii, p. 361). Brehm concluded that the gorilla is polygamous (A. E. Brehm, *Tierleben*, vol. i, p. 65). He regarded the evidence collected from native hunters by Winwood Reade as the most reliable which was available at the time he wrote. Reade says: 'The gorilla is polygamous, and the male frequently solitary; in fact I never saw more than one track at a time, but there is no doubt that both gorillas and chimpanzees are found in bands' (W. Winwood Reade, "The Habits of the Gorilla," *The American Naturalist*, vol. i, p. 179; cf. *Idem, Savage Africa*, p. 214). Dr. R. L. Garner says, 'It is certain that the gorilla is polygamous' (R. L. Garner, *Gorillas and Chimpanzees*, p. 224). The air of mystery formerly surrounding the gorilla and the uncertainty of our information concerning the animal have now been dissipated, and we know that, as Winwood Reade observes, 'there is nothing remarkable in the habits of the gorilla, nothing which broadly distinguishes it from other African apes' (W. Winwood Reade, "The Habits of the Gorilla," *The American Naturalist*, vol. i, p. 180). Mr. F. Guthrie, a gentleman who resided for many years in the Cameroons, and who was on intimate terms with native hunters, collected their evidence in a very careful manner, and checked it by the testimonies of various tribes. 'The gorilla of the Cameroons,' he states, 'live in small companies, scarcely to be called families. The smaller companies consist of one male with his one, two or three wives, and some small children' (A. E. Jenks, "Bulu Knowledge of the Gorilla and Chimpanzee," *The American Anthropologist*, N. S. xiii, pp. 52 *seq.*). Herr G. Zenker saw one male accompanied by several females and young. Von Gertzen describes the traces of a troop which, he says, must have consisted of about ten individuals (Brehm-Strassen, *Tierleben,* 1920, vol. xiii, pp. 684 *seq.*). Grenfell found gorillas in parties (H. H. Johnson, *George Grenfell and the Congo,* p. 344). Captain Dominick found the gorilla in the Cameroons in much larger troops; according to him, 'the gorilla in the Cameroons is a thoroughly gregarious animal, and, as with the baboon, several adult males are found in each troop' (T. Zell, "Das Einfangen ausgewachsener Gorillas," *Die Gartenlaube,* 1907, p. 880). Mr. T. A. Barns has also found the gorillas in the eastern Congo living in large troops consisting of 'quite a number of gorillas,' each troop including at least two females with several young of varying ages (T. A. Barns, *The Wonderland of the Eastern Congo,* pp. 84 *seq.*). Mr. Akeley found gorillas in polygamous bands (C. E. Akeley, *In Brightest Africa,* p. 247).

"As will be seen, our present information entirely disposes of any supposition as to monogamous habits among gorillas. Other stories concerning the animal have likewise become relegated to their proper sphere. No instance has been reported of a male gorilla defending his 'family.' The animal is most fierce and dangerous not when in the company of females and young, but when solitary; old, solitary gorillas are the only ones that have been known to attack man unprovoked" (Duke A. F. von Mecklenburg-Strelitz, *From the Congo to the Niger and the Nile,* vol. ii, p. 106).

I have quoted from Briffault at such great length here because the argument is so important and pertinent, since the apelike animals, in particular the gorilla, have been used by every variety of scholar following Westermarck to illustrate the monogamous instincts of our simian progenitors. But we know, for instance, that T. S. Savage and J. Wyman, A. E. Brehm, and Duke A. F. von Mecklenburg-Strelitz, have all attested to the chimpanzee's non-monogamous habits. The same abundance of evidence is present in reference to the absence of monogamy among the gibbons and orangutangs. In other words, the manlike apes are not monogamous. Why did Westermarck, then, claim that the gorilla was monogamous, and that monogamy prevailed almost exclusively "among the menlike apes"? Because certain of the evidence that we possess to-day was lacking when he originally wrote his *History of Human Marriage?* Not at all. At the very time that he was at work on his thesis evidence existed to prove that the gorilla was polygamous—or promiscuous—rather than monogamous. It is true that still more evidence has been collected since then, which has made Westermarck effect certain modifications in his statements about gorillas in later editions of his work. But why should he originally have argued for the monogamous habits of the gorilla—and for the anthropoid apes in general—when the evidence leaned in the opposite direction, or at best was highly uncertain? [1] The only answer is the one which we have given. Influenced by the middle-class culture of his day, and the necessity of defending its institutions by every device of logic, his mind reverted to that evidence which tended to justify those institutions, and endow them with a *natural* origin and continuity. Morgan and his followers, equally a part of that culture, did not seek such defenses, as we pointed out before, for their doctrines in themselves did not assail the institutions of their day. On the contrary, the so-called evolutionary anthropologists, like Spencer, were convinced that monogamy was the ultimate in ethical progress, and, therefore, needed no defense or protection. It was the rising influence of the radical critics, who used Morgan's doctrine as a revolutionary weapon, as we noted earlier in this analysis, that had to be rebutted. *The History of Human Marriage* provided just this rebuttal. If it could prove, as it essayed to do, that the "apelike animals" were monogamous, then it had already established its case, namely, that of the existence of a "monogamous instinct" and, therefore, a natural tendency to monogamy in all the higher species. It was thus that the prevailing institutions could be protected and the enemies of civilization, that is of nineteenth century civilization, confuted and destroyed.

It is not surprising, therefore, that Westermarck, in his zeal, distorted evidence out of all proportion, and threw his whole emphasis, to the exclusion of all contradictions, upon those materials which tended to prove his case. In trying to show that even among the lower animals sexual unions assume "a more durable character," resembling that of marriage, and foreshadowing the later development of the family, he makes actual citations from Brehm which seem to illustrate his contention. He notes, among the animals evincing this tendency, the whale, the seal, the hippopotamus, the reindeer, "a few cats and martens," and "possibly the wolf." Upon careful examination of his material,[2] however, it becomes clear at once that he has again garbled facts and exaggerated evidences. Whales, as Brehm himself stated, and Westermarck used Brehm as his main support, do not reveal monogamous tendencies—nor, as far as present evidence shows, do seals, reindeer, cats, or wolves. Brehm's evidence as to the tendency toward monogamy among hippopotami is contradicted by that of every other observer. Despite these facts, Westermarck's statement about these animals was uncritically accepted by most of his contemporaries during the generation that followed.

Again we are driven to the conclusion that it was because his doctrines supplied a need of the time, a protection against those doctrines that threatened middle-class supremacy in the field of ethics and economics, that they became at once part of the cultural defense of the era.

Let us turn for a moment to another aspect of his thesis, wherein he states that "the family, not the tribe, formed the nucleus of every social group, and, in many cases, was itself perhaps the only social group." Here Westermarck has trimmed down his thesis to its fundamental point. The family, and not the group, or the tribe, is the basic unit of primitive society. As in the case of the animals, the same justificatory mechanisms are operative here. If the family and not the group provides the unit structure of social organization, then it follows that the family is an inde-

structible part of social life. Destroy the family and social
life is ended. Or, expressed in an antipodal vein, since
social life cannot be destroyed, the family must always remain. And again, in order to fortify his case, Westermarck
has abused both evidence and observation. Among the
Yakut, for example, there is no word for the concept of
family, the clan having so absorbed all forms of relationship.
Moreover, it is a well-known fact that among many primitive
groups, the so-called husband and wife are not allowed to
live together, and hence the development of the family,
as Westermarck envisions, could only follow and not precede such a custom. Among the peoples of the Banks Islands,
the New Hebrides, in Northern Papua, New Caledonia, to
cite instances, family-organization does not exist. Kindred
relationships obtain, but they cannot be described in the
·same terms as we describe the family, or as Westermarck
describes it, in which a male and female and their progeny
act as the center of social organization. In fact among almost
all early primitive groups it is "love of the clan [which] is
greater than love between husband and wife." Indeed, the
very submergence of the individual within the group made
the dominance of the family impossible in primitive times.
More than that, the absence of the knowledge of paternity
certainly did not strengthen family-organization at the expense of social. In addition, the superiority of sister-brother
love over wife-husband love, evidenced in many tribes and
among many peoples, finding a striking illustration as late
as in Sophocles' play *Antigone,* is but further proof of the
fallacy of the Westermarckian thesis. In fact, as Briffault has
pointed out in great detail, the organization of the family-
group is "found to stand in direct conflict with the primal
social impulses of humanity in its simpler stages, and to
be in sharp opposition to the primitive organization which
it has tended to break up." Family-organization is by its
very nature, when it assumes a patriarchal form, individual·
istic instead of social in character. Consequently, it is highly
unlikely that primitive man could ever have effected his

early social organization upon a familial basis. At all events, whatever information we have to-day concerning the origins of social organization does not confirm Westermarck's thesis. On the contrary, it tends to weaken it, and, on the whole, to destroy it.

Nevertheless, Westermarck's theory has been swallowed *in toto* by our social scientists. What does this illustrate, then, we ask once more? Simply the fact that our social scientists are not interested in objective facts, but in theses that will justify existing attitudes and institutions.

Nor do we find an exception in Westermarck's attempt to carry the family-thesis further, and show that its origins among humans were monogamic. The social scientists have been just as gullible here as before. In the light of what is known to-day, I am guilty of no hyperbole when I say that few more inaccurate conclusions in the social sciences have ever been drawn than that which is to be found in Westermarck's contention that it is probable "that monogamy prevailed almost exclusively among our earliest ancestors." We have already seen how inaccurate Westermarck's conclusions were about the monogamous habits of higher animals. And when we turn to his third proposition—of monogamy among our earliest ancestors—we are confronted again with the same kind of inaccuracies and misinterpretations.[3] (Cf. the long analysis from Briffault's *The Mothers* in this footnote.) In many cases Westermarck used evidence that was contradicted by other evidences, more numerous and more authentic than his own, without ever mentioning the controversial nature of the material. His frequent recourse to the observations and comments of Jesuit fathers and missionaries instead of to other sources when other sources were available is but another index to the nature of his outlook and method. Wherever Christian influences crept primitive customs changed, especially where conversions were frequent, and even where the Christian influence made little advance, the observations of the Christian missionaries were usually of a kind that tended to interpret primitive culture in terms of Christian morality rather than in terms of the mores of the tribe itself. Even where Westermarck actually discovered tribal monogamy, he refused to see it in relationship with poverty as a cause, a connection that was obvious to almost all other observers, but insisted upon interpreting it as an evidence of the "monogamous instinct." His contention, for instance, that polygamy and polyandry tend to revert to monogamy, loses all its meaning when we realize that in the history of most primitive groups the tendency to monogamy invariably sets in whenever economic conditions are on the decline. In other words, the so-called reversion to monogamy does not arise out of a "monogamous instinct" but out of an economic condition. The very fact that Westermarck neglects almost entirely the latter factor, and its importance as a basic causation, reveals the weakness in his analysis. And furthermore, the fact that for every monogamous tribe that he could adduce there were many more examples of non-monogamous, illustrated the untenableness and absurdity of his thesis. Marriage in many primitive communities, we should remember, resembles so little marriage as we with our modern categories of consciousness conceive it that it is practically a misnomer to use the same word to describe both conditions. Among the aboriginal tribes of Malaya, for example, individuals often *marry* forty or fifty times; the Cherokee-Iroquois "commonly changed wives three or four times a year"; among the Hurons, "women (were) purchased by the night, week, month or winter." Now, while in a certain loose sense you may describe all these relationships as marital, there is a great danger of misapprehension in this type of nomenclature. It would be a highly intelligent procedure if we coined a new word for our anthropological vocabulary so that this kind of confusion could not occur. Especially is this confusion pronounced in the case of monogamy. And Westermarck, by way of his loose definition, confuses rather than clarifies the nature of these relationships by applying our concept to practices that have very faint resemblances in our culture at all. There is certainly a distinct difference between the attitude of a primitive people who has been forced to monogamy by economic pressure, and as soon as prosperity sets in, as in the case of its kings and chiefs, will revert to polygyny, and that of a civilized community which has adopted monogamy as an institution, and has set up a score of psychological devices to justify it as an evidence of progress. In the case of the primitive people the condition obviously is one of necessity and not of choice; in the case of the civilized community the condition assumes the aspect of choice and not of necessity. Even though we know that monogamy among civilized communities had its main origins likewise in economics, strengthened by a religion closely conjoined with economic tendency the cultural defenses erected in recent centuries have successfully obscured that origin and made the institution seem to be the result of cultural choice, a testimony to advance in civilized behavior and cultural wisdom. This "seeming to be," this cultural camouflage, has been so effective, however, that until recent days this attitude toward monogamy was viewed as fundamental and not derivative. Westermarck nowhere notes these differences in attitude between monogamy as practiced by a primitive and by a civilized group, nor does he anywhere interpret monogamy in the Christian world as the result of an environmental rather than an innate spiritual fact.

The wholesale manner in which the altogether inextensive and dubious evidence of Westermarck was adopted by scientists in every field: biological, psychological, sociological, was the best proof of the fact that the evidence was of more than purely theoretic value. Even to-day this manner of 'adoption has not entirely ceased. No less distinguished a biologist than Herbert Spencer Jennings, for example, in his essay on The Biological Basis of The Family, writes as follows:

"The tendency toward a permanent coöperative life career on the part of two parents is powerfully reënforced by the long period of dependence of the young. . . .

"There is no time when the two parents can separate without breaking in upon the functions they have undertaken in relation to the young. *Such is the situation we find in the higher anthropoids, the orang, and the gorilla; such is the situation found at its highest development in man. . . .* Marriage is life-long, even though the care of the offspring is not. Permanent monogamous marriage has arisen independently through similar functional requirements, in the mammals and the birds; *the biological needs giving origin to it being much the more numerous and powerful in the higher mammals."*

But the citations do not stop here. Jennings is quoted in this reference by a score of other authorities, anxious to prove the same point, and as always Westermarck is brought in to give the touch of final authority. The late Thomas Walton Galloway, another well-known biologist, in an article on Monogamic Marriage and Mating, points out that *"the trends in both (men and animals) have been toward permanent as against temporary relations of the mates* and toward monogamous as against promiscuous or polygamous unions." In a recent study entitled *Twenty-four Views of Marriage,* for example, both Jennings and Westermarck are alluded to upon frequent occasions. In the concluding pages of the study such passages as these appear:

"That monogamy is the basic form of human marriage is recognized by most anthropologists. As Professor Jennings said before the Conference on Family Life in America To-day at Buffalo in 1927, 'the monogamous family, with life-long union of the mates, appears as the final term in a long evolutionary series!' "

"Westermarck in his *Short History of Marriage* says that monogamy is the only form of marriage that is permitted among every people."

Similar quotations can be found in almost any social science text that one opens to-day. Our whole intellectual culture in fact is permeated with the same attitude, the same conviction. It is part of the prevailing ideology.

Now if this attitude were the product alone of some myth, some religious belief harking back into an antediluvian past, one might interpret it as an illustration of a cultural lag, and classify it with such phenomena. But such is not the case, for science rather than religion, as we have seen, has been its main support in recent generations. And not only Westermarck and Jennings have been conspicuous in its defense. Almost every modern anthropologist—the exceptions have been very few and without influence—has rallied to its support. Malinowski, Thomas, Lowie, for instance, have all lent their aid to the cause.

If we look a little more closely at the arguments of these men, we shall be able to discern, in a more definite way, the nature of the defense-mechanism at work in their logic. Malinowski is not less guilty than Westermarck or Jennings in his conclusions about the sexual life of the primates and primitive man. In his volume on *Sex and Repression in Savage Society,* he states that the family is the only type of grouping that man has carried over from the animal stage. Not only does he thus assume that the family existed among the primates, but continuing this logic, he goes further and, in line with Westermarck, denies the possible existence of a period of sexual promiscuity, in which gregariousness antedated the familial state. Indeed he goes so far as to say that "no type of human organization can be traced back to gregarious tendencies." It was the family, then, in his opinion, and not the group, which served as the creative continuum of culture. In keeping with this contention, one of his main suppositions is that man thus could have inherited from his ancestors among the primates the tendency to live in families but not in the form of the promiscuous horde. All this, as is obvious, is in agreement with the Westermarckian contentions which we have discussed and only adds further strength to the arguments of Jennings and the social scientists in general.

An examination of Malinowski's position, however, reveals the same weakness that we found before in that of Westermarck. While Malinowski does not stumble into the same specific errors as did his teacher, his general conclusions fall into the same category. In his study: *Some Elements of Sexual Behavior in Primates and Their Possible Influence on the Beginnings of Human Social Development*,[4] Gerrit S. Miller, Jr., has shown conclusively that "Malinowski's work is all based on widespread popular misconceptions about the primates with which man is compared; misconceptions which arise from wrongly attributing to these animals patterns of sexual behavior which are familiar from observation of domestic ungulates and carnivores." Dr. Miller, whose work in the field of mammalogy is inexhaustibly exacting and thorough, then goes on to show by consideration of all the known facts about the behavior of primates the absurdity of the statements of this whole school of thought. Instead of our primate precursors being monogamous, and living in family groups, as Westermarck, Lowie, and Jennings maintained, Dr. Miller points out that the exact opposite is the case. "The young monkey clings to the female," Dr. Miller writes, "and can be adequately reared by her sole administrations; the help of the male is not required, and I have not been able to find convincing evidence that a true family bond is established." But mammalogists, who are certainly in a better position to observe the sexual behavior of mammals than are anthropologists or social scientists, not only deny the existence of monogamy among the apes; they even go so far as to show the presence of promiscuous horde tendencies among them instead of the familial ones referred to by Westermarck and his followers. Dr. Miller's words in reference to this point are very important:

"When we look into the life histories of the Old World monkeys and apes as revealed by field studies we find that existence in loosely organized bands is the general rule. This type of association is well known to occur in gibbons, baboons, macaques, langurs, proboscis, monkeys, gnemons, and guerezas. Apparently the same is true of the great apes, and though the difficulty of making exact observations on these animals in their nature haunts has interfered with the collecting of reliable evidence, nothing that I have been able to find in print concerning the behavior of any non-human primate, either monkey or great ape, would justify the assumption that the sexual tendencies of the members of a free band in the forest differ essentially from those which Dr. Hamilton observed in his macaques roving at large among the live oaks at Montecito (*i.e., promiscuity*). *Life in sexually promiscuous bands can, therefore, not be dismissed from the possibilities of ancestral human conditions as the basis of known evidence derived from the habits of primates in general.* On the contrary the common possession by men and monkeys of a type of sexual behavior which perfectly harmonizes with the need of promiscuous life throws a heavy burden of proof on those who insist that the forerunners of existing men lived under a group formation totally different from that which appears to be the prevalent one among non-human primates. Furthermore, when human sexual behavior is looked at as it is and not as it is conventionally supposed to be, we have little difficulty in detecting beneath the surface of the cultural structure unmistakable traces of the framework of the promiscuous horde."

We are now in a position to see the necessity for an entire revaluation of the old point of view concerning the origin of human tendencies and institutions. Man is not as radically different from the animals [5] as we have been all too prone to conclude. *Human tendencies not only go back far beyond the family; they extend to the simian horde.* As Dr. Gerrit Miller declares in another part of his study, "it seems reasonable to believe that a state of simian horde life with its attendant sexual promiscuity lies somewhere in the ancestry of the human social systems which exist to-day." To understand man, therefore, which is the obvious task of anthropology, we need to consider, without evasion or euphemism, the ante-human and primitive impulses and motivations which governed his behavior. We can never do that if we insist upon trying to make him behave as we think a primitive gentleman should.

Now, what is apparent from these criticisms, and those that preceded, is that the whole Westermarckian superstructure of moral ideas has no foundation in fact at all. It is wish-fulfillment thought, superimposed upon an anthropological edifice. It was so widely accepted for just that reason. The social sciences have always been prone to accept such protective logic. In the days when *laissez-faire* was orthodox theory, economists and sociologists were its *uncritical* advocates; only to-day, when *laissez-faire* has lost its influence, do economists and sociologists criticize and at times cease to defend it. *Only the breakdown of a principle or an institution makes it possible for its former advocates to view it objectively.* For that reason, and that reason mainly, it has been possible for the reaction against Westermarck to gain force and momentum to-day. The complete breakdown of nineteenth century ethics and economics, hastened as it was by the World War, shattered the middle-class myth of perfection. The absolutistic concept of evolution had to be abandoned. And, as a consequence, the relativistic concept has steadily gained in power. The development of the relativity concept in the physical sciences no doubt has contributed to this change in emphasis also in the social sciences.

But this does not mean that anthropologists and social scientists will have to go back to Morgan now for their materials and interpretations. Just the contrary! Morgan's evolutionary theories, as we indicated in an earlier section of this essay, can no longer be defended either. Not that Morgan was not much closer to the truth than Westermarck in his conclusions about the nature of morality and marriage in primitive society. He was. But we cannot say, as he did that the marital institution passed through certain stages definitely evolved out of certain others in the history of every tribe. The existence of sexual communism among a certain number of tribes does not furnish us with sufficient evidence to make a sweeping deduction about the entire history of early mankind. No more than the existence of monogamy among certain primitive tribes provided Westermarck with enough material to draw the illation that our early ancestors were almost universally inclined to monogamous habits. If we have enough evidence to show that the family, as we think of it, could not possibly have functioned in the early stages of social organization, or even have developed in such stages, we do not have enough evidence to trace adequately the development of sexual relations through any precise evolutionary stages, common to all primitive groups. In other words, there are more things that can be said not to be true about primitive life as a whole than there are things that can be said to be true. Morgan's error lay in not recognizing that fact. He found many things that were true in particular but not true in general. His weakness, intensified by the dogmas of the evolutionary school, grew out of his attempt to make the two synonymous.

Now, what conclusions can be drawn from this analysis of anthropological doctrine? It is at this point that I want to advance a theory that will explain, I believe, what has happened in terms of sociological fact. This theory, in brief, endeavors to elucidate the conflict that has been described (between Westermarck and Morgan) as an expression of those social forces which tend to develop what I shall call *cultural compulsives*—or a *vested interest in a cultural complex*. The influence of the *milieu* is at work in the formulation of all doctrines and interpretations, but its presence can be seen more easily and obviously in the nature of the response to these doctrines and interpretations than in the nature of their origin. In other words it is the response to Westermarck's doctrine that is more important from a sociological point of view than their origin. The same is true of the doctrines of Morgan. The response to the doctrines of both of these men became a living, dynamic thing, as much a part of the prevailing culture as a political election or a scientific invention. *The accuracy or inaccuracy of their theories was unimportant beside the influence they exerted over their own field and the field of the social sciences in general.* This influence was a direct result of this response— a response that revealed the social meaning implicit in the doctrines as a whole.

The radicals had not seized upon the doctrines of Morgan because they represented the final word in anthropological science. They adopted them because they fitted in so well with their own doctrine of social evolution, with the triadic theory of thesis, antithesis, and synthesis, and lent themselves so excellently to the Marxian interpretation of culture as an economic unit. They supplied a historic illustration of the Marxian dialectic. They gave new historic meaning to the cause of the proletariat. Westermarck's doctrines, on the other hand, were adopted in the same way by the intellectuals of middle-class conviction. Westermarck's doctrines fitted in so well with the moral ideals of the middle class. They afforded a so-called scientific justification of middle-class mores. Hence their adoption by middle-class intellectuals, and their rejection by radical intellectuals, and hence their popularity in universities and with university professors and their lack of popularity in radical centers.

In both cases we have a clear illustration of a *cultural compulsive.* Class factors were at work as an obvious determinant. Westermarck was so uncritically accepted by the middle-class intellectuals because his work provided a defense of middle-class ethics. Morgan was so uncritically accepted by the radical intellectuals, Engels, Kautsky, Plechanov, because his work supplied the dynamite for the fortification of the proletarian position. Once accepted thus, Westermarck and Morgan became immediate authorities for the classes whose logic their doctrines defended. The work of each man became *a cultural compulsive—the cultural compulsive* being determined by the class factors involved. The work of neither man, as a result, could be viewed objectively. As in the case of all cultural drives, the emotive aspect overrode the intellectual. Criticism of either man was reserved for his enemies and not his followers. The presence of the vested interest factor blinded both sides to the weaknesses in their authority. The motive element involved precluded the kind of scientific analysis which was needed for the classes whose logic their doctrines defended. The work of each man thus became a rallying point for a *cultural compulsive,* and not an objective contribution to social science. It was removed from the sphere of abstract science into the field of living culture. Westermarck's superior influence was not due to any intrinsic superiority of logic, but to the fact that the middle-class advocates he immediately won were connected mainly with universities and other institutions of learning, while those who upheld Morgan, being radicals, had no such connections. Westermarck dominated the scene because all the educators, being middle-class, supported his doctrine. In this way, his work became a *cultural compulsive*—a *cultural compulsive* of the middle class.

But it should not be thought that the radicals did not let their thought be equally bound by the vested interest factor only in the direction of an opposite *cultural compulsive.* Morgan became as inviolable with them as Westermarck with the middle class. Any one who criticized Morgan was denounced as "bourgeois." Blinded by the vested interest motivation, the radicals were—and to an extent still are— as uncritical of Morgan as the middle-class intellectuals were of Westermarck. Here again we have a *cultural compulsive* at work, exacting affirmation at the expense of criticism.

As we stated before, such affirmation is weakened only when the principles and institutions affirmed have begun to break down and decay. If middle-class morals had not started to disintegrate with marked rapidity after the World War, and the family gone through a process of unprecedented change, equivalent almost to a revolution, Westermarck's ideas would never have been challenged in recent years. Briffault's criticisms of Westermarck's doctrines might have been appreciated by a few, that is, if they had been written at all—but they would never have gained any vogue. Only the general decay of middle-class moral doctrine and economic theory could have prepared the way for the weakening and passing of Westermarck's influence in the social sciences in general, and in anthropology in particular.

In conclusion, I should like to add, that there is no other way, as far as I know, of explaining idea-sets or fixations of a social character such as are represented in the influence of Westermarck and Morgan, than by resort to what I have called the theory of *cultural compulsives*. By use of this theory we are better able, I believe, to understand something of the social mechanism at work in the rise and fall of ideas and their authors. *It is not what has usually been called the truth of their doctrine which makes them so powerful, but their adaptability to other interests, class interests in the main, which they subserve.* It is these other, these more basic, interests that turn these ideas into *cultural compulsives,* invest them with social meanings which are more important than their intrinsic content.

Social history is full of such *cultural compulsives.* The influence of Rousseau is just as excellent an illustration as that of Westermarck or Morgan. *The cultural compulsive represents the group interest in its psychological form.* It is a compulsive because the ideas it represents are dependent for their influence upon the strength of the interests they represent, and not upon the abstract accuracy or inaccuracy of their sequence or structure. Its content, as we stated before, is more emotive than intellectual. It can be destroyed only by the removal of the interests which constitute its origin. But since those interests will be with us until we organize a new kind of society in which they can no longer function, and since we are all affected by those interests, however objective we may try to be, the task that confronts us is not to deny the presence of such *cultural compulsives,* but to attempt to keep them from blinding us to facts that are of importance to our intellectual heritage.

The *cultural compulsive* has had many antecedents in the field of social theory. The Marxians have been the most expert in this analysis. By use of their radical dialectic, they were early able to show just how classes utilized ideas and doctrines for their own protection and perpetuation. In recent years, in addition to the work of the radicals, a number of liberal sociologists have gone so far as to argue for the presence of class-factors in certain ideological mechanisms pertaining to such problems as race, neo-malthusianism and eugenics. They have seen such mechanisms as part of a rationalization-process. What they have not seen—nor many of the radicals either—and what is important, I believe, to an understanding of the nature of social thought, is that their own thought, as well as the thought they have analyzed, is governed just as distinctly by the presence and pressure of *cultural compulsives*. What I am trying to stress, then, by the theory of *cultural compulsives,* is that all social thought is colored by such compulsives, reactionary as well as radical, and that those who think they can escape them are merely deceiving themselves by pursuing a path of thought that is socially fallacious. The radical is just as caught by such cultural compulsives as the reactionary. The radical will point out the compulsive thought on the part of the reactionary but will never discern the same compulsive mechanism, only directed toward a different end, active in his own thought. The liberal sociologist will write about ideological mechanism, the influence of classes upon thought, but always as if he himself were free of such mechanisms and influences. The purpose of this analysis is to show that that is not the case. The liberal sociologist has merely been deceived by the myth of neutrality—the belief that he can be above the battle, as it were, aloof from the criss-cross of conflicting interests. The very fact that the liberal sociologist in most instances is connected with a university, and is dependent upon a middle-class environment for his survival, is a sufficient reason why such aloofness in the social sciences must of necessity rest upon false premise.

The existence of cultural compulsives, then, makes objectivity in the social sciences impossible. Indeed, the actual claim to objectivity in the social sciences has been largely a defense-mechanism, an attempt unconsciously to cover up the presence of compulsive factors and convictions. No mind can be objective in its interpretation and evaluation of social phenomena. One can be objective only in the observation of detail or the collection of facts—but one cannot be objective in their interpretation. Interpretation necessitates a mind-set, a purpose, an end. Such *mind-sets,* such purposes, such ends, are controlled by cultural compulsives. Any man living in any society imbibes his very consciousness from that society, his way of thought, his prejudice of vision. The class he belongs to in that society in turn gives direction to his thought and vision. It is only in the physical sciences, where his method is quantitative and not comparative, and where the issues do not strike at the essential structure of social life, that he can escape something of that dilemma.

Cultural compulsives are necessary to social thought. Without them social thought would lack unity and integration, and become as meaningless as doctorate theses in the weak "e's" in Chaucer. Anthropology becomes of value not because it collects facts about primitive peoples, but because those facts have meaning to our civilization. *Anthropology for anthropology's sake is even more absurd than art for art's sake.* And anthropological doctrine, as we have seen, is as full of cultural compulsives as any other social science. By being aware of the presence of cultural compulsives we are not able to free ourselves from them—to do that would be to say that the individual mind is greater than the social mind from which it has originated and by which it is controlled—but we are better able to protect ourselves from the more absurd, because too uncritical, extremes, that such compulsives may drive us to. Those of us who are radical cannot expect to view society from an objective point of view—our very objective makes such objectivity impossible. Nor, for the same reason can those who are middle-class view society with any more objectivity. One can be objective only about those matters which do not involve the crucial issues of society, and those are the matters that are not important to social thought. At the same time, however, the radical can be on his guard against accepting Morgan, or any future Morgan, unquestioningly simply because he has become part of his cultural compulsive, and the middle-class sociologist can be on his guard against accepting Westermarck, or any future Westermarck, because he has become part of his cultural compulsive. In other words, the awareness of the compulsive nature of social thought should make it possible for the development of a little more flexibility and a little more criticism within the radius of the *cultural compulsive* itself.

After all, knowledge has come in the social sciences through the very process of social conflict, and the task that faces us is that of realizing the conflict, and the compulsives that it creates, but at the same time of gaining as much flexibility as possible within its limits. In this, as in other fields, the radical should take the lead.

NOTES

[1] The observations of H. von Koppenfels were ridiculed with finality by Burton (*Two Trips to Gorilla Land* and *The Cataracts of the Congo*) and Du Chaillu's even more dubious testimony as to the monogamousness of the gorilla was shattered by Winwood Reade who "showed conclusively that Du Chaillu has never set eyes on a gorilla."

[2] "Among these animals (whales, seals, hippopotamus, etc.)," Westermarck states, "the sexes are said to remain together even after the birth of the young, the male being the protector of the family." The latter statement is certainly untrue for every one of the animals mentioned, and there is not, except as regards the hippopotamus, a word to suggest it in the authority whom he cites. Of whales, Brehm says (vol. iii, pp. 677 *seq.*) that they live in large flocks and that very little is known concerning their breeding habits. At breeding time "it would appear," he says, "that the herds break up into single pairs, which remain longer together." In the new edition that vaguely worded statement is withdrawn and a less ambiguous one substituted from the observations of Guldberg, to the effect that after sexual congress the sexes "separate entirely" (vol. xii, p. 502). This is in accordance with the experience of whalers, who know that only cowwhales are found with schools of young, and that they retire with these to the shallower waters, where the males are never seen (see A. W. Scott, *Seals,*

Dugongs, Whales, pp. 132 *seq.*). Seals, whose reproductive habits are better known than those of most mammals, certainly do not "remain together even after the birth of the young," nor does Brehm make any such statement. They are among the most typically polygamous of animals, and the females pass from one male to another as the first males become spent. The young which are born just before the rut are those of the previous season, and the sexes separate as soon as those young are able to take to the waters. Of the hippopotami, which always live in considerable herds, Brehm says that he "thinks he may venture to assume" that the father protects the young. No other observer, as far as I know, has received that impression; on the contrary, according to the best accounts, "the mother ... is sedulous in her attention to her offspring, but the male is apt to be evilly disposed towards it" (R. Lyddeker, *Toyal Natural History,* 1894, vol. ii, p. 450). The hippopotamus is a herding, promiscuous, and not a pairing animal (cf. J. A. Nichols and W. Eglington, *The Sportsman in South Africa,* p. 65; F. V. Kirby, *In Haunts of Wild Game,* p. 538; Brehm-Strassen, *Tierleben,* vol. xiii, p. 41; D. Livingstone, *Missionary Travels,* pp. 241 *seq.;* E. Pechuel-Loesche, in *Die Loango-Expedition,* part iii, p. 213). The reindeer of which Brehm speaks in the passage referred to by Professor Westermarck is the semi-domesticated Norwegian animal. "The life of the domesticated reindeer differs," he says, "in almost every respect from that of the wild reindeer." At rutting time, "the Lapps allow their reindeer to enjoy their freedom, provided no wolves are about, and the domesticated animals mix with the wild herds, much to the joy of the owner, whose stock is thereby improved" (Brehm-Strassen, *Tierleben,* vol. xiii, p. 115).

[3] In the recent remodeled edition of his work, Dr. Westermarck has considerably modified his former statements and has eliminated several examples which he formerly adduced as evidence of "primitive monogamy." Thus, for example, the Iroquois were formerly represented by Dr. Westermarck as "monogamous"; the impression was indeed conveyed that they were so strictly and rigorously; they were said to be "purely monogamous," and were repeatedly appealed to as a favorite and conspicuous instance (E. Westermarck, *The History of Human Marriage,* 1901, pp. 435, 500, 506). Those statements have now been entirely withdrawn and Dr. Westermarck acknowledges that they are opposed to our information (E. Westermarck, *The History of Human Marriage,* 1921, vol. iii, p. 4). Of the Apaches it is asserted by Dr. Westermarck that "formerly" only one woman was deemed the proper share of one man (E. Westermarck, *The History of Human Marriage,* vol. iii, p. 5). His authority is Major Cremony who says that an Apache once told him so and descanted upon the evils of polygamy. "These recitals," comments Major Cremony, "will serve to show that the Apaches have pondered over some of the most abstruse and perplexing social problems" (J. C. Cremony, *Life Among the Apaches,* pp. 249 *sq.*). The sociological speculations of the Apaches, "the most barbarous people thus far discovered in these parts," (P. de Castaneda de Nacera, "Relacion de la Jornada de Cibola," in *Fourteenth Annual Report of the Bureau of Ethnology,* part i, p. 448) did not prevent them from showing honor and respect to a man in proportion to the magnitude of his matrimonial establishment; and the women were "by no means averse to sharing the affection of their lords with other wives" (J.

32   THE MAKING OF MAN

C. Cremony, *op. cit.*, p. 249). Among the Apaches "a man will marry his wife's younger sisters as fast as they grow to maturity. Polygamy is the nuptial law" (J. C. Bourge, "Notes on the Gentile Organization of the Apaches of Arizona," *Journal of American Folk Lore*, iii, p. 118; cf. H. H. Bancroft, *Native Races of the Pacific States*, vol. v, p. 641; E. Domensch, *Journal d'une mission au Texas at au Mexique*, p. 135). Dr. Morse reported polygamy to be general among all the eastern tribes of North America which he knew (J. Morse, *A Report to the Secretary of War of the United States on Indian Affairs*, p. 349); and Catlin reports the same thing of the more southern tribes. "Polygamy," he says, "is countenanced amongst all of the North American Indians, so far as I have visited them" (G. Catlin, *Illustrations of the Manners, Customs and Conditions of the North American Indians*, vol. i). Among the Guaranti tribes, according to Dr. Westermarck, "chiefs alone are allowed to have more than one wife" (E. Westermarck, *The History of Human Marriage*, vol. iii, p. 2). The statement is given on the authority of Father Charlevoix, whose remark refers to Christian Indians (P. F. X. de Charlevoix, *The History of Paraguay*, vol. i, p. 202): "The men among them who have embraced the Christian religion never marry among their relations, even within the degree which the Church readily dispenses. But Caciques have more wives than one," but it is quite unnecessary to have recourse to his casual and second-hand remark for information concerning the Guaranis. Dr. Westermarck adds a reference to Father Hernandez. What Father Hernandez has to say concerning the monogamy of the Guarani is as follows: "The Guarani family, in their state of heathenism, suffered from a fundamental defect, for polygyny reigned amongst them, and they thus violated the natural law which is the basis of marriage" (P. Hernandez, *Misiones del Paraguay, Organization social de las doctrinas Guaranies de la Compania de Jesus*, vol. i, p. 84; cf. p. 85). Father Ruiz de Montoya loudly laments the unrestricted and ineradicable polygamy of the Guaranis; some of them had as many as twenty and even thirty wives (A. Ruiz de Montoya, *Conquista espiritual hecha por los religiosos de la Compania de Jesus en las Provincias del Paraguay, Prana, Uruguay, y Tape*, p. 14). D'Orbigny, summing up our information on the subject, says: "The customs of the Guaranis are almost identical in all sections of the race.... All of them practice polygamy" (A. Dessalines d'Orbigny, *L'homme américain*, vol. ii, pp. 306, 307). The Chiriguanos, another Carib race of the eastern interior, are also referred to by Dr. Westermarck as "allowing" chiefs only to have more than one wife (E. Westermarck, *The History of Human Marriage*). Colonel Church says that among the Chiriguanos, "polygamy was customary," though at the present day, they being mostly Catholics, it is "not often met with"; "bigamy is more common" (G. E. Church, *Aborigines of South America*, p. 238). Mr. Whiffen, to whom Dr. Westermarck refers, and who in truth refers to Dr. Westermarck for theories of primitive monogamy, says that in some tribelets south of the Tikie, chiefs have not more than one wife, but makes the curious statement that "it is extremely hard to distinguish at first between wives, concubines, and 'attached wives'" (T. Whiffen, *The North West Amazons*, p. 159; cf. W. E. Hardenburg, "The Indians of the Putumayo," *Man*, x, p. 135).

The eastern Sahara derives considerable wealth from the salt trade and from traffic with caravans; the western, or Moroccan, region is, with the exception of a few of the lower valleys of the Atlas and some patches of oasis, a land of such poverty and desolation that the inhabitants have difficulty in keeping body and soul together. So precarious are the means of existence that most of the natives live from year's end to year's end on dates alone; the men are haggard with hunger, and whole populations are decimated by famine (S. Nouve, *Nomads et Sodentaires au Maroc,* i, p. 107). In those conditions it would not be surprising if large households were not common. Nevertheless, there is little definite evidence of general monogamy, with the exception of a few communities, such as Dr. Dads' of the lower Atlas, and polygamy is found in every district. Dr. Westermarck cites Chavanne, who refers to Vincent as stating that he "did not meet a single man who had a plurality of wives" (E. Westermarck, *op. cit.,* vol. iii, p. 25). Dr. Rohlfs met one at Tafilet, in the heart of the same region, who had three hundred (G. Rohlfs, *op. cit.,* p. 65); and Mr. W. B. Harris, who perhaps knows that region better than any other Englishman, speaks of the harems and of the large polygamous households and slavegirls of the Sharifian families.

From India, Dr. Westermarck has not succeeded in culling a dozen instances of tribes concerning which monogyny has been predicated. Among these are the Khasis. "The practice of polygamy," says Mr. Gait, "is usually said to be uncommon among them"; but he adds: "an educated Khasi whom I consulted assures me that polygamy is by no means unknown. It was formerly considered meritorious for a Khasi to beget offspring by different wives" (E. A. Gait, *Census of India,* 1901, vol. i, p. 199). Among the Nagas, who are also adduced as an example of Indian monogamy, "polygamy is very common, and is limited only by the men's resources" (J. McSwiney, "Assam," *Census of India,* 1911, vol. iii, p. 79). Concerning the Meches, the Rev. S. Endle, who gives a somewhat idealized account of his parishioners, does not claim that they are monogamous, but merely makes the usual statement that polygyny is not common except among the well-to-do (S. Endle, *The Kacharis,* p. 30). A less tender account states that they "place few restrictions upon their natural appetites" (*The Imperial Gazetter of India,* vol. iv, p. 44). The Mikirs, who are cited by Dr. Westermarck as monogamous, are expressly stated by Mr. Stack in his monograph of them to be polygamous (E. Stack, *The Mikirs,* p. 19). The Kukis are first stated to be "strictly monogamous" on the authority of an account which is then admitted to be in contradiction with all others, the claim that "polygyny and concubinage are strictly forbidden," being next restricted to the Old Kukis, and finally to "some of them." That residue consists, in fact, according to Colonel Shakespear, of the Kohlen clan, whose sexual laxity strongly savors of promiscuity (J. Shakespear, *The Lushei Kuki Clans,* pp. 155, 166). Colonel Cole, the late superintendent of the Lushai Hiils, says that among them polygamy is merely "uncommon," and that chiefs usually have two or three concubines in addition to their principal wife (H. W. G. Cole, "The Lushais," in *Census of India,* 1911, vol. iii, p. 139). The Nayadis and the Kavaras of Southern Malabar, whom Dr. Westermarck states to be "strictly monogamous," have, according to Mr. Stuart, barely emerged from a condition difficult to distinguish from promiscuity; they are "monandrous with great freedom of divorce" (H. A. Stuart, in *Census of India,* 1891, vol. xiii, p. 151).

"The early discoverers of the Philippines," says Dr. Westermarck, "found legal monogamy combined with concubinage" (E. Westermarck, *op. cit.*, vol. iii, p. 15, after S. de Mas, *Informe sobre el estado de las Islas Filipinas en 1842*, vol. i, p. 20). What the early discoverers of the Philippines found was, according to one of the oldest account, that the natives "marry as many wives as they can afford to keep" (De Moluccis Insulis, Rome, 1523); translation in E. H. Blair and K. A. Robertson, *The Philippine Islands,* 1493-1808, vol. i, p. 330); what Magellan found was that "they have as many wives as they wish" (A. Pigafette, *Primo Viaggio intorno al Mondo,* 1525, vol. xxxiii, p. 173); what de Legazpi found was that "the men are permitted to have two or three wives if they have money enough to buy and support them" (Miguel Lopez de Legazpi, *Relation of the Philipinas Islands and of the Character and Conditions of Their Inhabitants,* 1569). What the discoverers found in the Bisayan, or Middle Islands, was that "all the men are accustomed to have as many wives as they can support. The women are extremely lewd, and they even encourage their own daughters to live a life of unchastity" (Miguel de Loarca, *Tracado de las yslas Philipinas,* 1582, vol. v, p. 119; cf. F. Cartelli, *Viaggi racontati in dodici ragionamenti,* p. 145). The greatest difficulty encountered by the Friars and Jesuits in converting the natives was that of inducing them to part with their wives (Father Pedro Chirino, *Relacion de las Islas Filipinas i de lo que en ellas an trabaiado los padres dae la Compania de Jesus,* Rome, 1604; translation in *op. cit.,* vol. xii, pp. 291, 317 *seq.;* vol. xi, p. 52), and a special council was even held with the express object of suppressing polygamy among the natives (Juan de la Concepción, *Historia general de Philipinas,* vol. i, pp. 409, *sq.*). Mention is made of one valuable convert who had three wives, all noble and of equal rank—and therefore not "concubines" (P. Chirino, *op. cit.,* vol. xii, p. 291); and of many more men who "encountered great difficulty in putting away their many wives" (*Ibid.,* vol. xiii, p. 162). Father Chirino assures us that "we are gradually uprooting that hindrance to conversion so common among these people and so difficult to remove the practice of having several wives" (*Ibid.,* vol. xiii, p. 98). "Among the Bagobo and some other tribes of Southern Mindanao," says Dr. Westermarck, "a man may not take a second mate until a child has been born to the first union." Since pregnancy usually precedes marriage, there is nothing very remarkable about the rule; and it can only be for the sake of rhetorical effect that Dr. Westermarck refrains from quoting the first part of the sentence from his authority, namely, that "a man may have as many wives as he desires and can afford" (F. C. Cole, *The Wild Tribes of Davao District, Mindanao,* p. 103). "Among the Subanu," he proceeds to tell us, "a plurality of wives is permissible but not 'common.' " Velarde found the Subanu "worse than Noors," and "married to several wives" (Pedro Murillo Velarde, "Historia de la Provincia de Philipinas," in E. H. Blair and J. A. Robertson, *op. cit.,* vol. xliv, p. 91), and Combes informs us that they were in the habit of exchanging wives (Francisco Comes, S.J., "Historia de las islas de Mindanao, etc.," in vol. xl, p. 164). They were moreover much addicted to homosexual practices. Concerning the Italons, Dr. Westermarck cites a highly edifying passage from Father Arzaga, who gives us much more incredible information concerning them (cited by Mozo, "Noticia de los gloriosos triumphos, etc.," p. 19); but Father Diaz, on the contrary, complained that they were polygamous (Casimiro Diaz, "Conquest of the Filipinas Islands and Chronicles of the Religious of our Father St. Augustine," in Blair and Robertson. vol. xlii, p. 255). The Tinguianes, we are informed, "are monogamists" (on the authority of J. Foreman, *Philippine Islands,* p. 216). Mr. Foreman's is a most charming book on the Philippines, but on matters of ethnology, except as regards the writer's personal observations of the Tagalog, entirely worthless and unreliable. They are most certainly nothing of the kind. Mr. Cole, the only authority concerning the tribe who need be taken into account, tells us, on the contrary, that there is amongst them no objection to a man having two wives, and that "from the first time" to the present a man might have as many concubines as he could secure. Pre-nuptial cohabitation is, as with all other tribes, the rule and a man is not bound to marry a girl even if he has had several children from her, and can leave her without incurring any reproach (F. C. Cole, "Traditions of the Tinguian, a Study of Philippine Folk-lore," *Field Museum of Natural History, Anthropological Series,* vol. xiv, no. i, pp. 12, 54, 59, 111, 120). "Generally the Negritos of the Philippines are strictly monogamists." Among the Negritos "a man may marry as many wives as he can buy. . . . Polygamy is allowed throughout the Negrito territory, and it is not uncommon for a man to marry several sisters" (W. A. Reed, *Negritos of Zambales,* Ethnological Survey Publications, vol. ii, part ii, p. 61). Finally, we are told by Dr. Westermarck that "the wild Tagbanuas of Palawan do not allow polygyny" (on the very doubtful authority of Dean Worcester, *The Philippine Islands,* p. 108). But we are informed by the official authority on the region that both polygyny and polyandry are permitted by their customs, although not much practiced at the present day (E. Y. Mil, *The Bataks of Alawan,* Ethnological Survey Publications, vol. ii, p. 184).

Among the Mantras, a tribe of the Jakuns, polygyny, Dr. Westermarck tells us, "is said to be forbidden" (E. Westermarck, *op. cit.,* vol. iii, p. 11). But he omits to give the context of the statement, which is anything but edifying. "It is nothing rare," says Father Bourien, "to meet individuals who have been married fifty times"; and, in spite of the alleged prohibition, some nevertheless live in simultaneous polygamy (M. Bourien, "On the Wild Tribes of the Interior of the Malay Peninsula," *Transactions of the Ethnological Society,* n.s. iii, p. 80). "Most of the Binua, according to Logan," says Dr. Westermarck, "have only one wife, whilst other authorities inform us that polygyny is not permitted among them"; Favre met one who had two wives, but "he was censured and despised by the whole tribe." But what is actually stated by Logan is: "Most of the Binuas have one wife, but some have two, and there does not appear to be any rule on the subject"; and he adds that separation is most easy, that husbands commonly exchange wives, and that adultery is frequent and unresented (J. R. Logan, "The Orang Binua of Johore," *Journal of the Indian Archipelago,* i, pp. 20, 268). The opinion of the "other authorities," namely, Father Favre, that the tribes of Malaya "have kept marriage in the purity and unity of its first institution," does not, therefore, appear to be borne out.

"The Central African Pygmies," says Dr. Westermarck, "seem to be mostly monogamous, in spite of Sir Johnston's statement that polygamy among them "depends on the extent of their barter goods" (E. Westermarck, *op. cit.*, vol. iii, p. 22; H. H. Johnston, *The Uganda Protectorate*, p. 539). The statement made twenty years ago by Sir Harry Johnston is almost literally repeated by the Gaboon Pygmies themselves, when questioned on the subject. They say that a Pygmy "may have as many as two or three wives; it depends on the man's being able to pay the head-money" (F. W. H. Migeod, "A Talk with Some Gaboon Pygmies," *Man*, xxii, p. 18).

Dr. Westermarck has not been able to discover any suggestion of monogamy in Polynesia or in Melanesia. There is no trustworthy evidence of any native monogamous institution in New Guinea. Polygamy, commonly very considerable in extent, is reported from every part of the country (D. L. White, in *Annual Report on British New Guinea*, 1893-4, p. 75). Dr. Westermarck reproduces the statement of Dr. Finsch that in the Geelvink Bay district, the oldest missionary settlement in Dutch New Guinea, "not only is polygamy forbidden, but concubinage and adultery are unknown" (E. Westermarck, *op. cit.*, vol. iii, p. 16; O. Finsch, *Neu-Guinea und seine Bewohner*, p. 101). Other and more authoritative reports give no countenance to such a statement. An account drawn up by a commission of Dutch investigators states that "a man is permitted to marry two women; although this happens but seldom" (*Nieuw Guinea ethnographisch en naturkundig onderzocht en beschreven in 1858 door een Nederlandsch Indische Commissie*, p. 161). Heeren Von der Lith and Snellman say that in the Doreh districts, the chief missionary center, "if they are able to pay for them, they can marry several wives," and in other parts of Geelvink Bay, "each man is permitted to take as many wives as he can pay for, and the majority have more than one wife" (P. A. Von der Lith and J. F. Snellman, in *Encyclopaedie van Nederlandsch-Indie*, vol. iii, p. 212).

Dr. Westermarck says that Mr. Curr "has discovered some truly monogamous tribes" (E. Westermarck, *op. cit.*, vol. iii, p. 20). But nobody else has; and Dr. Malinowski, Dr. Westermarck's disciple, is compelled to contradict him, and to admit that "polygyny seems to be found in all the tribes" (B. Malinowski, *The Family Among the Australian Aborigines*, p. 387).

[4] *Journal of Mammalogy*, vol. ix.

[5] Another interesting instance of this same type of rationalization, in an endeavor to differentiate man from the animals, exalting the former, as it were, at the expense of the latter, is Malinowski's argument as to the presence of the rutting season among primates and the absence of it among men. All evidence to-day shows the fallacy of this distinction. The evidence which Malinowski used as his main support is refuted to-day by laboratory investigations. Hamilton in his "Sexual Tendencies of Monkeys and Baboons" (*Journal of American Animal Behavior*, vol. iv, October, 1914) shows that "females do not have rutting seasons but accept males at all times. Males are sexually attracted by any adult or adolescent female at any time. Also interested in females of other species, snake, puppy, human infant, etc." E. Kempf in his study of "Social and Sexual Behavior Infra-Human Primates" (*Psychoanalytic Review*, vol. iv, April, 1917) observed "no period of heat was observed in female . . . healthy male monkey ready to respond to sexual attraction at any time." Sokolowsky in his study of "The Sexual Life of Anthropoid Apes" (*Urologic and Cutaneous Review*, October, 1923)

reported that he discovered no period of rut; male practices repeated inter-course every day with his females. Yerkes (Genetic Psychology Monograph, November, 1927), Bingham (Comparative Psychological Monograph, May, 1927), Hartman (*Journal of Mammalogy*, August, 1928); all corroborate these same observations (for more detail and further reference see Gerrit Miller's article, "Some Elements of Sexual Behavior in Primates and Their Possible Influence on the Beginnings of Human Social Development").

I

FOSSIL AND PREHISTORIC MAN

FOSSIL MEN *

By MARCELIN BOULE

By virtue of a supreme law of life, Mankind as a whole has had to pass through the phases of intellectual and physical evolution which to-day characterize the development of each individual in the human mass. In the beginning, the child is lulled by tales or songs of marvels: poetry is his first instructress. Later, his faculties of observation and reason awaken: truth compels him, and poetry is superseded by science.

So, regarding the "supreme question" of its origin, Mankind in its infancy had at first no source of information other than fairy tales, legends and stories of the miraculous. Then human intelligence developed; in certain bright spirits genius was made manifest; next calm observation, freed from all preconceptions, played its part; and finally, but only in later centuries when the reign of science began, there dawned some rays of Truth.

Our knowledge of Man's existence on the earth in prehistoric times is a conquest of modern science.

Neither in ancient times nor in the Middle Ages does there seem to have been expressed any but imaginary conceptions of the origin of Mankind. In the Greek poets and philosophers of the pre-Christian era, vague references occur bearing on the low estate of the first Men. And so also in the Latin poets; every one is familiar with the oft-quoted verses of Lucretius:

"Arma antique manus, ungues dentesque fuerunt,
Et lapides, et item sylvarum fragmina rami,
Et flammæ atque ignis postquam sunt cognita primum
Posterius ferri vis est, ærisque reperta.
Sed prior æris erat, quam ferri, cognitus usus." [1]

* *Historical Summary*. Edinburgh: Oliver and Boyd.

Similar views were expressed by Horace, Pliny, Strabo, Diodorus and others. Probably all these notions were purely intuitive, but it may be that they owed something to the persistence of ancient traditions. In any case they do not seem to have been based on true interpretations of relics of former days, for even though stone axes and weapons, called *ceraunia* (Greek,—thunder), were already well known, their origin or real significance was unrecognized. They were regarded as produced or launched by lightning, and extraordinary powers were attributed to them.

Such primitive ideas became widespread: with slight variations they have persisted to our own day in the popular superstitions of almost every country.[2]

And yet it is to a considered study of these ancient objects, it is to archæology, that we owe the first positive concrete facts of the great antiquity of Mankind.[3]

In regaining contact with Nature, lost since the time of the ancient Greeks, the scientific spirit reawoke with the Renaissance. Two great artists, Leonardo da Vinci and Bernard Palissy, propounded correct views regarding the nature of fossils. Yet although various authors, Agricola (1558), Gesner (1565) and others, described or figured polished stone axes and stone arrow-heads, they regarded them simply as curiosities. They still considered these objects, together with so many other "fossils," as sports of Nature, of which they gave more or less quaint explanations.

At the end of the sixteenth century, Michael Mercati, whose writings were not published till 1717, more than a century after his death (1593), discovered the true nature of the so-called thunder-bolts or *ceraunia*. "Most men," he says, "believe that *ceraunia* are produced by lightning. Those who study history consider that they have been broken off from very hard flints by a violent blow, in the days before iron was employed for the follies of war; for the earliest men had only splinters of flint for knives." And in this connection he quotes the verses of Lucretius.[4]

In 1636 Boetius de Boot, regardless of being "dubbed a

fool," rejected the commonly accepted ideas; but he believed that he was dealing with implements of iron transformed into stone through process of time.

Various writers, however, Aldrovandus in 1648, Hassus in 1714, A. de Jussieu in 1723, Lafitau the Jesuit in 1724, and Mahudel in 1730, compared the old stone weapons of our countries with the stone weapons of living native tribes, notably the American Indians, and so initiated an excellent working method based on comparative ethnography, giving at the same time "the finishing blow to the erroneous beliefs regarding ceraunia."

In 1750, Eccard, after investigating old German burials, established a succession of different prehistoric ages; and in 1758, a learned magistrate, Goguet, published a remarkable work on the "Origin of Laws," in which he declared that a Stone Age had been followed by an Age of Copper and of Bronze, and then by an Iron Age. Later this classification was firmly established and developed by the Danish archæologists Thomsen and Worsaac.

Thus the hesitating science of the eighteenth century arrived at the same ideas as the ancient poets or philosophers; but these ideas were now based on the observation of material evidences. Nevertheless, although it was recognized that the historic civilization had been preceded by an uncivilized or crudely barbarous period, the great antiquity of these primitive times was not suspected. The theories had first of all to be accommodated to the demands of biblical chronology. The new idea of Mankind beginning in a state of primitive destitution seemed incompatible with the idea of the physical and moral perfection of the terrestrial paradise. Hence arose these heated discussions, fierce battles of words, which to-day seem so naïve and ridiculous, specially when we consider, as M. Cartailhac has pointed out, that the most widely differing opinions regarding the date of the creation of Man did not diverge by more than 1500 years.

Buffon, who first suspected the immense duration of geological time, although he sought to interpret the Scriptures "soundly," was familiar with the stones which "were believed to have fallen from the clouds and to have been formed by thunder, but which nevertheless are really the first relics of the art of Man in a state of nature." Yet, to his mind, the epoch of Man was only the seventh and last of his "Epochs of Nature," much later than the fifth epoch, characterized by the remains of the Elephant, the Rhinoceros and the Hippopotamus, which he found in the superficial soil.[5]

With the nineteenth century Natural History sprang into sudden life and vigor. To the new sciences of Geology and Palæontology it fell to throw light on the great antiquity of Man. Up to that time it had been a question only of objects dating· no further back than modern geological times, objects which to-day are known as Neolithic. But now attention had to be turned to stone implements much more ancient found in the very heart of deposits which dated from a geological period preceding our modern period, and which were distinguished by the presence of remains of animals no longer existing to-day.

As early as 1715, Conyers, a pharmacist and antiquary of London, had found near that city, in the gravels of a former river and near the skeleton of an elephant, a flint worked after the manner now known as Acheulean. Bagford, a friend of Conyers, made the suggestion that the flint was a weapon used by a Briton to kill the elephant, brought over by the Romans in the reign of the Emperor Claudius!

In 1797, another Englishman, John Frere, made a similar discovery at Hoxne in Suffolk. He collected some dressed flints at a depth of four meters in a deposit containing bones of large extinct animals. He was able to give his find a much more correct interpretation than Bagford, stating that it must certainly belong to a "very distant period, much more remote in time than the modern world." This observation, so full of judgment, almost of genius, passed unnoticed. It was brought to light again by John Evans only after the memorable conflicts of Boucher de Perthes, of whom John Frere must be considered the forerunner.[6]

In 1823, a French geologist, Ami Boue, presented Cuvier with a human skeleton, exhumed near Lahr on the banks of the Rhine, from an ancient mud or loess containing also remains of extinct animals. This discovery was set aside by the famous palæontologist. "All the evidence leads us to believe," he said,[7] "that the human species did not exist at all in the countries where the fossil bones were found, at the period of the upheavals which buried them."

For these words the great naturalist has often been reproached; but it is easy to excuse him.[8] Cuvier had, as a matter of fact, examined all the evidences sent from various parts as remains of "antediluvian Man." Some were really human bones, such as those from Canstadt, from different German caves, from Lahr and from Guadeloupe; but no accurate observation, no delusive geological evidence justified the assertion of their high antiquity.

As for the other remains, Cuvier had recognized that the bones from Belgium were those of elephants; from Cerigo, fragments of a cetacean; from Aix, remains of a chelonian; from Œningen, the skeleton of a salamander (the famous *Homo diluvii testis* of Scheuchzer). Such statements were well calculated to arouse skepticism, the more so as not the least trace of any fossil Ape had yet been discovered. Cuvier prudently added: "But I do not wish to conclude that Man did not exist at all before this period (that of the 'last upheavals of the globe'). He might have inhabited certain circumscribed regions whence he repeopled the earth after these terrible events; perhaps even the places he inhabited had been entirely swallowed up and his bones buried in the depths of the present seas, except for a small number of individuals who carried on the race."

Cuvier died in 1832, just at the time when discoveries were imminent. "Perchance had he lived," wrote de Quatrefages, "he would have repeated the words he addressed one day to his fellow-worker Duméril: "My dear friend, we have been mistaken."

About the year 1830, several naturalists in the Midi of France, Tournal in the Department of Aude, Emilien Dumas, de Christol and Marcel de Serres in the Departments of the Gard and of Herault, continued in France such researches as Buckland had begun in England in 1820, by excavating the deposits accumulated in grottos and caves in their respective regions. There they found human bones, associated with numerous remains of animals belonging to species which had migrated or become extinct, bears, hyænas, reindeer, and others, the bones of which sometimes showed traces of cutting instruments. So clearly did Tournal recognize the importance of these observations that in 1829 he had no hesitation in writing: ". . . Geology, in supplementing our brief history, will at length awaken the pride of Man by revealing to him the antiquity of his race; for henceforth it lies in the power of geology alone to help us to some knowledge of the period when man first made his appearance on the globe." [9] These words assuredly mark a very great step in advance.

Again the Belgian author Schmerling published in 1833 an important work entitled *Recherches sur les ossements fossiles des cavernes de la province de Liége*. In this he not only demonstrated the co-existence of Man with the rhinoceros, bear, hyæna, and other animals, but further, he entitled his concluding chapter: "Relics worked by the hand of Man." These relics consisted of shaped bones, and in particular of an arrow-head and some flints. "Everything considered," he says, "it must be admitted that these flints have been cut by the hand of Man, and that they may have been used to make arrows or knives. . . . Even if we had not found human bones in circumstances strongly supporting the assumption that they belonged to the antediluvian period, proof would have been furnished by the worked bones and the shaped flints."

Some years later, in 1840, Godwon-Austen, continuing

McEnery's studies of Kent's Cavern in England, arrived at the same conclusions.

Proof of the geological antiquity of Man was thus firmly established by these pioneers; but that is not to say that it was accepted by professional scientists, save perhaps by Constant Prévost.[10] To Boucher de Perthes belongs the merit of impressing it upon the learned world, of giving it common currency as well.

Boucher de Perthes (1788-1868) was Controller of Customs at Abbeville.[11] He was a learned and prolific writer in diverse fields, a great lover of antiquities, "accustomed from childhood to listen to talk of fossils." Having devoted himself to the collecting of all sorts of ancient human remains, he had, towards the end of 1838, the good fortune to find "in diluvial beds" the "first diluvial axes," which he submitted to his fellow-members of the "Société d'émulation d'Abbeville." In 1846 he published the first volume of his *Antiquites celtiques et antédiluviennes* entitled *De l'industrie primitive ou des arts à leur origine*. In this work, Boucher de Perthes declared that the ancient alluvial soils, *diluvial* as he called them, in the suburbs of Abbeville, contained many stones worked by *"antediluvian"* Man buried at various depths along with bones of large animals belonging to extinct species. "In spite of all their imperfection," he says, "these rude stones prove the existence of Man as surely as a whole Louvre would have done."

This assertion, although founded on minute observations and on excellent evidence, at first met with the utmost disfavor. "Contradictions, jeers, scorn, were unsparingly heaped upon the author," wrote M. de Saulcy. He was regarded as a dreamer, as a kind of visionary, and the scientific world, priding itself on its detachment, allowed him to talk without further concerning itself with facts which, he maintained, he had forcefully introduced into the domain of practical science.[12]

Far from being discouraged, Boucher de Perthes continued, with fine perseverance and good nature, to combat this systematic and often sarcastic opposition. Soon two camps were formed in the learned world. The first included several naturalists of independent spirit, among them A. Brongniart and Constant Prévost, who, while maintaining a certain caution, supported Boucher de Perthes. In the second and by far the largest camp, that of the extremists, with Elie de Beaumont at their head, were to be found the more academic scientists, the disciples and successors of Cuvier, who, while repudiating any suggestion of prejudice, nevertheless exaggerated their master's scruples. "Before the intervention of English geologists and archæologists had deprived this great question raised and solved by a Frenchman, of its wholly French bearing, for so long the entire French Academy followed the lead of its Permanent Secretary, like a flock of sheep on the heels of the shepherd." [13]

In 1854, Dr. Rigollot of Amiens, having found in the sandpits at Saint-Acheul "axes" similar to those from the gravels of Abbeville, was the first to associate himself wholeheartedly with the views of Boucher de Perthes, which till then he had strenuously opposed. Further, a distinguished naturalist of the Midi, Dr. Noulet, brought forward favorable evidence when he announced the occurrence at Clermont, near Toulouse, of an "alluvial deposit containing remains of extinct animals, mingled with stones shaped by human hands."

In 1859, after repeated study of the facts on the spot, several distinguished English scientists, the palæontologist Falconer, the stratigrapher Prestwich, the archæologist John Evans, the anatomist Flower, and the famous geologist Lyell, who soon afterwards published his celebrated work, *The Antiquity of Man Proved by Geology,* all clearly and decidedly declared their adherence to the theory.[14]

In the same year Albert Gaundry, a palæontologist then at the outset of a brilliant career, went to Amiens to study the deposits and to carry out excavations. Having made up his mind never to leave his workmen, he himself succeeded in extracting, along with teeth of a large ox, "nine axes"

from the "diluvium" at a depth of 4½ meters, and at a
level from which, a short distance off, had been obtained
bones of the Rhinoceros, Elephant and Hippopotamus.[15]
Gaundry's evidence made a deep impression upon the minds
of several independent scholars, but opposition continued in
the Institute, which held to the old conception of the deluge,
and had absolute faith in the chronology of the Bible, according to which the creation of the world dated no further
back than 4,000 years before Christ. This opposition was
carried to such a point that, on 18th May, 1863, a geologist
in the highest official position, Member and Permanent
Secretary of the Academy, Elie de Beaumont, went so far
as to say: "I do not believe that the human race was contemporary with *Elephas primigenius*. M. Cuvier's theory
is born of genius; it is still undemolished."[16] He even won-
dered if the dressed flints were not of Roman origin. . . .[17]

Academic immortality is but a senile illusion. Permanent
Secretaries pass away and their names fall into oblivion; but
the name of Boucher de Perthes will shine forever in the
firmament of Science.

A very great advance in Science had been made by the
discovery that beyond the limits of History stretched a vast
Prehistory, which is finally lost in the obscurity of geological time. Henceforth the origin of Man became a problem for palæontology, on a par with the problems of the
origins of the animals. The impulse was given; everywhere
zealous workers devoted themselves to investigations, with
good results. A new science, that of "Human Palæontology,"[18] was on the point of being definitely established.

Edouard Lartet, who was born and died in Gers (1801-
1871), was the chief founder of this new science. At first
a lawyer by profession, he awoke to his true calling on seeing
a molar tooth of a Mastodon, found by a peasant in his village. Deeply interested, he read Cuvier's works, studied
osteology, and devoted himself to the investigation of fossil
bone-remains, which abounded in the ground about his
family estate. From 1836 onwards, he explored and made

famous the rich beds of Sansan, which date from Mid
Tertiary times. There he discovered, among other strange
forms entirely new to science, remains of an anthropoid
ape, an ancestor of the modern Gibbons, and this he named
Pliopithecus.

P. Fischer, author of one of the biographies of E. Lartet,
points out the importance of this discovery from the point
of view of the question of fossil Man: "Cuvier, in an enlightened and needful criticism of the so-called bone-remains
of man and of contemporary monkeys of extinct species,
exposed their lack of authenticity. He accordingly inferred
that monkey and man were late in appearing. 'What aston-
ishes me,' said he, 'is that, amongst all these mammals, the
majority of which have at the present day congeners in warm
regions, there is not a single Quadrumana; and also that
there has been found not a single bone, not a single tooth, of
a Monkey, even of any extinct species. Neither is there
any Man: all the bones of our species which have been collected along with those I have referred to were present by
accident.' "

"In thus associating the date of Man's appearance with
that of monkeys," Fischer continues, "Cuvier prepared the
way for the great reception accorded to the discovery of the
Sansan Ape, and it could be foreseen that the discovery of
a fossil Ape would be followed by that of fossil Man." [19]

The insight of Etienne Geoffroy Saint-Hilaire did not err.
Cuvier's distinguished adversary had pointed out "the important bearing on natural philosophy" of Lartet's discovery,
destined "to inaugurate a new era of knowledge relating
to human life." But he added, "the time for philosophical
research is not yet."

Even in 1845, Lartet boldly admitted the possibility of
Tertiary Man. "This corner of ground," he said, speaking
of Sansan, "once supported a population of mammals of
much higher degree than those here to-day. . . . Here are
represented various degrees in the scale of animal life, up
to and including the ape. A higher type, that of the human

kind, has not been found here, but we must not hastily conclude from its absence in these ancient deposits that it did
not exist. . . ." These were prophetic words. It seems as if
Lartet had "a presentiment of the important part he was to
play later, in the scientific discussion regarding the co-
existence of Man with the large Quaternary mammals."

About the year 1850, E. Lartet went to Paris to continue
his researches. He settled near the Museum, the scientific
treasures of which attracted him, and where he found none
but friends. In 1856, he described the jaw of a new anthropoid
ape, *Dryopithecus*. Three years later he published a comprehensive monograph on the fossil Proboscidians. But his
writings on the animals of former times constantly led him
back to the great problem of fossil Man. With great sympathy and interest he followed the efforts of Boucher de
Perthes.

On the 19th of March, 1860, E. Lartet sent to the Académie
des Sciences a note on the occurrence of Man in Western
Europe in geological times, entitled, "Sur l'ancienneté géologique de l'espèce humaine dans l'Europe occidentale." The
Académie has been accused of refusing to print this memoir,
and the fact is that only the title appears on p. 599 of Volume L of the *Comptes rendus*. For the text, reference must
be made to the *Archives des Sciences de la Bibliothèque
universelle de Genève,* or to the *Quarterly Journal of the
Geological Society of London,* which received it with enthusiasm." [20]

Now, this memoir was of prime importance. Along with
a description of the celebrated cave of Aurignac, which the
author had just explored, it contained certain suggestions of
great significance, which were renewed and developed the
following year (1861) in the *Annales des Sciences naturelles* under the title: "New researches on the coexistence
of Man and of the large fossil Mammals regarded as characteristic of the last geological period." [21]

It would seem that even from the time of his first purely
geological writings, E. Lartet had been an opponent of the

cataclysmic theory of the world's development. It required a great deal of independence and true courage to challenge a theory held by the scientific pundits. This courage he showed, a fact which sufficiently explains the hostile attitude of Elie de Beaumont.

In 1858, in his note "On the Ancient Migrations of Mammals of the Present Period," [22] he had already assailed the idea of deluges or other catastrophes. "The day is perhaps not far distant," he said, "when the erasure of the word *cataclysm* from the vocabulary of practical geology will be proposed." Or again: "It is an abuse of the technical language of science to use such high-sounding expressions as *upheavals of the globe, cataclysms, universal disturbances, general catastrophes,* and so on, for they immediately give an exaggerated significance to phenomena geographically very limited. . . . The great harmony of physical and organic evolution on the surface of the globe has in no case been affected. Aristotle perfectly understood these alternating movements of the earth, which have at different times changed the relations of continents and seas; he knew equally well how to reduce to its proper regional proportions the Deucalian Deluge, exaggerated and embellished by poetic fiction. Apparently this great naturalist also had to combat the fantastic ideas of the cataclysmic philosophers of his time, and the severe reproach he flung at them, might just as well, after 2,000 years, be applied to certain of our geologists or palæontologists of the present day: 'It is absurd, on account of small and transitory changes, to invoke the upheaval of the whole universe.' " [23]

The memoir contains another new and suggestive idea. The history of Man, like that of animals or like any geological history, is indeed a continuous story, and demands a chronological method. "Were it possible to establish that the disappearance of the animal species characteristic of the last geological period was successive and not simultaneous, a means would be discovered of establishing, at one and the same time, the relative chronology of the unstratified fossil

FOSSIL AND PREHISTORIC MAN 53

deposits and their time relations with these diluvial beds whose geognostic bearings are well defined." Accordingly, Lartet proposed a "palæontological chronology," which for the first time allowed a classification to be made of the beds in which traces of fossil man had been found up to that time. "Thus, in the period of Primitive Man there would be the Age of the Great Cave Bear, the Age of the Elephant and of the Rhinoceros, the Age of the Reindeer and the Age of the Aurochs; much after the manner recently adopted by archæologists in their divisions of Stone Age, Bronze Age, and Iron Age."

This classification could not be perfect, but its actual existence was of great value, in that it asserted the geological nature of the problem of Man's existence, showed how the history of our ancestors must be sought for in bygone ages, and fixed some milestones on the long journey. So a broad path was thrown open to investigators. In his eulogy of Lartet, Hamy has well said: "To the doctrine of the antiquity of Mankind, Aurignac converted a number of disciples, who were the more valuable in that they translated enthusiasm into productive activity."

Soon after, in 1864, E. Lartet discovered the famous engraved mammoth from La Madeleine, where, in delightful fashion, one of our distant forebears had himself inscribed decisive proof of his geological antiquity. Along with Christy, an Englishman, he undertook the investigation of the deposits of the Vézère Valley, the fame of which is now world wide. Thus he succeeded in revealing the astonishing artistic culture of the men of the Reindeer Age. The work in which so many fine discoveries were to have been described and expounded has unfortunately never been completed.[24]

In 1869 Lartet was chosen to succeed d'Archiac in the Chair of Palæontology in the French National Museum of Natural History. He was then sixty-eight years of age, and he died some months later, without having delivered his first lecture.

If I have spoken at length of Edouard Lartet, it is, first, from admiration for so independent and disinterested a man of science; secondly, to show the outstanding part which, through him, France played in the creation of the science of Human Palæontology; and, finally, because the achievement of our illustrious countryman has not always been sufficiently understood. To the public at large it is unknown, and the scientist has not appraised it at its true value. And yet the passing of the years only adds to the fame of Edouard Lartet.

Lartet's example was followed in France by numerous scholars and investigators, P. Gervais, de Vibraye, A. Milne-Edwards, Louis Lartet, Piette and others; whilst, in Belgium, Dupont took up and completed the work of Schmerling; and in England, where a good fight had also been waged, Lubbock, John Evans, and Boyd Dawkins published very valuable works on Prehistory.[25]

In 1864, in order that the progress of the science might be recorded, Gabriel de Mortillet founded a special Review, *Matériaux pour l'histoire naturelle et primitive de l'Homme,* which he soon placed under the able and liberal editorship of Emile Cartailhac. Keeping the archæological standpoint especially in view, G. de Mortillet revised Lartet's classification. With a lucidity that appealed to the comprehension of every investigator, he grouped systematically the innumerable facts of a science whose birth he had seen, and to the development of which he had largely contributed.

It was not long before prehistorians began to hold international congresses, where results in one country were compared with those in others, where general questions were discussed, and where interdependent labors were planned, for discoveries had meantime spread to every continent. So, step by step, we reach the present day, when researches in prehistoric archæology have become the fashion, when every one grubs in the most ancient of our archives, too often, alas, with an utterly inadequate scientific training.

Thus arose the science of Prehistory or Prehistoric

Archæology, founded on facts which, although supplied by all kinds of material things, nevertheless throw a tolerably clear light on the intellectual and moral character of the Men regarding whom History is silent.

In the meantime what progress had been made in research regarding the physical and zoölogical characters of Man himself? What steps had marked the progress of Human Palæontology in the strict sense of the words, the sense in which they are mainly used in this work?

• After the discovery by Ami Boue, in 1823, of a human skeleton in the loess of the Rhine Valley, a discovery the significance of which Cuvier utterly repudiated, there followed a barren period. Every find of human bones was now regarded *a priori* with suspicion. But when the great antiquity of Man was demonstrated by means of dressed flints and proved by geology, discoveries of human bones seemed more natural: they increased in number.[26] No fewer than eighty have been recorded from the beginning of the nineteenth century to our own day. Palæontology would thus seem to have been provided with material sufficient to enable it to attain to great results and to frame important conclusions.

Unfortunately these discoveries are far from being of equal value because of uncertainty regarding the age or even the authenticity of many of them. It is very easy to fall into error in dealing with such material. In many a place the earth is but human dust. Nothing, alas! is more common in superficial soils than the skeletons of our fellows. Of course, the physical characters of the bones vary according to the date of their burial; and the burials of historic times present features which would hardly deceive a practiced eye. In the case of prehistoric burials or of bone-remains of the Quaternary Period, one important character must be taken into account, that of fossilization, by which is meant the physical and chemical transformation of a bone, which having lost its organic substance has become pervaded by mineral matter and so more dense. But this character is not sufficient; the degree of fossilization may vary according to certain conditions of the environment, independent of age. Appeal must then be made to the conditions of the soil deposit, to geological and palæontological criteria. When a discovery is made, however, a competent observer is rarely on the spot, ready to make the necessary investigation. At the present day, now that the attention of an enlightened public has been directed to such events and their importance is understood, the assistance of professional scientists is usually invited; and several recent discoveries have also been made following upon systematic excavation conducted by experts. Formerly this was not the case, for then the geology and the palæontology of the Quaternary formations had barely been outlined. Many human skulls and skeletons, carelessly exhumed without scientific investigation, have been placed in museums, where anthropologists study them without sufficiently inquiring into the record of remains the origin and exact bearings of which cannot now be accurately determined.

As the question of age is a factor of prime importance in palæontology, scientific accuracy demands a courageous elimination of all those osteological evidences the high antiquity of which is not assured. After close scrutiny of all the discoveries recorded up to the present day, I retain for consideration in this book only those whose authenticity and age are beyond dispute. Here it is better to err through excess rather than through lack of prudence.

The first and one of the most important stages centered in the discovery, in 1856, of the famous brainpan or cranium at Neanderthal in Rhenish Prussia. This object was examined in succeeding years by various naturalists. With its considerable dimensions, its receding forehead, its enormous orbital ridges and its flattened brainbox, the skull presented an extraordinary appearance. Schaaffhausen in Germany, and Huxley in England, declared it "the most bestial of all known human skulls," and emphasized its simian or monkey-like characters.

This happened at a time when the scientific world was in a state of effervescence. Evolutionist ideas had begun to spread. Lamarck, who, long before Darwin, had not hesitated to attack the formidable problem of the origin of Man, and who conceived it as occurring through the modification of a Quadrumane, had been forgotten before he had even been understood or appreciated. But now Darwin published *The Origin of Species,* Boucher de Perthes began to gain ground, and Albert Gaundry made public the results of his first researches on the transformations of fossil mammals; Broca founded the Société d'Anthropologie de Paris, and Huxley wrote his celebrated memoir on the *Evidence as to Man's Place in Nature* (1863), which was followed soon after by Carl Vogt's excellent *Vorlesungen über den Menschen* (1863).

The Neanderthal skull, by reason of characters obviously of low type, and a conformation resembling that of the skulls of certain large Apes, supported the evolutionist theory; in the eyes of philosophic naturalists it appeared to be a sort of primitive form lessening the depth of the gulf which now separates the Apes from Men.

But this interpretation was not to the liking of anti-evolutionists of the old school. The scientific value of the skull was disputed and denied. As it had been found by workmen, geologists and palæontologists took exception to the obscurity of its origin. Eminent anthropologists, among them Virchow, regarded it as a pathological specimen of the skull of an idiot. I shall say nothing of the zealous and often foolish intervention of the defenders of religion, in a debate to which religion could only contribute arguments animated by sentiment, by tradition or by prejudice. It was an intervention of this kind which provoked the famous epigram of Huxley, that it was better to be a perfect Ape than a degenerate Adam.

Just at this time there occurred the notorious episode of the jawbone of Moulin-Quignon. In 1863, Boucher de

Perthes, desirous at all costs of discovering the fossil bones of the Man who had dressed the flints of Amiens and of Abbeville, found a human jawbone in conditions which stirred up lengthy polemics and caused floods of ink to flow. It would indeed seem as if on this occasion the famous and worthy archæologist had been the victim of a fraud. The English scientists who had so emphatically supported his views regarding the dressed flints, refused to believe in the authenticity of the jawbone; and one of them, John Evans, pronounced upon it a *Requiescat in pace,* of which the echoes have not yet died away. This, clearly, was not calculated to add to the credit of the new theory.

But in 1865, Ed. Dupont, in the course of scientific explorations organized by the Belgian Government in the caves of that country, found a human lower jaw in one of the excavations on the left bank of the Lesse, the *Naulette pit.* The circumstances of its deposit left no loophole for criticism. Now, this jaw, taken from a deep bed, where it lay along with bones of the Mammoth, Rhinoceros, Reindeer, etc., differed from the jaws of all modern Men in one important character which struck the observer at first glance, the absence of a chin. Here again was the stamp of the ape, associated none the less with other characters which were purely human. One was tempted to associate the jaw from La Naulette with the Neanderthal skull, as belonging to a similar lowly type.

In 1868, Louis Lartet, following with distinction in his father's footsteps, described the rock-shelter of Cro-Magnon on the banks of La Vézère, in the Dordogne, from which several human skeletons had already been obtained. On this occasion the skeletons presented all the features of modern Man; so much so indeed, that their great antiquity was not acknowledged by most anthropologists, who could not bring themselves to abandon their preconceived notions and to throw so far back into the past the physical type of *Homo sapiens.* So it was also with the skeleton found in 1872 by M. Rivière in one of the caves of Grimaldi. The

"Mentone Man," closely resembling the Cro-Magnon type, was considered to be Neolithic. The geological bearings were, however, perfectly definite.

On the other hand, far too much importance was laid on some skeletons obtained, about the same time, from more or less ancient and more or less disturbed river deposits of the Seine, at Clichy, Grenelle, and elsewhere.

In 1870, Hamy [27] published a summary of the state of the science at this time, in a book which may still be consulted with profit. In the following year, Darwin,[28] tackling the great problem of the descent of Man, published a work in which palæontological facts do not and could not as yet play any but a secondary part, but in which the famous naturalist expounded in all its bearings the theory of the animal origin of Man, formerly precisely stated by the great Lamarck.[29] To this theory the German naturalist Haeckel had just given his strong support in his *Generelle Morphologie der Organismen* (Berlin, 1866).[30]

About the same time, Broca [31] published some excellent studies on the comparative morphology of Apes and Man, and thus placed his great craniological knowledge at the service of human palæontology. During the years 1873 to 1882, de Quatrefages and Hamy contributed to this branch of science a great work,[32] in which descriptions of the principal cranial types of modern Man were preceded by long systematic discussions on all the fossil or pseudo-fossil evidences then known.

The year 1887 was marked by an interesting discovery of two human skeletons in a cave at Spy in the province of Namur. This was an event of considerable scientific importance, fortunate in two respects: first, in that the Quaternary Age of the deposit, investigated by geologists, was not open to question; secondly and especially, because the Spy skulls resembled in every way the Neanderthal skull. The hypothesis of the pathological nature of the latter was definitely destroyed by the fine report of Fraipont and Lohest, which helped to confirm the opinion of those who believed in the actual existence of an ancient human type very different from, and of lower nature than, modern types.

This opinion was notably strengthened some years later, in 1894, by the work of Dubois on the remains of Pithecanthropus, discovered in Java in 1891. It is sufficient at present to state the indisputable fact that the skull-cap of *Pithecanthropus* really embodies a morphological type ideally intermediate between the skulls of anthropoid apes, such as the Chimpanzee or the Gibbon, and a human skull.

These fine discoveries instigated others. A positive fever took hold of investigators; and excavations carried out in almost every part yielded many evidences, but of very unequal value.

Amongst the most important of the later discoveries, first in order of time must be mentioned that at Krapina in Croatia, which brought to light many human remains of Neanderthal type.

Next come the results of the important explorations undertaken by the Prince of Monaco, Albert I, in the Grimaldi Caves. Several human skeletons were exhumed in the Grotte des Enfants: some belonged to the Cro-Magnon type, the Palæolithic Age of which was here definitely established; while another, the most ancient, revealed to Professor Verneau the existence of a different type, of negroid character, the "Grimaldi type."

In 1907, a new fact of prime importance was brought forward. Up to that date, the Man of the oldest dressed flints was known only by the products of his handiwork—no authentic relic of his skeleton had been obtained. Then Schoetensack described a jawbone found in the ancient gravels of Mauer near Heidelberg. And this jawbone, very much older than those from La Naulette, from Spy, or from Krapina, presented a still more primitive appearance.

By systematic excavations carried out in France, the Abbés Bouyssonie and Bardon, Capitan and Peyrony, and Henri Martin, discovered in human settlements, deep in the caves or shelters of La Chapelle-aux-Saints in the Department of

Corrèze, of La Ferrassie in the Dordogne, and of La Quina in Charente, several skeletons and portions of skeletons of men of Neanderthal type.

Human palæontology has thus been furnished with records of exceptional value, which have enabled us to gain a fuller knowledge of this ancient type than we possess of many modern savages.[33]

After a considerable period of relative inactivity in the sphere of human palæontology, England, which claims a most honorable part in the foundation and development of the science, was seized with new enthusiasm for it. In addition to some recent discoveries, the importance of which was overestimated, such as that of the Ipswich skeleton, considered to belong to a period more remote than the Quaternary, but in reality barely prehistoric, there occurred the Piltdown find, studied from the anatomical point of view by the palæontologist Smith Woodward. Although its particular and general significance are still disputed, it is certainly a most important discovery, as we shall see later.

So far, I have spoken only of Europe, a very small part of the globe, yet the rest is almost unknown from the point of view which interests us here. Researches carried out in the two Americas, especially noteworthy being those of Ameghino in South America, have not yet produced any conclusive discovery. Asia, the outstanding importance of which will one day become apparent, has yielded no results to speak of, except of an archæological nature. Quite recent discoveries at Boskop in South Africa [34] as well as at Talgai in Australia show that, whenever investigations are undertaken with sufficient resources in these different parts of the globe, great results will be forthcoming.

NOTES

[1] The passage is thus rendered in English by Creech (1714).

"And Rage and furnish'd yet with Sword nor Dart;
With Fists, or Boughs, or Stones the Warriours fought;
These were the only Weapons Nature taught:

But when Flames burnt the Trees, and scorch'd the Ground,
Then Brass appeared, and Iron fit to wound.
Brass first was us'd."

[2] Cartailhac, E., *L'âge de pierre dans les souvenirs et superstitions populaires* (Paris, 1878).

[3] See for the whole of the first part of this history: Hamy, E. T., *Précis de Paléontologie humaine* (Paris, 1870). Id., "Matériaux pour servir à l'Histoire de l'archéologie préhistorique" (*Revue archéologique*, 1906). Evans, Sir John, *Ancient Stone Implements*, 2nd ed. (London, 1897). Cartailhac, E., *La France préhistorique* (Paris, 1889). Reinach, S., *Description raisonée du Musée de Saint-Germaine-en Laye*, I (Paris, 1889). Macalister, R. A. S., *A Text-book of European Archæology*, vol. i. *The Palæolithic Period* (Cambridge, 1921).

[4] Mercati, M., *Metallotheca, opus posthumum*, Rome, 1717, p. 243. See on this subject, Vayson, "Les précurseurs de la préhistoire" (*L'Anthropologie*, xxxi, p. 357).

[5] Buffon, *Epoques de la Nature* (Paris, 1778).

[6] Evans, Sir John, *loc. cit.*, p. 573. John Frere's account is to be found in *Archæologia*, vol. xiii, 1800, p. 204.

[7] "Discours sur les révolutions de la surface du globe" (in *Recherches sur les ossements fossiles*, 4th ed., vol. i., p. 217).

[8] Cartailhac, E., "Georges Cuvier et l'ancienneté de l'Homme" (*Matériaux pour l'Hist. nat. et primitive de l'Homme*, 1884, p. 27).

[9] *Annales des sciences naturelles*, vol. xviii, 1829, p. 258.

[10] Gosselet, J., *Constant Prévost*, Lille, 1896, p. 165.

[11] See Ledieu, A., *Boucher de Perthes, sa vie, ses œuvres*, Abbeville, 1885.

[12] See Meunier, Victor, *Les Ancêtres d'Adam*, Thieullen Ed., Paris, 1900. This failure was probably due in part to the fact that Boucher de Perthes associated with true primitive instruments, as if they were of the same significance, other stone *figures* or *symbolic* stones which were only "sports of Nature," and which are now recognized as of no account. But how was it possible at that time to separate the tares from the wheat?

[13] Meunier, V., *loc. cit.*, p. lx.

[14] For an account of this intervention, see Falconer, H., *Palæontological Memoirs*, vol. ii, p. 596; Prestwich, "On the Occurrence of Flint Implements, Associated with the Remains of Extinct Mammalia" (*Proc. Roy. Soc.*, 1859).

[15] Gaundry, A., "Contemporanéité de l'espèce humaine et de diverses espèces animales aujourd'hui éteintes" (*Comptes rendus de l'Académie des Sciences*, 3rd October, 1859).

[16] *Comptes rendus de l'Académie des Sciences*, 18th May, 1863.

[17] The persistence of this injurious influence, which continues even to our own day in a more or less feeble or unconscious form, is shown by the following facts: At the death of Boucher de Perthes, his works were withdrawn from sale by decision of his family and sold for waste paper. Some years afterwards Victor Meunier wrote his book, *Les Ancêtres d'Adam, Histoire de l'Homme fossile*. The book was printed in 1875, but was never published. It gave an account of the "martyrdom" of Boucher de Perthes, and the publisher, afraid of incurring the displeasure of the

Academy, suppressed the whole issue. In 1900 the firm of Fischbacher published a new edition edited by A. Thieullen, a warm admirer of Boucher de Perthes. It is a work of great interest.

[18] The expression is due to Serres—"Notes sur la Paléontologie humaine" (*C. R. Ac. Sci.,* xxxvii, 1853, p. 518).

[19] Fischer, P., "Note sur les travaux scientifiques d'Edouard Lartet" (*Bull. de la Soc. géoïog. de France,* 2nd ser., xxix, p. 246).

[20] "It was too soon to announce these truths to the Académie des Sciences; it did not understand that, in refusing to publish the forecast of E. Lartet, it was placing itself in the backwash of geological and anthropological progress, and that a day would come when it would be a cause for deep regret to find in a foreign publication seven pages so creditable to French science, rejected by the Institute of France."—E. Cartailhac, *in litt.*

[21] "Nouvelles recherches sur la co-existence de l'Homme et des grands Mammifères fossiles réputés caractéristiques de la dernière époque géologique."

[22] "Sur les migrations anciennes des Mammifères de l'époque actuelle."

[23] "Ridiculum enim est, propter parvas et momentaneas permutationes, movere ipsum totum" (γελοιδον γαρ, etc., Aristotle, *Meteorol.,* i, I, c. 2).

[24] Lartet, E., and Christy, H., *Reliquiæ aquitanicæ:* being contributions to the archæology and palæontology of Périgord (Paris, 1866-1875, vol. i, in 4to, with 102 plates).

[25] Lubbock, John, *Prehistoric Times* (London, 1867, 7th ed., 1913); French translation by Barbier, under the title *L'Homme avant l'Histoire* (Paris, 1867, 2nd ed., 1871). Evans, John, *Ancient Stone Implements* (London, 1872, 2nd ed., 1897). Dawkins, W. Boyd, *Cave Hunting* (London, 1874); *Early Man in Britain* (London, 1880).

[26] See Quatrefages, A. de, and Hamy, E. T., *Crania ethnica: Les Crânes des races humaines* (Paris, 1882). Première partie. *Races humaines fossiles.*

[27] Hamy, E. T., *Précis de Paléontologie humaine* (Paris, 1870).

[28] Darwin, C., *The Descent of Man* (London, 1871).

[29] Lamarck, *Philosophie Zoologique,* 1809, i, p. 337.

[30] See also Haeckel, E., *Histoire de la Création* (Fr. trans., Paris, 1874). *Anthropogénie ou histoire de l'évolution humaine* (Fr. trans., Paris, 1877). *Etat actuel de nos connaissances sur l'origine de l'Homme* (Paris, 1900). (English editions of these works appeared as follows: *The History of Creation* (1st Eng. ed., London, 1875; 3rd, 1883); *The Evolution of Man* (Eng. ed., London, 1879); *Our Present Knowledge of the Descent of Man* (1898).

[31] Broca, P., "L'ordre des Primates" (*Bull. de la Soc. d'Anthrop. de Paris,* 2nd series, vol. iv, 1869).

[32] Quatrefages, A. de, and Hamy, E. T., *Crania ethnica.*

[33] Boule, M., "L'Homme fossile de La Chapelle-aux-Saints" (*Annales de Paléontologie,* 1911-1913).

[34] And at Broken Hill Mine, Rhodesia.

THE STRUCTURE OF PREHISTORIC MAN *

By WILSON D. WALLIS

A NUMBER of human skeletons, or parts of skeletons, have been found which undoubtedly are of great age. Their antiquity is attested by the geological evidence of undisturbed superimposed strata beneath which these skeletal parts reposed, or by association with remains of animals now extinct—incontrovertible evidence of great age. The oldest of these remains is that of a skeleton found in Java, called *Pithecanthropus erectus,* or "ape-man erect," indicating that it was believed to be a type intermediate between man and ape, and a creature who walked erect. It belonged to the last part of the pliocene period, or, more probably, to the early pleistocene and is probably half a million years old.

Only portions of a skeleton were found, these being in separate places, though within the radius of a few feet and at the same geological horizon. The bones generally are assumed to belong to the same skeleton, although this view may be challenged. They consist of a calvarium, or skull cap, with prominent brow ridges and low frontal region, suggesting small brain capacity, a capacity estimated as 850-900 cubic centimeters, some 200-300 c.c. more than the brain capacity of the gorilla; a femur, undoubtedly human but with anthropoid characteristics and possessing a large third trochanter (a protuberance below the great trochanter on the upper part of the shaft), a femur indicating that its possessor walked with knees flexed; three molar teeth of a type bordering on that of the apes. The find was made by Dubois in 1891 and was exhibited to scientists in 1894. It was not until 1923 that fellow-scientists were again allowed to examine the remains. Hrdlicka reports them more human-

* *An Introduction to Anthropology.* New York: Harper & Brothers.

like than the casts had indicated. This is in accordance with the recent description which Dubois has given of the brain cast. The dentition, likewise, is human in type. The pulp cavity is not large and the roots of the teeth are fairly long— in contrast with the teeth of the Heidelberg man. As in the apes and in the more primitive races of man, however, the roots are widely separated. Though the crowns of the teeth are large, they have a transverse diameter in excess of their sagittal diameter, which is a trait of human teeth in distinction from those of the apes, in whom the width of the molar is less than the anteroposterior length. Although the upper wisdom tooth is large, it is smaller than the other molars, as in the orang and in contemporary man.

The frontal fissure, associated in modern man with the function of speech, is developed more than in the apes, though not so extensively as in modern man from which fact Dubois draws the conclusion that Pithecanthropus was in possession of speech. But it is very doubtful that such an inference can be made from a study of the skull cap. All that one can say, at most, is that the potentiality for speech was there so far as brain development is concerned. The anatomist cannot tell from an examination of the skull of modern man whether or not the possessor had speech, much less from fossil skulls.

In 1890 Dubois had discovered in another part of the island of Java remains of a large-brained early man of pleistocene date, represented by portions of two individuals. One of these men, known as Wadjak II, had a brain volume estimated at 1,650 c.c., which is very large. The brain size of the other individual, Wadjak I, is estimated at 1,550 c.c. (The average for European males is about 1,450 c.c.)

These, like the Talgai remains found in Queensland, Australia, suggest a type ancestral to the modern aborigines of that continent. The proportions are similar, the characteristics are much the same, but they are present in these fossils in more pronounced form. The estimated cranial capacity of the Talgai skull is 1,300 c.c., which is probably less than the average for adults of the type, for the individual who left us his brain case on the Darling Downs was a lad some fourteen to sixteen years of age and had not attained full development.

The Rhodesian skull, found in a quarry in South Africa in 1921, has been the subject of much interest among anatomists. Unfortunately, all geological evidence of age is lacking, though the circumstances of the find do not preclude the possibility of great age. It is one of the most primitive of fossil human remains, with large facial area, large beetling brow ridges, and large teeth. The form of the palate is human, for it has the horseshoe shape found only in man. The skull resembles that of Neanderthal man, but in some respects is more primitive.

Next in age, perhaps, is the Piltdown skull, found in 1912 in the county of Essex, southern England. The mandible is of primitive form, so primitive that more than one anatomist has pronounced it that of a chimpanzee, though now it is generally accepted as human and as belonging to the Piltdown skull. Cranial capacity has been variously estimated at from 1,170 c.c. to 1,400 c.c. The skull is that of a woman and, if we accept the estimate of 1,400 c.c., is large for a female.

The Heidelberg mandible, found in 1907 in gravel pits at Mauer, near Heidelberg, Germany, is admittedly human.[1] The jaw is massive, containing large teeth of primitive form, with molars ranging in size as in the gorilla, rather than as in contemporary man; the chin region is little developed and is receding. The ascending ramus is of the type found in the apes—broad, thick, with shallow sigmoid notch.

Remains of Neanderthal man have been found many times in western and southwestern Europe, in some cases nearly complete skeletal remains. The skulls are characterized by heaviness, roughness of outline, large occipital protuberance, heavy eyebrow ridges, large jaw and teeth.

Among English finds of Neanderthal age, at least 25,000

to 30,000 years ago, may be mentioned the Dartford skeleton, found in the third river terrace of the Thames, a terrace which lies from forty to sixty feet above the level of the river. If a thousand years be allowed for the wearing down of one foot of terrace, the deposits are from forty thousand to sixty thousand years of age. In the sixty-foot terrace were found remains of three species of rhinoceros, two species of elephant, one of lion, one of reindeer; the associated animal remains corroborating the geological testimony of great age. The skeleton is that of a male, the cranial capacity being about 1,750 c.c. The skull is long; glabella and superciliary ridges are prominent. The chin is feebly developed. The last molar is as large as or larger than the first. The head of the femur is large. All of these characteristics are primitive and suggest membership with the continental Neanderthal type.

Neanderthal man was followed, probably dispossessed, by Cro-Magnon man, whose type is more like that of modern man. He was of tall stature, erect, and had a large cranial capacity, his brain being larger than that of the average modern European. The vault of the skull is high—hypsicephalic. The face is broad, the orbits large, square, and angular. The nose is narrow, long and pointed. The upper alveolar border, containing the teeth, projects. The lower jaw is large, but there is a well-developed chin.

Not so old as the Dartford skeleton is the Tilbury skeleton, found at the Tilbury Docks, on the north bank of the Thames, about halfway between London and the mouth of that river, on flat marshy land. Its date is late paleolithic or early neolithic. This skull is more like that of modern man. The chin is projecting; the capacity of the skull is about that of the average Englishman, 1,500 c.c. The tibia is flattened from side to side, having an index of 55, whereas that of the average Englishman is 62. Otherwise there are no important differences between these remains and those of contemporary man.

Last may be mentioned the Essex skeleton, found along the coast line of Essex in 1910. It was uncovered below a prehistoric floor which was under eight to ten feet of clay, lying amid a mass of neolithic stone implements and pottery. The period of the deposits is neolithic, and has been estimated as about 2000 B.C. The skeleton is that of a woman, about five feet four inches in height. The capacity of the skull is 1,260 c.c., almost the average for London women (1,300 c.c.), and the length, width, and height of the skull are each about the average of London women. The teeth are regular and well formed, the incisors meet, instead of the lower passing behind the upper, as in contemporary man, thus permitting a side-to-side grinding which our incisors seldom allow. The humerus and the bones of the forearm indicate that the lady was right-handed. The remains show a close approximation to modern type.

Many anatomists have attributed man's evolution to the increase in the size and convolutions of his brain. But, as the above examples have frequently indicated, many of these early men had larger brains than the average contemporary European. The average of Neanderthal and more particularly that of Cro-Magnon exceeded the average of the present-day European. Taking into account all of the evidence, it can scarcely be said that man's brain has increased in size throughout the period of prehistoric times, nor is there evidence that his brain is likely to increase in size.[2]

The gradation in type from the oldest to the most recent finds is by no means complete and continuous, yet if all the skulls and skeletal portions of prehistoric times are arranged in order of age, they represent, with exceptions, a transition in type, a series in which the oldest is most like the apes, tapering down with modernity into greater similarity to civilized man. The evidence of geology and of palæontology is to the effect that our ancestors resembled the apes more than do our contemporaries, and that there has been through the millennia a gradual but undoubted transition from more to less apelike human type. The import of these changes is, however, not so clear.

Do the Characteristics of Prehistoric Human Remains Imply A Common Ancestry for Man and Apes?

Resemblance to the apes increases as we trace back man's ancestry into neolithic times, the later paleolithic, the earlier paleolithic, and those still earlier stages represented by the remains from Heidelberg, Piltdown, and Java. This increasing resemblance has been accepted as demonstrating a common ancestry for man and apes. Other abundant evidence indicates a common ancestry, but the evidence of prehistoric human remains does not in itself justify the inference, though, of course, it does not discountenance it. We base this conclusion on the fact, if fact it be, that practically all of the changes in man's structure traceable through prehistoric remains are the result of changes in food and habits. Let us see what these changes are and what shifts in man's diet and habits would account for them.

The most notable changes are found in the skull. Briefly, the story of change is to: a higher frontal region; increased bregmatic height; smaller superciliary ridges; increased head width; less facial projection; decreased height of orbits and a shifting of the transverse diameter downward laterally; a more ovoid palate; smaller teeth; diminished relative size of third molar; shorter, wider, and more ovoid mandible; decrease in size of condyles; decrease in distance between condylar and coronoid process; in general, greater smoothness, less prominent bony protuberances, less of the angularity and "savageness" of appearance which characterize apes. There is evolution in type, but the evolution is result rather than cause. The change in type is notable, but there is reason to assign it to change in function, to use and disuse.

Practically all of the above-mentioned features of the skull are intimately linked together, so that scarcely can one change without the change being reflected in the others, some features, of course, reflecting the change more immediately and more markedly than do others. If we suppose that man's diet and his manner of preparing food have changed, we have an index to most of the skull changes, provided the dietary change has been from uncooked or poorly cooked to better cooked food, from more stringent to less stringent diet. Development of stronger muscles concerned with chewing will bring about the type of changes which we find as we push human history further back into the remote past.

Change is most marked in the region in which the chewing muscles function. With tough food and large chewing muscles is associated a large mandible with broad ramus, large condyles, heavy bony tissue. The larger teeth are accommodated to the tougher food and their greater specialization is an adaptation to the needs of the masticator. Larger teeth demand more alveolar space, and there results an elongated alveolar region with greater sagittal diameter, and a more prognathous and more angular mandible. The increased width of ramus has a mechanical advantage in the leverage given the coronoid process. The larger condyle affords a better resisting fulcrum and is associated with the greater side-to-side play correlated with longer mandible and with the chewing of tougher food. The more forward projection of teeth in both upper and lower alveolar region is in accordance with the characteristics of animals which use the teeth for the mastication of tough food and no doubt is a function of vigorous mastication. The palate conforms to the mandible, with which it forms a physiological unit, however separate morphologically the two may be, hence is long and less arched. Zygomatic arches stand out for the accommodation of the large chewing muscles which pass beneath them. The adjacent walls of the skull are flattened and forced inward by the pull of muscles which of necessity is inward as well as downward, producing elongation of the skull. The temporal muscles reach far up on the skull, giving rise to a high temporal ridge; they extend forward as well as backward, giving a more prominent occipital region and a more constricted forward region, resulting, on the forehead region of the skull, in the elevation of the superciliary ridges and intervening glabellar region. Projecting brow ridges are associated with stout temporal and masseter muscles and large canines.

The facial region is constricted laterally and responds in a greater forward projection, one result being that the transverse diameter of the orbits is thrust upward outwardly, giving the horizontal transverse diameter which characterizes the apes and which is approximated in prehistoric man and some contemporary dolichocephalic peoples. In young anthropoid apes, when chewing muscles are little developed and there is little constriction in the lateral region posterior and inferior to the orbits, the transverse diameter of orbits is oblique, as in man, being elevated to the horizontal when temporal muscles develop and function more vigorously, thrusting in and upward the outer margins of the orbits. Construction of outer margins of orbits produces the high orbits which we find in apes, and to a less marked degree, in prehistoric human remains.

Elongation of the skull increases the distance between bregma and nasion, producing a low retreating forehead and a low head height-breadth index.

That muscular pull has this result is suggested by the laboratory experiments of Arthur Thomson conducted on inflated canvas bags the shape of a skull with attachments corresponding to the chewing muscles and with variations in the pressures and pulls applied. It is further indicated by the fact that the Eskimos, a people living on raw food, have almost all of the "primitive" characteristics in a more pronounced degree than do other contemporary peoples. Again, in the Australians, a people whose cooking of animals has attained little development—they cook the animals whole over an open fire—there are these "primitive" features. On the other hand, similar food conditions do not prevail among the negroes, who constitute a third group exemplifying these "primitive" traits.

As to other skeletal characters, we have no evidence for

the earliest remains, excepting only the femur of Java man, though there is abundant material from the much later, though still early, Neanderthal and Cro-Magnon types. Here the most notable differences have to do with the flexure of the knees and the larger posterior diameters of the lumbar vertebræ, both apelike characteristics. A stooping posture can be inferred from the shift in plane of articular surfaces at the head and on the lower surface of the femur, the upper surface of the tibia, and the articulation of the tibia with the subjacent astragalus. That these differences exist is clear, but that they have evolutionary significance beyond reflecting change in form associated with change in function is not clear. They are common in contemporary peoples of the lower cultures, such as Africans, Australians, and others. The explanation of these traits is the absence of chairs. The position of rest is that of squatting on the heels, or of sitting on the haunches with knees flexed, or other similar pose, different from that which Europeans assume when they sit. This throws the articular surface of the head of the femur further forward, throws back the articular surfaces of the lower end of the femur and the upper end of the tibia, and throws forward the articular surface at the inferior end of the tibia and gives rise to a forward articular surface on the subjacent astragalus. The greater posterior diameter and lessened anterior diameter of the vertebræ of the lumbar region are a function of the more frequent and forcible bend forward of the vertebral column. Similar differences are found in savage tribes whose culture lacks chairs.

If the above interpretations are correct, it follows that a return to the conditions of diet and of life which characterized prehistoric man would be followed by a return to his physical type. Yet if there were this transition to a type more simian, one could not say we were approaching a common ancestor, for, if we have one, we would of necessity be getting farther away, no matter how similar the types might become.

The similarity would not be due to the transmission of qualities from a common ancestor of a remote past. If this be true, it is equally true that an increase in similarities as we push back the time period does not imply common ancestry if the changes are due to changes in function, following changes in diet and posture. Since, in a given group, the male of the human species resembles the anthropoid ape in nearly all of these characteristics more than does the female, though of necessity both sexes must be equally remote from simian-like ancestry, it seems clear that mere resemblance cannot constitute an argument for phylogenetic descent. These sex differences, moreover, are in support of the above implications, seeing that the more muscular male has the same simian attributes, though in modified form, which are characteristic of early man. If he is more conservative of the type—though this attribute usually is assigned to the female —this is because his bodily activity is more nearly that of prehistoric man and that of his supposedly near relations, the anthropoid apes.

Though this is not a critique of the theory of evolution, but merely of the argument that change of type shows common ancestry with a zoölogically similar species, we would point out that man, if descended from an ancestor common to him and the apes, should in type more nearly approach that remote ancestor as we go back to earlier simian types, whereas commonly we are content to insist that the earlier human types approximate contemporary anthropoid apes. It is essential to the theory of common ancestry that earlier simian types approach the types of earlier human forms.

Yet they do not approach the types of earlier human forms. The resemblances of prehistoric man hark forward to modern apes rather than back to prehistoric anthropoid ancestry. Prehistoric anthropoid forms help us as little in supplying the missing link as do those prehistoric human forms on which we have placed too much reliance, because an age with its mind made up to evolution of a unilinear type has seen what it has looked for. In unraveling the past we cannot do better than follow the methods of the geologist, who infers past changes from a study of existing forces and infers the existence of no force with which he is unacquainted. In so far as prehistoric human remains are concerned, it is not so much evolution which has given us modern man, as man who has given us his type by evolving it through physiological or functional changes growing out of changes in culture, an evolution which he is still continuing. If the cause lies within the species, the changes do not imply common ancestry with a morphologically and anatomically similar species, even as they are not an argument against such ancestry.

What, then, shall we conclude with regard to the relationship between men and apes? Briefly this: A review of the similarities in structure, in blood, in use of limbs, points to the apes as man's nearest relations in the animal kingdom, his first cousins, if he has any. That some creature is his nearest relation is a conclusion to which we are driven by a consideration of animal life. As regards prehistoric human remains we cannot conclude that the increasing resemblance to apes as we go back in time implies simian ancestry, seeing that these changes may be due to changes in food and posture, representing the acquisition of form growing out of function, or closely correlated with function. In that case, prehistoric man's increasing resemblance to apes has other explanation than descent from a common ancestor, being, if our interpretation is correct, a case of convergence, the response of similar form to similar function.

As a matter of fact, the change from long-headedness to short-headedness from earliest man to more recent man of the prehistoric past, is a change to greater resemblance with the apes. Round-headedness is a characteristic of apes much more than of modern man. Here the resemblance is due to different factors: in the case of round-headed man to the decrease in chewing muscles; in the case of the apes the occiput is flattened to provide attachment for strong muscles reaching up from the neck to support the head. Man's upright posture obviates the need for such marked occipital support; the ensuing posterior projection of the occiput accounts largely for the greater length of his head in comparison with that of the apes. But this is only to repeat that mere resemblances do not count for much; they must be interpreted in the light of the causes and occasions which give rise to them.

This is not the place to discuss the relative merits of Darwinism, Weissmannism, or Lamarckianism; but there is nothing in the above view which would not fit into any one of those schemes. The modification of form through function can proceed from generation to generation by the principles of Darwinian selection, if that is the doctrine of evolution to which one is committed. It can proceed, of course, with the mechanism represented by Weissmann. Likewise it is susceptible of Lamarckian interpretation if one be a Lamarckian. But in any case we cannot afford to close our eyes to facts, because we may shy from their implications. A good case is not strengthened by adducing poor reasons in support of it, and no fear of giving comfort to the enemy should lead us to suppose that a partial concealment of truth, which arises from a concealment of part of the truth, can compensate for the loss of unprejudiced consideration of the facts of life, whether they seem to fit into our schemes of evolution or fail to fit. Since the day of Darwin the evolutionary idea has largely dominated the ambitions and determined the findings of physical anthropology, sometimes to the detriment of the truth. The duty of the anatomist, however, is not to plead a cause, but to play judicial advocate, willing to hear and consider all evidence bearing on the case.

The human has been differentiated from the simian type for a much longer period than we have been accustomed to suppose. We are constantly lengthening the vistas of the past, and it may be that we must extend them beyond our present wont in order to find the point where human and simian forms have diverged into their present types. Cer-

tainly one can no longer accept Java man as common ancestor, nor do any of the Tertiary remains of fossil apes
suggest common ancestry. Our present evidence is insufficient. We must not convict the prisoner at the bar simply
because we do not know who else committed the crime.
The issue is, Can we prove him guilty? And so with regard
to a common ancestor. "Positive facts," as Lamarck finely
says, "are the only solid ground for man; the deductions
he draws from them are a very different matter. Outside the
facts of nature all is a question of probabilities, and the most
that can be said is that some conclusions are more probable
than others."

NOTES

[1] G. Elliot Smith suggests, however, that the time may come when we
shall have to classify it as outside the human species.

[2] If we take the weight of the brain as equal to 1, the weight of the body
among fishes averages about 5,688. Among reptiles it is about 1,321;
among birds about 212; for anthropoids 60 to 100; and for mankind 22
to 36.

THE TASMANIANS *

By W. J. SOLLAS

THE Tasmanians, though recent, were at the same time a Palæolithic or even, it has been rashly asserted, an Eolithic race; and they thus afford us an opportunity of interpreting the past by the present—a saving procedure in a subject where fantasy is only too likely to play a leading part. We will, therefore, first direct our attention to the habits and mode of life of this isolated people, the most unprogressive in the world, which in the middle of the nineteenth century was still living in the Palæolithic epoch.

As regards clothing, the Tasmanians dispensed with it. They habitually went about in a state of nakedness, except in winter, when the skins of kangaroos were sometimes worn. To protect themselves from rain they daubed themselves over with a mixture of grease and ochre. Yet they were not without their refinements; the women adorned themselves with chaplets of flowers or bright berries, and with fillets of wallaby or kangaroo skin, worn sometimes under the knee, sometimes around the wrist or ankle; the men, especially when young, were also careful of their personal appearance—a fully dressed young man wore a necklace of spiral shells and a number of kangaroos' teeth fastened in his woolly hair.

They paid great attention to their hair; it was cut a lock at a time with the aid of two stones, one placed underneath as a chopping-block, the other used as a chopper. A sort of pomatum made of fat and ochre was used as a dressing. Tattooing was not practiced, but a more barbarous kind of decoration, produced by gashing the arm so as to give rise to cicatrices, was not uncommon.

* *Ancient Hunters.* New York: The Macmillan Company.

The Tasmanians had no houses, nor any fixed abode; they wandered perpetually from place to place in search of food, and their only protection from wind and weather, in a climate sometimes bitingly cold, was a rude screen made by fixing up strips of bark against wooden stakes.[1]

Their implements were few and simple, made of wood or stone; their weapons, whether for the chase or war, were of wood. Of these the spear was the most important; it was fashioned out of the shoots of the "ti" tree, which are distinguished for their straightness. To convert one of these into a spear was an operation demanding considerable skill and care: the stick was first warmed over a fire to render it limber, and if not quite straight was corrected by bending with both hands while held firmly between the teeth. Thus the human jaw was the earliest "arrow-straightener." The end was hardened by charring in the fire, and sharpened by scraping with a notched flake of stone. With a similar implement the bark was removed and the surface rendered round and smooth. When finished it was a formidable weapon; a good spear balanced in the hand as nicely as a fishing-rod; it could be hurled for a distance of sixty yards with sufficient force to pass through the body of a man. The aim of the Tasmanian was good up to forty yards. To keep spears in good condition, when not in use, they were tied up against the trunk of a tree, selected for its straightness.

The only other weapon was the club or waddy, about two feet in length, notched or roughened at one end to give a grip, and sometimes knobbed at the other; the shaft was scraped smooth in the same manner as the spear. Its range was over forty yards.

The stone implements, which served a variety of purposes, were made by striking off chips from one flake with another; in this occupation a man would sit absorbed for hours at a time. Flint is not known in Tasmania, and a fine-grained sandstone or "phthanite" served as a substitute; it is not so tractable as flint, however, and this may partly account for the inferior finish of much of the Tasmanian workmanship.

A double interest attaches to the notched stone or "spokeshave," used for scraping the spear. The spear itself is perishable, for wood soon decays, and until quite recently no wooden implements were known to have survived the Palæolithic period; but the stone spokeshave, which implies the spear, and in its smaller forms the arrow, may endure for an indefinite time. Many excellent examples of such implements are known under the name of hollow scrapers or "racloirs en coches," both from Palæolithic and Neolithic deposits.

A large, rough tool, delusively similar to the head of an axe, was made by striking off with a single blow a thick flake from a larger block of stone, and dressing the side opposite the surface of fracture by several blows directed more or less parallel to its length. This is not altogether unlike the ancient Palæolithic implement which the French call a "coup de poing" and the Germans a "Beil" (axe) or "Faust Keil" (fist wedge). In English it has no name, though it was at one time inappropriately spoken of as a celt, a term never used now in this sense. Many anthropologists are of opinion that the Palæolithic "coup de poing" was not provided with a haft, but was held directly in the hand; and that it was not used simply as a "chopper": some support for this view is afforded by the fact that the Tasmanians had no notion of hafting [2] their homologue, or rather analogue, of the "coup de poing," and that it served a variety of purposes, among others as an aid in climbing trees. It was the women who were the great climbers: provided with a grass rope which was looped round the tree and held firmly in the left hand, they would cut a notch with the chipped stone [3] and hitch the great toe into it; then adjusting the rope they would cut another notch as high, it is said, as they could reach; again hitch themselves up, and so on till they attained the requisite height—sometimes as much as 200 feet. In this way they pursued the "opossum" up the smooth

trunk of the gum-tree. Many stories are told of their expert-
ness: on one occasion a party of lively girls chased by sailors
made a sudden and mysterious disappearance; on looking
round a number of laughing faces were descried among the
branches of the trees, into which the girls had swarmed in
the twinkling of an eye.

There is a great inconvenience in having no special name
for the "coup de poing"—greater perhaps than attaches to
the introduction of a new word; I propose, therefore, to
call it a "boucher," thus honoring the memory of Boucher
de Perthes, who was the first to compel the attention of the
scientific world to these relics of the past. This kind of
nomenclature has already been introduced by physicists, as,
for instance, in the terms volt, joule, watt, and others. Its
great recommendation lies in its complete independence of
all hypothesis.[4]

Another implement was an anvil, formed of a plate of
stone chipped all round into a circle, about 7 in. in diameter,
1.5 in. thick in the middle, and 1 in. thick at the edge. On
this the women broke the bones left after a meal to extract
the marrow, using another stone about 6 in. in diameter, as
a hammer. M. Rutot has described several such anvils
(*enclumes*), but of a ruder make, from early Palæolithic
deposits.

One of the commonest tools was the scraper, a flake of
about 2 in. in diameter, carefully dressed by chipping on one
side only to a somewhat blunt edge. The edge was not
serrated, and great skill was required to keep the line of
flaking even: it was used for flaying animals caught in the
chase, and as well, no doubt, for other purposes. To test its
powers Sir Edward Tylor sent a specimen to the slaughter
house requesting the butcher to try his skill in flaying with
it. The notion was rather scornfully received, but on trial
the flake was found to be admirably adapted to the task,
removing the skin without damaging it by accidental cuts.

The country seems to have afforded the Tasmanians a
fair amount of game. Kangaroos, wallaby, opossums, bandi-

coots, the kangaroo rat, and the wombat were all excellent eating, especially as cooked by the natives. The animals were roasted whole in the skin and cut up with stone knives; the ashes of the wood fire were sometimes used as a seasoning in default of salt. Cooking by boiling was unknown to this primitive people, and when introduced by us they expressed their disapproval of it as an inferior method.

They hunted several kinds of birds, such as the emu, now extinct in Tasmania, black swans, mutton birds, and penguins. The eggs of birds were collected by the women and children. Snakes and lizards were put under contribution, as well as grubs extracted from hollow trees, and said by Europeans to be dainty morsels, with a nutty flavor reminiscent of almonds.

Fish the Tasmanians did not eat, simply because they were ignorant of the art of fishing, nets and fishhooks being unknown to them; but cray-fish and shell-fish were an important article of diet. The women obtained the shell-fish by diving, using a wooden chisel, made smooth by scraping with a shell, to displace those, such as the limpets, which live adherent to the rocks.

The shell-fish were roasted; and the empty shells, thrown away near the hearths, grew into enormous mounds or kitchen middens, which still afford interesting material to the anthropologist. Most of the shells found in them belong to genera which are universally eaten by mankind, such as oysters, mussels, cockles, limpets, periwinkles (Turbo and Purpura), and earshells (Haliotis). The periwinkles were broken by a stone hammer on a stone anvil, and these implements, as well as stone knives, are also found in the kitchen middens.

Several kinds of plants furnished the natives with vegetable food—the young roots of ferns, roots of bulrush, the ripe fruit of the kangaroo apple (*Solanum laciniatum*), a fungus with a truffle-like growth, and sea-wrack. These were cooked by broiling.

Water was their usual but not their only drink, for they

well understood the virtues of fermented liquor. A species of gum-tree (*Eucalyptus resinifera*) yields when tapped a slightly sweet juice, resembling treacle; this they allowed to collect in a hole at the bottom of the trunk, where it underwent a natural fermentation and furnished a kind of coarse wine.

Fire was obtained either by the simple plan of rubbing the pointed end of a stick to and fro in a groove cut in another piece of wood, or by the drill method, i.e., by rotating one stick in a hole sunk in another. Each family kindled its own fire at its own hearth, the hearths being separated by intervals of fourteen to twenty yards.[5]

The following statement of Backhouse [6] is of interest in connection with the discovery of marked stones in some European caves. He writes: "One day we noticed a woman arranging stones; they were flat, oval, about two inches wide, and marked in various directions with black and red lines. These we learned represent absent friends ('plenty long way off'), and one larger than the rest a corpulent woman on Flinders Island, known as Mother Brown." This description recalls the painted stones found by E. Piette [7] in the cave of Mas d'Azil, Ariège, on an horizon (Azilian) which marks the conclusion of the Palæolithic age. These also are "flat, oval and about two inches wide," and "they are marked in various directions with red and black lines," or other bands, but on not a few of them more complex characters occur which in a few instances simulate some of the capital letters of the Roman alphabet. The resemblance is indeed so startling that, on the one hand, doubts, certainly illfounded, have been expressed of their genuineness, and on the other, theories have been propounded attributing to them some connection with the Phœnician script. There can be no doubt as to their genuineness. M. Cartailhac [8] has confirmed the original observations of Piette, and M. Boule has found additional examples in another locality; but their meaning remains obscure. M. Hoernes remarks that they offer one of the darkest problems of prehistoric times. I am tempted to think that some light is thrown on this problem by the Tasmanian stones,[9] but here we have to lament one of our many lost opportunities; the Tasmanians have disappeared, and these stones with them; not a single specimen, not even a drawing, is preserved in any of our museums.

It is said that rude attempts were sometimes made to represent natural objects by drawings. Very poor sketches of cattle, kangaroo, and dogs done in charcoal are mentioned; but cattle and dogs suggest the possibility of European influence. The fact that large pieces of bark have been found with rudely marked characters like the gashes the natives cut in their arms is of more importance. These are not unlike some of the marks incised on Palæolithic implements.

The Tasmanians are said to have been unacquainted with boats or canoes, but they possessed a useful substitute, half-float, half-boat, which recalls in a striking manner the "balsa" of California or the rafts made of papyrus or of the leaf stalks of the ambatch tree, which are still to be met with on the Nile and Lake Nyanza. Similar rafts are said to have been used by some Melanesian islanders.

The Tasmanian raft was made of the bark of more than one kind of tree, but usually it would seem some species of Eucalyptus. The bark having been removed was rolled up into something like a colossal cigar, pointed at each end. Three such rolls were required, a larger one to form the bottom and two smaller ones to form the sides of the raft. They were firmly lashed together, side by side; a tough coarse grass serving for cord. The completed raft was not unlike in general form a shallow boat, being broadest in the middle and tapering away to a pointed extremity at each end. It was of considerable size, attaining sometimes a length of between 9 and 10 ft., with a breadth of about 3 ft., a height of $1\frac{1}{4}$ ft., and a depth inside of 8 to 9 ins. It would carry comfortably three or four persons, and at a pinch as many as five or six. In shallow water it was punted with poles, and the same poles, devoid of any blade-like expansion

at the end, were used as paddles on the open sea. Nevertheless the Tasmanians were able to make their rafts travel at
a fair pace through the water—"as fast as an ordinary English whale-boat"; it must have been hard work, and they
seem to have thought so: "after every stroke they uttered a
deep 'ugh' like a London pavior." A fire, carried on a hearth
of earth or ashes, was kept burning at one end of the raft.

How far the Tasmanians ventured out to sea in these
frail craft is unknown; they certainly visited Maatsuyker
island, "which lies three miles from the mainland in the
stormy waters of the South Sea," and they were observed
to make frequent crossings to Maria Island off the east
coast during calm weather. The rafts have been known to
live in very rough seas, and an old whaler asserted that he
had seen one of them go across to Witch Island, near Port
Davey, in the midst of a storm. The natives on the north
coast of Tasmania are said not to have made use of rafts.[10]

The "balsa" of the Seri Indians in Sonora (California)
closely resembles the Tasmanian raft, differing mainly in
the substitution of bundles of reeds for rolls of bark; but it
attained a much greater size, being sometimes as much as
30 ft. in length.[11] With only one passenger aboard it rose
too high out of the water, "rode better with two, carried
three without difficulty, even in a fairly heavy sea, and would
safely bear four adults . . . in moderate water." European
observers who have seen this craft afloat have admired "its
graceful movements and its perfect adaptation to variable
seas and loads," curving "to fit the weight . . . and to meet
the impact of swells and breakers."

The Seri Indians are in the habit of crossing in their
balsas from the mainland to the outlying island, and occasionally even complete the passage across the gulf to the
opposite shore of Lower California.[12]

The facts we have thus briefly summarized include almost
all that I can discover bearing directly on our subject. For
the sake of completeness it may be as well to give some

account of the bodily characters of this interesting people, and a few words as to their history.

The Tasmanians were of medium stature, the average height of the men being 1,661 mm., with a range of from 1,584 to 1,732 mm. the average height of the women was 1,503 mm., with a range of from 1,295 to 1,630 mm. The color of the skin was almost black, inclining to brown. The eyes were small and deep-set beneath strong overhanging brows; the nose short and broad, with widely distended nostrils; the mouth big; and the teeth large, disproportionately large indeed for the size of the jaw.

The hair was black and grew in close corkscrew ringlets. The men had hair on their faces—whiskers, mustache, and beard—and on the borders of the whiskers it assumed the form of tufted pellets like pepper-corns.

It is a commonplace amongst biologists that characters of apparently the most trivial significance are precisely those which are of the greatest value as a means to classification, and it is on the degree of curliness or twist in the hair that the most fundamental subdivision of the human race is based. We thus recognize three groups; one in which the hair is without any twist—that is, perfectly straight—the Lissotrichi; another in which it is twisted to an extreme, as in the Negro or Bushman—the Ulotrichi; and a third in which the hair is only twisted enough to be wavy, as in many Europeans—the Cymotrichi. The Tasmanian is ulotrichous, like the Negro and most other races with very dark skins.

The bony framework, being more resistant to decay than the rest of the body, is more likely to be preserved in the fossil state, and has therefore a certain amount of importance in our study. We shall restrict our description, however, to the skull, as more is to be learnt from this than from any other portion of the skeleton.

The skull of the Tasmanian is of a characteristic form, so that a practiced eye can readily distinguish it from that of other races. Looked upon directly from above its outline is oval or more or less pentagonal; its greatest breadth lies considerably behind the middle line. The crown rises into a low keel, bordered by a groove-like depression on each side; the sides of the skull are wall-like, but swell out into large parietal bosses.

It is long (dolichocephalic), and the ratio of its breadth to its length (cephalic index) is 74.9, as determined from measurement of eighty-six examples.[13] Its height is about 5 mm. less than its breadth; the Tasmanians may therefore be called flat-headed (platycephalic). The cranial capacity is the lowest yet met with among recent races, measuring on the average 1,199 c.c., or, in round numbers, 1,200 c.c.; in the men the average rises to 1,306 c.c., in the women it falls to 1,093 c.c.[14]

The face is remarkably short, and presents a peculiarly brutal appearance; the brow-ridges and glabella are strongly marked, and there is a deep notch at the root of the nose. The jaws project, but not to the extreme degree which is characteristic of the Negro, nor even so much as in some Australians. The lower jaw is small, disproportionately so when compared with the teeth, which, as already observed, are comparatively large. In consequence of this misfit the natives suffered grievously from abnormalities of dentition.

In endeavoring to discover the people to whom the Tasmanians were most closely related, we shall naturally restrict our inquiries to the Ulotrichi, for, as we have seen, the Tasmanians belonged to this group. Huxley thought they showed some resemblance to the inhabitants of New Caledonia and the Andaman Islands, but Flower was disposed to bring them into closer connection with the Papuans or Melanesians. The leading anthropologists in France do not accept either of these views. Topinard states that there is no close alliance between the New Caledonians and the Tasmanians, while Quatrefages and Hamy remark that "from whatever point of view we look at it, the Tasmanian race presents special characters, so that it is quite impossible to discover any well-defined affinities with any other existing race," and this probably represents the prevailing opinion of the present day.[15]

The Tasmanians appear to have been an autochthonous people, native to the soil, the surviving descendants of a primitive race, elsewhere extinct or merged into a preponderant alien population. Frequenting the coast, and yet destitute of sea-going craft capable of making long voyages it is scarcely likely that they reached Tasmania from any of the remote Pacific islands; and it is far more probable, as our foremost authorities now maintain, that they crossed over from Australia.

The primitive ancestors of the race may have been widely distributed over the Old World: displaced almost everywhere by superior races, they at length became confined to Australia and Tasmania, and from Australia they were finally driven and partly perhaps absorbed or exterminated by the existing aborigines of that continent, who were prevented from following them into Tasmania, because by that time Bass Strait was wide enough to offer an insuperable barrier to their advance.

A notion exists that the natives entered Australia and Tasmania by dry land, at a time antecedent to the formation of Torres Strait and Bass Strait, but the well-known distinction between the Australian and Oriental faunas present some difficulty to this view. It would appear that man must have possessed some special means by which he could enter Australia unaccompanied by other animals. The rafts of the Tasmanians thus acquire an unexpected importance; they were capable, as we have seen, of making voyages across channels at least three miles in width. It is true that much wider channels than this now break up the road from New Guinea to Tasmania; but there seems to have been a time, probably geologically recent, when these channels did not exist and the Australian cordillera stretched as a continuous mountain chain from the one great island to the other. It was only by repeated subsidence that it became broken down, in the region of Torres Strait on the north and Bass Strait on the south. Subsidence has also probably enlarged the seas between the islands of the East Indies. Thus at some past epoch the channels which afterwards confined the Australians and the Tasmanians to their respective lands may have been sufficiently narrow to have been crossed by rafts and yet wide enough to have barred the way to the rest of the Oriental fauna.

When the more civilized nations of the north had succeeded in subjugating the sea to their enterprise, even the ocean itself failed in its protection to the unfortunate Tasmanians, and with the arrival of English colonists their doom was sealed. Only in rare instances can a race of hunters contrive to coexist with an agricultural people. When the hunting ground of a tribe is restricted, owing to its partial occupation by the new arrivals, the tribe affected is compelled to infringe on the boundaries of its neighbors: this is to break the most sacred "law of the Jungle," and inevitably leads to war: the pressure on one boundary is propagated to the next, the ancient state of equilibrium is profoundly disturbed, and intertribal feuds become increasingly frequent. A bitter feeling is naturally aroused against the original offenders, the alien colonists: misunderstandings of all kinds inevitably arise, leading too often to bloodshed, and ending in a general conflict between natives and colonists, in which the former, already weakened by disagreements among themselves, must soon succumb. So it was in Tasmania.

The estimates which have been given of the number of the population at the time Europeans first became acquainted with the country differ widely: the highest is 20,000, but this is probably far in excess of the truth. After the war of 1825 to 1831 there remained scarcely 200. These wretched survivors were gathered together into a settlement, and from 1834 onwards every effort was made for their welfare but "the white man's civilization proved scarcely less fatal than the white man's bullet," and in 1877, with the death of Truganini, the last survivor, the race became extinct.

It is a sad story, and we can only hope that the replacement of a people with a cranial capacity of only about 1,200 c.c. by one with a capacity nearly one-third greater may prove ultimately of advantage in the evolution of mankind.

The world certainly needs all the brains it can get: at the same time it is not very flattering to our own power of intelligence to find that we allowed this supremely interesting people, the last representatives of one of the earliest stages of human culture, to perish, without having made any serious effort to ascertain all that could be known about it. What we do know is very little indeed: a book of about three hundred pages contains almost every scrap of trustworthy information.[16]

If any other nation than our own had shown the same disregard for a human document of such priceless value, we should be very outspoken in our censure. Even now, in this twentieth century, it cannot be said that the British Government takes such an intelligent interest in the numerous primitive peoples which it has taken into its charge as we have a right to expect, at least from a state having any regard for the advancement of learning.

The first to call attention to the resemblance between the stone implements of the Tasmanians and those of Palæolithic man was Sir Edward Tylor.[17] Subsequently Mr. R. M. Johnston[18] compared them with the "eoliths" figured by Ribiero already alluded to. Sir Edward Tylor[19] has repeatedly returned to the subject; and in 1905 when he exhibited specimens before the Archæological Institute, he made the following statement: "I am now able to select and exhibit to the Institute from among the flint implements and flakes from the cave of Le Moustier, in Dordogne, specimens corresponding in make with such curious exactness to those of the Tasmanian natives, that were it not for the different stone they are chipped from, it would be hardly possible to distinguish them."[20]

Subsequently Sir Edward Tylor was led to believe that an even closer resemblance could be traced between the so-called plateau implements and the Tasmanian. A similar view has also commended itself to M. Rutot and Dr. H. Klaatsch.[21] If this could be established it would invest the Tasmanian implements with peculiar interest.

The plateau "implements" are so called because they are found in gravels capping the high plateaux of Kent and elsewhere. They were first discovered by Mr. B. Harrison, of Ightham, who brought them before the notice of Sir Joseph Prestwich; and this observer, famous for the caution and sagacity of his judgment, expressed in unqualified terms his conviction that they showed signs of the handiwork of man.[22] Sir John Evans, a fellow-worker with Prestwich, and equally distinguished for his acumen, and insight, was unable, however, to share this opinion, and the question is still involved in controversy.

The plateau gravels are no doubt very ancient. Prestwich spoke of them as glacial or pre-glacial; M. Rutot assigns them to the Pliocene.

The problem presented by the supposed implements is no doubt a difficult one. Some of the Tasmanian forms are so rude and uncouth that, taken alone, we might have little reason to suspect that they had been chipped by man; a great number, on the other hand, show signs of very skillful working, and leave us in no doubt. It is on these last that our judgment should be based in a study of the Tasmanian art. As to the rest, "noscitur a sociis." They are distinguished by two very definite characters. In the first place their fundamental form is that of a flake which has been split off from a larger fragment. They never commence their existence as fragments already existing in a natural state. And next, the finer dressing of the stone is always confined to one face; if a boucher, there is one face obtained by a single blow which detached it from the parent mass, and an opposite face with secondary flaking; if a scraper, the marginal dressing is produced by the removal of chips always struck off in the same direction, and in a manner not greatly differing from that of characteristic Mousterian scrapers.

If we judge the Tasmanian implements by the best

examples, we should in fairness extend the same treatment to the plateau "implements." Some of the best of these show some superficial resemblance to the Tasmanian, but only in general form: this is particularly true of the hollow scrapers. In connection with these we may cite the following statement made by Prestwich when speaking of the plateau implements. He says: "A very common form is a scraper in the shape of a crook, sometimes single, sometimes double, such as might have been used *for scraping round surfaces like bones or sticks.*" The part we have placed in italics shows remarkable insight, but unfortunately these supposed scrapers will not scrape and, if artefacts, had presumably some other function.

Again, the comparison is scarcely sustained when we enter into a minute investigation. To begin with, the fundamental form of the plateau "implement" is rarely—so far as I know, never—artificial. On the hypothesis that these fragments were used by man, we must suppose that, to begin with, he simply selected such bits of flints, lying scattered about, as he thought would serve his ends, and then merely improved their existing edges by additional chipping. This supposed chipping, though often confined to one side of the fragment, has not the closeness or regularity that distinguishes Tasmanian scrapers. The confused and clumsy chipping of the plateau "hollow-scraper" does not produce an efficient edge, and it seems hard to believe that a being with sufficient intelligence to conceive the idea of a spokeshave should not have succeeded in making a better one.[23]

Mr. Henry Balfour, one of the first to study Tasmanian implements and to recognize their Palæolithic affinities, regards them as representing a separate industry. While agreeing with Mr. Balfour on the existence of special features characteristic of the Tasmanian implements—possibly due to the peculiar character of the stone [24] from which they were made—I am still inclined to think that Sir Edward Tylor made a closer approach to the truth in his earlier than in his later comparisons. Some resemblance to Mousterian implements may indeed be recognized, but scarcely any to the problematical flints of the Kent plateau. This is also the opinion of Professor Paul Sarasin [25] and of the Abbé Breuil, who considers that the Tasmanian implements find their closest alliance with the quartzite implements of Mousterian age which occur in the north of Spain.

The Tasmanians may therefore be regarded with great probability as representing an ancient race, which, cut off from free communication with the surrounding world, had preserved almost unchanged the habits and industrial arts which existed in Europe during the later days of the Lower Mousterian age.

Though in its bodily characters this race differed considerably from the Mousterian Europeans—they are of different species—yet it retained so much that is primitive and was at the same time so pure or homogeneous that we may fairly include it among those interesting relics known to biologists as surviving archaic types. Our knowledge of the Tasmanians is but small, yet the little we possess is of fundamental importance, providing analogies for our guidance in the study of Palæolithic man.

NOTES

[1] There is reason to suppose that they sometimes made use of cave shelters. See H. Ling Roth, "Cave Shelters and the Aborigines of Tasmania," *Nature*, 1899, lx, p. 545. Backhouse states that on the west coast they made huts for their winter quarters. The construction of these was simple and ingenious. A circular space was cleared in a thicket of young and slender Ti trees and the tops of the encircling bushes (? trees) were drawn together and thatched with leaves and grass (James Backhouse, *Narrative of a Visit to the Australian Colonies*, 1843, p. 104).

[2] R. M. Johnston (*Systematic Account of the Geology of Tasmania*, 1888, p. 334) asserts that a heavy stone used as a tomahawk was provided with a handle: "being fastened to it in the same way as a blacksmith fastens a rod to a chisel, and afterwards well secured by the sinews of some animal." This is denied by those best acquainted with the Tasmanians.

[3] Sir Edward Tylor describes this as a quoit-like stone, 4 to 6 in. across, and chipped about two-thirds round the edge (*Journ. Anthr. Inst.*, 1893, xxiii, p. 142).

[4] The name "hand-axe," which has been suggested, is a question-begging term, involving two assumptions, each of which is open to discussion.

Boucher de Perthes thought that some were hafted and some not (B. de
Perthes, *Antiquites celtiques et antediluviennes*, ii, 1857, p. 171; iii, 1864,.
p. 74). G. de Mortillet (*Le Prehistorique*, 1885, p. 142), that none were
hafted, and D'Acy (*Bull. Soc. d'Anthr.*, 1887), that all were hafted. There
is much to be said for D'Acy's view, and respect for the opinion of those
that agree with him leads me to think that an indifferent name has its
advantages. M. Commont does not admit that these implements, "denomme
improprement coup de poing," were axes at all, whether hafted or not.

⁵ That the Tasmanians were acquainted with the fire-drill is open to
doubt.—H. Ling Roth, "Tasmanian Firesticks," *Nature*, 1899, lix, p. 696,
and *The Aborigines of Tasmania*, Halifax, 1899.

⁶ James Backhouse, *op. cit.*, p. 104.

⁷ E. Piette, "Les Galets colories du Mas d'Azil," *L'Anthr.*, 1895, vi,
p. 276, and 1897, vii, p. 385.

⁸ E. Cartailhac, *L'Anthr.*, 1891, ii, p. 147.

⁹ "Palæolithic Races," *Science Progress*, 1909, p. 504. M. Salomon Reinach has since made a similar suggestion, *L'Anthr.*, 1909, xx, p. 605. Mr.
A. B. Cook has compared the painted pebbles of Mas d'Azil with the
Australian "churinga," *L'Anthr.*, 1905, xiv, p. 655, and Prof. F. Sarasin has
expressed his approval of this view, "Des Galets colories de la Grotte
de Birseck pres Bale," C. R. de la XIVe Session, *Congres International*
d'Anthropologie, Geneva, 1912, p. 569. The Tasmanian stones may also
have been "churinga," but this is very doubtful and difficult to reconcile
with the fact that in Australia such objects are "taboo" to the women.

¹⁰ H. Ling Roth, *The Aborigines of Tasmania*, Halifax, England, 1899.

¹¹ A similar craft, but provided with sails, is used in Peru. Mr. H. Balfour informs me that balsas are used all along the West Coast of America.

¹² W. J. McGee, *The Seri Indians*, pp. 215-221.

¹³ R. J. A. Berry, A. W. D. Robertson, and K. S. Cross, "A Biometrical
Study of the Tasmanian, Australian and Papuan," *Proc. Roy. Soc. Edin.*,
1910, xxxi, pp. 30-31. The mean length obtained is 180.30 ± 0.51, and
the mean breadth 135.14 ± 0.35 mm.

¹⁴ In computing these numbers I made use of all the observations
accessible up to 1910. Sir W. Turner obtains a mean capacity of between
1,200 and 1,300 c.c. for Tasmanian men. "The Aborigines of Tasmania,"
pt. 2, *Trans. Roy. Soc. Edin.*, 1910, xlvii, p. 451.

¹⁵ Sir W. Turner, "The Aborigines of Tasmania," *Trans. Roy. Soc.*
Edin., 1908, xlvi, pt. 2, p. 365, in particular pp. 385-394; 1910, xlvii, pt.
3, p. 411. See also R. J. A. Berry, A. W. D. Robertson, and K. S. Cross,
"A Biometrical Study of the Relative Degree of Purity of Race of the
Tasmanian, Australian and Papuan," *Proc. Roy. Soc. Edin.*, 1910, xxxi,
pp. 17-40. R. J. A. Berry and A. W. D. Robertson, "The Place in Nature
of the Tasmanian Aborigine," pp. 41-69; and H. Basedow, "Der Tasmanier Schadel ein Insulartypus," *Zeits. f. Ethn.*, 1910, xlii, pp. 175-227.
A different view is held by H. von Luschan, "Zur Stellung der Tasmanier,
ein anthropologie die System," *Zeits. f. Ethn.*, 1910, xlii, p. 287.

¹⁶ H. Ling Roth, *The Aborigines of Tasmania*, Halifax, England, 1899.

¹⁷ E. B. Tylor, *The Early History of Mankind*, London, 1865, p. 195.

¹⁸ R. M. Johnston, *Systematic Account of the Geology of Tasmania*, 1888,.
p. 334.

¹⁹ E. B. Tylor, in Preface to H. Ling Roth,. *The Aborigines of Tasmania*,

1st ed., 1890; 2nd ed., 1899. "On the Tasmanians as Representatives of Palæolithic Man," *Journ. Anthr. Inst.*, 1893, xxiii, pp. 141-152, 2 pls. "On the Survival of Palæolithic Conditions in Australia and Tasmania," *Journ. Anthr. Inst.*, 1898, xxviii, p. 199. "On Stone Implements from Tasmania," *Journ. Anthr. Inst.*, 1900, xxx, p. 257.

[20] *Journ. Anthr. Inst.*, 1895, xxiv, p. 336.

[21] A. Rutot, "La Fin de la Question des Eolithes," *Bull. Soc. Geol. Belg.*, 1907, xxi, p. 211; H. Klaatsch, *Zeits. f. Ethn.*, 1907.

[22] J. Prestwich, *Quart. Journ. Geol. Soc.*, 1889, xlv, pp. 270-294, pls.; 1890, xlvi, p. 166; 1891, xlvii, pp. 126-160, pls.; *Journ. Anthr. Inst.*, 1889, xxi, pp. 246-270, pl.; see also W. J. Lewis Abbott, *Nat. Sci.*, 1894, iv, pp. 256-266, and T. Rupert Jones, *Nat. Sci.*, 1894, v, pp. 269-275.

[23] Through the kindness of Mr. Harrison I have now examined a large number of his best specimens: several of them have a remarkably artificial look and may possibly have been shaped by man.

[24] It has a marked tendency to split in one direction.

[25] P. Sarasin, *Vh. d. Nf. Ges. Basel*, Bd. xxiii, and *Zeits. f. Ethn.*, Bd. xl, 1908, p. 248.

THE ART OF THE REINDEER EPOCH *

By JOSEPH DECHELETTE

§ I. HISTORY OF THE DISCOVERIES.

MOVABLE objects carved of stone, ivory, bone, and horn by Magdalenian artists had been known for a number of years when unexpected discoveries brought to light new revelations concerning the art of the primitive reindeer hunters. In some of the deep caves at the entrance of which these primitive men had installed their hearths, there were discovered drawings, often very numerous, of animals and several faces carved or painted upon walls and ceilings. The question arose at once as to whether these unusual designs were contemporary to the quaternary inhabitants of the caves. A Spaniard, Don Marcelino de Sautuola, the first to call the attention of investigators to these discoveries, did not hesitate to affirm this hypothesis, without, however, succeeding in dissipating the doubts which the novelty and strangeness of his discoveries had rightly evoked. In 1880, he published a summary description of the paintings of animals which he had recognized the year before on the ceiling of the cave of Altamira (township of Santillana del Mar, province of Santander). An engineer, M. Edouard Harlé, however, after studying these paintings, denied their antiquity. Later, even though Vilanova Y Piera, professor of paleontology in Madrid, took the same position as did his compatriot, and maintained firmly that these paintings were contemporary to the fireplaces of the later quaternary age, numerous circumstances seemed to favor the incredulity of the others. How could one explain the remark-

---

* Chapter x of part i of volume i of *Manuel d'archéologie Préhistorique, Celtique et Gallo-romaine.* Published by Libraire Alphonse Picard et Fils. Paris. The material here reproduced was translated by Frida Ilmer.

95

ably fine state of preservation of these frescoes, supposed to be many thousands of years old, if the walls were constantly moist and in places even covered by stalagmitic formations? Besides, what could be the meaning of these animal figures occupying completely obscure points of the cave that were, moreover, difficult of access? Objections were also raised against the complete absence of any trace of smoke on the walls. This circumstance seemed to exclude the hypothesis of a prolonged habitat in these dark subterranean passages. Nonetheless, certain of the facts which M. Harlé himself had observed were irreconcilable with the supposition that these designs had been faked and also made it difficult to attribute a recent date to them. Several figures were covered by a stalagmitic layer. Furthermore, the entrance to the grotto had remained obstructed and unknown until 1868. It was therefore impossible to consider all of these designs as recent works, without encountering serious difficulties.

Nevertheless, MM. de Sautuola and Vilanova did not succeed in dissipating the doubts, and the discoveries at Altamira fell into oblivion until, in 1895, M. Emile Rivière, the successful explorer of the grottoes of Mentone, in his turn, came across designs engraved upon the walls of the grotto de la Mouthe, in the commune of Tayac (Dordogne). Prior to M. Rivière's excavations paleolithic and neolithic deposits had completely obstructed the entrance to this cave. A bit of clay of unknown date revealed certain lines of the lower part of designs, whose authenticity was by no means incontestable. In the grotto of Pair-non-Pair, township of Marcamps (Gironde), M. Daleau had begun excavations in 1883. In 1897, stimulated by the discoveries of La Mouthe, he published the valuable wall paintings of that grotto, which he had known for several years previous. There the designs were completely uncovered. The last doubts were thus dissipated and, since then, the attention of archeologists has been focussed upon the walls of the caves. They ceased denying the authenticity and importance of the discoveries of Sautuola. Finally the engravings of the grotto of Charbot, at Aiguèze (Gard) announced by M. Chiron, instructor since 1889, could be classed as belonging to the quaternary and not to a later, and relatively recent period, as had at first been supposed.

§ IV. ROCK ENGRAVINGS AND PAINTINGS OF AUSTRALIA AND CALIFORNIA, AND INSCRIBED STONES OF NORTH AFRICA.

Building upon erroneous information, investigators generally held modern primitives to be incapable of producing any works of painting and sculpture other than timid and malformed essays. The earliest accounts of travelers who described the designs found on rocks in Australia met with the same incredulous audience which later rejected M. de Sautuola's reports concerning the paintings in the caves of Altamira. About 1840, George Grey had discovered in the northwest of the Australian continent several caves adorned with colored designs.[1] It was contested at first whether these finds really represented the work of natives. But the observations multiplied and it appeared that the designs on rocks, sculptured bas-reliefs, and paintings were, to the contrary, very frequently to be met with in the North of Australia. Stokes has published some reproductions of them.[2] Since then, scientists have been busy classifying and interpreting these interesting data which, as we shall see, bear an interesting relationship to primitive totem cults. It was by a fortunate coincidence that, at the precise moment when sociology turned its attention to the written documents of these uncivilized regions, prehistoric archeology rediscovered the ornamented grottoes of Perigourdia and the Pyrenees. The comparative study of these two groups of documents throws their close analogy into strong relief. From time to time there were discovered new and strange images of hands, reproduced in series upon the walls of caves or (in one part of Australia) upon huge rocks. They not only bore a great resemblance to each other, but also appeared to be executed by the same processes. Occasionally a realistic

art was found, often advanced enough to reproduce faithfully both form and movement, and bringing preferably
drawings of animals—although with modern savages scenes
of hunting and of combat with human beings or of human
beings either alone or in company of animals are by no
means absent. In the Clacks (northwest coast of Australia)
there is a rock bearing upon a background of red ochre more
than 150 figures painted in white: sharks, turtles, sea stars,
clubs, canoes, kangaroos, dogs, etc. On the island of Cape
York, among numerous paintings applied upon a background of red ochre, there was found upon the wall of a
rock, the image of a man covered with yellow patches that
were reminiscent of the spotted animals found at Mar-
soulas and Altamira.[3] Among the most curious paintings
of Australia are those published by M. Mathews. They
represent hands, tools, human beings, and animals painted
in different colors upon rocks forming a natural shelter.
Thus an excavation at the township of Coolcalwin in Philip
County, yielded 64 hands painted in red, clearly visible,
as well as more or less distinct traces of a number of others.
One large rock of sandstone alone, found in the township
of Coonbaralbe in Hunter County, bears 38 drawings of
hands executed in white, red, or yellow.[4] As was the case
with certain designs of the quaternary period, the arms of
these drawings are always depicted to the elbows. Other
English travelers discovered in the island of Chasm (Gulf
of Carpentaria) a grotto ornamented with designs painted
in red and black and representing kangaroos, turtles, *one
hand,* a kangaroo followed by 32 men, one of whom is
holding a kind of sword.[5]

   The rock engravings of lower California, as well as those
of the Australian continent, point to the same conclusions.
One of their discoverers, M. Léon Diguet, found drawings
of hands, of suns, of various symbols, of animals, etc.,
painted in red upon large bowlders. Drawings of human
figures pierced by spears, which were found in the grotto
of San Borgita, are reminiscent of the buffaloes pierced by

harpoons, found in the cave of Niaux. A profound study of these relics would, no doubt, enable us to note other points of comparison. However, attention must be called to the fact that the paintings in the Californian grottoes generally occupy an open place near the entrance to the cave.[6]

Various explorers have discovered petroglyphs, both engraved and painted, in other sections of North America,[7] employing similar motifs. And these examples can easily be multiplied.

Similarly, stone engravings, some of which resemble our wall paintings, have been discovered in Northern Africa, particularly in South Orange. Their discovery dates back as far as 1847,[8] but they owe the publicity which they received chiefly to Flammand.[9] These objects, designated as "Inscribed Stones," *Hadjrat mektoubat,* by the Arabs, appear to differ from each other at various periods. M. Flammand distinguishes between prehistoric and Libyco-Berberian stone engravings. The former, which are carved more deeply, chiefly represent the elephant, the rhinoceros, and the big-horned buffalo (*bubalus antiquus*), in other words, animals that are to-day extinct in the Sahara. Upon Libyco-Berberian stone carvings, which are executed by means of simple pointillage, there appear alphabetic inscriptions and animals still to be found in those regions. . . . Although the date at which the *bubalus antiquus* disappeared is uncertain, his fossil remains have been found in the upper deposits of the recent quaternary on the high plateaux of Algiers.[10] At Keragda (district of Geryville) a human figure, holding a neolithic hatchet with a handle, was found. This figure is placed among these rock designs where, among other things, polished hatchets, arrows, javelins, and shields [11] were found.

§ V. TOTEMISM AND MAGIC.

The resemblance which exists between the wall paintings of Australia and of North America and those of Gaul of

the quaternary period is one of the most striking illustrations of the lessons which prehistoric archeology may draw
from a judicious study of ethnography. Since modern sociology has shed light upon the origin and true character
of the first artistic attempts of primitives, we can now recognize without difficulty that all of these drawings may be
explained in one and the same manner, that is, as belonging to a group of primitive beliefs, known to scientists as
"totemism."

The word, *totem*, signifying "sign," "marking," "family,"
was borrowed from the North American Indians. The concepts, however, which are attached to this term are singularly universal, as has been attested by many observers. In
Australia as well as in America, the clans believe that they
are under the protection of a guardian being, ordinarily an
animal, which they must persuade by means of favors to
shield the interests of the clan. This totem animal becomes
in the course of time the object of a constant cult, in which
may be found the roots to a large number of the ancestral
superstitions of primitives, and even of civilized peoples.
The clan affix the image of their totem upon their weapons
of offense and defense. Multiplication of the tribe can also
be obtained from the totem animal through the intervention
of magic. Spencer, Gillen, and Frazer have described
the curious ceremonies which the Australians perform toward that end, at the foot of cliffs, ornamented with zoömorphic designs. Many details of these magic rites recall some
of the observations made in the grottoes of Perigourdia and
the Pyrenees. Salomon Reinach, who is equally well versed
in the literature of the totem as in the science of prehistory,
was the first to disclose very remarkable facts that have
direct bearing upon this question.[12]

As we have seen, the paintings of our caves are usually
remote from the entrance. At Niaux the visitor must pass
through a subterranean gallery, 800 meters long, in order
to find them. At Combarelles, the first figures are at least
120 meters from the entrance. Furthermore, Spencer and

Gillen state that in a great number of cases the Australian paintings which they have considered to be of
totemistic origin "are traced upon rocky walls in localities
that are strictly *taboo* to women, children, and uninitiated
youths." [13] Certain designs found in our ornamented
grottoes also occupy hidden recesses in the walls and inaccessible, bulging surfaces which it must have cost the artist
great difficulty to reach. It would, therefore, be impossible to
view these designs, which are so well hidden from the sight
of the uninitiated, as mere ornamental decorations or as
the products of a pastime occupation of idle Troglodytes.

The devotees of the cult of the emou in Australia paint
the image of this totem upon the earth, to the accompaniment of intricate rites. Around it the men of the clan dance
and sing. Now, in the Pyrenean grotto of Niaux, MM.
Cartailhac and Breuil discovered animal designs not only
upon the walls, but to their great surprise, also upon the
clayey ground of the gallery. Various symbols, painted or
scratched upon the figures, conform to these findings. The
tectiform sign of the hut is the symbol of ownership affixed
by the hunter upon the animal which he should bring back
with him to the camp; but its success is assured by special
rites. The magic value of arrow-heads is emphasized even
better. "The clan lived on meat," wrote S. Reinach. "In re-
producing the likeness of the animals which furnished their
food, they believed they increase their number and stimulate their multiplication, just as the Australian savages believe they stimulate the multiplication of the kangaroos
by performing the dance of the kangaroo. The practice of
bewitching a living person by inflicting injury or destruction upon his image with the intent of harming the living
is a phenomenon of the same kind, only inspired by an opposite sentiment. The notion that art is a form of play is
perhaps nothing but a modern prejudice; art began as a
ritual or act of magic. And when we speak to-day of the
'magic of art,' we do not know how truly right we are." [14]

The same author has also called attention to the fact that

the most useful animals are found most abundantly depicted in these wall paintings and the recent discovery of rare images of carnivorous animals has in no way weakened the value of his observation.

It would doubtless be stretching the facts too far to attempt to attribute a religious or symbolic significance to every quaternary design. The various instincts of human nature, as well as the love of ornamentation, have, most likely, rivaled religious beliefs in stimulating art among primitives. It must be recognized, however, that the totemistic interpretation, based upon solidly established facts, explains better than any other hypothesis the origin of the art of the reindeer epoch. Furthermore, it accounts also for its sudden disappearance, which is no less surprising than its brilliant flourish, since the primitive concepts from which these paintings have sprung have been at home among the hunting nomads. During the neolithic period the totemistic superstitions no longer exercised the same hold upon the inhabitants of Gaul, henceforth tillers of the soil and shepherds, and it never again gave rise to the same plastic arts.[15]

If we turn our attention again to the engravings and sculptures carried out upon small objects of durable material, recalling at the same time the resemblance of their numerous animal drawings to the wall paintings, it will appear logical to assume that one part at least of these objects owes its origin to concepts of the same nature. The toothed arrowheads which the bisons of the grotto of Niaux bear on their flanks explain to us the similar arrow-heads engraved upon the prairie dogs of Sorde, and the interpretation of the batons as magic wands seems to us more acceptable than any other conjecture.

The progress of science has gravely undermined the ancient theory of prehistorians, who, in accordance with the doctrine of G. de Mortillet, refused to concede any religious concept to quaternary man. For, as we have seen, the reindeer hunters did have their sanctuaries and the discovery of these mysterious galleries, revealing the vast distribution, if not the universality, of certain beliefs of primitive man, will count among the greatest prehistoric discoveries.

NOTES

1 George Grey, *Journals of Two Expeditions of Discovery in the North-West and Western Australia,* 1841, i, p. 203; cf. Grosse, *Débuts de Clack,* 1902, p. 128.

2 Stokes, *Discoveries in Australia.*

3 Cf. Grosse, *ibid.,* p. 131.

4 R. H. Mathews, *Gravures et paintures sur rochers* (Rock engravings and paintings), BSA, 1898, p. 429; also *Journal of the Anthropological Institute,* London, xxv, p. 147.

5 Grosse, *ibid.,* p. 131.

6 Léon Diguet, *Note sur la pictographie de la Basse-California, Anthropologie,* 1895, p. 160.

7 Cf. the recent work of M. Dellenbaugh, *The North Americans of Yesterday,* 1901, pp. 42-43, in which petroglyphs depicting hands, feet, animals, etc., are reproduced. One quadruped unearthed in Brown's Cave, Wisconsin, bears a tectiform sign engraved upon its flanks (p. 41).

8 This discovery was made by Captain Koch and Dr. Jacquot who accompanied Cavaignac on his South Orangian expeditions (*L'Illustration,* July 3, 1847). Since that date many explorers have followed in their tracks (cf. Hamy, R. E., March-April 1882, and Flammand, *Anthropologie,* 1892, p. 145).

9 Flammand, *Notes sur les status nouvelles de pierres écrites du Sud-Oranais, Anthropologie,* 1892, p. 145; *ibid., Anthropologie,* 1897, p. 284; *ibid., Les pierre écrites (Hadjrat mektoubat) du nord de L'Afrique et specialement de la region d'In-Salah,* CIA, Paris, 1900, p. 265; *ibid., R. C. Acad. Inscr.,* July 12, 1899, p. 437, and *Bull. Soc. Anthrop.,* Lyon, 1901, p. 181; cf. also a summary by Capitan, REA, 1902, p. 168.

10 Flammand, *Atlas,* Paris, 1900, i, p. 211.

11 Flammand, *ibid.,* p. 210.

12 "L'Art et la Magie," *Anthropologie,* 1903, p. 257. This article has been employed in the account quoted in the following note.

13 S. Reinach, *Cultes, mythes, et religions,* vol. i, p. 131, Paris, 1905. Cf. in this important collection of 35 memoirs and articles a synthetic description of the general phenomena of animal totemism (*Phenomènes généraux du totémisme animal*), pp. 9-29. Our readers may refer to this work for sources.

14 Salomon Reinach, *Chronique des arts,* Feb. 7, 1903

15 The date of certain paintings, traces of which have been discovered upon the walls of Portuguese dolmens (*Leite de Vascoucelles,* HP, 1907, p. 33), cannot be easily established. It is difficult to align them with the works of the quaternary age.

THE PEKING MAN *

By J. H. McGREGOR

NEW discoveries of prehistoric man always have popular news interest. Reports of them are often distorted or exaggerated, but occasionally they are based upon finds of importance and permanent scientific value. The latest case, the discovery last December [1929] of an ancient human skull near Peking, has been widely heralded as marking a notable advance in our knowledge of early humanity. When Professor G. Elliot Smith of London acclaims this fossil as "certainly the most illuminating fragment of early man ever found," it may be assumed that it is something more than merely "another prehistoric skull," even though it should fall short of meriting this superlative characterization.

I shall attempt here to present briefly the more notable features of this discovery with a minimum of technical detail, to evaluate it in relation to present knowledge, and to answer some of the questions people are asking about it.

Some two years ago Dr. Davidson Black, professor of anatomy in the Peking Union Medical College, had the temerity, or the foresight, to establish a new genus and species of early man upon the meager basis of a lower molar tooth, found in 1927 in a cave deposit of the early Pleistocene age, at Chou Kou Tien, thirty-seven miles southwest of Peking. He called it *Sinanthropus pekinensis*—Chinese man of Peking. (Time will show whether the creation of a new genus was justified; at present there is difference of opinion on this point.) Some other human teeth had been found previously in the same deposit, and further excavations in 1928 and 1929 yielded additional ones as well as two fragments of lower jaws and a few small pieces of other

* This article was published in *The New Republic*, August 13, 1930.

skull bones, all showing certain primitive features. On December 2, 1929, Mr. W. C. Pei, a young Chinese paleontologist, on the staff of the Cenozoic Laboratory of the Geological Survey of China, found in this Chou Kou Tien deposit a human skull which unquestionably belongs to the same type. The skull is incomplete, lacking the facial region, but the brain case is uncrushed and almost intact.

One especially gratifying feature of the discovery is the completeness of its geological and paleontological documentation. In a preliminary report on the geology and paleontology of the Chou Kou Tien deposit, the authors, Père Teilhard de Chardin and Dr. C. C. Young, present abundant evidence for regarding it as belonging to very early Pleistocene (Basal Lower Quaternary), a period comparable to the very beginning of the Ice Age of Europe. The finding of human bones in a deposit proved to be so old as this is a discovery of the first magnitude in human paleontology. As the beginning of the Pleistocene period is variously estimated at from 500,000 to 1,200,000 years ago, a fair guess as to the age of the Peking man might be *perhaps upwards of a million years!* Associated with the human fossils are numerous mammalian bones of various species, which establish the geologic age, as they are clearly distinguishable from the species of the preceding Late Pliocene period (Tertiary), and also from those of the subsequent loess, which is of Middle and Later Pleistocene age.

The fossilized bones are found in certain fissures at the base of low hills formed largely of limestone. In the days of *Sinanthropus* these were open clefts or caves, but during the course of ages they became gradually filled with deposits of red clay, limestone and bones, which finally became cemented together by secondary limestone infiltration. Some of the bones, even the human remains, may have been brought into these rock clefts by animals. As remarked by the authors of the report, *"Sinanthropus* itself may once have sheltered within the Chou Kou Tien cave"; but it is impossible to say definitely whether or not the Peking man was a cave dweller, and as there is complete absence of worked flints or other implements nothing whatsoever is yet known of his cultural status. The definite placing of *Sinanthropus* in the very early Pleistocene has important bearing on its possible relationship to other ancient types, for this skull may well be the oldest human fossil thus far found. It clearly antedates the Neanderthal race, and is apparently somewhat older than the Heidelberg man.

The Java "ape-man," *Pithecanthropus,* which was formerly believed by Dr. E. Dubois, who discovered it, to be of Late Tertiary age, is now rather generally regarded, upon strong evidence, as a fairly early Pleistocene form, which implies that it is no more ancient than the Peking man and perhaps not so old. The remains of the Piltdown "dawn man," *Eoanthropus,* found in England in 1911-13, are poorly documented as to geologic age, but are commonly held to be also Early or Middle Pleistocene; though Professor H. F. Osborn has recently advanced the opinion that this type lived as early as Late Pliocene time, which would make him an example of the long sought, but hitherto more or less hypothetical, Tertiary man. But whether older or more recent, the Piltdown type with its apelike teeth and jaws, rounded cranium and absence of brow ridges, is not, in my opinion, so nearly related to Peking man as are *Pithecanthropus* and especially the Neanderthal species, but belongs to another and widely divergent branch of our family tree.

The discovery of human remains of such great antiquity in China, while highly important, is not in itself very surprising. Central Asia has long been regarded as the presumptive "cradle of humanity," as also of humanity's nearest relatives. Paleontology affords cogent evidence for this view which need not be reviewed here. Expeditions from the American Museum of Natural History have been diligently seeking man's ancestors in China and Mongolia for several years. The Neanderthal species, widely distributed through

Europe, has recently (1925) been found as far eastward as Palestine. Flint implements, similar to those of the Mousterian (Neanderthal) culture of Europe, have been found in Shensi province in China near the upper Yellow River and also in the Ordos desert in Mongolia. Thus it appears probable that Neanderthal man may have been a widespread Eurasian race rather than limited to the western or European portion of that vast continent. For some years past I have frequently expressed the opinion that the discovery in Asia of Neanderthal man, or a pre-neanderthaloid such as the Heidelberg race, would not be surprising. Therefore, the finding of *Sinanthropus,* which, as Professor Black truly says, "might well be regarded as pre-neanderthaloid in type," although a discovery of outstanding importance, can hardly be said to revolutionize our ideas regarding early man, but rather to confirm previous theories. The proving of a theory by new evidence is quite as important, and scientifically more constructive, than overturning it by similar means.

Fortunately, Professor Black and his colleagues, instead of withholding the details of their discovery until they could publish a complete description, have generally presented the facts in well-illustrated preliminary reports. The skull, which was partly embedded in hard travertine, has been carefully freed from this matrix, and its main features are clearly exhibited in a series of life-sized photographs recently sent to this country. In size it somewhat exceeds the cranium of *Pithecanthropus,* but is not quite so large as the female Neanderthal from Gibraltar. In profile view it is almost exactly like the skulls of the well-known Neanderthal species, with the heavy brow ridge overhanging the eyes, so strikingly characteristic of that race, but the crown is even a trifle lower. Seen in top view also the outline is completely neanderthaloid, but when examined from the rear a marked difference is apparent in that the broadest part of this skull is very low, only slightly above the ear openings, the skull becoming narrower above this region. This relative narrowing of the upper part of the skull, which is found also in *Pithecanthropus* (and in the *Eoanthropus* skull as restored), must be regarded as an extremely primitive feature, which in correlation with the very flat low crown proves that the brain was less voluminous than in a typical Neanderthal skull of equal length and width. As the cranial capacities of *Pithecanthropus* and the Gibraltar skull are respectively about 940 and 1,280 cubic centimeters, one might tentatively estimate that of the new skull as somewhere between 1,100 and 1,200 cubic centimeters, which is well above the minimum capacity of modern normal crania. The capacity will eventually be determined with approximate accuracy, as a cast of the interior will surely be made, and as the brain case is so nearly complete, only a small portion of the base will require restoration.

It is regrettable that nothing is positively known regarding the cranium of *Homo* (*Paleoanthropus*) *heidelbergensis* (of which a lower jaw only was found in Germany in 1907), as the new Peking skull realizes so admirably the guess one might make as to what the Heidelberg cranium would probably be like. Though the *Sinanthropus* skull lacks the facial bones, the numerous teeth and two jaw fragments give us some idea of this region. Thus one piece, the anterior part of a jaw containing several teeth, demonstrates the complete absence of any chin prominence. This, together with the dental features, marks additional resemblance to the Neanderthal and Heidelberg types, except that the molars do not show a certain specialized condition known as "taurodonty," which is observable in some, though not in all, Neanderthal teeth. The canines are not enlarged, nor in any sense apelike, as are those of the Piltdown "dawnman," and in general the teeth, though primitive and generalized, are completely human. The skull is that of an individual of early adult or adolescent age, and from its general shape and modeling Professor Black considers it to be that of a female, but in the absence of other skulls for comparison it is impossible to be certain of the sex. The great development of the brow ridge would rather indicate that it is a male.

In brief, *Sinanthropus* is an extremely early human type, apparently at least as old as any other hominid thus far known, and probably the oldest. Belonging at the beginning of the Pleistocene, its age, as I have said, may be a million years! Its closest anatomical affinities are with the somewhat later Neanderthal race, and it seems well qualified to be regarded as a pre-neanderthaloid and probably ancestral to the true Neanderthals. Complete knowledge of the more nearly contemporary Heidelberg species might reveal a still closer relationship to that type, but any kinship to the Piltdown man must be quite remote. As for the cultural status of *Sinanthropus,* there is thus far no evidence whatsoever. This new discovery does not overthrow previous theories, but rather confirms them, as there has been ample reason to anticipate the finding of very early man in Asia, and especially man of neanderthaloid affinities. The possible relation of *Sinanthropus* to our own species is far more doubtful. We know nothing about it, but regarding this point we may quote with approval Professor Black's cautious statement that "Its dental characters certainly would seem to indicate that *Sinanthropus* could not have been far removed from the type of hominid from which evolved both the extinct Neanderthaler and the modern *Homo sapiens.*" This is far from being a definite assertion that Peking man *was* our ancestor.

The fact that *Sinanthropus* lived in China carries no possible implication that he was a pre-mongoloid. A type so ancient that it antedates the emergence of *Homo sapiens* by hundreds of millenniums can have no special relationship to any particular racial subdivision of "Wise Man," so we may be sure that this venerable fossil is no more eligible to ancestor worship by the yellow race than by the white or black.

Fortunately, the Chou Kou Tien cave deposits are not yet depleted. An additional skeletal discovery has already been reported, and we have the right to hope that there will be cultural ones as well.

II
RACE AND LANGUAGE

THE PROBLEM OF RACE *

By FRANZ BOAS

In the present cultural conditions of mankind we observe, or observed at least until very recent time, a cleavage of cultural forms according to racial types. The contrast between European and Japanese began to introduce European patterns. Still greater appeared the contrasts between Europeans, native Australians, African Negroes and American Indians. It is, therefore, but natural that much thought has been given to the problem of the interrelation between race and culture. Even in Europe cultural differences between North Europeans and people of the Mediterranean, between West and East Europeans, are striking and are correlated with differences in physical appearance. This explains why numberless books and essays have been and are being written based on the assumption that each race has its own mental character determining its cultural or social behavior. In America particularly fears are being expressed of the effects of intermixture of races, of a modification or deterioration of national character on account of the influx of new types into the population of our country, and policies of controlling the growth of the population are being proposed and laws based on these assumptions have been passed.

The differences of cultural outlook and of bodily appearance have given rise to antagonisms that are rationalized as due to instinctive racial antipathies.

There is little clarity in regard to the term "race." When we speak of racial characteristics we mean those traits that are determined by heredity in each race and in which all members of the race participate. Comparing Swedes and Negroes, lack of pigmentation of skin, eye and hair ar

* *Anthropology*. New York: W. W. Norton & Co.

113

hereditary racial characteristics; or the straight or wavy hair of the Swede, the frizzly hair of the Negro, the narrowness and elevation of the nose among the Swedes, its width and flatness among the Negroes, all these are hereditary racial traits because practically all the Swedes and Negroes participate in them.

In other respects it is not so easy to define racial traits. Anatomists cannot with certainty differentiate between the brain of a Swede and of a Negro. The brains of each group vary so much in form that it is often difficult to say, if we have no other criteria, whether a certain brain belongs to a Swede or to a Negro.

The nearer two races are related the more traits they will have in common. A knowledge of all the bodily traits of a particular individual from Denmark does not enable us to identify him as a Dane. If he is tall, blond, blue-eyed, long-headed and so on he might as well be a Swede. We also find individuals of the same bodily form in Germany, in France and we may even find them in Italy. Identification of an individual as a member of a definite, local race is not possible.

Whenever these conditions prevail, we cannot speak of ˉacial heredity. In a strict sense racial heredity means that *all* the members of the race partake of certain traits,—such as the hair, pigmentation and nose form of the Negro, as ʳompared to the corresponding features among the North ːuropean. All those forms that are peculiar to some membeːʳ of the race, not to all, are in no sense true hereditary racial characteristics. The greater the number of individuals exhibiting these traits the less is their racial significance. North Italians are round-headed, Scandinavians long-headed. Still, so many different forms are represented in either series, and other bodily forms are so much alike that it would be impossible to claim that an individual selected at random *must* be a North Italian or a Scandinavian. Extreme forms in which the local characteristics are most pronounced might be identified with a fair degree of probability, but intermediate forms might belong to either group. The bodily traits of the two groups are not racial characteristics in the strict sense of the term. Although it is possible to describe the most common types of these groups by certain metric and descriptive traits, not all the members of the groups conform to them.

We are easily misled by general impressions. Most of the Swedes are blond, blue-eyed, tall and long-headed. This causes us to formulate in our minds the ideal of a Swede and we forget the variations that occur in Scandinavia. If we talk of a Sicilian we think of a swarthy, short person, with dark eyes and dark hair. Individuals differing from this type are not in our mind when we think of a "typical" Sicilian. The more uniform a people the more strongly are we impressed by the 'type." Every country impresses us as inhabited by a certain type the traits of which are determined by the most frequently occurring forms. This, however, does not tell us anything in regard to its hereditary composition and the range of its variations. The "type" is formed quite subjectively on the basis of our everyday experience.

Suppose a Swede, from a region in which blondness, blue eyes, tall stature prevail in almost the whole population, should visit Scotland and express his experiences naïvely. He would say that there are many individuals of Swedish type, but that besides this another type inhabits the country, of dark complexion, dark hair, and eyes, but tall and long-headed. The population would seem to represent two types, not that biologically the proof would have been given of race mixture; it would merely be an expression due to earlier experiences. The unfamiliar type stands out as something new and the inclination prevails to consider the new type as racially distinct. Conversely, a Scotchman who visits Sweden would be struck by the similarity between most Swedes and the blond Scotch, and he would say that there is a very large number of the blond Scotch with whom he is familiar, without reaching the conclusion that his own type is mixed.

We speak of racial types in a similar way. When we see American Indians we recognize some as looking like Asiatics, others like East Europeans, still others are said to be of a Jewish cast. We classify the variety of forms according to our previous experience and we are inclined to consider the divergent forms that are well established in our consciousness as pure types, particularly if they appear as extreme forms.

Thus the North European blond and the Armenian with his high nose and his remarkably high head, which is flat behind, appear as pure types.

Biologically speaking, this is an unjustifiable assumption. Extreme forms are not pure racial types. We do not know how much their descendants may vary among themselves and what their ancestry may have been. Even if it were shown that the extreme types were of homogeneous descent, this would not prove that the intermediate types might not be equally homogeneous.

It is well to remember that heredity means the transmission of anatomical and functional characteristics from ancestors to offspring. What we call nowadays a race of man consists of groups of individuals in which descent from common ancestors cannot be proved.

All we know is that the children of a given family represent the hereditarily transmitted qualities of their ancestors. Such a group of brothers and sisters is called a fraternity.

Not all the members of a fraternity are alike. They scatter around a certain middle value. If the typical distribution of forms in all the groups of brothers and sisters that constitute the race were alike, then we could talk of racial heredity, for each fraternity would represent the racial characteristics. We cannot speak of racial heredity if the fraternities are different, so that the distribution of forms in one family is different from that found in another one. In this case the fraternities represent distinctive hereditary family lines. Actually in all the known races the single family lines as represented by fraternities show a considerable amount of variation which indicates that the hereditary characteristics of the families are not the same, a result that may be expected whenever the ancestors have distinct heritable characteristics. In addition to this we may observe that a fraternity found in one race may be duplicated by another one in another race; in other words, that the hereditary characteristics found in one race may not belong to it exclusively, but may belong also to other races.

This may be illustrated by an extreme case. If I wish to know "the type" of the New Yorker, I may not pick out any one particular family and claim that it is a good representative of the type. I might happen to select a family of pure English descent; and I might happen to strike an Irish, Italian, Jewish, German, Armenian or Negro family. All these types are so different and, if inbred, continue their types so consistently that none of them can possibly be taken as a representative New Yorker. Conditions in France are similar. I cannot select at random a French family and consider its members as typical of France. They may be blond Northwest Europeans, darker Central Europeans or of Mediterranean type. In New York as well as in France the family lines are so diverse that there is no racial unity and no racial heredity.

Matters are different in old, inbred communities. If a number of families have intermarried for centuries without appreciable addition of foreign blood they will all be closely related and the same ancestral traits will appear in all the families. Brothers and sisters in any one family may be quite unlike among themselves, but all the family lines will have considerable likeness. It is much more feasible to obtain an impression of the general character of the population by examining a single family than in the preceding cases, and a few families would give us a good picture of the whole race. Conditions of this type prevail among the landowners in small European villages. They are found in the high nobility of Europe and also among some isolated tribes.

The Eskimos of North Greenland, for instance, have been isolated for centuries. Their number can never have exceeded a few hundred. There are no rigid rules proscribing marriages between relatives, so that we may expect that unions were largely dictated by chance. The ancestors of the tribe were presumably a small number of Eskimos who happened to settle there and whose blood flows in the veins of all the members of the present generation. The people all bear a considerable likeness, but unfortunately we do not know in how far the family lines are alike.

We have information of this kind from one of the isolated Tennessee valleys in which people have intermarried among themselves for a century. The family lines in this community are very much alike.

In cases of this kind it does not matter whether the ancestry is homogeneous or belongs to quite distinct races. As long as there is continued inbreeding the family lines will become alike. The differences of racial descent will rather appear in the differences between brothers and sisters, some of whom will lean towards one of the ancestral strains, others to the other. The distribution of different racial forms in all the various families will be the more the same, the longer the inbreeding without selection continues. We have a few examples of this kind. The Bastaards of South Africa, largely an old mixture of Dutch and Hottentot, and the Chippewa of eastern Canada, descendants of French and Indians, are inbred communities. Accordingly, the family lines among them are quite similar, while the brothers and sisters in each family differ strongly among themselves.

In modern society, particularly in cities, conditions are not favorable to inbreeding. The larger the area inhabited by a people, the denser and the more mobile the population, the less are the families inbred and the more may we expect very diverse types of family lines.

The truth of this statement may readily be demonstrated. Notwithstanding the apparent homogeneity of the Swedish nation, there are many different family lines represented.

Many are "typical" blond Swedes but in other families dark hair and brown eyes are hereditary. The range of hereditary forms is considerable.

It has been stated before that many individuals of Swedish types may be duplicated in neighboring countries. The same is true of family lines. It would not be difficult to find in Denmark, Germany, Holland or northern France families that might apparently just as well be Swedes; or in Sweden families that might as well be French or German.

In these cases hereditary characteristics are not "racially" determined, but belong to family lines that occur in many "racial" groups. Just as soon as family lines of the same form are found in a number of racial groups the term "racial heredity" loses its meaning. We can speak solely of "heredity in family lines." The term "racial heredity" presupposes a homogeneity of lines of descent in different races, that do not exist.

In short, if we wish to discuss racial traits we have to recognize that a great diversity of these occurs in every race and that they are inherited not racially, but in family lines. Characteristics of this type do not belong to the race as a whole.

Another important problem confronts us. We have seen that our concept of types is based on subjective experience. On account of the preponderance of "typical" Swedes we are inclined to consider all those of different type as not belonging to the racial type, as foreign admixtures. There is a somewhat distinct type in Sweden in the old mining districts which were first worked by Walloons and it is more than probable that the great darkness of complexion in this region is due to the influence of Walloon blood. We are very ready to explain every deviation from a type in this way. In many cases this is undoubtedly correct, for intermingling of distinct types of people has been going on for thousands of years; but we do not know to what extent a type may vary when no admixture of foreign blood has occurred. The experience of animal breeders proves that even with intensive inbreeding of pure stock there always remains a considerable amount of variation between individuals. We have no evidence to show to what extent variations of this kind might develop in a pure human race and it is not probable that satisfactory evidence will ever be forthcoming, because we have no pure races. The history of the whole world shows us mankind constantly on the move; people from eastern Asia coming to Europe; those of western and central Asia invading southern Asia; North Europeans sweeping over Mediterranean countries; Central Africans extending their territories over almost the whole of South Africa; people from Alaska spreading to northern Mexico or vice versa; South Americans settling almost over the whole eastern part of the continent here and there,—in short, from earliest times on we have a picture of continued movements, and with it of mixtures of diverse people.

It may well be that the lack of clean-cut geographical and biological lines between the races of man is entirely due to these circumstances. The conditions are quite like those found in the animal world. Local races of remote districts may readily be recognized, but in many cases they are united by intermediate forms.

We have seen that on account of the lack of sharp distinctions between neighboring populations it happens that apparently identical family lines occur in both, and that an individual in one may resemble in bodily form an individual in another. Notwithstanding their resemblances it can be demonstrated that they are functionally not by any means equivalent, for when we compare their children they will be found to revert more or less to the type of the population to which the parents belong. To give an example: the Bohemians have, on the average, round heads, the Swedes long heads. Nevertheless it is possible to find among both populations parents that have the same head forms. The selected group among the Swedes will naturally be more round-headed than the average Swede, and the selected Bohemians will be more long-headed than the average Bohemians. The children of the selected group of Swedes are found to be more long-headed than their parents, those of the selected group of Bohemians more short-headed than their parents.

The cause of this is not difficult to understand. If we pick out short-headed individuals among the Swedes, short-headedness may be an individual nonhereditary trait. Furthermore the general run of their relatives will be similar to the long-headed Swedish type and since the form of the offspring depends not only upon the parent, but also upon the characteristics of his whole family line, at least of his four grandparents, a reversion to the general population may be expected. The same is true among the Bohemians.

We must conclude that individuals of the same bodily appearance, if sprung from populations of distinct type, are functionally not the same. For this reason it is quite unjustifiable to select from a population a certain type and claim that it is identical with the corresponding type of another population. Each individual must be studied as a member of the group from which he has sprung. We may not assume that the round-headed or brunette individuals in Denmark are identical with the corresponding forms from Switzerland. Even if no anatomical differences between two series of such individuals are discernible they represent genetically distinctive strains. Identity can occur in exceptional individuals only.

If we were to select a group of tall, blond Sicilians, men and women, who marry among themselves, we must expect that their offspring in later generations will revert more or less to the Sicilian type, and, conversely, if we select a group of brunette, brown-eyed Swedes, their offspring will revert more or less to the blond, blue-eyed Swedish type.

We have spoken so far only of the hereditary conditions of stable races. We imply by the term racial heredity that the composition of succeeding generations is identical. When one generation dies, the next one is assumed to represent the same type of population. This can be true only if random matings occur in each generation. If in the first generation there was a random selection of mates, due to chance only, the same condition must prevail in the following generations. Any preferential mating, any selective change in group mortality or fertility, or brought about by migration, must modify the genetic composition of the group.

For these reasons none of our modern populations is stable from a hereditary point of view. The heterogeneous family lines in a population that has originated through migration will gradually become more homogeneous, if the descendants continue to reside in the same spot. In our cities and mixed farming communities, on account of changes in selective mating, constant changes in the hereditary composition are going on, even after immigration has ceased. Local inbreeding produces local types; avoidance of marriages between near relatives favors increasing likeness of all the family lines constituting the population; favored or proscribed cousin marriages which are customary among many tribes establish separate family types and increase in this sense the heterogeneity of the population.

Another question presents itself. We have considered only the hereditary stability of genetic lines. We must ask ourselves also whether environmental conditions exert an influence over races.

It is quite obvious that the forms of lower organisms are subject to environmental influences. Plants taken from low altitudes to high mountains develop short stems; leaves of semi-aquatic plants growing under water have a form differing from the subaerial leaves. Cultivated plants transform their stamens into petals. Plants may be dwarfed or stimulated in their growth by appropriate treatment. Each plant is so organized that it develops a certain form under given environmental conditions. Microörganisms differ so much in different environmental settings that it is often difficult to establish their specific identity.

The question arises whether the same kind of variability

occurs in higher organisms. The general impression is that their forms are determined by heredity, not by environment. The young of a greyhound is a greyhound, that of a shorthorn a shorthorn; that of a Norway rat a Norway rat. The child of a European is European in type, that of a Chinaman of Mongolic type, that of an African Negro a Negro.

Nevertheless detailed study shows that the form and size of the body are not entirely shaped by heredity. Records of the stature of European men that date back to the middle of the past century show that in almost all countries the average statures have increased by more than an inch. It is true, this is not a satisfactory proof of an actual change, because improvement in public health has changed the composition of the populations, and although it is not likely that this should be the cause of an increase in stature, it is conceivable. A better proof is found in the change of stature among descendants of Europeans who settle in America. In this case it has been shown that in many nationalities the children are taller than their own parents, presumably on account of more favorable conditions of life.

It has also been observed that the forms of the body are influenced by occupation. The hand of a person who has to do heavy manual labor differs from that of a musician who develops the independence of all the muscles of his hand. The proportions and form of the limb are influenced by habitual posture and use. The legs of the oriental who squats flat on the ground are somewhat modified by this habit.

Other modifications cannot be explained by better nutrition or by the use of the muscles. Forms of the head and face are not quite stable, but are in some way influenced by the environment in which the people live, so that after a migration into a new environment the child will not be quite like the parent.

All the observed changes are slight and do not modify the essential character of the hereditary forms. Still they are not negligible. We do not know how great the modifications may be that ultimately result from such changes, nor have we any evidence that the changes would persist if the people were taken back to their old environment. Although a Negro will never become a European, it is not impossible that some of the minor differences between European populations may be due to environment rather than to heredity.

So far we have discussed solely the anatomical forms of races with a view of gaining a clearer understanding of what we mean by the term race. It may be well to repeat the principal result of our discussion.

We have found that the term "racial heredity" is strictly applicable only when all the individuals of a race participate in certain anatomical features. In each race taken as a whole the family lines differ considerably in their hereditary traits. The distribution of family lines is such that a considerable number of lines similar or even identical in one or many respects occur in contiguous territories. The vague impression of "types," abstracted from our everyday experience, does not prove that these are biologically distinct races, and the inference that various populations are composed of individuals belonging to various races is subjectively intelligible, objectively unproved. It is particularly not admissible to identify types apparently identical that occur in populations of different composition. Each individual can be understood only as a member of his group.

These considerations seem necessary, because they clear up the vagueness of the term "race" as usually applied. When we speak of heredity we are ordinarily concerned with family lines, not with races. The hereditary qualities of families constituting the most homogeneous populations differ very much among themselves and there is very little, if anything, that these family lines have in common and they are not sharply set off from neighboring populations that may give a quite distinctive impression.

The relation of racial types may be looked at in another way. It may be granted that in closely related types the identification of an individual as a member of each type cannot be made with any degree of certainty. Nevertheless the distribution of individuals and of family lines in the various races differs. When we select among the Europeans a group with large brains, their frequency will be relatively high, while among the Negroes the frequency of occurrence of the corresponding group will be low. If, for instance, there are 50 per cent of an European population who have a brain weight of more than, let us say, 1,500 grams, there may be only 20 per cent of Negroes of the same class. Therefore 30 per cent of the large-brained Europeans cannot be matched by any corresponding group of Negroes.

It is justifiable to compare races from this point of view, as long as we avoid an application of our results to individuals.

On general biological grounds it is important to know whether any one of the human races is, in regard to form or function, further removed from the ancestral animal form than another, whether the races can be arranged in an ascending series. Although we do not know the ancestral form with any degree of certainty, some of its characteristics can be inferred by a comparison of the anatomical forms of man and of the apes. Single traits can be brought into ascending series in which the racial forms differ more and more from animal forms, but the arrangement is a different one for each independent trait.

The ancestral form had a flat nose. Bushmen, Negroes and Australians have flat, broad noses. Mongoloids, Europeans and particularly Armenians have narrow, prominent noses. They are in this sense farthest removed from the animal forms.

Apes have narrow lips. The lips of the Whites are thin, those of many Mongoloid types are fuller. The Negroes have the thickest, most excessively "human" lips.

The hair coat of apes is moderately strong. Among human races the Australians, Europeans and a few scattered tribes among other races have the amplest body hairs; Mongols have the least.

Similar remarks may be made in regard to the forms of

the foot, of the spinal column, of the proportions of the limbs. The order of the degree to which human races differ from animals is not the same in regard to these traits.

Particular stress has been laid on the brain, which also differs in various races. Setting aside the pygmy Bushmen and other very small races, the negroid races have smaller brains than the Mongoloids, and these in general smaller ones than the Europeans, although some Mongoloid types, like the Eskimo, exceed in size of the brain many European groups.

The brain in each race is very variable in size and the "overlapping" of individuals in the races is marked. It is not possible to identify an individual as a Negro or White according to the size and form of the brain, but serially the Negro brain is less extremely human than that of the White.

We are apt to identify the size of the brain with its functioning. This is true to a limited extent only. Among the higher mammals the proportionate size of the brain is larger in animals that have greater intelligence; but size alone is not an adequate criterion. Complexity of structure is much more important than mere size. Some birds have brains much larger proportionately than those of the higher mammals without evidencing superior intelligence.

The size of the brain is measured by its weight which does not depend upon the nerve cells and fibers alone, but includes a large amount of material that is not directly relevant for the functioning of the central nervous system.

Superior intelligence in man is in a way related to size of the brain. Microcephalic individuals whose brains remain considerably under normal size are mentally defective, but an individual with an exceptionally large brain is not necessarily a genius. There are many causes that affect the size of the brain. The larger the body, the larger the brain. Therefore well-nourished people who have a larger bulk of body than those poorly nourished have larger brains, not because their brains are structurally more highly developed, but because the larger bulk is a characteristic feature of the entire bodily form. Eminent people belong generally to the better nourished class and the cause of the greater brain is, therefore, uncertain. The variation in the size of the brain of eminent men is also very considerable, some falling way beneath the norm.

The real problem to be solved is the relation between the structure of the brain and its function. The correlation between gross structure in the races of man and function is so slight that no safe inferences may be drawn on the basis of the slight differences between races which are of such character that up to this time the racial identification of a brain is impossible, except in so far as elongated and rounded heads, high and low heads and similar gross forms may be distinguished which do not seem to have any relation to minute structure or function. At least it has never been proved to exist and it does not seem likely that there is any kind of intimate relation.

The differences between races are so small that they lie within the narrow range in the limits of which all forms may function equally well. We cannot say that the ratio of inadequate brains and nervous systems, that function noticeably worse than the norm, is the same in every race, nor that those of rare excellence are equally frequent. It is not improbable that such differences may exist in the same way as we find different ranges of adjustability in other organs.

Without further proof the serial arrangement in brain size cannot be identified with a higher racial intelligence. If the anatomical structure of the brain is a doubtful indication of mental excellence, this is still more the case with differences in other parts of the body. So far as we can judge the form of the foot and the slight development of the calves of the Negro; the prominence of his teeth and the size of his lips; the heaviness of the face of the Mongol; or the difference in degree of pigmentation of the races have no relation to mentality. At least every attempt to prove such relation has failed.

In any attempt to place the human races in an evolutionary series we must also remember that modern races
are not wild but domesticated forms. In regard to nutrition
and artificial protection the mode of life of man is like that
of domesticated animals. The artificial modification of food
by the use of fire and the invention of tools were the steps
that brought about the self-domestication of man. Both belong to a very early period, to a time before the last extensive glaciation of Europe. Man must be considered the
oldest domesticated form. The most characteristic features
of human races bear evidence of this. The loss of pigmentation in the blond, blue-eyed races; the blackness of the
hair of the Negro are traits that do not occur in any wild
mammal form. Exceptions are the blackness of the hair
coat of the black panther, of the black bear and of the subterranean mole. The frizzliness of the Negro hair and the
curliness of the hair of the other races, the long hair of the
head do not occur in wild mammals. The permanence
rather than periodicity of the sexual functions and of the
female breasts; the anomalies of sexual behavior are also
characteristics of domesticated animals. The kind of domestication of man is like that of the animals raised by primitive
tribes that do not breed certain strains by selection. Nevertheless, forms differing from the wild forms develop in
their herds.

Some of the traits of man that might be considered as
indicating a lower evolutionary stage may as well be due
to domestication. Reduction or unusual lengthening of the
face occurs. The excessive reduction of the face in some
White types and the elongation of the mouth parts of the
Negro may be due to this cause. It may be a secondary
development from an intermediate form. The brain of
domesticated forms is generally smaller than that of wild
forms. In exceptional cases it may be larger. Pygmy forms
and giants develop in domestication. In short, the "primitive
traits" of races are not necessarily indications of an early

arrest. They may be later acquisitions stabilized in domestication.

All this, however, has little to do with the biologically determined mentality of races, which is often assumed to be the basis of social behavior. Mental behavior is closely related to the physiological functioning of the body and the problem may be formulated as an investigation of the functioning of the body, in the widest sense of the term "functioning."

We have seen that the description of the anatomical traits of a race in general terms involves a faulty generalization based on the impression made by the majority of individuals. This is no less true in regard to the functions of a population. Our characterization of the mentality of a people is merely a conceptionalization of those traits that are found in a large number of individuals and that are, for this reason, impressive. In another population other traits impress themselves upon the mind and are conceptionalized. This does not prove that, if in a third population both types are found, it is mixed in its functional behavior. The objective value of generalizations of this type is not self-evident, because they are merely the result of the subjective construction of types, the wide variability of which is disregarded.

Actually the functions exhibited by a whole race can be defined as hereditary even less than its anatomical traits, because individually and in family lines the variations are so great that not all the members of the race react alike.

When the body has completed its growth its features remain the same for a considerable length of time,—until the changes due to old age set in. It does not matter at what time we examine the body, the results will always be nearly the same. Fluctuations of weight, of the amount of fat, of muscle do occur, but these are comparatively slight, and under normal conditions of health, nutrition and exercise insignificant until senility sets in.

It is different with the functions of the body. The heart beat depends upon transient conditions. In sleep it is slow;

in waking, during meals, during exercise more rapid. The range of the number of heart beats for the individual is very wide. The condition of our digestive tract depends upon the amount and kind of food present; our eyes act differently in intense light and in darkness. The variation in the functions of an individual is considerable. Furthermore, the individuals constituting a population do not all function in the same way. Variability, which in regard to anatomical traits has only one source, namely, the differences between individuals, has in physiological functions an added source, the different behavior of the individual at different times. It is, therefore, not surprising that functionally the individuals composing a population exhibit a considerable variability.

The average values expressing the functioning of various races living under the same conditions are not the same, but the differences are not great as compared to the variations that occur in each racial group. Investigations of the functioning of the same sense organs of various races, such as Whites, Indians, Filipinos and people of New Guinea, indicate that their sensitiveness is very much the same. The popular belief in an unusual keenness of eyesight or hearing of primitive people is not corroborated by careful observations. The impression is due to the training of their power of observation which is directed to phenomena with which we are not familiar. Differences have been found in the basal metabolism of Mongols and Whites and there are probably differences in the functioning of the digestive tract and of the skin between Whites and Negroes. Much remains to be done in the study of physiological functions of different races before we can determine the quantitative differences between them.

The variability of many functions is well known. We referred before to the heart beat. Let us imagine an individual who lives in New York and leads a sedentary life without bodily exercise. Transport this person to the high plateaus of the Bolivian Andes where he has to do physical work. He will find difficulties for a while, but, if he is healthy, he will finally become adjusted to the new conditions. His normal heart beat, however, will have changed. His lungs also will act differently in the rarefied air. It is the same individual who in the new environment will exhibit a quantitatively different functioning of the body.

We pointed out before that environmental conditions cause in general but slight modification of anatomical form. Their effect upon most functions of the body is intense, as is the case in lower organisms which are in bodily form subject to important modifications brought about by the environment. The functions of the organs are adjustable to different requirements. Every organ has—to use Dr. Meltzer's term—a margin of safety. Within limits it can function normally according to environmental requirements. Even a partly disabled organ can be sufficient for the needs of the body. Inadequacy develops only when these limits are exceeded. There are certain conditions that are most favorable, but the loss of adequacy is very slight when the conditions change within the margins of safety.

In most cases of the kind here referred to the environmental influence acts upon different individuals in the same direction. If we bring two organically different individuals into the same environment they may, therefore, become alike in their functional responses and we may gain the impression of a functional likeness of distinct anatomical forms that is due to environment, not to their internal structure. Only in those cases in which the environment acts with different intensity or perhaps even in different directions upon the organism may we expect increased unlikeness under the same environmental conditions. When, for instance, for one individual the margin of safety is so narrow that the environmental conditions are excessive, for another one so wide that adequate adjustment is possible, the former will become sick, while the other will remain healthy.

What is true of the physiological functioning of the body is still more true of mental reactions. A simple example may illustrate this. When we are asked to react to a stimulus, for instance by tapping in response to a signal given by a bell, we can establish a certain basal or minimum time interval between signal and tapping which is found when we are rested and concentrate our attention upon the signal. As soon as we are tired and when our attention is distracted the time increases. We may even become so much absorbed in other matters that the signal will go unnoticed. Environmental conditions determine the reaction time. The basal time for two individuals may differ quite considerably, still under varying environmental conditions they will react in the same way. If the conditions of life compel the one to concentrate his attention while the other has never been required to do so, they may react in the same way, although structurally they represent different types.

In more complex mental and social phenomena this adjustment of different types to a common standard is of frequent occurrence. The pronunciation of individuals in a small community is so uniform that an expert ear can identify the home of a person by his articulation. Anatomically the forms of the mouth, inner nose and larynx of all the individuals participating in this pronunciation vary considerably. The mouth may be large or small, the tongue thin or thick, the palate arched or flat. There are differences in the pitch of the voice and in timbre. Still the dialect will be the same for all. The articulation does not depend to any considerable extent upon the form of the mouth, but upon its use.

In all our everyday habits imitation of habits of the society to which we belong exerts its influence over the functioning of our minds and bodies and a degree of uniformity of thought and action is brought about among individuals who differ considerably in structure.

It would not be justifiable to claim that bodily form has no relation whatever to physiological or mental functioning. I do not believe that Watson is right when he claims that the whole mental activities of man are due to his individual experiences and that what is called character or ability is due to outer conditions, not to organic structure. It seems to me that this goes counter to the observation of mental activities in the animal world as well as among men. The mental activities of a family of idiots will not, even under the most favorable conditions, equal those of a highly intelligent family, and what is true in this extreme case must be true also when the differences are less pronounced. Although it is never possible to eliminate environmental influences that bring about similarity or dissimilarity, it seems unreasonable to assume that in the mental domain organically determined sameness of all individuals should exist while in all other traits we do find differences; but we must admit that the organic differences are liable to be overlaid and overshadowed by environmental influences.

Under these conditions it is well-nigh impossible to determine with certainty the hereditary traits in mental behavior. In a well-integrated society we find people of most diverse descent who all react so much in the same way that it is impossible to tell from their reactions alone to what race they belong. Individual differences and those belonging to family lines occur in such a society, but among healthy individuals these are so slightly correlated to bodily form that an identification of an individual on the basis of his functions as belonging to a family or race of definite hereditary functional qualities is also impossible.

In this case, even more than in that of anatomical form, the range of variation of hereditary lines constituting a "race" is so wide that the same types of lines may be found in different races. While so far as anatomical form is concerned Negroes and Whites have racially hereditary traits, this is not true of function. The mental life of each of the individuals constituting these races is so varied that from its expression alone an individual cannot be assigned to the one or the other. It is true that in regard to a few races, like the Bushmen of South Africa, we have no evidence in regard to this point, and we may suspend judgment, a' though I do not anticipate that any fundamental differences will be found.

So far as our experience goes we may safely say that in any given race the differences between family lines are much greater than the differences between races. It may happen that members of one family line, extreme in form and function, are quite different from those of a family line of the opposite extreme, although both belong to the same race; while it may be very difficult to find individuals or family lines in one racial type that may not be duplicated in a neighboring type.

The assumption of fundamental, hereditary mental characteristics of races is often based on an analogy with the mental traits of races of domesticated animals. Certainly the mentality of the poodle dog is quite different from that of the bulldog, or that of a race horse from that of a dray horse.

This analogy is not well founded, because the races of domesticated animals are comparable to family lines, not to human races. They are developed by carefully controlled inbreeding. Their family lines are uniform, those of man diverse. They are parallel to the family lines that occur in all human races, which, however, do not become stabilized on account of the lack of rigid inbreeding. In this respect human races must be compared to wild animals, not to selected, domesticated breeds.

All these considerations are apparently contradicted by the results of so-called intelligence tests which are intended to determine innate intellectuality. Actually these tests show considerable differences not only between individuals but also between racial and social groups. The test is an expression of mental function. Like other functions the responses to mental tests show overlapping of individuals belonging to different groups and ordinarily it is not possible to assign an individual to his proper group according to his response.

The test itself shows only that a task set to a person can

be performed by him more or less satisfactorily. That the result is solely or primarily a result of organically determined intelligence is an assumption that has to be proved. Defective individuals cannot perform certain acts required in the tests. Within narrower limits of performance we must ask in how far the structure of the organism, in how far outer, environmental conditions may determine the result of the test. Since all functions are strongly influenced by environment it is likely that here also environmental influences may prevail and obscure the structurally determined part of the reaction.

Let us illustrate this by an example. One of the simplest tests consists in the task of fitting blocks of various forms into holes of corresponding forms. There are primitive people who devote much time to decorative work in which fitting of forms plays an important part. It may be appliqué work, mosaic, or stencil work. Others have no experience whatever in the use of forms. We have no observations on these people, but it seems more than likely that those who are accustomed to handling varied forms and to recognize them, will respond to the test with much greater ease than those who have no such experience.

Dr. Klineberg has investigated the reactions to simple tests of various races living under very different conditions. He found that all races investigated by him respond under city conditions quickly and inaccurately, that the same races in remote country districts react slowly and more accurately. The hurry and pressure for efficiency of city life result in a different attitude that has nothing to do with innate intelligence, but is an effect of a cultural condition.

An experiment made in Germany, but based on entirely different sets of tests, has had a similar result. Children belonging to different types of schools were tested. The social groups attending elementary schools and higher schools of various types differ in their cultural attitudes. It is unlikely that they belong by descent to different racial groups. On the contrary, the population as a whole is uniform. The responses in various schools were quite different. There is no particular reason why we should assume a difference in organic structure between the groups and it seems more likely that we are dealing with the effects of cultural differentiation.

In all tests based on language the effect of the linguistic experience of the subject plays an important part. Our whole sense experience is classified according to linguistic principles and our thought is deeply influenced by the classification of our experience. Often the scope of a concept expressed by a word determines the current of our thought and the categories which the grammatical form of the language compels us to express keep certain types of modality or connection before our minds. When language compels me to differentiate sharply between elder and younger brother, between father's brother and mother's brother, directions of thought that our vaguer terms permit will be excluded. When the terms for son and brother's son are not distinguished the flow of thought may run in currents unexpected to us who differentiate clearly between these terms. When a language states clearly in every case the forms of objects, as round, long or flat; or the instrumentality with which an action is done, as with the hand, with a knife, with a point; or the source of knowledge of a statement, as observed, known by evidence or by hearsay, these forms may establish lines of association. Comparison of reactions of individuals that speak fundamentally distinct languages may, therefore, express the influence of language upon the current of thought, not any innate difference in the form of thought.

All these considerations cause us to doubt whether it is possible to differentiate between environmental and organic determination of responses, as soon as the environment of two individuals is different.

It is exceedingly difficult to secure an identical environment even in our own culture. Every home, every street, every family group and school has its own character which is difficult to evaluate. In large masses of individuals we may assume a somewhat equal environmental setting for a group in similar economic and social position, and it is justifiable to assume in this case that the variability of environmental influence is much restricted and that organically determined differences between individuals appear more clearly.

Just as soon as we compare different social groups the relative uniformity of social background disappears and, if we are dealing with populations of the same descent, there is a strong probability that differences in the type of response are primarily due to the effect of environment rather than to organic differences between the groups.

The responses to tests may be based on recognition of sensory impressions, on motor experience, such as the results of complex movements; or on the use of acquired knowledge. All of these contain experience. A city boy who has been brought up by reading, familiar with the conveniences of city life, accustomed to the rush of traffic and the watchfulness demanded on the streets has a general setting entirely different from that of a boy brought up on a lonely farm, who has had no contact with the machinery of modern city life. His sense experience, motor habits and the currents of his thoughts differ from those of the city boy.

Certainly in none of the tests that have ever been applied is individual experience eliminated and I doubt that it can be done.

We must remember how we acquire the manner of acting and thinking. From our earliest days we imitate the behavior of our environment and our behavior in later years is determined by what we learn as infants and children. The responses to any stimulus depend upon these early habits. Individually it may be influenced by organic, hereditary conditions. In the large mass of a population these vary. In a homogeneous social group the experience gained in childhood is fairly uniform, so that its influence will be more marked than that of organic structure.

The dilemma of the investigator appears clearly in the

results or mental tests taken on Negroes of Louisiana and Chicago. During the World War the enlisted men belonging to the two groups were tested and showed quite distinct responses. There is no very great difference in the pigmentation of the two groups. Both are largely mulattoes. The Northern Negroes passed the tests much more successfully than those from the South. Chicago Negroes are accustomed to city surroundings. They work with Whites and are accustomed to a certain degree of equality, owing to similarity of occupation and constant contact. All these are lacking among the Louisiana rural Negroes It is gratuitous to claim that a more energetic and intelligent group of Negroes has migrated to the city and that the weak and unintelligent stay behind, and to disregard the effect of social environment. We know that the environment is distinct and that human behavior is strikingly modified by it. We do not know that selection plays an important part in the migration of the Southern Negro to Northern cities. It is quite arbitrary to ascribe the difference in mental behavior solely to the latter, doubtful cause and to disregard the former entirely. Those who claim that there is an organic difference must prove it by showing the difference between the two groups before their migration.

Even if it were true that selection accounts for the differences in the responses to tests among these two groups, it would not have any bearing upon the problem of racial characteristics, for we should have here merely a selection of better endowed individuals or family lines, all belonging to the same race, a condition similar to the often quoted, but never proved, result of the emigration from New England to the West. The question would still remain, whether there is any difference in racial composition in the two groups. So far as we know the amount of Negro and White blood in the two groups is about the same.

Other tests intended to investigate differences between the mental reactions of Negroes, Mulattoes, and Whites due to the racial composition of the groups are not convincing, because due caution has not been taken to insure an equal social background. The study of mental achievement of a socially uniform group undertaken by Dr. Herskovits does not show any relation between the intensity of negroid features and mental attainment. Up to this time none of the mental tests gives us any insight into significant racial differences that might not be adequately explained by the effect of social experience. Even Dr. Woodworth's observations on the Filipino pygmies are not convincing, because the cultural background of the groups tested is unknown.

A critical examination of all studies of this type in which differences between racial groups in regard to mental reactions are demonstrated, leaves us in doubt whether the determining factor is cultural experience or racial descent. We must emphasize again that differences between selected groups of the same descent, such as between poor orphan children often of defective parentage, and of normal children; and those between unselected groups of individuals representing various races are phenomena quite distinct in character. In the former case the results of tests may express differences in family lines. Similar peculiarities might be found, although with much greater difficulty, when comparing small inbred communities, for inbred communities are liable to differ in social behavior. For large racial groups acceptable proof of marked mental differences due to organic, not social, causes has never been given.

Students of ethnology have always been so much impressed by the general similarity of fundamental traits of human culture that they have never found it necessary to take into account the racial descent of a people when discussing its culture. This is true of all schools of modern ethnology. Edward B. Tylor and Herbert Spencer in their studies of the evolution of culture, Adolf Bastian in his insistence on the sameness of the fundamental forms of thought among all races, Friedrich Ratzel, who followed the historical dissemination of cultural forms—they all have carried on their work without any regard to race. The general experience of ethnology indicates that whatever differences there may be between the great races are insignificant when considered in their effect upon cultural life.

It does not matter from which point of view we consider culture, its forms are not dependent upon race. In economic life and in regard to the extent of their inventions the Eskimos, the Bushmen and the Australians may well be compared. The position of the Magdalenian race, which lived at the end of the ice age, is quite similar to that of the Eskimo. On the other hand, the complexities of inventions and of economic life of the Negroes of the Sudan, of the ancient Pueblos, of our early European ancestors who used stone tools, and of the early Chinese are comparable.

In the study of material culture we are constantly compelled to compare similar inventions used by people of the most diverse descent. Devices for throwing spears from Australia and America; armor from the Pacific Islands and America; games of Africa and Asia; blowguns of Malaysia and South America; decorative designs from almost every continent; musical instruments from Asia, the Pacific islands and America; head rests from Africa and Melanesia; the beginning of the art of writing in America and in the Old World; the use of the zero in America, Asia and Europe; the use of bronze, of methods of firemaking, from all parts of the world cannot be studied on the basis of their distribution by races, but only by their geographical and historical distribution, or as independent achievements, without any reference to the bodily forms of the races using these inventions.

Other aspects of cultural life are perhaps still more impressive, because they characterize the general cultural life more deeply than inventions: the use of standards of value in Africa, America, Asia, Europe and on the islands of the Pacific Ocean; analogous types of family organization, such as small families, or extended sibs with maternal or paternal succession; totemic ideas; avoidance of close relatives; the exclusion of women from sacred ceremonials; the formation of age societies; all these are found in fundamentally similar forms among all races. In their study we are compelled to disregard the racial position of the people we study, for similarities and dissimilarities have no relation whatever to racial types.

It does not matter how the similar traits in diverse races may have originated, by diffusion or independent origin. They convince us of the independence of race and culture because their distribution does not follow racial lines.

LANGUAGE, RACE, AND CULTURE *

By EDWARD SAPIR

LANGUAGE has a setting. The people that speak it belong to a race (or a number of races), that is, to a group which is set off by physical characteristics from other groups. Again, language does not exist apart from culture, that is, from the socially inherited assemblage of practices and beliefs that determines the texture of our lives. Anthropologists have been in the habit of studying man under the three rubrics of race, language, and culture. One of the first things they do with a natural area like Africa or the South Seas is to map it out from this threefold point of view. These maps answer the questions: What and where are the major divisions of the human animal, biologically considered (e.g., Congo Negro, Egyptian White; Australian Black, Polynesian)? What are the most inclusive linguistic groupings, the "linguistic stocks," and what is the distribution of each (e.g., the Hamitic language of northern Africa, the Bantu languages of the south; the Malayo-Polynesian languages of Indonesia, Melanesia, Micronesia, and Polynesia)? How do the peoples of the given area divide themselves as cultural beings? what are the outstanding "cultural areas" and what are the dominant ideas in each (e.g., the Mohammedan north of Africa; the primitive hunting, non-agricultural culture of the Bushmen in the south; the culture of the Australian natives, poor in physical respects but richly developed in ceremonialism; the more advanced and highly specialized culture of Polynesia)?

The man in the street does not stop to analyze his position in the general scheme of humanity. He feels that he is the

---

* *Language*. New York: Harcourt, Brace & Co.

representative of some strongly integrated portion of humanity—now thought of as a "nationality," now as a "race" —and that everything that pertains to him as a typical representative of this large group somehow belongs together. If he is an Englishman, he feels himself to be a member of the "Anglo-Saxon" race, the "genius" of which race has fashioned the English language and the "Anglo-Saxon" culture of which the language is the expression. Science is colder. It inquires if these three types of classification— racial, linguistic, and cultural—are congruent, if their association is an inherently necessary one or is merely a matter of external history. The answer to the inquiry is not encouraging to "race" sentimentalists. Historians and anthropologists find that races, languages, and cultures are not distributed in parallel fashion, that their areas of distribution intercross in the most bewildering fashion, and that the history of each is apt to follow a distinctive course. Races intermingle in a way that languages do not. On the other hand, languages may spread far beyond their original home, invading the territory of new races and of new culture spheres. A language may even die out in its primary area and live on among peoples violently hostile to the persons of its original speakers. Further, the accidents of history are constantly rearranging the borders of culture areas without necessarily effacing the existing linguistic cleavages. If we can once thoroughly convince ourselves that race, in its only intelligible, that is, biological, sense, is supremely indifferent to the history of languages and cultures, that these are no more directly explainable on the score of race than on that of the laws of physics and chemistry, we shall have gained a viewpoint that allows a certain interest to such mystic slogans as Slavophilism, Anglo-Saxondom, Teutonism, and the Latin genius but that quite refuses to be taken in by any of them. A careful study of linguistic distributions and of the history of such distributions is one of the driest of commentaries on these sentimental creeds.

That a group of languages need not in the least correspond to a racial group or a culture area is easily demonstrated. We may even show how a single language intercrosses with race and culture lines. The English language is not spoken by a unified race. In the United States there are several millions of Negroes who know no other language. It is their mother-tongue, the formal vesture of their inmost thoughts and sentiments. It is as much their property, as inalienably "theirs," as the King of England's. Nor do the English-speaking whites of America constitute a definite race except by way of contrast to the Negroes. Of the three fundamental white races in Europe generally recognized by physical anthropologists—the Baltic or North European, the Alpine, and the Mediterranean—each has numerous English-speaking representatives in America. But does not the historical core of English-speaking peoples, those relatively "unmixed" populations that still reside in England and its colonies, represent a race, pure and single? I cannot see that the evidence points that way. The English people are an amalgam of many distinct strains. Besides the old "Anglo-Saxon," in other words North German, element which is conventionally represented as the basic strain, the English blood comprises Norman French,[1] Scandinavian, "Celtic," [2] and pre-Celtic elements. If by "English" we mean also Scotch and Irish,[3] then the term "Celtic" is loosely used for at least two quite distinct racial elements—the short, dark-complexioned type of Wales and the taller, lighter, often ruddy-haired type of the Highlands and parts of Ireland. Even if we confine ourselves to the Saxon element, which, needless to say, nowhere appears "pure," we are not at the end of our troubles. We may roughly identify this strain with the racial type now predominant in southern Denmark and adjoining parts of northern Germany. If so, we must content ourselves with the reflection that while the English language is historically most closely affiliated with Frisian, in second degree with the other West Germanic dialects (Low Saxon or "Plattdeutsch," Dutch, High German), only in third degree with Scandinavian, the specific

"Saxon" racial type that overran England in the fifth and sixth centuries was largely the same as that now represented by the Danes, who speak a Scandinavian language, while the High German-speaking population of central and southern Germany [4] is markedly distinct.

But what if we ignore these finer distinctions and simply assume that the "Teutonic" or Baltic or North European racial type coincided in its distribution with that of the Germanic languages? Are we not on safe ground then? No, we are now in hotter water than ever. First of all, the mass of the German-speaking population (central and southern Germany, German Switzerland, German Austria) do not belong to the tall, blond-haired, long-headed [5] "Teutonic" race at all, but to the shorter, darker-complexioned, short-headed [6] Alpine race, of which the central population of France, the French Swiss, and many of the western and northern Slavs (e.g., Bohemians and Poles) are equally good representatives. The distribution of these "Alpine" populations corresponds in part to that of the old continental "Celts," whose language has everywhere given way to Italic, Germanic, and Slavic pressure. We shall do well to avoid speaking of a "Celtic race," but if we were driven to give the term a content, it would probably be more appropriate to apply it to, roughly, the western portion of the Alpine peoples than to the two island types that I referred to before. These latter were certainly "Celticized," in speech and, partly, in blood, precisely as, centuries later, most of England and part of Scotland was "Teutonized" by the Angles and Saxons. Linguistically speaking, the "Celts" of to-day (Irish Gaelic, Manx, Scotch Gaelic, Welsh, Breton) are Celtic and most of the Germans of to-day are Germanic precisely as the American Negro, Americanized Jew, Minnesota Swede, and German-American are "English." But, secondly, the Baltic race was, and is, by no means an exclusively Germanic-speaking people. The northernmost "Celts," such as the Highland Scotch, are in all probability a specialized offshoot of this race. What these people spoke before they were Celticized nobody knows, but there is nothing whatever to indicate that they spoke a Germanic language. Their language may quite well have been as remote from any known Indo-European idiom as are Basque and Turkish to-day. Again, to the east of the Scandinavians are non-Germanic members of the race—the Finns and related peoples, speaking languages that are not definitely known to be related to Indo-European at all.

We cannot stop here. The geographical position of the Germanic languages is such [7] as to make it highly probable that they represent but an outlying transfer of an Indo-European dialect (possibly a Celto-Italic prototype) to a Baltic people speaking a language or a group of languages that was alien to Indo-European.[8] Not only, then, is English not spoken by a unified race at present but its prototype, more likely than not, was originally a foreign language to the race with which English is more particularly associated. We need not seriously entertain the idea that English or the group of languages to which it belongs is in any intelligible sense the expression of race, that there are embedded in it qualities that reflect the temperament or "genius" of a particular breed of human beings.

Many other, and more striking, examples of the lack of correspondence between race and language could be given if space permitted. One instance will do for many. The Malayo-Polynesian languages form a well-defined group that takes in the southern end of the Malay Peninsula and the tremendous island world to the south and east (except Australia and the greater part of New Guinea). In this vast region we find represented no less than three distinct races —the Negro-like Papuans of New Guinea and Melanesia, the Malay race of Indonesia, and the Polynesians of the outer islands. The Polynesians and Malays all speak languages of the Malayo-Polynesian group, while the languages of the Papuans belong partly to this group (Melanesian), partly to the unrelated languages ("Papuan") of New Guinea.[9] In spite of the fact that the greatest race cleavage in this region lies between the Papuans and the Polynesians, the major linguistic division is of Malayan on the one side, Melanesian and Polynesian on the other.

As with race, so with culture. Particularly in more primitive levels, where the secondarily unifying power of the "national" [10] ideal does not arise to disturb the flow of what we might call natural distributions, is it easy to show that language and culture are not intrinsically associated. Totally unrelated languages share in one culture, closely related languages—even a single language—belong to distinct culture spheres. There are many excellent examples in aboriginal America. The Athabaskan languages form as clearly unified, as structurally specialized, a group as any that I know of. [11] The speakers of these languages belong to four distinct culture areas—the simple hunting culture of western Canada and the interior of Alaska (Loucheux, Chipewyan), the buffalo culture of the Plains (Sarcee), the highly ritualized culture of the southwest (Navaho), and the peculiarly specialized culture of northwestern California (Hupa). The cultural adaptability of the Athabaskan-speaking peoples is in the strangest contrast to the inaccessibility to foreign influences of the languages themselves. The Hupa Indians are very typical of the culture area to which they belong. Culturally identical with them are the neighboring Yurok and Karok. There is the liveliest intertribal intercourse between the Hupa, Yurok, and Karok, so much so that all three generally attend an important religious ceremony given by any one of them. It is difficult to say what elements in their combined culture belong in origin to this tribe or that, so much at one are they in communal action, feeling, and thought. But their languages are not merely alien to each other; they belong to three of the major American linguistic groups, each with an immense distribution on the northern continent. Hupa, as we have seen, is Athabaskan and, as such, is also distantly related to Haida (Queen Charlotte Islands) and Tlingit (southern Alaska); Yurok is one of the two isolated Californian languages of the Algonkin stock, the center of gravity of which lies in. the region of the Great Lakes; Karok is the northernmost member of the Hokan group, which stretches far to the south beyond the confines of California and has remoter relatives along the Gulf of Mexico.

Returning to English, most of us would readily admit, I believe, that the community of language between Great Britain and the United States is far from arguing a like community of culture. It is customary to say that they possess a common "Anglo-Saxon" cultural heritage, but are not many significant differences in life and feeling obscured by the tendency of the "cultured" to take this common heritage too much for granted? In so far as America is still specifically "English," it is only colonially or vestigially so; its prevailing cultural drift is partly towards autonomous and distinctive developments, partly towards immersion in the larger European culture of which that of England is only a particular facet. We cannot deny that the possession of a common language is still and will long continue to be a smoother of the way to a mutual cultural understanding between England and America, but it is very clear that other factors, some of them rapidly cumulative, are working powerfully to counteract this leveling influence. A common language cannot indefinitely set the seal on a common culture when geographical, political, and economic determinants of the culture are no longer the same throughout its area.

Language, race, and culture are not necessarily correlated. This does not mean that they never are. There is one tendency, as a matter of fact, for racial and cultural lines of cleavage to correspond to linguistic ones, though in any given case the latter may not be of the same degree of importance as the others. Thus, there is a fairly definite line of cleavage between the Polynesian languages, race, and culture on the one hand and those of the Melanesians on the other, in spite of a considerable amount of overlapping.[12] The racial and cultural divisions, however, particularly the former, are of major importance, while the linguistic division is of quite minor significance, the Polynesian languages constituting hardly more than a special dialectic subdivision of the combined Melanesian-Polynesian group. Still clearer-cut coincidences of cleavage may be found. The language, race, and culture of the Eskimo are markedly distinct from those of their neighbors;[13] in southern Africa the language, race, and culture of the Bushmen offer an even stronger contrast to those of their Bantu neighbors. Coincidences of this sort are of the greatest significance, of course, but this significance is not one of inherent psychological relation between the three factors of race, language, and culture. The coincidences of cleavage point merely to a readily intelligible historical association. If the Bantu and Bushmen are so sharply differentiated in all respects, the reason is simply that the former are relatively recent arrivals in southern Africa. The two peoples developed in complete isolation from each other; their present propinquity is too recent for the slow process of cultural and racial assimilation to have set in very powerfully. As we go back in time, we shall have to assume that relatively scanty populations occupied large territories for untold generations and that contact with other masses of population was not as insistent and prolonged as it later became. The geographical and historical isolation that brought about race differentiations was naturally favorable also to far-reaching variations in language and culture. The very fact that races and cultures which are brought into historical contact tend to assimilate in the long run, while neighboring languages assimilate each other only casually and in superficial respects,[14] indicates that there is no profound causal relation between the development of language and the specific development of race and of culture.

But surely, the wary reader will object, there must be some relation between language and culture, and between language and at least that intangible aspect of race that we call "temperament." Is it not inconceivable that the particular collective qualities of mind that have fashioned a culture are not precisely the same as were responsible for the growth of a particular linguistic morphology? This question takes us into the heart of the most difficult problems of social psychology. It is doubtful if any one has yet attained to sufficient clarity on the nature of the historical process and on the ultimate psychological factors involved in linguistic and cultural drifts to answer it intelligently. I can only very briefly set forth my own views, or rather my general attitude. It would be very difficult to prove that "temperament," the general emotional disposition of a people,[15] is basically responsible for the slant and drift of a culture, however much it may manifest itself in an individual's handling of the elements of that culture. But granted that temperament has a certain value for the shaping of culture, difficult though it be to say just how, it does not follow that it has the same value for the shaping of language. It is impossible to show that the form of a language has the slightest connection with national temperament. Its line of variation, its drift, runs inexorably in the channel ordained for it by its historic antecedents; it is as regardless of the feelings and sentiments of its speakers as is the course of a river of the atmospheric humors of the landscape. I am convinced that it is futile to look in linguistic structure for differences corresponding to the temperamental variations which are supposed to be correlated with race. In this connection it is well to remember that the emotional aspect of our psychic life is but meagerly expressed in the build of language.

Language and our thought-grooves are inextricably interwoven, are, in a sense, one and the same. As there is nothing to show that there are significant racial differences in the fundamental conformation of thought, it follows that the infinite variability of linguistic form, another name for the infinite variability of the actual process of thought, cannot be an index of such significant racial differences. This is only apparently a paradox. The latent content of all languages is the same—the intuitive *science* of experience. It is the manifest form that is never twice the same, for this form, which we call linguistic morphology, is nothing more or less than a collective *art* of thought, an art denuded of the irrelevancies of individual sentiment. At last analysis, then, language can no more flow from race as such than can the sonnet form.

Nor can I believe that culture and language are in any true sense causally related. Culture may be defined as *what* a society does and thinks. Language is a particular *how* of thought. It is difficult to see what particular causal relations may be expected to subsist between a selected inventory of experience (culture, a significant selection made by society) and the particular manner in which the society expresses all experience. The drift of culture, another way of saying history, is a complex series of changes in society's selected inventory—additions, losses, changes of emphasis and relation. The drift of language is not properly concerned with changes of content at all, merely with changes in formal expression. It is possible, in thought, to change every sound, word, and concrete concept of a language without changing its inner actuality in the least, just as one can pour into a fixed mold water or plaster or molten gold. If it can be shown that culture has an innate form, a series of contours, quite apart from subject-matter of any description whatsoever, we have a something in culture that may serve as a term of comparison with and possibly a means of relating it to language. But until such purely formal patterns of culture are discovered and laid bare, we shall do well to hold the drifts of language and of culture to be non-comparable and unrelated processes. From this it follows that all attempts to connect particular types of linguistic morphology with certain correlated stages of cultural development are vain. Rightly understood, such correlations are rubbish. The merest *coup d'œil* verifies our theoretical argument on this point. Both simple and complex types of language of an indefinite number of varieties may be found spoken at any desired level of cultural advance. When it comes to linguistic form, Plato walks with the Macedonian swineherd, Confucius with the head-hunting savage of Assam.

It goes without saying that the mere content of language is intimately related to culture. A society that has no knowledge of theosophy need have no name for it; aborigines that had never seen or heard of a horse were compelled to invent or borrow a word for the animal when they made his acquaintance. In the sense that the vocabulary of a language more or less faithfully reflects the culture whose purposes it serves it is perfectly true that the history of language and the history of culture move along parallel lines. But this superficial and extraneous kind of parallelism is of no real interest to the linguist except in so far as the growth or borrowing of new words incidentally throws light on the formal trends of the language. The linguistic student should never make the mistake of identifying a language with it dictionary.

There is perhaps no better way to learn the essential nature of speech than to realize what it is not and what it does not do. Its superficial connections with other historic processes are so close that it needs to be shaken free of them if we are to see it in its own right. Everything that we have so far seen to be true of language points to the fact that it is the most significant and colossal work that the human spirit has evolved—nothing short of a finished form of expression for all communicable experience. This form may be endlessly varied by the individual without thereby losing its distinctive contours; and it is constantly reshaping itself as is all art. Language is the most massive and inclusive art we know, a mountainous and anonymous work of unconscious generations.

NOTES

[1] Itself an amalgam of North "French" and Scandinavian elements.

[2] The "Celtic" blood of what is now England and Wales is by no means confined to the Celtic-speaking regions—Wales and, until recently, Cornwall. There is every reason to believe that the invading Germanic tribes

(Angles, Saxons, Jutes) did not exterminate the Brythonic Celts of England nor yet drive them altogether into Wales and Cornwall (there has been far too much "driving" of conquered peoples into mountain fastnesses and land's ends in our histories), but simply intermingled with them and imposed their rule and language upon them.

3 In practice these three peoples can hardly be kept altogether distinct. The terms have rather a local-sentimental than a clearly racial value. Intermarriage has gone on steadily for centuries and it is only in certain outlying regions that we get relatively pure types, e.g., the Highland Scotch of the Hebrides. In America, English, Scotch, and Irish strands have become inextricably interwoven.

4 The High German now spoken in northern Germany is not of great age, but is due to the spread of standardized German, based on Upper Saxon, a High German dialect, at the expense of "Plattdeutsch."

5 "Dolichocephalic."

6 "Brachycephalic."

7 By working back from such data as we possess we can make it probable that these languages were originally confined to a comparatively small area in northern Germany and Scandinavia. This area is clearly marginal to the total area of distribution of the Indo-European-speaking peoples. Their center of gravity, say 1000 B.C., seems to have lain in southern Russia.

8 While this is only a theory, the technical evidence for it is stronger than one might suppose. There are a surprising number of common and characteristic Germanic words which cannot be connected with known Indo-European radical elements and which may well be survivals of the hypothetical pre-Germanic language; such are *house, stone, sea, wife* (German *Haus, Stein, See, Weib*).

9 Only the easternmost part of this island is occupied by Melanesian-speaking Papuans.

10 A "nationality" is a major, sentimentally unified, group. The historical factors that lead to the feeling of national unity are various—political, cultural, linguistic, geographic, sometimes specifically religious. True racial factors also may enter in, though the accent on "race" has generally a psychological rather than a strictly biological value. In an area dominated by the national sentiment there is a tendency for language and culture to become uniform and specific, so that linguistic and cultural boundaries at least tend to coincide. Even at best, however, the linguistic unification is never absolute, while the cultural unity is apt to be superficial, of a quasi-political nature, rather than deep and far-reaching.

11 The Semitic languages, idiosyncratic as they are, are no more definitely ear-marked.

12 The Fijians, for instance, while of Papuan (negroid) race, are Polynesian rather than Melanesian in their cultural and linguistic affinities.

13 Though even here there is some significant overlapping. The southernmost Eskimo of Alaska were assimilated in culture to their Tlingit neighbors. In northeastern Siberia, too, there is no sharp cultural line between the Eskimo and the Chukchi.

14 The supersession of one language by another is of course not truly a matter of linguistic assimilation.

15 "Temperament" is a difficult term to work with. A great deal of

what is loosely charged to national "temperament" is really nothing but customary behavior, the effect of traditional ideals of conduct. In a culture, for instance, that does not look kindly upon demonstrativeness, the natural tendency to the display of emotion becomes more than normally inhibited. It would be quite misleading to argue from the customary inhibition, a cultural fact, to the native temperament. But ordinarily we can get at human conduct only as it is culturally modified. Temperament in the raw is a highly elusive thing.

III

SOCIAL ORGANIZATION

DAS MUTTERRECHT *

By J. BACHOFEN

INTRODUCTION

THE purpose of the present work is to discuss a historical phenomenon that has hitherto been regarded by few
and which no one has as yet fully examined. Students of
antiquity fail to mention the matriarchy. The very word is
new, as is the type of family life to which it refers. We not
only lack extensive preparatory work, but to date no investigator has made any effort to interpret that stage of
•civilization to which the matriarchy belongs. In discussing
it, we are, therefore, entering upon entirely unexplored
ground. This study will lead us from the known ages of
antiquity into earlier periods and from the world of ideas
that has been so familiar to us in the past into an older
milieu, wholly unknown. Those peoples with whose names
the greatness of antiquity is almost exclusively associated
must recede into the background, while others, who nevei
attained the heights of classical culture, occupy their places.
An unknown world is suddenly revealed to us. And, the
farther we penetrate into this world, the more strange does
everything about us become. Everywhere we meet antitheses
to the ideas of an advanced civilization, everywhere older
views, for we are entering into an era with a character of
its own and a morality that can be judged only on the basis
of its own principles. The gynæcocratic law of the family
is strange not only when we view it. The Ancients already
looked upon it as peculiar. Beside the Hellenic form of life
that older law to which the matriarchy belongs, from which
it has proceeded, and by which alone it can be explained,

* *Das Mutterrecht.* The material here reproduced was translated by
Frida Ilmer.

seems strange, indeed. It will be the aim of the following investigation to present the vital principle underlying this gynæcocratic epoch. I wish to show it in its true relationships with the lower stages of culture on the one hand, and the more advanced on the other. I fully realize that I have set myself a task that is more inclusive than the title I have chosen would indicate. It will extend to all phases of gynæcocratic ethics, illuminating both its individual traits and the fundamental principle uniting them. Thus I hope to reconstruct the picture of a stage of culture that has been arrested, and in places even completley halted, by the advance of the classical era. My aim may seem too ambitious. But only by thus expanding our vision to its widest limits is it possible to gain true understanding and to extend the scientific idea with that clarity and precision which constitute the essence of knowledge.

Of all reports that testify to the existence of the matriarchy in its intrinsic form, those concerning the Lykians are the clearest and most valuable. The Lykians, so reports Herodotus, named their children not after their fathers, as did the Hellenes, but after their mothers. In all genealogical reports they stressed only the maternal line of descent and determined the rank of the child solely by that of its mother. Nicholas of Damascus strengthened this statement by calling attention to the exclusive inheritance rights of daughters. These rights he traced back to a traditional law of the Lykians, that is, an unwritten law, which, according to Socrates' definition must be regarded as given by the gods themselves. Although Herodotus sees in them nothing more than a strange deviation from Hellenic custom, the observation of their inner unity must lead us to a profounder interpretation. What we meet is not incoherent, but systematic; it is not arbitrary, but seems to have arisen from necessity. Since, in addition, any influence of a written law-code is emphatically denied, the assumption that these customs represent but an insignificant anomaly, loses its last semblance of justification. The Hellenic-Roman father principle is

hereby contrasted with a code of family ethics that is its
direct opposite both in its fundamental principles and in
their resultant development. This concept is further affirmed
by the discovery of similar codes among other races. According to an Egyptian custom, testified to by Diodorus,
daughters alone are responsible for the support of their aged
parents. This corresponds well to the exclusive inheritance
rights of the Lykians. But even though this practice seems
to complete the Lykian system, a report of Strabo's concerning the Cantabrians leads us to still further variants of the
same principle. Among the Cantabrians, so Strabo reports,
brothers are elocated and equipped with dowries by their
sisters. In addition to presenting a remarkably complete
picture, these facts also justify the assumption that the
matriarchy is not merely an unusual development peculiar
to one nation, but is characteristic of an entire cultural stage.
Granted the uniformity of human nature, we must conclude
that the matriarchy is not conditioned nor limited by racial
lines. Finally, we must turn our attention not so much to
the internal harmony prevailing in the various forms discovered, as to the identity of the fundamental idea governing the entire system.

To this series of general facts the Polybrian reports concerning the 100 aristocratic Locrian families which are
characterized by maternal genealogy adds even more intrinsically related material, the correctness and significance of
which will be proven in the course of this investigation.
The matriarchy belongs to an earlier stage of civilization
than the patriarchal system and its full and unlimited
strength crumbled before victorious paternity. That this was
so is corroborated by the fact that the gynæcocratic forms
of society are found principally among those nations that
are older than the Hellenic peoples. They are an essential
part of that original culture whose peculiarities are as
closely linked up with the predominance of the matriarchy
as Hellenism is with the rule of the father.

The marked coherence evidenced by gynæcocratic culture points clearly to the existence of one governing principle, whose every outward expression is of the same substance. They suggest a self-sufficient stage in the development of the human mind. The dominance of the maternal element cannot be conceived of as an individual phenomenon. Such a morality, for instance, as that displayed by the Hellenic civilization at its height, cannot be associated with it. The same contrast that governs the patriarchal and matriarchal principles must of necessity permeate every phase of life in these two cultures.

The consistency of the gynæcocratic principle is borne out in the preference of the left over the right, commonly found among matriarchic peoples. The left direction belongs to the passive nature of woman, while the right is characteristic of the active male. To clarify this point, we need but recall the part which the left hand of Isis plays in the Nile region, one of the strongholds of matriarchy. Once we have become aware of this tendency, other facts soon appear in great numbers, testifying to its significance and universality, and assuring its freedom from philosophic speculation. In manners and usages of civil life as well as of ritual, in peculiarities of garment as well as of hairdress, no less than in the meaning of certain idiomatic turns of speech, the same fundamental principle finds repeated expression. It is the principle of the *major honos lævarum partium,* closely associated with the matriarchy.

By no means less significant is a second expression of the same fundamental law, that of the predominance of night over the day born of her maternal womb. An opposite conception would be decidedly in conflict with the gynæcocratic point of view. In antiquity already has the preference of night been associated with that of the left, and both have been placed in line with a dominant maternal influence. In this instance, too, hoary customs and usages, such as the reckoning of time by nights, the selection of the night for battles, council and court assemblies, that is, the preference of darkness for the exercise of social functions, show that we are not dealing with a philosophic theory of a later origin, but with an actual, primary mode of life. Pursuing this line of reasoning, we shall easily recognize the preference of the moon over the sun and of the receptive earth over the fertilizing ocean as the integral characteristics of an epoch that was primarily matriarchic. Added to these observations comes the preference of the sinister aspect of life, death, over its bright aspect of creation, the predominance of the dead over the living and of sorrow over joy. In the course of this investigation they will receive a deeper affirmation and significance. At this point we find ourselves involved in an ideology to which the matriarchy appears no longer as a strange and incomprehensible phenomenon, but as a homogeneous entity. Nevertheless, our picture still shows many gaps and vague patches. But every discovery that rests upon a solid foundation possesses the unusual power of rapidly attracting everything related to it into its own sphere, thus pointing readily the way from the obvious to hidden facts.

A faint hint made by an author of antiquity often suffices, then, to disclose new vistas. Such an example is offered by the distinction of the sister and of the youngest-born child. Both of these usages belong to the maternal principle, displaying its fundamental law in a new guise. The significance of the sister relationship is hinted at by a remark which Tacitus makes concerning the corresponding German practice. A similar report of Plutarch's concerning Roman usages reveals the fact that here, too, we are not confronted by an accidental, localized custom, but by the effects of a universal principle. The preference for the youngest child is fully recognized by Philostrates in his *Heroic Tales*. And even though this work falls into a somewhat later period, it is nonetheless of the greatest significance in the interpretation of the oldest ideas. A great number of disconnected examples, gleaned in part from mythical traditions and in part from historical reports, soon gather about these two practices, proving their universal application as well as their originality. It is not difficult to see with which phase of the gynæcocratic idea each of these phenomena is associated. The preference of the sister over the brother merely lends a new expression to that of the daughter over the son. The preference of the youngest-born child attaches the prolongation of life to that offspring of the maternal stem, which, because it was the last to spring into being, will also be the last to be reached by death.

The family that is based upon patriarchic law soon solidifies into one individual organism, while the matriarchic family bears that typically collective character which stands at the commencement of all civilization. It is this collective character which distinguishes the material aspects of life from the higher, spiritual ones. Herself the mortal image of the Mother of Earth, Demeter, every woman gives birth to children who are the brothers and sisters of every other woman's child. The native country under matriarchy will know only brothers and sisters, and this will last until an exclusively patriarchal era will have superseded it, dissolving the unity of the mass and supplanting all with the smaller units of the family. In matriarchic communities this phase of the maternal principle frequently finds legal expression; indeed it is often affirmed by law. Upon it rests that principle of liberty and equality which we shall often meet as a fundamental trait in the life of gynæcocracies. It is also the source of opposition to limiting barriers of any kind. It is the cause of the far-reaching significance of certain concepts, which, not unlike the Roman *paricidium,* were slow to exchange their natural and general meaning with their individual, i.e., limited application. Finally it is the source of the special praise bestowed upon a sense of closeness and συμπάβεια, which knows no bounds and includes all members of the race without distinction. The absence of strife and aversion to warfare are characteristics that are repeatedly lauded in accounts of matriarchic states.

The elevation of the human race and the progress of ethics are closely linked up with the rule of woman. In like manner the introduction of regularity and the cultivation of the religious sense. The enjoyment of every higher pleasure must be closely associated with the matriarchy. The longing for a purification of life arises earlier in woman than in man, and she also possesses to a higher degree the natural faculty of effecting it. The entire ethic code that follows upon barbarism is the work of woman. Her contribution to society is not only the power to give life, but also the ability to bestow all that which makes life beautiful. Hers is the earliest knowledge of the forces of nature, hers is also the presentiment and the hope that conquers the pain of death. Viewed from this angle, the gynæcocracy appears as a testimony to the progress of civilization. It is the source and guarantee of its benefits, as well as a necessary educational period in the history of man. It is therefore in itself the realization of natural law whose patterns must be observed by entire races as well as by individual beings.

The circle in which my ideas have developed has now been completed. I began by stressing the independence of matriarchy from all written laws and deduced from this its universal nature. I am now able to affirm its genuine position among family ethics and to complete its description.

Originating with the life-giving power of maternity, whose physical image it reflects, the gynæcocracy is completely under the influence of matter and of the natural phenomena from which it has derived its laws. Woman is more keenly aware of the unity pervading all life. She is more closely linked to the harmony of the universe, of which she still is a part. She is more sensitive to the pain of man's mortal fate and to that frailty of the earthly existence to which woman, and especially the mother, devotes her sorrow. She seeks with greater longing a higher consolation and finds it in the phenomena of nature. But these, too, she links up closely with the life-giving womb, the receptive, protecting, and nourishing mother's love. Obedient in every respect to the laws of material existence, she prefers to direct her glances down to the ground, placing the χτονίc powers above those of the Uranic light. She identifies male potency preferably with inland water, subordinating the procreative fluidum to the *gremium matris, the* ὀκεάνος to the earth. Her own existence being grounded in the soil, she bestows all her care and labor upon the beautification of the material life, the πραχτιχὴ ἀρετή. In agriculture, which woman was the first to develop, and in the construction of walls, which the Ancients very closely associated with the cult of the chthonic, she achieves a perfection that has often been admired by later generations. In no other period than during the matriarchy has there been such an emphatic stress placed upon the external appearance and the protection of the body, while spiritual beauty was scarcely emphasized. Nor has there ever been another era that carried out so consistently the maternal dualism and a *de facto* realistic spirit. No other period has been equally concerned to further lyric enthusiasm, that primarily feminine mood, rooted in the love of nature. In other words, the gynæcocratic form of life is a well-ordered naturalism, its laws of thought are materialistic, its development is chiefly physical. It is a stage of culture that is just as necessary in matriarchy as it is strange and incomprehensible in a patriarchic age.

·   ·   ·   ·   ·   ·   ·

Those who believe in the necessary primacy of permanent sexual unions cannot be spared a humiliating surprise. The ruling thought of antiquity is not only different from theirs; it is its perfect antithesis. The Demetrian principle [of marriage] appears at first as the limitation of a more original principle that was directly opposed to it. Marriage itself seems as the violation of a religious commandment. This condition, incomprehensible as it may appear to our ideology, is nevertheless supported by historical testimony. It alone is able to explain to our satisfaction a series of most peculiar phenomena that have never been appreciated in their true light. It alone can account for the belief that marriage requires the propitiation of the godhead whose law it violates by its exclusive character. Nature has not endowed woman with all her charms merely to let her fade in the arms of one man. The law of materialism abhors all limitations; it hates all bonds, and considers exclusiveness of any kind as a sin against its divine power. This fact, then, explains all usages that cause marriage itself to appear in association with rites of religious prostitution. Though varied in form, they are nevertheless similar in their fundamental idea. The deviation from natural law which is implied in marriage must be expiated by temporary prostitution, thus winning anew the favor of the god. The two institutions that appear to be mutually exclusive, prostitution and rigid marriage laws, now appear to be linked by the closest bonds: prostitution itself becomes a security for marital chastity, and the worship of this chastity becomes a condition to which woman's calling as wife is bound. It is obvious that the progress toward a higher morality could at best be very slow during the struggle against this attitude which, moreover, was shielded by religious sanction. The variety of intermediate stages which we discover prove, indeed, how fluctuating were the fortunes of the struggle that was waged on this behalf for thousands of years. The Demetrian principle advances but slowly toward victory. In the course of the ages the expiation which the married woman must pay was reduced to a smaller amount and to an easier service. The gradual emergence of these individual stages deserves our most careful understanding. At first the annual payment gives place to one single tribute. Instead of the matron it is the unmarried girl who serves as hetæra; prostitution, instead of being practiced after marriage, is now practiced before. Instead of unquestioning surrender to any male, only a certain few men are now selected. In connection with these limitations there appears the consecration of hierordulas. This step has become of special significance, since it places the payment of the expiation upon the shoulders of one particular class, thereby freeing the matron entirely from her duty and contributing toward the elevation of society. The lightest form of individual expiation is found in the sacrifice of the woman's hair at marriage. Hair has in many instances been named as the equivalent of the body in the prime of life. The Ancients, especially, have associated it closely with the irregularity of hetæric procreation, particularly with the vegetation of the morast, its prototype in nature. All of these phases have left numerous traces in their wake, not only in mythology, but also in the history of different peoples; they have found verbal expression even in the names of places, gods, and tribes.

It seems strange to us, who are accustomed to different modes of thought, to see conditions and events which we are wont to relegate to the intimacy of the family circle exerting such a far-reaching influence upon the entire state, its rise and its decline. That aspect of the internal development of Ancient man with which we are now concerned has not been given the slightest attention by past investigators. Still, it is precisely this connection which exists between the attitude toward the relationship of the sexes and the entire lives and destinies of nations that brings the following study into immediate contact with the primary questions of history. The encounter of the Asiatic world with that of the Greek is represented as a struggle between the Aphroditic-Hetæric and the Hereic-monogamous principles. Likewise, the cause of the Trojan War is led back to the violation of the marital couch. In continuation of the same idea, the finally complete conquest of Aphrodite, the mother of the Æneads, by the matronal Juno, is placed in the era of the second Punic War, that is, that period in which the inner strength of the Roman people had attained its apex.

The connection that exists between all these phenomena cannot be overlooked. History has imposed the task upon the Occident to lead the higher, Demetrian principle to victory because of the purer and chaster nature of its peoples thus freeing mankind from the bondage of the lowest telluricism in which the magic power of the Oriental culture has held it captive. It is to the political idea of the imperium with which it entered into the arena of world history that Rome owes the power which enabled it to end forever a complete culture that had once been prevalent in antiquity.

ORGANIZATION OF SOCIETY UPON THE BASIS OF SEX *

By LEWIS H. MORGAN

In treating the subject of the growth of the idea of government, the organization into gentes on the basis of kin naturally suggests itself as the archaic framework of ancient society; but there is a still older and more archaic organization, that into classes on the basis of sex, which first demands attention. It will not be taken up because of its novelty in human experience, but for the higher reason that it seems to contain the germinal principle of the gens. If this inference is warranted by the facts it will give to this organization into male and female classes, now found in full vitality among the Australian aborigines, an ancient prevalence as widespread in the tribes of mankind as the original organization into gentes.

It will soon be perceived that low down in savagery community of husbands and wives, within prescribed limits, was the central principle of the social system. The marital rights and privileges (jura conjugalia),[1] established in the group, grew into a stupendous scheme, which became the organic principle on which society was constituted. From the nature of the case these rights and privileges rooted themselves so firmly that emancipation from them was slowly accomplished through movements which resulted in unconscious reformations. Accordingly it will be found that the family has advanced from a lower to a higher form as the range of this conjugal system was gradually reduced. The family, commencing in the consanguine, founded upon the intermarriage of brothers and sisters in a group, passed into the

* *Ancient Society.* New York: Henry Holt & Co.

second form, the punaluan, under a social system akin to the Australian classes, which broke up the first species of marriage by substituting groups of brothers who shared their wives in common, and groups of sisters who shared their husbands in common,—marriage in both cases being in the group. The organization into classes upon sex, and the subsequent higher organization into gentes upon kin, must be regarded as the results of great social movements worked out unconsciously through natural selection. For these reasons the Australian system, about to be presented, deserves attentive consideration, although it carries us into a low grade of human life. It represents a striking phase of the ancient social history of our race.

The organization into classes on the basis of kin now prevails among that portion of the Australian aborigines who speak the Kamilaroi language. They inhabit the Darling River district north of Sydney. Both organizations are also found in other Australian tribes, and so widespread as to render probable their ancient universal prevalence among them. It is evident from internal considerations that the male and female classes are older than the gentes: firstly, because the gentile organization is higher than that into classes; and secondly, because the former, among the Kamilaroi, are in process of overthrowing the latter. The class in its male and female branches is the unit of their social system, which place rightfully belongs to the gens when in full development. A remarkable combination of facts is thus presented; namely, a sexual and a gentile organization, both in existence at the same time, the former holding the central position, and the latter inchoate but advancing to completeness through encroachments upon the former.

This organization upon sex has not been found, as yet, in any tribes of savages out of Australia, but the slow development of these islanders in their secluded habitat, and the more archaic character of the organization upon sex than that into gentes, suggests the conjecture, that the former may have been universal in such branches of the human family as afterwards possessed the gentile organization. Although the class system, when traced out fully, involves some bewildering complications, it will reward the attention necessary for its mastery. As a curious social organization among savages it possesses but little interest; but as the most primitive form of society hitherto discovered, and more especially with the contingent probability that the remote progenitors of our own Aryan family were once similarly organized, it becomes important, and may prove instructive.

The Australians rank below the Polynesians, and far below the American aborigines. They stand below the African Negro and near the bottom of the scale. Their social institutions, therefore, must approach the primitive type as nearly as those of any existing people.[2]

The Kamilaroi are divided into six gentes, standing with reference to the right of marriage, in two divisions, as follows:

I. 1. Iguana, (Duli). 2. Kangaroo, (Murriira).[3] 3. Opossum, (Mute).

II. 4. Emu, (Dinoun). 5. Bandicoot, (Bilba). 6. Blacksnake, (Nurai).

Originally the first three gentes were not allowed to intermarry with each other, because they were subdivisions of an original gens; but they were permitted to marry into either of the other gentes, and *vice versa*. This ancient rule is now modified, among the Kamilaroi, in certain definite particulars, but not carried to the full extent of permitting marriage into any gens but that of the individual. Neither males nor females can marry into their own gens, the prohibition being absolute. Descent is in the female line, which assigns the children to the gens of their mother. These are among the essential characteristics of the gens, wherever this institution is found in its archaic form. In its external features, therefore, it is perfect and complete among the Kamilaroi.

But there is a further and older division of the people

into eight classes, four of which are composed exclusively of males, and four exclusively of females. It is accompanied with a regulation in respect to marriage and descent which obstructs the gens, and demonstrates that the latter organization is in process of development into its true logical form. One only of the four classes of males can marry into one only of the four classes of females. In the sequel it will be found that all the males of one class are, theoretically, the husbands of all the females of the class into which they are allowed to marry. Moreover, if the male belongs to one of the first three gentes the female must belong to one of the opposite three. Marriage is thus restricted to a portion of the males of one gens, with a portion of the females of another gens, which is opposed to the true theory of the gentile institution, for all the members of each gens should be allowed to marry persons of the opposite sex in all the gentes except their own.

The classes are the following:

Male	Female
1. Ippai.	1. Ippata.
2. Kumbo.	2. Buta.
3. Murri.	3. Mata.
4. Kubbi.	4. Kapota.

All the Ippais, of whatever gens, are brothers to each other. Theoretically, they are descended from a supposed common female ancestor. All the Kumbos are the same; and so are all the Murris and Kubbis, respectively, and for the same reason. In like manner, all the Ippatas, of whatever gens, are sisters to each other, and for the same reason; all the Butas are the same, and so are all the Matas and Kapotas, respectively. In the next place, all the Ippais and Ippatas are brothers and sisters to each other, whether children of the same mother or collateral consanguinei, and in whatever gens they are found. The Kumbos and Butas are brothers and sisters; and so are the Murris and Matas, and the Kubbis and Kapotas respectively. If an Ippai and Ippata meet, who have never seen each other before, they address each other as brother and sister. The Kamilaroi, therefore, are organized into four great primary groups of brothers and sisters, each group being composed of a male and a female branch; but intermingled over the areas of their occupation. Founded upon sex, instead of kin, it is older than the gentes, and more archaic, it may be repeated, than any form of society hitherto known.

The classes embody the germ of the gens, but fall short of its realization. In reality the Ippais and Ippatas form a single class in two branches, and since they cannot inter-marry they would form the basis of a gens but for the reason that they fall under two names, each of which is integral for certain purposes, and for the further reason that their children take different names from their own. The division into classes is upon sex instead of kin, and has its primary relation to a rule of marriage as remarkable as it is original.

Since brothers and sisters are not allowed to intermarry, the classes stand to each other in a different order with respect to the right of marriage, or rather, of cohabitation, which better expresses the relation. Such was the original law, thus:

> Ippai can marry Kapota, and no other.
> Kumbo can marry Mata, and no other.
> Murri can marry Buta, and no other.
> Kubbi can marry Ippata, and no other.

This exclusive scheme has been modified in one particular, as will hereafter be shown: namely, in giving to each class of males the right of intermarriage with one additional class of females. In this fact, evidence of the encroachment of the gens upon the class is furnished, tending to the overthrow of the latter.

It is thus seen that each male in the selection of a wife is limited to one-fourth part of all the Kamilaroi females. This, however, is not the remarkable part of the system. Theoretically every Kapota is the wife of every Ippai; every Mata is the wife of every Kumbo; every Buta is the wife of every Murri; and every Ippata of every Kubbi. Upon this material point the information is specific. Mr. Fison, before mentioned, after observing that Mr. Lance had "had much intercourse with the natives, having lived among them many years on frontier cattle-stations on the Darling River, and in the trans-Darling country," quotes from his letter as follows: "If a Kubbi meets a stranger Ippata, they address each other as Goleer—Spouse. . . . A Kubbi thus meeting an Ippata, even though she were of another tribe, would treat her as his wife, and his right to do so would be recognized by her tribe." Every Ippata within the immediate circle of his acquaintance would consequently be his wife as well.

Here we find, in a direct and definite form, punaluan marriage in a group of unusual extent; but broken up into lesser groups, each a miniature representation of the whole, united for habitation and subsistence. Under the conjugal system thus brought to light, one-quarter of all the males are united in marriage with one-quarter of all the females of the Kamilaroi tribes. This picture of savage life need not revolt the mind because to them it was a form of the marriage relation, and therefore devoid of impropriety. It is but an extended form of polygyny and polyandry, which, within narrower limits, have prevailed universally among savage tribes. The evidence of the fact still exists, in unmistakable form, in their systems of consanguinity and affinity, which have outlived the customs and usages in which they originated. It will be noticed that this scheme of intermarriage is but a step from promiscuity, because it is tantamount to that with the addition of a method. Still, as it is made a subject of organic regulation, it is far removed from general promiscuity. Moreover, it reveals an existing state of marriage and of the family of which no adequate conception could have been formed apart from the facts. It affords the first direct evidence of a state of society which had previously been deduced, as extremely probable, from systems of consanguinity and affinity.[4]

Whilst the children remained in the gens of their mother,

they passed into another class, in the same gens, different from that of either parent. This will be made apparent by the following table:

Male	Female	Male	Female
Ippai marries Kapota.		Their children are Murri and Mata.	
Kumbo marries Mata.		Their children are Kubbi and Kapota.	
Murri marries Buta.		Their children are Ippai and Ippata.	
Kubbi marries Ippata.		Their children are Kumbo and Buta.	

If these descents are followed out it will be found that, in the female line, Kapota is the mother of Mata, and Mata in turn is the mother of Kapota; so Ippata is the mother of Buta, and the latter in turn is the mother of Ippata. It is the same with the male classes; but since descent is in the female line, the Kamilaroi tribes derive themselves from two supposed female ancestors, which laid the foundation for two original gentes. By tracing these descents still further it will be found that the blood of each class passes through all the classes.

Although each individual bears one of the class names above given, it will be understood that each has in addition the single personal name, which is common among savage as well as barbarous tribes. The more closely this organization upon sex is scrutinized, the more remarkable it seems as the work of savages. When once established, and after that transmitted through a few generations, it would hold society with such power as to become difficult of displacement. It would require a similar and higher system, and centuries of time, to accomplish this result; particularly if the range of the conjugal system would thereby be abridged.

The gentile organization supervened naturally upon the classes as a higher organization, by simply enfolding them unchanged. That it was subsequent in point of time, is shown by the relations of the two systems, by the inchoate condition of the gentes, by the impaired condition of the classes through encroachments by the gens, and by the fact that the class is still the unit of organization. These conclusions will be made apparent in the sequel.

From the preceding statements the composition of the

gentes will be understood when placed in their relations to the classes. The latter are in pairs of brothers and sisters derived from each other; and the gentes themselves, through the classes, are in pairs, as follows:

Gentes   *Male*   *Female*   *Male*   *Female*
1. Iguana. All are Murri and Mata, or Kubbi and Kapota.
2. Emu. All are Kumbo and Buta, or Ippai and Ippata.
3. Kangaroo. All are Murri and Mata, or Kubbi and Kapota.
4. Bandicoot. All are Kumbo and Buta, or Ippai and Ippata.
5. Opossum. All are Murri and Mata, or Kubbi and Kapota.
6. Blacksnake. All are Kumbo and Buta, or Ippai and Ippata.

The connection of children with a particular gens is proven by the law of marriage. Thus, Iguana-Mata must marry Kumbo; her children are Kubbi and Kapota, and necessarily Iguana in gens, because descent is in the female line. Iguana-Kapota must marry Ippai; her children are Murri and Mata, and also Iguana in gens, for the same reason. In like manner Emu-Buta must marry Murri; her children are Ippai and Ippata, and of the Emu gens. So Emu-Ippata must marry Kubbi; her children are Kumbo and Buta, and also of the Emu gens. In this manner the gens is maintained by keeping in its membership the children of all its female members. The same is true in all respects of each of the remaining gentes. It will be noticed that each gens is made up, theoretically, of the descendants of two supposed female ancestors, and contains four of the eight classes. It seems probable that originally there were but two male, and two female, classes, which were set opposite to each other in respect to the right of marriage; and that the four afterward subdivided into eight. The classes as an anterior organization were evidently arranged within the gentes, and not formed by the subdivision of the latter.

Moreover, since the Iguana, Kangaroo and Opossum gentes are found to be counterparts of each other, in the classes they contain, it follows that they are subdivisions of an original gens. Precisely the same is true of Emu, Bandicoot and Blacksnake, in both particulars; thus reducing the six to two original gentes, with the right in each to marry into the other, but not into itself. It is confirmed by the fact that the members of the first three gentes could not originally intermarry; neither could the members of the last three. The reason which prevented intermarriage in the gens, when the three were one, would follow the subdivisions because they were of the same descent although under different gentile names. Exactly the same thing is found among the Seneca-Iroquois.

Since marriage is restricted to particular classes, when there were but two gentes, one-half of all the females of one were, theoretically, the wives of one-half of all the males of the other. After their subdivision into six the benefit of marrying out of the gens, which was the chief advantage of the institution, was arrested, if not neutralized, by the presence of the classes together with the restrictions mentioned. It resulted in continuous in-and-in marriages beyond the immediate degree of brother and sister. If the gens could have eradicated the classes this evil would, in a great measure, have been removed.[5] The organization into classes seems to have been directed to the single object of breaking up the intermarriage of brothers and sisters, which affords a probable explanation of the origin of the system. But since it did not look beyond this special abomination it retained a conjugal system nearly as objectionable, as well as cast it in a permanent form.

It remains to notice an innovation upon the original constitution of the classes, and in favor of the gens, which reveals a movement, still pending, in the direction of the true ideal of the gens. It is shown in two particulars: firstly, in allowing each triad of gentes to intermarry with each other, to a limited extent; and secondly, to marry into classes not before permitted. Thus, Iguana-Murri can now marry Mata in the Kangaroo gens, his collateral sister, whereas originally he was restricted to Buta in the opposite three. So Iguana-Kubbi can now marry Kapota, his collateral sister. Emu-Kumbo can now marry Buta, and Emu-Ippai can marry Ippata in the Blacksnake gens, contrary to original limitations. Each class of males in each triad of gentes seems now to be allowed one additional class of females in the two remaining gentes of the same triad, from which they were before excluded. The memoranda sent by Mr. Fison, however, do not show a change to the full extent here indicated.[6]

This innovation would plainly have been a retrograde movement but that it tended to break down the classes. The line of progress among the Kamilaroi, so far as any is observable, was from classes into gentes, followed by a tendency to make the gens instead of the class the unit of the social organism. In this movement the overshadowing system of cohabitation was the resisting element. Social advancement was impossible without diminishing its extent, which was equally impossible so long as the classes with the privileges they conferred remained in full vitality. The *jura conjugalia,* which appertained to these classes, were the dead weight upon the Kamilaroi, without emancipation from which they would have remained for additional thousands of years in the same condition, substantially, in which they were found.

An organization somewhat similar is indicated by the *punalua* of the Hawaiians. Wherever the middle or lower stratum of savagery is uncovered, marriages of entire groups under usages defining the groups have been discovered either in absolute form or such traces as to leave little doubt that such marriages were normal throughout this period of man's history. It is immaterial whether the group, theoretically, was large or small, the necessities of their condition would set a practical limit to the size of the group living together under this custom. If then community of husbands and wives is found to have been a law of the savage state, and, therefore, the essential condition of society in savagery, the inference would be conclusive that our own savage ancestors shared in this common experience of the human race.

In such usages and customs an explanation of the low condition of savages is found. If men in savagery had not been left behind, in isolated portions of the earth, to testify concerning the early condition of mankind in general, it would have been impossible to form any definite conception of what it must have been. An important inference at once arises, namely, that the institutions of mankind have sprung up in a progressive connected series, each of which represents the result of unconscious reformatory movements to extricate society from existing evils. The wear of ages is upon these institutions for the proper understanding of which they must be studied in this light. It cannot be assumed that the Australian savages are now at the bottom of the scale, for their arts and institutions, humble as they are, show the contrary; neither is there any ground for assuming their degradation from a higher condition, because the facts of human experience afford no sound basis for such an hypothesis. Cases of physical and mental deterioration in tribes and nations may be admitted, for reasons which are known, but they never interrupted the general progress of mankind. All the facts of human knowledge and experience tend to show that the human race, as a whole, have steadily progressed from a lower to a higher condition. The arts by which savages maintain their lives are remarkably persistent. They are never lost until superseded by others higher in degree. By the practice of these arts, and by the experience gained through social organizations, mankind have advanced under a necessary law of development, although their progress may have been substantially imperceptible for centuries.

The Australian classes afford the first, and, so far as the writer is aware, the only case in which we are able to look down into the incipient stages of the organization into gentes, and even through it upon an anterior organization so archaic as that upon sex. It seems to afford a glimpse at society when it verged upon the primitive. Among other tribes the gens seems to have advanced in proportion to the curtailment of the conjugal system. Mankind rise in the scale and the family advances through its successive forms, as these rights sink down before the efforts of society to improve its internal organization.

The Australians might not have effected the overthrow of the classes in thousands of years if they had remained un-discovered; while more favored continental tribes had long before perfected the gens, then advanced it through its successive phases, and at last laid it aside after entering upon civilization. Facts illustrating the rise of successive social organizations, such as that upon sex, and that upon kin, are of the highest ethnological value. A knowledge of what they indicate is eminently desirable, if the early history of mankind is to be measurably recovered.

Among the Polynesian tribes the gens was unknown; but traces of a system analogous to the Australian classes appear in the Hawaiian custom of punalua. Original ideas, absolutely independent of previous knowledge and experience are necessarily few in number. Were it possible to reduce the sum of human ideas to underived originals, the small numerical result would be startling. Development is the method of human progress.

In the light of these facts some of the excrescences of modern civilization, such as Mormonism, are seen to be relics of the old savagism not yet eradicated from the human brain. We have the same brain, perpetuated by reproduction, which worked in the skulls of barbarians and savages in by-gone ages; and it has come down to us laden and saturated with the thoughts, aspirations and passions, with which it was busied through the intermediate periods. It is the same brain grown older and larger with the experience of the ages. These outcrops of barbarism are so many revelations of its ancient proclivities. They are explainable as a species of mental atavism.

Out of a few germs of thought, conceived in the early ages, have been evolved all the principal institutions of man-kind. Beginning their growth in the period of savagery,

fermenting through the period of barbarism, they have continued their advancement through the period of civilization. The evolution of these germs of thought has been
guided by a natural logic which formed an essential attribute of the brain itself. So unerringly has this principle
performed its functions in all conditions of experience, and
in all periods of time, that its results are uniform, coherent
and traceable in their courses. These results alone will in
time yield convincing proofs of the unity of origin of
mankind. The mental history of the human race, which is
revealed in institutions, inventions and discoveries, is presumptively the history of a single species, perpetuated
through individuals, and developed through experience.
Among the original germs of thought, which have exercised the most powerful influence upon the human mind,
and upon human destiny, are these which relate to government, to the family, to language, to religion, and to property.
They had a definite beginning far back in savagery, and a
logical progress, but can have no final consummation, because they are still progressing, and must ever continue
to progress.

NOTES

[1] The Romans made a distinction between *connubium* which related
to marriage considered as a civil institution, and *conjugium*, which was
a mere physical union.

[2] For the detailed facts of the Australian system I am indebted to the
Rev. Lorimer Fison, an English missionary in Australia, who received a
portion of them from the Rev. W. Ridley, and another portion from T. E.
Lance, Esq., both of whom had spent many years among the Australian
aborigines, and enjoyed excellent opportunities for observation. The facts
were sent by Mr. Fison with a critical analysis and discussion of the system,
which, with observations of the writer, were published in the *Proceedings
of the Am. Acad. of Arts and Sciences* for 1872. See vol. viii, p. 412 A
brief notice of the Kamilaroi classes is given in McLennan's *Primitive
Marriage,* p. 118; and in Tylor's *Early History of Mankind,* p. 288.

[3] Padymelon: a species of kangaroo.

[4] "Systems of Consanguinity and Affinity of the Human Family," *Smith
sonian Contributions to Knowledge,* vol. xvii, pp. 420, *et seq.*

[5] If a diagram of descents is made, for example, of Ippai and Kapota
and carried to the fourth generation, giving to each intermediate pair
two children, a male and a female, the following results will appear. The
children of Ippai and Kapota are Murri and Mata. As brothers and sis-

ters the latter cannot marry. As the second degree, the children of Murri, married to Buta, are Ippai and Ippata, and of Mata married to Kumbo, are Kubbi and Kapota. Of these, Ippai marries his cousin Kapota, and Kubbi marries his cousin Ippata. It will be noticed that the eight classes are reproduced from two in the second and third generations, with the exception of Kumbo and Buta. At the next or third degree, there are two Murris, two Kumbos, and two Butas; of whom the Murris marry the Butas, their second cousins, and the Kubbis the Matas, their second cousins. At the fourth generation there are four each of Ippais, Kapotas, Kubbis, and Ippatas, who are third cousins. Of these, the Ippais marry the Kapotas, and the Kubbis the Ippatas; and thus it runs from generation to generation. A similar chart of the remaining marriageable classes will produce like results. These details are tedious, but they make the fact apparent that in this condition of ancient society they not only intermarry constantly, but are compelled to do so through this organization upon sex. Cohabitation would not follow this invariable course because an entire male and female class were married in a group; but its occurrence must have been constant under the system. One of the primary objects secured by the gens, when fully matured, was thus defeated: namely, the segregation of a moiety of the descendants of a supposed common ancestor under a prohibition of intermarriage, followed by a right of marrying into any other gens.

[6] *Proc. Am. Acad. Arts and Sciences*, viii, 436.

MOTHERRIGHT *

By E. S. HARTLAND

IN the contemplation of peoples in the lower culture birth is a phenomenon independent of the union of the sexes. By this it is not meant that at the present time everywhere among such peoples physiological knowledge is still in so backward a condition that the coöperation of the sexes is regarded as a matter of indifference in the production of children. That would be to contradict the facts. To-day the vast majority of savage and barbarous nations are aware that sexual union is ordinarily a condition precedent to birth. Even among such peoples, however, exceptions are admitted without difficulty; and there are peoples like certain Australian tribes who do not yet understand it. Their stage of ignorance was probably once the state of other races and indeed of all humanity. The history of mankind so far as we can trace it, whether in written records or by the less direct but not less certain methods of scientific investigation, exhibits the slow and gradual encroachments of knowledge on the confines of almost boundless ignorance. That such ignorance should once have touched the hidden springs of life itself is no more incredible than that it should have extended to the cause of death. There are plenty of races who even yet attribute a death by anything else than violence to the machinations of an evil-disposed person or spirit, no matter how old or enfeebled by privation or hardship the deceased may have been. Nor do they omit anything which may render their ignorance on this point unambiguous; they proceed to discover and punish the sorcerer; they expel the malicious spirit; they appease the enraged or arbitrary divinity.

* *Primitive Paternity.* London: David Nutt.

Death has a character mysterious and awful, of which no familiarity has been able to divest it, and which not even the latest researches of physiologists have been able to dispel. Ignorance of the real cause of birth, it might be thought, on the other hand would not long survive the habitual commerce of men and women and the continual reproduction of the species. It would not, in our stage of civilization and with our social regulations. But the theory of the evolution of civilization postulates the evolution of man, mentally and morally as well as physically. At the moment when the anthropoid became entitled to be properly denominated man his intellectual capacity was not that of a Shakespeare, a Newton, a Darwin, or even of an average Englishman of the twentieth century. He was only endowed with potentialities which, after an unknown series of generations and thanks to what we in our nescience variously dub a fortunate combination of circumstances or an overruling Providence, issued in that supreme result. The savage who has not been thus favored is still by comparison undeveloped. His intellectual faculties are chiefly employed in winning material subsistence, in gratifying his passions, in fighting with his fellow-man and with the wild beasts, often in maintaining a doubtful conflict against inclement skies, unfruitful earth or tempestuous seas. Many of them, therefore, are dormant, like a bud before it has unfolded. His attention, not habitually directed to the problems of the universe, is easily tired. His knowledge is severely limited; his range of ideas is small. Credulous as a child, he is put off from the solution of a merely speculative question by a tale that chimes with his previous ideas, though it may transcend his actual experience. Hence many a deduction, many an induction, to us plain and obvious, has been retarded, or never reached at all: he is still a savage.

During many ages the social organization of mankind would not have necessitated the concentration of thought on the problem of paternity. Descent is still reckoned exclusively through the mother by a number of savage and barbarous peoples. This mode of reckoning descent is called by a useful term of German origin—Motherright. It would be impossible to undertake an exhaustive enumeration of the peoples among which motherright prevails. The civilized nations of Europe and European origin reckon descent and consequently kinship through both parents. A few others, chiefly more civilized nations like the Chinese and the Arabs, agree with them. Apart from these it may be roughly said that motherright is found in every quarter of the globe. Not that every people is in the stage of mother-right: on the contrary, many reckon through the father. But even where the latter is the case vestiges of the former are commonly to be traced. And the result of anthropological investigations during the past half-century has been to show that motherright everywhere preceded fatherright and the reckoning of descent in the modern civilized fashion through both parents.

This past universality of motherright points to a very early origin. It must have taken its rise in a condition of society ruder than any of which we have cognizance. Let us consider what social organization it implies. Kinship is a sociological term. It is not synonymous with blood-rela-tionship: it does not express a physiological fact. Many savage peoples are organized in totemic clans, each clan bearing usually the name of an animal or plant often sup-posed to be akin to the human members of the clan. Every member of the clan recognizes every other member as of the kin. Inasmuch as these clans extend frequently through whole tribes and even to distant parts of a vast continent like North America or Australia, it is practically impossible that the members can be in a physiological sense blood-rela-tions. Notwithstanding this, every member of the totem-clan, wherever he may be found, is entitled to all the privileges and subject to all the disabilities incident to his status. He is entitled to protection at the hands of his fellow-clansmen. He is liable to be called on to take part in the blood-feud of the clan, and to suffer by an act of vengeance for a wrong committed by some other member of the clan. Foremost among his disabilities is the prohibition to marry or have sexual relations with any woman within the kin. Consequently his children must all be children of women belonging to a different kin from his own.

Though kinship, however, is not equivalent to blood-relationship in our sense of the term, it is founded on the idea of common blood which all within the kin possess and to which all outside the kin are strangers. A feeling of solidarity runs through the entire kin, so that it may be said without hyperbole that the kin is regarded as one entire life, one body, whereof each unit is more than metaphorically a member, a limb. The same blood runs through them all, and "the blood is the life." Literally they may not all be descended from a common ancestry. Descent is the normal, the typical, cause of kinship and a common blood. It is the legal presupposition: by birth a child enters a kin for good and ill. But kinship may also be acquired; and when once it is acquired by a stranger he ranks thenceforth for all purposes as one descended from the common ancestor. To acquire kinship a ceremony must be undergone: the blood of the candidate for admission into the kin must be mingled with that of the kin. This ceremony, no less than the words made use of in various languages to describe the members of the kin and their common bond, renders it clear that the bond is the bond of blood.

The mingling of blood—the Blood-covenant as it is called —is a simple though repulsive rite. It is sufficient that an incision be made in the neophyte's arm and the flowing blood sucked from it by one of the clansmen, upon whom the operation is repeated in turn by the neophyte. Originally, perhaps, all the clansmen, assembled as witnesses if not as actual participants of the rite; and even yet participation by more than one representative is frequently required. The exact form is not always the same. Sometimes the blood is dropped into a cup and diluted with some other drink. Sometimes food eaten together is impregnated with the blood. Sometimes a species of inoculation is practiced or it is enough to rub the bleeding wounds together, so that the blood of both parties is mixed and smeared upon them both. Among certain tribes of Borneo the drops are allowed to fall upon a leaf, which is then made up into a cigar with tobacco and lighted and smoked alternately by both parties.[1] But whatever may be the exact form adopted the essence of the rite is the same, and its range is extraordinarily wide. It is mentioned by classical writers as practiced by the Arabs, the Scythians, the Lydians and Iberians of Asia Minor and apparently the Medes. Many passages of the Bible, many of the Egyptian *Book of the Dead,* are inexplicable apart from it. Odin and Loki entered into the bond, which means that it was customary among the Norsemen— as we know in fact from other sources. It is recorded by Giraldus of the Irish of his day; and it still lingered as lately as two hundred years ago among the western islanders of Scotland. It is related of the Huns or Magyars and of the mediæval Roumanians. Joinville ascribes it to one of the tribes of the Caucasus; and the Rabbi Petachia of Ratisbon, who traveled in Ukrainia in the twelfth century, found it there. In modern times every African traveler mentions it; many of them have had to undergo the ceremony. In the neighboring island of Madagascar it is well known. All over the eastern Archipelago, in the Malay peninsula, among the Karens, the Siamese, the Dards on the northern border of our Indian empire and many of the aboriginal tribes of Bengal and Central India, the wild tribes of China, the Syrians of Lebanon and the Bedouins, and among various autochthonous peoples of North and South America, the rite is or has been within recent times in use.[2] Nor has it ceased to be practiced in Europe by the Gypsies and the Southern Slavs. In the French department of Aube, when a child bleeds he puts a little of his blood on the face or hands of one of his playfellows and says to him: "Thou shalt be my cousin." In like manner in New England, when a school-girl not many years since pricked her finger so that the blood came, one of her companions would say: "Oh! let me suck the blood; then we shall be friends." Something more than vestiges of the rite remains among the Italians of the Abruzzi. And the band of the Mala Vita, a society for criminal purposes in Southern Italy only broken up a few years ago, was a brotherhood formed by the blood-covenant. Indeed many secret societies both civilized and uncivilized have adopted an initiation-rite of which the blood-covenant forms part, either actually or by symbol representing an act once literally performed.

That the blood-covenant, whereby blood-brotherhood is assumed, is not a primeval rite is obvious from its artificial character. At the same time its barbarism and the wide area over which it is spread point with certainty to its early evolution, and the fact that it is in union with conceptions essentially and universally human. It has its basis in ideas which must have been pre-existent. Even among races like the Polynesians, and the Turanian inhabitants of Northern Europe and Asia, where the rite itself may not be recorded, there are unmistakable traces of the influence of those ideas. On the other hand where, as among some of the peoples included above, it has ceased to be used for the purpose of admission to a clan, the rite or some transparent modification of it, has continued in use for the reconciliation of ancient foes or the solemnization of a specially binding league.[3]

In a society organized by the bond of blood, and where descent is reckoned through females only, the father is not recognized as belonging to the kin of the children. Among matrilineal peoples exogamy, or marriage outside the kin, is usually if not always compulsory. So far is this carried that the artificial tie of the blood-covenant is a barrier to marriage. When Cuchulainn in the Irish saga of *The Wooing of Emer* wounded his love, Dervorgil, in the form of a sea-bird with a stone from his sling, he became her blood-brother by sucking from the wound the stone with a clot of blood round it. "I cannot wed thee now," he said, "for I have drunk thy blood. But I will give thee to my companion here, Lugaid of the Red Stripes." And so it was done.[4] This tale beyond doubt reflects the custom among the ancient Irish. The islanders of Webar in the East Indies, to select only one other example, represent even an earlier stage in the development of the custom. They live in hamlets the inhabitants of which are usually related to one another, and often at odds with the inhabitants of adjacent hamlets. But sometimes these quarrels are made up and a blood-covenant is entered into, after which no intermarriage can take place.[5]

The alien position of the father with regard to his children, and consequently the small account taken of him, has never been more vividly illustrated than by Miss Kingsley. She relates that on landing in French Congo she went to comply with the tiresome administrative regulations by reporting herself and obtaining a permit to reside in the colony. While she was waiting in the office of the *Directeur del Administration* a black man was shown in. "He is clad in a blue serge coat, from underneath which float over a pair of blue canvas trousers the tails of a flannel shirt, and on his feet are a pair of ammunition boots that fairly hobble him. His name, the interpreter says, is Joseph. 'Who is your father?' says the official. Clerk interprets into trade English. 'Fader?' says Joseph. 'Yes, fader,' says the interpreter. 'My fader,' says Joseph. 'Yes,' says the interpreter, 'who's your fader?' 'Who my fader?' says Joseph. 'Take him away and let him think about it,' says the officer with a sad sardonic smile. Joseph is alarmed and volunteers name of mother; this is no good; this sort of information any fool can give; Government is collecting information of a more recondite and interesting character. Joseph is removed by Senegal soldiers, boots and all." [6] Nobody on the west coast of Africa reckons descent through his father. Whether he knows who is his father or not is very often of no consequence to his social or legal position. The native law of the

Bavili (and the same is true of other tribes) draws no distinction between legitimate and illegitimate children. "Birth," we are told by a keen observer who has lived for many years in intimate converse with the natives, "sanctifies the child"; [7] birth alone gives him status as a member of his mother's family. The French cast-iron regulations, made for a different race and a different latitude, puzzled and confounded poor Joseph by the unexpected and absurd questions they required to be put to him. Miss Kingsley sarcastically observes: "As he's going to Boma, in the Congo Free State, it can only be for ethnological purposes that the French government are taking this trouble to get up his genealogy." Joseph does not understand the French government any more than the French government understands him; and he has never traced his genealogy along those lines before.

Joseph was a member of a Bantu tribe; but the case is the same among the Negroes. The Fanti of the Gold Coast may be taken as typical. Among them, while an intensity of affection, accounted for partly by the fact that the mothers have the exclusive care of the children, is felt for the mother, "the father is hardly known or [is] disregarded," notwithstanding he may be a wealthy and powerful man and the legal husband of the mother.[8] In North America Charlevoix says that among the Algonkin nations the children belonged to and only recognized their mother. The father was always a stranger, "so nevertheless that if he is not regarded as father he is always respected as the master of the cabin." [9] In Europe among the Transylvanian Gypsies "a man enters the clan of his wife, but does not really belong to it until she has borne a child. He never during his life shows the slightest concern for the welfare of his children, and the mother has to bear the whole burden of their maintenance. Even if the father is living, the son often never knows him, nor even has seen him." [10] Among the Orang Mamaq of Sumatra the members of a *suku,* or clan, live together, and the feeling of kinship is

very strong. As marriage within the clan is forbidden, husband and wife rarely dwell under one roof; when they do,
it is because the husband goes to the wife's home. But he
does not become a member of the family, which consists
merely of the mother and her children. The latter belong
solely to their mother's clan; the father has no rights over
them; and there is no kinship between him and them. In
consequence of the spread of foreign influences the true
family has begun to develop in a section of these people
inhabiting the district of Tiga Loeroeng. The husband and
wife usually live together, but the home is with the wife's
clan. Though the husband is considered a member of the
family he exercises little power over the children. They
belong to their mother's *suku,* and the *potestas,* as usual
in such cases, is in the hands of her eldest brother.[11]

A corollary of the principle that the father is not akin to
his children is that children of the same father by different
mothers are not reckoned as brothers and sisters. This is
the rule of the Papuan tribe settled about Mowat on the
Daudai coast of British New Guinea,[12] and indeed wherever motherright is pure and uncomplicated by rules which
prescribe or presume the marriage of two or more sisters
respectively to two or more brothers. Such children may
accordingly intermarry. This permission however sometimes tends to be restricted, as among the Bayaka, of whom
we are told that "marriage between children of the same
mother is prohibited; between children of the same father
it occurs, but is considered unseemly." [13] On the other hand
it sometimes persists for a time, even a considerable time,
among patrilineal peoples. By the laws of Athens children of
the same father, but apparently not of the same mother,
were allowed to intermarry. The same rule prevailed in
Japan.[14] According to Hebrew legend Sarah was the daughter of Abraham's father, but not of his mother. And when
Amnon, King David's son, sought to ravish his half-sister
Tamar, in the course of her protest and struggles she said:
"Now therefore I pray thee, speak unto the king; for he

will not withhold me from thee." [15] That is: while she resented the indignity offered by her brother out of mere passing lust, marriage with him would have been legitimate and honorable. It is not necessary to contend that these stories are narratives of literal fact. There is no trustworthy evidence that they are. At the same time they are of high antiquity, and must have originated in a social condition where the incidents were not so far removed from daily life as to be incredible or even surprising. In that social condition kinship must have been counted only through the mother, or matrilineal having passed into patrilineal descent certain vestigial customs must have remained over from the prior stage. The incidents cited are therefore justly regarded as among the witnesses preserved to us that before the dawn of history the ancient Hebrews had traversed the stage of motherright.

Enough has now been said to exhibit the alien position occupied among matrilineal peoples by the father in regard to his children. It remains to complete the picture by showing how the duties of head of the family are fulfilled, and in whom the authority—or, according to the technical term, the *potestas*—is vested. Among many of the African peoples the mother's brother has greater rights over a child than the father, and the duty of blood-revenge falls to him, even against the father. Wherever progress has been made in the organization of the family, and motherright is still the basis of organization, as over perhaps the greater part of the African continent, the supreme power is vested in the mother's brother or maternal uncle. In Loango the uncle is addressed as *Tate* (father). He exercises paternal authority over his nephew, whom he can even sell. The father has no power; and if the husband and wife separate the children follow the mother as belonging to her brother. They inherit from their mother; the father's property on the other hand goes at his death to his brother (by the same mother) or to his sister's sons. [16]

The customs of the peoples of the Lower Congo are

the same. Around the missionary settlement of Wathen
a woman is married by means of a bride-price, the bulk
of which is paid to her mother's family, though the father
receives a portion. But the wife is not bought as a slave
is bought. The husband acquires merely the right to her
companionship, and in case of her death to another wife
in her place. He has no control over his children by her.
They belong to their mother's family; and as they grow
up they go to live with their uncles.[17] Among the Igalwas
the father's authority over his children is very slight.
"The really responsible male relative," says Miss Kingsley, "is the mother's eldest brother. From him must leave
to marry be obtained for either girl or boy; to him and
the mother must the present be taken which is exacted
on the marriage of a girl; and should the mother die, on
him and not on the father, lies the responsibility of rearing the children; they go to his house, and he treats them
as nearer and dearer to himself than his own children,
and at his death after his own brothers by the same
mother, they become his heirs."[18] Two kinds of marriage are known among the Bambala. The first is child-
marriage. "A little boy of his own free will may declare
that a certain little girl is his wife; by this simple act he
acquires a prescriptive right to her. He visits his future
parents-in-law and takes them insignificant presents.
When he is of mature age he gives a larger present, of
the value of about 2000 *djimbu* (a small shell of the
species *Olivella Nana*), and then he is allowed to cohabit
with her. Their children belong to the eldest maternal
uncle. This form of marriage is attended by no special
ceremony. If the girl, when of age, is unwilling, he cannot
coerce her; but if she marries another man, the latter
must make him a present of several thousand *djimbu*."
The other form of marriage is contracted between adults.
The man pays a bride-price from 10,000 to 15,000 *djimbu*
to the father or maternal uncle of the bride. In this case
the children belong to the father; but "parents have little

authority over their children, who leave them at a very early age." "A man's property is inherited by the eldest son of his eldest sister, or in default by his eldest brother." The mother's brother is the guardian of his sister's children. Here, as we have already seen reason to think, fatherright is beginning to make inroads on the original organization. This is confirmed by the further statement that "kinship is reckoned very far on the female side," but "in the male line not beyond the uncle and grand-father,"[19] indicating that some kinship is now reckoned on the paternal side. The Bayaka, neighbors of the Bambala, and like them a Bantu people, dwell in small villages, often consisting of not more than two or three huts, presided over by a chief. "Each married woman has a separate hut where she lives with her children, and the husband moves from one to the other; unmarried men live together, several in a hut." "A child belongs to the village of his maternal uncle." The inhabitants of a village regard themselves as akin. It is added that "relationship on the female side is considered closer than that on the male side."[20] Among the Bangala of the Cassange Valley the chieftainship is elective. This is not unusual where female kinship prevails, for primogeniture has not yet developed, and among a band of equal brothers he who has proved himself the most capable is often preferred. Our information as to the Bangala is very defective. We are told: "The chief is chosen from three families in rotation. A chief's brother inherits in preference to his son. The sons of a sister belong to her brother; and he often sells his nephews to pay his debts."[21] It may be said generally that motherright prevails throughout Angola. "The closest relation is that of mother and child, the next that of nephew or niece and uncle or aunt. The uncle owns his nephews and nieces; he can sell them, and they are his heirs, not only in private property, but also in the chiefship, if he be a chief."[22] The father has, among the Kimbunda, no power over his children, even when they are young. Only his children by slaves are considered his property and can inherit from him.[23]

To avoid further repetition we may leave the foregoing to stand as examples of the organization of the western Bantu. They exhibit the mother's brother or maternal uncle as the head of the family with almost absolute power over his sister's children, in which authority of the father is however beginning to make breaches. Among the Negroes I have already referred to the Alladians. It may be added that the eldest of the *etiocos,* whether man or woman, is the head of the family. Although during the father's lifetime the children reside with their mother in his house, on his death the sons go to live with their mother's brother, unless he consent to her retaining them while very young; the daughters remain with her, but under their uncle's tutelage. Polygamy prevails, but the children of the same father by different mothers scarcely consider that there is any tie between them. Marriages are arranged by the *etiocos* in council; and apparently unless the bride be a mere child the bride-price is paid to them.[24] The Ewhe-speaking peoples also trace kinship through females, except the upper classes of Dahomey, among which male kinship is the rule. "The eldest brother is the head of the family, and his heir the brother next in age to himself; if he has no brother his heir is the eldest son of his eldest sister.... Members of a family have a right to be fed and clothed by the family head; and the latter has in his turn a right to pawn and in some cases to sell them. The family collectively is responsible for all crimes and injuries to person or property committed by any one of its members, and each member is assessable for a share of the compensation to be paid. On the other hand, each member of the family receives a share of the compensation paid to it for any crime or injury committed against the person or property of any of its members. Compensation is always demanded from the family instead of from the individual wrong-doer, and is paid to the family instead of to the individual wronged." [25]

Among the Ewhe of Anglo in Upper Guinea the maternal uncle has more authority over his sister's sons than their father. Since they succeed to him at his death he requires from them labor and support in his lifetime. The nephew accompanies his uncle on trading journeys, carrying provisions, cowries, and merchandise. Under his uncle's tuition he thus gradually learns to trade, besides other useful work such as weaving and so forth. By-and-by he begins to trade on behalf of his father or uncle, accounts to him for the proceeds and receives a share of the profit. And at length his father and uncle together negotiate a bride for him. The mother has naturally the charge and teaching of her daughter; but the father is consulted as to her marriage and cheerfully takes his share of the brandy and other gifts furnished by the bridegroom.[26] The Fanti Customary Laws have been expounded by Mr. Sarbab, a native barrister, in an elaborate treatise which throws much light on the present condition of the Fanti family. Without discussing details, many of which are foreign to our present purpose, it may be stated generally that the Fanti are matrilineal. The head of the family is usually (but not always) the eldest male member in the line of descent. He has control over all the members; he is their natural guardian; he alone can sue or be sued, as the representative of the family, respecting claims on the family possessions. Within his compound the head of a family reigns supreme not only over his younger brothers and sisters and the children of the latter but also over his own wives and children. But he cannot pawn his child without the concurrence of the mother's relations; and children who have left his compound to reside with their maternal uncle are no longer under his power: they are wholly subject to their uncle.[27] The Negro has carried these customs in even a more archaic form to South America. The Bush Negro husband in Surinam does not live with his wife and often has wives in several different places. The maternal uncle supplies his place in the family.[28]

Turning now to the true Negroes we find in Buna on the Ivory Coast a social condition in which fatherright is predominant, but has not yet succeeded in stamping out all vestiges of the more archaic stage. The family is strongly organized, its head being the eldest male, who is absolute master. All the children born during a marriage are the husband's property, even those who are the fruit of adultery. In case of divorce where the wife is known to be pregnant the child subsequently born belongs to the husband; if, however, her pregnancy be not then known she retains the child.[29] In Seguela parentage runs in the paternal line by preference, and the family is similarly organized. Every child born during the marriage belongs to the husband. In case of lengthened absence of the husband the wife is authorized to live in concubinage with another man, preferably a member of the family. At his return the husband takes her back, together with any children born during his absence.[30] The Krumen of Sassandra reckon descent on both sides, but we are told that the female side is of little importance. The descendants of a common ancestor in the male line dwell together in the same village and form a clan. Since polygamy is here as elsewhere among the Negroes practically unlimited, infidelity to one wife leads to no more serious consequence than little tiffs. Adultery by the wife herself is hardly graver, the French official report tells us; and everything is comfortably arranged, if she only share with her husband the presents she has received from her lover. Some husbands, indeed, especially old chiefs who are inclined to violence, revenge themselves; but it is rare to find a really jealous husband. Sometimes, but very seldom, the husband demands a divorce when the wife is thoroughly abandoned. Conformably with these easy-going morals the law declares no distinction between legitimate, illegitimate, and adulterine children. *Is pater quem nuptiæ demonstrant* admits of no exception. The husband is considered the

father, even though he has been absent for ten years, of any
children his wife may have borne in the meantime.[31] The
Krumen of Cavally reckon descent only on the male side.
There is no distinction between legitimate and illegitimate
children. The children are the wealth of the family and
they are always welcome, even when the husband knows
he is not the real father. They belong to him in all cases.
He may however inflict corporal punishment on his adulter-
ous wife, or even send her back to her family and obtain
repayment of the bride-price. He may also institute a palaver
against the adulterer for damages, which may be settled if
he so please by an exchange of wives. The *patria potestas*
vests in the eldest male of the highest generation living, and
devolves with the property on his next brother at his death.
When there are no brothers the eldest son inherits.[32] In
the foregoing cases the marriage rites are of the most restricted character. On the other hand, among the Andon·
of Southern Nigeria (if I am right in thinking them
patrilineal) an elaborate ceremony is performed. Two stout
sticks of a certain wood called *odiri,* about four feet long,
are supplied by the Juju priests from the sacred grove. They
are sharpened at the end and first laid on the ground in a
corner of the bridegroom's house by the priests. The bride
and bridegroom are then made to place their feet on them.
The priest kills a goat and sprinkles its blood on their feet
and on the sticks. The stakes are then driven by their
sharpened ends into the ground in the corner of the house,
and there they remain until they fall to pieces. From that
moment the wife and all the children she may bear, by
whomsoever begotten, are the husband's property. The marriage is indissoluble Even if she leave her husband and
have children by chiefs or kings they must be delivered up
to him on his demand. When she dies she cannot be buried
save by him; any other person undertaking this important
function would incur heavy punishment; before the days
of British rule it was death.[33]

Islam is not necessarily a religion of high civilization. It has made extensive conquests in Africa by reason of its power of adaptation to lower stages of culture. By Mohammedan law kinship is reckoned through both lines; but such preponderant importance is attached to the paternal side that semicivilized African populations professing Islam may for our purpose be regarded as patrilineal. Just as among patrilineal peoples where fatherright is carried out to its logical term, great importance is attributed to the purity of Mohammedan women. On the other hand the law, by the aid of the physiological ignorance of the early doctors who framed it, stretches beyond all probability the presumption of legitimacy in its doctrine of the possibility of very lengthened gestations. A famous Maghribin saint named Sidi Nail left his home and went on pilgrimage to Mecca where he abode for two years and a half. At length he returned to find that his wife Cheliha had only a short time before given birth to a son. Even the credulity of the faithful, supported by the law, has had the greatest difficulty in digesting the legitimacy of this child. Yet the saint himself seems to have accepted him, and his sonship has been duly attested by heaven; for it is especially among his descendants that the gift of miracles possessed by Sidi Nail has been perpetuated.[34] In the same way the Bayazi, an heretical sect of which the bulk of the Arab population of Zanzibar consists, allow legitimacy to children born within two years after the husband's death. The Shafei, another sect, extend the period to four years.[35] Mohammedan law, exaggerated by these heretical sects, seems indeed a device for gathering into the husband's kin all the children of his wives to whom any semblance of a claim can be made. Among the Galla of northeastern Africa, who are Moslem, the illegitimate children of a woman married by the solemn rite of the rakko are legally descendants of the husband.[36]

Customs similar to those prescribed in the ancient Indian law-books have even been in use in Europe. A Spartan law attributed to Lycurgus required an old man who had a young wife to introduce to her a young man whose bodily and mental qualities he approved, that he might beget children on her.[37] The primary object indeed of this law of others fathered on the same law-giver was said to be what is called in modern scientific jargon Eugenics. However that may have been as regards the form in which they are reported to us, there can be little doubt that they are formulations of preëxisting custom which enabled the continuance of the husband's family by another man. At all events at Athens a law ascribed to Solon was in force which provided that if the next-of-kin who had in accordance with law successfully claimed an heiress for himself were impotent, his place should be supplied by some of his relatives (*cum mariti adgnatis concubito*). This as McLennan points out is identical with the law of Manu cited above. In both cases the object was to provide heirs; and the children took the estate as soon as they were able to perform the duties to their legal ancestors.[38] The old peasant custumals of Germany, especially of Westphalia, lay it down that an impotent husband shall perform the ceremony of taking his wife on his back over nine fences and then calling a neighbor to act as his substitute. If he cannot find one who is able and willing, he is to adorn her with new clothes, hang a purse at her side with money to spend and send her to a *kermess,* in the hope of finding some one there to help her.[39] Grimm, commenting on these curious prescriptions, admits that there is no historical record of any such actual transaction, but observes that they are plainly and seriously prescribed and that their memory lingers in tradition, instancing an old poem of Saint Elizabeth. He suggests that in the custumals all the details are not mentioned, that probably the rite was only performed where serious detriment would result from the want of an heir, and that the husband's choice of a substitute was not unlimited. In any case he holds the custom to be very archaic, though in the records it appears adapted to the circumstances of mediæval peasant-proprietors.

The foregoing examples are all chosen from peoples

among whom fatherright is the rule, or who deduce kinship through both parents with preference for the father, as in the highest civilization. Where these customs are in vogue the husband cannot be sure of the paternity of the children born of his wife. On the contrary he is often sure that the children belonging to him, reckoned of his kin and inheriting his property, are not in fact heirs of his body. They may even be born long after his death as the result of intercourse between his wives and other men. The list might be indefinitely lengthened if the customs of peoples among whom fatherright though predominant is imperfectly developed were considered. Thus in Madagascar motherright has left much more than traces. The hindrances on marriage of relatives are greater on the mother's side than on the father's. Children of two sisters by the same mother cannot intermarry, nor can their descendants. On the other hand children and grandchildren of a brother and sister by the same mother may intermarry on the performance of a slight ceremony prescribed to remove the disqualification of consanguinity. The royal family and nobles trace their lineage, contrary to the general practice, through the mother and not through the father. Yet so great a calamity is it counted that a man should die without posterity that if an elder brother die childless his next brother must take the widow and raise up seed to the deceased.[40] This involves sexual relations only after the husband's death between the widow and his brother. But the Malagasy customs are further-reaching still; for all the children of a married woman belong to her husband, whoever may beget them. Divorce is a frequent occurrence and for trivial causes. When it takes place, not only are the children previously born retained by the husband, but any whom the wife may afterwards bear to another man belong to the husband who has divorced her. And he hastens to secure them by taking a present to each one as it is born; a ceremony which appears to constitute a formal claim to them. In the ceremony of divorce the husband's final word to his wife is an injunction to remember that though she is now at liberty to marry any one else, all her future children will belong to him, the husband divorcing her.[41]

Motherright then is found not merely where paternity is uncertain, but also where it is practically certain. Fatherright on the other hand is found not merely where paternity is certain, but also where it is uncertain and even where the legal father is known not to have begotten the children. Nay, the institutions of fatherright often require provision for, and very generally permit, the procreation by other men of children for the nominal father. It follows therefore that the uncertainty of paternity cannot be historically the reason for the reckoning of descent exclusively through the mother. Some other reason must be discovered.

NOTES

[1] Roth, *Sarawak*, ii, 206.

[2] So far as I am aware it is expressly recorded only of the Seminoles in North America (Featherman, *Aoneo-Mar.*, 172), a tribe in Yucatan and a tribe in Brazil (Trumbull, 54, 55, citing authorities); but practices in other tribes point to the underlying idea.

[3] There is one doubtful account of its use among the descendants of Genghis Khan for this purpose (see the passage quoted and commented on by M. René Basset, *Rev. Trad. Prop.*, x, 176). As to the subject generally, see Robertson Smith (*Kinship;* and *Rel. Sem.*); Trumbull, *The Blood Covenant* (London, 1887); Strack, *Das Blut* (München, 1900).

[4] Eleanor Hull, *The Cuchullin Saga*, 82.

[5] Riedel, 446.

[6] Kingsley, *Trav.*, 109.

[7] Dennett, *Journ. Afr. Soc.*, i, 265.

[8] *J. A. I.*, xxvi, 145.

[9] Charlevoix, *Histoire de la Nouvelle France*, v, 424.

[10] Potter, 116, citing von Wlislocki, *Vom wandernde Zigeunervolke*.

[11] *Bijdragen*, xxxix, 43, 44.

[12] Haddon, *J. A. I.*, xix, 467. The Yorubas of the Slave Coast of West Africa now reckon descent through the father. They perhaps owe the change to intercourse with the Mohammedan tribes of the interior. Be this as it may, so strong even yet is the influence of uterine kinship that children of the same father by different mothers are by many natives hardly considered true blood-relations (Ellis, *Yoruba*, 176).

[13] *J. A. I.*, xxxvi, 45; 14. McLennan, *Studies*, i, 223, quoting the *Leges Atticæ*.

[14] *Rev. Hist. Rel.*, I, 328, *note;* Aston, *Shinto*, 249. Traces are also found among the Slavs (Kovalevsky, 13).

[15] *Gen.* xx, 12; 2 *Sam.*, xiii, 13.

[16] Bastian, *Loango-Kuste,* i, 166.

[17] Bentley, ii, 333.

[18] Kingsley, *Trav.,* 224.

[19] *J. A. I.,* xxxv, 410, 411.

[20] *Ibid.,* xxxvi, 43, 45.

[21] Livingstone, *Miss. Trav.,* 434.

[22] Chatelain, 8.

[23] Post, *Afr. Jur.,* i, 23, citing Magyar.

[24] Clozel, 391, 392, 393, 394, 397. As to the Yoruba and the Egbas see Ellis, *Yoruba,* 176; *Journ. Afr. Soc.,* i, 88.

[25] Ellis, *Ewhe,* 207, 208, 209.

[26] *Zeits. f. Ethnol.,* xxxviii, 43.

[27] Sarbab, 5, 9, 31, 39, 50, 86.

[28] Potter, 115, citing *Zeits. vergl. Rechtsw.,* xi, 420.

[29] Clozel, 308-312.

[30] *Ibid.,* 330, 331. Women may inherit in certain cases (*Id.,* 335).

[31] *Ibid.,* 495, 497, 498.

[32] *Ibid.,* 507, 511, 512, 515.

[33] *Journ. Afr. Soc.,* iv, 414; Leonard, 414.

[34] *Rev. Hist. Rel.,* xli, 315.

[35] Burton, *Zanzibar,* i, 403.

[36] Paulitschke, ii, 142. As to the *rakko* see *Ibid.,* 47. _ am not aware whether the Boni, a subject people among the Galla and Somali, are Mohammedans, or whether they are, as has been suggested, of Galla origin. "There is no divorce among these people, all the children of one woman, by whatever father, are the property of the woman's original husband, if alive; if dead, of her brother" (Capt. Salkeld, *Man,* 1905, 169, par. 94).

[37] Xenophon, *Rep. Laced.,* i, 9; Plutarch, *Lycurgus.*

[38] Plutarch, *Solon;* McLennan, *Studies,* i, 223; Seebohm, *Greek Tribal Soc.,* 23.

[39] Grimm, *Rechtsall,* 443. The details of the ceremony vary in different places.

[40] Ellis, i, 164; Sibree, 246.

[41] Verbal information to me by Rev. T. Rowlands, L.M.S., Missionary to the Betsileo. The information does not agree with that in Ellis, *Hist. Mad.,* i, 173. Possibly the latter refers to (or includes) children of tender age who are necessarily left with their mother for the time.

GROUP-MARRIAGE
AND SEXUAL COMMUNISM *

By ROBERT BRIFFAULT

IT is a widespread principle in uncultured societies that when a man marries a woman he thereby acquires marital rights over all her sisters. Thus in Australia, on the Penne-feather and Tully Rivers in Queensland, a man is under-stood to have the same sexual rights over all his wife's sisters as over his wife, whether they happen to be married to other men or not. Among the Kurnai of South-East Australia, when a man obtains a wife from another tribe by eloping with her, her parents, after their anger has blown over and the matter has been amicably settled, hand over her sister also to their son-in-law. Among the tribes of Gippsland, the men cannot be made to understand the distinction between a wife and a sister-in-law—the latter, they insist, are just as much their wives as the former. In Western Australia, "where there are several sisters of a family, they are all regarded as the wives of the man who marries the eldest of them." In Melanesia, it is likewise a general usage that when a man takes one woman as his individual partner, he thereby becomes the husband of all her actual sisters. So also in the western islands of Torres Straits, before the conversion of the natives to Christianity, a man's wives were all sisters or cousins, and even at the present day a man, there is little doubt, normally has marital relations with all his wife's sisters. The traditional tales of the natives of northern New Guinea represent a man as

---

* *The Mothers.* New York: The Macmillan Co. Because of pressure for space, it was necessary to omit the voluminous references with which Briffault documents his work. The references can all be secured in this chapter in Briffault's three-volume study. [Editor.]

being married as a matter of course to all the sisters of his wife. Like the rule of cross-cousin marriage, the principle is a translation in terms of family-relationship of the sexual claim of a man to all the women of the group with which his own group has entered into a marriage agreement.

Among the North American tribes it was an almost universal rule that when a man married a woman he thereby acquired marital rights over her sisters. For example, among the Ojibwa "it was usual for them, when an Indian married one of several sisters, to consider himself as wedded to all; and it became incumbent upon him to take them all as wives." Among the Pawnees "a man," says Murray, "having married the elder sister has a right to marry all the younger ones as they successively attain puberty. Nor is this at all unusual; on the contrary it is a common practice." "It is a custom," says a missionary, "that when a savage asks a girl in marriage and gets her to wife, not only she, but all her sisters belong to him and are regarded as his wives." Among the Natchez, when a man marries a woman, "if she has many sisters he marries them all, so that nothing is more common than to see four or five sisters, the wives of a single husband." Similarly, among the tribes of California "the common custom is when a man marries that he takes the whole of the sisters for wives." The custom "prevailed from the earliest ages among all the Dacota family as well as among the Algonkin and other tribes of the Great Lakes." Morgan found it in operation in forty different tribes, and it has been reported of practically every tribe of the North American continent.

The usage appears to have been equally general in Central and South America. Thus among the natives of New Granada it was customary for a man to marry all his wife's sisters. Among the Caribs, "very often the same man will take to wife three or four sisters, who will be his cousins-german or his nieces." In British Guiana and among the tribes of the Orinoco a man commonly had three sisters living with him as his wives. Among the Araucanians, "when an Indian is able to obtain several sisters together as wives, they prefer it to marrying women who are not related to one another, because this accords with their laws." Among the tribes of the Amazon and Rio Negro a man commonly married all the sisters of a family. Among the Canebo of the Upper Amazon "a man must marry all the sisters of the family as soon as they are old enough"; and the same obligation is imposed upon the Jivaros. Among the Guaranis, the men "often marry several sisters." So also among all the tribes of the Gran Chaco "a man has frequently two or more sisters as wives at the same time." The Chriguanos commonly marry two sisters. Among the Fuegians it was customary for a man to marry several sisters.

Among the Guanches of the Canary Islands it was customary for a man to marry several sisters. The practice is very common in Africa, more especially among the more primitive races and in those whose social organization has undergone least modification. Among the Bushmen of the Kalahari a man usually marries several sisters or female cousins, that is, tribal sisters. The custom is an old established principle among all the Kaffirs of South Africa and is very regularly observed by the Zulus. Among the eastern South African tribes of Mozambique a man has a claim to his wife's sisters as they reach maturity; and among the natives of Portuguese East Africa a man has a recognized right over all his wife's sisters, though the practice is said to be falling into disuse at the present day. Similarly, among the Herero of western South Africa a man cannot marry a younger sister without marrying her elder sister also. Sororal polygyny is observed as a matter of course by the tribes of the Upper Congo. Among the Ba-Congo "a man who has bought a woman has thereby a right to all her marriageable sisters in turn. To what extent a man would exercise the right it is difficult to say, but in theory he could go on as long as there remained an eligible girl in the family." Sororal polygyny has been reported among the Bangala, and the

Wabemba. In East Africa, among the Basoga, the bride is accompanied to ,her husband's home by a sister, who joins the household as a secondary wife. Among the Bagesu of Uganda it is usual for a man to marry all his wife's sisters, and the same is the practice of the Banyoro. Among the tribes of Kavirondo the younger sisters of a man's wife join her as they become of age. The same usages are observed by the tribes of northern Nigeria, and of the French Sudan.

The practice of sororal polygyny is usual among the more primitive races of Siberia, such as the Chukchi, the Kamchadals, the Ostyak. It is an old-fashioned custom among both the eastern Mongols and the western Mongols, or Kalmuks. Jinghis Khan married two sisters, and the practice was taken for granted among his warriors and khans. The same usage was observed in ancient times by the Chinese. We read of the famous emperor Yao bestowing both his daughters on the Chinese prince Shuenn, and accompanying them himself with great formality on their journey to their appointed bridegroom, bidding them to "fulfill all their duties with respect and diligence in the home of their husband." In a Chinese novel the hero is rewarded for his exemplary virtue by his protector bestowing upon him the hands of both his daughters. The same usage obtained among the ancient Japanese: "to wed two or more sisters at the same time was a recognized practice." We find the same practice in Tibet. Among the primitive Moi of Indo-China it is usual to take the first wife's sisters as co-wives; and the same usage is observed in Cambodia. It is likewise the custom in Siam. Among the Malays of the Patani States the most common form of polygny is the simultaneous marriage of several sisters. The custom prevails among the tribes of Upper Burma and of Manipur. It is observed by the Garos of Assam. Sororal polygyny was in vogue among the ancient Indo-Aryans; one of the most illustrious of the Rishis is reported to have married no less than ten sisters at the same time. The practice is common in the Panjab. We find it among the tribes of the Rajmahal Hills, and among the Gonds, and it prevails among several other native tribes of Central India. It is likewise prevalent in Mysore and Southern India. We know from the account of the marriage of Jacob that it was a recognized usage among the ancient Jews.

In Ceram in a polygynous family the wives are almost invariably sisters; and in Central Celebes a man cannot marry a younger sister unless he first marries the elder. In the Philippine Islands a man usually took as wives all the sisters of a family. The same practice is common among the Negritos of Zambales. In the Marshall Islands "when a man marries a woman he is regarded as married to all her sisters." The same view obtains in the Gilbert Islands, and among the Mortlock Islanders. In the Kingsmill or Line Islands, "if a woman has sisters, then the sisters become the wives of her husband on her own marriage, and no other man can ever take them as wives." According to the same authority, if the husband does not find it convenient to take charge of all the sisters, there is no alternative for the latter than to contract casual alliances; they become, in fact, what we should call prostitutes.

In New Zealand it was common for a man when he married a woman to take her sisters also. When the sailor Rutherford, who was adopted into a Maori tribe, was requested to select a wife, the father of the young woman called her sister, and he "advised me," says Rutherford, "to take them both." In Samoa "it was a common practice in the old days for a woman to take her sister or sisters with her, and these became practically the concubines of her husband." It does not appear, however, to be quite correct to call them "concubines" for each younger sister brought her dowry with her in the same manner as her elder sister. If a sister was not available, the wife brought with her a cousin or some other near relative. Even long after the conversion of the natives to Christianity it was considered that the husband of the elder sister had the disposal of the younger sisters, and intending suitors applied to him and not to her parents. Similarly, in the Hervey Islands a bride was followed to her husband's home by all her sisters, who became his co-wives. In the Marquesas a man had marital rights over all his wife's sisters, whether these married other men or not.

The same causes which tend to limit every kind of polygamy restrict sororal polygyny in practice; it is sometimes a severe strain on a man's resources to marry a whole family. That difficulty is, however, often relieved by the fact that, since in primitive society girls usually marry at puberty, the younger sisters are not marriageable at the time of their elder sisters' marriage; and by that time the man's circumstances may have improved so as to enable him to maintain a larger family. From those usages follows the rule which is observed in most parts of the world, that it is unlawful for a younger sister to be married before her elder sister. That rule, on which Laban insisted when he gave his daughters to Jacob, namely that "it must not be done so in our country to give the younger sister before the first-born," is a matter of fundamental morality, not only in most of the lower phases of culture, but in societies so highly civilized as that of China, and it has left traces at the present day even in England and in Scotland.

If the husband does not wish, or cannot afford, to exercise his claim on his wife's sisters, he allows them to marry other men, but in order to do so his consent is necessary; when a bride-price is due it is sometimes to him and not to the girl's relatives that it is paid. An additional sister is given as a matter of course if the first sister proves barren; the younger sister either replacing her, or joining her in her husband's household. The woman whom a man has married may be exchanged for another sister for no other reason than incompatibility of temper, or simply because the man wishes it. Of the Indians of the Oregon, for example, it is remarked that "the parents do not seem to object to a man's turning off one sister and taking a younger one," that prerogative being "a custom handed down from time immemorial." In Australia, however, among the Gourn-ditch-mara, if a man has repudiated his wife he loses his claim to her sisters, being regarded as having divorced the whole family. Among the Tartars, if the wife dies before the payment of the bride-price is completed, the sum already paid goes toward the acquisition of her sister; but if there is no sister to take the wife's place the whole of the deposit is lost. In other instances the husband or bridegroom may demand a refund of the bride-price, should the family refuse to supply the widower with another wife. A deceased wife's sister is supplied to the widower without extra payment, or at a reduced rate. Among the Kalmuks the right to marry a deceased wife's sister is regarded as a claim which a man is entitled to enforce. Should the father be unwilling to yield the younger sister to the widower, the latter calls on him, places bread and salt on the table, whereupon the father is held bound to give up the younger sister. Among the Kirghis failure to hand over the deceased wife's sister is an offense punishable by law. So strong is the claim that among the Flat-heads and other Oregon tribes, if the deceased wife's sister is already married to another man, she is obliged to leave him and marry the widower. Among the Wabemba of the Congo, if a man's wife dies, and all her sisters are married, the husband of one of them must allow his wife to cohabit for one or two nights with the widower. Unless this is done the latter cannot marry another woman. The same rule is observed by the Baholoholo; so essential is the observance accounted that if the surviving sister be a mere infant, the widower goes through the form of imitating the sexual act and pretending to have connection with the infant, although he does not marry her. In the last instances the usage of sororal succession has become a mere ritual. We shall see that similar ritual survivals abound in relation to the corresponding custom of fraternal succession, or the levirate. The observance of the ritual derives its obligatory or beneficial character from its formal conformity with established custom; for to comply with an established custom is always lucky, and to omit its observance unlucky. With the Wabemba, when the sister happens to be an infant she is nevertheless handed over to the widower, but a slave-girl is sent with her to act as a substitute until the girl grows to nubile age. Similarly among the Assiniboins if, when a man's wife dies, her sister is still immature, she is kept for him until she attains puberty. The same rule as to age must, however, be observed in marrying a deceased wife's sister as when marrying her during the wife's lifetime. Thus among the Kaikari of central India, a man may marry his deceased wife's younger sister, but may not marry her elder sister.

Marriage with a deceased wife's sister is sometimes regarded in the light of a moral obligation rather than as a claim or privilege. Thus the Iroquois widower who failed to do so was subjected to such abuse on the part of the insulted lady that he seldom failed to comply. Among the Shuswap of British Columbia the widower was actually kept a prisoner by the deceased wife's family until the period of mourning was over, and was released from his imprisonment on condition only that he married the deceased lady's sister. On the island of Engano the widower who failed to marry his deceased wife's sister was punished with a heavy fine. The abnormal notion that it is reprehensible to marry one's deceased wife's sister is a rare anthropological curiosity which appears to be found only among the natives of New Britain, some Chinese tribes, and some natives of Ashanti.

The rule that when a man's wife dies he marries her sister, which is often the only survival of sororal polygyny, is thus clearly an attenuated relic of the widespread claim of a man to all the sisters of a family when he marries one of them, and it would be difficult to find any two social facts the connection between which is so manifest and so fully exhibited by every possible transition and similarity in the mode of their observance. Nevertheless, in accordance with an even more general rule, those people who observe the

rule of marrying their deceased wife's sister, but who have
given up simultaneous sororal polygyny, do not admit that
they at present practice the former custom because they
once practiced the latter, and that their present usage is
derived from one which they now condemn, but justify
their practice by independent considerations of sentiment or
expediency. Thus the natives of the Hervey Islands, who
until quite lately practiced as a matter of course sororal
polygyny, are all at the present day good Christians and
their heathen customs have entirely ceased; but "a woman
feels herself to be deeply injured if her brother-in-law does
not, on the death of his wife, ask her to become a mother
to his children." Similarly, some Omaha Indians, among
whom sororal polygyny was a time-honored practice, but
who now conform to Christian usages, are reported to submit that marriage of a deceased wife's sister is expedient
because "the children bereft of their own mother ... would
come under the care of her close kindred, and not fall into
the hands of a stranger," or that the usage "shows a respect
for the dead." In like manner writers on anthropological
subjects to whom the application of the theory of evolution
to the human race is repugnant, have no hesitation in declaring that they cannot "find any reason for the assumption
that the custom of marrying a deceased wife's sister is derived from the custom of marrying her other sister in her
lifetime."

The peoples who practice sororal polygyny and the missionaries and other writers who interpret their customs have
likewise good reasons to offer for the origin and observance
of the usage. The favorite explanation given by travelers
and missionaries who report the custom as a peculiarity of
the peoples they are describing is that it is desirable in a
polygynous family that the wives should be sisters, because
sisters are more likely to live together in harmony. The
wives of an American Indian are said to live together "in
the greatest harmony." If, however, a man marries into
two different families, "the wives," it is alleged, "do not

harmonize well together, and give the husband much in-
quietude." But there is an overwhelming mass of testimony
to the perfect harmony obtaining between wives in polygynous families, whether the wives be sisters or not. Where
polygyny obtains, the women are the most persistent advocates of the practice, and additional wives are in most
instances acquired at the desire of a man's wife or wives,
and are very commonly selected by them. There is nothing
to indicate that the wives in a polygynous family are more
prone to quarrel among themselves than other persons who
live together, or that wives who are sisters are less liable
to disagree than those who are not. In contradiction to the
assumption of several writers, La Potherie asserts that sisters
among the North American Indians are often particularly
quarrelsome, and that their disputes are sometimes so lively
that they attack one another with knives. The value of the
psychological suppositions as to the greater harmony between wives who are sisters offered by uncultured peoples
when pressed to account for their customs, is pointedly
illustrated by the opinion of the Ostyak on the subject. Although it is their immemorial custom to marry several sisters, and they say that the observance of the usage brings
luck, they nevertheless state that the arrangement is unsatisfactory and that they would prefer to marry women
who are unrelated, "because experience shows that sisters
are particularly liable to disagree in such marriage."

The practice of sororal polygyny, like every other traditional custom, presents, there can be no doubt, many advantages that could be adduced in its defense or serve as an
inducement for its observance; but usages and customs do
not generally owe their origin to the careful a priori weigh-
ing of fine points of psychology. It may be doubted whether
Melanesian savages are much concerned about the amicable
nature of the relation between their wives, about respect
for their deceased wives, or proper qualifications in the
nurses of their children. None of those alleged beneficial
effects of the practice is applicable to ethnological facts as

we find them; they do not account for a man naving to marry his wife's sisters against his will or for his collecting the bride-price when they marry other men, or for his having to wait, with a slave-girl as a substitute, when those sisters are still infants in arms, or for his having a recognized right of access to them whether he marries them or not. With peoples in the lowest stage of social organization the practice of sororal polygyny and of sororal succession is, like that of cross-cousin marriage, the automatic effect of the principles which constitute the foundation of their social organization, namely, the rule of marriage between intermarrying groups. Like the principle of cross-cousin marriage, that of sororal polygyny in its narrower sense is a translation in terms of family relationship of the wider conceptions of clan relationship. In the one case the cross-cousins and the sisters are what we, in accordance with the family system, call "actual," or "own" cousins, and "own" sisters; in the other they are cousins and sisters in the tribal sense, and according to the system of relationship obtaining in more primitive societies. If relationship be reckoned from the point of view of the clan-group, the term "wife" includes all the women of the corresponding marriage-group, and all those women are "sisters"; that a man's wives should be sisters is not a right or claim, or a matter of policy, but a consequence of primitive organization to which there exists no alternative. According to the clear and oft-quoted description of Dr. Codrington, "speaking generally, it may be said that to a Melanesian man all women, of his own generation at least, are either sisters or wives; to the Melanesian woman all men are either brothers or husbands.... It must not be understood that a Melanesian regards all women who are not of his own division as in fact his wives, or conceives himself to have rights which he may exercise in regard to those women of them who are unmarried; but the women may be his wives by marriage, and those who cannot be so stand in a widely different relation to him; and it may be added that all women who may become wives by marriage and are not yet appropriated, are to a certain extent looked upon by those who may be their husbands as open to more or less legitimate intercourse. In fact, appropriation of particular women to their husbands, though established by every sanction of native custom, has by no means so strong a hold in native society, nor in all probability so deep a foundation in the history of the people, as the severance of either sex by divisions which most strictly limit the intercourse of men and women to those of the section or sections to which they do not themselves belong." Translated into terms of the relationship set up by the smaller family-group, those principles imply that a man has a right to all the women of the group into which he marries. The true reason for the principle of sororal polygyny in its various forms is very clearly stated by the Omaha woman who, according to the Rev. J. Owen Dorsey, says to her husband: "I wish you to marry my brother's daughter, as she and I are one flesh." Instead of "brother's daughter," she may say her sister or her aunt.

The converse or complementary aspect of the rule that when a man contracts a marriage with a family he marries all the marriageable females of that family is the principle that when a woman contracts a marriage with another family she marries all the marriageable males of that family. The simultaneous observance of the two rules constitutes a marriage between the several individuals composing them. The one-sided observance of sororal polygyny and perhaps also of fraternal polyandry are, however, at the present day much more common than the combination of the two practiced as complete group-marriage. The reason of this is, on consideration, plain. The combination of the two practices is, as we have already noted, an unstable arrangement; for unless the groups to which the men and the women respectively belong be supposed to be broken up and a new grouping of men and women substituted for the original groups, the arrangement can only operate in an unmodified form where sexual relations do not entail permanent cohabi-

tation. As soon as marriage involves not only sexual relations, but also economic interdependence and association,
such an arrangement becomes almost impracticable in an
unmodified form; for no economic association can take
place between a man and a woman or group of women
unless the labor of those women is in some degree specially
allotted to the man, unless, therefore, he has an individual
right to their labor. Unmodified group-marriage is, thus, a
practicable arrangement so long only as sexual relations
remain completely independent of economic relations between the associates; and directly such economic factors
enter into that relation the organization must of necessity
break up into one or the other of its constituent aspects,
into sororal polygyny or fraternal polyandry. But the whole
development of individualism, of individual property, and
of personal economic interests has taken place mainly in
the hands of the men and not of the women, and in human
societies as they exist at the present day the economic advantages are generally in favor of the men. Since it is those
very factors which constitute the chief difficulty in the
practical operation of unmodified group-marriage, it is
naturally to be expected that when that organization breaks
up, it will do so in the form of sororal polygyny rather than
in that of fraternal polyandry. And in fact fraternal polyandry, although scarcely less widespread in its distribution
than sororal polygyny, is found to be considerably less
common.

Not only is it less common, but pure fraternal polyandry
is, in point of fact, even more rare than it is generally supposed and currently stated to be. For if those customs which
are usually described as fraternal polyandry be more closely
inquired into, it will be found in a large proportion of instances that, in addition to the rule of fraternal polyandry,
that of sororal polygyny is either actually observed also or
that there are strong indications that it was until lately
observed. In other words, although primitive group-marriage
customs frequently assume the modified form of sororal

polygny without polyandry, when fraternal polyandry sur
vives, the converse aspect of the collective relation survives
also; and most instances of fraternal polygamous marriage
are in reality examples of complete group-marriage and
not of its decay in the form of fraternal polyandry. Accordingly, instead of reviewing separately reported instances of
fraternal polyandry and of group-marriage, we shall consider
together those survivals of primitive marriage institutions.

Collective Marriage Among the Peoples of Northern Asia

We will begin our survey in that region which includes
the northeastern portion of Asia and the adjoining northern
portion of the American continent, and which constitutes
a cultural and ethnical link between the old world and its
civilizations and the new world of America which has
remained comparatively isolated in its development.

The Gilyak are a palæo-Asiatic race inhabiting the region
of the lower Amur River, immediately north of Manchuria,
and the northern parts of the adjacent island of Sakhalin.
Our information concerning their customs illustrates the
confusion to which I have just referred. An old Japanese
traveler mentions incidentally that Gilyak women have several husbands. The more recent account of an able French
traveler gives us more specific details. Brothers have their
wives to some extent in common; when an elder brother is
absent on a journey his younger brother enjoys marital
rights over his wife, although the converse does not hold.
"Villages are inhabited as a rule by members of the same
family; every Gilyak comes into the world with so many
fathers and so many mothers that it is somewhat difficult
to understand their system of relationship." Another traveler
reports that their sexual relations are indiscriminate, and
that the circumstance is accounted for by the tradition that
"in earlier times cousins ('rus-er') had the juridic right
of collective use of cousins and even of the sisters of cousins."
Such information has, however, been greatly amplified by
the extensive investigations, including a census, conducted

among the Gilyak by Dr. Leo Y. Sternberg, the distinguished director of the Peter the Great Museum of Anthropology of the former Imperial Russian Academy of Science. The Gilyak are strictly organized into exogamic intermarrying classes, and every member, male and female, of one class marries into the corresponding marriage class to which he or she is allotted from birth. Those classes correspond exactly to the degree of relationship, and the terms used to denote these indicate at the same time the norms of their marriage regulations. Thus the woman whom a man is bound to marry is his cross-cousin; on the other hand all other cousins, the daughters of a father's brother or a mother's sister, are strictly barred even in the remotest degree, and are called "yoch," which implies that they are absolutely tabu and inviolable. The name given by a man to the women whom he may marry is "angej," and the name given by a woman to the men whom she may marry is "pu." Individual marriage takes place, that is, a woman becomes the particular economic associate of a man. But the economic husband possesses no exclusive sexual rights over the woman: "all people who are in the relation of 'angej' and 'pu' have really the right of sexual intercourse, not only before, but also after, individual marriage." When her husband is absent a wife is free to receive any man who is "pu" to her; his brothers (actual and tribal) living in the same village or neighborhood do customarily use that right, and every man who is "pu" to a woman has the right to claim his privilege. Sometimes a man from a distant part, hearing that an "angej" of his is living in a certain village will come to claim the right. In one respect the rules of group-marriage are different in the two principal divisions of the Gilyak nation; for among the western Gilyak of the interior all tribal brothers have marital rights over the wives of each other indifferently. Among the eastern Gilyak, on the other hand, the younger brothers have a claim to the wives of all their elder brothers, but the elder brothers have no right to the wives of the younger brothers. The terms of relationship are modified in accordance with those distinctions in the two divisions, the wives of younger brothers being "yoch," that is, forbidden, to the elder brothers. Dr. Sternberg sees in that rule of the eastern Gilyak, the significance of which will be perceived later on, a step from unmodified group-marriage towards the establishment of patriarchal rights.

The Yakut, the great Turki nation of which the Manchus are a branch, are divided into totemic clans. When the Russians first came upon them polygyny was general; the nature of that polygyny is clearly indicated by the fact that at the present day the sisters of the bride, as well as the bride herself, must carefully abstain from ever showing their faces, or even their hair to the bridegroom or any of his brothers or cousins. They have been for the last hundred years members of the Orthodox Russian Church, but their former organization still survives in a curiously modified form, for it is the established custom "that two brothers of one side marry two sisters of another." The same terms are employed to denote a man's own children or his brother's. Betrothals take place in infancy.

Among the Kamchadals it appears that the favorite marriage is between cousins, that is, presumably cross-cousins. Sororal polygyny was the recognized usage; when a man took a second wife she was his first wife's sister, or failing a sister her first-cousin, or tribal sister. A man frequently had two or three wives, either living in the same household or in separate dwellings. We are further told that it was customary between "friends," which expression usually means tribal brothers, to exchange wives, and the levirate rule was observed. In spite, therefore, of the imperfect and fragmentary character of our information, it seems fairly clear that their marital relations conformed to the principles of sororal and fraternal group-marriage.

The Tungus are, numerically, by far the most important race in northern Asia, extending from the borders of China in the east over the whole northern portion of the continent to the Ob River in the northwest. The organization of the Ochi tribe has been carefully investigated by Dr. Sternberg. Among them marriage is regulated by a classificatory system of relationship with wide age-grades, so that not only do those who stand in the relation of cross-cousins belong to reciprocal marrying classes, but also those who stand in the relation of uncle and niece, the daughter of a man's sister belonging to the class into which he is by birth married. Among the Tungus complete group-marriage relations obtain, for not only is sororal polygyny observed, but every man has marital rights over the wives of his elder brothers. Further, owing to the inclusiveness of their classificatory system, he has also marital rights over the wives of the younger brothers of his father.

A Russian traveler among the natives of the extreme northeast of the Asiatic continent, the Chukchi, mentions that, "among other customs, they have the usage of contracting so-called 'exchange-marriages.' Two or more men enter into an agreement whereby they have mutual rights to each other's wives. The right is exercised whenever the contracting parties come together, as for instance on the occasion of a visit. Even unmarried men or widowers can enter into an 'exchange-marriage,' which thus assumes the form of a veritable polyandry." We have, concerning the Chukchi, the elaborate monograph of Mr. Wlademar Bogoras, sumptuously published in the series of publications of the "Jesup North Pacific Expedition." The Chukchi are commonly betrothed in infancy to their first-cousins, that being the prescriptive marriage alliance. They moreover observe sororal polygyny; if a man desires or can afford to maintain several wives he has a right during her life-time as well as after her death to the sisters of his first wife. Further, not only have the Chukchi the common custom of exchanging wives, but Mr. Bogoras describes a regular system by which a number of men will solemnly bind themselves to mutual rights over their respective wives. Practically every Chukcha, we are told, belongs to such a marrying group. At first sight it would appear as if this group-marriage organization were an artificial one, that is to say, one formed by a pact into which the members deliberately enter by an individual contract, and not group-marriage in what we are led to regard as its typical and original form as a mutual relation arising from an established collective contract between the two groups. But the matter wears a different complexion when we are informed that "second and third cousins are almost invariably united by ties of group-marriage," and that it is indeed exceptional for any but cousins to belong to a group exercising those reciprocal marital rights. It is well to note, as a corrective to the ideas by which it is customary to judge those marriage organizations, that in this instance we have clear testimony that licentiousness has nothing to do with the institution. The Chukchi are indeed described as a sensual race, but their group-marriage organization is not taken advantage of for licentious purposes. In fact, they are careful not to form such an alliance if possible with dwellers in the same village, and they in general avoid exercising the rights conferred on them by the compact. It is, as in all instances where deliberate exchange of wives takes place with a friend or a guest, as a bond of brotherhood that the relation is regarded. A man will thus seek to bind himself to those of his relatives who dwell in other villages, and when he visits those villages his tribal cousin will yield to him his bed, presently returning the visit in order to make the obligation mutual; sometimes cousins will exchange wives for several months, for years, or permanently. So seriously is the arrangement regarded that children of the same marriage group are regarded as brothers and sisters; they are not allowed to marry among themselves, such a union being looked upon as incestuous. It appears, then, that although the group-marriage of the Chukchi is to a certain extent artificial and depends upon an individual compact, it nevertheless corresponds to, and is a direct derivative of, established marriage rights between two marrying classes or groups, modified by the necessities imposed by the isolated and scattered condition of those groups, who live in small communities ranging over wide areas.

That conclusion is confirmed the more we inquire into such reported instances of polyandrous arrangements. Passing to the bridge of islands which connects the Asiatic with the American continent across the Bering Sea, the majority of the reports which we have concerning the Aleuts are of the same character as those which are current concerning the Chukchi or the Gilyak, and represent them as given to loose polyandrous unions by "agreement" or from expediency. Thus Count Langsdorf says that a woman sometimes "lives with two husbands, who agree among themselves upon the conditions on which they are to share her." Father Veniaminoff, after stating that polygyny was usual among the Aleuts, adds that "in addition the custom of polyandry is practiced, a woman having the right to take, besides her principal husband, one who has the title of 'helper,' or 'partner' (in Russian, 'polovinschtchik'). Those supplementary husbands enjoyed all marital rights, and were under obligation of contributing towards the upkeep of the household. The women living in such double marriages were in no wise regarded as immoral, but on the contrary were rather honored for their industry in caring for two men besides their children." Three men sometimes lived together in one household with one woman "without suspicion of jealousy." Those multiple marriage arrangements were sometimes extended so as to include Russian settlers as accepted members in the partnership. All this might easily appear mere licentious depravity and laxity on the part of those savages, who were in the Stone Age when first visited by Europeans. Admiral Wrangell remarks that only a few years after the arrival of the Russians they had become Russianized, and had so entirely lost their native traditional customs, that it was quite useless to inquire what they really were. At the present day they have become as completely Americanized, and the appearance of many Aleutian villages and of their inhabitants differs little from that of a western township in the United States. To see the natives sitting on the verandas of their wooden cottages, the mother, maybe with her blouse-sleeves tucked up doing the week's washing, or putting the finishing touches to their children's toilet before they go to Sunday-school, one would consider those people to be no nearer to a primitive social state than the European immigrants in the little colonies. In those circumstances we should scarcely be entitled to hope that any investigation could bring to light more definite particulars concerning their social organization. Yet such an investigation has been successfully carried out under the auspices of the Russian Geographical Society by the well-known ethnologist, Mr. Wlademar Jochelson. To his intense surprise he found not only that in former times it was an established rule for younger brothers to have access to the wives of their elder brothers, but that even at the present day among these Europeanized natives "the institution is preserved among cousins, and—what is most remarkable—not as a facultative institution, but as an obligatory one. To participate in group marriage is the duty of cousins."

Sexual Hospitality

It will be well to pause here for a moment and consider how it is that participation in group-marriage, which we are in the habit of regarding as a form of licentious disorder, should be regarded not only in the light of a right and a privilege, but actually as a moral obligation. The reason is in reality quite clear and simple. Community of wives being originally part of the relation of tribal brotherhood, it was naturally regarded as an essential token of that relation—that is, a man could not be truly a tribal brother unless that reciprocal access to wives existed. To primitive man all men are either tribal brothers or strangers, and the latter term is equivalent in primitive society to "enemy"; there is no middle status between those two opposite relations. If a

man, not being by birth a tribal brother, is admitted into
the community, if he is found to be well-disposed, if he is
regarded with good will or affection or admiration—if,
in short, he is not an enemy—he must needs be a tribal
brother. Hence the sacredness of hospitality in all primitive
sentiment; a man who has been admitted to the relation of
guest is necessarily to be regarded and treated as a tribal
brother. If a man has touched the tent-rope of an Arab's
tent his life must be defended against all enemies, and to
tell an Arab that he has neglected his guest is the greatest
of insults. The hospitality of savages knows no bounds; if
they are on the verge of starvation they will give the little
that they have to the stranger who has been admitted to
their midst. The guest who is not by birth a tribal brother
must be made one, since he is not an enemy. The first
thought of the savage when a stranger to whom he feels
himself attracted is in his company, is to take the necessary
steps to make him a tribal brother. When a young American
naval officer won the good graces of Seri women, their first
anxiety was to paint on his face the tribal marks. The blood-
bond is insisted on whenever a traveler makes a stay in an
African, American or Polynesian tribe; an exchange of
blood must be effected so as to make the man who is not
treated as a stranger or enemy a tribal brother. In Australia,
if a member of a strange tribe refuses to drink the blood
of his hosts, it is forcibly poured down his throat. Among
the Koryak the guest is obliged to undergo a somewhat
strange rite of brotherhood with his host's wife before he
can avail himself of her hospitality. It follows that the
participation of the guest in his host's wife is a necessary
token of his friendship, a "friend" being necessarily a tribal
brother. The practice, very inaptly called "hospitality prostitution," is not a matter of misguided benevolence, but a
necessary pledge that the guest is a friend and not an enemy.
For the guest to refuse is equivalent to repudiating the
assumed brotherhood, and is thus tantamount to a declaration of war. The sedentary Koryak, for example, "look upon

it as the truest mark of friendship, when they entertain a friend, to put him to bed with their wife or daughter; and a refusal of this civility they consider as the greatest affront, and are capable of even murdering a man for such contempt. That happened to several Cossacks, before they were acquainted with the customs of the people." The same thing is reported of the Chukchi. In Madagascar a missionary closely escaped being murdered because he refused the proffered hospitality. I have heard of similar perils incurred by missionaries in New Zealand, in the early days, from the same cause. Even the very free sexual hospitality of the natives of Tahiti was, M. Lesson remarks, regarded in the light of a ceremony partaking of a religious character. The custom is very general in all primitive societies. From the manner in which it is regarded we may be as certain as we can be of any inference in social anthropology that wherever it is observed clan-brotherhood is, or was formerly, considered to imply sexual communism, for it is by assimilation to a clan-brother that the guest is treated as he is. All hospitality, which among primitive peoples organized in clans is so liberal and ungrudging as to excite the admiration of Europeans, has its foundation in the assimilation of the guest to a clan-brother. The practice of sexual hospitality has naturally tended to become modified and limited, in the same way as sexual communism has become modified and limited, with the development of individual marriage and its growing claims. All manner of transitional and attenuated modifications of the custom are accordingly found. Thus, the Missouri Indians were, like many North American tribes, so averse to any intercourse with members of another tribe, that they never offered their wives or daughters to strangers, not even to their close neighbors, the Mandans. Nevertheless, they regarded themselves as being under the obligation of offering sexual hospitality to a guest, and accordingly provided him with a captive from some other tribe. It may safely be concluded that this practice was a compromise between their strongly endogamic tribal principles and their equally strong conviction that a clan-brother was entitled to access to his fellow-clansman's or host's women. Among the Krumir Berbers a stranger visiting the tribe is received and lodged by one of the tribesmen, and is invited to spend the night in his tent in the company of his host's wife. The host leaves the tent, but he mounts guard outside it, armed with his gun, and should he hear the slightest suspicious movement on the part of his guest, he would have no hesitation in instantly shooting him. So-called "hospitality prostitution" has here dwindled down to an empty ceremonial which preserves the form of the social tradition, while safeguarding more advanced sentiments by abolishing the reality of the usage. Among the Arabs the cult of hospitality amounts to an article of religious faith, and, as is usually the case, is associated with an equally fervent devotion to the sentiment of clan-brotherhood and solidarity, which may be said to be the dominating passion of the Arab. At the same time the Arabs are at the present day, and have long been, intensely patriarchal in their conceptions, while passionately devoted to their women, and in the fullest sense of the term jealous of them and of their honor. From the importance of the conceptions of hospitality and clan-brotherhood among them we should, however, be disposed to infer, on comparative grounds, that at some former time hospitality amongst them included sexual hospitality, and that therefore sexual communism among clan-brothers was also at some former period a custom of their forefathers. In this instance we are able to check the inference, and we have evidence that it is, in fact, entirely justified. The learned Arab jurist, 'Ata ibn-Abi Rabah, states that the custom of offering one's wife to a guest was of old a universally sanctioned and recognized custom survived in historical times, and indeed, has survived amongst some down to the present, or quite recent, times. The Asir tribe, up to the time of the Wahhabites, lent their wives to their guest, and so also did the Dhahaban. Among the Merekedes, a tribe of the Yemen, "custom requires that the stranger should pass the night with his host's wife, whatever may be her age or condition. Should he render himself agreeable to the lady, he is honorably and hospitably treated; if not, the lower part of his 'abba,' or cloak is cut off and he is driven away in disgrace." Thus among a people whose notions of the exclusive nature of individual marriage are in general at the present day even more severe and more strict than our own, whose more civilized representatives veil their women and confine them to the sacred privacy of the harem, clan-organization entailed the same conceptions and usages as among the primitive savages of North America or of Australia.

It will, I think, be apparent from the above facts why it is that the Aleuts regard the ancient observance of community of wives between cousins as a moral duty and obligation. Neglect of it would be a dissolution and repudiation of the sacred bonds of clan-kinship. When a Chukcha claims his privilege from a tribal cousin, the latter makes a point of ceremoniously returning the visit, not on the principle that he is entitled to reciprocity, but because it would be as offensive not to return the token of brotherhood as to withhold his hand when another proffered his in friendship. When a Nayar of Travancore became converted to Christianity he refused to cohabit any longer with his brother's wife; the brother was mortally offended, and expressed his indignation at the unbrotherly conduct of the convert. Among the Eskimo of Davis Strait and Cumberland Sound the rite of reciprocal exchange of wives between tribal brothers is, as with the Aleuts, "commanded by religious law."

Collective Sexual Relations in America

There can be little doubt that the practice of exchanging wives temporarily, which is universal with all sections of the Eskimo race, is the survival of an organization of tribal sexual communism which, together with all clan and tribal organization, has become disintegrated through the dispersion of small communities in the icy habitat to which the race has been driven. Among the Eskimo of the Kadiak tribe the rules which were found by Mr. Jochelson among the Aleuts have been observed by M. Dawydoff. Among the Eskimo of Bering Straits "it is a custom," says Mr. E. W. Nelson, "for two men living in different villages to agree to become bond-fellows, or brothers by adoption. Having made the arrangement, when one of them goes to the other's village he is received as the bond-brother's guest, and is given the use of his host's bed with his wife during his stay. When the visit is returned the same favor is extended to the other, consequently neither family knows who is the father of the children." The children of each family call one another brother. Among the Eskimo of Baffin Land and Hudson Bay polygyny is combined with polyandry. In Repulse Bay "it is a usual thing among friends to exchange wives for a week or two about every two months," and Dr. Murdoch was informed that "at certain times there is a general exchange of wives throughout the village, each woman passing from man to man till she has been through the hands of all." In northern Greenland, as Dr. Bessels delicately puts it, "somewhat communistic tendencies seriously interfere with the sanctity of marriage."

The most important race of the extreme northwestern region of the American continent is the nation of the Tlinkit, or as the Russians called them, the Kolosh. They are divided into a number of totemic clans, which are grouped into two large divisions or exogamic marriage classes, and a man is strictly forbidden to marry in his own division, and must take his wives from the opposite marriage class. It would appear further that it is most usual for members of one clan to draw their wives from one particular clan only, for we are told that as a rule the wives are cousins of their husbands, which means that a man marries into the same clan or family from which his father, his grandfather, and all his forebears have been in the habit of taking their wives. Polygamy is very general and extensive, and a man of distinction may have as many as forty wives. In addition the Tlinkit are polyandrous. Their usages in this respect are interesting as illustrating once more the deceptive manner in which such an organization is apt to be reported. Some writers state that their customs allow "great looseness in sexual relations." Count Langsdorf, on the contrary, says that their decent and orderly behavior in this respect and the modesty of their women stand in striking contrast with the manners of neighboring races. The reason of this is, as usual, that the men are "very jealous"—that is to say, they are not disposed to allow the women any liberties. Girls are given in marriage as soon as they attain puberty. Adultery is very severely punished, the guilty parties, if discovered, being, we are told, usually killed on the spot, unless, indeed, the man is able to soothe the husband's feelings by the offer of an adequate monetary compensation. But the notable feature in the organization of the Tlinkit lies in what constitutes "adultery." It is a serious offense only if the seducer belongs to a clan other than the husband's; if he be a "relative" (by which term we are presumably to understand a "clan-brother") there is no offense and no punishment. The lover is, on the contrary, invited to continue his relations with the woman quite freely, subject to the reasonable proviso that he shall contribute his share towards the maintenance of the household. It is, in fact, customary for a woman to have several co-husbands, who exercise their rights during one another's frequent absences, and coöperate in the upkeep of the common home. The "secondary husbands," as they have been called, "are invariably either brothers or cousins of the principal husband." The rules governing the sexual organizations of the Tlinkit would seem, from those facts, to be fairly clear. The Russian bishop, Father Veniaminoff, to whom we owe our most valuable information concerning the populations of that region in their original state, thinks it, however, necessary to go to Sicily for a parallel to the customs of the natives, and many ethnological writers have used the hint, and affect to term these arrangements "cicisbeism." It does not appear that the customs of the Tlinkit bear any resemblance to the practices of the eighteenth-century Italian society, of which the relations between Nelson and Sir William and Lady Hamilton are a famous instance. Putting our information together it would seem that among the Tlinkit sexual relations with the wife of a clan-brother, or, what is the same thing, with a woman of the clan with which his was intermarried, did not constitute adultery, but that a man might always share such a woman with her individual husband; in other words, a man had the right of access to any woman of the corresponding marriage class, independently of any individual economic ties which she might have contracted, and could, in fact, become a co-partner in that economic marriage. Such rules resemble far more closely the scheme of what Mr. Fison described as group-marriage than any dissolute habits of eighteenth-century society in Sicily or elsewhere. It is to be noted that the marriages of the Tlinkit were commonly matrilocal; the households to which the various husbands contributed were therefore those of the women.

Still farther south, among the Salish Indians of British Columbia, "it was customary for a man to marry all his wife's sisters." As among most other American tribes, "the levirate prevailed among them, a man's widow or widows going to his surviving brother." Further, we are told that during the lifetime of the older brother his wives and his younger brothers "stood in the relation of 'skalpa' and 'kalapa' to one another. There is no equivalent in English for these terms." From what we have already seen of the relations between a man's wives and his brothers among kindred tribes, we may, I think, form a fairly accurate idea of the meaning of those special terms applied to that relationship.

Making due allowance for variations of statement and the great difficulty attending such observations, it would appear that from Manchuria on the Asiatic side to British Columbia on the American side the principles which govern collective sexual relations are substantially identical among all tribes, and that with the large majority reciprocal sexual rights between all the males and all the females of two intermarrying groups are recognized and used at the present day, or were so until quite recent times.

The general prevalence of those customs among the peoples of the ruder northern regions of eastern Asia and western America suggests that they may also have obtained among the American tribes, who, there is every reason to believe, originally passed over from Asia and southward from those northern regions. That presumption is strongly confirmed by several social characteristics common to all North American peoples. In the first place, the nomenclature of clan-relationship amongst them is that which is called "classificatory," and which corresponds to the relations established by such a sexual organization. The principles and practice of sororal polygyny is, as we have seen, universally observed among North American Indians. In conjunction with it levirate marriage is, as with the Alaskan and other tribes, a right and an obligation. Taken together, those facts are, to any one who admits the principle of evolution in social phenomena, in themselves conclusive evidence of a former sexual organization in groups. Not only did the wives pass, after the death of their economic associate, to his brother, but the practice of exchange of wives between clan-brothers was so general that sexual communism may be said to have, in fact, existed between the brothers of one group and the sisters of another. Among the Menomini Indians, between sisters-in-law and brothers-in-law on both sides sexual relations were permissible and lawful. Indeed, in many tribes even at the present day, according to a medical man thoroughly familiar with their conduct, "communism as to sexual relations seems to prevail." Among the Natchez, when a man married a woman, "if she has many sisters he marries them all, so that nothing is more common than to see four or five sisters the wives of a single husband." It appears, on the other hand, that they were not, after all,

confined in their sexual relations to a single husband, for
we are further informed that "jealousy has so little place in
their hearts that many find no difficulty in lending their
wives to their friends." As "their friends" obviously includes
their brothers, the marriage arrangements of the Natchez
must have been scarcely distinguishable from fraternal-
sororal group-marriages. Among the more secluded tribes
of the Dene, the northern branch of the great Athapascan
group, which includes the Navahos and the Apaches, those
collective relations were even more definite. As of other
American tribes, we are told that sororal polygyny, the
levirate, and the exchange of wives were usual; but among
the Sekanais "polyandry was in honor conjointly with
polygyny." "Brothers," in fact, "cohabit with one another's
women openly." Among the Beaver Indians, "one woman
is common to two brothers, and often to three." Among the
most primitive representatives of the American race, the
Seri Indians, it is practically certain that both sororal
polygyny and fraternal polyandry are, or were till recent
times, in force. Marriage with a woman gives a husband
marital rights over all her sisters. At the present time the
number of the women greatly exceeds that of the men,
owing to the constant losses from warfare; but Dr. McGee
is of opinion that when the tribe was more flourishing the
right of blood-relatives to one another's sexual mates was
mutual, if, indeed, it is not so at the present day. At any
rate, "among other privileges bestowed on the bride during
the probationary period are those of receiving the most intimate attentions from the clan-fellows of the bridegroom."
Zuñi traditions make distinct reference to fraternal polyandry
as an accepted custom; and from the traditional tales of
the Fox Indians we learn that among them also it was customary for brothers to share their elder brother's wives.
Those customs obtained among the Iroquois themselves.
After referring to the practice of sororal polygyny amongst
them, Father Charlevoix adds that among the Tsonnon-
touan—that is to say, the Senecas, the most important and

by far the most numerous of the confederated Iroquois nations—"there was a far greater disorder, namely, plurality
of husbands." The information is confirmed by Father
Lafitau, who adds that this "disorder" was regarded as a
perfectly regular form of marriage, and was, in fact, quite
"in order." There is thus ample evidence to confirm the
presumption that the marriage customs of the North American Indians at the time when they first became known to us,
were, like the breaking down of their clan exogamy, the
result of the decay of clan organization under the influence
of individual economic marriage;. and that the rules of
sororal polygyny and of the levirate were, like the terms of
kinship nomenclature, survivals of a collective sexual organization.

Similar principles would appear to have been widely current in South America. Thus of the natives of New Granada
or Colombia we are told that "brothers-in-law may marry
sisters-in-law, and two or three brothers will marry two or
three sisters jointly, and they regard this manner of contracting marriages as lawful." Of the tribes of Brazil with
which the Spaniards first came in contact, Herrera gives
the following account: "They observed no law or rule in
matrimony, but took as many wives as they would and
they as many husbands, quitting one another at pleasure
without reckoning any wrong done to either part. There was
no such thing as jealousy among them, all living as best
pleased them without taking offense at one another." Contrary to generally accepted notions of the evils inseparable
from a departure from European standards of morality, those
Indians, he says, "multiplied very much," and Herrera adds
the even more remarkable information that the men "were
very modest in conversing with the women." Of the Moxos
Indians it is reported that, "according to the ancient custom
of their nation, the women belong without distinction to all
their relatives." Among their neighbors, the Itonamas, the
men willingly lend their wives to one another, and the
women abandon themselves to all their relatives. The parents

designate at birth the children who shall intermarry. Polyandrous marriages are reported from the Paraguayan Chaco;
and among the Zaparos of Ecuador polyandry is usual, and
two men may have five wives between them. Baron von
Humboldt found that among the Avanos and among the
Maypures of the Orinoco brothers had often but one wife
between them. In Guiana at the present day polyandry is
common, and is practiced openly. A missionary endeavoring
to persuade a Guiana Indian to give up polygny, tried to
convince him of the wickedness of the practice by asking
him what he would think of a woman having several husbands. But the force of the argument was entirely lost upon
the Indian, who replied that both customs were equally honored in his tribe, and that both were practiced. Among the
western Fuegians, according to the testimony of the missionaries who are settled amongst them, polyandry is very
prevalent; it is quite common for several husbands to share
the same wife.

PROPERTY *

By W. H. R. RIVERS

The main problem with which I shall deal is how far in different human societies property is held by social groups, and how far it belongs to the individual. I shall also inquire into the nature of the group in which common ownership is vested when it is present.

We shall find that the matter is far from simple, and that in many societies where the institution of individual property is definite, there are, nevertheless, customs which show the existence of a group-interest in property at variance with individual rights. I may begin by going briefly through the different kinds of social groups that have been considered, and state briefly how they stand in relation to individualism and communism in respect of property.

We may lay it down as a definite proposition, that wherever we find the family (in the narrow sense) as the dominant feature of the social organization it is combined with the institution of individual property. The exact nature of ownership may differ, and variations such as those characterizing Primogeniture, Junior Right, or Borough English, and other forms of inheritance may be found, but in all cases in which society is founded mainly or altogether on the family, property is owned by individuals. The community has certain claims on these individual rights in the form of taxation, etc., but the prominent feature from the broad comparative point of view is the individual character of ownership.

Taking the various Indian forms of the joint family as instances of this form of social grouping, we find in most cases common ownership is a prominent feature. Thus, in

* *Social Organization.* New York: Alfred A. Knopf, Inc.

the joint family of Bengal, property is altogether in common, while in the *mitakshara* system of other parts of India only ancestral property is thus held in common, every member of the group having full rights over property acquired by his own exertions. Property is regarded as ancestral when it has been transmitted for two generations, and it is then regarded as inalienable. In the matrilineal joint family of Malabar property is held in common, being controlled by the senior male member of the group. In all these forms of the joint family we have a definite departure from individual ownership in the direction of communal ownership, the special feature of the communism being that common ownership is limited to a relatively small group bound together by close ties of genealogical relationship or kinship.

If now we pass to the bilateral group of the kindred, we find again this feature of communal ownership. There is evidence that in the kindreds of Northern Europe property was to a large extent in common,[1] and this is certainly the case in the modern example I have already cited more than once, the *taviti* of Eddystone Island in the Solomons. In this mode of social grouping land and other forms of property are held in common by the *taviti,* and where a person has individual rights in his land or other property these are subject to many claims on the part of other members of this *taviti.* I will not describe the nature of these claims here, because they are essentially of the same kind as those found in association with the clan-organization and can best be exemplified in connection with that form of social organization, to which I can now pass.

The study of the relation of the clan to property is complicated by the feature, which we have seen to produce complications of the other kinds, that the clan-grouping is always, so far as we know, complicated by the co-existence of a family grouping of some kind. Thus, in Melanesia where our information is more exact than in other parts of the world, not only is the family in the limited sense recognized, but there are still more definitely present examples, in one form or another, of the joint-family. Thus, in the island of Ambrim, where I was able to obtain a detailed account of the regulations concerning ownership, it was clear that the most important social group in relation to property was one called *vantinbül*. There was some doubt about the exact limits of this group, but it was certainly a kinship group consisting in the main of persons genealogically related in the male line, though it also included the daughters of members and their children, membership of the *vantinbül* in the female line then lapsing. In other parts of Melanesia the groups in which ownership is vested are kinship groups of this kind rather than moieties or clans. Thus, in Pentecost Island, which is the seat of the dual organization, the group which held property in common was the one called *verana,* which, so far as I could discover in a far too brief investigation, was a kinship group similar to the *vantinbül* of Ambrim.

I have given an account of the Ambrim mode of grouping because I do not think I can better illustrate the nature of the subject than by taking this island as an example of the ownership of a simple society. I will begin with the ownership of land. Here land was in one sense held to be the property of the clan. People of any *vantinbül* might clear patches in the uncultivated land, which would in time become the property of the *vantinbül* of the clearer. If a *vantinbül* died out, its land became the property of the village as a whole; it went out of cultivation and then shared the complete indifference of the people to the ownership of uncultivated land.

It was evident that in Ambrim there was no appearance even of the individual ownership of land. It was the custom in this island to indicate the nature of the ownership of an object by means of the possessive pronoun. Where there was individual ownership a man would indicate the fact by the use of the personal pronoun, and would speak of "my bow and arrow" or "my armlet," but, with one unimportant exception, he would never speak of "my land," and would always say "our land." Moreover, this mode of speech was no empty form. A man might clear a piece of ground entirely by his own labor, and might plant and tend it without help from any one, but any member of his *vantinbül* could nevertheless help himself to any of its produce without asking leave or informing the cultivator. Inhabitants of the village belonging to a *vantinbül* other than that of the cultivator might also take produce, but had to ask leave. Since such permission, however, was never refused, the communism extended in practice to the whole clan. For property of other kinds the case differed with the kind of object. The most frequent and important fact determining the nature of ownership in Ambrim is whether the object is indigenous or introduced, indigenous objects being owned by the *vantinbül* or other larger group, while introduced objects may be owned by individuals. A good example of the difference is presented by the weapons of Ambrim, of which there are four: the spear, club, bow and arrow, and sling. The first two are common property, and a man will always say "our spear" and "our club," but on the other hand, the bow and arrow and sling are individually-owned objects, and people said "my bow and arrow" and "my sling." Associated with this usage was a definite tradition that the people had always had the spear and club, while the sling and bow and arrow had been introduced from a neighboring island.

There was some reason to suppose that another factor which had influenced ownership was whether an object had been made by individual or common labor. Thus, one of the objects of Melanesian culture which is usually, if not always, the subject of common ownership is the canoe, and at one time I had the impression that this was because it was made by common labor of the community. It is highly doubtful whether this is the real explanation, whether it is not rather the result of rationalization of tradition, which must always be borne in mind as a possibility in the case of rude, or indeed of any explanation of social customs or institutions. For one of the objects most constantly made by communal effort in Melanesia is the house, and yet this is usually certainly in Ambrim an individual possession, or at least the possession of the family in the limited sense.

Such facts as those, however, fail to reveal the great extent to which communistic sentiments concerning property dominate the people of Melanesia. One who lives among Melanesians is continually impressed by little occurrences which indicate the strength and pervasiveness of these sentiments. I must be content with one example. When in the Banks Islands, a small group north of the New Hebrides, I worked out the history of a plot of land which was cleared about four generations ago. The greater part of the plot had been divided up between the children of the clearer, and had since been regarded as the individual property of their descendants, but part of the original plot had been left for the common use of all the descendants of the original clearers. I was told that disputes were frequent concerning the portions of the land which were owned individually, while there were never any quarrels concerning the part which had been left for the common use of all.

In one part of Melanesia, in Fiji, which differs from the rest in the greater definiteness of its chieftainship, and in several other respects, probably as the result of Polynesian influence, the communism is still more definite. Thus, there is a custom called *kerekere,* whereby persons may take the property of others, to such an extent that it has served as an effectual bar to the adoption of European methods of trading. A Fijian who sets up as a trader is liable to have his goods appropriated by any one who comes into his store, to such an extent as to make his success impossible.

About the Polynesian Islands of the Pacific our information is less definite, but here again it would seem that communism exists in a pronounced form. I must be content to give you an example from my own experience. I was traveling on a boat with four inhabitants of Niue or Savage Island, and took the opportunity of inquiring into their social organization. At the end of the sitting they said they would like now to examine me about my customs, and, using my own concrete methods, one of the first questions was directed to discover what I should do with a sovereign if I earned one. In response to my somewhat lame answers, they asked me point-blank whether I should share it with my parents and brothers and sisters. When I replied that I would not usually, and certainly not necessarily do so, and that it was not our general custom, they found my reply so amusing that it was long before they left off laughing. Their attitude towards my individualism was of exactly the same order as that which we adopt towards such a custom as the couvade, in which the man goes to bed when his wife has a child, and revealed the presence of a communistic sentiment of a deeply seated kind.

The ownership of property in Oceania has other points of interest, to which I shall return after sketching very briefly the state of affairs in other parts of the world.

The land-tenure of Africa differs from that of Melanesia in a very striking respect. In Melanesia chiefs have no functions in relation to land. If they possess land they own it in the same way, and subject to the same communal usages, as other persons, and, in one case at least, they are not even landowners, and only obtain land for their gardens by the grace of their subjects. Among the Bantu of Africa, on the other hand, the position of chiefs in this respect is very different. They hold the land and distribute it among their subjects, but they probably only act in this respect as the representatives of the people as a whole; for the Ba-Ila have a rule that the chief may only sell land after obtaining the permission of his people. In this case, and probably elsewhere among the Bantu, the chief seems to be the distributor of individual rights to the use of land rather than its owner.

According to the available accounts, land assigned by a Ba-Ila chief to one of his subjects is regarded as the assignee's individual property, but this individual ownership is subject to the restriction that any of his elder relatives on both sides have the right to take what they want. We have thus a form of common ownership, or rather common usufruct, which is similar to that of Melanesia in that the group concerned is a kinship-group, but there is the important difference that the right is limited to the members of the group senior to the owner. This rule also applies to other kinds of property, and Smith and Dale record how a Ba-Ila who has gained large sums by his industry in working for European settlers may be deprived of them all by his elder relatives.

As in Melanesia it would seem that the right of the elders, which is perhaps derived from a more extensive communism, is a privilege belonging to a kinship-group rather than to the clan.

In a recent paper Dundas gives an instructive case of pure individual ownership among a Bantu people. This occurs among the Wakarra, a tribe living on an island every acre of which is cultivated. Every piece of land is privately owned, and Dundas supposes that individual tenure has evolved owing to the high value which land possesses. This tribe is also exceptional in Africa, in that an owner may sell his land, but only after consulting his kinsmen in order to give them the first option. This right of the kin is of interest in relation to the common rights of kinship-groups elsewhere among the Bantu.

Dundas also records an interesting case among the Akikuyu. They have acquired their land from the earlier inhabitants. All the land thus bought by a man is held as the common property of his descendants. The senior member of the existing group of descendants is regarded as the owner, but only as representative of the group. Land is never sold, and Dundas says that the Akikuyu cannot comprehend the sale of land, by which I suppose he means that the sale of land is so foreign to their sentiments that they can hardly conceive what is meant when the idea of a sale is broached.

In West Africa there appear to be variations in different regions, the difference probably depending on the degree of influence of the peoples of higher culture who have for a long time been passing into the country from the north. Thus, in the northern parts of the region of the Gold Coast, individual property is, according to Cardinall, as definite an institution as among ourselves. On the coast itself, on the other hand, the land is regarded as the property of the tribe, but any member of the community is at liberty to clear and farm any portion of the untilled bush. The cleared part is regarded as his property so long as he cultivates it, and his right to it is still recognized if he should leave it untilled for a time in order that it may recover its fertility. In the intermediate region, farther inland, the individual retains rights in the trees growing on land which he has cleared but has then again allowed to fall into disuse, thus presenting a further step towards individual ownership.

Here, as in Melanesia, the chief has no special powers in connection with the land. As he has command over a larger number of laborers, he is able to cultivate more land than the rest, but otherwise he is no better off than any of his subjects. There is a native saying, "Chiefs command people, not the land." While the chiefs are thus devoid of special privileges in relation to the land, there is an official called the *tindana,* who has powers resting upon the tradition that he is the representative of the original owners of the soil, whose powers have persisted when people from elsewhere became the chiefs. The *tindana* assigns land to new settlers, and he is called upon to intercede with the local deity if, for any reason, such as the spilling of blood or other crime, the land has been polluted and there is the danger of its ceasing to yield its fruits. The *tindana* is, in fact, a priest, and receives for his services a basket of corn or other payment, which seems to correspond closely with the tithe of our own culture.

In North America there are many intermediate states between individual and communal ownership, but, as in Melanesia, where there is common ownership this seems to be vested in some form of the joint family, i.e., in a kinship-group rather than in the clan.

The case which has been supposed to point most definitely
to ownership by the clan is that of the Aztecs of Mexico,
where, according to some authorities, the group called *cal-*
pulli, which is usually supposed to have been a clan, though
its exact nature is doubtful, seems to have held land in
common. But the constitution of the *calpulli* is doubtful,
and there is reason to believe that it was a kinship-group
of some kind rather than a clan. Whatever the exact nature
of the tenure may have been, however, it seems certain that
it had one feature which distinguished it markedly from
the land-tenure of Melanesia and, at the same time, caused
it to resemble the early tenures of Europe. The land of the
calpulli was parceled out among the male members of the
group, each of whom had to cultivate his allotment, and
if any one failed in this duty the land was reallotted at the
end of two years and assigned to other members of the
calpulli. We have here a state intermediate between communal property and individual possession closely comparable
with that of our own history.

The ownership of other kinds of property in North America seems to have been individual rather than communal,
although we have singularly little information on the point.
Superficially there is little question that individual ownership is definite, but it is a question whether here, as in
other parts of the world, more detailed investigation would
not show the existence of rights of other members of the
group to objects which are said to be the individual property
of some members of the group. Dr. Paul Radin has given
me an interesting example pointing in this direction. When
buying an ancient pipe from a member of the Winnebago
tribe he found that a reluctance to sell was due to the sentiment of the rest of the group, in this case the joint-family.
It was acknowledged by all that the pipe was the property
of the vendor, and that he had a complete right to sell it,
but the whole group was animated by a sentiment towards
the object which was acting as a definite bar to alienation. It
is possible that in this case the sentiment was no more than

would exist in such a case among ourselves. Thus, to take a recent instance, the intention of the Duke of Westminster to sell Gainsborough's "Blue Boy" might be hindered by the existence among the Grosvenor family of a sentiment against the sale, and in some cases the sentiment might prove an effectual bar to alienation. In the case of our own society such rights have become the subject of definite social regulations, which make up what we call law. Where law is only customary, and has not been fixed in definite form by means of writing, there must always be an element of doubt as to whether a given act is definitely illegal or only an offense against a sentiment of the society, and Dr. Radin's case seems to be open to doubt of this kind.

I should like here to consider briefly a widespread case of ownership which has aroused much interest. I refer to the custom by which a person may own trees growing on land which belongs to another. This custom is frequent, for instance, in Melanesia. Thus, in Eddystone Island a person is allowed to plant a tree on the land of another, and this is regarded as the property of himself and his descendants. In other cases the separate ownership depends upon different laws of inheritance: while land on which trees are planted passes, according to ancient custom, to the children of the sister, the trees which a man has planted on this land may be inherited by his own children; and it seems clear that this forms a social mechanism by which the separate ownership of trees and land has come about. I believe that these customs in general are the result of the blending of peoples, patrilineal immigrants having succeeded in transmitting their trees to their children, while the land itself has to follow the laws of matrilineal inheritance of the indigenous inhabitants.

According to another Melanesian custom, an individual may obtain the sole right to use the fruit of certain trees by means of religious ceremonial. Thus, in the island of Ambrim in the New Hebrides, certain trees are assigned to individuals as part of the rites by which men rise from rank to rank of a graded organization called the *Mangge,* which plays a great part in the social organization of the people, and trees may also be appropriated to individual use by means of taboo marks, theft of the protected fruit being believed to bring sickness on the offender through the action of ancestral ghosts. Similarly, in Eddystone Island in the Solomons, the fruit of certain trees may only be used by an individual who pays one with the necessary powers to impose a taboo, infringement of the taboo being believed, as in Ambrim, to bring disease upon the thief. The nature of the trees thus protected suggests that they may have been introduced by immigrants who utilized religious beliefs, also introduced by them, to confine usufruct and ownership to themselves and their descendants. When I suggested this mode of origin of the practice at a meeting at which several African ethnographers were present, it was objected that such a mechanism could not apply to the separate owner-ship of trees in Africa, but I note a significant passage in Cardinall's account of the Gold Coast, which suggests that my explanation may also hold good there, at any rate in some cases. Cardinall notes that in one district certain trees, including the locust-bean, are owned by the chiefs. There is clear evidence that the chiefs are descendants of immigrants, and Cardinall expressly notes that the locust-bean is not indigenous to the country. He believes that the right of the chiefs was obtained from the *tindana,* but the foreign origin of the locust-bean suggests that its ownership by the chiefs may have had an origin similar to that to which I have referred the similar custom of Melanesia.

The general conclusion which can be drawn from the foregoing account is that both in Melanesia and Africa there is much evidence for an early state of communal ownership of land and of certain kinds of property, while in Melanesia there is reason to believe that individual ownership has come about as the result of influence from without. On the other hand, in those cases in which we have the most definite evidence of communal ownership, the group concerned is not the clan but a group within the clan or moiety, which consists of kin, of persons related to one another by kinship and not by sibship. Behind the definite regulations concerning ownership by these smaller groups there is often the tradition of ownership by the clan, and it seems probable that there was at one time common ownership by the clan or moiety which has been replaced, at any rate in practice, by ownership in which the common rights rest on kinship.

I have dealt in this chapter especially with the topics of communal and individual ownership, and I may now consider briefly whether the distinction between the two kinds of ownership can be correlated with different modes of inheritance. The problem is important, because if communal ownership was associated with the clan-organization, and if, as we have reason to believe, there is an association between this form of organization and motherright, we should expect to find a correlation between communal ownership and inheritance by the sister's children, rather than by the own children. Here, as in general, we are hampered by the paucity of evidence. In Melanesia the information given by Codrington would lead us definitely to the view that communal ownership and inheritance by the sister's children run together. On the other hand, Codrington's work was almost entirely confined to the matrilineal regions of Melanesia, and my own work has shown the existence of communal ownership of the most definite kind in two purely patrilineal societies. Nevertheless, there are facts pointing definitely to the close connection between communal ownership and fatherright on the other hand. Thus, it is significant that trees which, as we have seen, are owned individually, are in general inherited by the children, while the land on which they grow passes to the sister's children. Again, such organizations as the *Mangge* of Ambrim, through the agency of which men attain the individual ownership of trees, are certainly due to a patrilineal society which has been imposed upon an older matrilineal basis. While the evidence cannot be regarded as conclusive, there is much evidence from Melanesia of the association of communal ownership with motherright.

When we turn to Africa, on the other hand, evidence bearing on this problem is almost wholly lacking. Thus, Cardinall, who has given us the most explicit and complete account of land-tenure which we possess from any African Society, gives us no information whatever of the nature of descent, and none of those details of inheritance and ownership which so often enable us to infer the nature of earlier forms of social organization. His evidence makes it clear that communal ownership goes back to an early state of society of which the *tindana* is a survival, but we have no evidence by which we can infer of what kind this early society was.

I cannot leave the subject of communal ownership without a brief reference to its association with sexual communism. Here again our most satisfactory evidence comes from Melanesia, where there is a fairly definite association of the two kinds of communism. In several parts of Melanesia there is definite evidence for the association of communal ownership with customs which point to the existence in the past of organized sexual communism, which is still present here and there in Melanesia. The association is not, however, invariable. In Eddystone Island, which presents one of the most definite examples of communal ownership, the practice of monogamy exists in a degree which puts it far above that of our own society, but it may be noted that the very strict limitation of sexual relations only occurs after marriage, and that before marriage there is a state of organized communism which may be the survival of an earlier state in which this communism also existed after marriage.

I have confined my attention here almost exclusively to the topics of individual and communal ownership and the influence upon inheritance of the states of father- and

motherright. I may conclude by giving a few examples from
rude peoples of customs which exist or have existed among
ourselves. Thus, in Melanesia there are customs which resemble that known among ourselves as heriot. When, in
some parts of Melanesia, the owner of a tree growing upon
the land of another dies, the heir has to make a payment
to the owner of the land, or, when property passes to the
son of an owner, a similar payment is made by the heir to
the sister's children of the deceased.

Again, the custom of junior right, in which the youngest
son is the chief's heir, of which our own custom of Borough
English is an example, exists in many rude societies. In
some cases it has a feature which suggests the origin of
the practice. It is sometimes the rule that the youngest son
inherits the house, while the other kinds of property pass
to his eldest brothers, or are shared by all. This practice
seems to be the result of the custom by which the sons,
as they marry, set up establishments of their own, so that,
when the father dies, only the youngest son is still living at
home.

Problems of especial interest arise again in connection
with primogeniture. In Melanesia certainly, and probably
in other parts of the world, while the eldest son has no
special rights in relation to inheritance, he is the subject
of special ceremonial which does not take place in the case
of later children. There is reason to believe that in some
parts of the world these customs may be connected with the
belief in reincarnation—the belief that the ghost of the
father, or more frequently of the father's father, is rein-
carnated in the eldest child—and that this belief accounts
for the special treatment. The belief in such reincarnation
has a wide distribution and it therefore becomes possible
that the privileged position of the eldest child in other
societies, possibly even in our own, in relation to property
may be connected with a similar belief. In India, however,
the evidence is against any connection between primogeni-

ture and reincarnation: it is not necessarily the eldest son whom the ghost of the grandfather inhabits, but any son who is born soon after the death of the grandfather.

NOTE

1 Philpotts, *Kindred and Clan.*

THE SOLIDARITY OF THE INDIVIDUAL WITH HIS GROUP *

By LUCIEN LEVY-BRUHL

AFTER having studied the instances given in the Introduction we are, I consider, authorized in presuming that the primitive does not conceive the connection between a living being and its species quite as we do. When a leopard, or a mouse, for instance, is actually present to his sight or is imagined by him, the representation of it is not differentiated in his mind from another, a more general image which, though not a concept, comprises all similar beings. This grasps them in their ensemble, dominates them and frequently, if his mind dwells upon them, seems to engender them. The representation of it is characterized both by the objective qualities which the primitive perceives in beings of this kind, and by the emotions they arouse in him. It is somewhat analogous to the way in which, during the Great War, many people would talk of "the Boche," and as many colonists in Algeria talk of "the Arab," or many Americans of "the black man." It denotes a kind of essence or type, too general to be an image, and too emotional to be a concept. Nevertheless it seems to be clearly defined, above all by the sentiments which the sight of an individual of the species evokes, and the reactions it sets up.

Similarly, the idea which primitives have of plants and animals is both positive and also mystic. They are able to select the edible fruits and nearly always, when their condition is a sufficiently settled one, they know how to cultivate certain plants and how to treat those which, like the manioc, are originally noxious; they can hunt or lay traps for the

* *The Soul of the Primitive.* New York: The Macmillan Co.

larger animals, birds, fishes, etc. But on the other hand, as Gutmann has clearly shown, they have a great respect for the outstanding faculties of plants and animals, which so marvelously suffice unto themselves, and which therefore possess an ability, or rather, a power that man would gladly share with them. Hence their attitude with regard to them, not in any way like ours, that of a superior being, an irresponsible master. Hence, too, the complex sentiments of astonishment and admiration and sometimes even of veneration, and the need, as it were, of assimilating themselves to them, which lend the primitives' images of these beings a semi-religious character.

Such an aspect of them necessarily escapes our consciousness. It contains affective elements which we do not experience, and, on the other hand, we are not able to think unless definite concepts of plants and animals occupy our thoughts. As a matter of fact, the primitive's mind does not picture either the individual or the species exactly, but both at the same time, one within the other. As I have already recalled above, and as many observers have noted— A. R. Brown in the Andaman Islands, Junod and others among the Bantus—we can get some idea of what is in their minds through the personages of our old fairy stories of childhood. The bear, the hare, the fox, tortoise, and so on —and the personification of their species. Thus, whatever may happen to an animal in the story, if he is killed, for instance, it does not prevent him from reappearing alive, often in the same story. As far as the individual is concerned, he undergoes all possible catastrophes, and even death, but in so far as he is a type, he is imperishable, indestructible, comprising in himself the infinite multiplicity of the individuals of his species. Smith and Dale have noted this trait in the folk-lore of the Ba-ila. "To us there is a lack of coherence in many of the details, and explicit contradictions pull us up and spoil our pleasure; as when Fulwe, after being cooked and eaten, gives Sulwe his doom. But such things do not worry the Ba-ila or detract from their enjoyment. For one thing, Fulwe, though dead, lives in his face; it is a mere accident that one individual dies; it is the ideal Fulwe, not the Fulwe who merely breathes, but the Fulwe in the narrator's mind, and *he* is immortal." [1] To use the terms of Plato, the Ba-ila represent to themselves the "idea" of him.

It is not in stories alone, but also in everyday life that the primitive mind tends to confuse the individual and the species. As Miss Benedict remarks of the Bagobo: "The killing of a snake, though perhaps not carrying a direct prohibition, is regarded as unwise, in view of the attitude which the snake community might assume toward the offender. . . . They told me that if the snake had been put to death all its relatives and friends might have come to bite us." [2] (In this case a snake, encountered upon the road, had been carefully removed but not killed.) This solidarity among snakes implies that they are imagined, or rather, *felt,* to be all participating in the same essence.

Instead of snakes, it may be animals, of such a kind that man can hardly choose whether he is to spare or to kill them; he may be obliged to pursue them and take their lives that he may feed upon them. He will then take the greatest precautions not to offend his game, and, so that he may be forgiven the necessary slaughter, he will repudiate it. The invocations and charms before the departure and during the expedition (hunting or fishing), the excuses and supplications after the death of the animal, are not addressed solely to the one about to be pursued, or the one killed, but, through it, to all its species, and the species in its very essence or, as Smith and Dale express it, in the "idea" of it. The real individual is not such and such a stag or such and such a whale, but *the* Stag, *the* Whale.

This leads at once to two results. In the first place, a very close connection unites animals of the same species. Their individuality is but relative, and they are actually only multiple and transient expressions of a single and imperishable homogeneous essence. Offend one, and you incense

them all. Should you be so unwise as to speak ill of one
of them and irritate it, it is not that one alone of which
you must beware, for all will avenge the insult. Or again,
all will escape you. It is not one certain stag which will not
let you perceive or approach him; the unlucky hunter will
see none of them. So, too, if a forbidden word has been
uttered, all the trees of a certain species become invisible
to the eye. When at last the game has been captured he is
entreated thus: "Do not tell your companions or your
fellow-creatures that we have injured you, for it is not we
who have taken your life. On the contrary, we are offering
you food, fresh water, weapons, everything that can please
you. Tell the rest how well we have treated you," etc.

The hunter's concern in this particular is particularly
well-depicted in the *Relations de la Nouvelle-France*. "The
savages," says the missionary Le Jeune, "do not throw to the
dogs the bones of beavers or female porcupines—at any
rate, only certain specified bones; in short, they take very
good care that the dogs do not eat the bones of the birds or
any animals caught in the nets, for otherwise they would
have immense difficulty in catching others of the species.
Again, there are countless regulations to be observed in this
respect, for it does not matter if the vertebræ and the rump
are given to the dogs, but the rest must be thrown into the
fire. In any case, for the beaver which is ensnared it is best
to throw its bones into a river. It is remarkable that they
collect these bones and preserve them so carefully, that you
would think their hunt would be useless if they had con-
travened their superstitions.

"Whenever I laughed at them and told them that the
beavers did not know what happened to their bones, they
used to say: 'You don't know how to trap beavers, and yet
you want to tell us about them.' Before the beaver is actually
dead, they told me, his spirit would come and look round the
hut of the man who had taken him and he would notice
very carefully what had been done with his bones. If they
had been given to the dogs, the other beavers would have

been warned, and that would make it very difficult to snare
them, but they are quite content to have their bones thrown
into the fire or into the river, and the net which has ensnared
them is especially pleased about it. I told them that the
Iroquois, according to the report given by the one who was
with us, threw the bones of the beavers to the dogs, and yet
they caught a good many, and that our French hunters took
incomparably more than they did, nevertheless our dogs
ate the bones. 'There is no sense in what you say,' was their
reply; 'don't you see that both you and the Iroquois cultivate
the soil and reap the harvest, and we do not; therefore it is
not the same thing at all.' When I heard this irrelevant reply,
I began to laugh." [3]

No doubt the Indians wished the missionary to understand that the Iroquois and the French alike did not depend,
as they did, on living by the good will of the animals they
were hunting, and thus had not the same urgent need to
conciliate the species to which their victims belonged. In the
lines which follow the passage just quoted, Father Le Jeune
is deploring the fact that he knows so little of the Indians'
language. We may well ask ourselves, therefore, if the expression he uses really renders their thought when he is
speaking of the "spirit" of the beaver coming into the hut
to see what has become of its bones. What is certain is that
the other beavers, according to the Indians, have been told
about it. The treatment meted out to one animal is immediately known and resented by its companions. The
Indian is fully persuaded of this, and his actions bear it out.

As to the sum-total of plants or animals of a certain
species living at present, the primitive does not even attempt
to imagine it. To him it represents an indefinite multiplicity,
which he regards collectively as he would his own hair, or
the stars in the sky. He does not think of this as an abstract
idea, yet he needs to represent it in some form or other
to himself, since he feels it to be more real than the individuals composing it. His representation is reported to us
in varied forms, although these are all somewhat related to

each other. It is probable that their diversity depends, at any rate partially, on the greater or lesser degree of exactness in the observations made, according to whether the observers understand much or little of the language and the mentality of the natives studied, and whether these are more or less disposed to reveal what they really think, as well as the degree of capability they possess in doing so when their consent is obtained. For it often happens that the white man is asking them to define for him something that they have never yet formulated to themselves. We can therefore guess at the value of the reply he is likely to get.

It is once again Father Le Jeune, one of the best of the Jesuit observers of New France, from whom we borrow a fairly precise description of the idea we are now following up. "They say that all animals of every kind have an elder brother who is as it were the source and origin of all individuals, and that this elder brother is wondrously great and powerful. The beavers' elder brother, one of them told me, is about as big as our hut, whilst the young ones (by which I understand the ordinary beavers) are not quite as big as our sheep. It appears that the elders of all animals are the juniors of the Messou (the Manitou?). He is, therefore, well-connected, the worthy restorer of the universe is the elder brother of all the animals. If during sleep this eldest animal or principle of animal life is seen, the hunting will be successful; if the dreamer sees the senior of the beavers, he will trap beavers; if it be the senior moose-deer, he will catch them, and revel in the possession of the juniors by favor of the senior he has seen in his dreams. I asked them where these elder brothers were. 'We are not quite certain,' they said, 'but we believe that the senior birds are in the sky and the other seniors in the sea!' "

This principle, this "elder brother," then, is a kind of personified genius of the species, in whom individuals of the species, the younger brothers, participate, and which makes them what they are. Here it seems as if we can understand the primitive's thought without difficulty. The idea of genius of a species is familiar to us, and even natural. It has some affinity with the "archetypes" of the philosophers. Let us be cautious, however, lest we be deceived by words. When *we* speak of the genius of a species we have first represented to ourselves collectively the animals or plants which compose it, we have framed a general abstract idea of it. Later we interpret this concept of ours by a concrete, perceptible form, and thus the genius of the species is a more or less expressive and living symbol, according to the imaginations engaged upon it. In all cases, however, for us this personification of the species comes *after* the concept and presupposes it. The very language we speak would itself be enough to impose this order on us.

The process through which the primitive mind works is quite different, however. To it the genius of a species is not a more or less concrete symbol which follows after the concept, for primitive mentality has no abstract general ideas, or at any rate, if it possesses any, they are vague and indefinite. The representation of the genius takes their place. Since it is veritably the source, as Father Le Jeune puts it, and the substance of the individuals which participate in it, it is this which constitutes the element of generality, and this which is at the very center of the particular representation of each individual of the species.

It now becomes very difficult to locate ourselves at the point of view of primitive mentality. To tell the truth, we can hardly flatter ourselves that we ever really arrive there. We cannot expunge from our minds concepts which they have possessed from infancy, or suddenly do away with the use and the memory of words that we have always employed. How can we feel, as primitives do, that when an animal has been wounded or killed, not only are all the others of his species immediately warned, but that in reality it is not a particular individual but the very species personified in its essence and in its genius that has been struck down? If it were merely the case of a certain lion or a certain stag the hunter would not trouble any more about it. He would leave the wild beast there, he would eat the game, and there would be an end of the matter. But it is not solely a certain particular animal that he has killed; he has attacked the mystic essence of all lions or all stags, and this, as Father Le Jeune says, is "wondrously great and powerful," and hence indestructible. A mortal man's blows cannot endanger it. The Eskimo who slays an immense number of caribou does not imagine that these animals will ever disappear. If they become scarce and he finally sees none at all, he will account for the fact by some mystic reason. The caribou continue to exist and are no less numerous, even if they have been slain in thousands, but now they are refusing themselves, that is to say, the genius of their species has withdrawn his favor from the men whom he formerly permitted to track and slay them.

It is thus essential to retain his good graces at any price. If through some fault, such as the violation of a taboo, neglect of a rite or ceremony or incantation, a man has been unfortunate enough to lose them, it is absolutely necessary to regain them. The safety and well-being of the group depend upon its relations with these "genii," with the mystic principles of certain vegetable or animal species. If these relations are strained, he is in danger, and if they break, life is no longer possible for him. The hunter may then spend days and nights in the forest and the fisherman in his canoe; neither will catch anything. His wives, children, and he himself will die—unless the tribe is no longer nomadic, at any rate at certain seasons, or unless his wives know how to cultivate plantations and fields. It is thus easy to account for the unusual honors rendered by the hunter and his family to the animal slain—that is, in reality to the genius of its species. Since the rites have both a persuasive and a constraining influence, the primitive is sure that, if everything has been carried out as it should be, the relations between himself and this genius will remain satisfactory. Future hunting and fishing expeditions will once more turn out well.

In other regions, it is not of the genius of a species of plants or animals that a man talks, but of its ancestor, its chief, master, or king. He personifies the "mother of the rice" which bears it and makes it grow, and allows it to be gathered. Upon the subject of the "paddy spirit" Leslie Milne says: "His home is wherever the paddy is growing. He travels with the paddy as its bodyguard, and he is able to be in more than one place at the same time." [4] Kruijt relates that he was shown a "king of trees." On the east coast of Sumatra, the Bataks have planted large india-rubber trees. "At a place called Pematang Bandur, I found an enormous specimen of this kind of tree. They told me that this was the king of the heveas, and that it was forbidden to tap it except in times of the greatest need, for if this giant were ill-treated, the other trees would yield less latex." [5] This tree is to its congeners what the "mother of rice" is to the paddy.

Representations of the same kind are frequently encountered in the case of animal species. "Among the Atjeh natives, and in Macassar, Boegin, and with the Dayaks," says Kruijt too, "there is in each herd of buffaloes or cows one called 'the captain.' Most frequently it is an animal of a special form or color. It keeps the troop together, that is, it holds fast the principle (zielstof) of the others, so that they remain with one another and keep healthy. If this captain buffalo were to be slain, the others would certainly die or run away, and in any case the herd would be broken up." [6]

It is the same with wild animals. In Southern Nigeria, for instance, "among every thousand or so of bush-pig, one is to be found, of great size and very splendid, with a skin marked like that of a leopard.... Such animals are the kings of the bush-pig. They are never allowed to walk at all, but are carried everywhere by those of the common sort.... Never do they seek for their own chop. This is brought by the lesser pigs, at dawn and evening time.... Each year the King Boar is carried away to a new place amid very thick bush, so that the hunters should never find him." [7] This king-boar, like the buffalo-captain, the giant hevea-tree, the "mother of the rice," the elder brother of the beavers, like all the "genii" of this kind, is a personification, if we may put it thus, of the mystic essence of which all the individuals of the species partake. He is the true "unit" of them all.

With the Dschagga the word used to designate the bees of a hive is the singular, and perhaps we have here a linguistic trace of an idea akin to the foregoing. What interests the Dschagga especially is not any particular specimen of these insects, or their number: it is the Bee, the wonderful race that can produce wax and honey. It is certainly seen in a mass, but it is essentially a principle, genius mystic power of which it is natural to speak in the singular.

II

Does a man's representation of himself in his relations with his group differ considerably from that he pictures of the plant or animal with respect to its species? It is hardly possible that such should be the case if it be true that the difference between men, animals, plants, and even inanimate objects, is not one of nature but merely of degree, and that the faculties possessed by animals are in no whit inferior to those of men. Moreover, as we have already seen,[8] the idea that an individual has of himself, in primitive communities as in our own, must be differentiated from the subjective feeling he possesses of his states of consciousness, emotions, thoughts, actions and reactions, etc., in so far as he refers them to himself. From this latter point of view his personality is for him an individual clearly distinct from all the rest, opposed to them, and apprehended by him in a way that is unique and very different from that in which he perceives individuals and objects around him. But this direct apprehension, vivid and constant as it may be, forms only a small part of the idea he has of his own personality. The predominating elements of it are collective in origin, and the individual hardly grasps himself save as a member of his social group. There are very many facts which prove this, and I shall cite but a small number only, choosing those which most clearly demonstrate it.

"A man," says Elsdon Best, "thought and acted in terms of family group, clan or tribe, according to the nature or gravity of the subject, and not of the individual himself. The welfare of the tribe was ever uppermost in his mind; he might quarrel with a clansman, but let that clansman be assailed in any way by an extra-tribal individual, or combination of such, and he at once put aside animosity and took his stand by his side." [9] Again: "A native so thoroughly identifies himself with his tribe that he is ever employing the first personal pronoun. In mentioning a fight that occurred possibly ten generations ago he will say: 'I defeated the enemy there,' mentioning the name of the tribe. In like manner he will carelessly indicate 10,000 acres of land with a wave of his hand, and remark: 'This is my land.' He would never suspect that any person would take it that he was the sole owner of such land, nor would any one but a European make such an error. When Europeans arrived on these shores many troubles arose owing to the inability of the Maori to understand individual possession of land, and land selling." [10]

It is the same in French West Africa. "The individual," says Monteil, "whatever he or his position may be, is of no importance save as a member of the community; the community exists and progresses, he only exists and progresses by it and, to a great extent, for it." [11] In the Belgian Congo, "at the same age, every free Azanda seems to know just as much as his fellows; they give the same replies and manifest the same psychology. Thus it is an excessively stable and conservative psychology. The value of the social group seems to them to be inviolably fixed.... Therefore any revolutionary, any man who on account of personal experiences was differentiated from the collective thought, was at once pitilessly destroyed. Sasa had one of his own sons executed for having changed a legal decision which was the customary one. The Azanda who has been in contact with us, or who has acquired a different mental outlook, no longer has a place in the social group.... As a rule, what strikes one most in the answers given by the semicivilized with regard to their customs is the very slight importance attaching to individual opinion compared with the collective thought of the group. They do this or that, not because 'I' want it, but because 'we' desire it. Here, more than among Western peoples, whose individualization often masks a profound participation in the life of the community, we realize how intensely social the life of the Azanda is. All its rites, all its education tends to make the individual one with the community, to develop in him qualities exactly like those of the other individuals of his group." [12]

De Calonne-Beaufaict lays special stress upon the obligatory conformity which tends to make all the individuals of the same group alike. His testimony is supported by other witnesses, who show the subordination of the individual to his group, among the Bantus. For instance, a missionary tells us: "In studying Bantu institutions, it is necessary at the outset to eliminate our idea of the individual.... A man's rights and duties are born with him, being conditioned by his precedence in the family and the precedence of the family in the tribe. Nothing is further from Bantu thought than the doctrine that all men are endowed by nature with fundamental equality and an inalienable right to liberty (whatever the definition of the term).... They cannot admit for a moment that any man but a chief is born free, and they cannot conceive how any two men can be born equal. Everything in their political system is built on status, and status is a matter of birth. Well, all this means that the individual does not exist in Bantu society. The unit is the family." [13]

Smith and Dale say the same thing: "The clan is a natural mutual aid society, the members being bound to render their fellows all the help they can in life. Members of one clan are, if we may use the Biblical language, members also one of another. A member belongs to the clan; he is not his own; if he is wronged they will right him; if he does wrong the responsibility is shared by them. If he is killed the clan takes up the feud, for he belongs to them. If a daughter of the clan is to be married they have to give their consent first. Ba-ila who have ever met before will at once be friends if it turns out that they are of the same *mukoa*. If one has the misfortune to become a slave, his clansmen will contribute his redemption price," etc.[14]

Such a social organization at once involves a great difference between the idea of the individual animal and the human individual. Each animal is directly and immediately a participant in the mystic principle which is the essence of its species, and all have the same claim to it. Save for those which have something unusual about them, in which the primitive's mind suspects witchcraft, they all are, so to speak, similar and equivalent expressions of this "principle" or "genius." The human individual himself also exists by virtue of his participation in the essential principle of his group, but a community of human beings does not correspond at all points with an animal or vegetable species. First of all, it is not of an indefinite number in the same way as they are. Above all, it is articulated into sections and subsections. The individual occupies in turn several positions in his group. He attains them more or less quickly according to his birth and to his social importance during the course of his life. In short, in every human society there are ranks and a hierarchy, even if one of seniority only. The individual, whoever he may be, is dependent upon the group (except in the case of a chief where his absolute power has been accepted), but not in a way that is uniform.

The more deeply observers penetrate the minds of "primitive" or semicivilized peoples, the more important does the rôle of this hierarchy appear to be. Spencer and Gillen have demonstrated it in the Central Australian tribes, Dr. Thurnwald in the Banaro of New Guinea, and Holmes in other

Papuans of British New Guinea. The last-named relates the story of a man who kills his younger brother for having taken a place which belonged to the elder without asking permission.—Among the Bantus, the individual is both strictly subordinated to the social group and rigidly established in his own rank. The group, as we know, is composed of the living and of their dead, and the first place belongs to the latter. These must therefore be served first. It is to them that the first-fruits are offered, and none would fail in this obligation. "Bantus," as Junod observes, "do not think they dare enjoy the products of the soil if they have not first given a portion of them to their gods. Are these gods not those who make cereals grow? Have they not the power even of controlling the wizards who bewitch the fields? These rites are also evidently dictated by the sense of hierarchy."[15]— Among the Hereros, no one dare drink of the morning's milk just drawn from the cows until the ritual libations have been performed. The ancestors must drink first.

The "village," that is, the familial group, among the Thonga people studied by Junod, "is a little organized community having its own laws, amongst which the most important seems the law of hierarchy. The elder brother is the uncontested master, and no one can supersede him. He is the owner of the village.... No one must 'steal it' from him. Should any one do so, the whole community would suffer and no children would be born; the life of the organism would be deeply affected; this is the reason why the headman must go first with his principal wife to have relations with her in the new village, and thus to *take possession* of it or *tie* it. For this same reason, when the headman dies, the village *must* move. As long as the inheritance has not yet been distributed, it is still *his home;* but as soon as the ceremony has taken place, the villagers must go away, and close the door with a thorny branch."[16] As Junod says elsewhere: "There is a mystic tie between this man and the social organism which is under him."[17] Should he die, the village dies also. This intimate dependence on him is expressed by the Thonga, not in abstract terms, but in striking images. "The chief is the Earth. He is the cock ... he is the bull; without him the cows cannot bring forth. He is the husband; the country without him is like a woman without husband. He is the man of the village.... A clan without chief has lost its reason. It is dead... The chief is our great warrior; he is our forest where we hide ourselves, and from whom we ask for laws.... The chief is a magical being. He possesses special medicines with which he rubs himself or which he swallows, so that his body is taboo," etc.[18] Does not such a social organism recall—*mutatis mutandis*—a hive of bees? Is not the chief in certain respects to be compared with the captain buffalo that "keeps the herd together," and by its own power so assures its well-being and cohesion, that when it is slain the herd perishes or is broken up?

Moreover, and here again is another aspect of the intimate and almost organic solidarity uniting members of the same social group, the individual which does not belong to it counts for nothing. We know how much attention the group shows to its dead, and how it hastens to render them all the honors that are their due. But "when a *stranger* dies in a Thonga village, when no one knows him, 'he does not matter'" (says Junod's informant). "The grown-up men will bury him. They dig a hole and drag the corpse into it with a rope. They do not touch it. There is no contagion, therefore no ceremony of purification. Among the Malukele and the Hlengwe such a corpse is burnt." [19]

III

Melanesian and Micronesian languages nearly all present a remarkable peculiarity, which Codrington sums up as follows: "It is most important to understand that all nouns in Melanesian languages are divided in native use into two classes; those that take the personal pronoun suffixed, and those that do not.... In Melanesian languages, excepting Savo, the distinction is based upon the notion of closeness or remoteness of connection between the object possessed and the possessor, but the carrying out of this principle in detail is by no means easy to follow.... In some cases no doubt the same word may be used with or without the suffix; but never when the word is used in precisely the same meaning." [20]

The nouns which take this suffix, "according to a strict native use," are "nouns which generally signify members of the body, parts of a thing, equipments of a man, or family relationship." [21] In the Tami language of German New Guinea, for instance, "an important class of nouns is composed of those which take a possessive suffix; they are nouns denoting degrees of relationship and parts of the body." [22] In Neu Pommern, on the north coast of the Gazelle Peninsula, Father Bley remarks: "The possessive pronouns are also used to denote relationship, the connection (*Zugehörigkeit*) of the parts of the body itself, and they are placed after the noun, partly as suffixes." [23] At the same time, Father Bley points out some exceptions to this rule.— In the Roro, a Melanesian language of British New Guinea, "the possessive suffixes may be used with or without the personal pronoun preceding the thing possessed. The suffixes are used only with special nouns such as parts of the body and relations."— In the Mekeo language of a neighboring tribe "the possessive suffix is used in the case of parts of the body, relations, and a few other words." [24] We might cite other examples, but these will doubtless suffice to decide, as Codrington does, that this is an invariable rule in Melanesian languages.

Very often what seems to be an irregularity or an exception proceeds on the contrary from a very strict and precise application of the rule. This is so with the following irregularities, noted by Peekel: [25]

anugu tunan, my man (husband), instead of *tananagu;*
anugu hahin, my wife, instead of *hahinagu;*
a manuagu, my wound, instead of *anagu manua;*

a subanagu, the remains of my meal, instead of *anagu subana* (*gu* being the personal pronoun suffix of the first person).

From the natives' point of view, these are perfectly regular forms, and indeed the only correct ones. In fact, since exogamy is strictly observed in these tribes, husband and wife belong to different clans. Accordingly the husband is not and cannot be related to his wife, nor she to him, and it is quite natural that the possessive pronoun should not be suffixed after the nouns "husband" and "wife." These nouns are not among the class of substantives taking the pronominal suffix. Conversely the wound which involves a part of my body, and the skin of the banana that I have eaten are, to the primitive's way of thinking, things which "belong" to me in the strictest sense of the word. They are literally parts of myself; therefore the nouns "wound" and "remains of the meal" must be followed by the suffix.— By virtue of the same principle we can understand why the native says *anugu hahin* (my wife) without the suffix, when speaking of the woman he has married, for she is not of his family. But he will say: *hahin i gu* (my sister) with the suffix, for his sister is of the same clan as himself; she "belongs" to him, in the sense that she makes, with him, part of the same whole, like two limbs belonging to the same body.

In Micronesian languages we find, too, a class of nouns taking the personal pronoun as a suffix. According to Thalheimer, who has made a special study of the subject, these are nouns denoting: (1) the parts of the body and the divers functions of man's mental activity; (2) relationship; (3) relation of a position in space and time; (4) the dependent parts of an independent whole; (5) personal adornments, weapons and instruments, the house, the garden; (6) possessive nouns, i.e., nouns provided with possessive suffixes, which serve in certain cases as possessive pronouns in a special sense (*Pronomina ediva et potativa*).[26]

This instructive list helps us to comprehend how the Melanesians picture the relations of kinship to themselves. Thalheimer himself remarks on this: "The solidarity of relatives among themselves is denoted in the same way as that of the various parts of an individual," and he accounts for this fact by the construction of the Melanesian *gens,* saying: "The individual is to the family what the limb— head, arm, leg—is to the living body."

Thus the fact to be found in their languages throws light upon ideas of which we can hardly suppose that Melanesians have a clear consciousness. They do not think in abstract terms, nor reflect upon concepts. They have never had any notion of the organic finality manifested by the structure and functions of a living body, nor of the special way in which the parts are subordinated to the whole, and the whole in its turn depends upon its parts. Neither have they ever analyzed the solidarity uniting the individuals of the same family with one another. Nevertheless their languages testify that they do compare these. To them the familial group is a being which, by its unity, is like a living body. We too say: the "members" of a family, but to us it is a mere metaphor, though not an inapt one. To them, although they do not think about it, it is the literal expression of a fact. In their imaginings the individual does not depend less closely upon his familial group than the hand or foot depends upon the body of which it is part.

As Codrington has noted, the division of substantives into two classes one of which takes the possessive pronominal suffix, and the other not, is a feature peculiar to the languages of Melanesia and Micronesia. But in this very district, by way of exception, and in a good many others all over the world, one unvarying fact has been remarked. Certain substantives—usually the names of the parts of the body and the different relationships—are never used without a personal pronoun, whether it be prefixed or affixed or separated from the noun. Thus, in the Baining language, "there are words which are never used except conjoined with a personal pronoun. They are those which denote the parts of the body or the degrees of relationship. They are never to be met with standing alone ... the possessive pronoun is placed before the noun...." [27] In the other Melanesian and Polynesian languages known up to the present, he says, one is struck by finding a special possessive pronoun for a certain group of words denoting parts of the body and relationships. This kind of pronoun is used as a suffix for the nouns to which it refers. There is nothing like this in the Baining tongue. It knows no distinction between the possessive pronouns. It does not append a personal pronoun to any kind of substantive; the possessive pronoun is always placed *before* the substantive. Moreover, the Baining recognizes also certain substantives (precisely those denoting parts of the body and relationships), which he never uses without a possessive pronoun. Thus we see that Baining thought coincides on this point with that of the surrounding peoples, but the way in which it is expressed is different. [28]

This remark holds good for hundreds, perhaps thousands, of languages: Oceanic, American, African, Asiatic, European, in which one cannot, according to Powell's way of putting it, say simply "hand" or "head," but must always indicate at the same time whose hand or head it is; languages in which one cannot say "father," "mother," "son," "brother," etc. without mentioning whose father, mother, son, or brother is in question. The fact is universal, as it were, and it has been noted scores of times. Everywhere the rule applies equally to the nouns denoting degrees of relationship and parts of the body, and usually to these two categories only. This, it appears, allows us to conclude, especially after analyzing the more peculiar facts ascertained in Melanesian and Micronesian languages, and without being too bold in concluding, that in all parts of the world these two categories of nouns—names of relationships and names of parts of the body—make but one in reality. All proceeds as if, to those who speak these languages, the two relations are exactly alike. Not that they have ever taken this into account themselves. They apply this grammatical rule of theirs, of a grammar which is frequently so complex and so meticulous, with the same unreflecting rigidity and the same spontaneity as others. Yet the fact that the rule exists is only the more significant.

IV

How are we to understand the term "family relationship" in societies either "primitive" or "semicivilized"? It is not very long since ethnologists first thought of putting this question to themselves, yet as long as it had not been considered, dire confusion was inevitable in the matter. Up to a fairly recent period it has been accepted, as if it were a self-evident fact, that all existing human families were of essentially the same type as our own. Both history and observation seemed to agree with this instinctive conviction. What we knew of the Roman, Greek, Slav, Semitic, Chinese and other families seemed to confirm the idea that the fundamental structure of the family is everywhere the same.

Now to-day we know that in a great many of the social communities which are more or less "primitive," what we call the family, in the traditional and current sense of the word, does not exist. In its place ethnologists have found an institution that we can designate by the same name, but only on condition that we remember that it is radically different. A careful study of the vocabularies of these societies will suffice to establish this fact. Among the Banaro, as Dr. Thurnwald rightly remarks, "the absence of the family (in our sense of the word) is accompanied by the absence of the expressions which correspond with this idea." [29]

The family which is noted in these societies is of the type called "classificatory." We find it of the same kind in all its essential features in all latitudes, and in districts most remote from each other. It has been described in North America, where Morgan discovered it; in South America (among the Araucans, for instance); in Australia, Melanesia,

Papua, Equatorial and South Africa; among the Ashanti (where Captain Rattray recently confirmed its existence); among the Yakuts in Siberia, and so forth. In short, the classificatory "family" or system seems to have been no less widespread than our own type of family, which we held to be universal.

Its primary characteristic, as Howitt so aptly puts it, is that "the social unit is not the individual, but the group; and the former merely takes the relationships of his group, which are of group to group." [30] The individual does not form a part of a certain group because he has this or that tie of relationship; on the contrary, he has this or that tie because he forms part of a certain group. This family constitution is so different from our own and so foreign to ideas and sentiments which have been natural to us from childhood's days, that we can understand how it happened that it should have been unrecognized for so long, even by the observers who saw it daily. It demands a persevering effort to grasp the idea thoroughly. Nevertheless, if we do not accustom ourselves to the idea of "group relationship," the way in which many primitives picture to themselves their relations with other members of their familial group (known to the Germans as *Sippe*) will be unintelligible to us.

"It is absolutely essential," say Spencer and Gillen, "in dealing with these people to lay aside all ideas of relationship as counted amongst ourselves.... The primitive has no idea of relationships as we understand them. He does not discriminate between his actual father and mother and the men and women who belong to the group, each member of which might have lawfully been either his father or his mother." [31] Codrington says too: "It is the knowledge of this that forms probably the first social conception in the mind of the young Melanesian. It stands foremost in the native view of mankind, and is the foundation on which the fabric of society is built up. To the Melanesian man it may almost be said that all women, of his own generation at least, are either sisters or wives—to the Melanesian women, that all men are brothers or husbands." [32] In other words, all with whom marriage is forbidden her are her brothers; all the rest are her potential husbands.

Elsewhere Codrington has given a detailed description of this family constitution. Its fundamental feature is the following: "All of one generation, within the family connection, are called fathers and mothers of all who form the generation below them; a man's brothers are called fathers of his children, a woman's sisters are called mothers of her children.... This wide use of the terms father and mother does not at all signify any looseness in the actual view of proper paternity and maternity... the one who speaks has no confusion in his mind, and will correct a misconception with the explanation: 'my own child' *tur natuk; tur tasina,* his brother, not his cousin." [33]—A. R. Brown notes the same thing. "Although a given person applies the name *mama* (father) to a large number of individuals, if he is asked 'Who is your *mama?*' he immediately replies by giving the name of his actual father, unless his father died during his infancy, in which case he gives the name of his foster-father.... Each term, therefore, has what we may call a primary or specific meaning. The primary meaning of *mama* is father and that of *maeli* is father's father.... Just as we use the word 'cousin,' so the Kariera native uses his word *mama,* speaking of a large number of different related persons by the one name, but distinguishing in thought, though not in words, those of his 'fathers,' who are more nearly related to him from those who are more distantly related.... This distinction between nearer and more distant relatives of the same kind (that is, denoted by the same term) is of the greatest importance in the social life of the Kariera tribe. It seems probable that it is equally important in other tribes of Australia, though I do not know that it has been specifically pointed out by previous writers." [34]

With this reservation, and taking into account the special

affection that children nearly always feel permanently for their real mother, and frequently, too, for their father, it remains a fact that it is by no means from mere politeness, or in a purely conventional manner, that the primitive calls the brothers of his father "fathers," the sisters of his mother "mothers," and the children of his father's brothers and of his mother's sisters "brothers and sisters," and "wives" (at any rate potential ones), the women that he can lawfully marry, and so on. It is in this manner that family relations impose themselves on him, and his language testifies to the fact. In all the tribes of Queensland studied by Dr. Roth, for instance, "son, daughter, brother's son, brother's daughter, have no distinctive terms: every language has but one word to denote them all. Similarly, the sister's son and the sister's daughter are described by the same word." In these tribes, too, Roth shows that the father's father is denoted by the same word as the son's son, the mother's mother by the same word as the son's daughter. These extraordinary circumstances are explained when we study the classes and subclasses between which alone marriage is permitted. We cannot enter into details about these classes, but the nomenclature set forth by Roth suffices to show how greatly the group-relationship of the Australian aborigines differs from our own ideas of kindred.

Codrington lays considerable stress upon this difference. In a passage where it is so marked as to be difficult to follow, he notes that in certain Melanesian languages the words "mother," "husband," "wife" are plural in form. "In the Mota language the form is very clear; *ra* is the plural prefix; the division, side, or kin, is the *veve;* and mother is *ra veve; soai* is a member, as of a body, or a component part of a house or of a tree, and *ra soai* is either husband or wife. To interpret *ra* as a prefix of dignity is forbidden by the full consciousness of the natives themselves that it expresses plurality. The kin is the *veve,* a child's mother is 'they of the kin,' his kindred. A man's kindred are not called his *veve* because they are his mother's people; she

is called his *veve,* in the plural, his kindred, as if she were
the representative of the kïn; as if he were not the child
of the particular woman who bore him, but of the whole
kindred for whom she brought him into the world. By a
parallel use to this a plural form is given to the Mota word
for child, *reremera,* with a doubled plural sign; a single boy
is called not child, but children, as if his individuality were
not distinguished from the common offspring of his *veve.*
The same plural prefix is found in other Banks' Island words
meaning mother: *rave* in Santa Maria, *retve* in Vanua Lava,
reme in Torres Islands. The mother is called *ratahi* in
Whitsuntide, and *ratahigi* in Lepers' Island, i.e., the sisters,
the sisterhood, because she represents the sister members of
the social group who are the mothers generally of the children. Similarly the one word used for husband or wife has
the plural form. In Mota a man does not call his wife a
member of him, a component part of him, but his members,
his component parts; and so a wife speaks of her husband.
It is not that the man and his wife make up a composite
body between them, but that the men on the one side and
the women on the other make up a composite married
body. The Mota people know that the word they use means
this; it was owned to myself with a blush that it was so,
with a Melanesian blush! and a protestation that the word
did not represent a fact." [35] This is quite true. But it is not
less so that it was the missionary who had taught them to
blush about it. The existence of plural words to express
"husband," "wife," etc., would not be accounted for if they
had never corresponded with a reality to which we have
other testimony moreover. That there should be no word
of singular form in these languages to express mother, child,
husband, or wife, etc., is a feature (quite compatible, as we
have seen, with the natural feelings of maternal or filial
love) that of itself throws strong light upon the constitution
of the Melanesian family.

After this the facts related by Thurnwald in his study of
the Banaro of New Guinea will seem less singular. "Chil-

dren," says he, "except the one who is called the child of the 'spirit' (Geistkind) give each other names according to their respective ages, and their sex, and the sex of the speaker is also taken into account.... As *aia* and *nein* mean merely 'older' and 'younger,' special expressions to express fraternal relationship properly so called are altogether lacking. The entire generation of children regards itself as a unit for the two halves of the clan, and the only distinction between them is their relative age. The feeling of belonging to some kind of paternal or maternal family is not contained in it." [36] As a matter of fact, among the Banaro, lineage does not call for the conception of the fixed relation which two complementary terms, like father and son, would arouse in us. The charge of caring for the generation which is growing up is the concern of the familial group (*Sippe*) and of the clan. *The absence of a family in our sense of the word* is on all fours with the absence of the words corresponding with these ideas (of father and son). [37]

A study of the words denoting family relationships would lead to similar results. [38] Paternity is conceived in a very different fashion from ours, and one which, in certain cases, has nothing to do with the act of procreation. Just as in the Australian and Melanesian tribes of which we have already spoken, among the Banaro there are no clearly definite words to denote married pairs, that is, words which do not at the same time serve to denote other persons. The word for woman (wife) properly signifies "mother." The word *mu-mona* (husband) is also used for other quasi-marital relations. In all that relates to the etymology of this word, we should hardly be in error in assimilating it to *nram* or *nam:* the other, the stranger, i.e., the man who comes from the other clan. (The Banaro practice exogamy.)

Among them, as in all regions where the classificatory system is in existence, "we do not find any sharp boundary between relatives in the direct line and the collateral branches. No doubt this confusion of the two lines arises out of the circumstance that all social ties are conceived, not according to the relation of one individual to another, but according to *totals,* relations of groups and subgroups of individuals. Thus it is not a consequence of the principle of exogamy in itself, but indeed of the idea they hold of society. Yet this must not be interpreted to mean that the individual is wholly left out of account. Closely connected individuals who stand in a definite relation to one another are comprised in the same term" [39]—"The principle according to which these groups and subgroups are formed is moreover not unique. There is no characteristic which of itself determines it in a definite way. The predominating factor is the social relations between one person and another, for in the construction of the Banaro system these have had preponderating influence. Persons are afterwards grouped according to consanguinity and to age." [40] The young people who are growing up are ranked primarily and principally according to their age, and only afterwards according to their sex. "For adults, it is the sexual relations which are of the most importance. It is their position from the sexual point of view that determines the relation between two persons; it is decided according to whether sexual relations are allowed or prohibited between them, or with a certain third person. It is on these grounds that each individual is classed in a group relationship bearing a certain name." [41]

Before we leave the study of the Banaro I shall quote one more reflection of Dr. Thurnwald's which strikingly bears out what I have been trying to show here: "This method of grouping is closely bound up with the whole way of thinking of primitive peoples, and the latter is manifested in their general method of reckoning. In forming their groups the Banaro do not make use of general number-concepts as we do when we wish to distinguish the members of a family according to the universally applicable scheme of finding the distance between the degrees of relationship calculated from the precise number of births separating one person from another of the same blood. The number-concepts of the primitive are mere aids to memory, or else they are the image of a mass, as for instance a basket full of things, a bearer's load, a pack of wolves, a band of men, and these images are formed according to the impression made upon the imagination by external objects.... In their method of classing and grouping, the classificatory systems of relationship reflect the characteristic of primitive mentality, which at once seizes upon the concrete and is quite aloof from any theoretical abstraction." And finally, this concise summing-up: "Relationship is not a matter of calculation, but of grouping." [42]

Thurnwald knows and discusses the works of Codrington, of Rivers and others who have recently studied the classificatory system. It may perhaps be interesting to recall, after this description of his, one which was given more than twenty-five years ago by a Russian savant, Sieroshevski.[43] It shows that the earlier Yakuts possessed a familial constitution strikingly similar to that just related, without the author's having had, apparently, the slightest suspicion of the resemblance, or even of the existence of the classificatory system in general. "The ancient words for family relationships had different senses from what the same words have now. For instance, the Yakuts have no word for the general sense of brother or sister. . . . They have special names for older brothers, younger brothers, older sisters. These words, with some attributives which are generally omitted in vituperative speech, are used to address uncles, nephews, aunts, grandchildren of different grades, and even stepfathers and stepmothers, although the two latter are commonly called father and mother. It follows from this that the family falls into two groups—those who were born earlier and those who were born later. These groups form the background of the terminology for family relationship. . . . The author thinks that in the beginning the Yakuts had no words at all for brother or sister, and that the words used now for younger brother, younger sister, etc., were terms, not so much for family relationships, as for *sib* relationships, and meant simply older or younger *sib* comrades." Here we recognize the "group relationship" characteristic of the classificatory system.

"The Yakuts employ the term child or my child" (probably "child" is always accompanied by a possessive pronoun) "not only to their own proper children, but also to the children of brothers or of sisters, or even to brothers and sisters themselves, if they are very much younger. They have not, therefore, in their genealogical terminology, any words for son and daughter which testify directly to a blood relationship between specific persons. The word which we translate 'son' strictly means boy, youth, young person. It was formerly used as a collective for the body of warriors, or the young men of the tribe or *sib*. . . .

"This lack of words to distinguish between son and boy, daughter and girl, is not due to the poverty of the language; on the contrary, their genealogical terms astonish us by their abundance and variety." The same remark has often been made about Melanesia, Australia, and it applies almost everywhere where the existence of the classificatory system has been ascertained.[44] Not only do they distinguish those of earlier and later birth, but they have a special denomination for younger brothers which is only used by women. They have a special name for the wife of a husband's older brother, and other similar peculiarities, which seem incomprehensible not only to us, but also to the Yakuts of to-day.

"Accordingly . . . we infer beyond a doubt that, at the time when the present system of genealogical relationships took its origin amongst the Yakuts, *the precise genetic connection of any given boy with his parents had no especial denomination*. All the old people in the *sib* called all the young people in the *sib,* up to a certain point of growth, by the same denominatives."

So, too: "There is no word for father which admits of a natural and simple explanation, like the word for mother (procreatress)—the word for father should be translated 'old man.' This vagueness in regard to the male blood tie, side by side with the definiteness of the female connection with the offspring, is very significant.

"Unions between them, inside of the *sib,* were exceedingly free and non-permanent. The children could know only their mothers, and they could know them only up to a certain point of their age; after that they forgot this relationship. It was supplanted by a feeling of belonging to a certain group. Within that group there were only 'men' and 'women,' older or younger than the person in question. There are out-of-the-way places amongst them now where the current word of the language for 'wife' is unknown; they meet it with laughter. A word for 'husband' exists nowhere amongst the Yakuts. The current word means properly 'man.'"

To sum up on this point, in places where the classificatory system exists, relationship is "of the group" only. It is not individuals, but groups that are interrelated; individuals are related only because they belong to related groups. Thus the relationship is social rather than familial, in our sense of the word. In Western Australia, "When a stranger comes to a camp that he has never visited before, he does not enter the camp, but remains at some distance. A few of the older men, after a while, approach him, and the first thing they proceed to do is to find out who the stranger is. The commonest question that is put to him is: 'Who is your *maeli?*' (father's father). The discussion proceeds on genealogical lines until all parties are satisfied of the exact relation of the stranger to each of the natives present in the camp. When this point is reached, the stranger can be admitted to the camp, and the different men and women are pointed out to him, and their relation to him defined. . . . I took with me on my journey a native of the Talainji tribe, and at each native camp we came to the same process had to be gone through. In one case, after a long discussion, they were still unable to discover any traceable relationship between my servant and the men of the camp. That night my 'boy' refused to sleep in the native camp, as was his usual custom, and on talking to him I found that he was frightened. These men were not his relatives, and they were therefore his enemies." [45] The relationship in question here is evidently a social relationship and not, like our own, based mainly upon ties of blood.

The classificatory system also constitutes indeed, as Junod has pointed out, a hierarchy. No doubt natural sentiments are not stifled beneath this social structure, for all observers agree in telling us that "primitives" adore their children, that they indulge them and love to play with them. Filial, fraternal and conjugal affection exists among them as with us, though perhaps somewhat differently and with fine distinctions that it is often difficult to define precisely. But it is above all the implicit "idea" of the individual in his relations with his social group that differs from ours. To convince ourselves of this, we have only to remember the difficulty we experience in entering into the sentiments and ideas Codrington described for us, which appear so natural to the Melanesians.

NOTES

[1] Smith and Dale, *The Ila-Speaking Peoples of Northern Rhodesia*, ii, p. 344.
[2] L. W. Benedict, *Bagobo Ceremonial, Magic and Myth*, pp. 238-9.
[3] *Relations de la Nouvelle-France* (1634), pp. 87-9.
[4] Leslie Milne, *The Home of an Eastern Clan*, p. 2.
[5] A. C. Kruijt, *Het Animisme in den Indischen Archipel*, p. 155.
[6] *Ibid.*, p. 133.
[7] P. A. Talbot, *Life in Southern Nigeria*, pp. 92-3.
[8] F. A. Talbot, *Life in Southern Nigeria*, Introduction, pp. 1-2.
[9] Elsdon Best, *The Maori*, i, p. 342.
[10] *Ibid.*, pp. 397-8.
[11] Ch. Monteil, *Les Bambara du Segou et du Kaarta*, p. 220.
[12] A. de Calonne-Beaufaict, *Azande*, pp. 20-4.
[13] Rev. W. C. Willoughby, *Race Problems in the New Africa*, pp. 82-3.
[14] Smith and Dale, *The Ila-Speaking Peoples of Northern Rhodesia*, i, p. 296.
[15] H. A. Junod, *The Life of a South African Tribe*, i, p. 376.

[16] *Ibid.*, pp. 296-7.

[17] *Ibid.*, p. 289.

[18] *Ibid.*, i, pp. 356-7.

[19] *Ibid.*, i, p. 166.

[20] R. H. Codrington, *Melanesian Languages*, pp. 142-3.

[21] *Ibid.*, p. 128.

[22] Bamler, "Bemerkungen zur Grammatik der Tamisprache," *Zeitschrift für afrikanische und ozeanische Sprachen* (1900), v, p. 198.

[23] B. Bley, "Grundzuge der Grammatik der Neu-Pommerschen Sprache an der Nord-Kuste der Gazelle Halbinsel," *Zeitschrift für afrikanische und ozeanische Sprachen* (1897), iii, pp. 101-2.

[24] Strong, "The Roro and Mekeo Languages of British New Guinea," *Zeitschrift für Kolonialsprachen*, iv, 4, p. 304.

[25] Peekel, *Versuch einer Grammatik der Neu-Mecklemburgischen Sprache*, pp. 68-9.

[26] A. Thalheimer, *Beitrag zur Kenntniss der Pronomina personalia und possessiva der Sprachen Melanesiens*, pp. 52-7.

[27] Roscher, "Grundregeln der Baining Sprache," *Mitteilungen des Seminars für orientalische Sprachen*, vii, p. 38.

[28] *Ibid.*, p. 33.

[29] Dr. R. Thurnwald, *Die Gemeinde der Banaro*, pp. 133-4.

[30] A. W. Howitt, *The Native Tribes of South-East Australia*, p. 157.

[31] Spencer and Gillen, *The Northern Tribes of Central Australia*, p. 95.

[32] R. H. Codrington, "On Social Regulations in Melanesia," *J. A. I.*, xviii, 4, pp. 306-7.

[33] *Ibid.*, *The Melanesians*, pp. 36-7.

[34] A. R. Brown, "Three Tribes of Western Australia," *J. A. I.*, xliii (1913), p. 150.

[35] R. H. Codrington, *op. cit.*, pp. 28-9.

[36] R. Thurnwald, *Die Gemeinde der Banaro*, pp. iii, 115.

[37] *Ibid.*, p. 133.

[38] *Ibid.*, pp. 136, 145, 148.

[39] *Ibid.*, p. 149.

[40] *Ibid.*, p. 154.

[41] *Ibid.*, p. 158.

[42] *Ibid.*, pp. 123-4.

[43] W. G. Sumner, *The Yakuts*. Abridged from the Russian of Sieroshevski. *J. A. I.* (1901), p. 89.

[44] With the Ba-Ila, for instance. "The secret of understanding the system is first of all to rid one's mind of the terms one is used to, and to grasp firmly the principle that the words *tata* and *bama* do not mean what father and mother mean to us, but rather indicate certain positions in a table of genealogy; and the same with regard to *mwanangu, mukwesu,* etc.

"The terms applied vary as—

"(1) whether I am the person speaking, or spoken to, or spoken of;

"(2) whether I am directly addressing my relation, or referring to him or her;

"(3) whether I am speaking of myself as one person or including others with me;

"(4) whether the speaker is older or younger than the person spoken to; or of

"(5) whether the person speaking, or the person spoken to, is male or female.

"The vocabulary is equally extensive on the other points." Smith and Dale, *The Ila-Speaking Peoples of Northern Rhodesia,* i, pp. 316-7.

[45] A. R. Brown, "Three Tribes of Western Australia," *J. A. I.,* xliii (1913), p. 151.

INITIATION CEREMONIES *

By BALDWIN SPENCER and F. J. GILLEN

In every tribe there are certain ceremonies through which all of the youths must pass before they are admitted to the ranks of the men and allowed to see or take part in any of the performances which are regarded as sacred. The more important of these ceremonies are two in number, and are fundamentally similar in all of the tribes. They are those of circumcision and subincision. In this respect the central tribes differ markedly from those of the eastern and southeastern coastal districts, amongst whom the initiation ceremonies are, or rather were, of a very different nature.

Amongst these coastal tribes a very characteristic ceremony consisted in the knocking out of one or more of the upper incisor teeth. It is a curious fact that the central tribes very often performed this ceremony, but in this instance it has nothing whatever to do with initiation, and is not restricted to the men as of course it is amongst the tribes in which it is associated with initiation. It appears to be very probable that this was the older form of initiation common to the ancestors of the central, eastern, and southeastern tribes, and that in course of time it was, for some reason or another, superseded in the case of the central tribes by the ceremonies now in vogue. When once the latter became established, then the older ceremony lost all sacred significance, and came to be practiced indiscriminately by men and women alike. It is at all events a very suggestive fact that whilst amongst the central tribes we find traces of the customs associated with initiation in the eastern and southeastern coastal tribes, we do not, on the other hand, find amongst the latter even the slightest trace of the characteristic and im-

* *Northern Tribes of Central Australia.* London: Macmillan & Co.

281

portant ceremonies of the central and western natives.

In addition to the rites of circumcision and subincision, there are other ceremonies associated with initiation through which in some cases the youths and in others the adult men must pass. These are, however, really of secondary importance. One of them is associated with boys at an early age and the other with men of mature age, while the two important ones are always performed when the youth arrives at puberty. We tried in vain to find any satisfactory explanation of the ceremonies of circumcision and subincision, but so far as we could discover the native has no idea whatever of what these ceremonies mean. One thing is quite clear, and that is, they have not the slightest reference to keeping down the numbers of the tribe.[1] It must always, in regard to this matter, be borne in mind that in all of these tribes no one is allowed to have a wife until he has passed through the rites of subincision and circumcision, and that indeed the women look with contempt upon those who have not done so. Further still, if the natives do not wish a child to live, they adopt the very simple expedient of killing it as soon as ever it is born. This plan is by no means seldom adopted, and with this easy and well-recognized means of keeping down the population always to hand, it is scarcely likely that the men will submit to what is, after all, a very painful operation, for the purpose of achieving a result which not only can be, but normally is gained by that of infanticide. These initiations are of very ancient date, and their true meaning remains yet to be discovered. We tried hard to find among the traditions of the various tribes anything which might afford a clue to their meaning, but without success, and we know as little now as we did at the beginning of our work. The natives themselves have no idea in regard to their significance, and it is a rather curious fact that they have not invented some tradition to explain their meaning. All that they can tell you is that, in the Alcheringa, or the equivalent of the same in the different tribes, there was some ancestor or other who first of all performed one or both of the operations, usually upon himself first and later upon other individuals. Since that time the natives have continued to follow his example, but why their ancestor first of all performed the ceremony they have not the vaguest idea.

The ceremonies can never have had any reference directly to procreation, for the simple reason that the natives, one and all in these tribes, believe that the child is the direct result of the entrance into the mother of an ancestral spirit individual. They have no idea of procreation as being directly associated with sexual intercourse, and firmly believe that children can be born without this taking place. There are, for example, in the Arunta country certain stones which are supposed to be charged with spirit children who can, by magic, be made to enter the bodies of women, or will do so of their own accord. Again, in the Warramunga tribe, the women are very careful not to strike the trunks of certain trees with an ax, because the blow might cause spirit children to emanate from them and enter their bodies. They imagine that the spirit is very minute,—about the size of a small grain of sand,—and it enters the woman through the navel and grows within her into the child. It will thus be seen that, unless the natives have once possessed, but have since lost, all idea of the association between procreation and the intercourse of the sexes, which is extremely improbable, the elaborate and painful ceremonies of initiation cannot in their origin have had any direct relation to procreation.

There is one curious fact in regard to the distribution of the initiation ceremonies amongst the tribes in the northern part of the continent. Occupying the country in the Port Darwin district is a tribe called the Larakia, which apparently differs from all others in this part of the continent in regard to initiation. In connection with the latter this tribe practices neither the rite of knocking out of teeth nor that of circumcision and subincision. Unfortunately we could not work amongst them, and were only able to gather a little information from a member of the tribe—an elderly man—who happened to come down to the Macarthur River when we were there. The tribe has for long been under the influence of the white man, but the absence of ceremonies, so characteristic of the surrounding tribes, has nothing to do with this fact. The initiation of the Larakia youths takes the form of a series of more or less disagreeable tests, which are evidently designed to try the strength and endurance of those passing through them. A number of youths who have arrived at the age of puberty are taken to a retired spot under charge of certain old men, whose orders they have to obey implicitly. Here, as our informant told us, the old men do not give them too much to eat. A younger brother is provided by an elder brother with such food as he is allowed to have. Every now and again an old man, without any warning or reason, will bestow a hard blow or a kick upon one of the youths. The latter must neither resent nor show any sign of being hurt, which would only result in his receiving worse treatment. The old men also make the youths undergo severe manual labor, such as that of cutting down and rolling over heavy logs, and a favorite test is to order a few of them to go into the water and bring a crocodile to land. Finally, when the old men are satisfied with the conduct of the youths, they show them the sacred bull-roarer, which is called *Biddi-biduba,* telling them on no account to allow their younger brothers or any women to see it. The youths are each provided with one of these, which they take out into the bush and secrete in a safe place. Unlike what happens in most of the other tribes, the sacred stick is not kept, but at the end of two or three weeks it is broken and buried in the ground. The women call the stick, or rather the noise associated with it, Eruba, and believe that this is the voice of a spirit who has come down from the sky and is carrying the youths away into the bush from which they will return initiated men. With the exception of this tribe all of those occupying the central and northern central area of the continent practice the two important rites of circumcision and subincision.[2]

In the Urabunna tribes a man who stands in the relationship of *ḳadnini* (paternal grandfather) to the boy seizes
hold of him and puts his hand over the boy's mouth telling
him to remain silent. Placing string round the boy's neck,
the old man takes him away to the camp. Here he is made
to lie down, and is covered up while the lubras dance in
front of the men. All night long the old man keeps watch
over the boy, and at daylight, after the women have once
more danced, he ties the boy's hair up with string which
has been provided for the purpose by the father. Then the
boy is formally shown to the lubras, the old man with the
boy running round and round them shouting, *"Wo! Wo!"*
Suddenly they dart off into the scrub. That day the two
start away to visit distant groups and invite them to come in
to the ceremony. Each time they approach a camp [3] the
old man takes the boy by the arm and leads him up, while
the strangers, understanding exactly what is taking place,
shout out, *"Pau! Pau!"* On the way back they gather together the various groups, and for a time the lubras accompany them, but are left behind at a place some distance from
the main camp. On the way back the men, after the women
have been left behind, perform a few sacred ceremonies in
the camp at night-time. For the first time the boy sees one of
these and learns anything about the secret matters of the
tribe concerned with the totemic ancestors. Some miles away
from the home camp the old man tells the boy to make a
big smoke so as to let his father and the other men know
that he is returning. At the camp the women sit a little
distance behind the men, and the boy, approaching, walks
past the men and sits down close to the women. Then two
old men who are *ḳadnini* (grandfather) to the boy come up,
take the string from his head, and lead him off by a roundabout way to the men's camp. That night and the succeeding one singing goes on without ceasing, and totemic
ceremonies are performed, some associated with local groups
and others with those to which some of the strangers belong.
Then the boy is taken a little distance away while the stone

knife[4] is made ready by the *kawkuka* (mother's brother) and *nuthi* (elder brother). After this the boy is brought back, the singing is continued, and he is given a little food to eat.

After sunset three men, who stand in the relationship of *oknia* (father) to the boy, crouch down so as to form a kind of table on to which the boy is lifted by his *kawkuka* (mother's brother) and *kadnini* (grandfather). Fur-string is put into his mouth, and a *witiwa* (wife's brother) sits astride of his stomach. The foreskin is pulled up, the *kadnini* man makes the first cut, and this is rapidly completed by the *kawkuka*. Both the foreskin and the stone knife are handed over to the elder brother, who provided the knife, and he goes round and touches the stomach of every *nuthi* with the foreskin. The latter is then placed on a fire-stick and buried in the ground without any special ceremony, no further notice being taken of it.

An elder brother now takes the initiated youth away into the bush and makes a small plain wooden Churinga, which he gives the boy to carry about, telling him that it belonged to the Umbumbuninia (the equivalent of Alcheringa), and that he must keep swinging it. On no account is he to allow any lubra or child to see it. At times the elder brother watches over him and at others the *witiwa* (wife's brother). He is not allowed to eat *kadni,* the jew lizard (a favorite and fairly abundant food of the natives), or else it would make him sore and prevent his wound from healing. On the other hand he is supposed to make presents of it to the old men.

When he has recovered from the operation of circumcision he is brought into the men's camp, no women being allowed to see him. Early in the morning he is painted with red ochre, and later on a *kawkuka* (mother's brother) takes the string off his head. Then three men who stand to him in the relationship of *oknia* (father) crouch down so as to form a kind of table on which he is at once placed, another *oknia* performing the operation of subincision. A small piece of bark is inserted so as to keep the wound open, but is removed after a few hours, the blood being allowed to trickle down into a hole in the ground which is afterwards filled in with earth. That night he is shown more sacred totemic ceremonies, and men who are *witiwa* (wife's brother) and *kadnini* (grandfather) to him come up and tell him that he is now a man and not a boy. He must not attempt to have intercourse with lubras other than his *nupa* and *piraungaru* (lawful wives). If he does so then he will fall down dead like the stones. He is not on any account to interfere with other men's lubras.

In the morning the lubras light a fire and place green boughs upon it so as to make a smoke, in the midst of which the youth kneels down while his *kupuka* and *kakua* (younger and elder sisters) hit him on the back, the women who stand to him in the relationship of mother being close at hand to prevent, so they say, the sisters from hitting him too hard. After this he may have a wife and takes his place among the initiated men at the *urathilpi* or men's camp After a short time he must give a present of food, which is called by the special name of *katu,* to the men who assisted in the operation. These men put a little bit of meat up to his mouth, and in that way release him from the ban of silence.

The final ceremony of initiation in the Urabunna tribe is called Wilyaru, and is common to this, the Wonkgongaru, Dieri, and probably several other closely allied tribes. It does not occupy a great length of time, not being, in this respect, at all comparable to the Engwura or final initiation ceremony of the Arunta, but in both we meet with the placing of the men on the fire. In the Wilyaru an important part—in fact, the important part—consists in laying the man down on the ground with his back uppermost. All of the men present strike him hard (they must, of course, themselves be Wilyaru). Finally two men, one a *kawkuka* (mother's brother) and the other a *witiwa* (wife's brother), make a series of cuts, from four to eight in number, down each side of the spine and one median one in the nape of the neck. The scars left behind when the wounds heal up enable a man who has passed through the ceremony to be distinguished at a glance. No Wilyaru [5] man will, if he can avoid it, stand or sit with his back turned towards women and children. The cuts, according to tradition, are supposed to represent marks on the bell bird, and are made in commemoration of the time when, in the Alcheringa, the bell bird was instrumental in causing the death of a great hawk ancestor who used to kill and eat the natives. At the present day the natives will not eat that hawk in consequence of his cannibalistic habits in the Alcheringa. In connection with this it is not without interest to notice that in the Arunta the wild cat (*achilpa*) is not eaten, and that in the Alcheringa it also was especially associated with cannibalism. One ceremony in connection with the Engwura represented an attack by wild-cat ancestors on a native camp with the idea of getting human bodies to eat. Following closely on this was another ceremony representing the taming of the wild-cat men. In the one tribe the cannibal eagle-hawk is represented as being killed, and in the other the cannibal wild cats as being tamed. Neither animal is eaten by any one. The Arunta nowadays do not know why, though we may conjecture that originally the reason given was the same as that now given by the Urabunna people in regard to the hawk. Ceremonies associated with the cessation of cannibalism are represented during the final initiation ceremonies of both tribes, though in most other respects they are very different from one another. In the case of one of these ceremonies, they may perhaps be explained as commemorative of a reformatory movement which probably took place at some early time in regard to cannibalism.

In the Unmatjera tribe, as amongst the Arunta, the first ceremony, known as *alkira-kiuma,* consists in throwing a boy up in the air. When about twelve years of age, he is simply taken out into the bush by men of various relationships, and, without being painted or decorated in any way, is thrown up into the air and caught in the arms of the men. The *ikuntera,* his future wife's father, carries with him a stick, and if the boy has not been in the habit of presenting him with what he pleases to think a sufficient amount of food, in the form of small wallabies, etc., when he catches any, then it is so much the worse for the boy. As he rises and falls in the air the *ikuntera* strikes him repeatedly, emphasizing each stroke with the remark, "I will teach you to give me some meat." The warning is not lost upon the boy, and the unpleasant experience serves forcibly to remind him that he must very carefully regulate his conduct in respect to his *ikuntera,* for the latter, if dissatisfied with his behavior, has the power of taking away his wife and of bestowing her upon some other man. After having been thrown up, the boy is told that he must no longer go to the lubras' camp, but must stay with the men at the *ungunja* or men's camp, and during the day go out with them hunting, and not play about with the boys and girls.

The ceremony of circumcision, here spoken of as *pulla,* is very closely similar to that amongst the Arunta, so that we will only describe it very briefly. The boy who, after having been thrown up in the air, spends his time with the men at their camp and hunting with them out in the bush, is seized one night by men who stand in the relationship to him of elder brother, wife's brother, father's sister's son, and taken to the ceremonial ground, where all of the men and women are assembled. The women perform a dance, after which the boy's hair is tied up and a human hair-girdle wound round his waist. He is told that during the ceremonies about to be performed he must stay where he is placed, and remain covered up, so as not to see anything unless he is told to watch. Should he ever reveal any of the secrets which will soon be told to him, then the spirit Twanyirika will carry him away. His mother then presents him with a fire-stick, which he is told he must on no account lose, nor must he allow it to go out, or else he and his mother will be killed. After this is over he goes out into the bush for some days, accompanied by an elder brother, and on returning is brought on to the ceremonial ground, where meanwhile the men have been performing sacred ceremonies. Exactly as in the Arunta tribe, some of these are shown to him, and for the first time he learns the secrets of the totems and the history of his totemic ancestors. The exact nature of these ceremonies varies according to the men who are taking part in the performance. Each of the elder men has the right to perform certain of them which belong to his own totem, or to those of his father or elder brother, which he has inherited from them. In the Arunta tribe it is customary to perform one or more in which a sacred pole, called a *nurtunja* or a *waninga,* is used, but amongst the Unmatjera and Kaitish tribes the *waninga* is never and the *nurtunja* but seldom used. It is only very rarely that the latter is met with north of the Macdonnell Ranges, and its use appears to die out completely a little to the north of Barrow Creek. Amongst the Kaitish tribe we have only seen it used once, and that in the case of a ceremony of the water totem.

The actual operation of circumcision is conducted by the boy's father-in-law (*ikuntera*), and as soon as it is over he is presented by his elder brother with a Churinga belonging to his father. He is told that it is good, and will assist him to recover, and that on no account must he lose sight of it or leave it anywhere about in the bush, because if by any chance he should lose it then some one would kill both him and his mother. It must also on no account be shown to boys, or else they will have their eyes put out. He must hide himself away in the bush, and if by any chance he should see a lubra's track, he must be very careful to jump over it. If his foot should touch it, then the spirit of the louse which lives in the lubra's hair would go on to him, and his head would get full of lice. Not only this; but if he were to touch the track he would be sure sooner or later to follow up the lubra, who would ask him, "Why do you come and try to catch me?" and she would go back to the camp and tell her brother, who would come and kill him.

The foreskin is preserved for some time after the operation by the *ikuntera,* who, when it begins to smell offensively, gives it to the boy, along with some hair-string, saying, "This is your foreskin." Then the *ikuntera* goes back to his own camp, and a man who is *gammona* (mother's brother) to the boy comes up and ties the string round the latter's waist. The boy puts the foreskin on a shield, covers it up with a broad spear-thrower, and then, under cover of darkness, so that the lubras cannot by any chance see what he is doing, takes it away and puts it in a hollow tree, telling no one except an *unkulla* (father's sister's son) man where he has hidden it. There is no special relationship between the boy and the tree, though in times past there possibly may have been, for according to tradition the early Alcheringa ancestors always placed theirs in their *nanja* trees—that is, the trees specially associated with their spirits.

At an earlier stage than this, while the boy is out in the bush, he is visited by the men, and on one or more occasions he has to undergo the painful operation of *koperta kalkuma,* which consists in the biting of his scalp by a man who is his *gammona.* Though a comparatively unimportant ceremony, yet it is a very painful one, as the biter, urged to do his best by the men who are sitting around watching him, does not spare the boy, who often howls aloud with pain. . . . Amongst these tribes it is only men who themselves have very good heads of hair who are allowed to bite the boys, their bite being supposed to be of especial efficacy in making the hair grow.

When the boy has recovered from the operation of *pulla,* the *okilia* (elder brother) tells the other men that it is now time to perform the operation of *ariltha*—that is, subincision, or otherwise he will grow too big and it will be too hard to cut him. He is brought up by the *okilia* and *umbirna,* the latter being the brother of his future wife. These men have had charge of him out in the bush. The men are all gathered together at a spot some distance from the main camp, so as to be out of the way of the women. Here all night long they sit around small fires, while the father's elder brother and the boy's own elder brothers prepare and perform sacred ceremonies associated with their own totems, showing and explaining them to the boy. The latter sleeps with the men who are in charge of him a little way off from the rest, so that he does not see the preparations for the ceremonies, but when all is ready and the performers in position he is brought up to watch. Then, just before dawn—a very favorite time for the performance of many of their rites—the father himself prepares a ceremony—always, if possible, using a sacred pole or *nurtunja*. When it is over the elder brother leads the boy by the arm up to the pole, telling him that it is his own father's *nurtunja,* that it has made many young men, and that he must catch plenty of kangaroo and wallaby for his father. He is then told to embrace the *nurtunja*. Green boughs are now strewn upon the ground, a shield is placed on them, and the *nurtunja* on the top again of this; finally the boy's *umbirna* man lies down on the *nurtunja*. The boy himself is now seized and placed upon his back above the *umbirna;* fur-string is thrust into his mouth, one man sits astride his body while others hold his legs in case he should struggle. The man sitting upon him lifts up and stretches the penis, which is at once slit along its length with a stone-knife. In the Unmatjera tribe the actual operation is performed by an *ikuntera* of the boy, and in the Kaitish by an *okilia*. When all is over—and the operation seldom occupies more than a few seconds, though it must be an extremely painful one—the boy, who is usually more or less dazed, partly with pain and partly with fear and excitement, is raised to his feet, and his father gives him a Churinga, saying, "This is your *churinga alcheri* which had your *kurnah* in the Alcheringa,"—that is, it is the sacred stick with which his spirit was associated. "You must not go about the lubras' camp when you carry it; if you do, then you will lose your Churinga and your brother will kill you." His *ikuntera* and *okilia* then come up and repeat the same thing, telling him also that he must keep to the lubra whom his *ikuntera* gives him, and must not interfere with other men's lubras or go to another camp and steal one. If he were to do the latter, then sooner or later other black-fellows would come up from that camp and kill both him and his friends. He must be very careful always to pay attention to his *ikuntera,* and provide him with plenty of food. While out in the bush he must be sure to make the bull-roarer swing, or else another *arakurta,*[6] who lives up in the sky, will come down and carry him away. If this *arakurta* hears the *luringa*—that is, the noise of the bull-roarer —he says, "That is all right," and will not harm him.

The lubras and boys are taught to believe that the *luringa* is the voice of Twanyirika, who is supposed by the Kaitish to live in a particular rock, and that when a youth is initiated he comes forth in the form of a spirit and takes the boy away into the bush. He is further supposed to hobble along carrying one leg over his shoulder. Both women and children believe that in some way Twanyirika kills the youth and later on brings him to life again during the period of initiation.

The novice meanwhile gathers together a large amount of a grass seed called *idnimita,* and gives it to one of the men in charge of him, who takes it into the men's camp. It is finally handed over to the boy's mother, and at the same time the lubras are told that Twanyirika has been giving the boy *alpita.*[7]

When the wound is healed the fact is notified to the women, who make a fire close to their own camp. Then the youth is brought up by his *umbirna unjipinna*—that is, the actual man to whom his sister is either betrothed or married. He brings with him a supply of kangaroo flesh which he has himself secured. At the same time the mothers and elder sisters bring with them yams, which they place beside the fire on which green bushes are piled so as to give out great volumes of smoke. The youth kneels down on the bushes in the midst of the smoke. One or more of his *mias* (mothers) holds his arms while his sisters rub him all over and then touch his mouth with a yam, thereby releasing him from the ban of silence. At the same time the mother takes the forehead-band from his head and keeps it. Then the women return to their camp with the offering of meat which the boy has made to them, and he, together with his *umbirna,* goes to the *ungunja,* carrying the yams which are *ekekerinja* (tabooed) to him and must be handed over to the old men.

While the boy is out in the bush the mother wears *alpita* in her hair on the back of her head, and is careful also never to let her fire go out. The object of the former is to assist the boy to be watchful at night-time, so that no harm, such as damage from snake bite, shall come near to him. The *alpita* is the tail-tip of the rabbit-bandicoot, a small animal which is very lively during the night, so that, of course, according to native logic, the wearing of the *alpita* is a sure stimulus to wakefulness. Not only is it efficacious in the case of the actual wearer, but it is effectual when worn by some one closely related to the individual whom it is desired to influence in this particular way.

The actual operation of circumcision is performed by one or other of those men who stand to the boy in the relationship respectively of *auiniari* (wife's father), *turtundi* (wife's mother's father), or *tjurtalia* (wife's mother's brother). The foreskin, called *gnuru,* wrapped up in string, together with the stone knife by means of which the operation was performed, is taken by a *tjurtalia* man to the *naminni* (mother's brother) of the boy, who in return presents the *tjurtalia* with food. The foreskin is then placed in the hole by a witchetty grub in a tree, and served the purpose of causing a plentiful supply of the grub; or it may be put in the burrow of a ground spider, in which case it is supposed in some way to cause the penis to grow. The boy himself never sees the *gnuru* and is not aware of where it is placed.

When he has recovered from the operation it is customary

to perform that of subincision or *parra* within the course of the next month or two. Amongst the Warramunga this second operation is always carried out at a time when a large number of men are gathered together in camp performing a series of sacred ceremonies. Unlike what obtains in the Arunta tribe, it is the custom amongst the Warramunga not to perform odd ceremonies at different times, but to perform a long series, passing in review, as it were, the whole Alcheringa history of one totemic ancestor. At this particular time, for example, the men were gathered together, and more than a month had been spent in performing ceremonies relating to the Wollunqua, an important snake totem. It was decided by the old men that, towards the close of these, three young men should be subincised. Nothing, of course, was said to them, but one day, when a special and very elaborately decorated mound had been built representing the old Wollunqua, the three youths were suddenly seized and told that the time had come when they must be finally admitted to the ranks of the men. One of them was a Thakomara and the other two were Thungallas. The former was under the charge of a Thapungarti man who was his *naminni*—that is, his mother's brother— and the two latter under that of Thapanunga men who stood in the same relationship to them. Late at night, when all of the men in camp were gathered together singing and dancing round the mound, the three youths were brought up with their heads covered and told to sit down quietly and watch the proceedings. Their guardians explained to them what the mound meant; they were told that they must not quarrel with the men to whom it belonged, and especially must not throw boomerangs at them.

After the whole night, during the course of which the mound was destroyed, had been spent in singing and dancing, so that every one was more or less tired out, the guardians of the boys told them to get up, and they were taken to a spot right in the middle of the main camp. Here, just at sunrise, the older men sat down quietly in a group close to some bushes, behind which the three boys were crouching. Their guardians still kept careful watch over them to prevent any attempt to escape from the painful ordeal which they now knew that they had to pass through in a short time. The women had meanwhile been informed of what was about to take place, and ranged themselves in two groups about thirty or forty yards in front of the seated men, one to the right and the other to the left side. The Uluuru women were in one group and the Kingilli in another, and in turn each of them danced, jumping towards the men as if their ankles were tied together. At the same time they extended their arms and flexed their hands, with palms uppermost, up and down on their wrists. This curious hand movement is very characteristic of the women when they are taking part in ceremonies. Then, with the women standing only a short distance away, three Tjapeltjeri men, brothers of the future wife of one of the novices, came forward and extended themselves at full length on the ground immediately in front of the seated men. Two Thapungarti men led the Thakomara youth out from behind the bushes and placed him on the top of the Tjapeltjeri men. One Thapungarti man sat on his stomach, a pubic tassel belonging to his father was pressed down into his mouth, and while other men held his legs and arms the operation of subincision was performed by a Thapungarti man. As soon as it was over he was lifted up and, supported in the arms of the Thapungarti men, was placed between the knees of the old Tjupila man, his father, who tied a hair girdle round his waist. Then in turn he stroked the heads of Tjupila and Thapanunga men, his tribal fathers' and mothers' brothers, with the tassel used during the ceremony, and was led to one side, where he sat down on a *pitchi* into which the blood from the wound was allowed to flow. This blood was afterwards taken by a Thapungarti man to the camp of the youth's father and mother, and was drunk by them.

During the next few weeks sacred totemic ceremonies were

enacted daily, and the youths were always called up from their camp to watch them, each of them under the charge of a guardian, who stood with his arm round the boy carefully telling him what everything meant. At the close of a special series of ceremonies connected with the Thalaualla (black-snake) totem, the two Thungall boys were brought up and placed in the midst of the group of decorated men, who were seated on the top of a drawing made on the ground, representing the snake; the headdresses of the performers were taken off, and the stomachs of the boys repeatedly struck hard with them.

Ten days after the operation the Thakomara youth was presented with a boomerang, armlets, and forehead-band by a Tjunguri man, who was his tribal sister's son. He came onto the corrobboree ground wearing the armlets and forehead-band, and carrying the boomerang in his hand. Four men, who were respectively Tjapeltjeri, Thapanunga, Thapungarti, and Tjunguri,—that is, representative of all the groups in the moiety of the tribe to which he did not belong, —came up to him, and, in turn, he passed the boomerang through their waist-girdles. Each man then passed it in the same way through the novice's, the last man allowing it to remain in the position in which it is normally carried. This is emblematic of the fact that he has now entered the ranks of the men, and can take part in their occupations of hunting and fighting.

Towards the close of the series of ceremonies, some weeks after the operation of *parra,* a further little ceremony was enacted, the object of which was evidently to show that the boys had passed completely out of the hands of the lubras. At the same time it was possibly meant as a warning to the boys of what would happen if they disregarded the instructions which had been given to them and went near to the lubras' camp.

The natives had been busy all of the preceding day in getting ready for a special ceremony, the preparations for which were made by the men of one-half of the tribe, while the other men carefully kept away from the corrobboree ground until all was ready. The whole night long the former were singing and dancing on the ground, while the men of the other moiety came from their camps and slept, not far away, in the bed of the creek, from which they were summoned just at daylight. Meanwhile, acting under the instructions of the men in charge of them, the newly initiated youths had spent the night close by the lubras' camp, and as soon as ever the ceremony was over, which was just at sunrise, the guardians of the boys left the other men on the corrobboree ground and made a wide circuit so as to pass round behind the women's camp. The women meanwhile had deserted the latter, and had taken refuge on the far side of the creek. The guardians of the boys, who were lying concealed on the ground, came along rushing and yelling, in the direction of the lubras' camp. When they were about a hundred yards off, the boys sprang to their feet and raced along, as hard as ever their legs could carry them, towards the corrobboree ground. They were evidently anxious to lose no time, and were urged to do their best by the yells of the men, and still more by the boomerangs, which, thrown by the pursuers with all their might, came bounding after them. Once on the corrobboree ground they were safe, and here they joined the group of men who had been watching their headlong flight with amusement.

The only thing now remaining to be done was to release the boys from the ban of silence. This, of course, meant presents of food. In the first place the boys were decorated— the Thakomara by a Tjunguri man, and the Thungallas by Thapungarti men. Each of them was elaborately painted both back and front with designs in charcoal and red ochre. Bringing up the food in a *pitchi,* they knelt down on a few boughs which had been spread out for the purpose not far from the main camp. The Thakomara was in one place, and the two Thungallas side by side not far away from him. The women, decorated with red ochre and lines of yellow, approached them from behind, so as not to see their faces.

Those amongst them who were tribal mothers and sisters stroked and patted them with their hands, and then, still keeping their backs turned towards the lubras, the youths got up and walked away to join the men, who were seated some little distance off watching the ceremony. To this little ceremony, the performance of which enables the boys to speak once more to the women, the name of *barkamunda* is given. Later on still an offering of food must be made to the men. The Thakomara has to present this to Thapungarti and Tjapeltjeri, and the Thungallas to Thapanunga and Tjunguri men. Each of the men who receives food holds up his finger for the initiate to bite, and the ban of silence is thereby broken. This ceremony is called *thallateilbunthan.*

In the Mara tribe the operation of circumcision is called *gniarti,* that of subincision *marunku;* in the Anula tribe the equivalent terms are *taru* and *talkui.* The actual ceremonies are very closely similar in both tribes, and the following is an account of what took place in connection with the initiation of a Roumburia boy in the Anula tribe, the equivalent of a Tjulantjuka in the Binbinga.

The boy was caught by a Tjurulum man who stood to him in the relationship of *meimi* or mother's brother's son. He was told not to cry out or make any noise, for the time had come when he must no longer walk about a mere boy but become a young man. The father brought up a hair girdle (*wuthari*), tied it around his waist, and sent him to his mother, who told him not to cry out or run away, but go and bring in a big number of black-fellows, because they wanted to make him into a young man. Then, under the charge of the Tjurulum, he went out and visited distant camps in turn, the men being asked to come up and take part in the ceremonies. They said, "All right, we will come." From the different camps other men went on with them, but the boy was allowed to speak only to his guardian. For two moons they wandered about, the Tjurulum, Pungarinji and Yakomari men carrying him on their shoulders when he got tired. Meanwhile his father and mother, the latter assisted by other women, had been busy out in the bush collecting food supplies. The Tjurulum man and the boy traveled as far inland as a place now called Anthony's Lagoon, more than 200 miles away on the tableland country. On the return journey they lighted big fires as soon as they came within a day or two's march of the home camp, so as to let the father know that they were close at hand. These fires were made as usual by the boy himself, and the Tjurulum man left the others behind and went on ahead alone and said to the father, "I have left your son at my camp; to-morrow I will bring him in; are all of the men here?" The father told him that all was ready and he returned to his camp, carrying with him food sent to the boy by the father. That night the lubras danced in the male camp, in front of the men, who sang, and in the morning the boy, accompanied by the strangers, started for the home camp, the Tjurulum man again coming on by himself. All of the men and women had painted their bodies with red, white, and black, and were assembled on the ceremonial ground called *thamunki*. Seeing that all was ready, the Tjurulum man went back to bring the boy in. The father sat in the middle of the front row of men, and the women stood in a group behind. Then the strangers approached, shouting *"Ka! ka! ya-a!"* those from the hill country far away inland singing out also *"srr! srr!"* At first they held the boy by the hand, but on approaching close he was hoisted onto the shoulders of a Pungarinji man, who ran with him round and round the local mob, so that his father and mother could see him clearly. After this the Pungarinji, Tjuanaku, and Tjurulum men amongst the visitors came and placed spears, hair girdles, and other articles on a paper-bark dish at the feet of the father as a gift to him. The boy, who had been decorated with fur-string by his *meimi,* was brought up to his father, and the strangers leaving him there retired. After sitting for a short time by his father, he was sent to his mother, who embraced him and wept over him. The mother had brought up a supply of food which she had placed on the ground at the father's feet, and after a time this was handed over to the *meimi* man, who took it, accompanied by the boy, to the strangers. The *meimi* then painted a straight line across the backs of the Pungarinji, Tjuanaku, Tjurulum, Thungallum, and Yakomari men, and acting under his instructions the boy added three vertical lines below. The food was placed by the boy opposite to the Thungallum men, who were his future wife's brother, and when he had given it to them he went back to his father's camp. After the women had left the ground the men performed a sacred ceremony, and early the following morning the strangers returned and remained on the ground all day, a number of ceremonies being performed one after the other. The boy meanwhile had been sent to the *meimi* woman's camp, and told that he must not walk about, but lie down quietly and go to sleep. Later on in the afternoon the strangers painted themselves and at sundown came on to the ceremonial ground, where the local men stood in a single line with the women behind them. The *meimi* woman brought up the boy covered in paper bark, telling him not to look about but to keep his eyes fixed on the ground. He was handed over to the *meimi* man, who made two small fires, between which the boy had to lie down, covered over completely with sheets of paper bark. Then, standing on one side, the *meimi* struck his two *nulla nullas* (clubs) together, shouting out as he did so the names of the different countries from which the various parties had come. This over, he led up the painted men, who marched round and round, each of them waving a burning torch of paper bark, after which they returned to their camps and the lubras went away. Late at night the men were all recalled by whistling, and came onto the ground, each man having his legs decorated with bunches of twigs. Clanging boomerangs and waving paper-bark torches, the men marched round and round the boy, who was still hidden from view. Time after time they advanced and retired, singing loudly, until at length they all stood to one side. After a pause the *meimi* man, covering his eyes with his hands, brought up the Pungarinji man who had first of all carried the boy into camp on his shoulders, and at the same time the painted men came and placed themselves in front of the boy. The Pungarinji man stood behind the latter so that his face could not be seen, and then the boy, instructed as to what to do by the *meimi,* lifted up the bark under which he had lain concealed and gazed at the men. After a few minutes they ran away and the boy was told that what he had seen, and was about to see, was *kurta-kurta* (tabooed), and must on no account be spoken of to women or children. Sacred totemic ceremonies were then performed by Pungarinji, Tjuanaku, Thungallum, Tjurulum, and Yakomari men in turn, each of them being explained to the boy. At the same time songs referring to his own totem were sung. Just before dawn all of the men took their boomerangs and clashed them together; the *meimi* handed a knife to a Pungarinji man, asking him at the same time to perform the ceremony, and then, warming his hands at a fire, placed them on the thigh, leg, private parts, and head of the boy. Two Thungallum men who were *napi-napi*—that is, wife's brother to the boy—lay down full length on the ground. The *meimi* placed the boy on top of them, putting fur-string in his mouth, and telling him not to cry out or else the strangers would think that he was a coward. Then he seated himself astride the boy, pulled up the foreskin, and the Pungarinji man at once cut it off, laid the knife down on the ground, and retired to one side. The boy was lifted up, and standing above the two Thungallum men, allowed some of the blood to drip down on to their backs, thus establishing a special friendly relationship between himself and them. After this they brought up spears and boomerangs and presented them to the boy. Some of the blood was, as usual, placed in a paper-bark dish and, together with the spears and boomerangs, handed over by the father to one of the boys *tjakaka* (mother's eldest brother), whom he told to go and bury the blood in the bank of a water-hole where lilies grew. The foreskin, tied up in bark, was at first taken possession of by the *tjakaka* man, who subsequently handed it over to the *meimi,* his son, telling him to send it on to a tribal father of the boy living in a distant group. This man finally brought it back to the boy's father with a present of spears, and it was then handed once more to the *tjakaka* man, who, after cutting it in pieces, buried the remains in the ground by the side of a water-hole.

As amongst the Binbinga the ceremony of subincision was performed some time afterwards, when the final burial rites in connection with the bones of a dead man were carried out. After being shown the ceremonies connected with the totem of the dead man, the Tjulantjuka boy was subincised by a Yakomari man, the details of the ceremony being closely similar to those of the Binbinga tribe. When all was over the boy was presented with a sacred stick (bull-roarer) called *mura-mura* and told that it was made, in the first instance, by the whirlwind; that it was *kurta-kurta* (tabooed), and must on no account be shown to women or children, who think that its roaring is the voice of a great spirit called Gnabaia, who has come to swallow up the boy. He was then taken away into the bush by an elder brother, and kept there until the rain had fallen and the cool weather came, when he was brought back again to the camp, accompanied by men from other localities. Meanwhile the elder men in camp had been making preparations for the performance of certain special ceremonies concerned with the whirlwind totem. A hole had been dug in the ground large enough to hold two men easily, and into this a Paliarinji and a Tjulantjuka man went. Food was placed by the side of it, and then the older Tjurulum, Tjamerum, Yakomari, and Thungallum men came up and sang around it, after which they retired, taking the food with them. Later on the younger men were brought up and shown the hole, which they were told represented one of the *mungai* spots of the whirlwind when first he came out of the earth and wandered about over the country. Another and still larger pit was then dug some distance away, and in this whirlwind ceremonies were enacted. On a cleared space by its side a pole about fifteen feet high, made by lashing two long sticks together, was fixed upright in the ground. The whole pole was tied round and round with string, a bunch of white feathers ornamented the top, and beneath this a nose-bone was inserted. On the ground at its base whirlwind ceremonies were performed at night-time, and the young men were told that it represented the totem. Finally the recently initiated boy was hit on the back with the sacred *mura-mura* which he had carried about with him in the bush; the stick was then placed in the hole, the soil heaped over it, and there it was left. After having witnessed this ceremony the young men receive the special name of *wanjilliri,* and it may be noted that there is a curious resemblance in certain points between this final ceremony and that of the Engwura in the Arunta tribe. In each instance the ceremony includes the erection of a pole the decorations of which seem to indicate that it has some relation to a human being.[8] It is placed on a special ceremonial ground, and around it ceremonies connected with totems are performed in the presence of men, all of whom are already fully initiated, so far as the ordinary rites are concerned. Further still, in both cases the men, after having passed through the ceremony, receive a special designation, *uliara* in the Arunta tribe and *wanjilliri* in the Anula tribe.

NOTES

[1] This has been pointed out previously by Roth, *Ethnological Studies Among the Northwest-Central Queensland Aborigines,* p. 179, and also by ourselves, *N. T.,* p. 264.

[2] Curiously the Arunta tribe has a tradition relating to a number of individuals who were taken away to the north under the leadership of an Alcheringa ancestor named Kukaitcha. They traveled on until they came into the country of the salt water, and there they stayed and remained always uncircumcised.

[3] Traveling on an errand such as this the man and boy are perfectly safe. In regard to this immunity from attack, even in a strange country, there are certain fixed rules amongst the natives. Any one carrying a sacred

stick or Churinga is for the time being sacred and must on no pretense be injured. When an old man is seen with a youth traveling from place to place, the natives at once understand what is happening, and would not ;hink of molesting them. Since the advent of the white man a letter, or, as the natives call it, a "paper yabber," carried in a forked stick is as safe a passport as a Churinga.

4 This is often only a sharp chip of quartzite, or, when procurable, the natives prefer a splinter of glass.

5 The term is applied both to the ceremony and to the men who have passed through it.

6 *Arakurta* is the status term applied to a youth who has passed through the ceremony of circumcision, but not through that of subincision.

7 Tail-tips of the rabbit-kangaroo, *Perameles lagotis*, used as an ornament by the natives.

8 For a full description of the sacred pole called *Kauaua*, used by the Arunta, see *N. T.*, p. 370.

THE COMING OF THE WARRIORS *

By W. J. PERRY

THE Children of the Sun were closely connected with the archaic civilization. Their disappearance from the scene, which has so often happened, was accompanied by certain cultural transformations which will have to be discussed. In this chapter it will be shown that the sun-cult was a constant feature of the archaic civilization, and that it disappeared, the sun-god being replaced usually by a war-god. It will also be shown that this change in deities was accompanied by a change in the habits of such communities, by the adoption of a more warlike behavior.

Once established the sun-cult was always prominent in Egyptian religion. But later on, under the rule of Thebes, the sun-god became more definitely warlike than in the earlier stage.

In Babylonia and Assyria a definite transition to a war-god can be observed. Tammuz, the god of the Sumerians, was first connected with vegetation and fertility, and kings were identified with him. Very soon, however, in Sumerian history, he is associated with the sun-god Shamash, who is an important Babylonian god.[1] Although the religion of the Babylonians shows many signs of continuity with that of Sumeria, the religion of Assyria, a Babylonian colony, reveals traces of profound political changes. Ashur, the great god of the Assyrians, was a war-god.[2] He evidently was the product of a process of development such as produced Ramman or Rimmon, the Assyrian god of thunder, lightning, wind and storm, who was originally identified with Shamash, the Babylonian sun-god. The culture-sequences in the case of the Sumerians, Babylonians and Assyrians

---

* *The Children of the Sun.* London: Methuen & Co., Ltd.

show that the chief gods are first vegetation and fertility deities, then sun-gods, and then war-gods.

In India the transformation is from sun-god to war-god,[3] for there are no signs of the Tammuz-Osiris stage. The culture-sequences that can be observed are those between the Aryans and Asuras, and between the early and late stages of the Aryans themselves.[4] The sun was a great god of the Asuras, and has continued so in those parts of India under Dravidian influence. Peoples such as the Mundas of Chota Nagpur, who speak an Austronesian language, the Gonds, Khonds and other Dravidian tribes, have the sun-god as their chief deity. The sun is an important god among many of the Hindu sects of Southern India, the region where Dravidian influence is so powerful. The Aryan-speaking peoples, on the other hand, had Indra, a war-god, as their chief deity.[5] So, in the culture-sequence between Aryans and Dravidians, the sun-god is followed by a war-god. But it is possible to go farther, and to establish a culture-sequence among the Aryans themselves. It is known that Indra had, some time before the compilation of the Rig Veda, supplanted a group of sun-gods, headed by Varuna, who were the children of Aditi, the great mother of gods and men.[6] These sun-gods are common to the Aryans of India and those of Persia before the Zoroastrian reform, and among them is Mithra. So, among the Aryans themselves, a war-god had come to the front. Varuna himself lost his solar character, and became a creator god and god of waters. In Vedic India, as in Assyria, the sun-gods are transforming themselves, and also being supplanted by war-gods.

A culture-sequence can be established in Indonesia. For in Borneo, the Kayan, who have immigrated later than the Hindus, have no sun-god, and no ruling class of Children of the Sun. Their supreme god is Laki Tenganan, who is not endowed with special functions,[7] but is looked upon as a fatherly being who watches over their interests. He is identical with the supreme being of the Kenyah and Klemantan, tribes whom the Kayan have civilized. He is

apparently not the creator, but the Kayan are not clear on
this point; at any rate he does not figure in the creation
myth.[8] The most important of their ordinary gods is Toh
Bulu, the war-god.[9] The Kayan—this obviously means the
chiefs—claim descent from gods, especially Oding Lahang,
who acts as intermediary between men and Laki Tenganan.[10] Oding Lahang, they say, was a chief who lived
long ago. It is interesting to note his ancestry. "In the beginning there was a barren rock. On this the rains fell and
gave rise to moss, and the worms, aided by the dung-beetles,
made soil by their castings. Then a sword handle (*haup
malat*) came down from the sun and became a large tree.[11]
From the moon came down a creeper, which, hanging from
the tree, became mated with it through the action of the
wind. From this union were born Kaluban Gai and Kalubi
Angai, lacking the legs and lower half of their trunks, so
that their entrails hung loose and exposed. Leaves falling
from the tree became the various species of birds and winged
insects, and from the fallen fruits sprang the four-footed
beasts. Resin, oozing from the trunk of the tree, gave rise
to the domestic pig and fowl, two species which are distinguished by their understanding of matters that remain
hidden from all others, even from human beings. The first
incomplete human beings produced Pengok Ngai and Katira
Murei; the latter bore a son, Batang Uta Tatai, who married
Ajai Avai and begot Sijau Laho, Oding Lahang, Pabalan,
Pliban, and Tokong, who became the progenitors of the
various existing peoples. Oding Lahang is claimed by the
Kayans as their ancestor, and also by some of the Klemantan
tribes." [12]

This story raises an important point in mythology. The
history of the Kayan tends to connect them with the Hindus
of Java.[13] Their chiefs claim descent from the sky, and indirectly, from the sun. Their most prominent deity is a war-
god. But what is the function of Laki Tenganan, their
supreme being? What does he mean in their history? He is
identical with the supreme being of the Kenyah and Kleman-

tan tribes, whom the Kayan probably have civilized. This god means something in the past history of the Kayan, and possibly he was connected originally with the sun, from which the ancestors of Kayan chiefs seem originally to claim descent. If Oding Lahang, their great ancestor, were one of the Children of the Sun—he certainly is in the line of descent—and if he usurped the place of Laki Tenganan, then it is possible that the creation story presents history through a refracting medium that has distorted the original nature of Laki Tenganan.

The process may have been similar to that of India, where Varuna, originally a sun-god, has been pushed into the background by a war-god, and has lost his solar character. Were it not that other information exists about Varuna, it would not be possible to know that he was originally a sun-god. The case may be the same with Laki Tenganan. Another important tribe of Borneo, the Iban or Sea Dyak, have war-gods as their chief deities.[14] Borneo tribes thus show signs of contact, in the past, with the Hindu caste of the Children of the Sun; their chiefs seem originally to have claimed descent from the sun; their chief deity possibly changed from a sun-god into a vague supreme being with no cult; and war-gods have come into prominence.

The culture-sequence of sun-god and war-god can be established in the Pacific. The Carolines, or at least Ponape, formerly had the Children of the Sun as rulers. Then came invasions, and in Ponape the chief god is Tokata or Taukatau, which name is that of the king of Kusaie-Tokasa— whence came invaders who broke up the former civilization.[15] Another account, that of Christian, says that the Children of the Sun were wiped out by warlike peoples from the south, led by Icho-Kalakai, who became their war-god.[16]

With the exception of San Cristoval, New Britain, New Ireland, the Bismarck Archipelago and New Caledonia, the sun-cult is a thing of the past in Melanesia. It is said formerly to have existed in the southern part of the New Hebrides, representations of the sun having been found on

rocks in Anaiteum.[17] In New Zealand, along with traces of
the Children of the Sun, go certain indications of the former
existence of a sun-cult among the ancestors of the Maori,
who mention a sacred mountain in their homeland, which
is the abode of the Bird of the Sun, so well-known in connection with the sun-cult from Egypt to America.[18]

Although Melanesia and Polynesia possess traces of a
former sun-cult, yet most of the important Polynesian gods
are war-gods, who often have demonstrably displaced solar
gods.[19] The original rulers of Tau, that part of Manu'a
where originated the first ruling families of Samoa, were
Children of the Sun. Tagaloa Ui, the son of the Sun and
of Ui, a woman who came from a country that possessed
a sun-cult, had a son Taeotagaloa, whose sister was the wife
of the Tuafiti, that is, the ruler of Fiji.[20] Taeotagaloa married two girls. Each bore a son on the same day, and the
ruling power of the two parts of the island was divided
between them. When the sons had been instituted by Taeotagaloa in their offices, he said to his brother Le Fanonga,
"You stop here in the east and be the war-god of Fitiuta, but
I will go and be the war-god of Le-fale-tolu." [21] Taeotagaloa
was a son of the Sun: he changed himself deliberately into
a war-god. Henceforth the sun-god disappeared from the
active cult, and persists only in tradition and myth. Taeotagaloa was the last god of the sky-world who had intercourse with the Samoans: one authority claims that he was
the first man, and his son the first human king. It is significant that, at the moment when human dynasties are
inaugurated, the beings who previously had been Children
of the Sun became war-gods. It would be worth much to
know exactly what happened at this moment; some important historical event must have occurred to cause this
profound change. For Taeotagaloa evidently was a real
being, in that he is the traditional representative of the
Children of the Sun, who came to Tau of Manu'a in
Samoa to live. These Children of the Sun went back to
the sky, that is, back home, and left the ruling power in

the hands of the Ali'a family, members of which spread to Tahiti, Rarotonga and elsewhere.[22]

Oro, the god of the marae of Opoa in Raiatea, was the chief god of Tahiti and the Leeward Islands, and the kings of Tahiti in their coronation ceremony became his sons. The Tahitians claimed that Oro originated at Opoa, whence his worship spread to the neighboring islands, and throughout the Paumotu group. He was the great god of war in Eastern Polynesia,[23] and is equated to Rongo, the great god of Mangaia in the Hervey Group.[24] Rongo was the twin brother of Tangaroa in Mangaia.[25] Tangaroa was the elder and was connected with the sky. He is identical with Tangaloa of Samoa, and thus is really a sun-god. Rongo, on the other hand, is connected with the underworld, where lives the great mother of gods and men. On account of the favoritism shown for Rongo by his mother, Tangaroa went to Rarotonga and settled there, leaving Rongo in possession in Mangaia. So the sky-god has retired, leaving the war-god in possession.

The first king of Mangaia, where Rongo dispossessed Tangaroa, was Rangi, who is said to have come from Savai'i, a name of one of the islands of the Samoan group. Since Savai'i occurs so often in Polynesian tradition, and in connection with widely separated places, it is well not to rely on this. But Savai'i in Samoa is so closely connected with the underworld that Rongo, the god of war, whose son Rangi was the first king of Mangaia, might well, together with his son Rangi, be connected with it. The picture is completed by finding that, in Rarotonga, the island to which went Tangaroa, when disgusted with the favoritism shown to Rongo, the ruling family was founded by Kariki from Manu'a in Samoa, who was descended from the sky-gods. Thus the place with sky-gods is ruled over by people claiming descent from a sky-god, in fact, from the sun; while a place with a war-god, who rules in the underworld, has a king who comes from a place closely connected with the underworld, which in the case of the Samoan Savai'i, was ruled by families claiming descent from Manu'a, where the sun-god had changed into a war-god.

Behind all this mythology, therefore, a political revolution is being accomplished. The Children of the Sun have vanished, and their place is taken by other rulers; and the sun-gods give way to war-gods.[26] Thus it is natural to find that, as in New Zealand, all male children are dedicated to the war-god.[27]

The earliest great god of North America was the sun-god, who, in certain parts, reigned supreme to the end. But in Mexico he became partly superseded, but not so much as in Polynesia. Just before the arrival of Europeans, the Aztecs came from the north and seized power in Mexico. They differed in culture from the sedentary agriculturists whom they conquered, and this difference is shown in their pantheon. They had a war-god, the protector and leader of the tribe, who had come with them on their wanderings, named Huitzilopochtli. According to one account Huitzilopochtli was a deified man. It is said that when pushing their way to Mexico, the Aztecs had a leader named Huitziton, who, one night, was translated to the sky and presented to the god Tezauhteotl, the frightful god, who had the form of a horrible dragon. The god welcomed him, and thanked him for governing his people; and, saying that it was high time he was deified, told him to go to earth and tell the people of his impending departure, and to say that his skull and bones would be left with them for protection and consultation. This new deity was called Huitzilopochtli, for the Aztec thought that he was seated on the left hand of Tezcatlipoca. They took his relics with them to Mexico, whither he is said to have guided them. He directed the manner of sacrifice that he wished; for, some priests who had offended him having been found one morning with their breasts cut open and their hearts pulled out, this was adopted as the common mode of sacrifice. Thus in yet another culture-sequence does a war-god supersede a sun-god.

The Zuñi Indians of the Pueblo region afford a remarkable instance of the transition from a sun-god to a war-god. They are formed of the amalgamation of two peoples: a branch that probably descended from the old cliff dwellers, the people of the archaic civilization; and a branch from the west or southwest, less advanced in culture, who did not cultivate the soil to any extent before their arrival in Zuñi-land, who became the dominant branch of the tribe.[28]

The Zuñi have a long creation myth, which, according to Cushing, is that of the later and less civilized part of the nation. It is to the effect that the All-Father Father created himself as the Sun, "whom we hold to be our father." With his appearance came the water and the sea. With his substance of flesh outdrawn from the surface of his person, the sun-father formed the seed-stuff of twain worlds, impregnating therewith the great waters, and lo! in the heat of his light those waters of the sea grew green and scums rose upon them, waxing wide and weighty until, behold, they became Awitelin Teita, the "Four-fold containing Mother Earth," and Apoyan Tachu, the "All-covering Father Sky." These produced all life in the four-fold womb of the Earth. The earth-mother pushed apart from the sun-father, and man took form in the lowest cave-womb. Then a being called "the all-sacred master" appeared in the waters and arose to ask the All-Father for deliverance. The sun-father impregnated a foam-cap with his rays and incubated it, so that it finally gave birth to twins, the Beloved Preceder and the Beloved Follower, to whom the sun-father gave knowledge and leadership over men.[29]

With their magic knives the twins cleft asunder the Mountain of Generation, and went beneath into the underworld, to their subjects.[30] When they got on the earth they at once set out to find the "middle," the navel of the earth, where they should make their permanent settlement. It was in those days that war began. "At times they met people who had gone before, thus learning much of ways of war, for in the fierceness that had entered their hearts with fear, they deemed it not well, neither liked they to look upon strangers peacefully." [31] Finally, they met the dew-people, who claimed to be their elder brothers, and the two groups joined company.[32] After several stays in different places, "they sought more often than ever to war with all strangers (whereby they became still more changed in spirit)."

The twin Children of the Sun, well aware of the temper of the people, changed also in spirit. They founded the Society of the Knife, "the stout warriors of the Twain."

> "Of blood we have tasted the hunger,
> Henceforth by the power of war,
> And the hazard of omens and dance,
> Shall we open the ways for our people
> And guide them in search of the middle.
> And our names shall be known as the Twain
> Who hold the high places of Earth.
>
> . . . . . .
> Come forth, ye war-men of the knife,
>
> . . . . . .
> Our chosen, the priests of the bow.
>
> . . . . . .
> Ye shall changed be forever,
> The foot-rests of eagles
> And signs of our order." [33]

The twins were "strong now with the full strength of evil. . . . Twain children of terror and magic were they." [34] Finally, their wanderings ended, and they met the black people of the high buildings, their elder brethren, and amalgamated with them.[35]

This story, to my mind, is one of the most remarkable ever recorded. It is a piece of social psychology beyond price, showing, as it does, the change of behavior in a people as the result of warfare, and the consequent change in their gods. It is remarkable that the Zuñi priests should so accurately have analyzed the causes of this change of temper, and have recorded them so faithfully. It has already been claimed that a continuity exists between the archaic civilization and those that followed. In this case the signs of such a continuity are clear. A people begins with the Children of the Sun as their culture-heroes, the twain beloved, and ends with them in the guise of war-gods.

In the Mound area the sun-cult existed universally, and, as has been seen, the Children of the Sun were ruling over some tribes in post-Columbian times. But those tribes who got horses from the Spaniards, and went across the Mississippi after the buffalo, suffered many transformations in their material culture. Their religious and social organization also was much altered. The process varied with the tribes, so, in comparing the Plains Indians with those of the Mound area, it will be well to begin with the most extreme example. The great Siouan family of the Plains was split into several divisions. One of them, the Omaha, which possesses traditions of movement across the Mississippi from the eastern States, has lost much of its old culture. The tribe has two divisions, each of which plays an important part in the communal life. One half possesses the rites that appertain to the relationship between the individual and the cosmic powers, while the other has those that are more utilitarian, and those that pertain to war. In the course of the wanderings of the tribe, most of the first set of rites have disappeared, while the practical ones are retained. They now have no sacred chiefs, and the only approach to a god is the thunder being, so closely connected with war, who is in the sky, and is sometimes addressed as Grandfather. Certain ceremonies are performed for each individual, such as the Introduction of the Child to the Cosmos; Turning the Child; and the Consecration of the Boy to the Thunder, that is, to the war-god, who was invoked by the warriors.[36] No trace exists of the sun-cult among the Omaha, and no Children of the Sun rule over them.[37]

Evidence that the Siouan family once had the sun-cult is afforded by the fact that the chief deity of the Mandan, "The Lord of Life," is said to live in the sun.[38] It is important to note that the Mandan approximate closest in culture to the people of the eastern States, for they have retained maize cultivation to a considerable degree, and have not neglected it like the Omaha and others. Certain other cultural features also show them to be nearer to the archaic civilization than the Omaha, who have lost so much while wandering across the Mississippi. The old sun-cult has also not entirely died out among the Hidatsa, Tciwere, Winnebago and other Siouan tribes.

In North America, therefore, historical events have caused certain tribes to lose the sun-cult that their ancestors possessed. Thus the culture-sequence of the Indian tribes is similar to that of the rest of the region, namely, from sun-god to war-god.

This survey shows that the peoples who followed the archaic civilization, or were derived from it, in any spot, differ considerably from those of the archaic civilization, not only in material culture, in the absence of stone-working, irrigation and so forth, but in other ways; for they have often replaced sun-gods by war-gods; and also lack a ruling class of Children of the Sun.

The widespread existence of remains of the archaic civilization in places occupied by communities not capable of their construction shows that there must be a profound difference between the two cultural phases. There is every reason to believe that the later comers were intellectually equal to the peoples of the archaic civilization: they simply lacked the necessary organization. Why was that?

The answer to this question apparently lies partly in the fact that the later comers were more warlike than the peoples of the archaic civilization. In the days of the archaic civilization wars were not frequent, and time and energy were available for great works. But the later communities became educated in war, and gave up constructive work in favor of domination.

It is an error, as profound as it is universal, to think that men in the food-gathering stage were given to fighting. All the available facts go to show that the food-gathering stage of history must have been one of perfect peace. The study of the artifacts of the Palæolithic age fails to reveal any definite signs of human warfare. A critical analysis of the industry of this age in its various phases shows that the minds of the people were intent on their food supply and on art, which, itself, was probably connected with the food supply; and that the various inventions made in their flint industry were improvements in implements for preparing food, and in modeling tools and other means of exercising their artistic capacities, which were considerable. Such matters are, however, outside the scope of this book, for the great bulk of these remains are in Europe. Some are in India and Tasmania, and none of them indicate warlike activities.

The best evidence of the peaceful tendencies of early man is provided by existing food gathering communities in various parts of the region. In another place I have collected the descriptions of the early food-gathering communities in all parts of the world, and the unanimous testimony of the authorities leaves no room to doubt that these peoples are peaceful, and entirely lacking in any cruel mode of behavior.[39]

The coming of the archaic civilization into the outlying regions of the earth therefore meant the beginning of war. But only in the later phases did war become serious. The people of the archaic civilization were comparatively peaceful, as the following accounts show.

Professor Breasted describes the Egyptians as "usually unwarlike . . . naturally peaceful."[40] They became warlike as a consequence of the invasion, about 1688 B.C., of the Hyksos, who dominated the country for some time, but were ultimately driven out. "It was under the Hyksos that the conservatism of millennia was broken up in the Nile Valley. The Egyptians learned aggressive war for the first time, and introduced a well-organized military system, including the chariotry, which the importation of the horse by the Hyksos now enabled them to do. Egypt was transformed into a military empire. In the struggle with the Hyksos and with each other, the old feudal families perished, or were absorbed among the partisans of the dominant Theban family, from which the imperial line sprang. The great Pharaohs of the Eighteenth Dynasty thus became Emperors, conquering and ruling from Northern Syria and the upper Euphrates, to the fourth cataract of the Nile on the south." In the earliest phases of Egyptian history, the king had no regular army: each nome had its militia, commanded by civilians. There was no caste of officers. In case of serious war the militias were grouped together as well as possible and put under a leader chosen from the officials. "As the local governors commanded the militia of the nomes, they held the sources of the Pharaohs' dubious military strength in their own hands." [41]

In Babylonia the sequence in deities is that of Tammuz-Shamash-Ashur. No signs exist of warfare in connection with Tammuz; his attributes are the reverse of pugnacious or cruel. In connection with the sky-gods signs exist of war. But the Assyrians were extremely warlike, as is shown by the following statement: "The Assyrian was even more than most of the empires of antiquity a well-organized fighting machine, and, as all the statements about Ashur occur in inscriptions written after the era of conquest began, they necessarily represent Ashur as a god of war." [42] They thus differed entirely from the Sumerians and Egyptians. The story of Egypt, Babylonia and Assyria is thus one of education in warfare, and in Mesopotamia, along with this change in behavior, went a change in the ruling families, and in the gods connected with those families.

In India, as elsewhere, the old civilization succumbed to the onslaughts of conquerors who added but little to the cultural heritage of the country. India owes most of its civilization to people who were more peaceful than their conquerors. The Dravidian peoples were not warlike in the same way as the Aryans: they were agricultural, and lacked that element of mobility so characteristic of the great war rior peoples of history. Beyond doubt the break-up of civilization in India was due to the incursions of warlike peoples. Otherwise there appears to be no reason why this civilization should not have persisted indefinitely.

In Cambodia the downfall of the great Khmer civilization, of Dravidian origin, was due to the irruption of the Tai-Shan peoples from Yunnan, with a much inferior civilization but a more warlike behavior.[43]

Although the States of Southern Celebes have always possessed a military organization, the heads of which were princes of the royal blood, yet the warfare seems to have been of a half-hearted sort. These States had no real armies, which seems to suggest that only officers existed. "It is evident from this that the warfare must have been of a very different type from that of Europe." [44] The military organization is thus directly similar to that of ancient Egypt, being of the nature of a militia, and not a professional army, such as exist in later civilizations in Indonesia and elsewhere.

The great civilization in the Carolines owes its downfall to warlike invasions. It is said, in one set of traditions, that Yap was invaded by warriors, so that the people fled to Ponape. Then came a great fleet from Koto (?Kusaie) under a certain Ijokalakal, which captured Ponape; after this the old customs began to die out. Another tradition shows how the break-up of a community can be due to internal causes. Formerly, it is said, a single king ruled over Ponape. He lived at Metalanim at a place called Pankatara. This king sent his nobles to rule the provinces, and in time they became independent, his power was undermined, and probably wars between the different governors became frequent.[45]

If culture-heroes, who visit food-gatherers and civilize them, are representatives of the archaic civilization, and if the food-gatherers were peaceful before their arrival, it follows that peoples with culture-hero traditions would probably state that they got their warlike habits from these strangers. This is expressly so claimed in British New

Guinea. Oa Rove Marai, the culture-hero of the Mekeo people, having quarreled with the people of some other village, sent for the Mekeo people, gave them spears and black palmwood clubs, and sent battle, theft and adultery among them, and sorcerers to kill people. Thus death came among them.[46]

Similar traditions exist in Australia. For example, the great being of the Kurnai, Mungan-ngaua, is said to have given the people their weapons: "They are told that long ago he lived on the earth, and taught the Kurnai of that time to make implements, nets, canoes, weapons—in fact, everything that they know." [47]

Evidence exists with regard to the former peaceful nature of Oceania. With regard to the general question, I venture to quote the words of Mr. A. N. Hocart. He says: "My belief is that a highly civilized people with a theory of kingship akin to the Egyptians and of a peaceable nature occupied the South Sea Islands (with the possible exception of peaceful aborigines in the interior of the larger islands).[48] They were gradually pushed back towards the East by various peoples with whom warfare was a religious function; and who consequently were constantly fighting and killing. I should not like to say that the original civilized inhabitants never did fight, but they certainly did not make fighting a regular practice." He refers to the fact that the Tongans have traditions of the time when wars were not, and goes on to say, "Wars, or at least frequent wars, were certainly imported into Tonga from Fiji. In Fiji one can almost see the war-gods moving East."

The Tongan tradition is recorded by Mariner. "At the time when Captain Cook was at these islands the habits of war were little known to the natives; the only quarrels in which they had at that time been engaged were among the inhabitants of the Fiji Islands. . . . The bows and arrows which before that period had been in use among the people of Tonga were of a weaker kind, and fitted rather for sport than war—for the purpose of shooting rats, birds,

etc. From the fierce and warlike people of (Fiji) . . . however, they speedily learned to construct bows and arrows of
a much more martial and formidable nature; and soon became acquainted with a better form of the spear, and a
superior method of holding and throwing that weapon. They
also initiated them by degrees in the practice of painting their
faces, and the use of a peculiar head-dress in time of war,
giving them a fierce appearance, calculated to strike terror
into the minds of their enemies. These martial improvements
were in their progress at the time of Captain Cook's arrival,
but not in general practice, for having few or no civil dis-
sensions among themselves, the knowledge of these things
was confined principally to certain young chiefs and their
adherents, who had been to the Fiji Islands." [49]

The Fijians themselves seem originally to have been peaceful. "The ancient legends describe a peaceful immigration
of a few half-shipwrecked and forlorn people. . . . And so
far from being an entrance at that early period of a victorious host, it is not till long after that any serious war is
even hinted at; not, indeed, till several tribes had broken
away from the original stock and become independent."
The author quoted is confident that war on a considerable
scale is comparatively recent in Fiji, and that the introduction of firearms has had much to do with it. [50]

Manu'a, the earliest settlement of Samoa, was a land of
peace, and was neutral in intertribal wars. [51]

In Eastern Polynesia former times seem to have been
peaceful, and chiefs and their followers from all directions
assembled at Raiatea in Tahiti for certain ceremonies. This
delightful condition of affairs broke up because of quarrels
among the priests in charge of the ceremonies, and wars,
murders and strife ensued. [52] This is substantiated by the
traditions of the people of Hawaii, which state that the
Children of the Sun formerly lived in Tahiti and Hawaii.
In those days life was more peaceful, and a race of heroes,
probably such as the Eyeball of the Sun, the children of the
gods, ruled by subtlety and skill, and went to other islands

for courtship and barter. Then came a time when these chiefs, having to protect their property against their fellow-chiefs, gave up these long voyages: "Thus constantly in jeopardy from each other, sharpening, too, their observation of what lay directly about them and of the rational way to get on in life, they accepted the limits of a man's power and prayed to the gods, who were their great ancestors, for gifts beyond their reach." [53]

In later times warfare was not universal in Polynesia. For example, the people of Bowditch Island, who seem to have preserved much of the archaic civilization, were quiet and rarely fought.[54] Similarly the people of Funafiti in the Gilberts and those of Tikopia are described as peaceful. On the other hand, in Penrhyn Island, where are ruins of the archaic civilization far beyond the capacity of the present population, fighting is incessant. The ancestors of the people came from Rarotonga, like those of the Maori.[55]

Peace reigned in Mangaia in the days of Rangi, the son of Rongo, the war-god. The art of war is said to have been taught the people by denizens of the underworld,[56] that is, by followers of Rongo. It is also said that the Mangaians owe the development of their warfare to Tongans, who brought ironwood with them—so useful for weapons.[57] So the Tongans handed on what they had learned from Fiji.

The Maori found, in New Zealand, peoples with a civilization that seems to have been, in some respects, superior to theirs in material culture. These people were peaceful.[58] The cultural decadence of the Maori themselves is ascribed to their fighting habits. "In the centuries immediately after the first immigration all evidence points to the existence of large States, which occasionally were subject to one common head. There seems also to have been a religious center. This was the period of the national prosperity of the Maoris, when their workmanship also attained its highest perfection. Tasman alone saw in 1642 large and splendid double canoes in use among them; such canoes the Maori of the eighteenth century were no longer able to build. The decadence was universal. The ancient kingdoms broke up into small communities of bold incendiaries and robbers, who recognized no political center, but were engaged in fierce feud, one against another. . . . The national character, always inclined to pride and tyranny, ended by becoming more and more bloodthirsty, revengeful and cruel." [59] The Moriori of the Chatham Islands, the descendants of those driven out of New Zealand by the Maori, were peaceful. Their laws forbade killing, and they said that all fighting had been prohibited in the days of their ancestor Nunuku. They formerly used stone axes as weapons, but latterly had only a pole, 8 to 10 ft. long, for fighting.[60]

The evidence from the Pacific thus entirely bears out the contention of Mr. Hocart. Where culture-sequences can be established, it is found that the earlier phase was the more peaceful. The break-up of Polynesian society can now readily be understood. When communities give up their peaceful habits and take to fighting on a large scale, attention is diverted from one occupation to another. In the Pacific, the rise of warfare coincides with the degeneration of culture in the arts and crafts. It is thus legitimate to look upon warfare not, as many do, as a sign of strength, but of decay, from the standpoint of material culture.

The same story is told in America. The earliest known civilization, that of the Maya, shows signs of being comparatively peaceful.[61] The early beliefs of the Maya depict as the principal subject, a human figure, the divine ruler or priest, splendidly clad with the emblems of civil and religious authority. At Palenque, and elsewhere, religious ceremonies, sacrifices, self-torture, are depicted. Curiously enough, the more northerly Maya cities, which are of later date, contain traces of war. "At some of the northern cities the principal figures stand on the backs of crouched human beings who have been identified as captives, and at Piedras Negras captives, bound with ropes and stripped of all clothing and ornaments, appear huddled together before a ruler seated upon a throne, with attendants standing on either side; or, again, an elaborately dressed ruler with spear in hand and an attendant standing behind him faces kneeling captives or warriors, also armed with spears. These two monuments . . . have been interpreted, and probably correctly, as records of specific conquests, the captives representing the alien rulers, cities or tribes with their corresponding nemaglyphs on their shoulders or thighs. But at best these are only sporadic cases, and an overwhelming majority of the Old Empire sculptures portray religious ceremonies, deities, rulers and priests." [62] While the Maya in the center were living in a profound peace, those on the outskirts evidently fought with the surrounding tribes, which, on the hypothesis based on the study of the distribution of civilization of various stages, have been derived from them. That is to say, if it be granted that the Maya first settled peacefully among unwarlike food-gatherers, they brought with them something in their social and political organization that proved their ruin; that is to say, they ultimately produced warfare. This hardening process is at work in the later Maya settlements of Yucatan, where a certain ruling family, descended from the sacred priest-king of the early period, the Cocomes, evidently went the way of other ruling families. They ruled at Mayapan in Yucatan; and at the time when certain convulsions were taking place, "it would appear that they had begun to exercise a closer control over their vassals. To support the harsher methods which they introduced they commenced to employ the services of mercenaries, 'Mexicans,' recruited in Tabasco and Xilxicalance, and by their aid levied tribute upon the other members of the league to an extent which the latter were not prepared to suffer." [63] Thus a family, claiming descent from Kukulcan, a Son of the Sun, began to take on the aspect of a typical warrior aristocracy. The ruling class of Chichen-Itza, another Maya settlement in Yucatan, also constituted a warrior caste.[64]

So, in the case of the Maya, the story is one of education in warfare. The earliest cities show no trace of fighting;

then, on the outskirts, the later cities were engaged in war. The ruling class of the later cities probably were Children of the Sun. When the Maya left Guatemala and went to Yucatan, their rulers tended to become definitely warlike and to behave cruelly. Presumably, like the ancient Egyptians, they were educated in war. The growing aggression of the rulers of Mayapan seems itself to have caused much turmoil in Yucatan. Thus the phenomenon of the increasing warfare will probably find its explanation in that of the change of behavior of the ruling classes.

The warlike activities of Mexico in the time of the Aztecs are well known. According to Bandelier, speaking of the Aztecs: "War, at first *defensive,* afterwards offensive, became the life of the tribe." [65] The later civilizations certainly far surpassed, in this respect, the early civilization of the Maya. So, not only did the Maya become more warlike, but their successors, who surpassed them, went through the same process of education.

The hypothesis adopted with regard to North America was that the civilization of that region can be regarded as a unity, derived ultimately from Mexico and the south. The cultivation of maize, pottery making, the working of metals, the use of pearls and manufacture of polished stone implements, and the tales of culture-heroes, have been adduced as evidence of this unity. If it be true that the practice of warfare has been derived from the archaic civilization, that the people who brought in maize-cultivation to the food-gatherers also turned them into fighters, it will not be surprising to find further evidence of unity of culture. This evidence is forthcoming.

In North America in post-Columbian times the military organizations of the various tribes were similar. According to the Huguenot narratives, the tribes of North Florida and the adjacent region had a military system and marching order almost as exact as that of a modern civilized nation, the various grades of rank being distinguished by specific titles. The Indians who went into the Plains after the buffalo had military organizations so similar as to suggest a common origin.[66] Thus once again signs of unity run through the civilization of North America.

The post-Columbian Indians seem to have been more warlike than their predecessors for: "From what we know of the Indian character, there is every reason to believe that the non-sanguinary sun-worshiping tribes were conquered and rudely driven off" [67] by the ancestors of the post-Columbian Indians. In their place are warlike tribes such as the Iroquois, with war-gods as their chief deities.[68] This agrees with the Huron and Wyandot tradition that the sky-world, the place associated with the people of the archaic civilization, was peaceful.[69] Several of the Plains tribes were very warlike, especially the Pawnee, for whom war was business and pleasure. By it they amassed wealth, and gained credit and renown. They captured all the surrounding tribes, and claimed to hold the country from the Missouri to the Rockies, and from the Nebraska southwards to the Arkansas or the Canadian River.[70] They had given up the sun-god, which is shown by the fact that they came out of the southwest, where the sun-cult was universal; and also by the fact that the Skidi, a branch of the tribe, still retain some sort of sun-cult, although, even in this case, the sun is unimportant.[71]

The study of culture-sequences has led to the generalization that, in all parts of the region, the earlier civilization seems to be the more peaceful. The archaic civilization has spread out into countries inhabited by peaceful food-gatherers, and the earliest settlements were probably also peaceful, which accords with their apparent industrial nature. Men engaged in mining for gold would be more interested in that than in fighting. Moreover, such settlements would be sparse; India, for example, with the exception of Bellary, and one or two other places, does not seem to have possessed any great concentration of population in those early days, so that a pretext for warfare would hardly exist.

One fact points to warfare in this period—the building of

fortifications. What, it may be asked, would be the aim of such fortifications if no warlike peoples were feared? This difficulty tends to ignore the probable nature of these settlements. They were, according to the hypothesis, those of peoples with a fairly high degree of civilization, of whose provenance it will be necessary later to inquire. If it be assumed that they came from some country where war had already begun, where the building of fortresses was a habit, then, to account for the fortifications, it is only necessary to invoke the innate tendency for settlers to reproduce the culture of their homeland. Perhaps an instance from outside the region will help. The great ruins of Zimbabwe, south of the Zambesi, built by men working the goldfields, are fortresses. Yet, beyond doubt, they were built without reason. The warlike Bantu had not yet swarmed down from the north: the only possible inhabitants of the country were the peaceful Bushmen and Hottentots. This makes these great fortresses simply ridiculous. So, in places such as India, the habit of living on hilltops may have been brought by the people of the archaic civilization from their homes, and thus would have no reference to the conditions of the countries where they lived. It is further necessary to add that the more warlike peoples of the earth have not usually been given to the making of fortifications, and this makes the peaceful nature of the people of the archaic civilization more probable. At the same time these people must have had some warfare, and the habit of fighting must have developed. It must be remembered that the archaic civilization was based on agriculture, which implies a steady increase of population. A new world was created wherever these people settled; food-gathering gave place to food-producing, and new peoples came into being. In this way the chances of war must have increased in several ways.

The surveys of this chapter have shown that the loss of the sun-cult and of the Children of the Sun and the appearance in their place of warrior chiefs and war-gods, has been accompanied by an actual change in the behavior of peoples. This is the first example yet adduced of the relationship between various elements of civilization: a change in the ruling class is accompanied by a change in the deities of the community, and also by a change in the behavior of the community. Evidently one change caused the others. This raises one of the ultimate problems of social psychology, that of the interrelationship of institution and behavior in society. As the general argument proceeds, it will repeatedly be seen how close is this interrelationship. Once it is realized, it is obvious that the ultimate problem of all is that of explaining, in psychological terms, the process of all that is now being described in historical terms. Such a problem must be left on one side until the historical process is itself clear enough to make it possible to attempt its solution.

The aboriginal inhabitants of the region were peaceful food-gatherers with no social organization, wandering about in family groups. Then there came into existence at various points, India, Cambodia, Indonesia, the Carolines, Polynesia, Mexico and elsewhere, an advanced civilization based on irrigation, located near sources of wealth of various sorts, and characterized by stone-working and other arts and crafts. Some of these early settlements were obviously only there for the purpose of mining, and no attempt was made to colonize the country. But, in others, great cities sprang up, that must have numbered their populations by tens of thousands. These early civilizations were ruled over by divine kings, usually claiming descent from the sun. This archaic civilization gave rise to others, less advanced in the arts and crafts, but more warlike, with war-gods, which ultimately destroyed it. The rulers of these later communities were not divine beings.

The next task is that of determining what other circumstances attended this remarkable transformation. The archaic civilization contained some element destined to destroy it, in spite of its achievements in all parts of the world; it was rotten somewhere. This archaic civilization has exercised a tremendous influence upon all that followed;

even that of Western Europe is deeply rooted in it. Maybe that some of the problems that face us at the present day will find their solution in the determination of the reasons that brought to ruins this civilization that was so rich in material culture.

NOTES

1 Langdon, i, p. 31.
2 Barton, p. 221; Jastrow.
3 *Ibid.*, p. 224 *e.s.*
4 By "Aryans" is meant "peoples speaking Aryan languages." Similarly with "Dravidians" and "Austronesians."
5 Barnett, p. 22.
6 *Ibid.*, p. 18; Barth, p. 18.
7 Hose and McDougall, ii, p. 5.
8 *Ibid.*, ii, pp. 6-7.
9 *Ibid.*, ii, p. 5. Toh Bulu means "feather-spirit" or "spirit of feathers" (ii, p. 18).
10 *Ibid.*, ii, p. 10.
11 *Ibid.*, ii, p. 137.
12 *Ibid.*, ii, p. 138.
13 *Ibid.*, ii, p. 85.
14 *Ibid.*, ii, p. 85.
15 Hahl, i.
16 Christian, iv, p. 84.
17 Rivers, x, xii.
18 Best, x.
19 Formander mentions a former sun-cult in Tupai of the Society Group (44, n. 2).
20 Pratt, ii, p. 25.
21 *Ibid.*, ii, pp. 294-5. Le Fanonga and his brothers went to Upolu and became presiding deities (Stair, ii, p. 49).
22 From the time of disappearance of the Tagaloa family, Samoan chiefs are called Tui, a title similar to that found in Fiji and Tonga. These Tui chiefs are really war chiefs, for they take no part in the administration of the state.
23 Gill, i, p. 14.
24 *Ibid.*, ii, p. 635.
25 *Ibid.*, iv, pp. 10-11.
26 In Mangaia a king, Tiaio, became a war-god. The Mautara, a priestly tribe, gave up their ancient divinity, Tane, in favor of this new god. The greatness of Tiaio marks the political supremacy of that warlike clan, which is of recent origin (Gill, i, p. 30).
27 Best, vi, p. 456; xi, p. 128.
28 Cushing, ii, pp. 342-3.
29 *Ibid.*, pp. 379, 381-2.
30 *Ibid.*, pp. 382-3.
31 *Ibid.*, ii, p. 390.

[32] *Ibid.*, pp. 397-8.
[33] *Ibid.*, pp. 417-9.
[34] *Ibid.*, ii, pp. 422-3.
[35] *Ibid.*, p. 426.
[36] Fletcher and La Flesche, pp. 195, 299, 200, 382.
[37] J. O. Dorsey, ii, p. 430 *e.s.*
[38] *Ibid.*, pp. 506, 507.
[39] Perry, vi.
[40] Breasted, iii, pp. 193, 319.
[41] *Ibid.*, iii, pp. 19, 82.
[42] Barton, p. 221.
[43] Haddon, ii, pp. 30-2.
[44] Bakkers, iv, p. 80.
[45] Hahl, i.
[46] Seligman, i, p. 308.
[47] Howitt, p. 493.
[48] Cf. F. Kramer, i, p. 394, who says that doubtless in the earliest times peace reigned over Fiji, Samoa and Tonga and Western Polynesia in general. The quotation from Mr. Hocart is from a letter.
[49] Mariner, p. 67.
[50] Deane, p. 229.
[51] Ella, iii, p. 155.
[52] P. Smith, v.
[53] Beckwith, p. 303.
[54] Turner, p. 268.
[55] P. Smith, i, p. 96.
[56] Gill, i, p. 130.
[57] *Ibid.*, p. 288.
[58] Gudgeon, p. 209.
[59] Weule, p. 333.
[60] Shand, p. 76 *e.s.*
[61] Joyce, ii, pp. 364-5.
[62] Morley, ii, pp. 443-4.
[63] Joyce, ii, p. 205.
[64] Spence, p. 155.
[65] Bandelier, p. 98.
[66] Hand-Book: Art, Military Organization.
[67] Schoolcraft, v, p. 203.
[68] Tylor, ii, p. 308.
[69] Barbeau, i, p. 289; see Chapter 13 for sky-world.
[70] Grinnell, pp. 303, 306.
[71] *Ibid.*, p. 224; Wissler, iii, pp. 335, 337.

LAW AND ANTHROPOLOGY *

By HUNTINGTON CAIRNS

It is the object of this essay to examine the relationship
between anthropology and law and to show the importance
of this relationship. Within the past few years there has
been in the social sciences a marked trend towards synthesis,
and the idea of the social philosophers of the latter part
of the nineteenth century that the social studies were divided
by firm boundaries is regarded now as untrue. Formerly, and
to a considerable extent to-day, the efforts of social scientists
have been directed towards the discovery of a method of
investigation whose employment in the field of the social
sciences would lead to advances, such as have followed the
use of the inductive method in the field of the natural
sciences. Attempts so far to apply the inductive method to
research in the social sciences have not been marked by success; in addition, the question of the employment of the
inductive method has been complicated by the fact that investigators working in the field of the natural sciences have
awakened to the validity of Hume's criticism of this method
of research.[1] Thus, Mr. Bertrand Russell has recently
declared that the inductive method "is as indefensible intellectually as the purely deductive method of the Middle
Ages." [2] This raises the problem, the solution of which is
far from settled, of whether the inductive method should
continue to be employed even in the natural sciences. Thus
the social scientists in facing the problem of method have
been confronted with a task of the greatest complexity; no
Bacon, nor even an Aristotle, has yet appeared to contribute

* This article was first published with some minor changes in the
Columbia Law Review, January, 1931. Thanks are due to the Board of
Editors of this journal for their courteous permission to reprint.

331

his energy and vision to the solution of this problem. No method comparable to either the deductive or the inductive method has been developed for research in this field. A resulting stagnation of the social sciences has been averted by the realization at this stage of the need for coördination and synthesis of the data they have to offer; for not only have the natural sciences, as they have extended their frontiers, been found to overlap one another's territory, but the social sciences also have been found to be closely related and interdependent.

Attempts at synthesis in the past have revealed that it is an approach which must be handled with the utmost caution. Too often it leads to facile generalizations which have no scientific validity and to analogies which retard rather than advance the development of thought. Biology, for example, has been levied upon by political scientists for numerous analogies and concepts, and the foremost generalization born of the synthesis of these departments was the idea that the state was an organism. In the hands of Spencer this metaphor received its most complete expression and the analogies he drew, such as that of nerves paralleling arteries as telegraph wires parallel railroad tracks, were numerous and bizarre.[3] Nevertheless, for all the thought which has been lavished upon it, the metaphor has contributed nothing to our knowledge of the nature of the state but has instead led thinkers to false conceptions which have vitiated large portions of their work. Social scientists are apt to find in related fields resemblances which interpret without clarifying, and methods which work swiftly but only as a substitute for thought. Thus psychoanalysis, the most valuable instrument of psychological research yet devised, in the hands of skillful biographers and historians has revealed new depths of personality in such difficult figures, for instance, as Luther and Leonardo da Vinci,[4] but its uncritical use by psychologists and sociologists has produced sonorous and flexible explanations of social phenomena which, if examined, are meaningless. When there are discoveries in one field of science an effort is at once made to apply these discoveries to other fields without inquiring in what manner the application will lead to fruitful ends or wherein lies their real applicability. Evolution after 1859 became the shibboleth by which practically all problems were resolved; to-day it is the concepts of the new physics which, although of the greatest importance to scientists in every field, are likewise the subject of much unsound thinking. Subjects, however, such as sociology and history, anthropology and religion, political science and law so often meet on common ground that their synthesis along certain lines is natural and valuable.

Cultural anthropology was born in the latter half of the nineteenth century and to a few jurists of that time it was at once clear that a profitable field of research for the law had been opened. Sir Henry Maine in England,[5] and A. H. Post[6] and Josef Kohler[7] in Germany were the leaders in explorations into this new territory. Post and Kohler in particular were indefatigable workers in the field of anthropology and even to-day such essays as Kohler's *Zur Urgeschichte der Ehe*[8] possess considerable anthropological importance. Maine, it must be remembered, published his *Ancient Law* in 1861 when there were only a few anthropological works in print which could be of assistance to him, and he seems at that time to have been unaware even of such works as Morgan's *League of the Ho-de-no-san-nee*.[9] It is thus greatly to his credit that he should have turned for light upon juridical problems to early systems of law before the fever for anthropological research had really set in. But after the movement was under way he did not keep pace with it; the torch passed into the hands of Post and Kohler and the other writers whose chief medium of expression was the *Zeitschrift für vergleichende Rechtswissenschaft*. Moreover, J. F. McLennan,[10] a Scottish lawyer and a keen student of anthropology, soon placed his finger on Maine's weakest point—in view of our present knowledge—his patriarchal theory. Nor were Post and Kohler exempt from mistakes, which arose chiefly from the dearth of anthropological knowledge at that time. But what is more important than the errors of these early workers is the fact that the field of inquiry which they uncovered soon ceased to attract the attention of either jurists or anthropologists.[11]

For more than a quarter of a century research in anthropological jurisprudence, save for a few scattered and unrelated inquiries, has been at a standstill. To-day a recrudescence of interest in this field for the sociologist and the anthropologist —if not for the lawyer—appears to be taking place.[12] In a slim but admirable volume, Malinowski[13] has indicated the importance of primitive law for the anthropologist, and Lowie has similarly attempted in two brilliant papers[14] to attract the attention of the lawyer. Primitive law ceased to interest anthropologists, Malinowski has pointed out, because they had an exaggerated idea of its perfection; it also ceased to attract attention because—and mistakenly, as Malinowski has likewise shown—it was apparently easily explained.[15] Recent legal thinkers have neglected the study of the relationship of law and anthropology because in the hands of their nineteenth century predecessors it led to sterile conceptions and a false philosophy of law; the study has also been neglected because of the constant disinclination of jurists to seek help in adjoining fields. Law has been regarded as a subject which contains within itself the seeds of its own growth; but with the movement towards synthesis and the development of a functional attitude in jurisprudence and in anthropology it may well be that these departments by again combining will contribute to each other's advancement.

To-day in both jurisprudence and anthropology there has developed what is termed the functional attitude. This attitude, for jurisprudence at any rate, is closely related in contemporary thought to the instrumentalist or pragmatist movement. In jurisprudence it means simply that the jurist takes account, in Pound's phrase, of law in action as well as of law in books. No longer does the jurist regard law solely as a self-contained system of thought, comparable to mathematics or logic, which can be developed on paper from a few premises to meet all exigencies, as Whitehead and Russell in *Principia Mathematica*[16] developed symbolic logic. In the past the jurist has been content to frame his rules and test them by abstract principles of justice without concerning himself with the test of their applicability. Frequently the rules were unenforceable, absurd, and in practice unjust. From the functional point of view the attempt to frame legal precepts with respect to social interests and needs is more important than their logical or historical coherence on paper. The functional movement has given great vitality to legal thinking and has raised law to the status of social science.[17] In anthropology, Malinowski, who is responsible for the label "functional" in this field, has best stated the aims and principles of the functional method: "This type of theory," he writes, "aims at the explanation of anthropological facts at all levels of development by their function, by the part which they play within the integral part of culture, by the manner in which they are related to each other within the system, and by the way in which this system is related to the physical surroundings. It aims at the understanding of the nature of culture, rather than at conjectural reconstructions of its evolution or of past historical events."[18] Culture from the functional standpoint is regarded not only as dynamic but as an organic whole. Modern anthropology endeavors to study exogamy, totemism and other manifestations of primitive culture not solely with regard to the narrow field which these phases occupy but also to study them in relation to the entire field of social organization. Primitive culture is studied in action, and preconceived assumptions and paper schemes are banished. To-day law and anthropology are in their program one.

In marking out the boundaries of a new subject we are at once perplexed by the multitude of problems which immediately arise. So many questions press for an answer, so many lines of inquiry appear fruitful, that the risk of wan-

dering is great. This risk is no less real even when we are
dealing with a subject, such as the relationship of law and
anthropology, whose development must proceed along restricted lines. Anthropology, for all the achievements to its
credit, has in the hierarchy of thought only recently cast aside
its swaddling clothes and at present it is impossible to discern its ultimate contribution. The simplest criterion by
which to mark the present limits of the subject appears to be:
What discoveries and conclusions of the anthropologist are
of value to the jurist? With the assistance of this criterion
three lines of contact suggest themselves:

> (a) The nature of law;
> (b) Legal history and anthropology;
> (c) Law and anthropology in action.

In attempting to arrive at an understanding of the nature
of law we may first consider what is meant by the term
"law" and whether "law" exists in primitive cultures in the
sense that it is supposed to exist in advanced cultures. Jurists
from the Ancient Greeks to the present day have found it
a notoriously difficult task to define the term "law" and there
exists no definition which is satisfactory to all inquirers. Conceptions of the nature of the state have determined the view
jurists have taken of law and as these conceptions have
changed from time to time the definitions have been modified to meet current theories. It is the sociological theory
of the nature of the state, advanced by Small,[19] MacIver,[20]
Oppenheimer [21] and others, which is to-day one of the corner stones of modern political theory. No longer is political
science under bondage to the lawyers, as Beard [22] once complained, and definitions of law in terms of supreme authority
have been abandoned. The state, from the sociological standpoint, is viewed as a specific association, a product of social
growth and "perhaps the most important of several fundamental types of organs or agencies utilized by society to
insure that collective life shall be more safe, efficient and
progressive." [23] Judge Cardozo, in accord with general so-

ciological thought, has advanced what may be termed a sociological, or functional, definition of law. "A principle or rule of conduct so established as to justify a prediction with reasonable certainty that it will be enforced by the courts if its authority is challenged, is," he holds, "a principle or rule of law." [24] This statement is, of course, not strictly a definition of law. But it suggests a real criterion, as will presently be seen, by which to recognize law in advanced cultures.

It can be laid down, as a beginning, that principles or rules of conduct obtain in both primitive and advanced cultures. In all cultures we are confronted with the task of distinguishing rules of law from other rules of conduct, such as, for example, the rules of conduct regulating the behavior of communicants of the Roman Catholic Church or the rule that a man shall pay a debt incurred at cards. By Cardozo's criterion we are able to distinguish rules of law from other rules of conduct: rules of law are those rules of conduct which we are able to predict will be enforced by the courts. All other rules of conduct in legal theory are simply rules of conduct and nothing more. It is thus apparent that the essential element of the criterion is the element represented by the idea of "a court." Without this element Cardozo's criterion would be of no value, as it would not enable us to distinguish law from other rules of conduct. There is implied in this definition, it is necessary to add, the concept of the state, or, by its criterion, the decrees of the Rota would be law. Within the closed system of the Catholic hierarchy the decrees of the Rota may well be law; but they are not law in the sense we are considering it and it is the addition of the element of the state as the authority creating courts which excludes them. For advanced cultures Cardozo's definition is sufficient: we are able, by the criterion it postulates, to distinguish law from other rules of conduct.

When we attempt to apply this definition in certain primitive communities we discover that it will not work. In many primitive communities throughout the world we find no courts and no agencies for the administration of justice in any way comparable to courts. Justice in a case of violation of criminal rules of conduct is a private matter; redress is obtained by the individual affected, either unaided or with the assistance of his friends or kinsmen. Punishment may take form similar to the injury, or the offender may be killed or beaten, or the crime may be absolved by the payment of a fine.[25] This form of administration of justice is so widespread that two examples will suffice. Among the natives of Eddystone Island strict monogamy prevails and lapses on the part of the man, contrary to the custom in more civilized parts of the world, are regarded with an opprobrium equal to that with which lapses on the part of the woman are regarded. During a visit of Rivers to the Island, a wife discovered that her husband had been guilty of adultery. At once she put a knife into him, inflicting a severe but not a fatal wound. This procedure was regarded as orthodox and natural.[26] Again, the penalty for incest among these natives is death and, the event occurring, any machinery for the determination of guilt or punishment is held to be unnecessary. As soon as the crime is discovered the punishment follows automatically and the kinsmen of the offender take the leading part in its infliction.[27] In the field of primitive civil law, which Malinowski has been the first to discuss adequately, we also find Cardozo's definition to be of little assistance.[28] There exists in the Melanesian community inhabiting the Trobriand Archipelago a system of exchange whereby the villagers on the edge of the lagoon barter their catches of fish for vegetables from inland communities. This system, primarily economic, is conducted with great ceremony. In addition, as Malinowski has been able to show, a definite legal element enters into the arrangement. Fishermen must promptly and in full repay inland traders for the vegetables they receive, and so must the traders pay the fishermen. The dependence of the two communities upon each other for the exchange of food gives to each the weapon for the enforcement of the contract—reciprocity; although, as in civilized communities, the natives attempt, when there is no danger of loss of prestige, to evade their obligations. This system of mutualities, illustrated by the exchange of fish for vegetables, is an integral part of the Melanesian social organization. But it is the ceremonial manner in which certain of these transactions are carried out, and the feeling that the rules of conduct regulating the transactions are binding, that differentiate law in Melanesia from the remaining body of custom. Malinowski, upon these facts, has framed an anthropological definition of law: "Civil law, the positive law governing all the phases of tribal life, consists ... of a body of binding obligations, regarded as a right by one party and acknowledged as a duty by the other, kept in force by a specific mechanism of a reciprocity and publicity inherent in the structure of their society." [29]

Dr. Malinowski's definition, if applied to Melanesian rules of conduct, distinguishes "legal" rules of conduct from "non-legal" rules of conduct. But it is at once apparent that if the definition is applied in advanced cultures it fails to accomplish this purpose. Are we then to conclude that "law" in advanced cultures is something different from "law" in primitive cultures, since neither Cardozo's nor Malinowski's definition, both admirably satisfactory from the point of view of the cultures for which they were framed, is applicable to other and opposed civilizations? Assuming that Melanesian rules of conduct may be divided into two classes, and that Dr. Malinowski is justified from the Melanesian point of view (and it appears that he is) in terming one of those classes "law," then common sense suggests that as "law" in primitive communities apparently fulfills the same social needs that "law" fulfills in advanced cultures, the "law" of both cultures, from a societal standpoint, is functionally identical. But from the point of view of definition this conclusion does not follow. Logically, the element of "the courts" in Cardozo's definition indicates a real and not a verbal distinction; he has, to employ Ogden and Richards' conception, indicated a distinguishing attribute and has not proposed a symbol substitution.[30] If we substitute the "state" for the criterion the "court" our difficulty is not overcome although the definition is broadened without any corresponding loss of definiteness. For anthropologists and political scientists are by no means agreed as to the omnipresence of the state in society. MacIver, who as a political scientist is far removed from the strictly legal approach characteristic of the work of, say, W. W. Willoughby,[31] denies emphatically and with great cogency that the state exists in very rude cultures.[32] Lowie, with equal perspicacity, maintains a contrary position.[33] Unfortunately Lowie nowhere in his study defines exactly what he means by the state; but by implication it is apparent that he has in mind in discussing the state in advanced cultures a conception which would be correctly stated in the following definition of MacIver's: "The state is an association which, acting through law as promulgated by a government endowed to this end with coercive power, maintains within a community territorially demarcated the universal external conditions of social order." [34] This state, Lowie is quite prepared to demonstrate, has no existence in many primitive communities. What he does seek to prove is "that the germs of all possible political development are latent but demonstrable in the ruder cultures" and that a state of some type is everywhere a feature of human society.

The temptation to solve this perplexing problem upon the basis of some alluring hypothesis is almost irresistible. But the history of social theory is too largely a record of generalizations wrung from insufficient facts for us to-day to make similar errors. Anthropology has warned the jurist that his conception of law is perhaps egocentric but it has shown him that with its aid he may be able to work out a conception of law that will be adequate for all social requirements. Two obstacles stand at present in the way of the realization of this task: there is, first, a paucity of known facts concerning the simpler cultures and a lack of agreement among anthropologists with respect to the interpretation of such material as does exist; this is an obstacle which, as anthropological methods are refined, will disappear. There prevails, secondly, confusion with respect to the instrument—linguistics—with which the anthropologist, the jurist or the social scientist must pursue his investigations and through whose medium he must state his conclusions. Superficially, linguistics presents no difficulties; the anthropologist is able to describe what he sees in a primitive community in words that convey meaning, and the judge on the bench is able to sentence a housebreaker to jail without inquiring in any ultimate sense, except from the housebreaker's standpoint, whether he is following a rule of law. But once the social scientist passes from these simple aspects to the realm of theory, linguistics becomes a problem and it is in his struggle with this problem that he is most envious of the symbolism of the mathematician. Euclid may assume that through a point in a plane it is always possible to trace one and only one straight line parallel to a given straight line lying in the plane. Lobatchewski may deny this and assume that an indefinite number of non-intersecting straight lines can be drawn; and Riemann may deny both assumptions and assume that none can be drawn.[35] From these assumptions three geometries can be developed and the conclusions of all three are true within themselves although in conflict with one another. It is not possible to deny, for example, admitting the primary postulates, that in Euclid's geometry the sum of angles of any triangle is always equal to two right angles and that in Lobatchewski's and Riemann's geometries the value of this sum varies with the size of the triangles. Linguistics, which occupies in the social sciences a position analogous to mathematical symbolization in mathematics, is not remotely comparable in definiteness and utility to mathematical symbolization. Aristotle's postulate that man is a social animal is the oldest postulate known to the social sciences, but there is not one word in it upon the meaning of which social scientists can universally agree. It is this basic difficulty and nothing else which led F. H.

Bradley, perhaps the greatest of English philosophers, to remark, "on all questions, if you push me far enough, at present I end in doubts and perplexities." [36] Anthropology as it advances may throw light upon certain basic jural concepts, such as the nature of law, and by enlarging these concepts and giving to them a universal social significance it may also clarify the nature of some of the linguistic difficulties which at present are a barrier to any real advancement in the realm of theory.

When we pass to the question of the bearing of anthropological investigations upon certain aspects of legal history we see at once that in this field a connection between law and anthropology exists. Maitland long ago in a penetrating essay pointed out "that by and by anthropology will have the choice between being history and being nothing." [37] Prehistory, in its investigation of many manifestations of human culture, has accomplished much toward bridging the chasm between anthropology and history but in the field of social organization this chasm still exists. The origins of customs and institutions are irretrievably lost, even beyond the possibility of discovery by the prehistorian. We may know that Neolithic man domesticated sheep, cultivated various farinaceous crops and wore clothing made from the skin of animals, but it is extremely unlikely that we will ever be able to ascertain, except in the most fragmentary fashion—and from the standpoint of theory, valueless—the nature of Neolithic social organization. But anthropology can exhibit to us, in studies of ruder cultures, other forms of the customs and institutions which constitute the social organization of our particular civilization. When the facts of primitive social organization have been collected and compared on a more extensive scale than that with which the anthropologist at present works it may be possible to construct a scheme of social evolution which will be, if not history, at least the best available substitute for history. If to-day we are not warranted even in saying that the primitive customs and institutions which research discloses *may* be the early forms of Western customs and institutions we can at least recognize the value of the study of social manifestations in early societies similar to those which exist in advanced cultures. Upon at least two of the main problems of legal history—property and the family—research in primitive societies may ultimately shed considerable light. It will be unnecessary here to indicate in detail the findings of anthropologists with respect to these two phases of social life. Lowie,[38] Goldenweiser,[39] Rivers,[40] Malinowski,[41] Briffault[42] and others have summarized all that is at present known about these particular manifestations of culture. It will be sufficient for the purposes of this essay to point out the bearing upon law and legal history of the result of some investigations into the primitive nature of property and the family.

When we try to understand the basic ideas underlying property and the family we find that no other subject can compete with anthropology as an aid to their clarification. The wealth and variety of forms anthropology exhibits compel us to define our concepts, if they are to possess validity, from the standpoint of all cultures. Either the definition must work in every community or it is insufficient. To base the definition of a concept upon the necessities and peculiarities of each community, and thus to have many definitions of the same concept, is, in effect, to deny the existence of the concept. Furthermore, if concepts are defined from the standpoint of all cultures social inquiry will be greatly assisted in its efforts towards the realization of an adequate social theory. Holdsworth, for example, states that, "Early law does not trouble itself with complicated theories as to the nature and meaning of ownership and possession. . . . In fact, the earliest known use of the word 'owner' comes from the year 1340; the earliest known use of the word 'ownership' from the year 1583."[43] But he then shows that "the smallest degree of civilization will produce the phenomena of ownership divorced from possession. Owners will lend or deposit or lose their property. The law must lay down some rules as to the rights of owners on the one side, and as to the rights of the bailee or the finder on the other." [44] Anthropologists have shown that some notion of property—whether certain forms are privately or communally owned is a moot question—is everywhere a feature of human culture. The question at once arises how the word "ownership" shall be defined. Malinowski insists that it is "a grave error to use the word ownership with the very definite connotation given to it in our society . . . the term own as we use it is meaningless, when applied to a native society." [45] Lowie rightfully points out, however, that if we are to determine at what level of social development law distinguishes ownership and possession, "we cannot coin a special word for every shade of possessory right as locally defined in the far quarters of the globe. It is far more important to define all such rights conceptually than to devise an infinite series of labels for them." [46] In addition, new meaning will be added to many legal concepts if they are compared with the similar concepts held by the simpler peoples. Seisin, for example, in law means possession. The transference of a freehold interest in land was accompanied by livery of seisin, that is, the donee was put "into possession of the land, but the fact that it had thus been given was evidenced by handing over a stick, a hasp, a ring, a cross, or a knife." [47] This symbolic delivery of the land, known as livery of seisin, was an essential part of the conveyance. Livery of seisin is accounted for by the publicity attendant upon the act which prevented the perpetration of frauds by secret conveyances.[48] Etymologically "being seized" is connected with "seizing," that is, to grasp at, or to take; [49] but Pollock and Maitland are inclined also to connect it with "to sit" and "to set" and thus it would seem to have the same root as the German *Besitz* and the Latin *possessio*.[50] "The man who is seized is the man who is sitting on the land; when he was put in seisin he was set there and made to sit there." [51] Anthropology tends to support the view of Pollock and Maitland that the idea of seisin has more con-

nection with the idea of "set" or "sit" than with the etymological idea of taking by violence. Basically property
is conceived of as a part of the personality or self; it is a
relation between the person and the thing. Something that
the individual has touched or handled becomes imbued with
a portion of his personality. "That which I have touched
belongs to me; I put hand to it; it is mine. The property
I hold is the expansion of my own person." [52] In early German law it was necessary, in order to reclaim cattle found
in the possession of another, to place the right hand above
a relic, a fetish, and the left hand on the left ear of the
animal. The South African who touched a drinking cup
thereafter regarded it as his. The native of Baffin Bay and
the Eastern Eskimo pass the tongue over objects as they
are acquired.[53] It is an easy step from the idea that the thing
possessed is connected with the body to the idea that it is
necessary that there should be a physical contact of the
donee with the thing transferred before the transfer is actually complete. Sociologically, this concept seems to be
related to the idea of seisin, to the setting of the donee upon
the land. A justification of the practice is found in the publicity which accompanies it, but at bottom it appears to be
a development of the animistic conception of the relation
between the personality and the thing.

Long before Spencer had made fashionable the idea that
social development proceeded from "an indefinite, incoherent homogeneity to a definite, coherent heterogeneity," [54]
or, in other words, from simplicity to complexity, Blackstone
had attempted, by relying upon anthropological evidence, to
account for the rise of the idea of private property upon
the same principle. Originally mankind derived authority
over the things of the earth from the Creator.[55] "This,"
Blackstone held, "is the only true and solid foundation of
man's dominion over external things, whatever airy metaphysical notions may have been stated by fanciful writers
upon this subject." [56] In the early stages of society, according to Blackstone, property was held in common:

"And, while the earth continued bare of inhabitants, it is reasonable to suppose that all was in common among them, and that every one took from the public stock to his own use such things as his immediate necessities required.

"These general notions of property were then sufficient to answer all the purposes of human life; and might perhaps still have answered them had it been possible for mankind to have remained in a state of primeval simplicity: as may be collected from the manners of many American nations when first discovered by the Europeans; and from the ancient method of living among the first Europeans themselves, if we may credit either the memorials of them preserved in the golden age of the poets, or the uniform accounts given by historians of those times." [57]

But the notion that people of ruder cultures had undeveloped ideas of property was not confined to legal theory; it was a hypothesis that was also advanced by the earlier anthropologists. Morgan, for example, in his *Ancient Society,* distinguished three levels of social development: savagery, barbarism and civilization. Savages, he believed, had feeble ideas of property. "The property of savages was inconsiderable. Their ideas concerning its value, its desirability and its inheritance were feeble. Rude weapons, fabrics, utensils, apparel, implements of flint, stone and bone, and personal ornaments represent the chief items of property in savage life. A passion for its possession had scarcely been formed in their minds, because the thing itself scarcely existed." [58] But as Lowie has shown, even among the most "savage" societies in Morgan's sense—the Yamana, the most southerly of South American tribes, and the Seman, a negrito people of the Malay Peninsula—personal property is extensively held. [59] Though ownership of a particular piece of property does not in all cases vest the exclusive use in the owner, the line is, as Lowie shows, clearly drawn between what is one's actual due, and what is merely an ethical claim.

To-day the conception of primitive communism has been abandoned by legal historians and it has been found that real progress in the law lies in patiently working backward towards the source of legal rules instead of beginning with a hypothesis and working forward, attempting at the same time to make each apparent advance conform with the hypothesis. Here, again, anthropological evidence aids in the undertaking, not only by assisting in the clarification of the legal rules but by serving as a check on such generalizations as may be advanced as historical work progresses. Thus, Holdsworth regards the distinction between corporeal and incorporeal property as a characteristic of an advanced system of law: "The seignory of the feudal lord, rents, annuities, corodies, franchises, offices, advowsons, rights of common and other profits a prendre, easements, all are incorporeal things. What we must chiefly note is that all are treated (in medieval law) in many ways like corporeal things. The law can understand a corporeal tangible thing: it has hardly as yet arrived at a clear conception of an intangible right. The distinction between corporeal and incorporeal is not ready made. It is the mark of a mature system of law." [60] Maitland is even more positive in his opinion that the distinction between corporeal and incorporeal property is due to the genius of the law.

"The realm of medieval law is rich with incorporeal things. Any permanent right which is of a transferable nature, at all events if it has what we may call a territorial ambit, is thought of as a thing that is very like a piece of land. Just because it is a thing, it is transferable. This is no fiction invented by speculative jurists. For the popular mind these things are things. The lawyer's business is not to make them things but to point out that they are incorporeal. The layman who wishes to convey the advowson of a church will say that he conveys the church; it is for Bracton to explain to him that what he means to transfer is not that structure of wood and stone which belongs to God and the saints, but a thing incorporeal, as incorporeal as his own soul or the *anima mundi* . . . but we cannot leave behind us the law of incorporeal things, the most medieval part of medieval law, without a word of admiration for the daring fancy that created it, a fancy that was not afraid of the grotesque." [61]

But both the idea that the popular mind regards rights as things and the idea that the distinction between them is the mark of a mature system of law are open to doubt. The first belief was due probably to the once widespread notion that there is a strong tendency on the part of individuals to personify all objects and phenomena and that this tendency was particularly strong among primitive people. The child who turns and strikes the chair against which he has stumbled has been an often cited example. This hypothesis we know to-day is no longer tenable. Even Lévy-Bruhl, who has argued brilliantly, if unpersuasively, for the theory that primitive man possesses a type of mind different from that of the mind of civilized man, admits that primitive man employs concepts.[62] Primitive man does not always give concrete form to qualities or actions, or endow them with anthropomorphic characters; he conceives and recognizes the intangible as well as the tangible, though whether his conception of the distinction is as sharply verbalized as that of civilized man is, of course, another question. It is therefore of the highest interest to us when we learn that individuals in primitive communities own, sell and devise incorporeal property.[63] Examples of this form of ownership are numerous and are not confined to a particular geographical area but are well-developed among many primitive communities. A few instances of this form of ownership in the primitive social organization will illustrate its nature. Among the Central Eskimo the magical formulæ which the hunter sings to secure success in the chase are not communally owned but are the private property of the particular huntsman. Among the Greenland Eskimo the right to use spells is emphatically private property. There is, however, a limitation on the degree of ownership of this right. The owner of the right is not the absolute owner in the sense that the right is at his complete disposition: he cannot give it away Only if the right is transferred for a consideration will it retain its effectiveness—a rationalization which Lowie believes is transparent. The sale involves a rough equivalent of the modern purchase of "good-will." "When a woman sells an incantation, she must promise that she gives it up entirely, and that the buyer will become the only possessor of its mysterious power." [64] Among the Andaman Islanders the right to sing certain songs, among the North American Indians and the natives of the Eastern Torres Straits Islands the right to recount legends, and among the natives of British Columbia the right to use certain names and magical formulæ are all regarded as private property which cannot be appropriated or used by others. It thus appears that the existence of incorporeal property is a widespread feature of human culture. The recognition of the distinction between corporeal and incorporeal property by systems of law appears ultimately to be no more than a matter of form, though it is important to recognize that for a particular system of law the recognition may for certain periods of time have a profound effect upon its administration. In addition there is no reason, so far as is disclosed by present studies of primitive mentality, why primitive peoples should not recognize the distinction, though the present evidence is not clear on the point whether or not in fact they do so. Even if we should learn that the distinction between corporeal and incorporeal property is not recognized by primitive peoples, anthropology at least warns the legal historian that incorporeal property is not a development of advanced cultures but is a characteristic of all cultures.

When we consider another aspect of the problem of property—that of inheritance—we find that here also anthropology can be of material assistance. Maitland clearly recognized the importance of an adequate understanding of the rudiments of family law in connection with the unraveling of the mystery of the rules governing inheritance. "So long as it is doubtful whether the prehistoric time should be filled, for example, with agnatic *gentes* or with hordes which reckon by 'motherright,' the interpretation of many a historic text must be uncertain." [65] At the time he wrote, the concept of "motherright," particularly in Germany from whose scholars he derived much of his inspiration, exercised a powerful influence, and though he did not accept the concept, it had an appreciable influence on his thought. His consideration of this concept led him to the penetrating conclusion that "family-ownership" was really not the origin but the outcome of intestate succession.[66] This conclusion, with the modification that intestate succession is but one of the contributing factors, is accepted by anthropologists today. From this point Maitland, however, proceeded further and evolved a theory to account for the origin of the testament. He began by imagining "a time when testamentary dispositions are unknown and land is rarely given away." [67] A law of intestate succession becomes fixed and immutable. Each heir knows exactly what share of his ancestor's estate he will receive; the ancestor knows to whom the proper share of his possessions will pass. "What else should happen to it? He does not want to sell it, for there is no one to buy it; and whither could he go and what could he do if he sold his land? Perhaps the very idea of a sale of land has not yet been conceived." [68] But in course of time wealth is amassed, purchasers are desirous of acquiring the land, bishops will confer spiritual benefits for a gift, there is a struggle and law must decide whether or not the claims of expectant heirs can be defeated. There will be a compromise, a series of compromises, and then there will be a recognition of testamentary dispositions. This, in brief, is Maitland's theory which has also been adopted by Holdsworth who states it perhaps more explicitly.[69] Both Holdsworth and Maitland recognize the theory as a product of "bookland" and not of "folkland." What went on beneath the surface of the books in the world of actuality is hazy but the written records, in part at least, support the hypothesis. When we turn to anthropological evidence we find that the forms of inheritance are protean. First of all the practice of testation is not infrequent, though, as in modern times, there may be limitations upon it. Among the Fantis of West Africa the customary law does not permit any person to bequeath to an outsider a greater portion of his property than is left for his family. Among the Maoris land obtained by purchase or conquest may be given away or willed by the owner to anybody he thinks fit, but the case is different with patrimony.[70] A Plains Indian cannot transmit the rights acquired through fasting for a vision because of the principle that such rights can only be acquired by like visions or by purchase.[71] Among some tribes, such as the Maidu, the Assiniboin and the Pima, all of the decedent's effects are destroyed, thus greatly simplifying the rules of inheritance. Again, there is a principle that articles peculiarly applicable to a particular sex shall pass to that sex. Women's clothing, for example, passes to the female kin and a man's weapons pass to the male kin. Primogeniture, though rare, also occurs as does "borough-english" or "junior-right" as it is known ethnologically.[72] In short, the forms of inheritance are multitudinous and do not appear to follow a particular law of development. Many factors—religious, psychological, economic, historical,—all, briefly, but that of logic—contribute to the establishment of the particular form which obtains. It certainly does not seem to be satisfactory to account for the origin of inheritance and testamentary disposition by imagining "a time when testamentary dispositions are unknown and land is rarely sold or given away." From the anthropological facts now available it does not appear possible to account for either the various forms of inheritance or for the fact of inheritance itself. Westermarck has suggested that inheritance may have a psychological origin, and, though the theory he has developed to support the idea is not satisfactory, it is possible that we may ultimately recognize this as the true basis of the practice.[73]

In turning to the problems of family law we pass to a consideration of the most fundamental and universal of all societal institutions and one which occupies a central position in all legal systems. What form the earliest human groups assumed is one of the most difficult of anthropological problems. Briffault, who in recent times has most thoroughly investigated the problem, believes that the human group did not develop out of the animal herd and did not consist, in the first stages of its development, of small isolated groups corresponding to what we understand by families. His opinion is that the earliest human societies developed out of some form of animal assemblage and that they were, like all animal groups, primarily reproductive in function, and not, like existing human groups, coöperative organizations.[74] The most primitive form of marriage he believes to be group marriage which is exclusively sexual in its object.[75] Individual marriage, on the other hand, had its foundation in economic needs.

"What, in uncultured societies we call marriage, far from being a means of satisfying the sexual instincts, is one of the chief restrictions which have become imposed upon their operation. Those restrictions, being the effect of marriage, are necessarily non-existent before it; unmarried females, outside the prohibited classes or degrees, are accessible to all males. In all uncultured societies, where advanced retrospective claims have not become developed, and the females are not regularly betrothed or actually married before they have reached the age of puberty, girls and women who are not married are under no restrictions as to their sexual relations, and are held to be entirely free to dispose of themselves as they please in that respect. To that rule there does not exist any known exception." [76]

Primitive man's motive in entering into individual marriage is to obtain the economic advantage of personal service which a wife bestows upon him; the marriage is not entered into with a sexual object in view. With the development of agriculture in its higher forms, the accumulation of wealth became possible, women accordingly lost their economic value as workers and the economic need out of which individual marriage had grown ceased to exist.[77] Woman lost her status as chief producer, and became economically unproductive, destitute and dependent. Thus she turned to the cultivation of charm, and in the course of time, the sexual element again became the chief factor of marriage.[78] This, in brief, is Briffault's statement of social development. It is opposed in many vital points to the theory first advanced almost forty years ago by Westermarck, whose *History of Human Marriage* has ever since been generally accepted as the authoritative statement of the subject. Westermarck maintained that marriage had a biological origin, i.e., that it was an outgrowth of marriage habits which prevailed among animals.[79] Westermarck is an anthropologist of immense learning and the material which he collected to support his theory was overwhelming. His influence in the field of family research has been extensive and certain hypotheses which he endeavored to establish have been generally regarded as irrefutable. So great an authority as Havelock Ellis has stated that "a completely adequate history of marriage we can hardly expect to see. No one person could master all the disciplines of study that must go to the making of it, and the separate work of a group of experts, each in his own field competent, could not be fused into any living and harmonious whole," [80] and he believes that to-day the nearest approximation to such a completely adequate history is the work of Professor Westermarck. The fact that the field is too vast for any one single-handed to master accounts in large measure for the circumstance that Westermarck's supremacy has for so long remained unchallenged. A reëxamination of his material has appeared to be an undertaking which not only would occupy the major portion of a lifetime but would, in view of the great authority accorded his conclusions, perhaps lead to no advance. It is to the great credit of Briffault that he undertook such a reëxamination and brought it to a successful conclusion, with the result that the general conception of the development of the family and marriage has been modified in many important respects. In the works of Briffault and Westermarck we have the most complete and scientific studies, from the societal standpoint, of a subject which is of the most universal and fundamental importance.

It is important first to recognize that, historically, marriage is primarily a social or juridic institution.[81] Various definitions of marriage have been offered from time to time, but no definition yet proposed has been at the same time so flexible and yet so definite that it covers all forms. The task confronting the anthropologist is to understand what is meant by marriage, as distinguished from other sex relations, by the people who draw such a distinction.[82] In primitive communities the distinction appears to rest mainly upon the fact, whether or not children are born of the union.[83] The question of the degree of permanency of the union does not enter into the matter. With the passage of time other conditions were imposed until we reach the stage where it is held that a ceremony is necessary to establish the relationship. At first the relationships which are not juridic are not regarded as irregular nor subject to censure; but there is an inevitable tendency, as Briffault points out, apart from all other factors and considerations, "in a juridically established relation to cause a depreciation in the esteem in which relations not so established are held."[84] But the point of paramount importance which we must recognize is that there is in most communities a form of sexual relationship as distinguished from other forms which is invested with juridic attributes.

It is this form of sexual relationship which lies near the core of all legal systems. An adequate history of law and a sound philosophy of law cannot be written without an understanding of the social history of the institution and it is almost entirely upon anthropology that we must depend for this understanding. No one was more keenly aware than Maitland of the desperate need for sound anthropological evidence to complete the gaps in legal history which ordinary methods of research could not fill.[85] Marriage among the Anglo-Saxons appeared to consist of a sale of "mund" by the parents or guardians of a woman to the husband.[86]

Maitland's opinion was that the sale of the "mund" was not the sale of the woman as a chattel, but it was the sale of the protectorship over the woman. She assumed an honorable position as her husband's consort.[87] It is highly important historically to know whether a legal distinction existed between the purchase of property in the wife and the acquirement of authority over her. For many years it was disputed among anthropologists whether or not the sale of the "mund" was really "wife-purchase" or a sale of a protectorship. To-day the general view is that it was the sale of a protectorship.[88] But wife-purchase was not a practice peculiar to the Anglo-Saxons or the Teutons but was widespread among primitive tribes and even among peoples who have reached a high degree of culture such as the Chinese, the Semites, the ancient Arabs and Greeks, and the Hindus. Out of the practice of wife-purchase arose, by gradual steps, the practice which obtained in many communities of providing the wife with a dowry. It is of great value to us to understand a peculiar marriage practice in one legal system in relation to similar practices in other legal systems. And it is only by attaining universal perspective that we shall be able to understand the phenomena of social development in any adequate sense.

It is important to note that while anthropology may be of great assistance in expanding and clarifying legal concepts and practices it may also show that these concepts and practices have their origin in superstition, fear, vanity or some other ignoble source. This, however, as Sumner and Keller point out,[89] is no sufficient reason for condemning a concept or a practice. Astronomy grew out of astrology and medicine began with the exorcising of evil spirits. The test to apply is whether the concept or practice in its historical setting possesses social worth. And anthropology can aid not only in the enlargement of our comprehension of the legal concepts associated with property and the family, but it can also assist materially in determining the present value of those concepts.

When we turn from the historical and conceptual relation of law and anthropology to the problem of law and anthropology in action we pass to a question which may seem remote from problems of jurisprudence. Nevertheless, it is one of the gravest problems of world politics. It is the problem of the system of justice to be adopted by the dominating power in colonies populated by people of simpler culture. Lord Lugard's admirable volume, *The Dual Mandate in British Tropical Africa,*[30] well illustrates the difficulties accompanying this task and is the best text for this discussion. In the British African Tropical Dependencies the fundamental law, applicable alike to Europeans and natives, is the English common law and principles of equity, administered concurrently, and the statutes of general application which were in force in England at the time the administration was created. This body of law may be modified by Acts of the Imperial Parliament, by orders of His Majesty in Council, and by local ordinances. To apply this law to the exclusion of all other law would, it was found, result in inequities and hardships, and accordingly it was provided that the British Courts in civil cases affecting natives (and non-natives in their contractual relations with natives) should be guided by native law, religion and custom. This is contrary to the system prevailing in French Tropical Africa where if either party is a European French law is always applied to the exclusion of native law. It was found in practice that many native rules of law or custom were repugnant to European ideas of propriety and the further proviso was made that the rules would not be enforced if they were contrary to "natural justice and humanity." Thus a native law which compelled the destruction of twins would not be enforceable; indeed, if it were enforced the act of destruction would be regarded as an offense. In addition it was found necessary to change many procedural rules. Thus a Chief Justice, lately arrived from England to assume his duties, was greatly surprised when an accused man pleaded guilty of having turned himself into a hyena at night and devoured children, because there was a consensus of village opinion that he had done so. At present a plea of not guilty is entered on behalf of an illiterate accused, and in capital cases the evidence must, generally speaking, be sufficient for conviction irrespective of the assertions of the accused. Equally difficult of solution is the problem of punishment. The Koran prescribes death by stoning for the offense of adultery. This manifestly could not be enforced by a British court and as the Moslem judges insisted that, at least for the moral effect, there should be administered a light birching on the shoulders, a compromise was reached by which the person who inflicted the chastisement kept some cowrie shells under his armpit so as to prevent the raising of the arm to strike with force. If the cowries dropped the culprit was reprieved. This brief summary indicates the nature and extent of the problems confronting a nation assuming control of a native dependency.

But to leave the reconciliation of native and foreign law to the standard of "natural justice and humanity" is plainly inadequate for the simple reason that "natural justice and humanity" is a concept totally devoid of definite meaning. Even Lord Lugard admits, in connection with the question of infliction of corporal punishment upon a woman, that "it is questionable whether in the circumstances it could be said to be 'repugnant to natural justice and humanity.'" And when we approach the delicate problem of slavery we find, particularly in other parts of Africa, that as a criterion it is of no value at all. It is here that anthropology can render assistance of immediate and practical benefit. For administrators to enter territories with whose custom and law they are totally unfamiliar and to set up systems of justice which are expected to function equitably is absurd. It is to the anthropologist who is intimately acquainted not only with the peculiarities of the particular territory but with the principles of social organization which obtain in other primitive communities as well that the administrator must turn for help. With such assistance a system of justice adapted to the specific territory can be erected which will function with a minimum of friction.

We thus see, to return to our original problem, that although specialized, there is, along certain lines, a real relationship between law and anthropology and that anthropology can be of assistance in the solution of many legal problems. There is, though, one final warning which must be heeded if there is to be a genuine advance in the appreciation of the relationship of these two subjects. Anthropology has always been a fascinating subject from which to draw for many social theories. Hobbes'[91] idea of a state of nature was influenced by the contemporary knowledge of primitive life; Locke's[92] principal example in support of his contentions was the "Indian"; and Rousseau's[93] "Noble Savage" has become legendary. But as Professor Myers pointed out more than twenty years ago, "the very questions which philosophers have asked, the very questions which perplexed them, no less than the solutions which they proposed, melt away and vanish, *as problems,* when the perspective of anthropology shifted and the standpoint of observation advanced."[94] Not only is it important to ask the right question, as Bacon showed, but it is equally important to test conclusions based upon anthropological observation with all the available evidence and not merely to support them by facts selected to fit the problem.

NOTES

[1] *Treatise of Human Nature* (1817), pt. iii; *An Enquiry Concerning Human Understanding* (1750), sec. vi.

[2] Art. *Science* in *Whither Mankind* (1928), p. 65. The present position of induction is set forth, in addition to the above reference, in the following books and articles: Keynes, *A Treatise on Probability* (1921); Nicod, *Foundations of Geometry and Induction* (1930); *Book Review* (1925), 34 Mind 483; Nisbet, *The Foundations of Probability* (1926), 35 Mind 1; Russell, *The Analysis of Matter* (1927), pp. 167, 194; *Philosophy* (1927), chap. xxv.

[3] *Principles of Sociology* (1879), i, pt. ii; *Principles of Ethics* (1879), pt. iv.

[4] Preserved Smith, "Luther's Early Development in the Light of Psycho-

analysis" (1913), *Am. Jr. Psych.*, xxiv, p. 360; Freud, *Leonardo da Vinci* (1916).

⁵ *Ancient Law* (1861); *Lectures on the Early History of Institutions* (1875); *Village Communities in the East and West* (1871); *Dissertations on Early Law and Custom* (1883).

⁶ *Die Geschlechtsgenossen der Urzect und die Entstehung der Ehe* (1875); *Der Ursprung des Rechts* (1876); *Die Anfange des Staats- und Rechtslebens* (1878); *Bausteine für eine allegmeine Rechtswissenschaft auf vergleichend-ethnologischer Basis* (1880-81); *Die Grundlagen des Rechts* (1884); *Afrikanisch Jurisprudenz* (1887); *Studien zur Entwicklungsgeschichte des Familiensrecht* (1890).

⁷ *Zeitschrift für vergleichende Rechtswissenschaft*, passim.

⁸ *Ibid.* (1897), xii, pp. 187-353.

⁹ (1851).

¹⁰ *The Patriarchal Theory* (1885), passim; cf. Spencer, *Principles of Sociology*, i, pt. iii, chap. ix.

¹¹ Pound thus well summarizes the achievements in this field: "These interpretations have done something for the science of law as it is to-day. They have led us to a wider basis for philosophy of law. They have introduced thorough study of primitive social and legal institutions and thus have exploded many traditional false ideas that had come down from the days of the state-of-nature theory. They have given added impetus to the movement for unification of the social sciences by establishing connections with ethnology and anthropology and social psychology. Most of all they have suggested lines of preparatory work that must be carried on before we may achieve an adequate social theory and hence an adequate theory of law as a social phenomenon" (*Interpretations of Legal History* (1923), p. 91).

¹² Cf. Frank, "An Institutional Analysis of the Law" (1924), *Col. L. Rev.*, xxiv, p. 480; Cantor, "Law and the Social Sciences" (1930), *A. B. A. J.*, xvi, p. 385.

¹³ *Crime and Custom in Savage Society* (1926).

¹⁴ "Anthropology and Law," in *The Social Sciences* (1927), p. 50; "Incorporeal Property in Primitive Society" (1928), *Yale L. J.*, xxxvii, p. 551.

¹⁵ Malinowski, *op. cit., supra*, note 13, at 5.

¹⁶ (1912-13).

¹⁷ Cf. Pound, art. "Jurisprudence," in *The History and Prospects of the Social Sciences* (1925), pp. 463-4, and the same author's "Law in Books and Law in Action" (1910), *Am. L. Rev.*, xl, p. 12.

¹⁸ Art. "Social Anthropology," in *Encyclopedia Britannica* (14th ed., 1929); cf. his article, *Parenthood—The Basis of Social Structure* in the *New Generation* (1930).

¹⁹ *General Sociology* (1905).

²⁰ *Community* (a sociological study, 1924); *The Modern State* (1926).

²¹ *The State* (1914).

²² *New Republic*, xiii, Nov. 17, 1917, supp. 3.

²³ Barnes, *Sociology and Political Theory* (1924), p. 43.

²⁴ *The Growth of the Law* (1924), p. 52. Cf. p. 44. For a similar definition cf. John C. H. Wu, *Juridical Essays and Studies* (1928), p. 108. Dr. Wu adds, "Psychologically, law is a science of prediction *par excellence.*"

Cf. Meyerson, *Identity and Reality* (1930), p. 25. "Science, we have just seen, has an end, prevision. Its domain will thus include all that is capable of being foreseen, all of the facts subject to rules. Where there is no law, there is no science."

[25] Hobhouse, Wheeler, and Ginsberg, *The Material Culture and Social Institutions of the Simpler Peoples* (1915), p. 50 *et seq.;* Rivers, *Social Organization* (1924), p. 159 *et seq.;* Malinowski, *op. cit., supra,* note 13, passim.

[26] Rivers, *ibid.,* pp. 168-9.

[27] *Ibid.*

[28] Although published as late as 1924 E. Sidney Hartland's *Primitive Law,* while in many respects a valuable work, is based to a considerable degree upon older anthropological concepts.

[29] Malinowski, *op. cit., supra,* note 13, at 58. There is an ellipsis in this definition though the meaning is clear. A body of binding obligations cannot be regarded as a right or acknowledged as a duty. Perhaps the definition should be worded: "Civil law ... consists ... of a body of binding obligations which is recognized as specifying rights of one party and duties of the other. ..."

[30] *The Meaning of Meaning* (1923), chap. vi.

[31] *An Examination of the Nature of the State* (1896); *The Fundamental Concepts of Public Law* (1924).

[32] MacIver, *The Modern State,* pp. 40-42.

[33] *The Origin of the State* (1927), chap. vi.

[34] MacIver, *The Modern State,* p. 22.

[35] A. d'Abro, *The Evolution of Scientific Thought* (1927), p. 35. Cf. Edwin W. Patterson, "Can Law Be Scientific?" (1930), *Ill. L. Rev.,* xxv, p. 121.

[36] *Principles of Logic* (1920), p. vii.

[37] *Three Collected Papers* (1911), p. 295.

[38] *Culture and Ethnology* (1917); *Primitive Society* (1920); *Primitive Religion* (1924).

[39] *Early Civilization* (1922).

[40] *The Todas* (1906); *History of Melanesian Society* (1914); *Kinship and Social Organization* (1914); *Social Organization* (1924).

[41] *The Family Among the Australian Aborigines* (1913); *Argonauts of the Western Pacific* (1922); "The Natives of Mailu" (*Trans. of the R. Soc. of S. Australia,* Adelaide, 1915); *Myth in Primitive Psychology* (1926); *Crime and Custom in Savage Society, supra,* note 13; *The Father in Primitive Psychology* (1927); *Sex and Repression in Savage Society* (1927); *The Sexual Life of Savages* (1929).

[42] *The Mothers* (1927).

[43] *Hist. E. L.* (3rd ed., 1923), ii, p. 78.

[44] *Ibid.*

[45] *Argonauts of the Western Pacific,* p. 117.

[46] *Yale L. J.,* xxxvii, p. 55, *supra,* note 14.

[47] Holdsworth, *Hist. E. L.,* iii, p. 222.

[48] *Ibid.,* p. 224.

[49] Skeat, *Concise Etymological Dictionary* (1911), word "seize."

[50] Pollock and Maitland, *Hist. E. L.* (1895), ii, pp. 29-30. Skeat is also some authority for this view.

51 *Ibid.* Cf. Joün des Longrais, *La conception anglaise de ta saisine du XIIe au XIVe siècle* (1925), pp. 166-7.

52 Sumner and Keller, *Science of Society* (1927), i, § 108.

53 *Ibid.*

54 *First Principles* (1862), chap. xvii. Cf. *Principles of Sociology,* ii. p. 229.

55 "And God blessed them, and God said unto them ... have dominion over the fish of the sea, and over the fowl of the air, and over every living thing that moveth upon the earth" (*Gen.* 1:28).

56 *Bl. Comm.,* ii, * 3. "The airy metaphysical notions of fanciful writers" is perhaps a shaft aimed at Locke's theory of property. Cf. *Treatises of Government* (1690), ii, chap. v. Previously Blackstone had pointed out (though without naming him) that Locke's theory of the origin of political societies through a social contract was "too wild to be seriously admitted." *Bl. Comm.,* i, * 47.

57 *Bl. Comm.,* ii, * 3. Even at this stage Blackstone was careful to point out that community of ownership applied only to the substance and not to the "use." A man who lay in the shade of a tree could not be forcibly ejected, but having once abandoned the spot, another could occupy it unmolested by the original occupier or any one else. *Ibid.*

58 *Op. cit.* (1877), p. 527.

59 *Incorporeal Property in Primitive Society, supra,* note 14.

60 Holdsworth, *Hist. E. L.,* ii, p. 355.

61 Pollock and Maitland, *Hist. E. L.,* ii, pp. 123, 147-8.

62 *How Natives Think* (1926), p. 116.

63 Lowie, who has been especially interested in this point, has collected many examples. *Incorporeal Property in Primitive Society, supra,* note 14, and *Primitive Society,* pp. 235-43; cf. Wissler, *The American Indian* (1917), pp. 174-5; *Introduction to Social Anthropology* (1929), p. 77.

64 Jochelson, "Material Culture and Social Organization of the Koryak" (*Mem. Amer. Mus. Nat. Hist.,* 1908, x, p. 59). Quoted, Lowie, art., *supra,* note 14, at 555.

65 Pollock and Maitland, *Hist. E. L.,* ii, p. 237.

66 *Ibid.,* ii p. 247.

67 *Ibid.*

68 *Ibid.*

69 Holdsworth, *Hist. E. L.,* ii, p. 92 *et seq.*

70 Westermarck, *Origin and Development of the Moral Ideas* (1917), ii, p. 43.

71 Lowie, *Primitive Society,* pp. 243-4.

72 *Ibid.,* pp. 243-55.

73 Westermarck, *op. cit.,* ii, *supra,* note 70, at 53.

74 *The Mothers,* i, p. 194 *et seq.*

75 *Ibid.,* chaps. xi-xii.

76 Briffault, *The Mothers,* ii, p. 2 *et seq.*

77 *Ibid.,* p. 251.

78 *Ibid.,* p. 254.

79 *History of Human Marriage* (5th ed. 1922), li, chap. i.

80 *Studies in the Psychology of Sex* (1928), vii, p. 492.

81 MacIver has been one of the few sociologists to inquire the meaning of "institution." He defines it as "a form of order established within social life by some common will." *Community,* bk. ii, ch. iv.

[82] Briffault, *The Mothers,* ii, p. 93.

[83] *Ibid.,* pp. 69-88.

[84] *Ibid.,* p. 96.

[85] Cf. Pollock and Maitland, *Hist. E. L.,* ii, p. 237.

[86] *Ibid.,* pp. 362-3; Holdsworth, *Hist. E. L.,* ii, p. 87.

[87] *Ibid.*

[88] Westermarck, *History of Human Marriage,* ii, p. 412; Howard, *History of Matrimonial Institutions* (1904), i, p. 260.

[89] *Science of Society,* § 113.

[90] (1922), chaps. xxvii-xxviii; cf. Maine, *Village Communities in the East and West,* chap. "The Theory of Evidence."

[91] *Leviathan* (1651), chaps. xiii and **xx.**

[92] *Essay Concerning Human Understanding* (1690), bk. i, chaps. iii-iv; *Two Treatises of Civil Government* (1690), passim.

[93] *Discours sur l'Inégalité* (1754), pt. i.

[94] "The Influence of Anthropology on the Course of Political Science" (*Univ. Cal. Pub. Hist.,* 1916, iv, p. 75).

TOTEMISM

An Essay on Religion and Society

By *ALEXANDER GOLDENWEISER*

I. DEFINITION AND GEOGRAPHICAL DISTRIBUTION OF TOTEMISM

In the cultures of many primitive tribes, features of religion and social organization are combined in a peculiar way. Anthropologists call such tribes *totemic,* while designating as a *totemic complex* the sum-total of features, whether religious, ritualistic, social or artistic, which make up *totemism.*

Totemism is one of the most widespread institutions of primitive society. It is found in North America in several wide-flung areas; as our knowledge of South America increases, totemism there seems to be almost equally common; it is encountered in Africa throughout the enormous area south of the Sahara and north of the desert of Kalahari; in India we again discover it in numerous tribes, here in a crude, or perhaps, moribund form; in Australia totemism is practically universal, and it is found, in function or at least in traces, in several of the island clusters of Melanesia.

An institution so general in primitive society, and in it alone, is evidently tied to it by bonds far from casual. An understanding of totemism seems imperative if primitive life and thought are to be understood.

In his presidential address before Section H, Anthropology, of the *British Association for the Advancement of Science,* A. C. Haddon referred to totemism in the following terms: "Totemism, as Dr. Frazer and I understand it in its fully developed condition, implies the division of a people into several totem kins (or, as they are usually termed, totem clans), each of which has one or sometimes more than one totem. The totem is usually a species of animal, sometimes a species of plant, occasionally a natural object or phenomenon, very rarely a manufactured object. Totemism also involves the rules of exogamy, forbidding marriage between the kins. It is essentially connected with the matriarchal stage of culture (mother-right), though it passes over into the patriarchal stage (father-right). The totems are regarded as kinsfolk and protectors of the kinsmen, who respect them and abstain from killing and eating them. There is thus a recognition of mutual rights and obligations between the members of the kin and their totem. The totem is the crest or symbol of the kin."

Without endorsing this now somewhat antiquated statement, we may let it stand as a fairly accurate description of a common enough content of a totemic complex.

II. THEORIES OF TOTEMISM

In the *Fortnightly Review* for 1869-70, John Ferguson McLennan published two articles on "The Worship of Animals and Plants"; the first he called "Totems and Totemism," the second, "Totem-Gods Among the Ancients." Ever since, and especially after the appearance of J. G. (now Sir John) Frazer's initial study, *Totemism* (1887), this subject has persistently evoked theories not from anthropologists alone but from sociologists, psychologists, psychoanalysts and others. Some of these may now be passed in brief review.

In speculating about totemism some authors were primarily concerned with its origin while others attempted to place totemism against the background of primitive mentality or to indicate its place in the evolution of religion. Totemism was conceived as a "system of naming" by Major Powell,[1] a theory partially maintained also by Pikler and Somlo [2] and by Herbert Spencer. In the form given to it by the latter author the theory became known as the "misrepresentation of nicknames" theory. Spencer assumed that animal names were once given to individuals, that these names were subsequently confused with the animals themselves, owing to the vagueness of primitive languages, and that ultimately such animals came to be worshiped as ancestors. Andrew Lang in his *Secret of the Totem* (1905), partially subscribed to the naming theory with two important modifications. He held that, for one reason or another, the animal names were first applied to social groups, not to individuals, that later the origin of these names was forgotten, and speculative guesses were made by the primitives as to the provenience of the names. Thus the stage was set for a totemic origin. "No more than these three things—argued Lang— a group animal name of unknown origin; belief in a transcendental connection between all bearers, human and bestial, of the same name; and belief in the blood superstitions— were needed to give rise to all the totemic creeds or practices, including exogamy."

Frazer, who launched totemism upon its busy career and years later contributed to the subject his massive four-volume work, *Totemism and Exogamy* (1910), entertained at different times three different theories of totemic origin. The first became known as the "outward soul" or "bush soul" theory, the second as the "coöperative magic" theory, and the third as the "conceptional" theory. Initially, Frazer held that totemism developed out of the practice of tucking away human souls in animals, for preservation or safety.[3] This enhanced the religious status of the animals. As it was not known, moreover, in which particular animal of a species the "bush soul" had its abode, the custom in time led to the veneration of the entire species. Frazer's second hypothesis was suggeted by the *intichiuma* ceremonies described by Spencer and Gillen (1899) in their work on the Central Australians. These ceremonies, which have since been described and discussed so much, consist in somewhat dramatic rituals in which the natives dance and sing their magical rites for the multiplication of the totem animals. Each gens has the exclusive right to perform the *intichiuma* for its own totem animal. From the resulting enhancement of the species the gens itself does not, to be sure, derive any benefit, for the totem is taboo to its members, but the other gentes do benefit. "In short," writes Frazer,[4] "totemism among the Central Australian tribes appears, if we may judge from the *intichiuma* ceremonies, to be an organized system of magic intended to procure for savage man a plentiful supply of all the natural objects whereof he stands in need." Then, waxing enthusiastic, the author adds: "The thought naturally presents itself to us: 'Have we not in these ceremonies the key to the original meaning and purpose of totemism among the Central Australian tribes, perhaps even of totemism in general?'" Further pondering of the Australian material, meanwhile amplified by Spencer and Gillen's second study (1904), then led to the formulation of the third and final theory, the "conceptional" one (1905). It appeared that these natives ascribed conception, the physiology of which was obscure to them, to the impregnation of women by spirits or spirit carriers which they encountered, or thought they did, at the sacred totem spots (*oknanikilla*) haunted by the spirits. "If we use what in particular may have suggested the theory of conception which appears to be the tap-root of totemism," says Frazer, "it seems probable that, as I have already indicated, a preponderant influence is to be ascribed to the sick fancies of pregnant women, and that so far, totemism may be described as a creation of the feminine rather than of the masculine mind." With this contribution to the psychology of the sexes, Frazer's speculations about totemism come to an end.

Pater Schmidt, the then editor of the *Anthropos,* saw the origin of totemism, at least in Australia and certain parts of the South Seas region, in primitive trade. He observed first that in Mabuiag the two totems used in the magical fertilization ceremonies are also the principal, or perhaps only, articles employed in inter-tribal trade. Reflection over this fact led to a theory which deduced totemism "seemingly so mysterious" from a "relatively prosaic and simple source."[5] Here it is! Who does not know the familiar fact, writes the author in substance, that our peasants often

abstain from using in their own households the food products they cultivate, but export them mostly to the neighboring town? What we find here in rudimentary form may
develop everywhere under analogous conditions. Such conditions we find wherever the production and consumption
of food-articles are locally distinct, calling for supplementary
inter-tribal exchange of food-products. Local products intended for trade, are tabooed to the inhabitants of the district. The food interdict, an economic custom in origin,
becomes in time a moral law, and after a while the original
motive of the interdict is forgotten (it is to be noted how
Schmidt, and before him Lang, exploits the speculative possibilities of such an hypothesized amnesia). "There followed
a time of doubt and uncertainty," quoth the author, "conditions pregnant with metaphysical associations." In recognition of its importance in the life of the tribe, the animal or
plant becomes the mythical source of the life of the tribe,
its ancestor. And what could be more natural than that the
group should assume or be called by the name of the animal
or plant so plentiful in its district!

After advancing a further argument in favor of the priority of plant-magic over animal-magic, Schmidt concludes
that garden-culture was the cradle of the magical multiplication rites: "I believe that these things develop quite
naturally out of plant-cultivation followed by trade; starting
from this base, the subsequent developments in the sphere
of mythology explain equally naturally all the details of
the fertilization rites and of the peculiar totemism of the
Northern Australians." This theory, extravagant though it
might seem, does not stand alone, for it was anticipated by
A. C. Haddon, who in 1902 advanced a very similar theory,
even though less elaborately argued.[6]

There were other theories. Hill-Tout, basing his conclusions mainly on data from the Salish tribes of British Columbia, held that totemism grew out of the worship of
individual guardian spirits.[7] Ankermann, who worked
largely with African material, saw the basis of totemism in

a sort of compensation for the drabness of primitive life, accompanied by an urge to play with the man-animal relationship, to dramatize it.[8] Graebner, faithful to his diffusionistic principles, identified totemism with localization and paternal descent, forming a culture area; [9] and so on and on. For the sake of brevity I shall not consider these theories, turning instead to the more ambitious contributions of Emile Durkheim, Wilhelm Wundt and Sigmund Freud.

No adequate analysis of Durkheim's theory contained in his *Elementary Forms of the Religious Life, The Totemic System in Australia,* 1915 (French original, 1912), can be given here; a brief summary attempted elsewhere will have to suffice.[10] Religion is a complex of beliefs and activities referring to sacred things, and the characteristic fact in all religions is the division of beings, things and activities into sacred and profane. If Australian totemism is a genuine religion, it must be the most primitive type of religion, for the social organization of the Australians is the most primitive known to us, being based on the clan.

The totemic symbol or emblem is the expression of the social solidarity of the clanmates. The symbol as well as the name of the clan are derived from the animal or plant which happens to be most common in the locality where the clan congregates. Totemic rituals arise spontaneously, as a direct expression of certain wishes regarding the food supply, and, whether imitative or representative, these rituals arouse pleasurable sensations in the participants by raising their social consciousness. These feelings of satisfaction are projected into the realm of physical nature, giving rise to the belief in the efficacy of the ritual.

The unusual experiences accompanying the periodic ceremonial gatherings, when contrasted with the routine happenings of daily life, awaken in the mind of the totemite a sense of the sacred. Not being aware of the source of their exaltation, the individuals of the clan identify the sacred with the totemic symbols by which they find themselves surrounded on these ritualistic occasions. The true content of their beliefs, however, consists of a vague undifferentiated sense of an impersonal totemic principle, prototype of *mana;* but, unlike *mana,* the totemic principle, instead of becoming generalized, remains associated with the specific characteristics of the clans.

The totem represented in the symbol partakes of its nature and sacred character. The totemites having become identified with the totem the name of which they bear, are, as such, also sacred. The entire physical universe is classified in accordance with the phratries and clans, and the beings and objects thus classified with a certain totem share its sacred character.

Thus totemism must be regarded as a religion not of the clan but of the tribe, each clan being sympathetically aware of the beliefs and practices of the other clans which, moreover, strictly correspond to its own.

Individual totemism is a derivative of clan totemism, and sex totemism partakes of the nature of both.

The individual soul is an incarnation of the spiritual essence of a totemic ancestor. The souls of these mythical totemic personages live on as spirits, the more prominent among them developing into tribal gods.

Thus totemism is revealed as a genuine religion. It comprises a division of beings, things and activities into sacred and profane; it engenders the belief in souls, spirits and gods; it has its cosmology; and its elaborate rituals embrace a form of sacrifice and ascetic practices. At the root of this religion lies the belief in a totemic principle, a belief which expresses the reaction of an individual psyche to its experience of the social control exercised by the clan. Indeed, the totemic principle *is* the clan. Society is God.[11]

To Wundt totemism appears of interest from two angles. He places the origin of the institution in the period when the belief in a breath or shadow soul became differentiated from the earlier belief in a body soul. The first totem animals, therefore, were the soul-animals,—hawk, crow and lizard in Australia; eagle, falcon and snake in America—in which human souls were deposited.[12] As a culture historian, on the other hand, Wundt conceives of totemism as providing the socio-psychological and ideological background of nothing less than a "totemic era," one of the four or five great culture eras into which the history of mankind can be divided.[13] With the totemic era Wundt identifies clan organization, exogamy, chieftainship, animal and plant culture, nature myths, zoömorphic and phytomorphic cults and a number of other cultural features.[14]

And, finally, Freud's theory expounded in his book, *Totem and Taboo*. The theory runs, in brief, as follows: In very early times, before there was any definite social organization or religion, man lved in so-called Cyclopean families in which all the sex rights were monopolized by the dominant old man, while the younger men, his sons, had to submit to the restrictions imposed by him or be killed or expelled from the group. The great dominant male, the father, was revered by the others for his power and wisdom, but he was also hated on account of his monopolistic prerogatives. One day a great tragedy was enacted in such a primitive community. The brothers banded together—encouraged perhaps, adds Freud, by the invention of a new weapon—and dared to do openly together what each one had long secretly desired. They murdered the father. Then they consumed his body in the assurance of thus acquiring his prowess.

The patricidal act having been committed, the sons, tortured by remorse, reverted to a positive attitude toward the father. Obsessed by a belated desire to be obedient to him—"nachträglicher Gehorsam"—they decided to continue the taboo the oppressive character of which had led to the murder, and to abstain from sex contact with the women of the group. The consciousness of common guilt became the root of the new social bond. Thus arose the clan, protected and reinforced by the taboo on killing a clanmate, in order that the fate of the father might not befall any of the brothers. The totem of the clan is therefore but a transfigured image of the father, and the totemic sacrifice, an occasion for both joy and sorrow, but a dramatization of the remote tragedy in which the jubiliant brothers murdered their despot father, then, conscience-stricken, reimposed upon themselves the oppressive taboo in the name of which the murder had been committed.

Freud goes still further. In the central setting of Greek tragedies he discovers another cultural symbolization of the gruesome event of earliest antiquity. The hero's part is to suffer, for he is but the dramatized memory of the murdered father, whereas the responsive chorus stands for the patri-cidal brothers. In this new setting, however, their part in the original tragedy is disguised under the cloak of a positive attitude toward the hero, a psychological subterfuge with which, in the domain of the individual psyche, psychoanal-ysis has made us familiar.

Thus, four great institutions of mankind are ultimately reducible to one basic and pregnant event, a common psycho-sociological source. Common guilt lay at the root of the new social system, the clan, primitive Society. The con-sciousness of guilt expressed itself in a regard for the totem-father, the earliest Religion. In expiation of the crime came the self-imposed rule of exogamy, primal sex taboo and the earliest embodiment of Morality. In the domain of Art, finally, Greek tragedy reënacted the ancient deed in an expiatory disguise.

Details apart, a review of these theories leaves one with the impression that when we say "totemism" we have said all there is to be said about the history of human civilization. Give the speculator a thread and he will enmesh the world!

No systematic analysis of totemic theories can be under-taken here.[15] But a few remarks will be in order for the sake of orientation.

The totemic origin theories which seek the first origin of totemism in some one of its features—name, descent, zoölatry, trade, taboo, magic coöperation, ideas of conception —all suffer from dogmatic one-sidedness. With reference to

TOTEMIC COMPLEXES

AMONG THE TLINGIT AND HAIDA INDIANS, IN CENTRAL AUSTRALIA, AMONG THE BAGANDA (EAST AFRICA), AND IN MABUIAG ISLAND (WESTERN TORRES STRAITS)

	TLINGIT AND HAIDA	CENTRAL AUSTRALIA	BAGANDA	MABUIAG
EXOGAMY	Phratries clans (indirectly)	Phratries classes Gentes (indirectly) Fixed relationship groups	Gentes	Phratries (formerly) clans
GROUP NAMES	Phratries with eponymous totems (crests) clans with district names	Meaning of phratry and class names doubtful Gentes named after totems	Gentes not named after totems	Phratry names with totemic reference Clans with district names
TABOO	No totemic taboo	Strict taboo	Taboo even more strict	Taboo
DESCENT FROM TOTEM	Absent	Universal	Descent of gentes from human ancestors	Absent

Magical Ceremonies for Multiplication of Totem	Absent	Present	Absent	Present
Totemic Reincarnation	Absent	Present	Absent	Absent
Art	Saturated with totemic ideas (crest, not totem, is sacred)	Symbolic totemic art not differentiated according to gentes	No totemic art	Totemic art (in ornaments and on body)
Physical and Psychic Resemblance of Totem and Totemite	Absent	Absent	Absent	Marked
Rank	Crests differ in rank which reflects on totemites	No rank grading of totems or gentes	No rank grading of totems except in case of royal gentes	No rank grading
Number of Totems in Social Unit	Several crests (Haida) one crest (Tlingit)	One main, several associated totems in each gens	Two totems in each gens (with exceptions)	Several clans have one main totem and several subsidiary ones

a particular place one or another of these theories may prove correct, but no ground is forthcoming why almost any of the others might not apply at some other place. It must be granted, however, that the theories stressing the totemic clan name come nearer to the essence of the problem than do the others. Even though this feature is not universal in totemic complexes, it is exceedingly common and must have provided in many, if not most, instances the link between the mystical and the social elements in totemism. Through the name, the locus and limits of each particular totemic connection—a particular clan with a particular totem—must have been established, in numerous cases.

The theories stressing the rôle of totemism in religious evolution are in the wrong in so far as they overemphasize the religious aspect of totemism and assume its universality. This stricture applies particularly to F. B. Jevons' *Introduction to the History of Religion,* as has been pointed out by L. Marillier in his brilliant essay, "La place du totémisme dans l'évolution religieuse." [16] In Durkheim's sense, totemism certainly qualifies as a religion, a tribal not a clan religion, for it belongs to the domain of the sacred, not the profane, in primitive life. But it must never be forgotten that the intensity of the religious *attitude* toward the totem is scarcely ever pronounced; also, that totemism, in *no* instance, constitutes the whole or even the center of the religious aspect of a tribal culture. Animism, ancestor or nature worship, fetichism, idolatry, or even animal or plant worship, may each and all be present in a totemic tribe, side by side with totemism. Again, any of these features may become assimilated with a totemic complex in a particular place, so as to form an integral part of it, or they may not.

There is even something contradictory in the notion of a true religious regard and worship in connection with totemism. Primitives, it is true, have not as yet developed those extreme forms of religious partisanship and pugnacity so characteristic of later historic periods, but it may well be doubted whether totemic complexes could have sailed along as smoothly as they have if each family were divided against itself in point of its deepest religious attitudes. Equivalence of faith and practice in totemic clans and relative mildness of the specifically religious attitude seem equally important here.

Writers like Wundt, finally, and Lawrence Gomme in his *Folklore as a Historical Science,* who speak of a "totemic era" and the like, err in two important respects. On the one hand, they once more assume the universality of totemism of which, to say the least, there is no evidence. On the other, they identify with totemism, genetically or as historic coexistences, a variety of cultural features and tendencies [17] which have nothing whatsoever to do with totemism, either psychologically or culturally or historically, even though they will occur in totemic tribes and cultures.

III. TOTEMISM AS A CONVERGENT HISTORIC-PSYCHOLOGICAL COMPLEX

By contrast with the older theorists of totemism who were, as a rule, concerned with the similarity and unity of totemic phenomena, my own preoccupation in *Totemism, An Analytical Study* (1910) was with the diversity of totemic complexes and the psychological and historical heterogeneity of the features entering into these complexes.

The classified features of four totemic complexes (see Table, pp. 372-3) may serve as an example.

Exogamy among the Tlingit and Haida is a phratry affair: one may not marry in one's own phratry but must marry into the opposite phratry. The clans here are also exogamous but only in so far as, being subdivisions of a phratry, they partake of its exogamic nature. In Central Australia the exogamous situation is much more complex. The two phratries are here also exogamous, but so are their subdivisions, the classes (or, in the more northern tribes, sub-classes and classes), where the rule is that a class (or sub-class) of one phratry must intermarry with another specific class (or sub-class) of the other phratry. The gentes are, in a derivative way, also exogamous, although exceptions occur on account of the havoc wrought with gentile descent by the peculiar local theory of conception. Over and above all this, certain groups of blood relatives are taboo to each other matrimonially and certain others must intermarry. Such, at least, is the orthodox way. Among the Baganda the gentes are exogamous, and so are the clans at Mabuiag, where the phratries seem to have been exogamous in the past.

In re group names the phratries of the Tlingit and Haida have eponymous crests, not so the component clans which are known by local names. In Central Australia where the meaning of the phratry and class names is unknown— although some of these names seem to have been those of animals or birds—the gentes invariably bear the name of their totem. This is not the case among the Baganda, whereas at Mabuiag the phratry names refer in one or another way to the totem, whereas the clans bear district names.

As to totemic taboos, these are absent in the Indian tribes —no eating or killing prohibitions prevail—but present in the three other groups. Among the Baganda, in fact, the totemic taboo is preëminent in the totemic complex, as among many other Bantu speaking Negro tribes where the native term for "totem" often means "that which is forbidden."

The idea of totemic descent prevails in Central Australia, but does not occur either in the Indian tribes or in Mabuiag. The Baganda gentes trace their descent from a common human ancestor.

The Central Australians perform magical totemic fertilization or multiplication rites and so do the natives of Mabuiag, both groups falling within a larger area where this practice is common. On the other hand, such rites (with reference to the totems) are unknown among the Baganda or the Tlingit and Haida.

The Central Australians regard themselves as reincarnations, after a fashion, of their semi-human, semi-animal totemic ancestors. In ancient *alcheringa* times, so the myths tell, these entered the ground leaving behind their spiritual descendants, the *ratapa,* which ever since hover about the sacred spots. It is the *ratapa* which enter the bodies of women to be reborn as human totemites. In the other three groups no such totemic beliefs are known to occur.

Totemic art in Mabuiag takes the form of small ornaments or scarifications on the body; the Baganda seems to have none; whereas among the Indians, on the one hand, and the Central Australians, on the other, totemic art appears in two strikingly diverse forms. The Tlingit and Haida paint and carve their totem animals and birds pretty much all over the landscape. These paintings and carvings, moreover, are so specific for each animal or bird that no doubt can be entertained as to the identity of the representation. In Central Australia, on the contrary, the totemic designs—whether on the *churinga* or on the ground —are identical for *all* gentes (with a few exceptions), the specific totemic reference of the designs being *read into* them by the gentile mates whenever they make use of them.

In Mabuiag the totemite and his totem are of a kind: a "mystic affinity" obtains between them, which expresses itself in physical and psychic resemblance. Thus the men of the Kassowary, Crocodile, Snake and Shark clans—pugnacious animals all—are known as fighters, whereas the Skate, Ray and Sucker—fish people, are peaceable; and so on with the rest. In the other three groups the totem and totemite are not thus attuned to each other.

The rank grading of totem crests and, with them, of the clans that own them, occurs only among the Tlingit and Haida and the royal gentes of the Baganda, not in the other groups. The number of crests or totems allowed each clan or gens, as will be seen from the Table, also varies in the four groups.

There is thus considerable variability in content in totemic complexes. And if instead of taking four groups, we examined forty or four hundred, the range of variability would increase. The particular features entering a totemic complex are not always the same, nor is the part they play. in the ideology or practice of the totemites.

It is equally apparent that the individual features figuring in totemic complexes are not inherently and necessarily totemic. This applies to *all* the features. We know of totemic exogamy, but it also occurs in clans, gentes or phratries that are not totemic, as well as in families, local groups and elsewhere. Similarly with taboos. Killing and eating taboos may or may not refer to totemic animals, in one or another group, but they also occur with reference to creatures other than totems. Killing and eating taboos, moreover, constitute only one aspect of the phenomenon of taboo which is world-wide. As cultural traits, taboo and totemism merely overlap. The same applies to the other features.

What we mean, therefore, when we say that totemism is historically and psychologically complex is this. The features entering a totemic complex are not inherently totemic but become such in the particular context. As between complex and complex, the particular features composing one, vary. Also, the emphasis, the cultural or totemic status of a feature, varies as one passes from complex to complex.

This does not mean that all totemic features are equally rare, or common, in their occurrence. Far from it. An examination of a sufficient number of totemic complexes will show that exogamy, in one form or another, is almost always present. Also, that a relation between humans and the rest of nature, especially animals and plants, is involved here. It may take the form of a "mystic affinity," or a belief in descent, or a taboo on the totem, or a mere eponymous function of the latter without any associated beliefs or practices with reference to it. It must be remembered, however, that the very assumption of an animal or other such name by a group or its acceptance of one given it by others, implies a certain ideological, if not emotional, relationship between humans and the rest of nature. This is a phenomenon not unknown in modern days but incomparably more common, and therefore, more characteristic, in primitive society. As a background we discover a *Denkart*,[18] a certain way of looking at things which makes such developments as totemism possible.

In addition to exogamy and a certain relationship between man and nature, the latter usually taking a mystical form, there is still another aspect of totemic complexes which, in this case, is *universal*. In every totemic community the tribal group is divided into a set of social units which are equivalent. The totemic functions of these social units, while different specifically, are also equivalent or homologous, as between unit and unit. It seems obvious that any attempt to find a general formula for totemism must rest on these three features.

Before we venture on such a final formulation, a word must be said about totemism as a convergent phenomenon. The "origins" of historical facts of totemic complexes, as must have appeared from the preceding, must be assumed to have been varied. Nevertheless, totemic complexes reveal sufficient similarities in their structure, contents, and what might be called their psycho-sociological flavor, to justify the designation of such complexes by one descriptive term. The hypothesis of convergence reconciles this present similarity with genetic divinity. The theory of convergence may, in fact, be utilized to account for the distinct aspects of totemic complexes; the separate features in two or more complexes, in so far as they are comparable, must have often been due to convergence, for the objective and psychological history of such features must, in many instances, have been quite different. Again the totemic social structures with their features, which as a rule are strictly comparable, must be ascribed to convergence, for the order and specific mode of absorption of the features by the system, or their origin within the system, must also have been vastly different in the several instances; the totemic association in a convergent process. And, finally, the totemization of the complexes, the translation of the features of whatever derivation into totemic terms, must be regarded as a convergent process, which operates in the core of each complex with a psychologically lactogeneous aggregate of cultural features, and through a process of assimilation mold them into a totemic atmosphere providing all totemic complexes and constituting, perhaps, the prime basis of their comparability: the totemic assimilation is a convergent process.

IV. FINAL SYNTHESIS

Exogamy, a mystical man-nature relationship, and the splitting up of a tribe into a set of equivalent and functionally homologous social units are, one and all, traits appearing in totemism but also outside of it: they are not inherently totemic features. Also, these features cannot be brought into genetic relationship to each other, nor are they in any other way akin, socio-psychologically or otherwise. But these are the features which we find associated in totemism and about them grow up the other varying features.

How can this be accounted for?

The solution of the problem apparently lies in the fact that the three features become connected with the social structures underlying totemic complexes: with sib systems. For, once and for all, it must be understood that totemism or likenesses of it are so rare outside sib systems and that sib systems are so frequently totemic that the two institutions, sib system on totemism, must be regarded as adhesive phenomena, in Tylor's sense.

Is there then anything about a sib system that would attend exogamy, a mystical man-nature relationship and an emphatic functional homology of equivalent social units? I think there is.

That exogamy and functional homology of social units are prone to prosper in a sib system of hereditary unilateral social units seems fairly clear. If exogamous tendencies are taken for granted—as this anthropological experience justifies us in doing—clans or gentes appear as its ideal carriers. Once on the go, it persists and crystallizes automatically. As to homologous functions these always tend to develop in equivalent social units, and when these social units are as clean cut and stable as they are in hereditary unilateral sibs, the homologous functions are invited and spurred to multiply.

The problem is more complex in the case of the mystical man-nature relationship. Why should this be attracted to sib systems? The reason, I believe, can be discovered.

In a community subdivided into social units, such as clans, the first demand is for some kind of classifiers, preferably names, which would identify the separate units and yet signify their equivalence by belonging to one category. Again, hereditary kinship groups, such as clans, with a strong feeling of common interest and solidarity tend, so socio-psychological experience shows, to project their community spirit into some concrete thing which henceforth stands for the unity of the group and readily acquires a certain halo of sanctity. It often happens with such objects that certain rules of behavior develop with reference to them, both positive and negative rules, prescriptions and restrictions. Such objects thus become symbols of the social values of the groups. Their very objectivity as well as emotional significance lend themselves readily to artistic elaboration. All along the classificatory aspects remains a fixed requirement, so that whatever traits may develop in the social crucible appear as homologous traits. Then again, the sense of kinship between members of the individual clans, especially in view of the absence of precise degrees of relationship and sometimes supported by the genealogical tendency, will often express itself in hypothetical descent from a common ancestor. Also, it would obviously fit the needs of the situation if the above objectivations of the social values consisted of things congenial to man, the properties of which were near and dear to him, of things, however, that would not lie too closely within the realm of specifically human activities, as, in such a case, confusion might result, the sense of property might interfere with the smooth running of the system. Again, it would seem eminently desirable that the things should belong to classes, each one representing a homogeneous group, as this condition would ideally satisfy the requirement that they figure as symbols and objectivations of groups of individuals who, within each group, profess intense feelings of solidarity and homogeneity.

Such, in rough outline, would be the tendencies of a community subdivided into clans.

Now, if the individuals who are the psychic foci of these tendencies had nothing in their experience or psychic content to draw upon to satisfy the demands of the situation, some new creations might be expected to appear which would to some extent satisfy the demands of these social tendencies. But our hypothesis is contrary to fact. For there exists in all primitive communities a complex of experiences and attitudes which has produced values of just the sort needed in the above social situation, has produced them long before any totemic complex or any clan system has made its appearance among men. That complex comprises the experiences resulting from man's contact with nature and the attitudes flowing therefrom. Among these the experiences with and the attitudes toward animals occupy the foremost place, although those referring to plants and inanimate objects are of almost equal significance. Things in nature have at all times exercised multitudinous functions in human society, and the attitudes they have aroused, matter-of-fact as well as supernatural attitudes, range as far as does man himself. These things, animals in particular, are constantly used for naming purposes, for naming individuals; groups of all varieties, such as families, societies, clubs, game teams, political parties, houses, constellations. They are beautifully adjusted to the function of classifiers, as names or otherwise, for they contain many individuals belonging to the same or to several wide categories, they are familiar and congenial to man, yet lie outside the circle of specifically human things and activities, thus not being subject to the action of those disturbing agencies which abound within that realm. Again, animals, as well as other things in nature, are early drawn into the domain of art, they are painted, tattooed, carved, woven, embroidered, dramatized in dances; they figure in realistic as well as geometric representations, thus also rising into prominence as badges, signs and symbols. Primitive man almost everywhere regards himself as somewhat akin to the animal, and many mythologies abound in animals that were men and in men who are metamorphosed animals. Often descent is traced from animals. Again, it is hard to find a tribe where some sort of prescriptive or proscriptive rules do not exist referring to animals, or also plants or other things. Religious attitudes toward things in nature are as universal as religion itself. Moreover, to the eyes of men organized into mutually disparate and internally homogeneous units, the kingdom of animals and only to a less degree that of plants present a spectacle of strange congeniality: for just as in their own social system, these kingdoms embrace beings or things that belong to the same general kind, but are subdivided into categories that are disparate while internally homogeneous.

Now, it must be remembered that all of these experiences, relations and attitudes belong to the range of the common human: they are found in most primitive communities and many of them reach far into the historic period including modern life itself. Hence a community organized into definite hereditary social units, say, clans, finds itself already in possession of most or all of these experiences and attitudes. But we have seen how in such a community, on account of its sociological make-up, certain tendencies must and, as experience shows, almost invariably do arise. These tendencies point toward just such relations, attitudes, functions, as we have seen have everywhere arisen out of man's experience with nature, particularly with animals and only to a less degree with plants. If these cultural features—for such they are—were not there, the social situation might have created them, or something like them. But they are there. Hence, the demands of the social situation are readily satisfied out of this rich store of preëxisting psychological material. The precise how and when of the process is another story, nor does it particularly matter. The crucial and significant point is this: a group divided into hereditary clans spontaneously develops tendencies the limiting value of which is a totemic complex. For the realization of these tendencies certain psychological or cultural data are required. These are found available. In a situation which, were they absent, might have itself created them, they are utilized promptly and effectively. Thus a totemic complex arises.

It will thus be seen that there exists an inherent and most deep-rooted *fitness* between the supernaturalism referred to before, the mystical man-nature relationship, and the social system which absorbs it. It is, then, to be expected that the vast majority of groups divided into hereditary social units will develop some sort of totemic complexes. And such is found to be the case.[19]

To summarize: Exogamy, a mystical man-nature relationship and functional homology of equivalent social units become associated in totemism by adopting a sib system as their carrier. And they adopt a sib system as their carrier because such a system is admirably fitted to become a vehicle for the crystallization and enhancement of these features.

V. TOTEMIC COMPLEXES AND RELIGIOUS SOCIETIES

Totemic communities, as complexes of historically and psychologically heterogeneous features, display certain striking similarities to another form of socio-religious association fairly common in primitive groups, namely, religious societies. A religious society is a group of individuals who have a common name (often derived from an animal, bird, or thing), share a set of religious and mythological beliefs, and perform together certain ceremonies. Where the societies occur, there are always more than one society in the tribe, while often a large part of the tribesmen may be grouped in societies either permanently or, as among the Kwakiutl, periodically. While male societies are more common, female societies also occur, but the membership of a society is almost invariably restricted to either one or the other sex. The geographical distribution of religious societies suggests some relation to totemism. In a large number of totemic areas religious societies also occur; for example, in several large areas in North America, in at least one area in South America, in West Africa and Northern Melanesia.

On the basis of his Melanesian studies W. H. R. Rivers came to the conclusion that in Mota (one of the Banks Islands), the religious societies developed out of a pre-existing totemism which was, as it were, sucked up into these societies.[20] Hutton Webster [21] went further, representing secret societies, in all areas, as totemism in decay. In this version the societies appear as a normal stage of evolution from totemism to other forms of socio-religious organization.

In this sweeping form the theory must certainly be rejected but it may nevertheless contain a germ of truth. In individual instances—in Mota, for example, or, perhaps, in the American Southwest—religious societies may actually have developed in this way. Also, the two institutions, resting against a similar socio-psychological and ideological background, must certainly be regarded as compatible, even though not genetically linked, except incidentally. The case of the Southern Kwakiutl is instructive here, among whom societies or totemic clans alternate: in the summer (the profane season) the clans constitute the social organization; whereas in the winter (the season of the secrets) these are replaced or, more accurately, overshadowed by a system of religious societies. One would not expect such periodic fluctuation between a system of clans, and, say, one of castes.

Of even greater interest than the geographical and the possible genetic relations of totemism and societies, are the similarities and contrasts between the two institutions from a theoretical standpoint. In both cases the tribe comprises a set of homologous social units; these units exercise functions—ceremonial, religious, artistic—similar in kind but differing specifically in each clan or society. These functions, finally, cluster about or grow out of certain mystical attitudes towards creatures or objects in nature, the latter feature, however, being more nearly characteristic of totemism than it is of societies. In both cases, moreover, the institution—a totemic complex or a cluster of societies —must be regarded as an alloy of historically and psychologically disparate traits.

The similarity, from a theoretical angle, thus seems to be so close as almost to approach identity. But the contrasts are equally significant. While a society, like a clan, is a social unit, it is one solely by dint of the common functions of its members. Take away the functions and nothing remains but an aggregate of wholly disparate individuals. Not so in the clan. Here also the functions give the true cultural orientation of the social unit, but should the functions lapse, the unit remains; for a clan consists of related individuals (*de facto* or *de jure*)—it is a group of status, whereas a society is a purely functional group. While this contrast is, perhaps, most important, other differences are not lacking. The religious aspect is almost invariably more pronounced in a society than in a totemic clan. Societies, as we saw, are largely unisexual, but not clans: a totemic complex with its supporting skeleton of clans necessarily comprises *all* the individuals of the tribe, whereas a tribal cluster of societies at best includes some of the women and never more than a majority of the men. This, of course, flows from the fact that a clan is a hereditary unit, part of the tribal social system, whereas a society is merely a part of *a* social system within the tribe, even though some societies may tend to become hereditary or comprise hereditary officials.

While the two institutions—totemism and religious societies—present, from a theoretical standpoint, a set of similar problems, it seems imperative to keep them apart conceptually as well as for purposes of investigation.[22]

VI. THE PATTERN THEORY OF TOTEMIC ORIGIN

It will be seen that any attempt to derive totemism from any one of its features is doomed to failure. If the historic facts were known in a particular instance, one of the theories might prove to be correct. But so might any of several others, in other particular instances. Generalization here would be vain and futile. It may, on the other hand, be of interest to inquire whether we could not go a step further in attempting to visualize the process through which any totemic complex might have come into being.

Let us remember, then, that in all totemic communities we find a group differentiated into clans which display sets of totemic features different in specific content but homologous in form and function. Can it be conceived that these features developed in the different clans independently? When one considers that the clans of a totemic organization are so interwoven as to constitute, to all appearance, an integral system; and that the homology of the clans is objectively, for the observer, as well as subjectively, for the totemite, the most patent fact about a totemic organization, one cannot but realize that any such series of independent developments lies entirely beyond the range of probability. But if the assumption of the independent development of totemic clan features is rejected, we must accept the only alternative assumption of a process of diffusion. On the other hand, the totemic features cannot be regarded as a contemporaneous growth; as regards the order of their appearance in a totemic complex, the features must be conceived of as a temporal series. Guided by these two assumptions, we may now visualize the totemic process at an extremely early stage of its growth. The tribe is differentiated into a number of social units or clans. The psychic atmosphere (Thurnwald's *Denkart*) is saturated with totemic possibilities. The stage is set for a first origin of totemism. Most totemic origin theories may claim the right of supplying one, but it is not with them we are here concerned. The first origin—animal name, taboo, sacred animal, myth of descent—is assumed to have occurred in one, or in a few, of the clans. Still there is no totemism. But presently, with the psychological conditions remaining favorable, another clan adopts the feature. Then another, and another. Finally, all the clans have it. The features in the various clans are not identical but they are equivalent, and they become specific clan character-istics—become socialized. The totemic process has begun.[23] In the same way other features begin to develop. They may arise in one or another clan through "inner" growth, or they may come from the outside, through contact with other tribes. No sooner is a new feature evolved or adopted by a clan than it starts on its round of diffusion until all the clans have incorporated it. Thus the totemic organi-zation grows and increases in complexity. Meanwhile, each feature in a clan stands for functional solidarity, and as the number of features multiplies, the solidarity increases. On the other hand, the homology of the clans also gains in complexity and completeness, and the realization of such homology, at first no doubt unconscious, may tend to rise into the consciousness of the totemites. It need not be assumed that a new feature always appears in the same clan, but it does not seem improbable that such a tendency should develop. One or a few clans may thus assume the function of setting totemic fashion.

In the early days of a totemic complex the diffusion of a new feature throughout the clan system must be a slow process. But as each clan consolidates tnrough the continuous superposition of common functions, and as the equivalence of the clans progresses with the addition of every new feature with reference to which the clans become homologous, this process of diffusion must become increasingly rapid and smooth. As feature upon feature spring up in one or another clan, their spread to other clans becomes a traditionally approved procedure, and the course and direction of the diffusion may also become fixed and stereotyped.

The central point of the above theory of the origin of totemism lies in the conception that the building up of a totemic complex consists of a series of totemic features which appear one by one (or possibly in small groups), spread from clan to clan, become socialized in the clans and absorbed in the complex. Each new feature, on its appearance in a clan, becomes a pattern presently followed by other clans until the wave of diffusion has swept over them all. The theory may thus be fitly called the *pattern* theory of the origin of totemism. It may be regarded as a compromise between the views of those whose thirst for interpretations cannot be quenched by anything save a first origin, and the views of those who do not believe in any hypothetical reconstructions. Attempts at reconciliation by compromise are seldom successful in science, and the theory seems to be doomed to rejection by both camps. I may therefore be permitted to emphasize the two aspects of the theory which, to my mind, should commend it to the attention of totemizing ethnologists. Being convinced that the search for first origins is a vain pursuit, I eliminate from my theory all assumption as to the specific character of the first origin of a totemic complex. I simply assume one. The second important aspect of the theory is the conception of the waves of diffusion through which each new feature is assimilated by the complex. This conception is purely hypothetical, that is, it cannot be substantiated by anything we know as actually occurring in totemic complexes, but it is supported by what we know of the psychology of social processes. It seems, in fact, to formulate the only way in which a totemic complex can come into being.

The theory offers a ready explanation of various totemic "anomalies." When one finds that one totemic community has only animal totems and another only bird totems, the tendency is to look for deep-rooted causes. It cannot, of course, be denied that some peculiarity in the environment or beliefs of the group may lead to such special developments. The explanation, however, may also lie in the fact that in one community a few animal names, adopted by several clans, fixed the pattern, which was followed by the other clans; while in another instance, the same occurred with bird names. In still other numerous instances the character of the names did not become stereotyped until some animal, bird, and plant names were taken, resulting in the distribution of names most frequently found in totemic communities. Double totems, as among the Baganda, or linked quadruple totems, as among the Massim of New Guinea, can be accounted for along the same lines. Not that the double or quadruple totems need be assumed to have constituted the primary conditions in these communities. In the early stages of their development these totemic complexes may have had the normal one-clan one-totem aspect. But presently some unconventional "cause" doubled the totems in one or a few clans; other clans followed suit; and so on.[24]

VII. TOTEMIC ANALOGUES IN MODERN SOCIETY

Evidence is not lacking that mystical and social features, once components of totemism, persist in modern society, if in less integrated form.

Of all things in nature, animals, both wild and tame, stand closest to us, and we find it difficult not to think of them in anthropomorphic terms. Similarities of physical and psychic traits in man and animal are stressed in verbal usage. We speak of the eagle eye, the leonine neart, the bull's neck, dogged perseverance. The fox and beaver, bear and rabbit, cat and cow, hog and ass, ape and shark, all figure in our scene in human disguise. The layman and the amateur naturalist as well find it difficult not to ascribe to animals qualities of intellect, affection, understanding, sensitiveness, vastly in excess of what sober judgment would allow.

While our attitude here is not strictly mystical, it leans dangerously in that direction.

Similarly with social tendencies. In modern as in primi- tive society, equivalent social units are known to adopt as classifiers names, badges, pins, flags, tattoo marks, colors. One thinks of high-school and college classes, baseball and football teams, political parties, the degrees of Elks and Masons, and the regiments of our armies.

The names and things thus used as classifiers rest against a background charged with potential emotion. In the case of regimental banners the emotional heat can, on occasion, become intense. Even the animal or bird- mascots cultivated by military units become, under appropriate conditions, such as war, immersed in a complex of attitudes and rites so exotic as to suggest an exaggerated analogy with totemism.

In one form or another the mystic and social tendencies of totemic days linger on in modern society. But we miss them on its highways. Here and there, under specially favorable conditions, these tendencies may flare up in a sort of totemic glow, presently to go out again, for lack of fuel. In primitive society the same tendencies, quickened and integrated by their association with sib systems, reach great heights of complexity and elaboration.

NOTES

[1] *Man*, 1902.
[2] *The Origin of Totemism*, 1901.
[3] *Golden Bough*, vol. ii.
[4] *Totemism and Exogamy*, vol. i.

[5] *Zeitschrift für Ethnologie,* vol. xli, 1909.

[6] Presidential Address to the Anthropological Section, *British Association for the Advancement of Science.*

[7] "The Origin of the Totemism Among the Aborigines of British Columbia," *Transactions of the Royal Society of Canada,* Second Series, vol. vii, 1901-2.

[8] "Ausdrucks- und Spieltätigkeit als Grundlage des Totemismus," *Anthropos,* vols. x-xi, 1915-16.

[9] In the sense of the "Culture Historical School"; cf. his "Totemismus als Kulturgeschichtliches Problem," *ibid.*

[10] See *Anthropos,* vols. x-xi, pp. 9669-70.

[11] For a more extended exposition and criticism of Durkheim's extraordinary book, see my "Religion and Society: A Critique of Emile Durkheim's Theory of the Origin and Nature of Religion," *Journal of Philosophy, Psychology and Scientific Methods,* vol. xiv, 1917.

[12] Cf. Frazer's "bush-soul" theory.

[13] *Elements of Folk-Psychology,* and *Völkerpsychologie,* vol. ii.

[14] Cf. the somewhat similar approach of Lawrence Gomme in his *Folklore as a Historical Science.*

[15] Cf., in this connection, my "Totemism, an Analytical Study," *Journal of American Folklore,* 1910; also the section "Early Life and Thought" in my *Early Civilization,* 1922; and "The Views of Andrew Lang and J. G. Frazer and E. Durkheim on Totemism," *Anthropos,* vols. x and xi, 1915-16.

[16] *Revue de l'Histoire des Religions,* vols. xxxvi and xxxvii, 1897-98.

[17] *Vide* Wundt.

[18] Thurnwald.

[19] This section is reproduced from my article, "Form and Content in Totemism," *American Anthropologist,* N.S., vol. xx, 1918.

[20] *History of Melanesian Society,* vol. ii, and "Totemism in Polynesia and Melanesia," *Journal of the Royal Anthropological Institute,* vol. xxxix, 1909.

[21] In his *Primitive Secret Societies,* 1908, and "Totem Clans and Secret Associations in Australia and Melanesia," *Journal of the Anthropological Institute,* vol. xli, 1911.

[22] This section is reproduced, with some omissions and additions, from my article, *Totemism,* in the New International Encyclopædia, Second Edition, vol. xxii.

[23] It must further be noted that the diffusion of the feature does not here proceed from individual to individual merely, which is, indeed, the way in which any custom spreads through a community. The individuals, to be sure, are the ultimate units to whom refer the functions for which the totemic features stand. But the diffusion of totemic features proceeds from clan to clan; and the individuals of each clan, when their turn arrives, do not adopt the feature itself but its homologue.

[24] The section on "The Pattern Theory" is reproduced in somewhat abbreviated form, from my "The Origin of Totemism" (*American Anthropologist,* N.S., vol. xiv, 1912, pp. 603-607).

THE INFLUENCE OF ANCIENT EGYPTIAN CIVILIZATION IN THE EAST AND IN AMERICA

By G. ELLIOT SMITH

In the lectures which in former years I have delivered at the John Rylands Library I discussed the problems of the gradual diffusion of Egypt's influence to the neighboring parts of Africa, Asia, and the Eastern Mediterranean Islands and Coasts, which began at a very early historical period. On the present occasion I am calling attention to a mass of evidence which seems to prove that, towards the close of the period of the New Empire, or perhaps even a little later, a great many of the most distinctive practices of Egyptian civilization suddenly appeared in more distant parts of the coastlines of Africa, Europe, and Asia, and also in course of time in Oceania and America; and to suggest that the Phœnicians must have been the chief agents in initiating the wholesale distribution of this culture abroad.

The Mediterranean has been the scene of so many conflicts between rival cultures that it is a problem of enormous complexity and difficulty to decipher the story of Egyptian influence in its much-scored palimpsest. For the purposes of my exposition it is easier to study its easterly spread, where among less cultured peoples it blazed its track and left a record less disturbed by subsequent developments than in the West. Mr. W. J. Perry has shown that once the easterly cultural migration has been studied the more complicated events in the West can be deciphered also.

The thesis I propose to submit for consideration, then, is (a) that the essential elements of the ancient civilizations of India, Further Asia, the Malay Archipelago, Oceania, and America were brought in succession to each of these places by mariners, whose oriental migrations (on an extensive scale) began as trading intercourse between the Eastern Mediterranean and India some time after 800 B.C. (and continued for many centuries); (*b*) that the highly complex and artificial culture which they spread abroad was derived largely from Egypt (not earlier than the XXI Dynasty), but also included many important accretions and modifications from the Phœnician world around the Eastern Mediterranean, from East Africa (and the Soudan), Arabia, and Babylonia; (*c*) that, in addition to providing the leaven which stimulated the development of the pre-Aryan civilization of India, the cultural stream to Burma, Indonesia, the eastern littoral of Asia and Oceania was in turn modified by Indian influences; and (*d*) that finally the stream, with many additions from Indonesia, Melanesia, and Polynesia, as well as from China and Japan, continued for many centuries to play upon the Pacific littoral of America, where it was responsible for planting the germs of the remarkable Pre-Columbian civilization. The reality of these migrations and this spread of culture is substantiated (and dated) by the remarkable collection of extraordinary practices and fantastic beliefs which these ancient mariners distributed along a well-defined route from the Eastern Mediterranean to America. They were responsible for stimulating the inhabitants of the coasts along a great part of their extensive itinerary (*a*) to adopt the practice of mummification, characterized by a variety of methods, but in every place with remarkable identities of technique and associated ritual, including the use of incense and libations, a funerary bier and boat, and certain peculiar views regarding the treatment of the head, the practice of remodeling the features and the use of statues, the possibility of bringing the dead to life, and the wanderings of the dead and its adventures in the underworld; (*b*) to build a great variety of megalithic monuments, conforming to certain well-defined types which

present essentially identical features throughout a consider
able extent, or even the whole, of the long itinerary, and in
association with these monuments identical traditions, beliefs, and customs; (*c*) to make idols in connection with
which were associated ideas concerning the possibility of
human beings or animals living in stones, and of the petri-
faction of men and women, the story of the deluge, of the
divine origin of kings, who are generally the children of
the sun or of the sky, and of the origin of the chosen people
from incestuous unions; (*d*) to worship the sun and adopt
in reference to this deity a complex and arbitrary symbolism
representing an incongruous grouping of a serpent in conjunction with the sun's disc equipped with a hawk's wings,
often associated also with serpent-worship or in other cases
the belief in a relationship with or descent from serpents;
(*e*) to adopt the practices of circumcision, tattooing, mas-
sage, piercing and distending the ear-lobules, artificial
deformation of the skull, and perhaps trephining, dental
mutilations, and perforating the lips and nose; (*f*) to practice
weaving linen, and in some cases to make use of Tyrian
purple, pearls, precious stones, and metals, and conch-shell
trumpets, as well as the curious beliefs and superstitions attached to the latter; (*g*) to adopt certain definite metal-
lurgical methods, as well as mining; (*h*) to use methods
of intensive agriculture, associated with the use of terraced
irrigation, the artificial terraces being retained with stone
walls; (*i*) to adopt certain phallic ideas and practices; (*j*)
to make use of the swastika symbol, and to adopt the idea
that stone implements are thunder-teeth or thunderbolts and
the beliefs associated with this conception; (*k*) to use the
boomerang; (*l*) to hold certain beliefs regarding "the
heavenly twins"; (*m*) to practice couvade; (*n*) to adopt the
same games; and (*o*) to display a special aptitude for, and
skill and daring in, maritime adventures, as well as to
adopt a number of curiously arbitrary features of boat-
building.

Many of the items in this list I owe to Mr. W. J. Perry,

to whose coöperation and independent researches the conclusiveness of the case I am putting before you is due. But above all the credit is due to him of having so clearly elucidated the motives for the migrations and explained why the new learning took root in some places and not in others.

That this remarkable cargo of fantastic customs and beliefs was really spread abroad, and most of them at one and the same time, is shown by the fact that in places as far apart as the Mediterranean and Peru, as well as in many intermediate localities, these cultural ingredients were linked together in an arbitrary and highly artificial manner, to form a structure which it is utterly impossible to conceive as having been built up independently in different places.

The fact that some of the practices which were thus spread abroad were not invented in Egypt and Phœnicia until the eighth century B.C. makes this the earliest possible date for the commencement of the great wandering.

In some of the earliest Egyptian graves, which cannot be much less than sixty centuries old, pottery has been found decorated with paintings representing boats of considerable size and pretensions. The making of crude types of boats was perhaps one of the first, if not actually the earliest, manifestations of human inventiveness: for primitive men in the very childhood of the species were able to use rough craft made of logs, reeds, or inflated skins, to ferry themselves across sheets of water which otherwise would have proved insuperable hindrances to their wanderings. But the Egyptian boats of 4000 B.C. probably represented a considerable advance in the art of naval construction; and before the Predynastic period had come to a close the invention of metal tools gave a great impetus to the carpenter's craft, and thus opened the way for the construction of more ambitious ships.

Whether or not the Predynastic boatmen ventured beyond the Nile into the open sea is not known for certain, although the balance of probability inclines strongly to the conclusion that they did so.

But there is positive evidence to prove that as early as 2800 B.C. maritime intercourse was definitely established along the coasts of the Eastern Mediterranean, bringing into contact the various peoples, at any rate those of Egypt and Syria, scattered along the littoral. Egyptian seamen were also trafficking along the shores of the Red Sea; and there are reasons for believing that in Protodynastic times such intercourse may have extended around the coast of Arabia, as far as the Sumerian settlement at the head of the Persian Gulf, thus bringing into contact the homes of the world's most ancient civilizations.

More daring seamen were venturing out into the open sea, and extending their voyages at least as far as Crete: for the geographical circumstances at the time in question make it certain that Neolithic culture could not have reached that island in any other way than by maritime intercourse.

The Early Minoan Civilization, as well as the later modifications of Cretan burial customs, such as the making of rock-cut tombs and the use of stone for building, were certainly inspired in large measure by ideas brought from Egypt.

Long before the beginning of the second millennium B.C. the germs of the Egyptian megalithic culture had taken deep root, not only in Crete itself, but also throughout the Ægean and the coasts of Asia Minor and Palestine.

In course of time, as the art of ship-building advanced and the mariners' skill and experience increased, no doubt more extensive and better-equipped enterprises were undertaken.[1] Instances of this are provided by the famous expedition to the land of Punt in Queen Hatshepsut's reign and the exploits of the Minoan seamen of Crete.

Such commercial intercourse cannot fail to have produced a slow diffusion of culture from one people to another, even if it was primarily of the nature of a mere exchange of commodities. But as the various civilizations gradually assumed their characteristic forms a certain conventionalism and a national pride grew up, which protected each of these more cultured communities from being so readily influenced by contact with aliens as it was in the days of its uncultured simplicity. Each tended to become more and more conscious of its national peculiarities, and immune against alien influences that threatened to break down the rigid walls of its proud conservatism.

It was not until the Minoan state had fallen and Egypt s dominion had begun to crumble that a people free from such prejudices began to adopt all that it wanted from these hidebound civilizations. To its own exceptional aptitude for and experience in maritime exploits it added all the knowledge acquired by the Egyptians, Minoans, and the peoples of Levant. It thus took upon itself to become the great intermediary between the nations of antiquity; and in the course of its trafficking with them, it did not scruple to adopt their arts and crafts, their burial customs, and even their gods. In this way was inaugurated the first era of really great sea-voyages in the world's history. For the trafficking with these great proud empires proved so profitable that the enterprising intermediaries who assumed the control of it, not only of bartering their merchandise one with the other, but also of supplying their wants from elsewhere, soon began to exploit the whole world for the things which the wealthy citizens of the imperial states desired.

There can be no doubt that it was the Phœnicians, lured forth into the unknown oceans in search of gold, who first broke through the bounds of the Ancient East and whose ships embarked upon these earliest maritime adventures on the grand scale. Their achievements and their motives present some analogies to those of the great European seamen of the fifteenth and sixteenth centuries who raided the East Indies and the Spanish Main for loot. But the exploits of the Phœnicians must be regarded as even greater events, not only by reason of the earlier period in which they were accomplished, but also from their vast influence upon the history of civilization in outlying parts of the world, as well as for inaugurating new methods of commerce and extending the use of its indispensable instrument, gold currency.

Their doings are concisely set forth in the twenty-seventh chapter of the Book of Ezekiel, where Tyre is addressed in these words: "Who is there like Tyre, like her that is brought to silence in the midst of the sea? When thy wares went forth out of the seas, thou filledst many peoples: thou didst enrich the kings of the earth with the multitude of thy riches, and of thy merchandise."

Many circumstances were responsible for extending these wider ramifications of maritime trade, so graphically described in the rest of the same chapter of Ezekiel. As I have already explained, it was not merely the desire to acquire wealth, but also the appreciation of the possibilities of doing so that prompted the Phœnicians' exploits. Not being hampered by any undue respect for customs and conventions, they readily acquired and assimilated to themselves all the practical knowledge of the civilized world, whether it came from Egypt, Mesopotamia, Asia Minor, or the Ægean. They were sprung from a preëminently maritime stock and probably had gained experience in seamanship in the Persian Gulf: and when they settled on the Syrian Coast they were also able to add to their knowledge of such things all that the Egyptians and the population of the Levant and Ægean had acquired for themselves after centuries of maritime adventure. But one of the great factors in explanation of the naval supremacy of the Phœnicians was their acquaintance with the facts of astronomy. The other peoples of the Ancient East had acquired a considerable knowledge of the stars, the usefulness of which, however, was probably restricted by religious considerations. Whether this be so or not, there can be no doubt that the Phœnicians were not restrained by any such ideas from putting to its utmost practical application the valuable guide to navigation in the open sea which this astronomical learning supplied.

They were only able to embark upon their great maritime enterprises in virtue of the use they made of the pole-star for steering. This theme has been discussed in great detail by Mrs. Zelia Nuttall; and although I am unable to accept a great part of her argument from astronomy, the evidence in substantiation of the use made of the pole-star for navigation, not only in the Mediterranean, but also by seamen navigating along the coasts of Asia and America, cannot be questioned.

Within recent years there has been a remarkable reaction against the attitude of a former generation, which perhaps unduly exaggerated certain phases of the achievements of the Phœnicians.

But the modern pose of minimizing their influence surely errs too much in the other direction, and is in more flagrant conflict with the facts of history and archæology than the former doctrine, which its sponsors criticize so emphatically. Due credit can be accorded to the Egyptians, Minoans, and other ancient mariners, without in any way detracting from the record of the Phœnicians, whose exploits could hardly have attained such great and widespread notoriety among the ancients without very real and substantial grounds for their reputation. The recent memoirs of Siret, Dahse, Nuttall, and the writer have adduced abundant evidence in justification of the greatness of their exploits. Professor Sayce says: "They were the intermediaries of the ancient civilizations"; and that by 600 B.C. they had "penetrated to the northwest coast of India and probably to the island of Britain." "Phœnician art was essentially catholic . . . it as-similated the art of Babylonia, Egypt, and Assyria, super-adding something of its own. . . . The cities of the Phœnicians were the first trading communities the world has seen. Their colonies were originally mere marts and their voyages of discovery were taken in the interests of trade. The tin of Britain, the silver of Spain, the birds of the Canaries, the frankincense of Arabia, the pearls and ivory of India all flowed into their harbors."

These were the distinctive features of the Phœnicians' activities, of which Mr. Hogarth [2] gives a concise and graphic summary. But, as Mr. Perry has pointed out, they were led forth above all in search for gold. As he suggests, the Phœnicians seem to have been one of the first peoples to have assigned to gold the kind of importance and value that civilized people have ever since attached to it. It was no longer merely material for making jewelry: "it became a currency, which made the foundation of civilization not only possible but inevitable, once such a currency came into being."

The remarks addressed to Tyre in the Book of Ezekiel [3] give expression to these ideas: "All the ships of the sea with their mariners were in thee to occupy thy merchandise. . . . Tarshish was thy merchant by reason of the multitude of all kinds of riches; with silver, iron, tin, and lead, they traded for thy wares. . . . Syria was thy merchant by reason of the multitude of thy handy-works: they traded for thy wares with emeralds, purple, and broidered work, and fine linen, and coral [probably pearls], and rubies; they traded for thy merchandise wheat of Minnith, and Pannag, and honey, and oil, and balm. . . . The traffickers of Sheba and Raamah, they were thy traffickers: they traded for thy wares with chief of all spices, and with all precious stones, and gold. . . . The ships of Tarshish were thy caravans for thy merchandise; and thou wast replenished, and made very glorious in the heart of the seas. Thy rowers have brought thee into great waters: the east wind has broken thee in the heart of the seas."

The Phœnicians in fact controlled the commerce of most of the civilized world of that time; and they did so mainly because of their superior skill and daring in seamanship, their newly realized appreciation of the value of gold, and their desire for precious stones and pearls, for which they began to ransack every country near and far. So thoroughly did they, and their pupils and imitators, accomplish their mission that only one pearl-field in the whole world (the West Australian site at Broome) escaped their exploitation. Many of their great maritime adventures have been recorded by the ancient classical writers. The reality or others, for example, to India, which have not been specifically described, are none the less certain: not only was there most intimate intercourse between the Red Sea and India at the very time when the Phœnicians were displaying great activity in the Indian Ocean, but the methods and the motives, no less than the cargoes, of these energetic and skillful mariners, whose exploits are celebrated in the *Mahābhārata,* and whose achievements are indelibly impressed upon Indian culture, proclaim them unmistakably to be Phœnicians.

In the course of this trading there was not only an interchange of the articles of commerce provided by the Mediterranean countries and India, as well as by all the intermediate ports of call, but also there is the most positive evidence, in the multiude of western practices which suddenly made their appearance in India, at the very time when this free trafficking became definitely established, in demonstration of the fact that the civilizations of the West were exerting a very potent cultural influence upon the Dravidian population of India. Many of the customs which made their first appearance in India at that epoch, such as mummification, the making of rock-cut temples, and stone tombs (and many others of the long list of practices enumerated earlier in the present discourse) were definitely Egyptian in origin.

One of the most significant and striking of the effects of this maritime intercourse with Egypt was the influence exerted by the latter in the matter of ship-building.

The fact that such distinctively Egyptian practices were spread abroad at the same time as, and in close association with, many others equally definitely Mediterranean in origin (such as the use of Tyrian purple and of the conch-shell trumpet in temple services) is further corroboration of the fact that the Phœnicians, who are known to have adopted the same mixture of customs, were the distributors of so remarkable a cultural cargo.

This identification is further confirmed by the fact that additions were made to this curious repertoire from precisely those regions where the Phœnicians are known vigorously to have carried on their trafficking, such as many places in the Mediterranean, on the Red Sea littoral, Ethiopia, and Southern Arabia.

In this way alone can be explained how there came to be associated with the megalithic culture such practices as the Sudanese Negro custom of piercing and distending the ear-lobules, the Armenian (or Central Asiatic) procedure for artificial deformation of the head, the method of terraced cultivation, which was probably a Southern Arabian modification of Egyptian cultivation and irrigation on a level surface; certain beliefs regarding the "heavenly twins"; and perhaps such institutions as "men's houses" and secret societies, and the building of pile-dwellings, and customs such as trephining, dental mutilations, and perforating the lips and nose, which were collected by the wanderers from a variety of scattered peoples in the Ancient East.

Mrs. Nuttall has made a vast collection of other evidence relating mainly to astronomy, calendars, the methods of sub-dividing time, and questions of political and social organization, upon the basis of which she independently arrived at essentially the same conclusions as I have formulated, not only as regards the reality and the time of the great migration of culture, but also as to the identification of the Phœnicians as the people mainly responsible for its diffusion abroad. She failed to realize, however, that this easterly diffusion of knowledge and customs was merely incidental to commercial intercourse and a result of the trafficking.

In addition to all these considerations I should like once more to emphasize the fact that it was the study of the physical characteristics of the people scattered along the great megalithic track—and more especially those of Polynesia and the Eastern Mediterranean—that first led me to investigate these problems of the migrations of culture and its bearers to the Far East. For one cannot fail to be struck with the many features of resemblance between the ancient seamen who were mainly responsible for the earliest great maritime exploits in the Mediterranean and Erythrean seas and the Pacific Ocean respectively.

The remarkable evidence brought forward at the recent meeting of the British Association by Mr. W. J. Perry seems to me finally to decide the question of the identity of the wanderers who distributed early Mediterranean culture in the East.

His investigations also explain the motives for the journeyings and the reasons why the western culture took root in some places and not in others.

Throughout the world the localized areas where the distinctive features of this characteristic civilization occur—and especially such elements as megalithic structures, terraced irrigation, sun-worship, and practices of mummification—are precisely those places where ancient mineworkings, and especially gold-mines, or pearl-fisheries, are also found, and where presumably Phœnician settlements were established to exploit these sources of wealth. "But not only is a general agreement found between the distributions of megalithic influence and ancient mine-workings, but the technique of mining, smelting, and refining operations is identical in all places where the earliest remains have been found. . . . The form of the furnaces used; the introduction of the blast over the mouth of the furnace; the process of refining whereby the metal is first roughly smelted in an open furnace and afterwards refined in crucibles; as well as the forms of the crucibles and the substances of which they were made, are the same in all places where traces of ancient smelting operations have been discovered. . . . The conclusion to which all these facts point is that the search for certain forms of material wealth led the carriers of the megalithic culture to those places where the things they desired were to be found."

The distribution of pearl-shell explains how their course was directed along certain routes: the situations of ancient mines provide the reason for the settlement of the wanderers and the adoption of the whole of the megalithic culture-complex in definite localities.

From the consideration of all of these factors it is clear that the great easterly migration of megalithic culture was the outcome of the traffic carried on between the Eastern Mediterranean and India during the three or four centuries from about 800 B.C. onward, and that the Phœnicians were mainly responsible for these enterprises. The littoral populations of Egypt, Ethiopia, Arabia, the Persian Gulf, and India itself no doubt took a considerable part in this intercourse, for they all provided hardy mariners inured by long experience to such pursuits; but for the reasons already suggested (their wider knowledge of the science and practice of seamanship) the Phœnicians seem to have directed and controlled these expeditions, even if they exploited the shores of the Mediterranean, Red Sea, Arabia, and farther East for skilled sailors to man their ships. That such recruits played a definite part in the Phœnician expeditions is shown by the transmission to the East of customs and practices found in localized areas of the coasts of the Mediterranean and Black Seas, and especially of Ethiopia, Arabia, and the Persian Gulf. It is probable that expert pearl-fishers were recruited on the shores of the Red Sea and gold-miners in Nubia and the Black Sea littoral.

The easterly migration of culture rolled like a great flood along the Asiatic littoral between the end of the eighth and the beginning of the fifth century B.C.; and there can be no doubt that the leaven of western culture was distributed to India, China, Japan, Indonesia, and possibly even further, mainly by that great wave. But for long ages before that time, no doubt a slow diffusion of culture had been taking place along the same coastlines; and ever since the first great stream brought the flood of western learning to the East a similar influence has been working along the same route, carrying to and fro new elements of cultural exchange between the East and West.

The "Periplus of the Erythrean Sea" reveals to us how

closely the old routes were being followed and the same kina of traffic was going on in the first century of the Christian era; the exploits of other mariners, Egyptian, Greek, Arabic, Indian, and Chinese, show how continuously such intercourse was maintained right up to the time when Western European adventurers first intruded into the Indian Ocean. The spread of Brahmanism, Buddhism, and Islam are further illustrations of the way in which such migrations of new cults followed the old routes.

In the light of such knowledge it would be altogether unjustifiable to assume that the geographical distribution of similar customs and beliefs along this great highway of ancient commerce was due exclusively to the great wave of megalithic culture before the sixth century B.C. There is evidence of the most definite kind that many of the elements of western culture—such, for example, as Ptolemaic and Christian methods of embalming—were spread abroad at later times.

Nevertheless there is amply sufficient information to justify the conclusion that many of the fundamental conceptions of Indian, Chinese, Japanese, and American civilization were planted in their respective countries by the great cultural wave which set out from the African coast not long before the sixth century B.C.

One of the objections raised even by the most competent ethnologists against the adoption of this view is the assumption involved in such a hypothesis that one and the same wave carried to the East a jumble of practices ranging in dates from that of Predynastic Egypt to the seventh century B.C.—that at, or about, the same time the inspiration to build megalithic monuments fashioned on the models of the Pyramid Age and others imitating New Empire temples reached India.

But the difficulties created by this line of argument are largely illusory, especially when it is recalled that the sailors manning the Phœnician ships were recruited from so many localities. It is known that even within a few miles of the

Egyptian frontiers—Nubia, for instance—many customs and practices which disappeared in Egypt itself in the times of the New, Middle, or Old Empires, or even in Predynastic times, persist until the present day. The earliest Egyptian method of circumcision (which Dr. Rivers calls "incision") disappeared in Egypt probably in the Pyramid Age, but it is still practiced in East Africa; and no doubt it was the sailors recruited from that coast who were responsible for transmitting this practice to the East. When the first British settlement was made in America it introduced not only the civilization of the Elizabethan era, but also practices and customs that had been in vogue in England for many centuries; and no doubt every emigrant carried with him the traditions and beliefs that may have survived from very remote times in his own village. So the Phœnician expeditions spread abroad not only the Egyptian civilization of the seventh cenutry B.C., but also the customs, beliefs, and practices of every sailor and passenger who traveled in their ships, whether he came from Syria, or the Ægean, from Egypt or Ethiopia, Arabia or the Persian Gulf. The fact that many extremely old Egyptian practices, which had been given up for centuries in Egypt itself, had survived elsewhere in the Mediterranean area and in Ethiopia explains how a mixture of Egyptian customs, distinctive of a great variety of different ages in Egypt itself, may have been distributed abroad at one and the same time by such mixed crews.

In her great monograph Mrs. Nuttall refers to "the great intellectual movement that swept at one time, like a wave, over the ancient centers of civilization"; and she quotes Huxley's essay on "Evolution and Ethics" with reference to the growth of Ionian philosophy during "the eighth, seventh, and sixth centuries before our era" as "one of the many results of the stirring of the moral and intellectual life of the Aryan-Semitic population of Western Asia"; but Huxley was careful to add that "the Ionian intellectual movement is only one of the several sporadic indications of some powerful mental ferment over the whole of the area comprised between the Ægean and Northern Hindustan." She cites other evidence that points to the seventh century B.C. as about the time of the extension of Mediterranean influence to India [and Indian influence to the west] through the intermediation of the Phœnicians.

It was not, however, merely to India that this diffusion extended, but also to China and Mexico. In the light of my own investigations I am inclined to reëcho the words of Mrs. Nuttall: "As far as I can judge, the great antiquity attributed, by Chinese historians, to the establishment of the governmental and cyclical schemes, still in use, appears extremely doubtful. Referring the question to Sinologists, I venture to ask whether it does not seem probable that the present Chinese scheme dates from the lifetime of Lao-tze, in the sixth century B.C., a period marked by the growth of Ionian philosophy, one feature of which was the invention of numerical schemes applied to 'divine politics' and ideal forms of government."

To this I should like to add the query, whether there is any real evidence that the art of writing was known in China before that time? The researches of Dr. Alan Gardiner make it abundantly clear that the art of writing was invented in Egypt; and further suggest that the idea must have spread from Egypt at an early date to Western Asia and the Mediterranean, where many diversely specialized kinds of script developed. Discussing the cultural connection between India and the Persian Gulf "at the beginning of the seventh (and perhaps at the end of the eighth) century B.C.," my colleague Professor Rhys Davids adduces evidence in demonstration of the fact that the written scripts of India, Ceylon, and Burma were derived from that of "the pre-Semitic race now called Akkadians." [4]

Dr. Schoff, however, in his remarkable commentary on the "Periplus of the Erythrean Sea," claims a Phœnician origin for the Dravidian alphabet.

If then the knowledge of the art of writing reached India

with the great wave of megalithic culture, it might be profitable to inquire whether the development of Chinese writing was really as ancient as most Sinologists assume it to be, or, on the other hand, may not its growth also have been stimulated by the same "great intellectual ferment" which is recognized as having brought about the new development in India? There is, of course, the possibility that the knowledge of writing may have reached China overland even before it is known to have reached India.

Professor Rhys Davids also calls attention to "the great and essential similarity" between the "details of the lower phases of religion in India in the sixth century B.C., with the beliefs held, not only at the same time in the other centers of civilization—in China, Persia, and Egypt, in Italy and Greece—but also among the savages of then and now"; with reference to "a further and more striking resemblance," he quotes Sir Henry Maine's observation that "Nothing is more remarkable than the extreme fewness of progressive societies—the difference between them and the stationary races is one of the greatest secrets inquiry has yet to penetrate." [5]

But is it not patent that what we who have been brought up in the atmosphere of modern civilization call "progress," is the striving after an artificial state of affairs, like all the arts and crafts of civilization itself, created by a special set of circumstances in one spot, the Ancient East? There is no inborn impulse to impel other people to become "progressive societies" in our acceptation of that term: in the past history of the world these other communities only began to "progress" when they had been inoculated with the germs of this artificial civilization by contact with the peoples of the Eastern Mediterranean area.

My colleague does not view the problem in this light. For him it is the most "stupendous marvel in the whole history of mankind" that the four great civilizations which grew up in the river basins of the Nile and the Euphrates, the Ganges and the Yellow River—through real and progressive civilizations, whose ideas and customs were no doubt constantly changing and growing—maintained merely "a certain dead level, if not a complete absence of what we should call philosophic thought," and "did not build up any large and general views, either of ethics, or of philosophy, or of religion"; but then "suddenly, and almost simultaneously, and almost certainly independently, there is evidence, about the sixth century B.C., in each of these widely separated centers of civilization, of a leap forward in speculative thought, of a new birth in ethics, of a religion of conscience threatening to take the place of the old religion of custom and magic."

But Professor Rhys Davids' opinion that this profound transformation occurred "almost certainly independently" is hard to reconcile with the fact, which he clearly explained earlier in the same book, that for more than a century before the time of this "stupendous marvel" India had been in touch with the older civilizations of the West.[6] All of the difficulties of this, the most "suggestive problem awaiting the solution of the historian of human thought," [7] disappear once the extent of this cultural contact with the West is fully realized.

The evidence to which I have called attention here, and elsewhere, makes it appear unlikely that these momentous events in the history of civilization were independent one of the other; to me it seems to prove definitely and most conclusively that they were parts of one connected movement. The "powerful ferment" of which Huxley speaks was due to the action upon the uncultured population of India (and in turn also those of China, Japan, and America) of the new knowledge brought from the Eastern Mediterranean by the Phœnician mariners, or the passengers who traveled with them in their trading expeditions.

To quote Mrs. Nuttall again: "Just as the older Andean art closely resembles that of the early Mediterranean, an observation made by Professor F. W. Putnam (1899), so the fundamental principles, numerical scheme, and plan of the state founded by the foreign Incas in Peru, resembled those formulated by Plato in his description of an ideal state." [8] As one of the results of their intimate intercourse with Egypt the Phœnicians had adopted many of the Egyptian customs and beliefs, as well as becoming proficient in its arts and crafts. Perhaps also they recruited some of their seamen from the Egyptians who had been accustomed for long ages to maritime pursuits. In this way it may have come to pass that, when the Phœnicians embarked on their great over-sea expeditions, they became the distributors of Egyptian practices. They did not, of course, spread abroad Egyptian culture in its purest form: for as middlemen they selected for adoption, consciously as well as unconsciously, certain of its constituent elements and left others. Moreover, they had customs of their own and practices which they had borrowed from the whole Eastern Mediterranean world as well as from Mesopotamia.

The first stage of the oriental extension of their trafficking was concerned with the Red Sea and immediately beyond the Straits of the Bab-el-Mandeb.[9] In the course of their trading in these regions the travelers freely adopted the practices of the inhabitants of the Ethiopian coast and southern Arabia —customs which in many cases had been derived originally from Egypt and had slowly percolated up the Nile, and eventually, with many modifications and additions, reached the region of the Somali coast. Whether this adoption or Ethiopian customs was the result merely of intercourse with the natives in the Sabæan and East African ports, or was to be attributed to the actual recruiting of seamen for the oriental expeditions from those regions, there is no evidence to permit us to say: but judging from the analogies of what is known to have happened elsewhere, it is practically certain that the latter suggestion alone affords an adequate explanation of the potent influence exerted by these Ethiopian practices in the Far East. For such a complete transference of customs and beliefs from one country to another can occur only when the people who practice them migrate from their homeland and settle in the new country. It is, of course, well recognized that from the eighth century onward, if not before then, there has been some intercourse between East Africa and India, and the whole of the intervening littoral of Southern Asia.[10]

For reasons that I have explained elsewhere it is probable that, even as early as the time of the First Egyptian Dynasty, maritime intercourse was already taking place along the whole Arabian coast, and even linking up in cultural contact the nascent civilizations developing in the Nile Valley and near the head of the Persian Gulf. No doubt the following twenty-five centuries witnessed a gradual development and oriental extension of this littoral intercommunication: but from the eighth century onward the current flowed more strongly and in immeasurably greater volume. The western coast of India was subjected to the full force of a cultural stream in which the influences of Egypt and the Eastern Mediterranean world, Ethiopia, Arabia, and Babylonia were blended by the Phœnicians, who no doubt were mainly responsible for controlling and directing the current for their own pecuniary benefit.

This easterly stream, as I have already explained above, was responsible for originating in India and Ceylon, at about the same time, temples of New Empire Egyptian type, dolmens which represent the Old Empire type, rounded tumuli which might be regarded as Mycenean, and seven-stepped stone Pyramids as Chaldean, modifications of Egyptian Pyramids; and if the monuments farther east are taken into consideration, the blended influences of Egypt, Babylonia, and India become even more definitely manifested. In studying the oriental spread of Egyptian ideas and practices it must constantly be borne in mind that it was the rare exception rather than the rule for the influence of such things to be exerted directly, as for example when Cyrus definitely adopted Egyptian funerary customs and methods of tomb-construction. His successors even employed Egyptian craftsmen to carry out the work. In most cases an alien people, the Phœnicians, were responsible for transmitting these customs to India and the Further East, and not only did they modify them themselves, but in addition they, or the crews of their ships, carried to the East the influence of Egyptian practices which had been adopted by various other alien peoples and had suffered more or less transformation. In this way alone is it possible to explain how large a part was played in this easterly migration of culture by the customs of Ethiopia. For many centuries the effects of Egyptian civilization had been slowly percolating up the Nile amongst a variety of people, and ultimately, with many additions and modifications, made themselves apparent among the littoral population of East Africa. Such Ethiopian transformations of Egyptian ideas and customs form a very obtrusive element in the cultural wave which flowed to India, Indonesia, and Oceania.

It is instructive to compare the outstanding features of tomb and temple-construction in Egypt with those of the Asiatic and American civilization. In Egypt it is possible to study the gradual evolution of the temple and to realize in some measure the circumstances and ideas which prompted the development and the accentuation of certain features at the expense of others.

For example, the conception of the door of a tomb or temple as symbolizing the means of communication between the living and the dead was apparent even in Proto-dynastic times, and gradually became so insistent that by the time of the New Empire the Egyptian temple has been converted into a series of monstrously overgrown gateways or pylons, which dwarfed all the other features into insignificance. The same feature revealed itself in the Dravidian temples of Southern India; and the obtrusive gateways of Further Asiatic temples, no less than the symbolic wooden structures found in China and Japan (Torii), are certainly manifestations of the same conception.

Among less cultured people, such as the Fijians, who were unable to reproduce this feature of the Egyptian and Indian temples, the general plan, without the great pylons or gopurams, was imitated. The Fijians have a tradition that the people who built these great stone enclosures came across the sea from the West.

Other features of the Egyptian temples of the New Empire period, which were widely adopted in other lands, were the placing of colossal statues alongside the doorway, as in the Ramesseum at Thebes, the construction of a causeway leading up to the temple, flanked with stones, carved or uncarved, such as the avenue of sphinxes at Karnak, and the excavation of elaborate rock-cut temples such as that at Abu-Simbel. In the temples of India, Cambodia, China, and America such features repeatedly occur.

A whole volume might be written on the evidence supplied by Oriental and American Pyramids of the precise way in which the influences of Egypt, Babylonia, and the Ægean were blended in these monuments.

In the Far East and America the Chaldean custom obtained of erecting the temple upon the summit of a truncated Pyramid. In Palenque and Chiapas, as well as elsewhere in the Isthmus region of America, many temples are found thus perched upon the tops of Pyramids. In design they are essentially Egyptian, not only as regards their plan, but also in the details of their decoration, from the winged disc upon the lintel, to the reliefs within the sanctuary. For in the Palenque temples are depicted scenes strictly comparable to those found in the New Empire Theban temples.

I need not enter into the discussion of mummification and the very precise evidence it affords of the easterly spread of Egyptian influence, for I have devoted a special memoir to the consideration of its significance. I should like to make it plain, however, that it was the data afforded by the technique of the earliest method of embalming that is known to have been adopted in the Far East which led me to assign the age of the commencement of its migration to a time probably not earlier than the eighth century B.C.; and that this conclusion was reached long before I was aware of all the other evidence of most varied nature[11] which points to the same general conclusion. As several different methods of embalming, Late New Empire, Græco-Roman, and Coptic, are known to have reached India it is quite clear that at least three distinct cultural waves proceeded to the East: but the first, which planted the germs of the new culture on the practically virgin soil of the untutored East, exerted an infinitely profounder influence than all that came after.

In fact most of the obtrusive elements of the megalithic culture, with its strange jumble of associated practices, beliefs, and traditions, certainly traveled in the first great wave, somewhere about the time of, perhaps a little earlier or later than, the seventh century B.C.

Although in this lecture I am primarily concerned with the demonstration of the influence exerted, directly or indirectly, by Egyptian culture in the East, it is important to obtain confirmation from other evidence of the date which the former led me to assign to the great migration. I have already referred to the facts cited by Mrs. Nuttall in proof of her contention that Ionian ideas spread East and ultimately reached America. Since her great monograph was written she has given an even more precise and convincing proof of the influence of the Phœnician world on America by describing how the use of Tyrian purple extended as far as Mexico in Pre-Columbian times. The associated use of conch-shell trumpets and pearls is peculiarly instructive: the geographical distribution of the former enables one to chart the route taken by this spread of culture, while the latter (the pearl-fisheries) supply one of the motives which attracted the wanderers and led them on until eventually they reached the New World.

Professor Bosanquet has adduced evidence suggesting that Purpura was first used by the Minoans: in Crete also the conch-shell trumpet was employed in the temple services. No doubt the Phœnicians acquired these customs from the Mycenean peoples.

In his monograph on "The Sacred Chank of India" (1914) Mr. James Hornell has filled in an important gap in the chain of distribution given by Mrs. Nuttall. He has not only confirmed her opinion as to the close association of the conch-shell trumpet and pearls, but also has shown what an important rôle these shells have played in India from Dravidian times onward. His evidence is doubly welcome, not only because it links up the use of the Chank with so many elements of the megalithic culture and of the temple ritual in India, but also because it affords additional confirmation of the date which I have assigned for the introduction of the former into India.

In India these new elements of culture took deep root and developed into the luxurious growth of so-called Dravidian civilization, which played a great part in shaping the customs and practices of the later Brahmanical and Buddhist cults. From India a series of migrations carried the megalithic customs and beliefs, and their distinctively Indian developments, farther east to Burma, Indonesia, China, and Japan; and, with many additions from these countries, streams of wanderers for many centuries carried them out into the islands of the Pacific and eventually to the shores of America, where there grew up a highly organized but exotic civilization compounded of the elements of the Old World's ancient culture, the most outstanding and distinctive ingredients of which came originally from Ancient Egypt.

I do not possess the special knowledge to estimate the reliability of M. Terrien de Lacouperie's remarkable views on the origin of Chinese civilization, some of which seem to be highly speculative. But there is a sufficient mass of precise information, based upon the writings of creditable authorities, to discount in large measure the wholesale condemnation of his opinions in recent years. Whatever justification, or lack of it, there may be for his statements as to the early overland connection between Mesopotamia and China, his views concerning the later maritime intercourse between the Red Sea, Persian Gulf, India and Indo-China, and China are in remarkable accordance with the opinions which, in the absence of any previous acquaintance with his writings, I have set forth here, not only as regards the nature of the migration and the sources of the elements of culture, but also the date of its arrival in the far east and the motives which induced traders to go there.

There can be no reasonable doubt that Asiatic civilization reached America partly by way of Polynesia, as well as directly from Japan, and also by the Aleutian route.

The immensely formidable task of spanning the broad Pacific to reach the coasts of America presents no difficulty to the student of early migrations. "The islands of the Pacific were practically all inhabited long before Tasman and Cook made their appearance in Pacific waters. Intrepid navigators had sailed their canoes north and south, east and west, until their language and their customs had been carried into every corner of the ocean. These Polynesian sailors had extended their voyages from Hawaii in the North to the fringe of the ice-fields in the Far South, and from the coast of South America on the East to the Philippine Islands on the West. No voyage seems to have been too extended for them, no peril too great for them to brave."

Mr. Elsdon Best, from whose writings I have taken the above quotation, answers the common objection that the frailness of the early canoes was incompatible with such journeys. "As a matter of fact the sea-going canoe of the ancient Maori was by no means frail: it was a much stronger vessel than the eighteen-foot boat in which Bligh and his companions navigated 3,600 miles of the Pacific after the mutiny of the 'Bounty.'"

Thirty generations ago Toi, when leaving Raratonga to seek the islands of New Zealand, said, "I will range the wide seas until I reach the land-head at Aotearoa, the moisture-laden land discovered by Kupe, or be engulfed forever in the depths of Hine-moana."

It was in this spirit that the broad Pacific was bridged and the civilization of the Old World carried to America.

When one considers the enormous extent of the journey, and the multitude and variety of the vicissitudes encountered upon the way, it is a most remarkable circumstance that practically the whole of the complex structure of the megalithic culture should have reached the shores of America. Hardly any of the items in the large series of customs and beliefs enumerated at the commencement of this lecture failed to get to America in pre-Columbian times. The practice of mummification, with modifications due to Polynesian and other oriental influences; the characteristically Egyptian elements of its associated ritual, such as the use of incense and libations; and beliefs concerning the soul's wanderings in the underworld, where it undergoes the same vicissitudes as it was supposed to encounter in Pharaonic times [New Empire]—all were found in Mexico and elsewhere in America, with a multitude of corroborative detail to indicate the influence exerted by Ethiopia, Babylonia, India, Indonesia, China, Japan, and Oceania, during the progress of their oriental migration. The general conception, no less than the details of their construction and the associated beliefs, make it equally certain that the megalithic monuments of America were inspired by those of the ancient East; and while the influences which are most obtrusively displayed in them are clearly Egyptian and Babylonian, the effects of the accretions from the Ægean, India, Cambodia, and Eastern Asia are equally unmistakable. The use of idols and stone seats, beliefs in the possibility of men or animals dwelling in stones, and the complementary supposition that men and animals may become petrified, the story of the deluge, of the divine origin of kings, who are regarded as the children of the sun or the sky, and the incestuous origin of the chosen people—the whole of this complexly interwoven series of characteristically Egypto-Babylonian practices and beliefs reappeared in America in pre-Columbian times, as also did the worship of the sun and the beliefs regarding serpents, including a great part of the remarkably complex and wholly artificial symbolism associated with this sun and serpent-worship. Circumcision, tattooing, piercing and distending the ear-lobules, artificial deformation of the head, trephining, weaving linen, the use of Tyrian purple, conch-shell trumpets, a special appreciation of pearls, precious stones, and metals, certain definite methods of mining and extraction of metals, terraced irrigation, the use of the swastika-symbol, beliefs regarding thunder-bolts and thunder-teeth, certain phallic practices, the boomerang, the beliefs regarding the "heavenly twins," the practice of couvade, the custom of building special "men's houses" and the institution of secret societies, the art of writing, certain astronomical ideas, and entirely arbitrary notions concerning a calendrical system, the subdivisions of time, and the constitution of the state—all of these and many other features of pre-Columbian civilization are each and all distinctive tokens of influence of the culture of the Old World upon that of the New. Not the least striking demonstration of this borrowing from the old world is afforded by games.

When in addition it is considered that most, if not all, of this variegated assortment of customs and beliefs are linked one to the other in a definite and artificial system, which agrees with that which is known to have grown up somewhere in the neighborhood of the Eastern Mediterranean, there can no longer be any reasonable doubt as to the derivation of the early American civilization from the latter source.

All the stories of culture-heroes which the natives tell corroborate the inferences which I have drawn from ethnological data.

When to this positive demonstration is added the evidence of the exact relationship of the localities where this exotic Old World culture took root in America to the occurrence of pearl-shell and precious metals, the proof is clinched by these unmistakable tokens that the same Phœnician methods which led to the diffusion of this culture-complex in the Old World also were responsible for planting it in the

New some centuries after the Phœnicians themselves had ceased to be.

In these remarks I have been dealing primarily with the influence of Ancient Egyptian civilization; but in concentrating attention upon this one source of American culture it must not be supposed that I am attempting to minimize the extent of the contributions from Asia. From India America took over the major part of her remarkable pantheon, including practically the whole of the beliefs associated with the worship of Indra.

NOTES

[1] For a concise summary of the evidence see pp. 120, *et seq.*

[2] *Ancient East*, pp. 154-159.

[3] Xxvii: 9 *et seq.*

[4] *Buddhist India*, p. 116.

[5] *Ancient Law*, p. 22.

[6] *Buddhist India*, pp. 70 and 113 *et seq.*

[7] *Ibid.*, p. 239.

[8] Pp. 545-6.

[9] In his scholarly commentary on *The Periplus of the Erythrean Sea*, Dr. Schoff gives, in a series of explanatory notes, a most illuminating summary of the literature relating to all these early trading expeditions. The reader who questions my remarks on these matters should consult his lucid digest of an immense mass of historical documents.

[10] See Schoff's commentaries on the *Periplus*.

[11] Mentioned in the writings of Vincent Smith, Rhys-Davids, Crooke, Nuttall, Oldham, and many others.

CAUSALITY AND CULTURE *

By F. GRAEBNER

§ 1. In his Völkerkunde [1] Ratzel demands of the ethnologist that he observe various cultures not merely as local phenomena, but that he go beyond that and establish the temporal and causal relationships existing between them. In application of this principle I have shown that the origin of numerous cultural forms is conditioned by the meeting and interaction of various cultural phenomena. I demonstrated furthermore that this meeting of cultures, as well as the emergence of the individual elements of culture and entire cultural complexes is the result of migration, and that the course pursued by such migrations can be clearly traced. We meet with difficulty, however, when we attempt to establish the nature of these migratory movements. Were they large-scale migrations or merely the result of intercourse between tribes, accompanied by gradual intermarriage? Unfortunately the existing elements within a given culture fail to provide us with irrefutable criteria toward the solution of this question. It is only in the case of the feeble contemporary offshoots of these movements that we can observe the process at work. In problems such as this, anthropology can be of great aid to the ethnologist. Obviously enough, the reverse does not follow, since, aside from the possibility of a secondary absorption of the original traits, a strong indication of migratory movements is a definite linguistic relationship. Indeed, we know of not one instance in which a language has been transmitted over long distances without live personal contact between the people who spoke it.

* *Methode der Ethnologie*, appearing in *Kulturgeschichtliche Bibliothek* edited by W. Foy. First series, *Ethnologische Bibliothek*, published by Carl Winter's Universitätsbuchhandlung, Heidelberg.

An attempt has been made to distinguish between cultural elements that are easily transferable and those that are not. However, the supposition that mental culture is less freely transferable than material culture,[2] because the latter may be spread through commerce, is decidedly fallacious. To mention but one contradictory evidence, I need only cite the well-known spread of legends and adoption of foreign religious ceremonies, which has been proved to exist in Australia. A more appropriate method of establishing the transferability of a given cultural trait is Vierkandt's classification of cultural elements according to the amount of training required for their reception and to the degree of their attractiveness.[3] But, above all, let us beware of *a priori* judgments when we decide which cultural phenomena fall into any given category. We must draw individual inferences from the conditions surrounding each single case. The importance to us of this consideration lies therein that *the lower the receptivity of a given cultural element the less probable*—though not impossible—*is its external dissemination without the aid of migration.* As a final criterion we must bear in mind that the complete or nearly complete appearance of identical cultures in widely separated localities is hardly thinkable without the aid of migrations, for an external dissemination from tribe to tribe over long distances must result in the diversification and weakening of the complex, so that, near the outskirts of the movement, we may perhaps discern a few disconnected elements or weakened forms of the whole complex, but never the complex itself as a complete unit. The shorter the distance separating the two cultures in question, the less weight does this argument naturally carry. Nevertheless, we may safely assume that the more complete the reappearance of a cultural complex in another locality, the less credible appears its transfer without migration.

§ 2. It would be folly to deny the relative meagerness of information concerning external causality in ethnology, as compared with the varied sources open to the student of the strictly historical periods of mankind. Indeed, we lack bare records of the events themselves, not to mention a political history of the period into which they fall. Consequently, we can never expect to advance beyond a rough outline of such movements. Their individual traits must, perhaps, be forever lost to us. Their causes—overpopulation, the pressure of other races, and, in the case of the earliest history, perhaps the coming and disappearing of the diluvial ice age—we can only divine, but never prove. Nevertheless, so long as we are only concerned with external causation, we may quite objectively derive certain important causal relationships from the given facts.

The danger of fanciful interpretation is far greater in the problem of internal causation, that is, the question of what causes *any* cultural phenomenon to arise or undergo changes. In no historical criticism is a real understanding of causation and origins thinkable, without psychologic re-experience of the events depicted. There is a vast difference, however, between the position of the historian and ours. In the description of historic events in Europe we can not only see the events and their effects directly before us at the moment of occurrence, that is, in their immediate psychic reality, but, in addition, we can also meet the people who are their objects and subjects. In the observation of pre-historic migratory movements, on the other hand, we can perceive their effects alone. And the causes of these effects, moreover, date back to the remotest ages, while the people subjected to them can be nothing more to us than mere abstractions of man, conceived after the image of living races, and, at best, perhaps slightly modified by our vague concept of what constitutes primitive life. The only modification permissible, however, in view of the evidence at hand, would be an explanation growing directly out of the land and people who are the setting of these events. Such an explanation, the very supposition, if not actual proof, of widespread migrations of culture, renders impossible. This difficulty is yet complicated by our habit of viewing all cultural phenomena in the light of their present-day setting. But such an interpretation is permissible only in the case of those traits which can, according to culture-historical standards, be viewed as local phenomena. Thus, for instance, it is not improbable that the pronounced Central Australian form of magic totemism is conditioned in part at least by the climatic peculiarities of its place of occurrence.[4] It must be noted, however, that this limitation applies only to the origin of these phenomena and subphenomena. And even in the case of those elements which are local, we cannot always treat the natural environment as causal. For, in the first place, a phenomenon of culture—and this is particularly true of economic factors—can persist unaltered only under unaltered geographic conditions.[5] Furthermore, it can be safely assumed that a spreading culture will invade at first and most intensely those regions whose geographic conditions are most favorable to it. In both of these instances the geographic environment is but a factor and not a cause. Wherever it is not—or at least only partially—feasible to explain a cultural phenomenon from the geographic setting of its present place of occurrence, the paths of distribution of the individual complexes at least permit of fairly safe conclusions concerning the approximate place of origin of the entire complex-group. Sometimes one group, taken as a whole, may even point definitely to one land of origin. This, at least, was Frobenius' contention about the Malayo-Negritic culture.[6] I feel, however, that he was only partially justified. With conclusions of this nature, extreme caution is always in place. Indeed it is highly probable that we may never advance beyond the hypothesis stage in this subject, a circumstance which students of ethnology should never lose sight of.

.   .   .   .

§ 4. The question of cultural determinants fortunately permits more substantial conclusions that the above. To be sure, in this case, too, the knowledge of historic relationships

derived by our method is not able to give us a vivid picture
of the entire culture at the time when a new complex was
created or an old one changed, not to mention the individual
processes that led up to it. Thanks to our method, however,
we can at least determine the complex or group of which
the element in question is a part. This factor is capable of
so far narrowing down the number of possible explanations that it will in many instances actually permit of only
one interpretation. As an illustration of this we might consider the origin of burial in squatting position. It has frequently been asked whether this form of burial is supposed
to be an imitation of the fœtus stage or whether it was employed to shackle the dead.[7] The only acceptable reply in
this case is governed by the simple fact that the cultural
group in which this form of burial has been proved to have
appeared at first is not afraid of its dead. Similarly Pater W.
Schmidt contends that the chief gods of South-East Australia owe their origin neither to mythologic concepts, nor
to magic or animism.[8] He would no doubt be justified in
this contention, if he could prove the absence—or at least
very feeble development—of these three elements in the
cultural group in question. His proof fails, because these
suppositions are most likely unfounded. The principle in
question, briefly stated, is: A cultural phenomenon can be
interpreted only through the ideologies of those cultural
groups of which they are part. This principle will allow
a certain flexibility, to be sure, but this flexibility can at best
be only very slight; namely, the elements in question may
have been derived from an older culture. To be precise, the
origin of a phenomenon or form of culture can always be
assumed to fall into a period that is ended when the new
phenomenon or form is complete, but which begins when
the mother complex undergoes its first modification. The
roots, therefore, of the earliest manifestations of the daughter
complex must be sought in the conditions surrounding the
mother complex. Thus it appears that even seemingly new
phenomena do not spring full-clad from the head of a

Jupiter in imitation of Pallas Athena. They evolve gradually from earlier phenomena and ideas and must be viewed in the widest sense as nothing more than mutations and continuations of the older cultures.[9] It was in application of this point of view that M. Schmidt sought to interpret the highly developed forms of meander and spiral ornaments as results of the weaving technic practiced in a certain cultural region of America.[10] There no doubt exists the relationship between these forms which he mentions. Indeed the spiral ornaments actually belong to the same group in which the particular type of weaving technic is employed.[11] In so far his proof would appear to be incontestable. It falls down, nevertheless, because the more developed types of weaving, from which alone the later ornaments could have been derived, are younger than the spiral ornaments, not to mention the meander. On the other hand, we can conclude with certainty that the institution of head hunting is derived from *skull-worship*. Both practices belong to the same cultural group. Skull-worship, moreover, is also represented in an older sister group, thus also being chronologically the older of the two elements.

These last few cases offer a significant illustration of the general rule that no phenomenon of culture can be derived from a group or complex which is culture-historically younger than it. In particular, an explanation based upon local cultural conditions is admissible only in the case of those elements and forms which, from the culture-historical point of view, may be characterized as local peculiarities. It must be borne in mind, however, that their local character must be established beyond doubt. Thus, for instance, it had until recently seemed justified to look for the strange motif of *subincisio* in the sexual attitudes of those Australian tribes who alone were known to practice it.[12] This explanation was completely overthown by the discovery that the same operation is practiced by the Fiji Islanders, who motivate it quite differently.[13]

When we are dealing with the products of mixed cultures,

this general principle, naturally applies likewise, with the only distinction that, instead of one single complex, the several composing elements of the mixture must be taken into account.

§ 5. Since the far greater number of historic causalities are of a psychic nature, a thorough knowledge of human psychology is essential to the ethnologist. Psychology, individual as well as racial, must be one of the most prominent aids to ethnology. Obviously, the psychic determinants of a cultural phenomenon or culture-historical process can never fall outside general psychologic possibility. On the other hand, it is not necessary for the historian to wait until a certain problem has been solved by the psychologists before he can study it in the light of his own field. Nor is it improbable that the results of psychologic investigation, with its main emphasis upon the average, the typical, may in certain instances be inapplicable to the individual historical processes. What the ethnologist needs most of all, in view of these circumstances, is a thorough practical acquaintance with the human soul, an understanding of human nature in all of its most subtle ramifications. This ability cannot be acquired as can the knowledge of scientific data. It is a native gift, developed through careful cultivation. Those who possess it, however, will be capable of a highly versatile understanding. They will not be the slaves of their own intellectual environment. Able to grasp the great number of possibilities, they will not be very likely to draw one-sided conclusions.[14]

Such a versatility has, in addition, the power to make us feel and think as though we were part of the culture we are studying, no matter how foreign its terms may be to our own environment.

This gift is an indispensable prerequisite of all those who attempt to solve the problem of causality and to understand a phenomenon as part of its cultural background. It is most important, however, in all those cases in which the evidence at hand fails to point to unquestionable conclusions, that is, wherever we must resort to hypothesis in the absence of proof. Wherever the order of development of several forms or the cultural group to which a given phenomenon belongs cannot be objectively established, our problem becomes one of psychic causality. Our main task is to avoid one-sidedness. Wherever none of the given possibilities of solution is obviously dominant, we must apply the *ceterum censeo* of all unprejudiced science; we must by no means "force" a solution, but—while not relinquishing our personal opinion—we must dispassionately weigh all possibilities, and admit it honestly, if the present state of the science precludes a positive answer to our question.

NOTES

[1] Ratzel, *Geschichte, Völkerkunde und historische Perspective*, 1904, pp. 1 *ff.*

[2] This attitude has been particularly stressed by Pater W. Schmidt in *Globus*, xcvii, pp. 174, 176, 189.

[3] Vierkandt, *Die Stetigkeit im Kulturwandel*, pp. 118 *ff.*

[4] Cf. Spencer and Gillen, *The Northern Tribes of Central Australia*, pp. 283 *ff.*

[5] Leo Frobenius, *Naturwissenschaftliche Kulturlehre*, pp. 15 *ff.*

[6] Leo Frobenius, *Der Ursprung der Afrikanischen Kulturen*, pp. 245 *ff.*; *Das Zeitalter des Sonnengotts*, pp. 37 *ff.*

[7] Cf. Andree, *Ethnographische Betrachtungen über Höckerbestattung, Z. für Anthropologie*, Neue Folge, vi, pp. 262 ff.

[8] Pater W. Schmidt, *L'Origine de l'idée de Dieu*, in *Anthropos*, iii, pp. 125 *ff.*, 336 *ff.*, 559 *ff.*, 801 *ff.*, 1081 *ff.*; iv, pp. 207 *ff.*, 505 *ff.*, 1075 *ff.*; v, pp. 231 *ff.*

[9] Cf. Vierkandt, *Die Stetigkeit im Kulturwandel*, pp. 5 *ff.*

[10] M. Schmidt, *Indianerstudien in Zentralbrasilien*, pp. 330 *ff.*; *Peruanische Ornamentik, Z. für Anthropologie*, Neue Folge, vii, pp. 22 *ff.*

[11] Graebner, *Anthropos*, iv, pp. 769*ff.*, 1004, 1017, 1020*f.*, 1024, 1027*f.*

[12] Cf. Klaatsch, referred to by Pater W. Schmidt in *Z. für Ethnologie*, xli, p. 373. Incidentally, the attitude found there is not a sufficient motivation for this operation, because, as is well known, the *subincisio* is not indispensable in the carrying out of homosexual acts.

[13] Marzan, *Anthropos*, v, pp. 808 *f.*

[14] A good illustration of such a versatile treatment of a subject, a systematic sensing and analysis of all possibilities, can be found in Ehrenreich's recent work, *Allgemeine Mythologie*.

BANARO SOCIETY *

Social Organization and Kinship System of a Tribe in the Interior of New Guinea

By RICHARD THURNWALD

LOCATION

In the following pages I shall endeavor to give an account of the social institutions of the Bánaro tribe in New Guinea which seems to provide the clue to several problems connected with primitive social organization.

The tribe concerned lives along the middle course of the Kerám, the lowest tributary of the Sepík or Kaiserin Augusta river in the northern part of New Guinea. During the dry season, when the current is not too strong, the trip up the Kerám, with its endless meanderings, to the region of the native settlements can be made by a good motor launch in three days, provided that no stops are made on the way. As the crow flies, the distance from the junction of the Kerám and the Sepík to the native settlements is certainly not less than fifty kilometers.

The first village encountered as one goes up the Kerám still belongs to the linguistic and cultural area of the lower Sepík tribes. The second village, Kambót, a rather large one, belongs to a different culture area. This area is subdivided into two districts; the one includes Tjámbio (Kambót) (Kámboa), Engáleb (Iérambo) (Gorogopá), and Ka-

* The present paper is based on material obtained in 1912-15 in New Guinea, as part of the work of an expedition to the region of the Kaiserin Augusta river, otherwise called the Sepík. The expedition was sustained jointly by the German Colonial Office and the Berlin Ethnographical Museum. The outbreak of the war brought the work to a sudden close, and forced me to leave New Guinea. *Memoirs of the American Anthropological Association.*

mén (Kumbrágumbra); the other, the following tribes met with in traveling up the Kerám: Búegendum (Kauguiánum), Rámunga and Búnaram, and finally Banaro. The culture of this area is distinguished by the possession of bow and arrow, whereas the adjoining tribes of the lower Sepík use the dart, *Wurfpfeil*. The people of this region also practice the art of pottery, unknown on the lower Sepík. As the pottery of the lower Sepík is imported from the Kerám, this river is commonly known in New Guinea as "Potters' river," or *Toepferfluss*. Feuds are constantly in progress among the different tribes, including, of course, the Banaro.

TRIBE-NAME, VILLAGE-NAME AND SOCIAL GROUPS

Each of the villages has a name of its town. Different localities such as parts of the forest, of the grassland, big trees, creeks, hunting grounds, fishing pools, sago swamps, etc., are provided with special designations or proper names. These appellations are used as village-names. However, the name of the settlement must be carefully distinguished from that of the tribe. The tribe-name is the designation given to a tribe by its neighbors.

The difference between village-name and tribe-name is especially marked in cases where we can observe the migration of a tribe that occupies but a single village. This may perhaps be made more clear by the example of the Tjímundo tribe, inhabiting the first settlement met with on the Kerám, which has changed its dwelling place several times in the last twenty years. This tribe, consisting of one village, is called Tjímundo by the surrounding tribes, but the village the tribe inhabits at present is called, from its location, Bobónarum. It removed to this place about four years ago from Orómanum, where many deaths occurred, resulting probably from unhealthy conditions. The stay of these people at Orómanum was very short, lasting only for two or three years. They had there built up a new village on coming from Máienum, a place that they left because of attacks by their old enemies, the Móagem people. On account of these attacks they had already changed their former dwelling place on the mouth of the Kerám, called Yánumbui. Prior to that they had inhabited Amēbonum (Parám, to-day the Mission station Marienberg) on the left bank of the Sepík river. They quit this location on account of hostilities with their neighbors in the hinterland. The tribe-name, however, remained Tjímundo.

EXCHANGE SYSTEM

In the South Seas in general, two forms of arranging marriage prevail: (1) the exchange of woman for woman; (2) the buying of women with objects of value.

Mutual exchange of women probably originated as a pledge of good will in the establishment of friendly relations between two communities. This form seems to me the original one from which the second form has been derived. In cases where mutual exchange became impossible, return was made by objects of value.

Among the Banaro we find the exchange system in full operation, elaborately worked out in every detail. When a girl has reached the age of puberty and gone through the initiation ceremonies, she consults with her mother as to which of the marriageable youths suits her best. Of course, she often has an understanding with the boy beforehand. She may choose from among the boys of the several gentes of which her tribe is composed. Marriage within the gens is not permitted. It is only in exceptional cases that marriage into another tribe takes place, as an examination of native pedigree proves. For this reason we may call the gens exogamic, the tribe endogamic.

The girl's mother discusses the matter with her husband and if they agree, she prepares a pot of boiled sago, which they then carry in a basket to the parents of the chosen bridegroom. The families concerned confer with each other and come to a formal agreement. As compensation for the girl the sister of the bridegroom must be married to the bride's brother. But the sago is offered under the pretext of asking the bridegroom's sister in marriage for the bride's brother. If the other parents accept the sago, the case is settled, as far as the two sets of parents are concerned.

But the situation is now complicated further. Each gens is divided into two sibs. These two sibs are united by a bond of friendship for mutual protection and pleasure, as well as for purposes of revenge against outsiders. The two sibs are considered to be the best of friends. They "can never fight" against each other. It seems required, therefore, by a kind of active sympathy, that if one sib is going to celebrate a marriage, the other sib shall also have an opportunity for a feast. Moreover, the principle of requital implies that the other sib shall participate. Accordingly a bridegroom of the right side (*tan*) of the sib must take his bride from the same side of the other gens; a bridegroom of the left side (*bon*) takes his bride from a left sib.

After the parties have mutually agreed, each pair of parents confers with the paternal grandfather of each bridegroom. Each grandfather consults with his *mundū*, his special friend in the corresponding sib. If the grandfather is dead, his brother takes his place.

The *mundūs* of the grandfathers now confer with their sons, and the sons with their children, in order to arrange for two corresponding marriages further in the parallel sib. Thus we may count four pairs to be united by marriage. Two gentes each exchange one girl for a girl of the other gens, and this pair of girls is doubled by the parallel exchange in the corresponding sib of each gens.

This is the ideal system, but in reality it cannot always be carried out to its fullest extent. Defective cases will be dealt with later.

GIRLS' INITIATION

The marriage ceremony is connected with the initiation ceremony of the girls. Girls are provided with husbands on reaching the age of puberty. It would lead us too far to give a detailed account of the rather complicated festivities here.

The following, however, are some of their principal features.

Wild pigs are hunted, and domestic pigs slaughtered on different occasions, once by the fathers of the girls, once by their mothers' brothers. During a lapse of altogether nine months, the girls are confined to a cell in the family house, getting sago soup instead of water throughout that time. For the whole period their fathers are obliged to sleep in the goblin-house. At last their cell is broken up by the women, the girls released and allowed to leave the house. The women get cocoanuts laid ready beforehand, and throw them at the girls, whom they finally push into the water, again pelting them with cocoanuts. The girls crawl out of the water on to the bank, receive portions of sago and pork, and are now dressed, and adorned with earrings, nose-sticks, necklaces, bracelets, and aromatic herbs. After this a dance of the women takes place.

That same evening the orgies begin. When dusk breaks in, the men assemble on the streets of the village. The old men consult with each other, agreeing to distribute the girls according to their custom. This custom was explained to me in the following way: The father of the chosen bridegroom really ought to take possession of the girl, but he is "ashamed" and asks his sib friend, his *mundū,* to initiate her into the mysteries of married life in his place. This man agrees to do so. The mother of the girl hands her over to the bridegroom's father, telling her that he will lead her to meet the goblin.

The bridegroom's father takes her to the goblin-hall and bids her enter. His *mundū* has already gone into the goblin-hall, and awaits her within. When she comes in, he, in the rôle of the goblin, takes her by the hand and leads her to the place where the big bamboo pipes (three to six meters long) are hidden.

These musical pipes, by the way, play a most important part in many ceremonies, and their voice is supposed to be that of the goblin himself. Sight of them is forbidden to women, on pain of death.

Before these hidden gods the couple unite. Afterwards the girl is led out of the goblin-hall, where her bridegroom's father awaits her and brings her back to her mother. The *mundū* returns home in a roundabout way, for he is "ashamed" to meet anybody on his way back.

The bridegroom's father goes back to the goblin-hall, and it is now his turn to perform the rôle of goblin, his *mundū* bringing him his son's bride.

After that, the same rite is performed with the other two girls.

The bridegrooms and the other two boys, in the meantime, are confined in a house, set apart for this purpose, and watched by their mothers' brothers.

The fathers in their capacity of goblins are allowed to have intercourse with the brides on several subsequent occasions, but only in the goblin-hall.

The bridegroom is not allowed to touch her until she gives birth to a child. This child is called the goblin's child. When the goblin-child is born, the mother says, "Where is thy father? Who had to do with me?" The bridegroom responds, "I am not his father: he is a goblin-child"; and she replies, "I did not see that I had intercourse with a goblin."

After the birth of the child, the bridegroom is expected to have finished building a new house, and the bride, the plaiting of the big sleeping bag, used on the banks of the Kerám river, as well as on the Sepík river, as a shelter from mosquitoes. Then the couple are finally permitted to begin married life, without any further ceremonies, in the new house. On solemn occasions the goblin-father continues to exercise his "spiritual" function in the goblin-hall.

The avoidance between bride and bridegroom must be classed with a widely-spread custom appearing in the different forms of so-called "Tobias nights," and not unknown elsewhere in New Guineas, as, for instance, among the Massim people, and the Mekeo tribe.

When the first child, say a boy, comes to the age of puberty, and becomes a *guli,* as a child of about twelve years is called, he goes through initiation ceremonies which are somewhat similar to those of the girls described above.

BOYS' INITIATION

These ceremonies are also connected with the *mundū* institution. Boys of the two sibs are initiated together. First, their fathers consult with each other. The grandfathers, who acted reciprocally as goblin-fathers of the firstborn, confer with the brothers of the respective mothers, in order to plan for a hunt of wild pigs in the forest. The two goblin-fathers go in one party, the two mothers' brothers in another. After the hunt, the two parties meet outside the village, and now the respective fathers and uncles of the boys return home together with the pigs. The goblin-father cuts the pig into two halves, giving one side to the adopted father of the goblin-child, and retaining the other for himself. The mothers boil the pork and prepare sago. The next morning the men bring the head of the pig to the goblin-hall, and deposit it before the bamboo pipes. Later on, the two mothers' brothers and the two legal fathers eat the head of the pig. The other women of the village bring baked sago to the goblin-hall, where the men are assembled. After sunset a *mundū* festival takes place.

At this time the goblin-father ceases to exercise his right as representative of the goblin, ceding his power to his son, a man of the same age as the initiated woman's husband. The goblin-father, however, is formally invited, but he scratches his head and refuses. He might, for example, say, "No, I am too old now; my son had better take over the *mundū* rights." These rights are, as a matter of fact, usually inherited.

From this time forth the husband's sib-friend, his *mundū,* acts as goblin on festive occasions.

The initiation ceremony coincides in time with the refusal of the goblin-father to continue in his goblin rights toward his sib-friend's daughter-in-law. This indicates that the goblin-father is entering into another age-class, paralleled by the permission of his son to enter into the full privileges of sex life, and by the arrival of his own goblin-child at the age of puberty. The latter stage is used as a means of grading the age-class.

During these ceremonies in the goblin-hall, the boys are brought to another house, and there watched over by their mothers' brothers. When the father returns, he brings a burning brand from the goblin-hall with him, goes to his son and describes a circle of fire around the head of the boy.

The fathers' and mothers' brothers now pick up the boys and carry them on their shoulders to the goblin-hall. Here they wait outside on the veranda until all the men have entered. The men form a line across the hall and begin to dance. The other men blow the pipes from behind the row of dancers. The boys are now brought inside the hall. At this, the pipers break through the line of rhythmically dancing men, and press the pipes upon the navels of the boys. After further ceremonies, the boys are placed upon a piece of sago bark, and the fathers and mothers' brothers now take the bamboo pipes and blow upon them. Then they hand over the instruments to the boys and show them how to play them. After this, the boys continually practice playing the pipes.

Thereupon the boys are confined in cage-like cells (mo-múnevem), built for that purpose in the goblin-hall. The goblin-hall itself is surrounded during that time with a fence of sago leaves.

A good many other ceremonies are performed during the period the boys are interned, for instance, a ceremony connected with the bull-roarer. They also insert in the urinary passage two or three stems of Coix lacrima, a barbed grass. These stems they pull out suddenly, so that the walls of the passage are cut. After three months of confinement the initiates are "shown" the phenomena of the world that surrounds them,—animals, plants, high water, thunder and lightning,—which are presented as spirits in the shape of wooden idols. They are also introduced to the goblins of this world and the spirits of their ancestors.

Five months later, during new moon, the father and the mothers' brothers slaughter domestic pigs, as is usual at the conclusion of ceremonies. The mother now roasts the pork and cooks sago. The other women of the gens also prepare sago. The men of the related gentes bring taro, yams, bananas, sugar cane, tobacco, betel nut, and betel pepper. Then they sing and dance, day and night.

Finally the boys are girded, clothed in a kind of fringed sago leaf skirt, belted with hoops of rattan, and adorned with plaited bracelets, nose sticks, and ear ropes. Their waists are tightly bound with a wide band of rattan wickerwork, drawn so firmly together that they can hardly eat. It is the pride of the boys to have a slender waist.

Their father then offers them betel nut and betel pepper, and washes them in the water left from the filtration of the sago. The mothers' brothers shave their temples and the back of their heads, leaving a kind of crest.

The fathers in the meantime have carved small human figures (*bukámorom,* on the lower Sepík called *kandim-boan*) as a gift of mutual friendship between the inter-marrying gentes. With these figures a particular charm is performed. The father goes with the boy into the forest to search for a water liana, a particular species containing water in its stem. This liana is cut and the water allowed to flow over the figure, betel nut and betel pepper are laid upon it, and it is then wrapped up in bark. The figure is used as a love charm. If the boy should go into the bush with this, he would expect to meet a woman. When the women hear that such a charm has been executed, one of them, ordinarily the wife of the mother's goblin-initiator, *i.e.,* the wife of his grandfather's sib friend, complies with the wish expressed in the charm. This is the boy's initiation into sexual life.

At sunset the fathers' and mothers' brothers carry the boys with the pipes to the banks of the river, where they line up along the shore, the boys still on their shoulders. The other men stand in a line behind them, dancing and singing. The goblin-fathers, stationed at the two ends of the line, hold a rattan rope in their hands, with which they finally force the boys into the water, so that they may have a bath with the pipes. Afterwards the boys return to the goblin-hall. Meanwhile the women are sent to the forest, lest they should get a glimpse of the pipes.

The next morning another bathing ceremony takes place among the adults of the community. First the men, singing and dancing, form a line along the bank of the river; the women line up behind them. The mothers of the boys who are being initiated make a fire by rubbing a cord of rattan on firewood. The women begin to dance, the mothers drawing taut a long rope of rattan behind the men, by means of which they finally push them into the water. After this the women throw at the men cocoanuts previously laid ready. The men, in return, shoot back with bow and arrow, each man trying to hit his *mundū's* wife. The men now climb out of the water, and the reverse of the above ceremony takes place, the men pushing the women into the water with the rattan rope. This time the women shoot back from the water with arrows, aiming at their goblins.

While the bathing ceremony is going on, the boys are kept apart and watched over by their mothers' brothers.

On the same evening the festival in the goblin-hall is repeated, but this time is extended to the mothers' brothers and their *mundūs*. The latter also meet in the goblin-hall of the initiated boys.

After this the boys are brought home to their mothers. Here their hands are extended over a fire, and the joints of their fingers cracked over the flames.

These ceremonies conclude the festivities, and the boy is finally allowed to associate with women.

The initiation ceremonies, as we have seen, introduce the marriage rites and are intimately connected with them.

I should like to call attention to the fact that marriage

ceremonies are not differentiated from the ceremonies associated with puberty. The maturing of sex is ritually identified with the functioning of sex, and the possibility of the
function with its practical employment. This employment,
however, is restricted to a definite group of persons and to
certain fixed occasions, in the manner shown above.

THE SYSTEM AT WORK

If we try to sum up the system that results from these
various customs, we come to the following conclusions:

Each woman, as time goes on, has regular intercourse with
three men: (1) With the sib-friend of her bridegroom's
father, (2) with her husband; (3) with her husband's sib-
friend. And each man also has legal intercourse with three
women: (1) With his wife; (2) with his sib-friend's wife;
(3) with the bride of his sib-friend's son. This holds true if
we leave out of consideration the old woman who initiates
the boy.

There is no doubt that this results in greater probability
of conception, and that sterile marriages are prevented in a
higher degree. But I doubt whether this eugenic reason had
any influence in establishing these customs. However, in
case a marriage should prove to be sterile, the man is allowed
to take another wife; but then there are no ceremonies.

It must be borne in mind that if a child's extramarital
father is its mother's sib-friend, this man is the son of its
mother's goblin initiator. Thus the three men of the other
sib with whom the woman has to deal, besides her husband,
are a father and his son, and eventually this latter person's
grandson. A man, however, has to do first with a woman of
his grandmother's generation, hereafter with his female sib-
friend of his wife's age-class, later with this woman's son's
wife. A woman has intercourse with males who are lineal
descendants, a man with females who are not direct off-
springs in successive generations. A male will have union—
besides his initiation—with two persons of his age-class and
one of the following one, a female with one of the pre-

ceding age-class and two of her own, and eventually with her grandchildren's generation. It will be noticed that intercourse is avoided on the female side with the son's generation and correspondingly on the male side with the mother's age-class.

The offspring of the union with the goblin is called the goblin's child, *móro-me-m'an*. Although the child remains with the mother, we cannot speak of a female line of descent, for the child is adopted by his mother's husband, who cares for his further education, and practically acts as his foster father.

That the first child is known as the "goblin's child," might be associated with a religious usage which we find widely spread in some form or other in the custom of offering the first-born, the firstling, or first fruits, to the gods.

The psychological association of the "first" with the first cause and whatever is felt superior to man, is, of course, striking and suggestive, and explains the wide distribution of this custom.

Whether the husband happens to be the children's father or not, is of no importance in this scheme; he is the foster father of his wife's goblin-child, and of any children his wife might have with his own *mundū,* as well. These children of his wife may, perhaps, originate entirely from fathers of the other sib of the gens. But the man is the head of his wife's family. The family relation and the sexual relation rest each upon a different basis, as has been shown above.

SOCIALIZING INFLUENCE OF THE SYSTEM

The exchange system maintains a great socializing influence, for by its means all members of the tribe are connected with, and dependent on, each other. This appears in the different ceremonials where persons are assigned special functions, as well as in the marriage system, which has spread a network of all kinds of relationships, not only over the gens, but over the tribe itself.

The working of this system of ties could well be felt when

I tried to recruit a boy from the Banaro tribe for service with the expedition. Of the boys who served me as informants, one (Yómba) was a single man from a gens of the Banaro tribe, the other (Mánape) from the Rámunga tribe. It was impossible, however, to get another boy, in spite of friendly relations, for there was no one to spare, each man having his special part to play in the social system.

PSYCHOLOGICAL BASIS

The marriage regulations exist as a means of insurance against the disturbing influence of the emotions upon social life; for social life depends upon a certain established harmony between emotion and intellect. If the intellect encounters emotions with which it cannot successfully cope, social life is disturbed by internal friction, because of blunders committed by members of the social group. Now, whether this is because, in a particular case, the emotions are relatively too strong, or the intellect too weak, and therefore the presence of mind needed in adapting itself to unexpected situations is insufficient, the establishment of regulating forms, laws, and ceremonies is required. The more formulæ of the kind pervade life, the more we may expect to find a relative insufficiency of intellect in dealing with the emotions. The social group erects rigid barriers in order to lead emotional life into well-defined channels. This applies especially to all phenomena connected with sexual life, and with the reproduction of the race.

For this reason no external pressure is needed to enforce such customs; they are considered quite a matter of course, and not to be criticized.

COUNTING OF DESCENT AND THE ORIGIN OF EXOGAMY

Now, if we inquire how descent is counted, we notice a queer combination of both female and male influence. Practically the children are their mother's, and her husband seems to be selected only in order to protect her and her children. He is merely the protector of his wife's family.

Thus, the sibs and the gentes are organized upon the men, and it is through them that exogamic marriages are reckoned. This leads us to the theory already mentioned, that the exogamic regulations may have originated from an understanding between gentes, formerly hostile, but afterwards agreeing to peaceful relations. These were sealed by the exchange of women, and might thus be said to have had a political origin.

It seems to me, however, as if the much-discussed question regarding the origin of exogamy should be stated somewhat differently.

It has often been emphasized, and seems to be proved by psychological research, that a certain strangeness works as a sexual stimulus. The contempt visited upon incestuous unions is mostly based upon this fact. On the other hand, an exogamy in the form of an unlimited liberty of choosing the mate is never really found. What is particularly striking to us is the sharply restricted limitation in the number of groups united by a connubium.

As we have certain limitations to deal with here, it would seem preferable to speak of a "marriage regulation," rather than of an "exogamy." This "exogamy," regarded from the point of view of such limitations, would often be better classified as an "endogamy." We ought, therefore, to consider rather the origin of the marriage regulations. My solution of the problem has been suggested above.

There is no doubt that the regulation of marriage in the form of the so-called "exogamy" has important biological consequences. It gives us a hint as to how we may account for the many distinct types of man we encounter in relatively small areas. Whereas the physical types are conditioned by the intermarrying of a very limited number of small exogamic units, the various linguistic and cultured types find their explanation in the isolation of the groups practicing the exogamy. This "exogamy," within a very restricted number of small groups, is practically an "endogamy," resulting in inbreeding on account of an intermingling of a restricted set of persons throughout many generations.

The grouping of kinship depends upon the complex living conditions of the tribe. These conditions are again dependent upon the method of getting the food supply, and the perfection of the particular tools, *i.e.,* the economic status. In this way the whole system of relationship comes to be influenced by economic principles, based upon the possession of property.

Among the Banaro the economic unit is the sib. It is the sib that has definite claims to the sago places, hunting districts and plantation grounds. These localities are identified by certain names and the boundaries marked by creeks, swamps, big trees, grass limits, ravines, bends of the river, etc. The owners as well as the other members of the tribe know these localities and are aware of the traditional rights to them.

The ties of kinship are associated with the common holding of the land. The *connubium* tends to preserve the claims on a certain territory within a restricted number of people. In consequence of the marriage prescriptions the origin of the persons entitled to exploit the land is limited, so that the offspring derives its rights through kinship to members of the community. Individuals have no claim of ownership or rights of disposal over the ground. Therefore we cannot speak of a transmission by inheritance, as the sib is not, like a person, capable of death. The right of a person depends on his situation in the social complex. Hence the importance of stating the relationship.

Even the earnings of a boy recruited for service with the white man fall to his sib as a requital for the absence of his working power claimed by his sib. Whatever he brings home is distributed among his kinsfolk.

Individual property is confined to the products of the labor of the individual. The tree, for instance, that a man plants, or the fish that a man catches, or the weir that a man weaves, or the stone ax he puts together, belong to him as the fruit of his labor. This individual property is of a very temporary character, for the crops of the plantation are consumed when they are ripe, and the few tools are used up after a relatively short time. If a man should die, they are burned, and buried with him, for they are considered as a sort of personal appurtenance.

Under primitive conditions as dealt with here individual property is generally too transient to be transmitted. It is only on higher stages when the accumulation of property becomes important, that conditions change.

Especially if the population becomes dense in comparison with the area providing food, and a more intense exploitation of the soil becomes necessary, does the value of the land rise. Its possession then becomes an important factor, so that the transmission of inheritance rights is carefully watched and calculated.

If it is a question of valuables to be inherited, an exact reckoning, in either the male or the female line, must be considered, and one or the other system adopted.

If a *mundū* system were confronted with a development in the suggested direction, it is just as probable to suppose that the result would turn out patriarchy as mother-right, for the husband in the Banaro organization is, as we have seen, "the head of his wife's family." Certain modifying ideas or other influences might then tip the balance towards the establishment of the one or the other institution.

Real and efficient economic exploitation of resources cannot of course be carried through with primitive or even refined tools by any people. For civilized man, as well as the savage, is never an economic being alone, but in his desires and aims is "disturbed" by a great many other factors that have nothing to do with economics proper. Among these disturbing factors are many which we are inclined to call prejudices if we find them among other peoples, but which are generally clad in high-sounding names if we ourselves are concerned. However it may be that these spiritual motives, magic, ceremonies, customs (*e.g.,* exogamy), laws and so on, these systems growing out of simplifications, abstractions, and associations of phenomena nevertheless exercise their influence upon an efficient economic exploitation through the technical means of a given people.

I think, however, we ought not to forget the importance of the economic factor in considering primitive social systems. The individualization of an originally supposed group marriage has possibly been brought about by the importance of the labor of the women claimed by certain men, though, of course, I should not reject the influence of ideas, as introduced by migrating people. But I hold that such ideas, even if they do survive to some extent, may in the lapse of time be absorbed because of the necessity imposed by the conditions of life.

TECHNOLOGY *

By CLARK WISSLER

IF the reader visits a museum dealing with a living race, he finds exhibits of clothing, baskets, weapons, tools, foods, charms, etc., usually grouped according to the tribe from which they were obtained and intended to show its material culture. By comparing the exhibit for one tribe with that of another, individualities may be observed and regional similarities discovered. One advantage in having a museum collection is that the objects speak for themselves; all we need is accurate information as to the tribe producing them and a minimum of knowledge as to how they were used. Even the last can be dispensed with, for important conclusions can be drawn by comparing the objects as they stand. The archæologist, for example, cannot be sure of the uses of stone artifacts, but nevertheless, he determines their types and distributions. However, in securing collections from living peoples, the collector seeks the important data concerning the manufacture and use of the objects, or, to put the matter fairly, his purpose is to learn all he can about each phase of material culture, choosing such objects as will illustrate, or demonstrate, the subject. Thus, if he finds the women making baskets, he learns all he can about this: the types of baskets made and their uses; how the materials are gathered and prepared; the different weaves employed; and the decorations. To illustrate these points, a type series of baskets, materials, unfinished baskets to show the techniques of weaving, and a series of decorated baskets are collected. The museum ideal is to exhibit this material with explanatory labels and the whole is regarded as data on the basketry of tribe concerned.[1] In a similar manner, the field collector

* An Introduction to Social Anthropology. New York: Henry Holt & Co.

may undertake the study of hunting, fishing, agriculture, cooking, house building, etc., eventually covering all the tribal activities. The basic feature that makes such a study feasible is that in all such matters the tribe has a prevailing style for each type of object and process, and when once these styles have been determined for a large number of tribes, they can be classified, compared, and utilized like other scientific data. Such subjects as social organization, totemism, and animism are not easily represented in a museum collection, but the presentation of data on magic may be advantageously supplemented by an exhibit of charms and other accessories to magical procedures. But aside from the advantage of having before one authenticated objects for study, museum collections when well made serve as a partial substitute for a visit to the living tribes. If, for example, one walked through a large museum hall for the tribes of Africa, he might in this way realize something of what would appear if the villages of the tribes themselves were passed in review. Automatically, also the collections fall into certain classes, as those showing agriculture by the presence of hoes and other implements, those showing milking stools and pails in areas where cattle were raised, etc. All this could be quickly observed as one passed through the exhibit and would serve as a perspective outline to be carried in the mind and into which additional information can be incorporated.

HISTORY OF MUSEUMS

The collecting of curious objects from strange lands is an old, old weakness of mankind, which was greatly stimulated by the discovery of the New World, and so objects made by Indians, Eskimo, Polynesians, etc., found their way into collector's cabinets, and it is in these cabinets that the modern museum had its beginning. We cannot go into the history of the development of museums in general, for we are concerned chiefly with the part museum collections have played in the development of anthropology. For a long time, as we have said, the objects made by living primitive men were regarded as curios embodying no important problem. Eventually, it was shown that they could lend themselves to scientific treatment. This elevation of curios to the research level and the dignification of technology as a branch of anthropology should be credited to A. H. Pitt-Rivers (1827-1900). He entered upon the collection and the study of the objects made by living man on the theory that their genesis, or development, would be revealed in the objects themselves, just as structure in the bodies of animals and plants is taken as the evidence for their evolution. Before the time of Pitt-Rivers, as we have said, the objects made by savages and other peoples were collected as curios, but no one conceived that in them was to be found an empirical lead to a problem. If, as Pitt-Rivers assumed, the story can be read in the objects themselves, then a new world of inquiry is opened up to us. First, however, the collecting must be accurate as to the location and character of the tribe, and the use to which the objects were put. This done, it was conceived that then one might soon discover how each object came to have its present form.

In his *History of Mankind,* Tylor used the available material in the collections of Pitt-Rivers and others; one of his classical studies was that of fire-making, in which he defended the thesis that man first kindled fire by simple wood friction, passed through several successive steps in elaborating the fire drill, later discovered the use of flint and iron pyrites, and finally ending with the friction match.

A contemporary of Pitt-Rivers was the distinguished American anthropologist, O. T. Mason (1838-1908), who, though influenced by Tylor more than by Pitt-Rivers, showed great originality in the study of technology, placing greater stress upon geographical distribution than did either Tylor or Pitt-Rivers. His methods were of the laboratory type and, in large measure, laid the foundation for the study of material culture, a subject now occupying an important place in anthropology. Mason is best known for his studies of the American Indian collections in the United States National Museum at Washington, especially for his exhaustive work on basketry. He also gave attention to museum methods, using a tribal and geographical arrangement for his museum collections, but in addition sought to discover in these collections the origins of technological process.

At this point we may note an important matter. Pitt-Rivers, while the leader in this significant development, did not treat his museum collections tribally and geographically but arranged the objects in assumed chronological sequences. This is quite opposed to the usual point of view. We have gone to some length to emphasize that the community or the tribe is the recognized unit in anthropology, and consequently, when one visits a museum presenting collections from living peoples, he finds them arranged by tribes and not according to the form and structure of the objects themselves. Classification by tribes is considered scientific, because one can ordinarily be sure that the objects listed did come from the tribe to which they are attributed; at least such information is usually verifiable. On the other hand, when one arranges the fire-making appliances of the world in a series such as we have noted above, he is resorting to interpretation and drawing a conclusion, which, in the nature of the case, cannot be objectively verified. The tribal arrangement is now regarded as the proper one in a museum, since it records the association of the objects, as observed and observable; the student can then compare them at will, and draw his conclusions accordingly.

For the sake of completeness we should not close this historical sketch without noting the work of the great builder of anthropological museums, F. W. Putnam (1839-1915). He seems to have been a many-sided man, with a genius for leadership and a belief in the study of objects rather than books; he stood for true field work in anthropology as opposed to mere collecting, insisting that museums should become research institutions and not purchasers of the curios offered them by unscientific collectors. It was under his leadership that the Peabody Museum at Harvard University, the anthropological section of the American Museum of Natural History in New York, the Field Museum of Natural History in Chicago, and the anthropological section of the University of California, were established. In general, the rise of anthropological museums as research institutions, in Europe as well as in America, may be said to have come strongly to the fore by 1870 and these institutions continue to be productive of research.

TECHNOLOGICAL PROGRESS

A number of technological processes have wide distributions and have persisted over great periods of time. Flaking, or chipping stone is one of these; it is the oldest technique of which we have archæological record. Naturally, this does not mean that it is the first technological process devised by man, but merely that it is the first handicraft using materials sufficiently resistant to have survived. Whether work in wood or something equally perishable preceded work in stone, we may never know, but it can be demonstrated that, in so far as Palæolithic Europe is concerned, the working of bone came in long after work in stone. Wood is, therefore, about the only known material that might have preceded stone. Further, we find in the stone work of Palæolithic Europe, first, crude, simple forms, and later, much more elaborate implements. In fact, the early forms are so simple that the experts are not agreed as to where the line may be safely drawn between fractures of stone due to natural phenomena and those purposefully executed by man. However, as soon as the working of stone reaches a stage where the primitive technician has in mind a definite form of implement and a fixed procedure in striking off chips, then the close similarity of the artifacts found in a campsite and the wide distribution of the same form will reveal the character of the technique employed by the makers.

Thus, the distinction between true eoliths and accidental

fractures hinges upon the minimum human design, or pattern. Fractured flint, or similar stone, is not proof of human agency, because flints may be broken from pressure in the original bed. On the other hand, if broken by design to serve some purpose, the flints should closely follow a pattern, or type. The earliest forms of flints certainly the work of man are all made after one basic pattern: a pebble is selected and shaped by striking off flakes. The following is a rough outline of the development of their technique:

1. Eoliths—doubtful forms because not distinguished from pebbles fractured by other than human agencies, miocene, and pliocene finds.

2. Rostro-carinates—a series of large flints from pliocene beds in England. These are regarded as presenting the minimum of pattern and as an advance over eoliths. These rostro-carinates have a ridge extending their entire length and end in a kind of beak.

3. Coup-de-poing—large pebbles shaped by striking off large flakes from one end; age, pre-Chellean, of the pleistocene. In later divisions of the Chellean the butt of the original surface disappears.

4. Acheulean—the simplest forms follow the above lines but become thinner and the flakes smaller.

The preceding are made by trimming down a pebble, or by shaping what is technically known as the core. Yet, the occasional use of flakes begins to make its appearance in Chellean times and increases gradually to the end of the Acheulean period. The Mousterian horizon, however, comes in with a dominance of the use of flakes, the cores being discarded. The Aurignacian period shows flakes of greater length and delicacy and then comes the Solutrean with its fine "laurel-leaf" blades with surface chipping.

We note that these slow, simple developments extend over two geological periods variously estimated as many thousand years. We cannot help being impressed by the importance of the least possible technological step, and how great an achievement even the absolute minimum in pattern may represent.

It is easy for us to sense how a precise way of making a basket may be spread from tribe to tribe, but when we are confronted with a museum collection of artifacts from Chellean stone age horizons, in which occur such simple forms as the *grattoir,* or planing tool, it is difficult to see that here also the worker had a pattern in mind and attained it by a fixed chipping technique; yet, this will be clearly realized after careful study of many such specimens. Further, when we consider the long periods of time in Palæolithic Europe before anything more elaborate appears and begin to realize that these simple, and, to us, crude forms, represented the maximum achievements in stone, we see the problem of technology in a new light.

We sometimes hear that the art of working stone began to decline in the Bronze Age and disappeared altogether in the Iron Age, but primitive peoples were making stone points and knives when discovered in the fifteenth and sixteenth centuries and some of them are still doing it. And, of course, broadly viewed, the use of stone in some form, with many special techniques, survives in the most civilized countries. It is true, however, that the introduction of metal soon causes stone tools to disappear.

Students of stone tools have pointed out that they fall into a few classes, according to use, as striking, rubbing, scraping, cutting, sawing, piercing, and boring, and that these functions may be served, as in early Palæolithic times, by two or three simple forms, and that the development of stone tool technique has been in the direction of specialized forms. If, however, we turn to the processes used in making these tools, these are, in the main, flaking, pecking and grinding, and all the many special techniques used by living and extinct races fall, for the most part, under these heads. To come to a better understanding of what is meant, the reader should examine a well-ordered exhibit in a museum, but, if this is not feasible, read some of the special treatises on the subject.[2]

Ceramics, or pottery, is another important subject. Pottery does not appear in Europe until the Neolithic period and is not found among many primitive peoples. To the archæologist, however, as we have stated, it is as useful in establishing chronological and regional differences as are fossils in the work of the geologist, but the distinctions upon which the archæologist bases his chronology are the secondary details of surface finish and design, rather than gross structure.

In outline, the making of pottery includes the following steps:

1. The mixing of the clays and the introduction of granular tempering material, sand, crushed rock, etc.

2. Shaping the vessel. This may be done by squeezing masses of clay into the required shape; by coiling rolls of clay spirally; or by shaping on a wheel, and by molding.

3. Smoothing off the surface.

4. Drying.

5. If an ornamental surface is desired, an earthen slip is prepared and spread thinly over the surface; when glaze is desired, the necessary slip is added.

6. If designs are to be in color, these are painted on the surface; if they are incised or stamped into the surface, they are executed after the pot is shaped, but before it dries.

7. Firing.[3]

Shaping and decorating pottery being a plastic art, it has offered an easy road to expression and to tribal individuality, and so the study of tribal styles and regional patterns in the ceramic art has been carried to great detail.

Another technological process, as old or older than pottery, is weaving. The basic processes are found in such crude, but useful, forms as wattling, but are more clearly seen in basketry. Reference to any treatise on basketry will give illustrations of the important weaves as, plain, checker, twilled, twined, and coiled. Matting tends to follow the methods of basketry. Cloth is usually either plain or twill, differing from basketry only in that the materials are of cord, the production of which calls for a spinning technique.[4]

Another important aspect of technological research is that through it stand revealed the basic factors in industrial processes. The weaving of a carpet on a modern loom impresses one as an intricate procedure and it takes the uninitiated person a long time to comprehend it all, but a study of textile processes as a whole, primitive and civilized, makes it plain that the weaving of such a fabric is resolvable into a few simple processes known to primitive peoples. For example, in the matter of materials, the textile industry makes use of four types of fiber: wool, bast, cotton, and silk. Hair was used by the primitive Australians for twisting into string; many other peoples used the bark of plants for the same purpose. Cotton appears in aboriginal America at an early date. Silk, on the other hand, seems to possess a reasonable antiquity in the old civilization of eastern Asia. Naturally, the making of string is the foundation of cloth and, for materials, man has been limited to the animal and vegetable fibers that possessed the clinging properties necessary for spinning. Now, so far as the data in anthropology go, every people, however simple their culture, understand the principle of twisting string from animal or vegetable fiber; spinning may be accomplished with the fingers and thumb, unaided, by rolling the fiber on the skin of the leg under the palm of the hand, by twisting with a spindle whorl, by a spring wheel, etc. The more complicated appliances may increase the output, but really do nothing that cannot be turned out by the hands alone. The basic process thus underlies the production of cord from the beginning to the present and the mechanization of the process is seen to have begun in very early times.

When weaving is analyzed it is found to consist of little more than one concept, the most natural form being that of interlacing rods or cords at right angles to each other. This process is also known to most every people, though some may never use it except in interlacing a few sticks;

yet, again the process is always the same, the crossing rod or cord alternately passing over and under. Also, so far as the data go, matting and basketry tend to appear before cloth, using these terms in the modern sense; but the distinction here is chiefly in the materials used for weaving: coarse materials resulting in mats and baskets, fine materials in bags and cloth. Like the spinning process, weaving presents several types of mechanization, a simple frame, the addition of a beater to force the weft down on the woof, the heddle to give the pattern, the development of the shuttle, and finally, the use of foot and then of machine power to operate the loom.

In this same way we might analyze pottery, agriculture, stonework, metal work, woodwork, fire-making, etc., finding one or more simple fundamental process used throughout each cycle, some, which seem to have begun with man and to have been in continuous use to the present; others appear at various periods in human history. It was the discovery of this characteristic of civilized industry that inspired the leaders of research in technology and which, in large measure, led to the establishing of anthropological museums.

THE EVOLUTION OF TECHNOLOGICAL PROCESSES

Even brief sketches of a few widely distributed industrial processes, such as have been cited, and a cursory glance at a museum collection, suggest that there has been a more or less gradual evolution of these processes. Our experience in life and our traditions commit us to the belief that all our productive techniques have developed by accretions from very simple beginnings. This was fully recognized in the time of Tylor and Pitt-Rivers, but when collections of handwork from primitive peoples became available, this sequence at once assumed a worldwide and all-embracing character. Stone was not only worked by primitive peoples, but archæological researches in Europe made it clear that the earliest steps in the development of this art were simple and crude. As this idea seemed to be in agreement with the experience of civilized man, it was natural to assume that by arranging objects made by primitive and civilized men, according to their apparent logical sequences, the steps in the evolution of these processes would be revealed. In discussing the history of technology, we noted the formulation of this method of interpretation by which it was proposed to recover the whole story of man's culture achievements. Recalling our studies of animism and of social organization, we see that the development of these insights is parallel to that for technology. Further, as the study of technological collections continued, difficulties were encountered, similar to those noted for animism and social organization. It is often possible to arrange the objects in a collection in a sequence, or in steps, presenting what seems to be a plausible order of evolution, but, for one thing, one cannot be sure that he has a complete series of objects; in any case, a check is needed in the form of historical, geographical, or chronological data. Thus, the reason we can speak definitely of successive steps in chipping stone in early Europe is that by the method of stratification we can give the time order in which the various forms of chipping appear. Nevertheless, the pioneer studies of Pitt-Rivers and Mason led the way to the development of museum collections and the study of material culture, now an important line of anthropological research.

As the matter stands, then, the general problem as to the chronological steps in the history of weaving, pottery, etc., is still an objective and in the minds of many investigators the primary objective. The immediate problems are to analyze the regional data for these technologies, tribe by tribe. A good example of such studies is seen in the researches among the Indians of California conducted by the University of California.[5]

THE PROBLEM OF INVENTION

One of the important questions arising out of technological studies is whether the improvements in technological processes originate after the manner of modern inventions, or whether they are arrived at in a different way. In archæology this question can only be approached by a study of the specimens themselves; among living peoples, it is theoretically possible that the histories of changes in technique can be recovered, but in practice this is rarely attained. So, for the most part, this history must be read, if read at all, in the specimens themselves. Invention, as we generally conceive it, is a cumulative process, one step succeeding another. For example, we know how the steam engine was developed by many successive improvements and is still being changed. Watt, after all, did little more than start on the right track. So, seeing a series of stone tools from Palæolithic Europe, and noting that the early forms are nothing more than stones of convenient size, the ends of which have been rudely pointed by knocking off chips, and later examples in which slender long chips are struck off and these worked down to symmetrical forms by skillful, detailed chipping, we find little difficulty in seeing parallelism. Cave man after cave man, we think, improved the method and discovered better stone; finally, some one proved it better to use the chip than the original core and so on. This seems, on the face of it, the expected human way in which all that we see came about, and, if we stop there, it may appear that all men, savage or civilized, progress by invention, just as they all breathe, sleep, and eat.

And this is so matter of course that there would be no reason for questioning it were it not for the time element. A change of the simplest kind, extending over a period of seemingly thousands of years, is quite a different matter from the story of the steam engine. When an object like an arrow point reaches a high state of perfection, then one can understand its stability, but why, if invention is the order of the day, should stone technique have lagged so long in the beginning?

Our conception of invention assumes some previous knowledge of techniques and materials and the recognition of a desired objective. We are told that the whole matter may be accidental and unconscious, but it is difficult to account for the survival of a trick, unless the observer had a much-desired objective in mind and saw in the new method a suggestion of accelerating its attainment. We are also forced to concede that if invention among cave men proceeded as it does among ourselves, then a great deal of thought must have been given at one time and another to the nature of stone materials, the specific objectives, etc.; otherwise we could not account for what occurred; but we are told that we are assuming too much on the part of primitive man, or becoming too rationalistic. At the same time, it is claimed that the mind of primitive man works just like that of a Darwin or a Newton. What these confusing statements imply is that the last word has not been said respecting the primitive mind; those who insist that in the earliest stone age man had a mind capable of anything man does to-day, are asking us to believe that he not only came on the scene with an equipment equal to something a million years off, but that this equipment lay relatively idle for a long time. Yet, we are told that even if our Chellean predecessors possessed the minds of Edison and the like, there was no chance for them to function, and so nothing happened. While there is some sense to this argument, it does not satisfy, and so it seems wiser to leave the question open. But to return to the nature of the process itself; we might agree to the probability that stone tools began with taking a stone in the hand for pounding, scraping, etc. Then may have come the idea of selecting a stone of better shape, the idea of re-shaping, etc.; but we are merely reading our own experience and belief into the phenomena, just as is frequently done in explaining the acts of animals. However, to explain a technique or an invention we must assume existing experience and knowledge as the starting point.

The problem then resolves itself into an objective examination of stone-working technique and a comparison of the established sequences with those in the technological processes of modern times, which we know can be safely interpreted in the light of our experience. If the parallel seems close, then we have a strong case. The doubtful point is, as we have stated, that the time element in the cave period seems extraordinarily long, raising the question as to whether the changes in early stone technique came about as mere drifts, or by sudden insights after the mode of the present. No satisfactory answer to these questions can be given now. Penetrating research is necessary along this line

POTTERY AND AGRICULTURE

We turn now to some of the problems that have arisen in the study of museum collections and technological data. In the New World it was observed that the geographical distributions of agriculture and pottery were fairly coincident; in the Old World, also, the two arts seem to coincide. This raises the question as to the nature of this linkage. First, let us appraise the data. In America we do find some small exceptions, for pottery seems to have been known to a few tribes just beyond the margin of the agricultural area. These exceptions, however, do not negate the overlapping of agriculture and pottery in the great central area of the New World. However, we have an important exception, since the Eskimo west of Hudson Bay, and some of the non-agricultural Siberians, make a little pottery. Turning to archæology, we find the time of appearance for pottery tending to follow closely the appearance of agriculture; yet, there are but three areas in the world for which we have good working chronological outlines: southwestern United States, western Europe, Egypt and Mesopotamia.

In southwestern United States the earliest well-known culture is that of the Basket Makers who, as the term implies, made baskets, but no pots; yet, they possessed a simple form of agriculture. Following the Basket Makers, however, or in their later career, pottery appears, and from that time on, develops hand in hand with agriculture.[6] The minute chronologies for other areas in North and South America have not been worked out in sufficient detail to say more than that agriculture and pottery seem to appear synchronously.

Turning to the Old World, we find in Egypt and Mesopotamia again a close association between the two arts.

The problem here is similar to that raised by Hobhouse [7] and earlier by Tylor. Simply stated, it is whether certain arts and customs occur together more often than separately. So stated, the preliminary inquiry becomes statistical, or a matter of listing tribe after tribe until all the available data have been used. This was the method employed by Hobhouse, but he confined his inquiry to social and economic traits of culture, rather than to technology. Thus, he observed that polygamous marriages were far less frequent among hunters than among pastoral and agricultural tribes; also, that the frequency of wife purchase increased greatly as one passed from hunters to the more intense pastoral and agricultural cultures. These findings tend to support the statement frequently made that the more advanced cultures are responsible for the larger polygamous families and for the extreme commercialism of marriage. Or, to put the matter in another way, the organization and increased efficiency of agriculture went hand in hand with the development of marriage systems. This result does not throw light upon which appeared first, agriculture or polygamy, it merely links them or reveals a tendency to associate. In the case of pottery and agriculture we can approach the question of origin by direct archæological methods and speak definitely of the relative sequence in which agriculture and pottery appear; the only difficulty lies in the incompleteness of data, a defect which future archæological research may be expected to remedy.

However, the fundamental question involved here is whether culture traits are associated in this way because they are related or dependent in function, or whether they just happen to occur together. This is a problem we can best discuss when we come to a consideration of the distribution of cultures and their relations to each other.

INFLUENCE OF MATERIALS UPON FORM

While it is true that the first great impetus to the study of technology came in the attempt to solve one all-embracing problem, or to discuss the principle according to which technology as a whole evolved, there have arisen from time to time a number of special problems. One of these is the influence of the original form of the materials used in determining shape and design. For example, in weaving with coarse materials, as in matting and basketry, the surface takes on a checker appearance due to the crossing of the weaving elements. A splint basket will show this clearly and it is likely that when weaving is regular, all peoples, primitive or otherwise, find the symmetry pleasing. But color may be used to complicate the surface pattern, by using splints of wo colors, and in the more complicated schemes, several colors. Yet, the result is a series of angular geometric figures and not curved and realistic designs. In short, the weaving process tends to commit one to geometric design and this is why it is frequently assumed that the one is an outgrowth of the other and that whenever we meet with geometric designs upon pottery it is because basketry preceded pottery. There is some truth in this, but that geometric art never arose in any other way is, in the present state of our knowledge, an unjustifiable assumption.

On the other hand, a good case can be made for convergence in development, since in different parts of the world similar basketry materials, worked by similar weaves, do result in similar decorative patterns. In this case, it is safe to say that the materials and the processes determined the decorative forms evolved.

Pottery is often considered free from such determining factors because of the plasticity of its materials, and it is difficult to think of anything much more plastic than soft wet clay; yet time and again, attention has been called to the similarity in form between certain pottery vessels and gourds, shells, and baskets. If, as appears to be the usual sequence, basketry and the use of gourds, etc., precede pottery, then we can safely say that the pottery shapes observed were influenced by the forms of the containers displaced by pots. Further, as intimated above, we do often find painted designs upon pots, closely resembling those upon baskets and other textiles; this, however, might occur at any time, independent of sequence or use of the objects to be decorated, and so is not clearly an evidence of the direct influence of textile art upon that of pottery.[8]

The detailed study of moccasins is another interesting chapter in technology.[9] The simplest and probably the oldest form is that in which a single piece of skin is shaped over the foot, like a stocking. It is true this piece of skin is first cut according to a pattern, so that when the edges of the piece are sewed up, the resulting moccasin fits the foot. Certain moccasins from the peat bogs of Europe have come to light, dating back to the Bronze Age and beyond; some of these seem to have been formed from pieces of skin from the head of a deer, the shape of which was such as to require little trimming, offering the tantalizing suggestion that the peculiar pattern for the North American soft-soled moccasin was also derived from the natural shape of a head skin. This, however, cannot be proved; but when we turn to the decorations upon Indian moccasins we see every indication that the moccasin pattern employed by the tribe set the styles of decoration. For example, one pattern for a soft-soled moccasin requires a U-shaped insert over the instep and it is the practice of the tribes using this pattern to decorate this insert. Yet, a number of tribes use this same U-shaped decoration upon moccasins of a different pattern requiring no insert; in other words, to keep the same appearance of the moccasin as comes naturally in the old pattern, a fake insert is laid over the surface. If this were the only instance of such similarity it could be treated lightly, but parallel occurrences in other parts of moccasin patterns and decorative fields have been noted; also, we find similar correspondence in decoration and pattern in certain types of skin clothing. We may safely generalize, then, with the statement that the pattern, or the shape, of the material in shoe and garment, often exerts a determining influence upon the decoration, occasionally originating specified designs.

To show how the natural shape of skins may determine the style of a garment, one needs but study men's and women's shirts in a museum collection from the Indians of the Plains.[10] The older shirts for men in such collections are made of two mountain sheepskins, or from the skins of a small deer. These are placed back to back, with scarcely any trimming or cutting, thus making a shirt of peculiar pattern. The later shirts are made of large skins, and sometimes from cloth, but the material is now cut to simulate the original pattern. Thus, the peculiar sleeves and side pendants to the garment did not originate in the imagination of the designer, but were determined by the original materials. In these same collections the garments for women are of a different pattern, but were originally fashioned of two complete skins and so their peculiar pattern was also determined by the material itself.

Turning to woven garments we often find the same principle in operation. Ordinary hand-loom weaving gives a fabric that cannot be cut but must be used in "the square," as it were; so if a shirt is made, its body must be plainly rectangular, and if sleeves are added they must be uniformly rectangular; hence, the simple rigid lines of woven garments among the more primitive tribes are also largely determined by the material itself. Naturally, these limitations can be overcome, but such studies should warn us not to assume that styles and designs are pure fictions of the imagination, until there is good evidence upon which to base a judgment.

SUMMARY

Technology is a general term covering all mechanical processes involving the use of tools and the shaping of materials. Objects illustrating technology make up the collections in an anthropological museum. Material culture is the term frequently used to cover technology and economics among primitive tribes. Many studies are based exclusively upon museum collections. Also the history of museums is in part the history of anthropology. The evolution of technological processes and forms is one of the most interesting human problems in social science, involving the whole process of invention. One of the great leads in anthropological research was the idea that by the objective comparative study of museum collections, an objective procedure, one could arrive at conclusions as to how technological processes and objects evolved. This is a genetic point of view, though the order of progression is quite different from that in biological evolution.

NOTES

1 Otis T. Mason, *Aboriginal American Basketry: Studies in a Textile Art Without Machinery* (United States National Museum Report for 1902, Washington, 1904).

2 Otis T. Mason, *The Origins of Invention* (London, 1895); George Grant MacCurdy, *Human Origins: A Manual of Prehistory*, 2 vols. (New York and London, 1924); Henry Fairfield Osborn, *Men of the Old Stone Age, Their Environment, Life and Art* (New York, 1915).

3 Otis T. Mason, *The Origins of Invention* (London, 1895); A. C. Parker, *The Indian How Book* (New York, 1927); C. E. Guthe, *Pueblo Pottery Making: A Study of the Village of San Ildefonso* (New Haven, 1925).

4 Mary Lois Kissell, *Yarn and Cloth Making: An Economic Study* (New York, 1918).

5 A. L. Kroeber, *Handbook of the Indians of California* (Bulletin 78, Bureau of American Ethnology, Washington, 1925).

6 A. V. Kidder, *An Introduction to the Study of Southwestern Archæology, with a Preliminary Account of the Excavations at Pecos* (New Haven, 1924).

7 L. T. Hobhouse, G. C. Wheeler, and M. Ginsberg, *The Material Culture and Social Institutions of the Simpler Peoples, an Essay in Correlation* (London, 1915).

8 William H. Holmes, *Origin and Development of Form and Ornament in Ceramic Art* (Fourth Annual Report, Bureau of American Ethnology, Washington, 1886). Max Schmidt, *The Primitive Races of Mankind. A Study in Ethnology* (Boston, 1926).

9 O. T. Mason, *Primitive Travel and Transportation* (Report, United States National Museum for 1894, Washington, 1896); Gudmund Hatt, *Moccasins and Their Relation to Arctic Footwear* (Memoirs, American Anthropological Association, vol. iii, pp. 151-250, 1916); Clark Wissler,

Structural Basis to the Decoration of Costumes Among the Plains Indians (Anthropological Papers, American Museum of Natural History, vol. xvii. part iii, 1917).

[10] Clark Wissler, *Costumes of the Plains Indians* (Anthropological Papers, American Museum of Natural History, vol. xvii, part ii, 1915).

CANNIBALISM *

By WILLIAM GRAHAM SUMNER

Cannibalism. Cannibalism is one of the primordial mores. It dates from the earliest known existence of man on earth. It may reasonably be believed to be a custom which all peoples have practiced.[1] Only on the pastoral stage has it ceased, where the flesh of beasts was common and abundant.[2] It is indeed noticeable that the pygmies of Africa and the Kubus of Sumatra, two of the lowest out-cast races, do not practice cannibalism,[3] although their superior neighbors do. Our intense abomination for cannibalism is a food taboo, and is perhaps the strongest taboo which we have inherited.

Origin in food supply. It is the best opinion that cannibalism originated in the defects of the food supply, more specifically in the lack of meat food. The often repeated objection that New Zealanders and others have practiced cannibalism when they had an abundant supply of meat food is not to the point. The passion for meat food, especially among people who have to live on heavy starch food, is very strong. Hence, they eat worms, insects, and offal. It is also asserted that the appetite for human flesh, when eating it has become habitual, becomes a passion. When salt is not to be had the passion for meat reaches its highest intensity. "When tribes [of Australians] assembled to eat the fruit of the bunya-bunya they were not permitted to kill any game [in the district where the trees grow], and at length the craving for flesh was so intense that they were impelled to kill one of their number, in order that their appetites might be satisfied."[4] It follows that when this custom has become traditional the present food supply

* *Folkways,* New York: Ginn & Company.

may have little effect on it. There are cases at the present
time in which the practice of using human flesh for food
is customary on a large and systematic scale. On the island
of New Britain human flesh is sold in shops as butcher's
meat is sold amongst us.[5] In at least some of the Solomon
Islands human victims (preferably women) are fattened
for a feast, like pigs.[6] Lloyd [7] describes the cannibalism of
the Bangwa as an everyday affair although they eat chiefly
enemies, and rarely a woman. The women share the feast,
sitting by themselves. He says that it is, no doubt, "a
depraved appetite." They are not at all ashamed of it.
Physically the men are very fine. "The cannibalism of the
Monbutto is unsurpassed by any nation in the world." [8]
Amongst them human flesh is sold as if it were a staple
article of food. They are "a noble race." They have national
pride, intellectual power, and good judgment. They are
orderly, friendly, and have a stable national life.[9] Ward [10]
describes the cannibalism on the great bend of the Congo
as due to a relish for the kind of food. "Originating, apparently, from stress of adverse circumstances, it has become an acquired taste, the indulgence of which has created
a peculiar form of mental disorder, with lack of feeling,
love of fighting, cruelty, and general human degeneracy,
as prominent attributes." An organized traffic in human
beings for food exists on the upper waters of the Congo.
It is thought that the pygmy tribe of the Wambutti are
not cannibals because they are too "low," and because they
do not file the lower incisors. The latter custom goes with
cannibalism in the Congo region, and is also characteristic of the more gifted, beautiful, and alert tribes.[11] None
of the coast tribes of West Africa eat human flesh, but
the interior tribes eat any corpse regardless of the cause
of death. Families hesitate to eat their own dead, but they
sell or exchange them for the dead of other families.[12] In
the whole Congo region the custom exists, especially
amongst the warlike tribes, who eat not only war captives
but slaves.[13]

It is noteworthy that a fork [14] was invented in Polynesia for this kind of food, long before the fork was used for any other.

Cannibalism not abominable. Spix and Martius asked a chief of the Miranhas why his people practiced cannibalism. The chief showed that it was entirely a new fact to him that some people thought it an abominable custom. "You whites," said he, "will not eat crocodiles or apes, although they taste well. If you did not have so many pigs and crabs you would eat crocodiles and apes, for hunger hurts. It is all a matter of habit. When I have killed an enemy it is better to eat him than to let him go to waste. Big game is rare because it does not lay eggs like turtles. The bad thing is not being eaten, but death, if I am slain, whether our tribal enemy eats me or not. I know of no game which tastes better than men. You whites are really too dainty." [15]

In-group cannibalism. Cannibalism was so primordial in the mores that it has two forms, one for the in-group, the other for the out-group. It had a theory of affection in the former case and of enmity in the latter. In the in-group it was so far from being an act of hostility, or veiled impropriety, that it was applied to the closest kin. Mothers ate their babies, if the latter died, in order to get back the strength which they had lost in bearing them. Herodotus says that the Massagetæ sacrificed the old of their tribe, boiling the flesh of the men with that of cattle and eating the whole. Those who died of disease before attaining old age were buried, but that they thought a less happy fate. He says that the Padeans, men in the far east of India, put a sick man of their tribe to death and ate him, lest his flesh should be wasted by disease. The women did the same by a sick woman. If any reach old age without falling victims to this custom, they too are then killed and eaten. He mentions also the Issidones, in southeastern Russia, who cut up their dead fathers, mingle the flesh with that of sacrificed animals, and make a feast of the whole. The skull is cleaned, gilded, and kept as an emblem, to which they make annual sacrifices. They are accounted a righteous people. Amongst them women are esteemed equal with men.[16] Strabo [17] says that the Irish thought it praiseworthy to eat their deceased parents. The Birhors of Hazaribag, Hindus..n, formerly ate their parents, but "they repudiate the suggestion that they ate any but their own relations" [i.e., each one ate his own relatives and no others?].[18] Reclus [19] says that in that tribe "the parents beg that their corpses may find a refuge in the stomachs of their children rather than be left on the road or in the forest. The Tibetans, in ancient times, ate their parents," out of piety, in order to give them no other sepulcher than their own bowels. This custom ceased before 1250 A.D., but the cups made of the skulls of relatives were used as memorials. Tartars and some "bad Christians" killed their fathers when old, burned the corpses, and mingled the ashes with their daily food.[20] In the gulf country of Australia only near relatives partake of the dead, unless the corpse is that of an enemy. A very small bit only is eaten by each. In the case of an enemy the purpose is to win his strength. In the case of a relative the motive is that the survivors may not, by lamentations, become a nuisance in the camp.[21] The Dieyerie have the father family. The father may not eat his own child, but the mother and female relatives must do so, in order to have the dead in their liver, the seat of feeling.[22] The Tuare of Brazil (2 S. 67 W.) burn their dead. They preserve the ashes in reeds and mix them with their daily meals.[23] The Jumanas, on the head waters of the Amazon, regard the bones as the seat of the soul. They burn the bones of their dead, grind them to powder, mix the powder with intoxicating liquor, and drink it, "that the dead may live again in them." [24] All branches of the Tupis are cannibals. They brought the custom from the interior.[25] The Kobena drink in their *cachiri* the powdered bones of their dead relatives.[23] The Chavantes, on the Uruguay, eat their dead children to get back the souls. Especially young mothers do this, as they are thought to have given a part of their own souls to their children too soon.[27] In West Victoria "the bodies of relatives who have lost their lives by violence are alone partaken of." Each eats only a bit, and it is eaten "with no desire to gratify or appease the appetite, but only as a symbol of respect and regret for the dead." [28] In Australian cannibalism the eating of relatives has behind it the idea of saving the strength which would be lost, or of acquiring the dexterity or wisdom, etc., of the dead. Enemies are eaten to win their strength, dexterity, etc. Only a bit is eaten. There are no great feasts. The fat and soft parts are eaten because they are the residence of the soul. In eating enemies there appears to be ritual significance.[29] It may be the ritual purpose to get rid of the soul of the slain man for fear that it might seek revenge for his death.

Some inhabitants of West Australia explained cannibalism (they ate every tenth child born) as "necessary to keep the tribe from increasing beyond the carrying capacity of the territory." [30] Infanticide is a part of population policy. Cannibalism may be added to it either for food supply or goblinism. When children were sacrificed in Mexico their hearts were cooked and eaten, for sorcery.[31]

Judicial cannibalism. Another use of cannibalism in the in-group is to annihilate one who has broken an important taboo. The notion is frequently met with, amongst nature peoples, that a ghost can be got rid of by utterly annihilating the corpse, e.g., by fire. Judicial cannibalism destroys it, and the members of the group by this act participate in a ritual, or sacramental ceremony, by which a criminal is completely annihilated. Perhaps there may also be the idea of collective responsibility for his annihilation. To take the life of a tribe comrade was for a long time an act which needed high motive and authority and required expiation. The ritual of execution was like the ritual of sacrifice. In the Hebrew law some culprits were to be stoned by the whole congregation. Every one must take a share in the great act. The blood guilt, if there was any, must be incurred by all.[32] Primitive taboos are put on acts which offend the ghosts and many, therefore, bring woe on the whole group. Any one who breaks a taboo commits a sin and a crime, and excites the wrath of the superior powers. Therefore he draws on himself the fear and horror of his comrades. They must extrude him by banishment or death. They want to dissociate themselves from him. They sacrifice him to the powers which he has offended. When his comrades eat his corpse they perform a duty. They annihilate him and his soul completely.

Judicial cannibalism in ethnography. "A man found in the harem of Muatojamvos was cut in pieces and given, raw and warm, to the people to be eaten."[33] The Bataks employ judicial cannibalism as a regulated system. They have no other cannibalism. Adulterers, persons guilty of incest, men who have had sex intercourse with the widow of a younger brother, traitors, spies, and war captives taken with arms in their hands, are killed and eaten. The last-mentioned are cut in pieces alive and eaten bit by bit in order to annihilate them in the most shameful manner.[34] The Tibetans and Chinese formerly ate all who were executed by civil authority. An Arab traveler of the ninth century mentions a Chinese governor who rebelled, and who was killed and eaten. Modern cases of cannibalism are reported from China. Pith balls stained with the blood of decapitated criminals are used as medicine for consumption. Cases are also mentioned of Tartar rulers who ordered the flesh of traitors to be mixed with the ruler's own food and that of their barons. Tartar women begged for the possession of a culprit, boiled him alive, cut the corpse into mince-meat, and distributed it to the whole army to be eaten.[35]

Out-group cannibalism. Against members of an out-group, e.g., amongst the Maori, cannibalism "was due to a desire for revenge; cooking and eating being the greatest of insults."[36] On Tanna (New Hebrides) to eat an enemy was the greatest indignity to him, worse than giving up his corpse to dogs or swine, or mutilating it. It was believed that strength was obtained by eating a corpse.[37] A negro chief in Yabunda, French Congo, told Brunache [38] that "it was a very fine thing to enjoy the flesh of a man whom one has killed in a battle or a duel." Martius attributes the cannibalism of the Miranhas to the enjoyment of a "rare, dainty meal, which will satisfy their rude vanity, in some cases, also, blood revenge and superstition." [39] Cannibalism is one in the chain of causes which keeps this people more savage than their neighbors, most of whom have now abandoned it. "It is one of the most beastly of all the beast-like traits in the moral physiognomy of man." It is asserted that cannibalism has been recently introduced in some places, e.g., Florida (Solomon Islands). It is also said that on those islands the coast people give it up [they have fish], but those inland retain it. The notion probably prevails amongst all that population that, by this kind of food, *mana* is obtained, *mana* being the name for all power, talent, and capacity by which success is won.[40] The Melanesians took advantage of a crime, or alleged crime, to offer the culprit to a spirit, and so get fighting *mana* for the warriors.[41] The Chames of Cochin China think that the gall of slain enemies, mixed with brandy, is an excellent means to produce war courage and skill.[42] The Chinese believe that the liver is the seat of life and courage. The gall is the manifestation of the soul. Soldiers drink the gall of slain enemies to increase their own vigor and courage.[43] The mountain tribes of Natal make a paste from powder formed from parts of the body, which the priests administer to the youth.[44] Some South African tribes make a broth of the same kind of powder, which must be swallowed only in the prescribed manner. It "must be lapped up with the hand and thrown into the mouth . . . to give the soldiers courage, perseverance, fortitude, strategy, patience, and wisdom." [45]

Cannibalism to cure disease. Notions that the parts of the human body will cure different diseases are only variants of the notion of getting courage and skill by eating the same. Cases are recorded in which a man gave parts of his body to be eaten by the sick out of love and devotion.[43]

Reversions to cannibalism. When savage and brutal emotions are stirred, in higher civilization, by war and quarrels, the cannibalistic disposition is developed again. Achilles told Hector that he wished he could eat him. Hekuba expressed a wish that she could devour the liver of Achilles.[47] In 1564 the Turks executed Vishnevitzky, a brave Polish soldier who had made them much trouble. They ate his heart.[48] Dozy [49] mentions a case at Elvira, in 890, in which women cast themselves on the corpse of a chief who had caused the death of their relatives, cut it in pieces, and ate it. The same author relates [50] that Hind, the mother of Moavia, made for herself a necklace and bracelets of the noses and ears of Moslems killed at Ohod, and also that she cut open the corpse of an uncle of Mohammed, tore out the liver, and ate a piece of it. It is related of an Irish chief, of the twelfth century, that when his soldiers brought to him the head of a man he hated "he tore the nostrils and lips with his teeth, in a most savage and inhuman manner." [51]

In famine. Reversion to cannibalism under a total lack of other food ought not to be noted. We have some historical cases, however, in which during famine people became so familiarized with cannibalism that their horror of it was overcome. Abdallatif [52] mentions a great famine in Egypt in the year 1200, due to a failure of the inundation of the Nile. Resort was had to cannibalism to escape death. At first the civil authorities burned alive those who were detected, being moved by astonishment and horror. Later those sentiments were not aroused. "Men were seen to make ordinary meals of human flesh, to use it as a dainty, and to lay up provision of it. . . . The usage, having been introduced, spread to all the provinces. Then it ceased to cause surprise. . . . People talked of it as an ordinary and indifferent thing. This indifference was due to habit and familiarity." This case shows that the horror of cannibalism is due to tradition in the mores. Diodorus says that the ancient Egyptians, during a famine, ate each other rather than any animals which they considered sacred.[53]

Cannibalism and ghost fear. Human sacrifice and cannibalism are not necessarily conjoined. Often it seems as if they once were so, but have been separated.[54] Whatever men want ghosts want. If the former are cannibals, the latter will be the same. Often the notion is that the gods eat the souls. In this view, the men eat the flesh of sacrificed beasts and sacrifice the blood, in which is the life or soul, to the gods. This the Jews did. They also burned the kidneys, the fat of the kidneys, and the liver, which they thought to be the seat of life. These they might not eat.[55] When men change, the gods do not. Hence the rites of human sacrifice and cannibalism continue in religion long after they disappear from the mores, in spite of loathing. Loathing is a part of the sacrifice.[53] The self-control and self-subjugation enter into the sacrament. All who participate, in religion, in an act which gravely affects the imagination as horrible and revolting enter into a communion with each other. Every one who desires to participate in the good to be obtained must share in the act. As we have seen above, all must participate that none may be in a position to reproach the rest. Under this view, the cannibal food is reduced to a crumb, or to a drop of blood, which may be mixed with other food. Still later, the cannibal food is only represented, e.g., by cakes in the human form, etc. In the Middle Ages the popular imagination saw a human body in the host, and conjured up operations on the host which were attributed to sorcerers and Jews, which would only be applicable to a human body. Then the New Testament language about the body and blood of Christ took on a realistic sense which was cannibalistic.

Cannibalism, sorcery, and human sacrifice. Among the West African tribes sacrificial and ceremonial cannibalism in fetich affairs is almost universal.[57] Serpa Pinto[58] mentions a frequent feast of the chiefs of the Bihe, for which

a man and four women of specified occupations are required. The corpses are both washed and boiled with the
flesh of an ox. Everything at the feast must be marked
with human blood. Cannibalism, in connection with religious festivals and human sacrifice, was extravagantly
developed in Mexico, Central America, and British Columbia. The rites show that the human sacrifice was sacramental and vicarious. In one case the prayer of the person
who owned the sacrifice is given. It is a prayer for success
and prosperity. Flesh was also bitten from the arm of a
living person and eaten. A religious idea was cultivated
into a mania and the taste for human flesh was developed.[59]
Here also we find the usage that shamans ate the flesh of
corpses, in connection with fasting and solitude, as means
of professional stimulation.[60] Preuss emphasizes the large
element of sorcery in the eating of parts of a human sacrifice, as practiced in Mexico.[61] The combination of sorcery,
religious ritual, and cannibalism deserves very careful attention. The rites of the festival were cases of dramatic sorcery.
At the annual festival of the god of war an image of the
god was made of grain, seeds, and vegetables, kneaded with
the blood of boys sacrificed for the purpose. This image
was broken into crumbs and eaten by males only, "after
the manner of our communion." [62] The Peruvians ate sacrificial cakes kneaded with the blood of human victims, "as
a mark of alliance with the Inca." [63] In Guatemala organs
of a slain war captive were given to an old prophetess to
be eaten. She was then asked to pray to the idol which she
served to give them many captives.[64] Human sacrifices and
sacramental cannibalism exist amongst the Bella-coola Indians in northwestern British America. Children of the poor
are bought from their parents to be made sacrifices. The
blood is drunk and the flesh is eaten raw. The souls of the
sacrificed go to live in the sun and become birds. When the
English government tried to stop these sacrifices the priests
dug up corpses and ate them. Several were thus poisoned.[35]

Cult and cannibalism. The cases which have been cited

show how cult kept up cannibalism, if no beast was substituted. Also, a great number of uses of blood and superstitions about blood appear to be survivals of cannibalism or deductions from it. The same may be said of holiday cakes of special shapes, made by peasants, which have long lost all known sense. In one part of France the last of the harvest which is brought in is made into a loaf in human shape, supposed to represent the spirit of corn or of fertility. It is broken up and distributed amongst all the villagers, who eat it.[36]

A Mongolian lama reported of a tribe, the Lhopa of Sikkim or Bhutan, that they kill and eat the bride's mother at a wedding, if they can catch no wild man.[37]

A burglar in West Prussia, in 1865, killed a maid-servant and cut flesh from her body out of which to make a candle for use in later acts of theft. He was caught while committing another burglary. He confessed that he ate a part of the corpse of his first-mentioned victim "in order to appease his conscience." [38]

Food taboos. It is most probable that dislike to eat the human body was a product of custom, and grew in the mores after other foods became available in abundance. Unusual foods now cost us an effort. Frogs' legs, for instance, repel most people at first. We eat what we learned from our parents to eat, and other foods are adopted by "acquired taste." Light is thrown on the degree to which all food preferences and taboos are a part of the mores by a comparison of some cases of food taboos. Porphyrius, a Christian of Tyre, who lived in the second half of the second century of the Christian era, says that a Phœnician or an Egyptian would sooner eat man's flesh than cow's flesh.[39] A Jew would not eat swine's flesh. A Zoroastrian could not conceive it possible that any one could eat dog's flesh. We do not eat dog's flesh, probably for the same reason that we do not eat cat's or horse's, because the flesh is tough or insipid and we can get better, but some North American Indians thought dog's flesh the very best food. The Banziris, in the French Congo, reserved dog's flesh for men, and they surround meals of it with a solemn ritual. A man must not touch his wife with his finger for a day after such a feast.[70] The inhabitants of Ponape will eat no eels, which "they hold in the greatest horror." The word used by them for eel means "the dreadful one."[71] Dyaks eat snakes, but reject eels.[72] Some Melanesians will not eat eels because they think that there are ghosts in them.[73] South African Bantus abominate fish.[74] Some Canary Islanders eat no fish.[75] Tasmanians would rather starve than eat fish.[76] The Somali will eat no fish, considering it disgraceful to do so.[77] They also reject game and birds.[78] These people who reject eels and fish renounce a food supply which is abundant in their habitat.

Food taboos in ethnography. Some Micronesians eat no fowl.[79] Wild Veddahs reject fowl.[80] Tuaregs eat no fish, birds, or eggs.[81] In eastern Africa many tribes loathe eggs and fowl as food. They are as much disgusted to see a white man eat eggs as a white man is to see savages eat offal[82] Some Australians will not eat pork.[83] Nagas and their neighbors think roast dog a great delicacy. They will eat anything, even an elephant which has been three days buried, but they abominate milk, and find the smell of tinned lobster too strong.[84] Negroes in the French Congo have a "perfect horror of the idea of drinking milk."[85]

Expiation for taking life. The most primitive notion we can find as to taking life is that it is wrong to kill any living thing except as a sacrifice to some superior power. This dread of destroying life, as if it was the assumption of a divine prerogative to do so, gives a background for all the usages with regard to sacrifice and food. "In old Israel all slaughter was sacrifice, and a man could never eat beef or mutton except as a religious act." Amongst the Arabs, "even in modern times, when a sheep or camel is slain in honor of a guest, the good old custom is that the host keeps open house for all his neighbors."[86] In modern Hindustan food which is ordinarily tabooed may be eaten if it has been

killed in offering to a god. Therefore an image of the god
is set up in the butcher's shop. All the animals are slaughtered nominally as an offering to it. This raises the taboo,
and the meat is bought and eaten without scruple.[87] Thus
it is that the taboo on cannibalism may be raised by religion,
or that cannibalism may be made a duty by religion.
Amongst the ancient Semites some animals were under a
food taboo for a reason which has two aspects at the same
time: they were both offensive (ritually unclean) and sacred.
What is holy and what is loathsome are in like manner
set aside. The Jews said that the Holy Scriptures rendered
him who handled them unclean. Holy and unclean have a
common element opposed to profane. In the case of both
there is devotion or consecration to a higher power. If it
is a good power, the thing is holy; if a bad power, it is unclean. He who touches either falls under a taboo, and needs
purification.[88] The tabooed things could only be eaten sac-
rificially and sacramentally, i.e., as disgusting and unusual
they had greater sacrificial force.[89] This idea is to be traced
in all ascetic usages, and in many medieval developments
of religious usages which introduced repulsive elements, to
heighten the self-discipline of conformity. In the Caroline
Islands turtles are sacred to the gods and are eaten only
in illness or as sacrifices.[90]

Philosophy of cannibalism. If cannibalism began in the
interest of the food supply, especially of meat, the wide ramifications of its relations are easily understood. While men
were unable to cope with the great beasts cannibalism was
a leading feature of social life, around which a great cluster
of interests centered. Ideas were cultivated by it, and it
became regulative and directive as to what ought to be
done. The sentiments of kinship made it seem right and
true that the nearest relatives should be eaten. Further deductions followed, of which the cases given are illustrations.
As to enemies, the contrary sentiments found place in connection with it. It combined directly with ghost fear. The
sacramental notion seems born of it. When the chase was

sufficiently developed to give better food the taboo on human flesh seemed no more irrational than the other food taboos above mentioned. Swans and peacocks were regarded as great dainties in the Middle Ages. We no longer eat them. Snakes are said to be good eating, but most of us would find it hard to eat them. Yet why should they be more loathsome than frogs or eels? Shipwrecked people, or besieged and famine-stricken people, have overcome the loathing for human flesh rather than die. Others have died because they could not overcome it and have thus rendered the strongest testimony to the power of the mores. In general, the cases show that if men are hungry enough, or angry enough, they may return to cannibalism now. Our horror of cannibalism is due to a long and broad tradition, broken only by hearsay of some far-distant and extremely savage people who now practice it. Probably the popular opinion about it is that it is wicked. It is not forbidden by the rules of any religion, because it had been thrown out of the mores before any "religion" was founded.

NOTES

[1] See Andree, *Anthropophagie;* Steinmetz, *Endokannibalism, Mitt. Anthrop. Ges. in Wien,* xxvi; Schaffhausen in *Archiv für Anthrop.,* iv, p. 245. Steinmetz gives in tabular form known cases of cannibalism with the motives for it, p. 25.

[2] Lippert, *Kulturgesch.,* ii. p. 275.

[3] *Globus,* xxvi, p. 45; Stuhlmann, *Mit Emin Pascha,* p. 457; *J. A. I.,* xxviii, p. 39.

[4] Smyth, *Victoria,* i, p. xxxviii.

[5] *Aust. Ass. Adv. Sci.,* 1892, p. 618.

[6] *J. A. I.,* xvii, p. 99.

[7] *Dwarf-land,* p. 345.

[8] Schweinfurth, *Heart of Africa,* ii, p. 94.

[9] Keane, *Ethnology,* p. 265.

[10] *J. A. I.,* xxiv, p. 298.

[11] *Globus,* lxxxv, p. 229.

[12] Nassau, *Fetishism in West Africa.*

[13] *Globus,* lxxii, p. 120; lxxxvii, p. 237.

[14] Specimen in the Dresden Museum.

[15] *Brasilien,* p. 1249.

[16] *Herod.,* i, p. 216; iii, p. 99; iv, p. 26.

[17] *Ibid.,* iv, pp. 5, 298.

[18] *J. A. S. B.,* ii, p. 571.

[19] *Prim. Folk,* p. 249.
[20] Rubruck, *Eastern Parts,* pp. 81, 151.
[21] *J. A. I.,* xxiv, p. 171.
[22] *Ibid.,* xvii, p. 186.
[23] *Globus,* lxxxiii, p. 137.
[24] Martius, *Ethnog. Bras.,* p. 485.
[25] Southey, *Brazil,* i, p. 233.
[26] *Ztsft. für Ethnol.,* xxxvi, p. 293.
[27] Andree, *Anthropophagie,* p. 50.
[28] Dawson, *West Victoria,* p. 67.
[29] Smyth, *Victoria,* i, p. 245.
[30] Whitmarsh, *The World's Rough Hand,* p. 178.
[31] *Globus,* lxxxvi, p. 112.
[32] W. R. Smith, *Religion of the Semites,* p. 284.
[33] Oliveira Martins, *Racas Humanas,* ii, p. 67.
[34] Wilken, *Volkenkunde,* pp. 23, 27.
[35] Marco Polo, i, p. 266, and Yule's note, p. 275.
[36] *J. A. I.,* xix, p. 108.
[37] *Austral. Ass. Adv. Sci.,* 1892, pp. 649-663.
[38] *Cent. Afr.,* p. 108.
[39] *Ethnog. Bras.,* p. 538.
[40] *J. A. I.,* x, p. 305.
[41] Codrington, *Melanesians,* p. 134.
[42] *Bijdragen tot. T. L. en Vekunde,* 1895, p. 342.
[43] *Globus,* lxxxi, p. 96.
[44] *J. A. I.,* xx, p. 116.
[45] *Ibid.,* xxii, p. 111: cf. Isaiah lxv. 4.
[46] *Intern. Arch. f. Ethnol.,* ix, supp. 37.
[47] *Iliad,* xxii, p. 346; xxiv, p. 212.
[48] Evarnitzky, *Zaporoge Kossacks* (russ.), i, p. 269.
[49] *Mussulm. d'Espagne,* ii, p. 226.
[50] *Ibid.,* i, p. 47.
[51] Gomme, *Ethnol. in Folklore,* p. 149.
[52] *Relation de l'Egypte,* p. 360.
[53] Diodorus, i, p. 84.
[54] Ratzel, *Völkerkunde,* ii, p. 124. Martius, *Ethnog. Bras.,* p. 129; *Globus,* lxxv, p. 260.
[55] W. R. Smith, *Religion of the Semites,* p. 379.
[56] Lippert, *Kulturgesch.,* ii, p. 292.
[57] Kingsley, *Travels in W. Afr.,* p. 287.
[58] *Como Eu Atravassei Afr.,* i, p. 148.
[59] Bancroft, *Native Races of the Pacific Coast,* i, p. 170 (iii, p. 150); ii, pp. 176, 395, 689, 708; iii, p. 413.
[60] *Ibid.,* iii, p. 152.
[61] *Globus,* lxxxvi, pp. 109, 112.
[62] *Bur. Ethnol.,* ix, p. 523.
[63] *Ibid.,* p. 527.
[64] Brinton, *Nagualism,* p. 34.
[65] *Mitt. Berl. Mus.,* 1885, p. 184.
[66] *P. S. M.,* xlviii, p. 411.
[67] Rockhill, *Mongolia and Thibet.* p. 144.

[68] *P. S. M.*, liv, p. 217.
[39] *De Abstinentia*, ii, p. 11.
[70] Brunache, *Cent. Afr.*, p. 69.
[71] Christian, *Caroline Isl.*, p. 73.
[72] Perelaer, *Dyaks*, p. 27.
[73] Codrington, *Melanesians*, p. 177.
[74] Fritsch, *Eingeb. Südafr.*, p. 107.
[75] *N. S. Amer. Anthrop.*, ii, p. 454.
[76] Ling Roth, *Tasmanians*, p. 101.
[77] Paulitschke, *Ethnog. N. O. Afr.*, i, p. 155.
[78] *Ibid.*, ii, p. 27.
[79] Finsch, *Ethnol. Erfahr.*, iii, p. 53.
[80] *N. S. Ethnol. Soc.*, ii, p. 304.
[81] Duveyrier, *Touaregs de Nord*, p. 401.
[82] Volkens, *Kilimandscharo*, p. 244.
[83] Smyth, *Victoria*, i, p. 237.
[84] *J. A. I.*, xi, p. 63; xxii, p. 245.
[85] Kingsley, *West. Afr. Studies*, p. 451.
[86] W. R. Smith, *Religion of the Semites*, pp. 142, 283.
[87] Wilkins, *Mod. Hinduism*, p. 168.
[88] Bousset, *Relig. des Judenthums*, p. 124.
[89] W. R. Smith, *Religion of the Semites*, p. 290. Isaiah lxv. 4; lxvi. 3, 17; swine, dog, and mouse.
[90] Kubary, *Karolinen Archipel.*, p. 168.

IV

SEXUAL CUSTOMS AND SOCIAL PRACTICE

THE ORIGIN OF LOVE *

By ROBERT BRIFFAULT

SEXUAL HUNGER AND CRUELTY

It has been almost universally assumed that feelings of tenderness and affection are part and parcel of the attraction between the sexes. That attraction is commonly spoken of as "love," and the sentiment is identified with the sexual impulse. Sexual attraction throughout the animal kingdom, and even in the vegetable kingdom, is loosely spoken of as a manifestation of love; and love comes hence to be regarded as almost a "primordial quality of protoplasm." We say, quoting Schiller, that life is ruled by Hunger and Love. Scientific writers vie with the poets in describing Nature as pervaded with a hymn of love. The term is even extended to include molecular attractions. The apostle of materialism, Büchner, adopts the language of Empedocles, who described atoms as actuated in their attractions and repulsions by love and hate. "Just as man and woman attract one another," says the German philosophical writer, "so oxygen attracts hydrogen, and in loving union with it forms water. Potassium and phosphorus entertain such a violent passion for oxygen that even under water they burn, that is, unite themselves with the beloved object." "It is love," he says again, "in the form of attraction which chains stone to stone, earth to earth, star to star, and which holds together the mighty edifice on which we stand." Robert Burton, inspiring himself from Leo the Jew, used similar language. "How comes a lodestone," he says, "to draw iron? the ground to covet showers, but for love? No stock,

---

* *The Mothers*. New York: The Macmillan Co. Because of pressure for space, it was necessary to omit the voluminous references with which Briffault documents his work. [Editor.]

no stone that has not some feeling of love." The "primordial quality of protoplasm" is thus extended to the entire Universe, and we speak of it as moved by love, "the most ancient of the gods"—"L'amor che muove il sole e l'altre stelle."

Those widely current modes of speech and of thought are founded on a profound misconception of biological facts. The attraction between the sexes is not primarily or generally associated with the order of feelings which we denote as "tender feeling," affection, love. These have developed comparatively late in the course of organic evolution, and have arisen in relation to entirely different functions. The primitive, and by far the most prevalent, association of the sexual impulse is not with love, but with the opposite feelings of callous cruelty and delight in the infliction and the spectacle of pain.

Neither love nor hatred, kindness nor cruelty is connected with the fundamental impulses that move living things any more than with chemical reactions. The pain and suffering of another individual is primordially neither pleasant nor unpleasant but indifferent. The trend of animal evolution has, however, been to make the spectacle of suffering an object of pleasant and gratifying feeling. Animals are preying beings; the perception of a mangled, bleeding, or of a suffering, weak, and helpless creature means to the universal disposition of animal life a prey, food. That the suffering animal belongs to the same species, or is a close associate, makes no difference. All carnivorous animals and rodents are cannibalistic. Lions and tigers, which furnish favorite examples of mating among carnivora, commonly kill and devour their mates. Andersson describes how a lion, having quarreled with a lioness over the carcass of a springbok, "after killing his wife, had coolly eaten her also," and the same thing has been reported by other observers. A female leopard which had been wounded, but had got away, was found a few days later with her hind-quarters half eaten by her mate. Half-grown tiger cubs, orphaned by their mother being killed, are attacked and eaten by their father. A jaguar in the Zoölogical Gardens at New York, to whom it was desired to give a female companion, showed every sign of delight and extreme fondness for her while she was safely kept in an adjacent cage in order to habituate the animals to one another's company; the male jaguar purred, licked the female's paws, and behaved like the most love-sick admirer. When at last the partition between the cages was removed and the male was united with the object of his affection, his first act was to seize her by the throat and kill her. The same thing happened when a female was introduced to a grizzly bear. The danger of allowing the sexes to associate is a commonplace in menageries. Wolves commonly kill and eat their mates. Male mice have been observed to kill their females and eat them for no apparent reason. It is a rule with herding animals that any sick or wounded individual is driven from the herd, or gored and worried to death.

Sexual attraction, sexual "hunger," as it has been aptly called, is a form of voracity. The object of the male cell in seeking conjunction with the female cell is primarily to improve its nutrition, in the same manner, and by virtue of the same fundamental impulse, as it seeks food. The female does not in the primitive forms of life seek or desire the male; but with the establishment of sexual reproduction she also required the male as a substance necessary to her reproductive growth and nutrition, as an object of assimilation. And in the same manner as the ovum cell assimilates the sperm-cell, so in some forms of life, such as the rotifers and spiders, the female devours and assimilates the male.

With both the male and the female, "love," or sexual attraction, is originally and preeminently "sadic"; it is positively gratified by the infliction of pain; it is as cruel as hunger. That is the direct, fundamental, and longest established sentiment connected with the sexual impulse. The male animal captures, mauls and bites the female, who in turn uses her teeth and claws freely, and the "lovers" issue from the sexual combat bleeding and mangled. Crustaceans usually lose a limb or two in the encounter. All mammals without exception use their teeth on these occasions. Pallas describes the mating of camels: as soon as impregnation has taken place, the female, with a vicious snarl, turns round and attacks the male with her teeth, and the latter is driven away in terror. Renegger remarks that the sexual union of a pair of jaguars must be a formidable conflict, for he found the forest devastated and strewn with broken branches over an area of a hundred feet where the fierce "love-making" had taken place. The congress of the sexes is assimilated by the impulse to hurt, to shed blood, to kill, to the encounter between a beast of prey and its victim, and all distinction between the two is not infrequently lost. It would be more accurate to speak of the sexual impulse as pervading nature with a yell of cruelty than with a hymn of love. The circumspection which is exhibited by many animal females in yielding to the male, the haste which is shown by most to separate as soon as impregnation has taken place, would appear to be due in a large measure to the danger attending such relations rather than to "coyness."

So fundamental and firmly established is the association between the sexual impulse and cruelty that, as is well known, manifestations of it frequently break out, and are perhaps never wholly absent, in humanity itself. According to M. d'Enjoy, the kiss has developed out of the love-bite. In many parts of Europe women are not convinced of their lover's or husband's affection unless their own bodies bear the visible marks of it in the form of impressions from their teeth. Mr. Savage Landor relates a little love-affair he had with a young Ainu woman. As is the custom with those primitive peoples the young lady did most of the wooing. "I would not have mentioned the small episode," says Mr. Landor, "if her ways of flirting had not been so extraordinary and funny. Loving and biting went together with her. She could not do the one without doing the other. As we sat on a stone in the semi-darkness she began by gently biting my fingers, without hurting me, as affectionate dogs often do to their masters; she then bit my arm, then my shoulder, and when she had worked herself up into a passion she put her arms round my neck and bit my cheek." The young traveler had to cut the affair short; he was bitten all over. Among the Migrelians of Transcaucasia the betrothal of a girl is sealed by her lover firmly biting her breast. Among the ancient Egyptians the word which is translated by Egyptologists as "to kill" meant "to eat." The desire expressed by lovers to "eat" the object of their affection probably contains more sinister biological reminiscences than they are aware.

THE MATING INSTINCT

Sentiments of tenderness and affection between the sexes are not originally connected with the sexual impulse, but with an entirely different instinct, the mating instinct. The utmost confusion has resulted from failing to draw any distinction between the two. They have different origins and fulfill different functions. The operation of the sexual impulse does not demand anything beyond the performance of the sexual act; mating, or association between the sexes, is a special adaptation to the reproductive functions of the female. With the extension of maternal care the female is placed in a position of disadvantage as regards self-protection, and the procuring of food. When thus handicapped it becomes desirable, and even necessary, that she should obtain the coöperation and assistance of the male. The mating instinct, where the female is thus handicapped, comes into operation in both sexes during the period that maternal care is beneficial. The merely physical, and even cruel, impulse leading to impregnation has received, in exact correlation to the prolongation of care for the eggs and offspring, the superadded element of a transferred maternal tenderness leading to the association of the sexes during a longer or shorter period, to mating, instead of momentary congress ending in impregnation. That is more particularly the case where the eggs are hatched by brooding. The cooperation of the male while the female is sitting on the eggs is almost a necessity to provide for her sustenance and protection. Among the majority of nidicolous birds the mating instinct has accordingly attained to a degree of development unparalleled in any other class of the animal kingdom. The mating instinct of birds is strictly confined to those species which hatch their eggs by prolonged brooding; where no brooding takes place there is no mating. "There is no necessity for birds to pair, in the usual sense of the word, when they do not tend their young."

Among mammals the conditions are different. Although the pregnant and suckling female is at a certain disadvantage in the material struggle, she is able to fulfill her functions unaided. That coöperation which has led to the marked development of the mating instinct among nidicolous birds is accordingly not conspicuous among mammals.

With a large proportion of mammalian species the association between the male and the female does not extend beyond the primary purpose for which the sexes come together—the fecundation of the female. After that function is fulfilled there appears to be, as a general rule, an actual repulsion between the sexes. "As soon as pairing is over," says Brehm, speaking of mammals generally, "great indifference is shown towards one another by the sexes." Of antelopes Mr. Seton says: "The separation of the sexes seems to be due to an instinctive dislike of each other as the time approaches for the young to be born. It becomes yet stronger as the hour draws near. At that time each female strives to be utterly alone." This applies almost universally to herbivora. Among reindeer "the prospective mother goes entirely alone, avoiding her own kind even as she avoids man." During their migration the cows and the bulls of the American reindeer keep in separate herds. With the elk, and in fact all the deer and antelope tribe, the same rule obtains. Among buffaloes as September wanes the males lose interest in their partners, the clan becomes divided.

the males in one herd and the females in another. Their lives go on as before, but they meet and pass without mixing. Among bats the sexes live entirely separate; the males are driven off after sexual congress, and no male is ever found in a band of females. Elephant cows, after they have been impregnated, likewise form bands from which males are driven off; the cow, which carries for nearly two years, does not receive the male until eight or twelve months after calving. "The male and female elephants," observes Livingstone, "are never seen in one herd. The young males remain with their dams only until they are full-grown, and so constantly is the separation maintained that any one familiar with them, on seeing a picture with the sexes mixed, would immediately conclude that the artist had made it from his imagination and not from sight." Seals and walruses separate into male and female herds after the breeding season. The moose bull associates with cows during two months of the year. The wild boar consorts with the female at the breeding season only. Among squirrels the sexes often live separate. The same thing has been reported of the monkey, *Presbytis entellus,* "the males live apart from the females." Blyth noticed that in one locality males only were to be found, in another chiefly females. With the orang-utan the sexes never live together. In bands of gorillas the sexes keep separate, the females and young forming one group, the males keeping to themselves.

Among most carnivora cohabitation of the male with the female takes place for a short time only during the rutting season, and in many species there is no cohabitation at all. Weasels "continue together during the mating season for a week or more, then separate completely." Bears do not cohabit after sexual congress; "no one yet has found two adult black bears in one den; mother and half-grown cubs have been taken together in the same winter-quarters, but never two old ones." "I have never seen the two (male and female) together at any time of the year," says an experienced observer of the species; "they meet by chance and again separate." The same is reported of the Indian, and of the polar bear. The jaguar cohabits with the female during one month of the year only; and the cougar during a few weeks. The leopard male and female live entirely separate.

The male takes no share in rearing the young. The parental relation is, amongst mammals, confined to that be· tween the mother and her offspring; fatherhood does not exist, and no mammalian young looks to a male for protec tion or assistance. Among herbivorous animals the male sees the young for the first time when they have reached a state of independence. Among carnivora the female generally takes great pains to conceal herself and her brood from the male, and drives him off lest he should eat the cubs. "Some fathers are considered models when they refrain from doing bodily harm to their offspring, and are especially admired if they keep away altogether while the young are helpless." The lioness, like all other mammals, withdraws from the male when she is about to give birth. The beaver also is said to "drive away the male from the 'lodge,' who would otherwise destroy the young." Even where a fairly close association exists between the parents, the feeding of the young after they are weaned is attended to entirely by the female. The male lion is not infrequently represented as bringing his "kill" to the female while she remains with her cubs. But the lion drags his kill, often for long distances, to his lair, whether there are cubs or not. The leopard, which does not cohabit with the female, invariably does the same. The lioness forages for herself and for her young. The male does not exercise any protective function either towards the female or towards the young. Some members of the ox tribe are said to take an interest in the young and have been known to defend them; but this, if correct, is a collective, not an individual act. The almost universal rule among animals, birds and mammals, is that the female alone protects her offspring. In a number of instances she is the protector not only of her offspring, but also of the male. Among deer and antelopes the does watch over the safety of the bucks and interpose themselves between them and any source of danger. This has also been observed of elephants. "Many hunters, when they come across a lion and a lioness together, shoot the lioness first, on the assumption that if you kill the lion the lioness will charge at once, whereas if you shoot the lioness the lion will probably stand by, and, before making off, stop to smell the lioness, and, when he has satisfied himself that there is not much use in staying any longer, he may clear."

SEXUAL AND MATERNAL LOVE IN PRIMITIVE HUMANITY

The mating instinct appears to play in primitive humanity a scarcely more important part than among mammals generally. Cohabitation is, as will later be shown, very transient in the lower phases of human culture, and the sexes, as a rule, associate little with one another. The bulk of testimony concerning the sentiments which obtain in those relations among uncultured peoples is decidedly unfavorable. For example, it is said of the Eskimo, that, "like all other men in the savage state, they treat their wives with great coolness and neglect." Love, in our sense of the word, is said to be "unknown to the North American Indians." "If you wish to excite laughter," says Father Petitot, "speak to the Déné of conjugal affection. We have been obliged to create the sentiment, and we are now beginning to see it appear little by little." South American Indians are said to have no love for their wives. The Papuans are said to be entirely indifferent to their women's charms. In West Africa, it is reported, "love, as understood by the people of Europe, has no existence." "Not even the appearance of affection exists between husband and wife." "I have never witnessed any display of tenderness betwixt man and wife," says Mr. Ward of the Congo tribes. In East Africa the natives show "scant appearance of affection." "In all the long years I have been in Africa," says Monteiro, "I have never seen a negro manifest tenderness to a negress. I have never seen a negro put his arm round a woman's waist, or give or receive any caress whatever that could indicate the slightest loving regard or affection on either side." In New Zealand the Maori "in general appear to care little for their wives. In my own experience," says Mr. Brown, "I have only seen one instance where there was any perceptible attachment between husband and wife. To all appearance they behave as if they were not at all related, and it not infrequently happens they sleep in different places before the termination of the first week of marriage."

Statements like the above have been the subject of a good deal of somewhat futile controversy, and there are more favorable reports of affection between married people, particularly in reference to societies where the conditions of life are easy and culture somewhat advanced. But the real evidence, which we shall have an opportunity of viewing, that, namely, which is afforded by the whole sexual life of uncultured peoples and the principles which govern their sexual associations, makes it clear that sexual love as we conceive it is at best rudimentary in primitive humanity.

While there may be room for ambiguity or misunderstanding in regard to affection between the sexes among savages, there is none in respect of the love of primitive mothers for their offspring. With exceedingly few exceptions the testimonies on the point are uniform and emphatic. In reference to the same peoples who are described as being devoid of love between man and woman, the liveliness of maternal affection is constantly noted. Thus among the Eskimo, the coldness of whose sex relations is conspicuous, maternal love is said to be "lively and tender." "We are inferior to the savages," remarks Father Petitot in speaking of them, "as regards the sentiment of maternity." Reports are very unfavorable as regards affection between the sexes amongst the Déné; but "maternal love is developed among these peoples to the point of obliterating every suggestion of prudence and even every reasoned act of intelligence." Among the Ojibwa, says the Ojibwa Peter Jones, "I have scarcely ever seen anything like social intercourse between husband and wife"; but the same witness bears testimony to the fact that "no mother can be fonder of her children." "They love their children," says Father Theodat, speaking of the North American Indians generally, "more than we do ours." Among the Indians of Guiana the extreme love of the mothers for their children has been noted, while the father is said to take little notice of them. Similar manifestations of maternal tenderness are reported of the wild tribes of Brazil, among whom conjugal affection is not apparent. Among the Patagonians a child "is the object of the whole love of its parents, who, if necessary, will submit themselves to the greatest privations to satisfy its least wants or exactions." Their love for their children "is quite extravagant; they show such extreme compliance with regard to them that whole tribes have been known to leave a district or to remain there longer than was advisable simply to gratify the whim of a child." Among the Fuegians "conjugal affection," we are told, "does not exist"; but maternal love is conspicuously tender and lively.

The women of the Orinoco, when their children are ailing, perforate their own tongue with a skewer and cover the child's body with their blood, believing that this will promote its recovery. They repeat the process daily until the child has recovered or is dead. Similarly among the aborigines of New South Wales the mothers give their blood to bring about the recovery of their children when they are sick. Among the Omahas it was the practice in wartime, when they were overtaken by foes, for the women to dig a hole in the ground, and to conceal themselves there with their children, covering up the opening. It is related that a mother was overtaken by the enemy after she had placed her children in the "cache," but before she had had time to cover the opening; this she did with her body, pretending to be dead, and allowed herself to be scalped without stirring. During a tribal war in Samoa "a woman allowed herself to be hacked from head to foot bending over her son to save his life. It is considered cowardly to kill a woman, or they would have despatched her at once. It was the head of her little boy they wanted, but they did not get it." Among the Wagogo of East Africa, mothers besought the slave raiders to allow them to take the place of their sons. Bushmen women gave themselves up in like manner to redeem their children. The lack of affection between men and women among the Hottentots has frequently been referred to; but it is related that during a famine, when food was brought to them, the women would not touch it until their children had been fed. The same thing has been reported of the Aleuts, of the Indians of the Red River Colony, of the Tasmanians. With the natives of Madagascar "the idea of love between husband and wife is hardly thought of"; accounts agree in representing the relations between men and women as utterly destitute of sentiment or affection. But we are told at the same time that "the love of the parents for their children is intense"; that "nothing can exceed the affection with which the infant is treated; the indulgence is more frequently carried to excess than otherwise." So again among the Dayaks of Borneo the children are spoilt; their slightest whim is indulged in. The intensity of maternal affection in the savage is noted of the lowest races which we know, such as the Bushmen, Fuegians, the Seri Indians, the Andaman negritos, the Veddahs of Ceylon, the Sakai of the Malaccan forests, the Ainu, the New Hebrides Islanders. To an Australian woman her child is the object of the most devoted affection; "There is no bounds to the fondness and indulgence with which it is treated."

The practice of infanticide, which is very widespread among uncultured races, appears to us irreconcilable with the manifestations of maternal instincts in primitive women. The apparent inconsistency applies equally to the maternal instincts of most animals; and from what has been already noted it has little, if any, significance as an index of the power and reality of maternal affection. Infanticide takes place, as a rule, with the human as with the animal mother, directly after the birth of the child. Thus in the Society Islands infanticide, "if not committed at the time the infant enters the world, was not perpetrated at any subsequent period. If the little stranger was, from irresolution, the mingled emotions that struggled for mastery in the mother's bosom, or any other cause, suffered to live ten minutes or half an hour, it was safe; instead of a monster's grasp it received a mother's caress and a mother's smile, and was nursed with solicitude and tenderness." The missionary's language imports, as usual, the notions and sentiments of European tradition into primitive psychology. Infanticide is committed by primitive women without any compunction or "struggle" or feelings; but with them, as with animal mothers, it is the adoption of the offspring and not the relationship, intellectually viewed, which constitutes maternity. Death and the sacredness of life are not conceived in the same manner in primitive as in civilized societies. The killing of children, like the killing of aged people, may often be done with the most tender feelings and sentiments towards them. It is certain, in any case, that the practice of infanticide is no indication of deficient maternal tenderness. Among the Patagonians, whose extravagant affection for their·children has attracted the attention of every traveler, infanticide is habitual. Directly after its birth, the fate of each child is considered and decided; if allowed to live, it becomes at once the object of its parents' unbounded solicitude. American squaws are said to destroy their female children in order to spare them the arduous life which their mothers have to lead. The Arabs represent the extensive practice of female infanticide which obtained amongst them as arising from their love for their daughters, "the flesh of their flesh and blood of their blood," in order to shield them from poverty or dishonor. In the Cameroons, during the German invasion, the natives, who are noted as devoted parents, killed most of the new-born, "in pity for their sufferings and in the firm belief that their spirits would return to earth as soon as all was peaceful once more." Australian

mothers, if one of their children is weak and sickly, sometimes kill its infant brother or sister and feed the survivor
with its flesh in order to make it strong.

The maternal love of primitive women is much fiercer
and more unreasoning than that of civilized mothers. "Their
affection is not rational," observes Dr. Todd. Corporal punishment of children is unthought of in primitive society.
"All the savage tribes of these parts, and those of Brazil,
as we are assured," remarks Father La Jeune, "cannot chas-
tise a child or bear to see one chastised. What trouble this
will cause us in carrying out our intention of instructing
their young!" The Eskimo do not consider that white
people deserve to have children, since they are so heartless
as to strike them. Missionaries are constantly in trouble on
that score. "It would be well," says one of them, "if the
parents did not grow so angry when their children are now
and then slightly chastised for gross misdemeanor by order
of the missionary; but instead of bearing with patience such
wholesome correction of their sons and daughters, they take
great offense and become enraged, especially the mothers,
who will scream like furies; tear out their hair, beat their
naked breasts with a stone, and lacerate their heads with
a piece of wood or bone till the blood flows, as I have frequently witnessed on such occasions."

The maternal sentiment is, then, very much more primitive, fundamental and stronger than the mating instinct,
the love, as we term it, in the relations between the sexes.
The latter is primarily an extension of the maternal instinct.
The feelings of tenderness and affection of which the offspring is the direct object have become extended to the male
associate for the biological utilitarian purpose of enlisting
his coöperation in the discharge of maternal functions. Maternal affection and not sexual attraction is the original
source of love.

In mammals that extension of the maternal sentiment
generally consists rather in a tolerance which overcomes the
primary self-protective distrust and hostility of the female

towards the male than in active affection. After the birth of the offspring that solicitude for a vicarious object reverts to its natural channel, and the male tends to become an object of repulsion. In primitive woman the mating instinct does not differ greatly from that observed in mammals. The primitive mother is, apart from her fierce maternal tenderness, a wild enough creature with little about her of what we reckon as feminine gentleness. Primitive women commonly exceed the men in cruelty. Their attitude towards their mate, which at its worst is what we should term cynical, is at its best a loyalty such as binds the members of all primitive groups. It is invariably utilitarian, and has in view those functions of assistance, protection, economic coöperation which are expected of him in regard to herself and her offspring. The qualities which she looks for are those which will render him efficient in the discharge of those functions: strength, courage, endurance, ability, in short, the qualities that command success. A contemporary authoress, in emphasizing that character of the mating instinct in modern woman, goes so far as to defend the primitive practice of leaving the choice of a husband entirely to parents, on the ground that their experience and judgment will enable them to leave the choice of their mate to relatives. These, brothers, uncles, fathers, and mothers, apply the severest tests to prove the qualities of the aspirants; the woman sets the highest store on those tests of the intended mate's economic value. That mercenary attitude is not, as is commonly supposed, a corruption of civilization, a profanation of love; it is, on the contrary, the primal form, the source of the mating instinct in the female. The loyalty and devotion of primitive woman is no less real because her choice has been determined by deliberate utilitarian motives. It is subservient to the maternal instinct, and eventually uses in its interest the most powerful attraction, by transferring to the male associate some of the mothering tenderness which becomes the tender constituent of her relation to him. In certain conditions where the pressure of life's necessities is less acute, and the female's need for protection less pressing, that mothering character of feminine tenderness may go so far as to respond to the appeal of the weak, the suffering, the vanquished, of the gentle and effeminate. But the male's appeal to the female lies normally and overwhelmingly in his utilitarian worth, a value which has reference not to the sexual relation, but to economic coöperation, and grows therefore with the closeness and stability of that relation.

The gradual admixture of tenderness with the mating instinct, its transformation into love, is a process which has taken place in the psychological evolution of the female, and it appears probable that in the human species love was at first confined to woman. What sexual selection exists among the lower races is predominantly exercised by the women. In those races where the attitude of the men towards the women is one of indifference and even brutality, manifestations of strong and genuine attachment are shown by the women towards their tyrannous mates. North American squaws, notwithstanding the coldness with which they are treated, "are remarkable for their care and attachment to the men, continually watching over them with utmost solicitude and anxiety." Chippeway widows are truly inconsolable and pine with grief over the loss of their husbands. Aleut women often commit suicide on that account. Fijian women, who are among the most brutally treated, insist upon being killed on the graves of their husbands. It is highly probable that the widespread custom of "suttee" was originally voluntary. The numerous wives of an African chief, whom he uses as pillows and footstools, vie for the honor of being so employed, and genuinely worship their lord. The unmistakable gleam of devotion is seen in their eyes as they watch their master and seek to forestall his wishes.

TRANSFERENCE OF CHARACTERS FROM ONE SEX TO THE OTHER

Tender feelings are one and all derivatives of the maternal instincts and products of feminine evolution; they have developed, that is, in relation to the reactions of the female organism, and are feminine secondary characters. But characters developed in relation to the functions of one sex are, nevertheless, transmitted in some form to both. The cell produced by the fusion of a male and of a female cell inherits the characters and dispositions of both parents. This does not necessarily mean that those characters are blended in the corresponding character of the offspring, or even that they are reproduced at all; for a given hereditary disposition may result in a variety of structural reactions, any one of which may be incompatible with others. Where characters are mutually incompatible, or the disposition towards the one is more firmly fixed in heredity than the disposition towards the other, either the character of the male parent or that of the female parent will result, the one being prepotent over the other; thus will be produced the appearance of "unit characters" which has been interpreted in terms of the speculations of Weissmann on the basis of the conception of a complex structure of "determinants.", Similarly one character may manifest itself at one period of life, and another, derived from the other parent, at another period. But the organism, whether male or female, inherits equally dispositions corresponding to all the characters, physical and psychical, of both parents and of their ancestry. Every disposition developed in the race by the males is thus transmitted to the females, and every disposition developed by the females is transmitted to the males. Even the primary reproductive organs of each sex are in all their parts represented in the opposite sex; a rudimentary uterus and vagina in the male, a rudimentary penis in the female. The males of mammalian species possess mammary glands, which may even be functional; the pouches in which marsupial females carry their young after birth are found, in a

rudimentary condition, in the males also. By merely trans-
planting some ovarian tissue into young castrated rats
Steinach caused them to develop all the characters, psychical as well as physical, of the females. They developed
mammæ and nipples, their bones assumed the lighter structure characteristic of the females, and their hair the finer
and softer quality of the opposite sex. They developed "the
tail up reflex" peculiar to the females, and warded off the
males by kicking. "These feminized rats were followed by
males as if they were females."

Thus it is that in every race, although the two sexes may
lead different lives and both their environments and their
reactions to those environments may differ widely, different
structures and reactions resulting in each sex, yet the race
will combine the results of evolutions which have taken
place in the males and in the females. "In vast numbers of
species the individuals of opposite sex are so much alike
that it is difficult to distinguish them without examination
of their genital organs." The two sexes differ in so far only
as the common racial characters are held in abeyance or
modified by the functional characters of each sex. "The
secondary characters of each sex," as Darwin says, "lie
dormant or latent in the opposite sex, ready to be evolved
under peculiar circumstances." When females cease to be
reproductive male characters usually make their appearance.
Thus hens that have ceased laying crow like a cock, develop
a comb, hackles, spurs, and tail-feathers; pheasants, par-
tridges, pea-hens, and many other female birds assume the
secondary male plumage of the species, and a duck ten
years old has been known to put on the perfect winter and
summer plumage of the drake. Old ewes and does grow
horns and antlers, old lionesses manes. Mares that are old
or sterile frequently develop canine teeth, which normally
are rudimentary in the female. Cow giraffes, when old,
assume the darker coat which is characteristic of the bulls.
Female salmon develop the peculiar hook or knob on the
lower jaw which is distinctive of males at the breeding

season. Women who have passed the climacteric, or suffer from ovarian atrophies, assume male characters, such as changes in the larynx giving rise to a deeper voice, hair on the upper lip and chin. Similar symptoms and often the growth of a dense beard, are produced by disease of the adrenal glands in women, and the development of male characters is arrested by administration of the glandular substance.

Many characters which in some species are sexual secondary characters are in other species normal specific characters common to both sexes. Thus many of the markings and bright colors distinctive of male birds appear in the female, usually in a somewhat duller form, but sometimes, as in the guinea-fowl, in identical form. The larynx has probably developed as a male sexual character, but it is common to both sexes, and has become used by the female for the purpose of calling the young. Horns are grown by the females of goats, some breeds of sheep, and cattle, and by the female of the reindeer, though not usually by deer and antelopes.

So likewise many purely female characters manifest themselves in the males of animals. Darwin states that "with the bees, the pollen-collecting apparatus is used by the female for gathering pollen for the larvæ, yet in most species it is partially developed in the males to whom it is quite useless, and it is perfectly developed in the male of Bombus, the humble-bee." The most conspicuous example is the appearance of mammary glands and nipples in the male, which in early mammalia are thought to have been functional, and which are functional at birth even in the human infant, and are sometimes developed in the adult to the extent of being used for suckling. Steers, and even bulls, sometimes secrete milk. In pigeons a peculiar secretion developed from fatty degeneration of the lining of the crop a few weeks after the hatching of the young is used by both sexes to feed them.

The like holds true of psychical characters, the distinction between the two being but a concession to our forms of thought. Psychical reactions necessarily differ in the two sexes. The relations of life present themselves in the form of entirely different values, and their effect upon the complex of existing impulses and instincts varies according as they act upon the dispositions of the male or upon those of the female. The former is primarily concerned with activities directed to obtaining for the individual greater control over the conditions of active life and with securing the best advantages in the competition for food and favorable conditions. The female's organism is specialized for the production of offspring, and the impulses which are related to those racial interests predominate in her over those which have regard to the securing of the most advantageous present conditions. The forms which the reproductive impulse itself takes in the two sexes are dissimilar, and reactions and feelings are differentiated according to the divergent functions and dispositions of the two sexes.

The psychical development of the race thus takes place along two separate lines. Two psychical evolutions proceed side by side, a masculine and feminine evolution, each giving rise to different products, modifications of impulses, general and specialized instincts, affective values, and powers of cognition, control, and action. Some of those psychical products have come into existence as a result of the reactions of masculine impulses and instincts, others as a result of the reactions of the instincts and impulses of the female. But here also, as in the development and transmission of visible organic characters, the results of evolution in the one sex are transmitted to the other.

Darwin mentions the instance of a hen which had ceased laying and had assumed the plumage, voice, and warlike disposition of the cock. When opposed to an enemy she would erect her hackles and show fight. "Thus every character, even to the instinct and manner of fighting, must have lain dormant in the hen as long as her ovaria continued to act." Capons take up the brooding and nursing functions of the female. A cock by being kept for a time in enforced solitude and darkness could be taught to take charge of chickens. He uttered the peculiar cry and retained during his whole life the newly acquired (or rather, elicited) maternal instinct. The sterile male hybrids from pheasants and fowl take delight in sitting on eggs, and watch for the hens to leave their nests that they may have an opportunity of taking their place.

The development in the male of instincts and psychical modifications of female origin is widespread in the animal kingdom. Examples of maternal instincts in the male are found among reptiles and fishes whose parental instincts are not in general highly developed. It is, indeed, a somewhat startling fact that the earliest manifestations of parental instincts and care, as distinguished from purely physiological provisions, appear in the lowest vertebrates, the fishes, not in the female but in the male. "As a rule it is the male who acts as guardian nurse, the female troubling herself but little about the fate of her eggs or her offspring." Several male fishes carry the eggs in their mouth or pharynx until they hatch. In a species of sea-horse, *Hippocampus guttulatus,* the male develops a regular marsupial pouch in which it carries the eggs. In a number of species the male fish builds a more or less elaborate nest in which the female deposits her ova. The male stickleback uses for the purpose a mucous secretion which is specially produced by the kidneys at the rutting season. The Butter-fish, or Gunnel, rolls the mass of eggs into a ball and coils himself round them, the female in this instance also taking a share in the process of brooding. The male Lump-sucker (*Cyclopterus lumpus*) sedulously guards the eggs, which are affixed to rocks or piles, and the young fry, when hatched, attach themselves by their suckers to the body of their paternal nurse. The North American Catfish (*Ameiurus nebulosus*) also mounts guard with great solicitude over the eggs, and when they are hatched "leads the young in great schools near the shore, seemingly caring for them as the hen for

her chicks." It might thus be said that maternal instincts
have, in the first instance, originated in the male! The paradox is readily intelligible when it is borne in mind that with
fishes, except the elasmo-branchs and teleosteans, there
is no copulation, spawn and milt being shed in the water
without sexual congress. The sexual instincts of the male
are accordingly directed not so much towards the female
as towards the eggs; these, and not the female, are the
excitant to their operation. It follows that the male is even
more disposed than the female to take an interest in the
eggs, to segregate them in his own person, parental care
being here indistinguishable from the sexual impulse.

It appears not improbable that those dispositions in primitive vertebrate males have largely contributed to the development of parental instinct-interest in the care of eggs,
and consequently in the development of the mating instinct
in the immediate successors of the fishes in the vertebrate
scale. And, in fact, the males of some reptiles and batra-
chians show the same solicitude directed towards the eggs
rather than towards the females. Thus the male obstetric
frog (*Alytes obstetricans*) helps the female to discharge
her eggs, pushes its hind-limbs in the convoluted mass, thus
winding it round its legs, and, after tending them carefully
for three weeks, betakes itself to the water to hatch the
eggs. In *Rhinoderma Darwinii,* a small Chilian frog, a
purely male organ, the croaking-ratchet, is temporarily converted into a brood-pouch in which the eggs are carried
till hatched.

In the class of birds which presents the most conspicuous
development of the mating instinct in the male, those
instincts are connected with the eggs almost as much as with
the female. The male, as with fishes, is interested in the
protection of the eggs and in their hatching, and the reproductive impulse continues to operate in relation to that function, apart from the purely sexual impulse that leads to congress; while on the other hand, that mating instinct ceases,

in general, to operate as soon as the brood has left the nest. The male bird often relieves the female in brooding. This is the rule among all Rasores, in several other birds, such as godwits, the dotterel, and phalaropes. The psychology of mating birds has in all probability been entirely misconceived by interpreting it in terms of our own sentiments; it is not so much the female which is the object of interest to the male as the eggs. It is noteworthy that in those species in which the male assumes female functions, the female is considerably larger than the male and has a brighter and handsomer plumage. The most curious instance is presented by an Indian gallinaceous species, *Turnix taigoor*. In this bird the usual respective characters of male and female are almost completely reversed; "the males only sit on eggs, the females meanwhile calling and fighting, without any care for their obedient mates. The males and the males only tend their brood." While the males are of a tame and mild disposition, the females are most pugnacious, and it is indeed those females and not the males which are kept by the natives as "fighting cocks." The famous habit of the cuckoo which, as Gilbert White remarked, "is such a monstrous outrage on maternal affection, one of the first dictates of nature, and such violence on instinct that, had it only been related of a bird in the Brazils, or Peru, it would never have merited belief," illustrates the manner in which the correlated instincts of each sex are dependent upon combined inheritance from both sexes. For "the species consists predominantly of males. The preponderance is probably as five to one, though one observer makes it five times greater." So entirely identical are the males and the females that they are not to be distinguished by external appearance. With such a preponderatingly male heredity it is not surprising to find the maternal instincts atrophied in the female. There is no mating; sexual relations are "promiscuous, that is, both polyandrous and polygynous."

As with physical characters, the dispositions inherited by one sex from the other can become manifested and active only when not conflicting with the functional characteristics of the sex which inherits them, and when they perform a useful function in regard to the reproductive interests of the race.

Not only does each sex benefit by the products of the evolution which has taken place in the opposite sex—a uniform level of development being maintained in the race—but a further important consequence follows. Since in each sex the characters of the opposite sex are only held in abeyance by the functions peculiar to the sex of the individual, a mutual adjustment takes place between the sexual characters of the two sexes. These characters, both physical and psychological, are balanced within every organism of either sex—organization, functions, and instincts being adjusted and adapted in each to the corresponding characters of the other sex. The development of special impulses and instincts in the one sex, being transmitted by heredity to the other, calls forth a corresponding and complementary adaptation, in the same manner as correlation of physiological functions takes place in the individual. Mutual adjustment between the sexes in respect of the common racial interests is thus automatically established.

ANTAGONISM BETWEEN THE MATING AND THE SEXUAL INSTINCT

No greater inducement could be offered to the male to modify his sexual instincts in adaption to the mating instinct of the female than the latter's transferred affection, for it is the equivalent of the maternal tenderness and devotion under the ægis of which his development has taken place. The mating instinct leading to prolonged association is nevertheless entirely foreign to his sexual instincts. The sole function of the male in regard to reproduction is primarily the impregnation of the ova, and the instincts are limited to fulfilling that function. In most teleostean fishes, impregnation does not even necessitate the coming together of the sexes. In the majority of animals the contribution of the male to the reproductive process does not extend beyond the sexual act. The further functions of providing physiologically and psychologically for the development of the offspring devolve upon the female alone. Not only is the mating instinct, leading to prolonged association with the female and manifesting itself in tender sentiments and affection, unrelated to any function and instinct of the male, but that sentiment is in direct contrast and antagonism to the character of his sexual impulse. So much so that the two orders of impulses remain even in the higher forms of their development essentially distinct. The sadic hunger of the masculine impulse can never become entirely blended with the mating affection. Love and lust must remain antagonistic. "Il n'y a rien de si loin de la volupté que l'attendrissement," observes Lamartine. Although they may be directed towards the same object, the two forms of sexual attraction in the male, distinct as they are in function and origin, are not only opposed, but essentially incompatible; they may alternate, but can never completely blend. Love, tender feeling, is a common cause of "psychical" impotence. The high developments of the transferred maternal instinct in the male, the "sublimations" of the sexual impulse, tend to obliterate the impulse itself. It has been suggested that such transformations of the male instincts are in reality a manifestation, or an index, of diminished reproductive power, and that the high development of romantic love would tend ultimately towards the extinction of the race. The two instincts, the sexual and the mating instinct, may exist in the male quite independently of one another; and this, as we shall have occasion to note, is commonly the case in primitive humanity. The sexual impulse may have no trace of affection, while on the other hand, genuine and strong attachment, which quite commonly results from prolonged association, may be unattended with any manifestation of sexual instincts, such, for instance, as jealousy. It is not uncommon among savages for an old and decrepit wife to be tenderly loved and treated with gentle affection, whilst her place is taken, sexually, by younger wives. Throughout primitive societies the distinction between the two functions and instincts is, indeed, much more definitely and consciously recognized than in our own, where sentiments and institutions have deliberately tended to obliterate and ignore the distinction. Sexual relations do not, in primitive society, imply sexual association, and sexual association is not primarily regarded as a sexual relation.

Those utilitarian considerations which are paramount with the female have no place in the functional purpose of the male's sexual instincts. It is, of course, the interest of the male to obtain a capable mate; and in primitive marriage, as we shall see, the capacity and ability of the woman as a worker even is the chief, and often the sole, consideration in determining the economic association. But that order of considerations is, with the male, distinct from the sexual instinct, and not, as with the female, an intrinsic part of it. The economic motives of the male have regard to his individual interests, not to those of the offspring; they are conscious, not instinctive and subconscious; they are unconnected with the sexual impulse, and they do not imply, or even lead up to, tenderness and affection towards the woman. In the latter those economic values are the cause and standard of attraction; in man they are even antagonistic to that sexual attraction. In the sexual relations of man the sexual instinct itself is supreme; and when that instinct becomes discriminating, the discrimination has reference chiefly or solely to sexual values. These are physical qualities of youth and beauty, which are, ultimately, expressions of the suitability of the female for rearing offspring of the best type. Those moral qualities, such as courage, ability, character, which are supreme in the woman's sexual choice, have no place in the man's in so far as that choice is purely sexual. Hence the feminine taunt that a man may be attracted by a woman whom he neither esteems nor respects.

Since the mating instinct, or love, is in the female

founded on much more direct biological needs, and is much older in the order of development than with the male, it tends to retain even in advanced stages of culture its primitive character. That primitive character completely fulfills the purpose and function of the instinct, and does not require to be reinforced and sustained by adventitious motives. In the male, on the contrary, that transferred feminine instinct, destitute of any relation to purely masculine instincts, is to a very much greater extent apt to become an artificial product of cultural and social development. Hence, one of the most important grounds for the differences in the sentiment in man and in woman; it is deeper in the latter, without being so exalted and subject to cultural transfigurations as in man.

That cultural and social evolution is the all-important factor in the development of the sentiment in the male. So little does the emotional complex which we speak of as love bear any resemblance to a primary and universal impulse of life that even a cursory consideration suffices to show the greatest diversities in the forms of those sentiments within the range of familiar historical experience. It has frequently been remarked that "romantic love" is profoundly influenced by literature and tradition, and that no one would be subject to it in the same form had he never read a novel or seen a play. That social and cultural tradition varies so much that the contrast between its forms among the Greeks, the Romans, or the Arabs, the Hindus, and the modern European has thrust itself upon the notice of the least analytical psychology. Romantic love is by many regarded as a product of the Middle Ages and Renaissance, and as having been previously unknown. Early Victorian love is noticed to be not the same thing as twentieth-century love. The Italian's or the Spaniard's notions and sentiments of sexual love differ considerably from those of the Russian, the Norwegian, or the Englishman. If, then, the sentiment can assume so many different forms and variations within that narrow range of human observation, and if so many of its features are manifestly social products of different types of culture, it may be gauged how uncritical is the proceeding which treats all sexual impulses and sentiments, in primitive man, in animals, as though they were even roughly and substantially identical with those of cultured humanity.

Yet that is what is constantly and gravely done. Sexual love is spoken of as if it were a simple and irreducible emotion or impulse, whereas it is in reality the most composite and complex of sentiments. As Herbert Spencer pointed out, in addition to the sexual impulse and mating affection, which are quite distinct, it is made up of an almost boundless aggregate of feelings and sentiments. Love of approbation and self-esteem receive their most vivid gratification in the exclusive choice, the "blind" admiration and idealization of the male by the female, and her devotion to his chosen person; hence love is irresistibly bred by love—"amor a nullo amato amar perdona." To those sentiments are added the æsthetic feelings which are themselves highly complex products of culture, and which not only imply an "ideal of feminine beauty," but also of charm, of character, of elegance and taste. Few men, for instance, would have enough discrimination to detect, and be attracted by, physical beauty in a woman who was an habitual frump, or grotesque, sluttish, and disgusting or ridiculous in her attire. Admiration for the imaginative objectivation of all ideals of what is deemed desirable is incorporated, no less than æsthetic ideals, in romantic affection, the cultural results of mental and moral development thus forming part of the sentiment. Sympathetic participation, mostly imaginary, in common tastes; the release of conventions in the freedom of intimacy, the gratifications of proprietary feelings and of vanity must be added. The conception of some ideal of future happiness thought of, perhaps, as shaping the whole of life is blended with the sentiments that are regarded as holding out the promise of its realization. These all enter into the composition of what we speak of as "love," which, as Spencer says, "fuses into one immense aggregate most of the elementary excitations of which we are capable." So complex and comprehensive a sentiment may well become a dominant inspiration of emotional life and of art. The exaltation and intensity which are imparted to its varied components are derived from the strongest impulse of living organization. But such a complexity is not a biological character of the sexual impulse in the male. Nothing could be simpler than its simplicity. Complexity results from the permeation of all other activities by that impulse. Every aspect and product of human cultural and mental evolution can be directly or indirectly brought into relation with the reproductive impulse when its operation is diverted. Social restrictions and cultural associations have diverted the operation and diffused the energy of the sexual impulse, thus giving rise to highly complex emotional states; these are, in that form, the culmination of the long evolution which has brought about those associations.

While the sentiments which, deriving originally from the maternal instinct, have become associated with the sexual impulse owe much to cultural and social development, modifying influences even more important have taken place in the opposite direction. Just as the transferred affection of the female for the male is a direct derivative of maternal love, so likewise all feelings of a tender, compassionate, altruistic character, which are in direct contrast to primitive biological impulses, and while almost entirely absent in animals, have become distinctive of human psychology, are extensions and transformations of the maternal instinct and are directly derived from it. Apart from the relation between mother and offspring there is in competitive animality no germ of that order of feelings, and every form which they have assumed is a derivative product of maternal love. Sympathy for suffering, compassion, the placating of anger and hostility, benevolence, generosity, all those sentiments which are termed "altruistic," up to their most abstract and generalized developments, owe the mere possibility of their existence to the growth of mother-love, and have arisen through the transference of those maternal instincts to the male. That order of sentiments, being of female origin, is developed more spontaneously and more strongly in the female. The sympathetic, protective, compassionate, affectionate attitude, transferred by the female from the offspring to its father, tends to become still further extended. Woman becomes in general tender-hearted, merciful, compassionate towards all males, towards females also provided they are not possible rivals, towards animals and all living things, and even towards plants, flowers, inanimate things, possessions, which are handled gently, tenderly; whereas the male is disposed to be rough, to destroy and break. The development and extension of sentiments of that order are much more difficult, more unnatural in the male. They are too radically opposed to the character of his instincts and impulses. In spite of the accumulated force of heredity the male child is born cruel; to inflict suffering on other children, on his brothers and sisters, on animals, and to elicit the signs of pain, is his natural propensity. He is destructive, and to destroy even his own most valued possessions affords him pleasure. The operation of social and traditional education is required to enable the dispositions to tenderness inherited through the female line of evolution to attain a high degree of development in the male.

THE FILIAL INSTINCT

Those higher developments of maternal tenderness are for the most part phenomena of advanced culture, and have been comparatively late in making their appearance. But the maternal instincts have from the outset given rise to even more momentous derivative products. The sexual associate is not the first in whom the sentiment of affection is reflected. Long before the sexual impulse of the male becomes transformed by such a sentiment, maternal instincts produce an even stronger bond of attachment in their direct object, the offspring itself. The strong feeling of the child for the mother, his dependence and reliance on her affection, her help, her protection, founded upon fundamental experience during the first years of life, is in highly developed societies weakened by a number of causes which do not operate so strongly in the primitive grades of society. The primitive natural sentiment remains much stronger than the counteracting traditional sentiments of "manliness" and independence, and the "mauvaise honte" attaching to the notion of being tied to a woman's apron strings. Savages remain children. In this they closely resemble animals. "Among human beings," remarks Mr. Seton, "the maternal feeling continues longer than the filial; but in most (possibly all) of the lower animals it is the other way. The young could keep on indefinitely deriving sustenance and comfort from the mother, if allowed." That continued dependence upon the mother's affection is a fea-ture of primitive psychology.

"In the very lowest human society," remarks Schweinfurth, "there is a bond which lasts for life between mother and child, although the father may be a stranger to it." The Indians of California "scarcely acknowledge their father, but they preserve a longer attachment for their mother, who has brought them up with extreme tenderness." Filial and parental love is "the strongest affection that an Indian can experience." Among the Iroquois, "the crime which is regarded as most horrible and which is without example is that a son should be rebellious towards his mother. When she becomes old he provides for her." When the Russians first settled in the Aleutian Islands, two of the most intelligent natives were sent to St. Petersburg and earned a good deal of money by exhibiting on the Neva their skill in plying their canoes. They made many friends and were pressed to remain; but they answered that they could not think of staying longer away from their old and decrepit mother, and must return to look after her in her old age. In Melanesia, when engaging a boat's crew for a week or two, one comes upon grown men of forty who say that they are willing to join, but must first obtain the consent of their mother. One of the most conspicuous traits of the Dayaks of northern Borneo is said to be "their devotion to their mothers and the honor they pay them all their lives from the first moment they can understand. Their father they may like, or they may not; they recognize no duty towards him; but their mother is something holy to them, whatever she is like, and no one is ever allowed to breathe a word against her." The Japanese believe that the spirits of mothers look, from the other world, after the welfare of their children. "I have noticed," says M. Giraud in speaking of the natives of the Ivory Coast, "that children, even when grown up to manhood, retain their affection for their mothers. Their filial sentiments towards her are very much more developed than towards their father." The same thing is reported of the Ewe of Togoland and of the Bangala. Among the Mandingo, says Mungo Park, "the maternal affection, neither suppressed nor diverted by the solicitude of civilized life, is everywhere conspicuous, and creates a corresponding return of tenderness. The same sentiment I found universally to prevail, and observed in all parts of Africa that the greatest affront which could be offered to a negro was to reflect on her who gave him birth." "Strike me, but do not curse my mother," is a common saying among the Mandingo, and also among the Fanti and in the Congo. Lieut. Costermanns is doubtless right in remarking that with the Congo native's respect for his mother is mixed up a superstitious sentiment. In most countries the imprecations intended to be most offensive are directed against a man's mother. Quarrels between children among the Kru and among the Kaffirs are said to arise mostly from some child having insulted another's mother. The most solemn oath among the Damaras and among the Herero is "by the tears of their mother." In Loango

SEXUAL CUSTOMS AND SOCIAL PRACTICE 517

grown-up persons invariably call, when in pain or in difficulty, upon the name of their mother, and the mother always addresses her offspring, no matter how old, as "my children." They believe that even after death the mother watches over her children and protects them not only from evil men, but also against the influences of spirits and natural forces. "The strongest of all natural ties," says Wilson of the West African negroes, "are those between the mother and her children. Whatever other estimate we may form of the African, we may not doubt his love for his mother. Her name, whether dead or alive, is always on his lips and in his heart. To her he confides secrets which he would reveal to no other being on the face of the earth. He cares for no one else in time of sickness. She alone must prepare his food, administer his medicine, prepare his ablutions, and spread his mat for him. He flies to her in the hour of distress, for he well knows, if all the rest of the world turn against him, she will be steadfast in her love, whether he is right or wrong." Among the Ibo of Nigeria, "the mother's love for the child, and vice versa, are perhaps the most remarkable elements in the family relationships. The son may not always treat his mother kindly—although not to do so is abhorrent to the Ibo mind, and very seldom indeed is a mother neglected or treated disrespectfully—but the son never forgets his mother. Invariably she is the first in his affections, and she is his confidante in all serious affairs of life. In times of danger his mother is thought of before even wife and children. Wives are always to be had; he cannot get a second mother." "Throughout all the bush-tribes in West Africa," says Miss Kingsley, "this deep affection is the same; next to the mother comes the sister." The same deep affection of children for their mother is noted in Central Africa. Cameron in his travels across Africa was once led a very considerable distance out of his way by one of his guides; it turned out that he had led the expedition astray for hundreds of miles in order to meet his mother

A negro guide of Mr. Felkin resisted the temptation to do the same; "I feared if I saw my mother," he said, "I should want to stay with her, and I must not leave you." In the polygamous African home the husband's mother is generally the first person whom the traveler meets; she is the real head of the female part of the household, and the "family," so far as regards the bonds of affection, consists rather of mother and son than of husband and wives. The women, on the other hand, are more closely bound to their mother than to their husband; in Togoland "the bond between mother and daughter is so strong that both remain bound to one another until one dies. Never can love towards the husband displace in the heart of a daughter the love towards her mother. In Oriental as in African harems the mother, and not the chief wife, is usually the head of the household. Lord Cromer, who speaks rather severely of the Egyptians, remarks upon their affection towards their mothers; they often repeat the saying of the Kuran; "Paradise lies at the feet of the mother."

THE SOCIAL INSTINCTS

The attachment of the young to the mother differs considerably in its character from maternal love; it consists not so much in a sentiment of tenderness as in a sense of dependence which gives rise to panic fear when that protection is withdrawn and to a dread of solitude. The young of carnivorous animals, even when not hungry, invariably shriek and howl when left alone. Since it thus consists primarily of a sense of dependence the filial sentiment is particularly ready to accept a substitute. It is not primarily the mother as such that it requires—it is a protector, a guide, an individual upon whom it can lean. All young animals will attach themselves to the first creature, animal or human, that will look after them. New-born chickens will follow any moving object. When guided by the sense of sight alone "they seem to have no more disposition to follow a hen than to follow a duck or a human being." By attending to his chickens from birth, Mr. Spalding completely ousted their mother, and the chickens would, without any encouragement, follow him everywhere without taking the slightest notice of their own bereaved parent. "When Indians have killed a cow buffalo," says Hennepin, "the calf follows them and licks their hands." Mr. Selous mentions that having shot a female rhinoceros which had just dropped a calf, the latter at once trotted behind its mother's slayer and quietly followed him to his camp. The manner in which the domestication of animals first took place will be apparent from such instances. The reliance upon the mother extends to all companions, to all individuals who are recognized as not being hostile or dangerous, and results in a general disposition to friendliness and affection. "When wild animals become tame," says Dr. Chalmers Mitchell, "they are really extending or transferring to human beings the confidence and affection they naturally give to their mothers, and this view will be found to explain more facts about tameness than any other. Every creature that would naturally enjoy maternal care is ready to transfer its devotion to other animals or to human beings. The capacity to be tamed is greatest in those animals that remain longest with their parents and that are most intimately associated with them."

Herbivorous animals show scarcely any attachment or affection towards human beings. The carnivores become extremely attached to their keepers; lions and tigers brought up by Herr Hagenbeck showed excitement and joy when seeing him again after an interval of two or three years. Monkeys are the most affectionate of the lower animals towards those who have brought them up, and the anthropoids most of all. Mr. R. B. Walker, who had a large experience in bringing up young gorillas, states that they "become so much attached to their keeper or attendant that a separation from him almost invariably causes these affectionate apes to pine away and die."

Members of the same group, brothers and sisters, are naturally the first substitutes adopted in satisfying the sentiment of dependence, and in appeasing the fear of solitude created by maternal care. Those feelings are even more prone to assume the character of sympathy and tender affection when directed towards companions of the same age than in relation to the mother. An instinct of clannishness which draws a sharp distinction between members of the group, known and familiar individuals, and strangers, becomes a marked feature of such a group. Thus among American bison "each small group is of the same strain of blood. There is no animal more 'clannish' than the bison. The male calf follows the mother until two years old, when he is driven out of the herd, and the parental tie is entirely broken. The female calf fares better, as she is permitted to stay with her mother's family for life. In a broad sense it will be seen that the small local herd is a family, or rather a clan. Their leader is always an old cow, doubtless she is the grandmother of many of them. A pathetic sight was sometimes witnessed when the mother of one of these families was killed at the first shot. They were so devoted to her they would linger and wait until the last one could be easily slain." The same group sentiment has been observed by many as being very marked in the elephant. "If by any accident," says Sir E. Tennant, "an elephant becomes hopelessly separated from his herd, he is not permitted to attach himself to any other. No familiarity or intimate association is under any circumstances permitted. To such height is this exclusiveness carried that even amidst the terror of an elephant corral, when an individual, detached from his own party in the mêlée and confusion, has been driven into the enclosure with an unbroken herd, I have seen him repulsed in every attempt to take refuge among them." In those animals which have in numbers been together under the influence of prolonged maternal care, a tendency is observable among the young to continue together after they have left, or been expelled from, the maternal group. This is observed among crows, jackdaws, starlings, and other birds, and in some members of the deer tribe. Among primates the tendency is conspicuous. Monkeys are the only mammals in which a true social instinct may be said to be developed. Until sexual causes come into operation all young monkeys tend to remain associated in troops with the members of the same brood, and in that association are developed for the first time in the animal kingdom sentiments of sympathy. Sympathy is, as Romanes remarked, "more strongly marked in monkeys than in any other animal, not even excepting the dog." He mentions striking instances of that mutual interest which is a conspicuous feature of all associations of monkeys. A sick monkey is waited on with the utmost solicitude and anxiety by his companions, who even forgo dainties in order to offer them to him. A monkey on board a ship is said to have extended a rope overboard in order to save a drowning companion. Those social impulses are correlated with the prolonged association of infancy under maternal care.

The so-called instinct of sociability or of gregariousness is in reality the effect of the offspring's dependence upon maternal protection, and consequent dread or dislike of solitude on the part of the dependent young. It has been repeated since the time of Aristotle that "man is a social animal," and the origin of human society has been set down to the operation of such a supposed innate disposition to association. Modern psychologists have continued to refer to such a supposed primary instinct, and to regard it as an ultimate fact of paramount importance in determining human social organization. But in doing so they appear to have merely taken for granted a time-honored assumption. When any attempt is made to justify such an estimate, and to describe the manifestations of the supposed instinct, it is invariably found that other powerful motives are at work. Mr. Marshall is almost singular in judiciously maintaining that all social instincts appertain to a much more recent stratum than other mental tendencies. Dr.

Drever cautiously observes that "it is perhaps a matter for the biologist rather than for the psychologist to decide."

Biological facts give no support to the conception. The supposed "gregarious instinct" has, indeed, commonly been referred to as the cause of the associations or congregations of animals in much the same manner as the properties of opium are explained by Molière's physician by a reference to its "dormitive virtue." It has been supposed that such an instinct is one of the primary and fundamental impulses of life, and the theory formulated by Buffon in the eighteenth century, that the "forms of the social instinct" are the chief determining factor of the habits and groupings of animals, persists in many later biological writings. It is constantly suggested or assumed that an instinct of sociability is an innate impulse of all living protoplasm, and that living organisms are naturally attracted towards other living organisms. But those prevalent assumptions will not stand the test of critical examination. Primitive plasmophagous organisms are attracted towards others by hunger, or by the need for conjugation, which is a form of the same impulse. The congregation of microorganisms is determined, as is easily demonstrated by experiment, not by the presence or absence of other organisms, but by the most favorable conditions of nutrition and temperature. The broods of all organisms naturally accumulate in one spot and are therefore commonly found in groups. But far from there being any indication of a natural tendency to congregate together, the impulses of living organisms show, on the contrary, the opposite tendency. The broods which are accumulated by the reproductive process in the neighborhood of one spot tend invariably to scatter and spread abroad. The uniquity of life is the result of that tendency to dispersion. It is the natural consequence of the need for food which is liable to become exhausted where many claimants to it congregate, and must be sought farther afield. It is an advantage to organisms to wander away from the pressure of competition to fresh fields and pastures new.

That impulse of the individual to wander is far more conspicuously manifested among animals, from the lowest to the highest, than any "gregarious instinct." In the lower animals the tendency is almost invariably to wander as far afield as possible. Insects, among which the most perfect examples, outside humanity, of social communities are found, are nevertheless eminently solitary. "The majority of insects," says Mr. C. A. Ealand, "are solitary in their habits; each individual, or at most a pair of individuals, lives its life irrespectively of the activities of others of its kind." If a "socal instinct" were an original, or even a common and deep-seated, impulse of life, we should expect to find the majority of animals, especially the higher and more intelligent, aggregated in communities. But that is very far from being the case. On the contrary, the lower and least intelligent birds and the ruminants are found herding in large numbers, while the more highly developed nesting-birds, the birds of prey, and the carnivores are eminently solitary. Even the most typically herding animals have a tendency to segregate themselves and to disperse. Large herds are in reality subdivided into smaller groups of closely related animals, and it is the familial instinct, and not an undifferentiated gregarious instinct, which causes Galton's Damaraox to feel uneasy when separated from his group. Cattle, sheep, horses, when promiscuously herded together, sort themselves out into separate groups according to color and varieties, and such groups will hold no communication with one another, and will often segregate themselves in different territories. All animal groups, in the natural state, break up through the operation of the reproductive instincts. The females of nearly all animals seek solitude after impregnation, and in every species, even the most gregarious, the males have a tendency to wander in solitude. Of elephants, Mr. Sanderson remarks: "Much misconception exists on the subject of 'rogues' or solitary elephants. The usually accepted belief is that these elephants are turned out of the herds by their companions at times to roam by themselves

Sometimes they make those expeditions merely for the sake of solitude." The same remark doubtless applies to many of the males, which in all species are seen roaming by themselves, or in small groups of two or three. In old males, when both the infantile and the sexual instincts have ceased to operate, instinctive tendencies revert to the more primitive impulse towards dispersal and independence. Of bats it is noted that, "though most bats are gregarious in the summer, in the winter they prefer solitude and quiet. They go off singly, or at most in twos or threes." Those animals which mate in pairs separate after the functions of reproduction are discharged as commonly as do herding animals; and of the animals nearest to man the gorilla has been found alone most as frequently as in herds, and the orang-utan has scarcely ever been seen except alone or with young. All monkeys strongly resent the intrusion of a stranger in their troops, which are close corporations. Their gregarious instincts are towards the groups, not towards the species.

The truth is that there is neither an intrinsic social instinct nor any instinct of solitude; animal life does not, as an inherent impulse, love either society or solitude for its own sake. Such abstract predilections may operate in the realms of culture and conceptual thought, but they have no bearing on the behavior of unsophisticated life. Other impulses, such as the sexual impulse, or the infantile dependence of offspring, may keep or bring animals together; or they may, as does the competition for food, drive them apart; but whether they come together or seek segregation their behavior is not the effect of any "gregarious" or "antigregarious" disposition, but of a need for the satisfaction of which either aggregation or solitude is favorable.

The social instinct, the love of company which has developed in the very highest forms of life, is a special and specifically developed instinct. All familial feeling, all group-sympathy, the essential foundation, therefore, of a social organization, is the direct product of prolonged maternal care, and does not exist apart from it. The deep, self-protective instincts of timidity and distrust forbid, especially in the male, the extension of those sentiments beyond the group of companions. In regard to individuals that are not members of the family group, the original instincts of the cautious, competitive animal retain their full force; the stranger is regarded with spontaneous hostility and hatred.

To man absolute solitude is abhorrent; it is not good for man to be alone. But that is a very different matter from a "social instinct." The distress caused by solitude can usually be remedied by the company of an individual of the opposite sex. The "social instinct" is here no other than the sexual instinct. As in animals that need may, and commonly does, admit of all sorts of substitutes and extensions. In the absence of a congenial companion of the opposite sex, man, rather than suffer absolute isolation, will draw up even to uncongenial companions, or he will value the companionship of an animal, of a dog, of a horse, or even, as in the legend of Bruce, of a spider. A stranger in an unknown land will find comfort in the silent companionship of other human beings, though they may take no notice of him. In all circumstances he will desire, above all, the companionship, not only of a mate, but of his family, his children friends, of all who are dear to him.

Those feelings are the expression of the familial sentiment arising out of the operation of the maternal instincts, not of a generalized, indiscriminate "social instinct." Far from there existing any indication of such a general social instinct in primitive humanity, the attitude of an uncultured human being towards any individual who is not a member of their own restricted social group is one of profound distrust and generally of active hostility. "In primitive culture," observes Dr. Brinton, "there is a dual system of morals: the one of kindness, love, help, and peace, applicable to the members of our own clan, tribe, or community; the other of robbery, hatred, enmity, and murder, to be practiced against all the rest of the world; and the latter is regarded as quite as much a sacred duty as the former." Among all

primitive peoples small groups show the strongest indis-
position to fuse into larger ones, and the intrusion of
strangers is resented. In the Andaman Islands, before the
arrival of Europeans, the inhabitants of the small area of
those islands were divided into a number of tribelets which
had never held any intercourse with one another. When first
brought together they were unable to converse, their languages having during centuries of segregation diverged
completely, although they were members of the same race.
The island of Raratonga was in like manner inhabited, before the advent of Europeans, by tribes which had no knowledge of one another. When the Veddahs of Ceylon are
brought into contact with individuals belonging to another
tribelet, which, maybe, dwells only a few miles away, they
stand in silent embarrassment, refuse to speak, and scowl
at the strangers with a manifest disinclination to associate
with them. The attitude of the Fuegians, who live in small,
scattered communities, towards members of all other groups
is said to be one of strong hostility. Between the North
American tribes "there was no intermarriage, no social
intercourse, no intermingling of any kind, except that of
mortal strife." The most salient trait of the Seri Indians is
their implacable hostility towards every human being,
Indian or white, who is not a member of their tribe, and
even each clan views all others with suspicion. South American natives are divided into innumerable small groups and
tribelets who hate one another mortally. "The savages detest all who are not of their tribe, and hunt the Indians of
a neighboring tribe who are at war with their own, as we
hunt game." The rough huts of the wild Cashibo of southern
Peru are surrounded with pitfalls and concealed spikes. In
Australia it is a rule that no black fellow from one camp
may visit another camp without being invited; a messenger
or visitor from one clan to another must sit down at some
distance from the strange camp and wait until he has been
examined by some of the elders before he is asked to ap-

proach. "Every stranger who presents himself uninvited amongst them incurs the penalty of death." Among the ancient Britons no man could approach or pass a village without giving warning of his presence by blowing a horn. The same precaution was observed by the Guatos of South America, and by the Maori of New Zealand.

It is not in obedience to any generalized mutual attraction, to any "gregarious" or "social" instinct, that groups, whether of human beings or of animals, are formed or maintained. Wherever such a group exists it is the result of specific needs and instincts, and not of any attraction that impels individuals to association for its own sake. In the higher forms of animal life, what has commonly been called the "social instinct" is the direct outcome of the relation between mother and offspring, and of the reflection of the maternal instincts in the relations of mutual dependence and sympathy, between members of the same brood or brotherhood. Darwin, although he appeared to share some of the current misconceptions concerning so-called social instincts, perceived that "the feeling of pleasure from society is probably an extension of the parental or filial affection," and that those latter feelings and instincts "lie at the basis of social affections." The material out of which all human society had been constructed is the bond of those sentiments. These have undergone many extensions and transformations, sentiments of brotherhood towards all members of the same clan, and, in higher forms of culture, ideal loyalties, patriotic devotion, and religious altruisms. Those sentiments and social virtues which are necessary to the existence of any form of human society have their original root in the feeling which characterizes the relation between mother and offspring. Dr. Ferriani, in discussing the education and reformation of youthful delinquents, that is, of youths who are deficient in social sentiment and virtues, remarks that the most numerous and most hopeless cases are those where no opportunity has been afforded for the development of filial sentiments. On the other hand, "I never despair," he says, "of youths who honor their mother." The original of all social bonds, the only one which exists among the higher animals and in the most primitive human groups, is that created by mother-love.

HOMOSEXUAL LOVE *

By EDWARD WESTERMARCK

OUR review of the moral ideas concerning sexual relations has not yet come to an end. The gratification of the sexual instinct assumes forms which fall outside the ordinary pale of nature. Of these there is one which, on account of the rôle which it has played in the moral history of mankind, cannot be passed over in silence, namely, intercourse between individuals of the same sex, what is nowadays commonly called homosexual love.

It is frequently met with among the lower animals.[1] It probably occurs, at least sporadically, among every race of mankind.[2] And among some peoples it has assumed such proportions as to form a true national habit.

In America homosexual customs have been observed among a great number of native tribes. In nearly every part of the continent there seem to have been, since ancient times, men dressing themselves in the clothes and performing the functions of women, and living with other men as their concubines or wives.[3] Moreover, between young men who are comrades in arms there are liaisons d'amitie, which, according to Lafitau, "ne lassent aucun soupçon de vice apparent, quoiqu'il y ait, ou qu'il puisse y avoir, beaucoup de vice réel." [4]

Homosexual practices are, or have been, very prominent among the peoples in the neighborhood of Behring Sea.[5] In Kadiak it was the custom of the parent who had a girl-like son to try to dress and rear him as a girl, teaching him only domestic duties, keeping him at woman's work, and letting him associate only with women and girls. Arriving at the age of ten or fifteen years, he was married to some

* The Origin and Development of the Moral Ideas. London: Macmillan and Co.

529

wealthy man and was then called an *achnuchik* or *shoopan*.[6]
Dr. Bogoras gives the following account of a similar practice prevalent among the Chukchi: "It happens frequently
that, under the supernatural influence of one of their shamans, or priests, a Chukchi lad at sixteen years of age will
suddenly relinquish his sex and imagine himself to be a
woman. He adopts a woman's attire, lets his hair grow, and
devotes himself altogether to female occupation. Furthermore, this disowner of his sex takes a husband into the *Yurt*
and does all the work which is usually incumbent on the
wife in most unnatural and voluntary subjection. Thus it
frequently happens in a *Yurt* that the husband is a woman,
while the wife is a man! These abnormal changes of sex
imply the most abject immorality in the community, and
appear to be strongly encouraged by the shamans who
interpret such cases as an injunction of their individual
deity."

The change of sex was usually accompanied by future
shamanship; indeed, nearly all the shamans were former
delinquents of their sex.[7] Among the Chukchi male shamans who are clothed in woman's attire and are believed
to be transformed physically into women are still quite
common; and traces of the change of a shaman's sex into
that of a woman may be found among many other Siberian
tribes.[8] In some cases at least there can be no doubt that
these transformations were connected with homosexual
practices. In his description of the Koriaks, Krasheninnikoff
makes mention of the *ke'yev,* that is, men occupying the position of concubines; and he compares them with the Kamchadale *koe'kčuč,* as he calls them, that is, men transformed
into women. Every *koe'kčuč,* he says, is regarded as a
magician and interpreter of dreams; but from his confused description Mr. Jochelson thinks it may be inferred
that the most important feature of the institution of the
koe'kčuč lay, not in their shamanistic power, but in their
position with regard to the satisfaction of the unnatural
inclinations of the Kamchadales. The *koe'kčuč* wore

women's clothes, did women's work, and were in the position of wives or concubines.[9]

In the Malay Archipelago homosexual love is common,[10] though not in all of the islands.[11] It is widely spread among the Bataks of Sumatra.[12] In Bali it is practiced openly, and there are persons who make it a profession. The *basir* of the Dyaks are men who make their living by witchcraft and debauchery. They "are dressed as women, they are made use of at idolatrous feasts and for sodomitic abominations, and many of them are formally married to other men." [13] Dr. Haddon says that he never heard of any unnatural offenses in Torres Straits; [14] but in the Rigo district of British New Guinea several instances of pederasty have been met with,[15] and at Mowat in Daudai it is regularly indulged in.[16] Homosexual love is reported as common among the Marshall Islanders [17] and in Hawaii.[18] From Tahiti we hear of a set of men called by the natives *mahoos,* who "assume the dress, attitude, and manners, of women, and affect all the fantastic oddities and coquetries of the vainest of females. They mostly associate with the women, who court their acquaintance. With the manners of the women, they adopt their peculiar employments. . . . The encouragement of this abomination is almost solely confined to the chiefs." [19] Of the New Caledonians, M. Foley writes: "La plus grande fraternité n'est pas chez eux la fraternité utérine, mais la fraternité des armes. Il en est ainsi surtout au village de poepo. Il est vrai que cette fraternité des armes est compliquée de pédérastie." [20]

Among the natives of the Kimberley District in West Australia, if a young man on reaching a marriageable age can find no wife, he is presented with a boy-wife, known as *chookadoo.* In this case, also, the ordinary exogamic rules are observed, and the "husband" has to avoid his "mother-in-law" just as if he were married to a woman. The *chooka-doo* is a boy of five years to about ten, when he is initiated. "The relations which exist between him and his protecting *billalu,*" says Mr. Hardman, "are somewhat doubtful. There is no doubt they have connection, but the natives repudiate with horror and disgust the idea of sodomy." [21] Such marriages are evidently exceedingly common. As the women are generally monopolized by the older and more influential men of the tribe, it is rare to find a man under thirty or forty who has a wife; hence it is the rule that, when a boy becomes five years old, he is given as a boy-wife to one of the young men.[22] According to Mr. Purcell's description of the natives of the same district, "every useless member of the tribe" gets a boy, about five or seven years old; and these boys, who are called *mullawongghs,* are used for sexual purposes.[23] Among the Chingalee of South Australia, Northern Territory, old men are often noticed with no wives but accompanied by one or two boys, whom they jealously guard and with whom they have sodomitic intercourse.[24]

That homosexual practices are not unknown among other Australian tribes may be inferred from Mr. Howitt's statement relating to South-Eastern natives, that unnatural offenses are forbidden to the novices by the old men and guardians after leaving the initiation camp.[25]

In Madagascar there are certain boys who live like women and have intercourse with men, paying those men who please them.[26] In an old account of that island, dating from the seventeenth century, it is said: "Il y a quelques hommes qu'ils appellent Tsecats, qui sont hommes effeminez et impuissans, qui recherchent les garçons, et font mine d'en estre amoureux, en contrefaisons les filles et se vestans ainsi qu'elles leurs font des présents pour dormir avec eux, et mesmes se donnent des noms de filles, en faisant les honteuses et les modestes. . . . Ils Haïssent les femmes et ne les veulent point hanter." [27] Men behaving like women have also been observed among the Ondonga in German Southwest Africa [28] and the Diakité-Sarracolese in the French Soudan,[29] but as regards their sexual habits details are wanting. Homosexual practices are common among the Banaka and Bapuku in the Cameroons.[30] But among the natives of Africa generally such practices seem to be comparatively rare,[31] except among Arabic-speaking peoples and in countries like Zanzibar,[32] where there has been a strong Arab influence.

In North Africa they are not restricted to the inhabitants of towns; they are frequently among the peasants of Egypt [33] and universal among the Jbâla inhabiting the Northern mountains of Morocco. On the other hand, they are much less common or even rare among the Berbers and the nomadic Bedouins,[34] and it is reported that the Bedouins of Arabia are quite exempt from them.[35]

Homosexual love is spread over Asia Minor and Mesopotamia.[36] It is very prevalent among the Tartars and Karatchai of the Caucasus,[37] the Persians,[38] Sikhs,[39] and Afghans; in Kaubul a bazaar or street is set apart for it.[40] Old travelers make reference to its enormous frequency among the Muhammedans of India,[41] and in this respect time seems to have produced no change.[42] In China, where it is also extremely common, there are special houses devoted to male prostitution, and boys are sold by their parents about the age of four, to be trained for this occupation.[43] In Japan pederasty is said by some to have prevailed from the most ancient times, whereas others are of opinion that it was introduced by Buddhism about the sixth century of our era. The monks used to live with handsome youths, to whom they were often passionately devoted; and in feudal times nearly every knight had as his favorite a young man with whom he entertained relations of the most intimate kind, and on behalf of whom he was always ready to fight a duel when occasion occurred. Tea-houses with male *gheishas* were found in Japan till the middle of the nineteenth century. Nowadays pederasty seems to be more prevalent in the Southern than in the Northern provinces of the country, but there are also districts where it is hardly known.[44]

No reference is made to pederasty either in the Homeric poems or by Hesiod, but later on we meet with it almost as a national institution in Greece. It was known in Rome and other parts of Italy at an early period; [45] but here also it became much more frequent in the course of time. At the close of the sixth century, Polybius tells us, many Romans paid a talent for the possession of a beautiful youth.[46] During the Empire "il était d'usage, dans les familles patriciennes, de donner au jeune homme pubère un esclave du même âge comme compagnon de lit, afin qu'il pût satisfaire . . . 'ses premiers élans' génésiques"; [47] and formal marriages between men were introduced with all the solemnities of ordinary nuptials.[48] Homosexual practices occurred among the Celts,[49] and were by no means unknown to the ancient Scandinavians, who had a whole nomenclature on the subject.[50]

Of late years a voluminous and constantly increasing literature on homosexuality has revealed its frequency in modern Europe. No country and no class of society is free from it. In certain parts of Albania it even exists as a popular custom, the young men from the age of sixteen upwards regularly having boy favorites of between twelve and seventeen.[51]

The above statements chiefly refer to homosexual practices between men, but similar practices also occur between women.[52] Among the American aborigines there are not only men who behave like women, but women who behave like men. Thus in certain Brazilian tribes women are found who abstain from every womanly occupation and imitate the men in everything, who wear their hair in masculine fashion, who go to war with a bow and arrows, who hunt together with the men, and who would rather allow themselves to be killed than have sexual intercourse with a man. "Each of these women has a woman who serves her and with whom she says she is married; they live together as husband and wife." [53] So also there are among the Eastern Eskimo some women who refuse to accept husbands, preferring to adopt masculine manners, following the deer on the mountains, trapping and fishing for themselves.[54] Homosexual practices are said to be common among Hottentot [55] and Herero [56] women. In Zanzibar there are women who wear men's clothes in private, show a preference for masculine occupations, and seek sexual satisfaction among women who have the same inclination, or else among normal women who are won over by presents or other means.[57] In Egyptian harems every woman is said to have a "friend." [58] In Bali homosexuality is almost as common among women as among men, though it is exercised more secretly; [59] and the same seems to be the case in India.[60] From Greek antiquity we hear of "Lesbian" love. The fact that homosexuality has been much more frequently noticed in men than in women does not imply that the latter are less addicted to it. For various reasons the sexual abnormalities of women have attracted much less attention,[61] and moral opinion has generally taken little notice of them.

Homosexual practices are due sometimes to instinctive preference, sometimes to external conditions unfavorable to normal intercourse.[62] A frequent cause is congenital sexual inversion, that is, "sexual instinct turned by inborn constitutional abnormality toward persons of the same sex." [63] It seems likely that the feminine men and the masculine women referred to above are, at least in many instances, sexual inverts; though, in the case of shamans, the change of sex may also result from the belief that such transformed shamans, like their female colleagues, are particularly powerful.[64] Dr. Holder affirms the existence of congenital inversion among the Northwestern tribes of the United States,[65] Dr. Baumann among the people of Zanzibar; [66] and in Morocco, also, I believe it is common enough. But as regards its prevalence among non-European peoples we have mostly to resort to mere conjectures; our real knowledge of congenital inversion is derived from the voluntary confessions of inverts. The large majority of travelers are totally ignorant of the psychological side of the subject, and even to an expert it must very often be impossible to decide whether a certain case of inversion is congenital or acquired. Indeed, acquired inversion itself presupposes an innate disposition which under certain circumstances de-

velops into actual inversion.[67] Even between inversion and
normal sexuality there seems to be all shades of variation.
Professor James thinks that inversion is "a kind of sexual
appetite, of which very likely most men possess the germinal
possibility." [68] This is certainly the case in early puberty.[69]

A very important cause of homosexual practices is absence
of the other sex. There are many instances of this among
the lower animals.[70] Buffon long ago observed that, if male
or female birds of various species were shut up together,
they would soon begin to have sexual relations among themselves, the males sooner than the females.[71] The West
Australian boy-marriage is a substitute for ordinary marriage
in cases when women are not obtainable. Among the Bororo
of Brazil homosexual intercourse is said to occur in their
men-houses only when the scarcity of accessible girls is
unusually great.[72] Its prevalence in Tahiti may perhaps
be connected with the fact that there was only one woman to
four or five men, owing to the habit of female infanticide.[73]
Among the Chinese in certain regions, for instance Java,
the lack of accessible women is the principal cause of homosexual practices.[74] According to some writers such practices
are the results of polygamy.[75] In Muhammedan countries
they are no doubt largely due to the seclusion of women,
preventing free intercourse between the sexes and compelling the unmarried people to associate almost exclusively
with members of their own sex. Among the mountaineers
of northern Morocco the excessive indulgence in pederasty
thus goes hand in hand with great isolation of the women
and a very high standard of female chastity, whereas
among the Arabs of the plains, who are little addicted to
boy-love, the unmarried girls enjoy considerable freedom.
Both in Asia [76] and Europe [77] the obligatory celibacy of the
monks and priests has been a cause of homosexual practices,
though it must not be forgotten that a profession which
imposes abstinence from marriage is likely to attract a
comparatively large number of congenital inverts. The temporary separation of the sexes involved in a military mode

of life no doubt accounts for the extreme prevalence of homosexual love among warlike races,[78] like the Sikhs, Afghans, Dorians, and Normans.[79] In Persia [80] and Morocco it is particularly common among soldiers. In Japan it was an incident of knighthood, in New Caledonia and North America of brotherhood in arms. At least in some of the North American tribes men who were dressed as women accompanied the other men as servants in war and the chase.[81] Among the Banaka and Bapuku in the Cameroons pederasty is practiced especially by men who are long absent from their wives.[82] In Morocco I have heard it advocated on account of the convenience it affords to persons who are traveling.

Dr. Havelock Ellis justly observes that when homosexual attraction is due simply to the absence of the other sex we are not concerned with sexual inversion, but merely with the accidental turning of the sexual instinct into an abnormal channel, the instinct being called out by an approximate substitute, or even by diffused emotional excitement, in the absence of the normal object.[83] But it seems to me probable that in such cases the homosexual attraction in the course of time quite easily develops into genuine inversion. I cannot but think that our chief authorities on homosexuality have underestimated the modifying influence which habit may exercise on the sexual instinct. Professor Krafft-Ebing [84] and Dr. Moll [85] deny the existence of acquired inversion except in occasional instances; and Dr. Havelock Ellis takes a similar view, if putting aside those cases of a more or less morbid character in which old men with failing sexual powers, or younger men exhausted by heterosexual debauchery, are attracted to members of their own sex.[86] But how is it that in some parts of Morocco such a very large proportion of the men are distinctly sexual inverts, in the sense in which this word is used by Dr. Havelock Ellis,[87] that is, persons who for the gratification of their sexual desire prefer their own sex to the opposite one? It may be that in Morocco and in Oriental countries generally, where almost every individual marries, congenital inversion, through the influence of heredity, is more frequent than in Europe, where inverts so commonly abstain from marrying. But that this could not be an adequate explanation of the fact in question becomes at once apparent when we consider the extremely unequal distribution of inverts among different neighboring tribes of the same stock, some of which are very little or hardly at all addicted to pederasty. I take the case to be, that homosexual practices in early youth have had a lasting effect on the sexual instinct, which at its first appearance, being somewhat indefinite, is easily turned into a homosexual direction.[88] In Morocco inversion is most prevalent among the scribes, who from childhood have lived in very close association with their fellow-students. Of course, influences of this kind "require a favorable organic predisposition to act on"; [89] but this predisposition is probably no abnormality at all, only a feature in the ordinary sexual constitution of man.[90] It should be noticed that the most common form of inversion, at least in Muhammedan countries, is love of boys or youths not yet in the age of puberty, that is, of male individuals who are physically very like girls. Voltaire observes: "Souvent un jeune garçon, par la fraîcheur de son teint, par l'éclat de ses couleurs, et par la douceur de ses yeux, ressemble pendant deux ou trois ans à une belle fille; si on l'aime c'est parce que la nature se méprend." [91] Moreover, in normal cases sexual attraction depends not only on sex, but on a youthful appearance as well; and there are persons so constituted that to them the latter factor is of chief importance, whilst the question of sex is almost a matter of indifference.

In ancient Greece, also, not only homosexual intercourse, but actual inversion, seems to have been very common; and although this, like every form of love, must have contained a congenital element, there can be little doubt, I think, that it was largely due to external circumstances of a social character. It may, in the first place, be traced to the methods of training the youth. In Sparta it seems to have been the practice for every youth of good character to have his lover, or "inspirator," [92] and for every well-educated man to be the lover of some youth.[93] The relations between the "inspirator" and the "listener" were extremely intimate: at home the youth was constantly under the eyes of his lover, who was supposed to be to him a model and pattern of life; [94] in battle they stood near one another and their fidelity and affection were often shown till death; [95] if his relatives were absent, the youth might be represented in the public assembly by his lover; [96] and for many faults, particularly want of ambition, the lover could be punished instead of the "listener." [97] This ancient custom prevailed with still greater force in Crete, which island was hence by many persons considered to be the place of its birth.[98] Whatever may have been the case originally, there can be no doubt that in later times the relations between the youth and his lover implied unchaste intercourse.[99] And in other Greek states the education of the youth was accompanied by similar consequences. At an early age the boy was taken away from his mother, and spent thenceforth all his time in the company of men, until he reached the age when marriage became for him a civic duty.[100] According to Plato, the gymnasia and common meals among the youth "seem always to have had a tendency to degrade the ancient and natural custom of love below the level, not only of man, but of the beasts." [101] Plato also mentions the effect which these habits had on the sexual instincts of the men: "When they reached manhood they were lovers of youths and not naturally inclined to marry or beget children, but, if at all, they did so only in obedience to the law." [102] Is not this, in all probability, an instance of acquired inversion? But besides the influence of education there was another factor which, coöperating with it, favored the development of homosexual tendencies, namely, the great gulf which mentally separated the sexes. Nowhere else has the difference in culture between men and women been so immense as in the fully developed Greek civilization. The lot of a wife in Greece was retirement and ignorance. She lived in almost absolute seclusion, in a separate part of the house, together with her female slaves, deprived of all the educating influence of male society, and having no place at those public spectacles which were the chief means of culture.[103] In such circumstances it is not difficult to understand that men so highly intellectual as those of Athens regarded the love of women as the offspring of the common Aphrodite, who "is cf the body rather than of the soul."[104] They had reached a stage of mental culture at which the sexual instinct normally has a craving for refinement, at which the gratification of mere physical lust appears brutal. In the eyes of the most refined among them those who were inspired by the heavenly Aphrodite loved neither women nor boys, but intelligent beings whose reason was beginning to be developed, much about the time at which the beards began to grow.[105] In present China we meet with a parallel case. Dr. Matignon observes: "Il y a tout lieu de supposer que ce tains Chinois, raffinés au point de vue intellectuel, recherchent dans le pédérastie la satisfaction des sens et de l'esprit. La femme chinoise est peu cultivée, ignorante même, quelle soit sa condition, honnête femme ou prostituée. Or le Chinois a souvent l'âme poétique: il aime les vers, la musique, les belles sentences des philosophes, autant de choses qu'il ne peut trouver chez le beau sexe de l'Empire du Milieu."[106] So also it seems that the ignorance and dullness of Muhammedan women, which is a result of their total lack of education and their secluded life, is a cause of homosexual practices; Moors are sometimes heard to defend pederasty on the plea that the company of boys, who have always news to tell, is so much more entertaining than the company of women.

We have hitherto dealt with homosexual love as a fact; we shall now pass to the moral valuation to which it is subject. Where it occurs as a national habit we may assume that no censure, or no severe censure, is passed on it. Among the Bataks of Sumatra there is no punishment for it.[107] Of the *bazirs* among the Ngajus of Pula Patak, in Borneo, **Dr.** Schwaner says that "in spite of their loathsome calling they escape well-merited contempt." [108] The Society Islanders had for their homosexual practices "not only the sanction of their priests, but direct example of their respective deities."[109] The *tsekats* of Madagascar maintained that they were serving the deity by leading a feminine life; [110] but we are told that at Ankisimane and in Nossi-Bé, opposite to it, pederasts are objects of public contempt.[111] Father Veniaminof says of the Atkha Aleuts that "sodomy and too early cohabitation with a betrothed or intended wife are called among them grave sins"; [112] but apart from the fact that his account of these natives in general gives the impression of being somewhat eulogistic, the details stated by him only show that the acts in question were considered to require a simple ceremony of purification.[113] There is no indication that the North American aborigines attached any opprobrium to men who had intercourse with those members of their own sex who had assumed the dress and habits of women. In Kadiak such a companion was on the contrary regarded as a great acquisition; and the effeminate men themselves, far from being despised, were held in repute by the people, most of them being wizards.[114] We have previously noticed the connection between homosexual practices and shamanism among the various Siberian peoples; and it is said that such shamans as had changed their sex were greatly feared by the people, being regarded as very powerful.[115] Among the Illinois and Naudowessies the effeminate men assist in all the Juggleries and the solemn dance in honor of the *calumet,* or sacred tobacco pipe, for which the Indians have such a deference that one may call it "the god of peace and war, and the arbiter of life and death"; but they are not permitted either to dance or sing. They are called into the councils of the Indians, and nothing can be decided upon without their advice; for because of their extraordinary manner of living they are looked upon as *manitous,* or supernatural beings, and persons of consequence.[116] The Sioux,

Sacs, and Fox Indians give once a year, or oftener if they choose, a feast to the *Berdashe,* or *I-coo-coo-a,* who is a man dressed in woman's clothes, as he has been all his life. "For extraordinary privileges which he is known to possess, he is driven to the most servile and degrading duties, which he is not allowed to escape; and he being the only one of the tribe submitting to this disgraceful degradation, is looked upon as 'medicine' and sacred, and a feast is given to him annually; and initiatory to it, a dance by those few young men of the tribe who can ... dance forward and publicly make their boast (without the denial of the Berdashe).... Such, and such only, are allowed to enter the dance and partake of the feast."[117] Among some American tribes, however, these effeminate men are said to be despised, especially by the women.[118] In ancient Peru, also, homosexual practices seem to have entered in the religious cult. In some particular places, says Cieza de Leon, boys were kept as priests in the temples, with whom it was rumored that the lords joined in company on days of festivity. They did not meditate, he adds, the committing of such sin, but only the offering of sacrifice to the demon. If the Incas by chance had some knowledge of such proceedings in the temple, they might have ignored them out of religious tolerance.[119] But the Incas themselves were not only free from such practices in their own persons, they would not even permit any one who was guilty of them to remain in the royal houses or palaces. And Cieza heard it related that, if it came to their knowledge that somebody had committed an offense of that kind, they punished it with such a severity that it was known to all.[120] Las Casas tells us that in several of the more remote provinces of Mexico sodomy was tolerated, if not actually permitted, because the people believed that their gods were addicted to it; and it is not improbable that in earlier times the same was the case in the entire empire.[121] But in a later age severe measures were adopted by legislators in order to suppress the practice. In Mexico people found guilty of it were killed.[122] In Nicaragua it was punished capitally by stoning,[123] and none of the Maya nations was without strict laws against it.[124] Among the Chibchas of Bogota the punishment for it was the infliction of a painful death.[125] However, it should be remembered that the ancient culture nations of America were generally extravagant in their punishments, and that their penal codes in the first place expressed rather the will of their rulers than the feelings of the people at large.[126]

Homosexual practices are said to be taken little notice of even by some uncivilized peoples who are not addicted to them. In the Pelew Islands, where such practices occur only sporadically, they are not punished, although, if I understand Herr Kubary rightly, the persons committing them may be put to shame.[127] The Ossetes of the Caucasus, among whom pederasty is very rare, do not generally prosecute persons for committing it, but ignore the act.[128] The East African Masai do not punish sodomy.[129] But we also meet with statements of a contrary nature. In a Kafir tribe Mr. Warner heard of a case of it—the only one during a residence of twenty-five years—which was punished with a fine of some cattle claimed by the chief.[130] Among the Ondonga pederasts are hated, and the men who behave like women are detested, most of them being wizards.[131] The Washambala consider pederasty a grave moral aberration and subject it to severe punishment.[132] Among the Waganda homosexual practices, which have been introduced by the Arabs and are of rare occurrence, "are intensely abhorred," the stake being the punishment.[133] The Negroes of Accra, who are not addicted to such practices, are said to detest them.[134] In Nubia pederasty is held in abhorrence, except by the Kashefs and their relations, who endeavor to imitate the Mamelukes in everything.[135]

Muhammed forbade sodomy,[136] and the general opinion of his followers is that it should be punished like fornication—for which the punishment is, theoretically, severe enough [137]—unless the offenders make a public act of penitence. In order to convict, however, the law requires that four reliable persons shall swear to have been eye-witnesses,[138] and this alone would make the law a dead letter, even if it had the support of popular feelings; but such support is certainly wanting. In Morocco active pederasty is regarded with almost complete indifference, whilst the passive sodomite, if a grown-up individual, is spoken of with scorn. Dr. Polak says the same of the Persians.[139] In Zanzibar a clear distinction is made between male congenital inverts and male prostitutes; the latter are looked upon with contempt, whereas the former, as being what they are "by the will of God," are tolerated.[140] The Muhammedans of India and other Asiatic countries regard pederasty, at most, as a mere peccadillo.[141] Among the Hindus it is said to be held in abhorrence,[142] but their sacred books deal with it leniently. According to the "Laws of Manu," "a twice-born man who commits an unnatural offense with a male, or has intercourse with a female in a cart drawn by oxen, in water, or in the day-time shall bathe, dressed in his clothes"; and all these are reckoned as minor offenses.[143]

Chinese law makes little distinction between unnatural and other sexual offenses. An unnatural offense is variously considered according to the age of the patient, and whether or not consent was given. If the patient be an adult, or a boy over the age of twelve, and consent, the case is treated as a slightly aggravated form of fornication, both parties being punished with a hundred blows and one month's cangue, whilst ordinary fornication is punished with eighty blows. If the adult or boy over twelve resist, the offense is considered as rape; and if the boy be under twelve, the offense is rape irrespective of consent or resistance, unless the boy has previously gone astray.[144] But, as a matter of fact, unnatural offenses are regarded as less hurtful to the community than ordinary immorality,[145] and pederasty is not looked down upon. "L'opinion publique reste tout à fait indifférente à ce genre de distraction et la morale ne s'en émeut en rien: puisque cela plaît à l'opératéur et que l'opere est consentant, tout est pour le mieux; la loi chinoise n'aime guère à s'occuper des affaires trop intimes. La pédérastie est même considérée comme une chose de bon ton, une fantaisie dispendieuse et partout un plaisir élégant.... La pédérastie a une consécration officielle en Chine. Il existe, en effet, des pédérés pour l'Empereur." [146] Indeed, the only objection which Dr. Matignon has heard to be raised to pederasty by public opinion in China is that it has a bad influence on the eyesight. [147] In Japan there was no law against homosexual intercourse till the revolution of 1868. [148] In the period of Japanese chivalry it was considered more heroic if a man loved a person of his own sex than if he loved a woman; and nowadays people are heard to say that in those provinces of the country where pederasty is widely spread the men are more manly and robust than in those where it does not prevail. [149]

The laws of the ancient Scandinavians ignore homosexual practices; but passive pederasts were much despised by them. They were identified with cowards and regarded as sorcerers. The epithets applied to them—*argr, ragr, blandr,* and others—assumed the meaning of "poltroon" in general, and there are instances of the word *arg* being used in the sense of "practicing witchcraft." This connection between pederasty and sorcery, as a Norwegian scholar justly points out, helps us to understand Tacitus' statement that among the ancient Teutons individuals whom he describes as *corpore infames* were buried alive in a morass. [150] Considering that drowning was a common penalty for sorcery, it seems probable that this punishment was inflicted upon them not, in the first place, on account of their sexual practices, but in their capacity of wizards. It is certain that the opprobrium which the pagan Scandinavians attached to homosexual love was chiefly restricted to him who played the woman's part. In one of the poems the hero even boasts of being the father of offspring borne by another man. [151]

In Greece pederasty in its baser forms was censured, though generally, it seems, with not any great severity, and in some states it was legally prohibited. [152] According to an

Athenian law, a youth who prostituted himself for money lost his rights as a free citizen and was liable to the punish-ment of death if he took part in a public feast or entered the *agora*.[153] In Sparta it was necessary that the "listener" should accept the "inspirator" from real affection; he who did so out of pecuniary consideration was punished by the ephors.[154] We are even told that among the Spartans the relations between the lover and his friend were truly inno-cent, and that if anything unlawful happened both must forsake either their country or their lives.[155] But the uni-versal rule in Greece seems to have been that when decorum was observed in the friendship between a man and a youth, no inquiries were made into the details of the relation-ship.[156] And this attachment was not only regarded as per-missible, but was praised as the highest and purest form of love, as the offspring of the heavenly Aphrodite, as a path leading to virtue, as a weapon against tyranny, as a safe-guard of civic liberty, as a source of national greatness and glory. Phædrus said that he knew no greater blessing to a young man who is beginning life than a virtuous lover, or to the lover than a beloved youth; for the principle which ought to be the guide of men who would lead a noble life cannot be implanted by any other motive so well as by love.[157] The Platonic Pausanias argued that if love of youths is held in ill repute it is so only because it is inimical to tyranny; "the interests of rulers require that their subjects should be poor in spirit, and that there should be no strong bond of friendship or society among them, which love, above all other motives, is likely to inspire."[158] The power of the Athenian tyrants was broken by the love of Aristogei-ton and the constancy of Harmodius; at Agrigentum in Sicily the mutual love of Chariton and Melanippus pro-duced a similar result; and the greatness of Thebes was due to the Sacred Band established by Epaminondas. For "in the presence of his favorite, a man would choose to do any-thing rather than to get the character of a coward."[159] It was pointed out that the greatest heroes and the most warlike nations were those who were most addicted to the love of youths; [160] and it was said that an army consisting of lovers and their beloved ones, fighting at each other's side, although a mere handful, would overcome the whole world.[161]

Herodotus asserts that the love of boys was introduced from Greece into Persia.[162] Whether his statement be correct or not, such love could certainly not have been a habit of the Mazda worshipers.[163] In the Zoroastrian books "unnatural sin" is treated with a severity to which there is a parallel only in Hebrewism and Christianity. According to the Vendîdâd, there is no atonement for it.[164] It is punished with torments in the other world, and is capital here below.[165] Even he who committed it involuntarily, by force, is subject to corporal punishment.[166] Indeed, it is a more heinous sin than the slaying of a righteous man.[167] "There is no worse sin than this in the good religion, and it is proper to call those who commit it worthy of death in reality. If any one comes forth to them, and shall see them in the act, and is working with an ax, it is requisite for him to cut off the heads or to rip up the bellies of both, and it is no sin for him. But it is not proper to kill any person without the authority of high-priests and kings, except on account of committing or permitting unnatural intercourse." [168]

Nor are unnatural sins allowed to defile the land of the Lord. Whosoever shall commit such abominations, be he Israelite or stranger dwelling among the Israelites, shall be put to death, the souls that do them shall be cut off from their people. By unnatural sins of lust the Canaanites polluted their land, so that God visited their guilt, and the land spued out its inhabitants.[169]

This horror of homosexual practices was shared by Christianity. According to St. Paul, they form the climax of the moral corruption to which God gave over the heathen because of their apostasy from him.[170] Tertullian says that they are banished "not only from the threshold, but from all shelter of the church, because they are not sins, but monstrosities."[171] St. Basil maintains that they deserve the same punishment as murder, idolatry, and witchcraft.[172] According to a decree of the Council of Elvira, those who abuse boys to satisfy their lusts are denied communion even at their last hour.[173] In no other point of morals was the contrast between the teachings of Christianity and the habits and opinions of the world over which it spread more radical than in this. In Rome there was an old law of unknown date, called Lex Scantinia (or Scatinia), which imposed a mulct on him who committed pederasty with a free person;[174] but this law, of which very little is known, had lain dormant for ages, and the subject of ordinary homosexual intercourse had never afterwards attracted the attention of the pagan legislators.[175] But when Christianity became the religion of the Roman Empire, a veritable crusade was opened against it. Constantius and Constans made it a capital crime, punishable with the sword.[176] Valentinian went further still and ordered that those who were found guilty of it should be burned alive in the presence of all the people.[177] Justinian, terrified by certain famines, earthquakes, and pestilences, issued an edict which again condemned persons guilty of unnatural offenses to the sword, "lest, as the result of these impious acts, whole cities should perish together with their inhabitants," as we are taught by Holy Scripture that through such acts cities have perished with the men in them.[178] "A sentence of death and infamy," says Gibbon, "was often founded on the slight and suspicious evidence of a child or a servant, ... and pederasty became the crime of those to whom no crime could be imputed."[179]

This attitude towards homosexual practices had a profound and lasting influence on European legislation. Throughout the Middle Ages and later, Christian lawgivers thought that nothing but a painful death in the flames could atone for the sinful act.[180] In England Fleta speaks of the offender being buried alive;[181] but we are elsewhere told that burning was the due punishment.[182] As unnatural intercourse, however, was a subject for ecclesiastical cognizance, capital punishment could not be inflicted on the criminal unless the Church relinquished him to the secular arm; and it seems very doubtful whether she did relinquish him. Sir Frederick Pollack and Professor Maitland consider that the statute of 1533, which makes sodomy a felony, affords an almost sufficient proof that the temporal courts had not punished it, and that no one had been put to death for it for a very long time past.[183] It was said that the punishment for this crime—which the English law, in its very indictments, treats as a crime not fit to be named [184]—was determined to be capital by "the voice of nature and of reason, and the express law of God"; [185] and it remained so till 1861,[186] although in practice the extreme punishment was not inflicted.[187] In France persons were actually burned for this crime in the middle and latter part of the eighteenth century.[188] But in this, as in so many other respects, the rationalistic movement of that age brought about a change.[189] To punish sodomy with death, it was said, is atrocious; when unconnected with violence, the law ought to take no notice of it at all. It does not violate any other person's right, its influence on society is merely indirect, like that of drunkenness and free love; it is a disgusting vice, but its only proper punishment is contempt.[190] This view was adopted by the French "Code pénal," according to which homosexual practices in private, between two consenting adult parties, whether men or women, are absolutely unpunished. The homosexual act is treated as a crime only when it implies an outrage on public decency, or when there is violence or absence of consent, or when one of the parties is under age or unable to give valid consent.[191] This method of dealing with homosexuality has been followed by the legislators of various European countries,[192] and in those where the law still treats the act in question per se as a penal offense, notably in Germany, a propaganda in favor of its alteration is carried on with the support of many men of scientific eminence. This changed attitude of the law towards homosexual intercourse undoubtedly indicates a change of moral opinions. Though it is impossible to measure exactly the degree of moral condemnation, I suppose that few persons nowadays attach to it the same enormity of guilt as did our forefathers. And the question has even been put whether morality has anything at all to do with a sexual act, committed by the mutual consent of two adult individuals, which is productive of no offspring, and which on the whole concerns the welfare of nobody but the parties themselves.[193]

From this review of the moral ideas on the subject, incomplete though it be, it appears that homosexual practices are very frequently subject to some degree of censure, though the degree varies extremely. This censure is no doubt, in the first place, due to that feeling of aversion or disgust which the idea of homosexual intercourse tends to call forth in normally constituted adult individuals whose sexual instincts have developed under normal conditions. I presume that nobody will deny the general prevalence of such a tendency. It corresponds to that instinctive repugnance to sexual connections with women which is so frequently found in congenital inverts; whilst that particular form of it with which legislators have chiefly busied themselves evokes, in addition, a physical disgust of its own. And in a society where the large majority of people are endowed with normal sexual desires their aversion to homosexuality easily develops into moral censure and finds a lasting expression in custom, law, or religious tenets. On the other hand, where special circumstances have given rise to widely spread homosexual practices, there will be no general feeling of disgust even in the adults, and the moral opinion of the society will be modified accordingly. The act may still be condemned, in consequence of a moral doctrine formed under different conditions, or of the vain attempts of legislators to check sexual irregularities, or out of utilitarian considerations; but such a condemnation would in most people be rather theoretical than genuine. At the same time the baser forms of homosexual love may be strongly disapproved of for the same reasons as the baser forms of intercourse between men and women; and the passive pederast may be an object of contempt on account of the feminine practices to which he lends himself, as also an object of hatred on account of his reputation for sorcery. We have seen that the effeminate men are frequently believed to be versed in magic; [194] their abnormalities readily suggest that they are endowed with supernatural power, and they may resort to witchcraft as a substitute for their lack of manliness and physical strength. But the supernatural qualities or skill in magic ascribed to men who behave like women may also, instead of causing hatred, make them honored or reverenced.

It has been suggested that the popular attitude towards homosexuality was originally an aspect of economics, a question of under- or over-population, and that it was forbidden or allowed accordingly. Dr. Havelock Ellis thinks it probable that there is a certain relationship between the social reaction against homosexuality and against infanticide: "Where the one is regarded leniently and favorably, there generally the other is also; where the one is stamped out, the other is usually stamped out." [195] But our defective knowledge of the opinions of the various savage races concerning homosexuality hardly warrants such a conclusion; and if a connection really does exist between homosexual practices and infanticide it may be simply due to the numerical disproportion between the sexes resulting from the destruction of a multitude of female infants.[196] On the other hand, we are acquainted with several facts which are quite at variance with Dr. Ellis's suggestion. Among many Hindu castes female infanticide has for ages been a genuine custom,[197] and yet pederasty is remarkably rare among the Hindus. The ancient Arabs were addicted to infanticide,[198] but not to homosexual love,[199] whereas among modern Arabs the case is exactly the reverse. And if the early Christians deemed infanticide and pederasty equally heinous sins, they did so certainly not because they were anxious that the population should increase; if this had been their motive they would hardly have glorified celibacy. It is true that in a few cases the unproductiveness of homosexual love has been given by indigenous writers as a reason for its encouragement or condemnation. It was said that the Cretan law on the subject had in view to check the growth of population; but, like Dollinger,[200] I do not believe that this assertion touches the real root of the matter. More importance may be attached to the following passage in Pahlavi texts: "He who is wasting seed makes a practice of causing the death of progeny; when the custom is completely continuous, which produces an evil stoppage of the progress of the race, the creatures have become annihilated; and certainly, that action, from which, when it is universally proceeding, the depopulation of the world must arise, has become and furthered the greatest wish of Aharman." [201] I am, however, of opinion that considerations of this kind have generally played only a subordinate, if any, part in the formation of the moral opinions concerning homosexual practices. And it can certainly not be admitted that the severe Jewish law against sodomy was simply due to the fact that the enlargement of the population was a strongly felt social need among the Jews.[202] However much they condemned celibacy, they did not put it on a par with the abominations of Sodom. The excessive sinfulness which was attached to homosexual love by Zoroastrianism, Hebrewism, and Christianity, had quite a special foundation. It cannot be sufficiently accounted for either by utilitarian considerations or instinctive disgust. The abhorrence of incest is generally a much stronger feeling than the aversion to homosexuality. Yet in the very same chapter of Genesis which describes the destruction of Sodom and Gomorrah we read of the incest committed by the daughters of Lot with their father; [203] and according to the Roman Catholic doctrine, unnatural intercourse is an even more heinous sin than incest and adultery.[204] The fact is that homosexual practices were intimately associated with the gravest of all sins: unbelief, idolatry, or heresy.

According to Zoroastrianism, unnatural sin had been created by Angra Mainyu.[205] "Aharman, the wicked, mis-created the demons and fiends, and also the remaining cor, rupted ones, by his own unnatural intercourse."[206] Such intercourse is on a par with Afrasiyab, a Turanian king who conquered the Iranians for twelve years;[207] with Dahak, a king or dynasty who is said to have conquered Yim and reigned for a thousand years;[208] with Tur-i Bradar-vakhsh, a heterodox wizard by whom the best men were put to death.[209] He who commits unnatural sin is "in his whole being a Daeva";[210] and a Daeva-worshiper is not a bad Zoroastrian, but a man who does not belong to the Zoroastrian system, a foreigner, a non-Aryan.[211] In the Vendidad, after the statement that the voluntary commission of un-natural sin is a trespass for which there is no atonement for ever and ever, the question is put, When is it so? And the answer given is: If the sinner be a professor of the religion of Mazda, or one who has been taught in it. If not, his sin is taken from him, in case he makes confession of the religion of Mazda and resolves never to commit again such forbidden deeds.[212] This is to say, the sin is inexpiable if it involves a downright defiance of the true religion, it is for-given if it is committed in ignorance of it and is followed by submission. From all this it appears that Zoroastrianism stigmatized unnatural intercourse as a practice of infidels, as a sign of unbelief. And I think that certain facts referred to above help us to understand why it did so. Not only have homosexual practices been commonly associated with sor-cery, but such an association has formed, and partly still forms, an incident of the shamanistic system prevalent among the Asiatic peoples of Turanian stock, and that it did so already in remote antiquity is made extremely probable by statements which I have just quoted from Zoroastrian texts. To this system Zoroastrianism was naturally furiously opposed, and the "change of sex" therefore appeared to the Mazda worshiper as a devilish abomination.

So also the Hebrews' abhorrence of sodomy was largely due to their hatred of a foreign cult. According to Genesis, unnatural vice was the sin of a people who were not the Lord's people, and the Levitical legislation represents Canaanitish abominations as the chief reason why the Canaanites were exterminated.[213] Now we know that sodomy entered as an element in their religion. Besides *kedeshoth,* or female prostitutes, there were *kedeshim,* or male prostitutes, attached to their temples.[214] The word *kadesh,* translated "sodomite," properly denotes a man dedicated to a deity;[215] and it appears that such men were consecrated to the mother of the gods, the famous Dea Syria, whose priests or devotees they were considered to be.[216] The male devotees of this and other goddesses were probably in a position analogous to that occupied by the female devotees of certain gods, who also, as we have seen, have developed into libertines;[217] and the sodomitic acts committed with these temple prostitutes may, like the connections with priestesses, have had in view to transfer blessings to the worshipers.[218] In Morocco supernatural benefits are expected not only from heterosexual, but also from homosexual intercourse with a holy person. The *kedeshim* are frequently alluded to in the Old Testament, especially in the period of the monarchy, when rites of foreign origin made their way into both Israel and Judah.[219] And it is natural that the Yahveh worshiper should regard their practices with the utmost horror as forming part of an idolatrous cult.

The Hebrew conception of homosexual love to some extent affected Muhammedanism, and passed into Christianity. The notion that it is a form of sacrilege was here strengthened by the habits of the gentiles. St. Paul found the abominations of Sodom prevalent among nations who had "changed the truth of God into a lie, and worshiped and served the creature more than the Creator."[220] During the Middle Ages heretics were accused of unnatural vice as a matter of course.[221] Indeed, so closely was sodomy associated with heresy that the same name was applied to both. In "La Coutume de Touraine-Anjou" the word *herite,* which is the ancient form of *heretique,*[222] seems to be used in the sense of "sodomite"; [223] and the French *bougre* (from the Latin *Bulgarus,* Bulgarian), as also its English synonym, was originally a name given to a sect of heretics who came from Bulgaria in the eleventh century and was afterwards applied to other heretics, but at the same time it became the regular expression for a person guilty of unnatural intercourse.[224] In mediæval laws sodomy was also repeatedly mentioned together with heresy, and the punishment was the same for both.[225] It thus remained a religious offense of the first order. It was not only a "victim nefandum et super omnia detestandum," [226] but it was one of the four "clamantia peccata," or "crying sins," [227] a "crime de Majestie, vers le Roy celestre." [228] Very naturally, therefore, it has come to be regarded with somewhat greater leniency by law and public opinion in proportion as they have emancipated themselves from theological doctrines. And the fresh light which the scientific study of the sexual impulse has lately thrown upon the subject of homosexuality must also necessarily influence the moral ideas relating to it, in so far as no scrutinizing judge can fail to take into account the pressure which a powerful non-volitional desire exercises upon an agent's will.

NOTES

1 Karsch, "Päderastie und Tribadie bei den Tieren," in *Jahrbuch für sexuelle Zwischenstufen,* ii, p. 126 *sq.* Havelock Ellis, *Studies in the Psychology of Sex,* "Sexual Inversion," p. 2 *sqq.*

2 Cf. Ives, *Classification of Crimes,* p. 49. The statement that it is unknown among a certain people cannot reasonably mean that it may not be practiced in secret.

3 Von Spix and von Martius, *Travels in Brazil,* ii, p. 246; von Martius, *Von dem Rechtszustande unter den Ureinwohnern Brasiliens,* p. 27 *sq.;* Lomonaco, "Sulle razze indigene del Brasile," in *Archivio per l'antropologia e la etnologia,* xix, p. 46; Burton, *Arabian Nights,* x, p. 246 (Brazilian Indians); Garcilasso de la Vega, *First Part of the Royal Commentaries of the Yncas,* ii, p. 441 *sqq.;* Cieza de Leon, "La crónica del Perú (primera parte)," ch. 49, in *Biblioteca de autores españoles,* xxvi, p. 403 (Peruvian

Indians at the time of the Spanish conquest). Oviedo y Valdés, "Sumario de la natural historia de las Indias," ch. 81, in *Biblioteca de autores españoles,* xxii, p. 508 (Isthmians). Bancroft, *Native Races of the Pacific States,* i, p. 585 (Indians of New Mexico); ii, p. 467 *sq.* (Ancient Mexicans). Diaz del Castillo, "Conquista de Nueva-España," ch. 208, in *Biblioteca de autores españoles,* xxvi, p. 309 (Ancient Mexicans). Landa, *Relacion de las cosas de Yucatan,* p. 178 (Ancient Yucatans). Nuñez Cabeza de Vaca, "Naufragios y relacion de la jornada que hizo a la Florida," ch. 26, in *Biblioteca de autores españoles,* xxii, p. 538; Coreal, *Voyages aux Indes Occidentales,* i, p. 33 *sq.* (Indians of Florida). Perrin du Lac, *Voyage dans les deux Louisianes et chez les nations sauvages du Missouri,* p. 352; Bossu, *Travels Through Louisiana,* i, p. 303. Hennepin, *Nouvelle Découverte d'un très Grand Pays Situé dans L'Amérique,* p. 219 *sq.;* "La Salle's Last Expedition and Discoveries in North America," in *Collections of the New York Historical Society,* ii, p. 237 *sq.;* de Lahontan, *Mémoires de l'Amérique septentrionale,* p. 142 (Illinois). Marquetté, *Recit des Voyages,* p. 52 *sq.* (Illinois and Naudowessies). Wied-Neuwied, *Travels in the Interior of North America,* p. 351 (Manitaries, Mandans, etc.). McCoy, *History of Baptist Indian Missions,* p. 360 *sq.* (Osages). Heriot, *Travels Through the Canadas,* p. 278; Catlin, *North American Indians,* ii, p. 214 *sq.* (Sioux). Dorsey, "Omaha Sociology," in *Ann. Rep. Bur. Ethn.,* iii, p. 365; James, *Expedition from Pittsburgh to the Rocky Mountains,* i. p. 267 (Omahas). Loskiel, *History of the Mission of the United Brethren Among the Indians,* i. p. 14 (Iroquois). Richardson, *Arctic Searching Expedition,* ii, p. 42 (Cretes). Oswald, quoted by Bastian, *Der Mensch in der Geschichte,* iii, p. 314 (Indians of California). Holder, in *New York Medical Journal,* December 7, 1889, quoted by Havelock Ellis, *op. cit.,* p. 9 *sq.* (Indians of Washington and other tribes in the Northwestern United States). See also Karsch, "Uranismus oder Päderastie und Tribadie bei den Naturvölkern," in *Jahrbuch für sexuelle Zwischenstufen,* iii, p. 122 *sqq.*

[4] Lafitau, *Mœrs des sauvages amériquains,* i, pp. 603, 697, *sqq.*

[5] Dall, *Alaska,* p. 402; Bancroft, *op. cit.,* i, p. 92; Waitz, *Anthropologie der Naturvölker,* iii, p. 314 (Aleuts); von Langsdorf, *Voyages and Travels,* ii, p. 48 (Natives of Oonalaska); Steller, *Kamtschatka,* p. 289, *n.a.;* Georgi, *Russia,* iii, p. 132 *sq.* (Kamchadales).

[6] Davydow, quoted by Holmberg, "Ethnographische Skizzen über die völker des russischen Amerika," in *Acta Soc. Scientiarum Fennicæ,* iv, p. 400 *sq.* Lisiansky, *Voyage Round the World,* p. 109. Von Langsdorf, *op. cit.,* ii. p. 64. Sauer, *Billing's Expedition to the Northern Parts of Russia,* p. 176. Sarytschew, "Voyage of Discovery to the North-East of Siberia," in *Collection of Modern and Contemporary Voyages,* vi, p. 16.

[7] Bogoras, quoted by Demidoff, *Shooting Trip to Kamchatka,* p. 74 *sq.*

[8] Jochelson, *Koryak Religion and Myth,* pp. 52, 53, *n.* 3.

[9] *Ibid., op. cit.,* p. 52 *sq.*

[10] Wilken, "Plechtigheden en gebruiken bij verlovingen en hawelijken bij de volken van den Indischen Archipel," in *Bijdragen tot de taalland- en volkenkunde van Nederlandsch-Indie,* xxxiii (ser. v, vol. iv), p. 457 *sq.*

[11] Crawford, *History of the Indian Archipelago,* iii, p. 139. Marsden, *History of Sumatra,* p. 261.

[12] Junghuhn, *Die Battalander auf Sumatra,* ii, p. 157, *n.*

[13] Hardeland, *Dajacksch-deutsches Wörterbuch*, p. 53 *sq.* Schwaner, *Borneo*, i, p. 186. Perelaer, *Ethnographische beschrijving der Dajaks*, p. 32.

[14] Haddon, "Ethnography of the Western Tribe of Torres Straits," in *Jour. Anthr. Inst.*, xix, p. 315.

[15] Seligmann, "Sexual Inversion Among Primitive Races," in *The Alienist and Neurologist*, xxiii, p. 3 *sqq.*

[16] Beardmore, "Natives of Mowat, Daudai, New Guinea," in *Jour. Anthr. Inst.*, xix, p. 464. Haddon, *ibid.*, xix, p. 315.

[17] Hernsheim, *Beitrag zur Sprache der Marshall-Inseln*, p. 40. A different opinion is expressed by Senft, in Steinmetz, *Rechtsverhältnisse von eingeborenen Völkern in Afrika und Ozeanien*, p. 437.

[18] Remy, *Ka Moolelo Hawaii*, p. xliii.

[19] Turnbull, *Voyage Round the World*, p. 382. See: Wilson, *Missionary Voyage to the S. Pacific*, pp. 333, 361; Ellis, *Polynesian Researches*, i, pp. 246, 258.

[20] Foley, "Sur les habitations et les mœurs des Néo-Calédoniens," in *Bull. Soc. d'Anthrop. Paris*, ser. iii, vol. ii, p. 606. See: de Rochas, *Nouvelle Calédonie*, p. 235.

[21] Hardman, "Notes on Some Habits and Customs of the Natives of the Kimberley District," in *Proceed. Roy. Irish Academy*, ser. iii, vol. i, p. 74.

[22] *Ibid.*, pp. 71, 73.

[23] Purcell, "Rites and Customs of Australian Aborigines," in *Verhandl. Berliner Gesellsch. Anthrop.*, 1893, p. 287.

[24] Ravenscroft, "Some Habits and Customs of the Chingalee Tribe," in *Trans. Roy. Soc. South Australia*, xv, p. 122. I am indebted to Mr. N. W. Thomas for drawing my attention to these statements.

[25] Howitt, "Some Australian Ceremonies of Initiation," in *Jour. Anthr. Inst.*, xiii, p. 450.

[26] Lasnet, in *Annales d'hygiène et de médicine coloniales*, 1899, p. 494, quoted by Havelock Ellis, *op. cit.*, p. 10. Cf. Rencurel, in *Annales d'hygiène*, 1900, p. 562, quoted *ibid.*, p. 11 *sq.* See: Leguével de Lacombe, *Voyage à Madagascar*, i, p. 97 *sq.* Pederasty prevails to some extent in the island of Nossi-Bé, close to Madagascar, and is very common at Ankisimane, opposite to it, on Jassandava Bay (Walter, in Steinmetz, *Rechtsverhältnisse*, p. 376).

[27] De Flacourt, *Histoire de la grande isle Madagascar*, p. 86.

[28] Rautanen, in Steinmetz, *Rechtsverhältnisse*, p. 333.

[29] Nicole, *ibid.*, p. 111.

[30] *Ibid.*, p. 38.

[31] Munzinger, *Ostafrikanische Studien*, p. 525 (Barea and Kunáma). Baumann, "Conträre Sexual-Erscheinungen bei der Neger-Bevölkerung Zanzibars," in *Verhandl. der Berliner Gesellsch. für Anthropologie*, 1899, p. 668. Felkin, "Notes on the Waganda Tribe of Central Africa," in *Proceed. Roy. Soc. Edinburgh*, xiii, p. 723. Johnston, *British Central Africa*, p. 404 (Bakongo). Monrad, *Skildring of Guinea-Kysten*, p. 57 (Negroes of Accra). Torday and Joyce, "Ethnography of the Ba-Mbala," in *Jour. Anthr. Inst.*, xxxv, p. 410. Nicole, in Steinmetz, *Rechtsverhältnisse*, p. 111 (Muhammedan Negroes). Tellier, *ibid.*, p. 159 (Kreis Kita in the French

558 THE MAKING OF MAN

Soudan). Beverley, *ibid.*, p. 210 (Wagogo). Kraft, *ibid.*, p. 288 (Wapokomo).

32 Baumann, in *Verhandl. Berliner Gesellsch. Anthrop.*, 1899, p. 668, *sq.*

33 Burckhardt, *Travels in Nubia*, p. 135.

34 D'Escayrac de Lautre, *Afrikanische Wüste*, p. 93.

35 Burckhardt, *Travels in Arabia*, i, p. 364. See also Von Kremer, *Culturgeschichte des Orients*, ii, p. 269.

36 Burton, *Arabian Nights*, x, p. 232.

37 Kovalewsky, *Coutume contemporaine*, p. 340.

38 Polak, "Die Prostitution in Persien," in *Wiener Medizinische Wochenschrift*, xi, p. 627 *sqq*. *Idem, Persien*, i, p. 237. Burton, *Arabian Nights*, x, p. 233 *sq*. Wilson, *Persian Life and Customs*, p. 229.

39 Malcolm, *Sketch of the Sikhs*, p. 140. Havelock Ellis, *op. cit.*, p. 5, n. 2. Burton, *Arabian Nights*, x, p. 236.

40 Wilson, *Abode of Snow*, p. 420. Burton, *Arabian Nights*, x, p. 236.

41 Stavorinus, *Voyages to the East-Indies*, i, p. 456. Fryer, *New Account of East-India*, p. 97. Chevers, *Manual of Medical Jurisprudence for India*, p. 705.

42 Chevers, *op. cit.*, p. 708.

43 *Indo-Chinese Gleaner*, iii, p. 193. Wells Williams, *The Middle Kingdom*, i, p. 836. Matignon, "Deux mots sur la pédérastie en Chine," in *Archives d'anthropologie criminelle*, xiv, p. 38 *sqq*. Karsch, *Das gleichgeschlechtliche Leben der Ostasiaten*, p. 6 *sqq*.

44 Jways, "Nan sho k," in *Jahrbuch für sexuelle Zwischenstufen*, iv, pp. 266, 268, 270. Karsch, *op. cit.*, p. 71 *sqq*.

45 Dionysius of Halicarnassus, *Antiquitates Romanæ*, vii., p. 2. *Athenæus, Deipnosophistæ*, xii, p. 518 (Etruscans). Rein, *Criminalrecht der Römer*, p. 863.

46 Polybius, *Historiæ*, xxxii, 11, p. 5.

47 Buret, *La syphilis aujourd'hui et chez les anciens*, p. 197 *sqq*. Catullus, *Carmina*, lxi ("In Nuptias Juliæ et Manlii"), p. 128 *sqq*. Cf. Martial, *Epigrammata*, viii, 44, p. 16 *sq*.

48 Juvenal, *Satiræ*, ii, p. 117 *sqq*. Martial, *op. cit.*, xii, p. 42.

49 Diodorus Siculus, *Bibliotheca historica*, vol. xxxii, p. 7. Aristotle, *Politica*, ii, 9, p. 1269 b.

50 "Spuren von Konträrsexualität bei den alten Skandinaviern," in *Jahrbuch für sexuelle Zwischenstufen*, iv, p. 244 *sqq*.

51 Hahn, *Albanesische, Studien*, i, p. 168.

52 Karsch, in *Jahrbuch für sexuelle Zwischenstufen*, iii, p. 85 *sqq*. Ploss-Bartels, *Das Weib*, i, p. 517 *sqq*. Von Krafft-Ebing, *Psychopathia sexualis*, p. 278 *sqq*. Moll, *Die Conträre Sexualempfindung*, p. 247 *sqq*. Havelock Ellis, *op. cit.*, p. 118 *sqq*.

53 Magalhanes de Gandavo, *Histoire de la Province de Sancta-Cruz*, p. 116 *sq*.

54 Dall, *op. cit.*, p. 139.

55 Fritsch, quoted by Karsch, in *Jahrbuch für sexuelle Zwischenstufen*, iii, p. 87 *sq*.

56 Fritsch, *Die Eingeborenen Süd-Afrika's*, p. 227. Cf. Schinz, *Deutsch-Südwest-Afrika*, pp. 173, 177.

57 Baumann, in *Verhandl. Berliner Gesellsch. Anthrop.*, 1889, p. 668 *sq*

[58] Havelock Ellis, *op. cit.*, p. 123.

[59] Jacobs, *Eenigen tijd onder de Baliërs*, p. 134 *sq.*

[60] Havelock Ellis, *op. cit.*, p. 124 *sq.*

[61] See *ibid.*, p. 121 *sq.*

[62] Another reason for such practices is given by Mr. Beardmore (in *Jour. Anthrop. Inst.*, xix, p. 464), with reference to the Papuans of Mowat. He says that they indulge in sodomy because too great increase of population is undesired amongst the younger portion of the married people. Cf. *infra*, p. 484 *sqq.*

[63] Havelock Ellis, *op. cit.*, p. 1.

[64] Jochelson, *op. cit.*, p. 52 *sq.*

[65] Holder, quoted by Havelock Ellis, *op. cit.*, p. 9 *sq.*

[66] Baumann, in *Verhandl. Berliner Gesellsch. Anthrop.*, 1899, p. 668 *sq.*

[67] Cf. Féré, *L'instinct sexuel*, quoted by Havelock Ellis, *op. cit.*, p. 41.

[68] James, *Principles of Psychology*, ii, p. 439. See also Ives, *op. cit.*, p. 56 *sqq.*

[69] Dr. Dessoir ("Zur Psychologie der Vita sexualis," in *Allgemeine Zeitschrift für Psychiatrie*, i, p. 942) even goes so far as to conclude that "an undifferentiated sexual feeling is normal, on the average, during the first years of puberty." But this is certainly an exaggeration (cf. Havelock Ellis, *op. cit.*, p. 47 *sq.*).

[70] Karsch, in *Jahrbuch für sexuelle Zwischenstufen*, ii, p. 126 *sqq.* Havelock Ellis, *op. cit.*, p. 2 *sq.*

[71] Havelock Ellis, *op. cit.*, p. 2.

[72] Von den Steinen, *Unter den Naturvölkern Zentral-Brasiliens*, p. 502.

[73] Ellis, *Polynesian Researches*, i, p. 257 *sq.*

[74] Matignon, in *Archives d'anthropologie criminelle*, xiv, p. 42. Karsch, *op. cit.*, p. 32 *sqq.*

[75] Waitz, *Anthropologie der Naturvölker*, iii, p. 113. Bastian, *Der Mensch in der Geschichte*, iii, p. 305 (Dohomans).

[76] *Supra*, ii, p. 462. Karsch, *op. cit.*, pp. 6 (China), 76 *sqq.* (Japan), 132 (Corea).

[77] See Voltaire, *Dictionnaire philosophique*, "Amour Socratique" (Œuvres, vii, p. 82); Buret, *Syphilis in the Middle Ages and in Modern Times*, p. 88 *sq.*

[78] Cf. Havelock Ellis, *op. cit.*, p. 5.

[79] Freeman, *Reign of William Rufus*, i, p. 159.

[80] Polak, in *Wiener Medizinische Wochenschrift*, xi, p. 628.

[81] Marquette, *op. cit.*, p. 53 (Illinois). Perrin du Lac, *Voyage dans les deux Louisianes et chez les nations sauvages du Missouri*, p. 352. Cf. Nuñez Cabeza de Vaca, *loc. cit.*, p. 538 (concerning the Indians of Florida):—
"... tiran arco y llevan muy gran carga."

[82] Steinmetz, *Rechtsverhältnisse*, p. 38.

[83] Havelock Ellis, *op. cit.*, p. 3.

[84] Krafft-Ebing, *op. cit.*, p. 211 *sq.*

[85] Moll, *op. cit.*, p. 157 *sqq.*

[86] Havelock Ellis, *op. cit.*, p. 50 *sq.* Cf. *ibid.*, p. 181 *sqq.*

[87] *Ibid.*, p. 3.

[88] Cf. Norman, "Sexual Perversion," in Tuke's *Dictionary of Psychological Medicine*, ii, p. 1156.

[89] Havelock Ellis, *op. cit.*, p. 191.

[90] Dr. Havelock Ellis also admits (*op. cit.*, p. 190) that if in early life the sexual instincts are less definitely determined than when adolescence is complete, "it is conceivable, though unproved, that a very strong impression, acting even on a normal organism, may cause arrest of sexual development on the psychic side. It is a question," he adds, "I am not in a position to settle."

[91] Voltaire, *Dictionnaire Philosophique*, art. "Amour Socratique," (Œuvres, vii, p. 81). Cf. Ovid, *Metamorphoses*, x, p. 84 *seq.*

[92] Servius, *In Vergilii Æneidos*, x, p. 325. For the whole subject of pederasty among the Dorians see Mueller, *History and Antiquities of the Doric Race*, ii, p. 307 *sq.*

[93] Ælian, *Varia historia*, iii, p. 10.

[94] Mueller, *op. cit.*, ii, p. 308.

[95] Xenophon, *Historia Graca*, iv, p. 8.

[96] Plutarch, *Lycurgus*, xxv, p. i.

[97] *Ibid.*, xviii, p. 8. Ælian, *op. cit.*, iii, p. 10.

[98] Ælian, *op. cit.*, iii, p. 9. Athenæus, *Deipnosophistæ*, xiii, 77, p. 601.

[99] Cf. Symonds, "Die Homosexualität in Griechenland," in Havelock Ellis and Symonds, *Das Konträre Geschlechtsgefühl*, p. 55.

[100] *Ibid.*, p. 116. Döllinger, *The Gentile and the Jew*, ii, p. 244.

[101] Plato, *Leges*, i, p. 636. Cf. Plutarch, *Amatorius*, v, p. 9.

[102] Plato, *Symposium*, p. 192.

[103] "State of Female Society in Greece," in *Quarterly Review*, xxii, p. 172 *sqq.* Lecky, *History of European Morals*, ii, p. 287. Döllinger, *op. cit.*, ii, p. 234.

[104] Plato, *Symposium*, p. 181. That the low state of the Greek women was instrumental to pederasty has been pointed out by Döllinger (*op. cit.*, ii, p. 244) and Symonds (*loc. cit.*, pp. 77, 100, 101, 116 *sqq.*).

[105] Plato, *Symposium*, p. 181.

[106] Matignon, in *Archives d'anthropologie criminelle*, xiv, p. 41.

[107] Junghuhn, *op. cit.*, ii, p. 157, *n.*

[108] Schwaner, *op. cit.*, i, p. 186.

[109] Ellis, *Polynesian Researches*, i, p. 258. Cf. Moerenhout, *Voyages aux îes du Grand Océan*, ii, p. 167 *sq.*

[110] De Flacourt, *op. cit.*, p. 86.

[111] Walter, in Steinmetz, *Rechtsverhältnisse*, p. 376.

[112] Veniaminof, quoted by Petroff, *Report on Alaska*, p. 158.

[113] *Ibid.*, p. 158:—"The offender desirous of unburdening himself selected a time when the sun was clear and unobscured; he picked up certain weeds and carried them about his person; then deposited them and threw his sin upon them, calling the sun as a witness, and, when he had eased his heart of all that had weighed upon it, he threw the grass or weeds into the fire, and after that considered himself cleansed of his sin."

[114] Davydow, quoted by Holmberg, *loc. cit.*, p. 400 *sq.* Lisianski, *op. cit.*, p. 199.

[115] Bogoras, quoted by Demidoff, *op. cit.*, p. 75. Jochelson, *op. cit.*, p. 52 *sq.*

[116] Marquette, *op. cit.*, p. 53 *sq.*

[117] Catlin, *North American Indians*, ii, p. 214 *sq.*

[118] "La Salle's Last Expedition in North America," in *Collections of the New York Historical Society*, ii, p. 238 (Illinois). Perrin du Lac, *Voyage*

dans les deux Louisianes et chez les nations sauvages du Missouri, p. 352. Bossu, *op. cit.*, i, p. 303 (Choctaws). Oviedo y Valdés, *loc. cit.*, p. 508 (Isthmians). Von Martius, *Von dem Rechtszustande unter d. Urein-wohnern Brasiliens*, p. 28 (Guayeurius).

[119] Cieza de Leon, *Segunda parte de la Crónica del Perú*, ch. 25, p. 99. See also *idem, Crónica del Perú (primera parte)*, ch. 64. *Biblioteca de auteres españoles*, xxvi, p. 416 *sq.*).

[120] *Idem, Segunda parte de la Crónica del Perú*, ch. 25, p. 98. See also Garcilasso de la Vega, *op. cit.*, ii, p. 132.

[121] Las Casas, quoted by Bancroft, *op. cit.*, ii, p. 467 *sq.* Cf. *ibid.*, ii, p. 677.

[122] Clavigero, *History of Mexico*, i, p. 357.

[123] Squier, "Archæology and Ethnology of Nicaragua," in *Trans. American Ethn. Soc.*, iii, pt. i, p. 128.

[124] Bancroft, *op. cit.*, ii, p. 677.

[125] Piedrahita, *Historia general de las conquistas del nuevo reyno de Granada*, p. 46.

[126] See *supra*, i, pp. 186, 195.

[127] Kubary, "Die Verbrechen und das Strafverfahren auf den Pelau-Inseln," in *Original-Mittheilungen aus der ethnologischen Abtheilung der königlichen Museen zu Berlin*, i, p. 84.

[128] Kovalewsky, *Coutume contemporaine*, p. 340.

[129] Merker, *Die Masai*, p. 208. The Masai, however, slaughter at once any bullock or he-goat which is noticed to practice unnatural intercourse for fear lest otherwise their herds should be visited by a plague as a divine punishment (*ibid.*, p. 159).

[130] Warner, in Maclean, *Compendium of Kafir Laws*, p. 62.

[131] Rautanen, in Steinmetz, *Rechsverhältnisse*, p. 333 *sq.*

[132] Lang, *ibid.*, p. 232.

[133] Felkin, in *Proceed. Roy. Soc. Edinburgh*, xiii, p. 723.

[134] Monrad, *op. cit.*, p. 57.

[135] Burckhardt, *Travels in Nubia*, p. 135.

[136] *Koran*, iv, p. 20.

[137] Sachau, *Muhammedanisches Recht nach Schafitischer Lehre*, pp. 809, 818:—"Sodomita si muhsan (that is, a married person in possession of full civic rights) est punitur lapidatione, si non est *muhsan* punitur et flagellatione et exsilio."

[138] Burton, *Arabian Nights*, x, p. 224.

[139] Polak, in *Wiener Medizinische Wochenschrift*, xi, p. 628 *sq.*

[140] Baumann, in *Verhandl. Berliner Gesellsch. Anthrop.*, 1899, p. 669.

[141] Chevers, *op. cit.*, p. 708. Burton, *Arabian Nights*, x, p. 237.

[142] Burton, *Arabian Nights*, x, p. 222 *sq.*

[143] *Laws of Manu*, xi, p. 175. Cf. *Institutes of Vishnu*, liii, p. 4; *Apastamba*, i, 9, 26, p. 7; *Gautama*, xxv, p. 7.

[144] Alabaster, *Notes and Commentaries on Chinese Criminal Law*, p. 367 *sqq. Ta Tsing Leu Lee*, Appendix, no. xxxii, p. 570.

[145] Alabaster, *op. cit.*, p. 369.

[146] Matignon, in *Archives d'anthropologie criminelle*, xiv, pp. 42, 43, 52.

[147] *Ibid.*, p. 44.

[148] Karsch, *op. cit.*, p. 99.

[149] Jwaya, in *Jahrbuch für sexuelle Zwischenstufen*, iv, pp. 266, 270 *sq.*

[150] Tacitus, *Germania*, p. 12.

[151] "Spuren von Konträrsexualität, bei den alten Skandinaviern—Mitteilungen eines norwegischen Gelehrten," in *Jahrbuch für sexuelle Zwischenstufen*, iv, pp. 245, 256 *sqq.*

[152] Xenophon, *Lacedæmoniorum respublica*, ii, p. 13. Maximus Tyrius, *Dissertationes*, xxv, p. 4; xxvi, p. 9.

[153] Æschines, *Contra Timarchum*, p. 21.

[154] Ælian, *Varia historia*, iii, p. 10. Cf. Plato, *Leges*, viii, p. 910.

[155] Ælian, *op. cit.*, iii, p. 12. Cf. Maximus Tyrius, *op. cit.*, xxvi, p. 8.

[156] Cf. Symonds, *loc. cit.*, p. 92 *sqq.*

[157] Plato, *Symposium*, p. 178.

[158] *Ibid.*, p. 182.

[159] Hieronymus, the Peripatetic, referred to by Athenæus, *op. cit.*, xiii, 78, p. 602. See also Maximus Tyrius, *op. cit.*, xxiv, p. 2.

[160] Plutarch, *Amatorius*, xvii, p. 14.

[161] Plato, *Symposium*, p. 178.

[162] Herodotus, i, p. 135.

[163] Ammanianus Marcellinus says (xxiii, p. 76) that the inhabitants of Persia were free from pederasty. But see also Sextus Empiricus, *Pyrrhoniæ hypotyposes*, i, p. 152.

[164] *Vendidâd*, i, p. 12; vii, p. 27.

[165] Darmesteter, in *Sacred Books of the East*, lv, p. lxxxvi.

[166] *Vendidâd*, viii, p. 26.

[167] *Dînâ-i Maînôg-î Khirad*, xxxvi, p. 1 *sqq.*

[168] *Sad Dar*, ix, p. 2 *sqq.*

[169] *Leviticus*, xviii: 22, 24 *sqq.; xx: 13.*

[170] *Romans*, i: 26 *sq.*

[171] Tertullian, *De pudicitia*, p. 4 (Migne, *Patrologiæ cursus*, ii, p. 987).

[172] St. Basil, quoted by Bingham, *Works*, vi, p. 432 *sq.*

[173] *Concilium Elibertianum*, ch. 71 (Labbe-Mansi, *Sacrorum Conciliorum collectio*, ii, p. 17).

[174] Juvenal, *Satiræ*, ii, p. 43 *sq.* Valerius Maximus, *Facta dictaque memorabilia*, vi, 1, p. 7. Quintilian, *Institutio oratoria*, iv, 2, p. 69:—"Decem milia, quæ pœna stupratori constituta est, dabit." Christ, *Hist. Legis Scatiniæ*, quoted by Döllinger, *op. cit.*, ii, p. 274. Rein, *Criminalrecht der Römer*, p. 865 *sq.* Bingham, *op. cit.*, vi, p. 433 *sqq.* Mommsen, *Römisches Strafrecht*, p. 703 *sq.*

[175] Mommsen, *op. cit.*, p. 704. Rein, *op. cit.*, p. 866. The passage in *Digesta*, xlviii, 5, 35, p. 1, refers to *stuprum* independently of the sex of the victim.

[176] *Codex Theodosianus*, ix, pp. 7, 3. *Codex Justinianus*, ix, pp. 9, 30.

[177] *Codex Theodosianus*, ix, pp. 7, 6.

[178] *Novellæ*, p. 77. See also *ibid.*, p. 141, and *Institutiones*, iv, pp. 18, 4.

[179] Gibbon, *History of the Decline and Fall of the Roman Empire*, v, p. 323.

[180] Du Boys, *Histoire du droit criminel de l'Espagne*, pp. 93, 403. *Les Establissements de Saint Louis*, i, p. 90; ii, p. 147. Beaumanoir, *Coutumes du beauvoisis*, xxx, II; vol. 1, p. 413. Montesquieu, *De l'esprit des lois*, xii, p. 6 (*Œuvres*, p. 283). Hume, *Commentaries on the Law of Scotland*, ii, p. 335; Pitcairn, *Criminal Trials in Scotland*, ii, p. 491, *n.* 2. Clarus, *Practica criminalis*, book v. . . . . In the beginning of the nineteenth

century sodomy was still nominally subject to capital punishment by burning in Bavaria (von Feuerbach, *Kritik des Kleinschrodischen Entwurf's zu einem peinlichen Gesetzbuche für die Chur-Pfalz-Bayrischen Stäaten*, ii, p. 13), and in Spain as late as 1843 (Du Boys, *op. cit.*, p. 721).

181 Fleta, i, 37, 3, p. 84.

182 Britton, i, p. 10; vol. i, p. 42.

183 Pollock and Maitland, *History of English Law Before the Time of Edward I*, ii, p. 556 *sq.*

184 Coke, *Third Part of the Institutes of the Laws of England*, p. 58 *et seq.* Blackstone, *Commentaries on the Laws of England*, iv, p. 218.

185 Blackstone, *op. cit.*, iv, p. 218.

186 Stephen, *History of the Criminal Law of England*, i, p. 475.

187 Blackstone, *op. cit.*, iv, p. 218.

188 Desmaze, *Pénalités anciennes*, p. 211. Havelock Ellis, *op. cit.*, p. 207.

189 Numa Prætorius, *loc. cit.*, p. 121 *sqq.*

190 Note of the editors of Kehl's edition of Voltaire's *Prix de la justice et de l'humanité*, in *Œuvres complètes*, v. 437, *n.* 2.

191 Code Pénal, 330 *sqq.* Cf. Chevalier, *L'inversion sexuelle*, p. 431 *sqq.* Havelock Ellis, *op. cit.*, p. 207 *sq.*

192 Numa Prætorius, *loc. cit.*, pp. 131-133, 143 *sqq.*

193 See, *e.g.* Bax, *Ethics of Socialism*, p. 126.

194 See also Bastian, in *Zeitschr. f. Ethnol.* i, 88 *sq.* Speaking of the witches of Fez, Leo Africanus says (*History and Description of Africa*, ii, p. 458) that "they haue a damnable custome to commit vulawfull Venerie among themselves." Among the Patagonians, according to Falkner (*Description of Patagonia*, p. 117), the male wizards are chosen for their office when they are children, and "a preference is always shown to those who at that early time of life discover an effeminate disposition." They are obliged, as it were, to leave their sex, and to dress themselves in female apparel.

195 Havelock Ellis, *op. cit.*, p. 206.

196 Cf. *supra*, ii, p. 466 (Society Islanders).

197 *Supra*, i, p. 407.

198 *Supra*, i, p. 406 *sq.*

199 Von Kremer, *Culturgeschichte des Orients*, ii, p. 129.

200 Döllinger, *op. cit.*, ii, p. 239.

201 *Dadistan-i Dinik*, lxxvii, II.

202 Havelock Ellis, *op. cit.*, p. 206.

203 *Genesis*, xix, p. 31 *sqq.*

204 Thomas Aquinas, *Summa theologica*, ii, iii. 154, 12. Katz, *Grundriss des kanonischen Strafrechts*, pp. 104, 118, 120. Clarus, *Practica criminalis*, book v. #Sodomia, Additiones, i (*Opera omnia*, ii, p. 152): "Hoc vitium est majus, quam si quis propriam matrem cognosceret."

205 *Vendidad*, i, p. 12.

206 *Dînâ-î Maînôg-î Khirad*, viii, p. 10.

207 *Sad Dar*, ix, p. 5. West's note to *Dînâ-î Maînôg-î Khirad*, viii, p. 29 (*Sacred Books of the East*, xxiv, p. 35, *n.* 4).

208 *Sad Dar*, ix, p. 5. West's note to *Dînâ-î Maînôg-î Khirad*, viii, p. 29 (*Sacred Books of the East*, xxiv, p. 35, *n.* 3).

209 *Sad Dar*, ix, p. 5. West's note to *Dadistan-i Dinik*, lxxii, p. 8 (*Sacred Books of the East*, xviii, p. 218).

[210] *Vendidad,* viii, p. 32.

[211] Darmesteter, in *Sacred Books of the East,* iv, p. ii.

[212] *Vendidad,* viii, p. 27 *sq.*

[213] *Leviticus,* xx, 23.

[214] *Deuteronomy,* xxiii, 17. Driver, *Commentary on Deuteronomy,* p. 264.

[215] Driver, *op. cit.,* p. 264 *sq.* Selbie, "Sodomite," in Hastings, *Dictionary of the Bible,* iv, p. 559.

[216] St. Jerome, *In Osee,* i, pp. 4, 14 (Migne, *op. cit.,* xxv, 851). Cook's note to I *Kings,* xiv, 24, in his edition of *The Holy Bible,* ii, p. 571.

[217] *Supra,* ii, p. 444.

[218] Rosenbaum suggests (*Geschichte der Lustseuche im Alterthume,* p. 120) that the eunuch priests connected with the cult of the Ephesian Artemis and the Phrygian worship of Cybele likewise were sodomites.

[219] I *Kings,* xiv, 24; xv, 12; xxii, 46. II *Kings,* xxiii, 7. *Job,* xxxvi, 14. Driver, *op. cit.,* p. 265.

[220] *Romans,* i, 25 *sqq.*

[221] Littre, *Dictionnaire de la langue française,* i, p. 386. "Bougre." Haynes, *Religious Persecution,* p. 54.

[222] Littre, *op. cit.,* i, p. 2010, "Heretique."

[223] *Les Establissements de Saint Louis,* i, p. 90; ii, p. 147. Viollet, in his Introduction to the same work, i, p. 254.

[224] Littre, *op. cit.,* i, p. 386, "Bougre." Murray, *New English Dictionary,* i, p. 1160, "Bugger." Lea, *History of the Inquisition of the Middle Ages,* i, p. 115, note.

[225] Beaumanoir, *Coutumes du Beauvoisis,* xxx, II, vol. i, p. 413: "Qui erre contre le foi, comme en méscreance, de le quele il ne veut venir a voie de verité, ou qui fet sodomiterie, il droit estre ars, et forfet tout le sien en le manière dessus." Britton, i, p. 10, vol. i, p. 42. Montesquieu, *De l'esprit des lois,* xii, 6 (*Œuvres,* p. 283). Du Boys, *Histoire du droit criminel de l'Espagne,* pp. 486, 721.

[226] Clarus, *Practica criminalis,* book v. #Sodomia, I (*Opera omnia,* ii, p. 151).

[227] Coke, *Third Part of the Institutes of the Laws of England,* p. 59.

[228] *Mirror,* quoted *ibid.,* p. 58.

THE RELATIONS BETWEEN THE SEXES IN TRIBAL LIFE *

By BRONISLAW MALINOWSKI

MAN and woman in the Trobriand Islands—their relations in love, in marriage, and in tribal life—this will be the subject of the present study.

The most dramatic and intense stage in the intercourse between man and woman, that in which they love, mate, and produce children, must occupy the dominant place in any consideration of the sexual problem. To the average normal person, in whatever type of society we find him, attraction by the other sex and the passionate and sentimental episodes which follow are the most significant events in his existence, those most deeply associated with his intimate happiness and with the zest and meaning of life. To the sociologist, therefore, who studies a particular type of society, those of its customs, ideas, and institutions which center round the erotic life of the individual should be of primary importance. For if he wants to be in tune with his subject and to place it in a natural, correct perspective, the sociologist must, in his research, follow the trend of personal values and interests. That which means supreme happiness to the individual must be made a fundamental factor in the scientific treatment of human society.

But the erotic phase, although the most important, is only one among many in which the sexes meet and enter into relations with each other. It cannot be studied outside its proper context, without, that is, being linked up with the legal status of man and woman; with their domestic relations; and with the distribution of their economic functions. Courtship, love, and mating in a given society

* The Sexual Life of Savages. New York: Horace Liveright.

are influenced in every detail by the way in which the sexes face one another in public and in private, by their position in tribal law and custom, by the manner in which they participate in games and amusements, by the share each takes in ordinary daily toil.

The story of a people's love-making necessarily has to begin with an account of youthful and infantile associa tions, and it leads inevitably forward to the later stage of permanent union and marriage. Nor can the narrative break off at this point, since science cannot claim the privilege of fiction. The way in which men and women arrange their common life and that of their children reacts upon their love-making, and the one stage cannot be properly under-stood without a knowledge of the other.

This book deals with sexual relations among the natives of the Trobriand Islands, a coral archipelago lying to the northeast of New Guinea. These natives belong to the Papuo-Melanesian race, and in their physical appearance, mental equipment, and social organization combine a ma-jority of Oceanic characteristics with certain features of the more backward Papuan population from the mainland of New Guinea.[1]

I

THE PRINCIPLES OF MOTHER-RIGHT

We find in the Trobriands a matrilineal society, in which descent, kinship, and every social relationship are legally reckoned through the mother only, and in which women have a considerable share in tribal life, even to the taking of a leading part in economic, ceremonial, and magical activities—a fact which very deeply influences all the cus-toms of erotic life as well as the institution of marriage. It will be well, therefore, first to consider the sexual rela-tion in its widest aspect, beginning with some account of those features of custom and tribal law which underlie the institution of mother-right, and the various views and conceptions, which throw light upon it; after this, a short sketch of each of the chief domains of tribal life—domestic, economic, legal, ceremonial, and magical—will combine to show the respective spheres of male and female activity among these natives.

The idea that it is solely and exclusively the mother who builds up the child's body, the man in no way contributing to its formation, is the most important factor in the legal system of the Trobrianders. Their views on the process of procreation, coupled with certain mythological and animistic beliefs, affirm, without doubt or reserve, that the child is of the same substance as its mother, and that between the father and the child there is no bond of physical union whatsoever.

That the mother contributes everything to the new being to be born of her is taken for granted by the natives, and forcibly expressed by them. "The mother feeds the infant in her body. Then, when it comes out, she feeds it with her milk." "The mother makes the child out of her blood." "Brothers and sisters are of the same flesh, because they come of the same mother." These and similar expressions describe their attitude towards this, their fundamental principle of kinship.

This attitude is also to be found embodied, in an even more telling manner, in the rules governing descent, inheritance, succession in rank, chieftainship, hereditary offices, and magic—in every regulation, in fact, concerning transmission by kinship. Social position is handed on in the mother-line from a man to his sister's children, and this exclusively matri-lineal conception of kinship is of paramount importance in the restrictions and regulations of marriage, and in the taboos on sexual intercourse. The working of these ideas of kinship can be observed, breaking out with a dramatic intensity, at death. For the social rules underlying burial, lamentation, and mourning, together with certain very elaborate ceremonies of food distribution, are based on the principle that people joined by the tie of maternal kinship form a closely knit group, bound by an identity of feelings, of interests, and of flesh. And from this group even those united to it by marriage and by the father-to-child relation are sharply excluded, as having no natural share in the bereavement.

These natives have a well-established institution of marriage, and yet are quite ignorant of the man's share in the begetting of children. At the same time, the term "father" has, for the Trobriander, a clear, though exclusively social, definition: it signifies the man married to the mother, who lives in the same house with her, and forms part of the household. The father, in all discussions about relationship, was pointedly described to me as *tomakava,* a "stranger," or, even more correctly, an "outsider." This expression would also frequently be used by natives in conversation, when they were arguing some point of inheritance or trying to justify some line of behavior, or again when the position of the father was to be belittled in some quarrel.

It will be clear to the reader, therefore, that the term "father," as I use it here, must be taken, not as having the various legal, moral, and biological implications that it holds for us, but in a sense entirely specific to the society with which we are dealing. It might seem better, in order to avoid any chance of such misconception, not to have used our word "father" at all, but rather the native one *tama,* and to have spoken of the *"tama* relationship" instead of "fatherhood"; but, in practice, this would have proved too unwieldy. The reader, therefore, when he meets the word "father" in these pages, should never forget that it must be defined, not as in the English dictionary, but in accordance with the facts of native life. I may add that this rule applies to all terms which carry special sociological implication, that is to all terms of relationship, and such words as "marriage," "divorce," "betrothal," "love," "courtship," and the like.

What does the word *tama* (father) express to the native? "Husband of my mother" would be the answer first given by an intelligent informant. He would go on to say that his *tama* is the man in whose loving and protecting company he has grown up. For, since marriage is patrilocal in the Trobriands, since the woman, that is to say, moves to her husband's village community and lives in his house, the father is a close companion to his children; he takes an active part in the cares which are lavished upon them, invariably feels and shows a deep affection for them, and later has a share in their education. The word *tama* (father) condenses, therefore, in its emotional meaning, a host of experiences by early childhood, and expresses the typical sentiment existing between a boy or girl and a mature affectionate man of the same household; while socially it denotes the male person who stands in an intimate relation to the mother, and who is master of the household.

So far *tama* does not differ essentially from "father" in our sense. But as soon as the child begins to grow up and take an interest in things outside the affairs of the household and its own immediate needs, certain complications arise, and change the meaning of *tama* for him. He learns that he is not of the same clan as his *tama,* that his totemic appellation is different, and that it is identical with that of his mother. At the same time he learns that all sorts of duties, restrictions, and concerns for personal pride unite him to his mother and separate him from his father. Another man appears on the horizon, and is called by the child *ḳadagu* ("my mother's brother"). This man lives in the same locality, but he is just as likely to reside in another village. The child also learns that the place where his *ḳada* (mother's brother) resides is also his, the child's, "own village"; that there he has property and his other rights of citizenship; that there his future career awaits him; that there his natural allies and associates are to be found. He may even be taunted in the village of his birth with being an "outsider" (*tomaḳava*), while in the village he has to call "his own," in which his mother's brother lives, his father is a stranger and he a natural citizen. He also sees, as he grows up, that the mother's brother assumes a gradually increasing authority over him, requiring his services, helping him in some things, granting or withholding his permission to carry out certain actions; while the father's authority and counsel become less and less important.

Thus the life of a Trobriander runs under a two-fold influence—a duality which must not be imagined as a mere surface play of custom. It enters deeply into the existence of every individual, it produces strange complications of usage, it creates frequent tensions and difficulties, and not seldom gives rise to violent breaks in the continuity of tribal life. For this dual influence of paternal love and the matrilineal principle which penetrates so far into the framework of institutions and into the social ideas and sentiments of the native, is not, as a matter of fact, quite well adjusted in its working.[2]

It has been necessary to emphasize the relationship between a Trobriander and his father, his mother, and his mother's brother, for this is the nucleus of the complex system of mother-right or matriliny, and this system governs the whole social life of these natives. The question is, moreover, especially related to the main theme of this book: love-making, marriage, and kinship are three aspects of the same subject; they are the three facets which it presents in turn to sociological analysis.

II

A TROBRIAND VILLAGE

We have so far given the sociological definition of fatherhood, of the mother's brother's relation, and of the nature of the bond between mother and child; a bond founded on the biological facts of gestation and the extreme close psychological attachment which results from these. The best way to make this abstract statement clear will be to display the inter-working of the three relationships in an actual community in the Trobriands. Thus we can make our explanations concrete and get into touch with actual life instead of moving among abstractions; and, incidentally, too, we can introduce some personalities who will appear in the later parts of our narrative.

The village of Omarakana is, in a sense, the capital of Kiriwina, the main district of these islands. It is the residence of the principal chief, whose name, prestige, and renown are carried far and wide over the Archipelagoes, though his power does not reach beyond the province of Kiriwina.[3] The village lies on a fertile, level plain in the northern part of the large, flat coral island of Boyowa. As we walk towards it, from the lagoon anchorages on the western shore, the level road leads across monotonous stretches covered with low scrub, here and there broken by a tabooed grove, or by a large garden, holding vines trained on long poles and looking, in its developed form, like an exuberant hop-yard. We pass several villages on our way; the soil becomes more fertile and the settlement denser as we approach the long ridge of raised coral outcrop which runs along the eastern shore and shuts off the open sea from the inland plains of the island.

A large clump of trees appears at a distance—these are the fruit trees, the palms and the piece of uncut virgin jungle which together surround the village of Omarakana. We pass the grove and find ourselves between two rows of houses, built in concentric rings round a large open space. Between the outer ring and the inner one a circular street runs round the whole of the village, and in it, as we pass, we see groups of people sitting in front of their huts. The outer ring consists of dwelling-houses, the inner of store-huts in which the *taytu,* a variety of yam, which forms the staple food of the natives, is kept from one harvest to the next. We are struck at once by the better finish, the greater constructive elaboration, and the superior embellishment and decoration which distinguish the yam-houses from the dwellings. As we stand on the wide central space we can admire the circular row of storehouses in front of us, for both these and the dwellings always face the center. In

Omarakana a big yam-house belonging to the chief stands in the middle of this space. Somewhat nearer the ring, but still well in the center stands another large building, the chief's living hut.

This singularly symmetrical arrangement of the village is of importance, for it represents a definite sociological scheme. The inner place is the scene of the public and festive life. A part of it is the old-time burial ground of the villagers, and at one end is the dancing ground, the scene of all ceremonial and festive celebrations. The houses which surround it, the inner ring of store-huts that is, share its quasi-sacred character, a number of taboos being placed upon them. The street between the two rows is the theater of domestic life and everyday occurrence. Without overlaboring the point, the central place might be called the male portion of the village and the street that of the women.

Let us now make preliminary acquaintance with some of the more important inhabitants of Omarakana, beginning with the present chief, To'uluwa. Not only are he and his family the most prominent members of the community, but they occupy more than half of the village. As we shall see, the chiefs in the Trobriands have the privilege of polygamy. To'uluwa, who lives in the large house in the middle of the village, has a number of wives who occupy a whole row of huts. Also his maternal kinsmen, who belong to his family and sub-clan called Tabalu, have a separate space in the village for themselves. The third section is inhabited by commoners who are not related to the chief either as kinsmen or as children.

The community is thus divided into three parts. The first consists of the chief and his maternal kinsmen, the Tabalu, all of whom claim the village as their own, and consider themselves masters of its soil with all attendant privileges. The second consists of the commoners, who are themselves divided into two groups: those claiming the rights of citizenship on mythological grounds (these rights are distinctly inferior to those of the chief's sub-clan, and the claimants

remain in the village only as the chief's vassals or servants);
and strangers in the hereditary service of the chief, who
live in the village by that right and title. The third part
consists of the chief's wives and their offspring.

These wives, by reason of patrilocal marriage, have to
settle in their husband's village, and with them, of course,
remain their younger children. But the grown-up sons are
allowed to stay in the village only through the personal influence of their father. This influence overrules the tribal
law that every man ought to live in his own—that is his
mother's—village. The chief is always much more attached
to his children than to his maternal kinsmen. He prefers
their company; like every typical Trobriand father, he takes,
sentimentally at least, their side in any dispute; and he invariably tries to grant them as many privileges and benefits
as possible. This state of affairs is naturally not altogether
appreciated by the chief's legal successors, his maternal kinsmen, the children of his sister; and frequently considerable
tension and sharp friction arise between the two sections
in consequence.

Such a state of tension revealed itself recently in an acute
upheaval which shook the quiet tribal life of Omarakana
and for years undermined its internal harmony.[4] There
was a feud of long standing between Namwana Guya'u,
the chief's favorite son, and Mitakata, his nephew and third
in succession to the rule. Namwana Guya'u was the most
influential man in the village, after the chief, his father:
To'uluwa allowed him to wield a great deal of power, and
gave him more than his share of wealth and privilege.

One day, about six months after my arrival in Omarakana,
the quarrel came acutely to a head. Namwana Guya'u, the
chief's son, accused his enemy, Mitakata, the nephew and
one of the heirs, of committing adultery with his wife,
brought him before the White Resident Magistrate, and
thereby caused him to be imprisoned for a month or so.
The news of this imprisonment reached the village from
the Government compound, a few miles distant, at sunset,

and created a panic. The chief shut himself up in his personal hut, full of evil forebodings for his favorite, who had thus rashly outraged tribal law and feeling. The kinsmen of the imprisoned heir to chieftainship were boiling with suppressed anger and indignation. As night fell, the subdued villagers settled down to a silent supper, each family over its solitary meal. There was nobody on the central place. Namwana Guya'u was not to be seen, the chief To'uluwa remained secluded in his hut, most of his wives and their children staying indoors also. Suddenly a loud voice rang out across the village. Bagido'u, the heir apparent and eldest brother of the imprisoned man, standing before his hut, cried out, addressing the offender of his family:

"Namwana Guya'u, you are a cause of trouble. We, the Tabalu of Omarakana, allowed you to stay here, to live among us. You had plenty of food in Omarakana. You ate of our food. You partook of the pigs brought to us as a tribute, and of the flesh. You sailed in our canoe. You built a hut on our soil. Now you have done us harm. You have told lies. Mitakata is in prison. We do not want you to stay here. This is our village! You are a stranger here. Go away! We drive you away! We drive you out of Omarakana."

These words were uttered in a loud, piercing voice, which trembled with stronge emotion: each short sentence was spoken after a pause; each, like an individual missile, was hurled across the empty space to the hut where Namwana Guya'u sat brooding. Next, the younger sister of Mitakata rose and spoke, and then a young man, one of their maternal nephews. Their words were in each case almost the same as Bagido'u's, the burden being the formula of dismissal or driving away, the *yoba*. These speeches were received in deep silence. Nothing stirred in the village. But, before the night was over, Namwana Guya'u had left Omarakana for ever. He had gone over and settled a few miles away, in Osapola, his "own" village, whence his mother came. For weeks she and his sister wailed for him with loud lamentations as for the dead. The chief remained for three days in his hut, and when he came out he looked aged and broken by grief. All his personal interest and affection were on the side of his favorite son, yet he could do nothing to help him. His kinsmen had acted strictly within their rights, and, according to tribal law, he could not possibly dissociate himself from them. No power could change the decree of exile. Once the words "Go away"— *bukula*, "we drive thee away"—*kayabaim*, had been pronounced, the man had to go. These words, very rarely uttered in earnest, have a binding force and an almost ritual power when pronounced by citizens against a resident outsider. A man who would try to brave the dreadful insult involved in them and remain in spite of them, would be dishonored forever. In fact, anything but immediate compliance with a ritual request is unthinkable for a Trobriand Islander.

The chief's resentment against his kinsmen was deep and lasting. At first he would not even speak to them. For a year or so, not one of them dared to ask to be taken on overseas expeditions by him, although they were fully entitled to this privilege. Two years later, in 1917, when I returned to the Trobriands, Namwana Guya'u was still resident in the other village and keeping aloof from his father's kinsmen, though he frequently visited Omarakana in order to be in attendance on his father, especially when To'uluwa went abroad. His mother had died within a year after his expulsion. As the natives described it: "She wailed and wailed, refused to eat, and died." The relations between the two main enemies were completely broken, and Mitakata, the young chieftain who had been imprisoned, had repudiated his wife, who belonged to the same sub-clan as Namwana Guya'u. There was a deep rift in the whole social life at Kiriwina.

This incident was one of the most dramatic which I have ever witnessed in the Trobriands. I have described it at length, as it contains a striking illustration of the nature of mother-right, of the power of tribal law, and of the passions which work against and in spite of these. It shows also the deep, personal attachment which a father feels for his children, the tendency which he has to use all his personal influence to give them a strong position in the village, the opposition which this always evokes among his maternal kinsmen, and the tension and rifts thus brought about. Under normal conditions, in a smaller community where the contending powers are humbler and less important, such tension would merely mean that, after the father's death, the children would have to return to his maternal kinsmen practically all the material benefits they had received from him during his lifetime. In any case a good deal of discontent and friction and many roundabout methods of settlement are involved in this dual play of paternal affection and matrilineal authority: the chief's son and his maternal nephew can be described as predestined enemies.

This theme will recur in the progress of the following narrative. In discussing consent to marriage, we shall see the importance of paternal authority and the functions of the matrilineal kinsmen. The custom of cross-cousin marriage is a traditional reconciliation of the two opposing principles. The sexual taboos and prohibitions of incest also cannot be understood without a clear grasp of the principles discussed in this section.

So far we have met To'uluwa, his favorite wife Kadamwasila, whose death followed on the village tragedy, their son Namwana Guya'u, and his enemy Mitakata, son of the chief's sister, and these we shall meet again, for they were among my best informants. We shall also become acquainted with the other sons of the chief, and of his favorite wife, and with some of his maternal kinsmen and kinswomen. We shall follow several of them in their love affairs, and in their marriage arrangements; we shall have to pry into their domestic scandals, and to take an indiscreet interest in their intimate life. For all of them were, during a long period, under ethnographic observation, and I obtained much of my material through their confidences, and especially from their mutual scandal-mongering.

Many examples will also be given from other communities, and we shall make frequent visits to the lagoon villages of the western shore, to places on the south of the island, and to some of the neighboring smaller islands of the Archipelago. In all these other communities more uniform and democratic conditions prevail, and this makes some difference in the character of their sexual life.

III

FAMILY LIFE

In entering the village we had to pass across the street between the two concentric rows of houses. This is the normal setting of the everyday life of the community, and thither we must return in order to make a closer survey of the groups of people sitting in front of their dwellings. As a rule we find that each group consists of one family only—man, wife, and children—taking their leisure, or engaged in some domestic activity which varies with the time of day. On a fine morning we would see them hastily eating a scanty breakfast, and then the man and woman preparing the implements for the day's work, with the help of the bigger children, while the baby is laid out of the way on a mat. Afterwards, during the cool hours of the forenoon, each family would probably set off to their work, leaving the village almost deserted. The man, in company with others, may be fishing or hunting or building a canoe or looking for timber. The woman may have gone collecting shell-fish or wild fruits. Or else both may be working in the gardens or paying a visit. The man often does harder work than the woman, but when they return in the hot hours of the afternoon he will rest, while the woman busies herself with household affairs. Towards evening, when the descending sun casts longer, cooler shadows, the social life of the village begins. At this time we would see our family group in front of their hut, the wife preparing food, the children playing, the husband, perhaps, seated amusing the smallest baby. This is the time when neighbors call on one another, and conversation may be exchanged from group to group.

The frank and friendly tone of intercourse, the obvious feeling of equality, the father's domestic helpfulness, especially with the children, would at once strike any observant visitor. The wife joins freely in the jokes and conversation; she does her work independently, not with the air of a slave or a servant, but as one who manages her own department. She will order the husband about if she needs his help. Close observation, day after day, confirms this first impression. The typical Trobriand household is founded on the principles of equality and independence of function: the man is considered to be the master, for he is in his own village and the house belongs to him, but the woman has, in other respects, a considerable influence; she and her family have a great deal to do with the food supply of the household; she is the owner of separate possessions in the house; and she is—next to her brother—the legal head of her family.

The division of functions within the household is, in certain matters, quite definite. The woman has to cook the food, which is simple, and does not require much preparation. The main meal is taken at sunset, and consists of yams, taro, or other tubers, roasted in the open fire—or, less frequently, boiled in a small pot, or baked in the ground—with the occasional addition of fish or meat. Next morning the remains are eaten cold, and sometimes, though not regularly, fruit, shell-fish, or some other light snack may be taken at mid-day.

In some circumstances, men can and do prepare and cook the food: on journeys, oversea voyages; fishing or hunting expeditions, when they are without their women folk. Also, on certain occasions, when taro or sago dumplings are cooked in the large clay pots, men are required by tradition to assist their wives. But within the village and in normal daily life the man never cooks. It would be considered shameful for him to do so. "You are a he-cook" (*to-kakabwasi yoku*) would be said tauntingly. The fear of deserving such an epithet, of being laughed at or shamed (*kakayuwa*), is extreme. It arises from the characteristic dread and shame, found among savages, of not doing the proper thing, or, worse still, of doing something which is intrinsically the attribute of another sex or social class.

There are a number of occupations strictly assigned by tribal custom to one sex only. The manner of carrying loads is a very noteworthy example. Women have to carry the special feminine receptacle, the bell-shaped basket, or any other kind of load upon their heads; men must carry only on the shoulder. It would be with a real shudder, and a profound feeling of shame, that an individual would regard carrying anything in the manner proper to the opposite sex and nothing would induce a man to put any load on his head, even in fun.

An exclusive feminine department is the water supply. The woman has the water bottles of the household in her charge. These are made out of the woody shell of a mature cocoanut, with a stopper of twisted palm leaf. In the morning or near sunset she goes, sometimes a full half-mile, to fill them at the water-hole: here the women forgather, resting and chatting, while one after another fills her water-vessels, cleans them, arranges them in baskets or on large wooden platters and just before leaving, gives the cluster a final sprinkling of water to cover it with a suggestive gloss of freshness. The water-hole is the woman's club and center of gossip, and as such is important, for there is a distinct woman's public opinion and point of view in a Trobriand village, and they have their secrets from the male, just as the male has from the female.

We have already seen that the husband fully shares in the care of the children. He will fondle and carry a baby, clean and wash it, and give it the mashed vegetable food which it receives in addition to the mother's milk almost from birth. In fact, nursing the baby in the arms or holding it on the knees, which is described by the native word *ƙapo'i,* is the special rôle and duty of the father (*tama*). It is said of the children of unmarried women who, according to the native expression, are "without a *tama*" (that is, it must be remembered, without a husband to their mother), that they are "unfortunate" or "bad" because "there is no one to nurse and hug them (*gala taytala biƙopo'i*)." Again, if any one inquires why children should have duties towards their father, who is a "stranger" to them, the answer is invariably: "because of the nursing (*pela ƙopo'i*)," "because his hands have been soiled with the child's excrement and urine."

The father performs his duties with genuine natural fondness: he will carry an infant about for hours, looking at it with eyes full of such love and pride as are seldom seen in those of a European father. Any praise of the baby goes directly to his heart, and he will never tire of talking about and exhibiting the virtues and achievements of his wife's offspring. Indeed, watching a native family at home or meeting them on the road, one receives a strong impression of close union and intimacy between its members. Nor, as we have seen, does this mutual affection abate in later years. Thus, in the intimacy of domestic life, we discover another aspect of the interesting and complicated struggle between social and emotional paternity, on the one hand, and the explicitly acknowledged legal mother-right on the other.

It will be noticed that we have not yet penetrated into the interior of a house, for in fine weather the scene of family life is always laid in front of the dwelling. Only when it is cold and raining, at night, or for intimate uses, do the natives retire into the interior. On a wet or windy evening in the cooler season we should find the village streets deserted, dim lights flickering through small interstices in the hut walls, and voices sounding from within in animated conversation. Inside in a small space heavy with dense smoke and human exhalation, the people sit on the floor round the fire or recline on bedsteads covered with mats.

The houses are built directly on the ground and their floors are of beaten earth. The main items of their very simple furniture are: the fireplace, which is simply a ring of small stones with three large ones to support a pot; wooden sleeping bunks, placed one over another against the back and side walls opposite the fireplace and one or two shelves for nets, cooking pots, women's grass petticoats, and other household objects. The chief's personal dwelling is built like an ordinary house, but is larger. The yam houses are of somewhat different and more complicated construction, and are slightly raised above the ground.

A normal day in a typical household forces the family to live in close intimacy—they sleep in the same hut, they eat in common and spend the best part both of their working and leisure hours together.

IV

THE DIVISION OF PROPERTY AND DUTIES ACCORDING TO SEX

Members of the household are also bound together by community of economic interest. On this point, however, a more detailed statement is necessary, as the subject is important and complicated. To begin with the right of ownership, it must be realized that personal possession is a matter of great importance to the native. The title *toli* ("owner" or "master," used as a prefix to the object possessed) has a considerable value in itself as conferring a sort of distinction, even when it does not give a claim to rights of exclusive use. This term and the conception of ownership are, in every particular case, very well defined, but the relationship varies with different objects, and it is impossible to summarize it in one formula covering all cases.[5]

It is remarkable that in spite of the close union within the household, domestic utensils and the many objects littering the hut are not owned in common. Husband and wife have each his or her own possessions. The wife owns her grass petticoats, of which there are usually some twelve or twenty in her wardrobe, for use on various occasions. Also she relies on her own skill and industry to procure them. So that in the question of toilet, a Kirwinian lady depends solely upon herself. The water vessels, the implements for dressmaking, a number of articles of personal adornment, are also her own property. The man owns his tools, ax and adze, the nets, the spears, the dancing ornaments, and the drum, and also those objects of high value, called by the natives *vaygu'a,* which consist of necklaces, belts, armshells, and large polished ax-blades.

Nor is private ownership in this case a mere word without practical significance. The husband and the wife can and do dispose of any article of their own property, and after the death of one of them the objects are not inherited by the partner, but distributed among a special class of heirs. When there is a domestic quarrel a man may destroy some of his wife's property—he may wreak his vengeance on the water bottles or on the grass petticoats—and she may smash his drum or break his dancing shield. A man also has to repair and keep his own things in order, so that the woman is not the housekeeper in the general European sense.

Immovable goods, such as garden-land, trees, houses, as well as sailing-vessels, are owned almost exclusively by men, as is also the live stock, which consists mainly of pigs. We shall have to touch on this subject again, when we speak of the social position of women, for ownership of such things goes with power.

Passing now from economic rights to duties, let us consider the partition of work according to sex. In the heavier type of labor, such as gardening, fishing, and carrying of considerable loads, there is a definite division between man and woman. Fishing and hunting, the latter of very slight importance in the Trobriands, are done by men, while only women engage in the search for marine shell-fish. In gardening, the heaviest work, such as cutting the scrub, making fences, fetching the heavy yam supports, and planting the tuber, is done exclusively by men. Weeding is the women's special duty, while some of the intermediate stages, in which the plants have to be looked after, are performed by mixed male and female labor. Men do such tending as there is to be done of the coco- and areca-nut palms and of the fruit trees, while it is chiefly the women who look after the pigs.

All overseas expeditions are made by men, and the building of canoes is entirely their business. Men have to do most of the trading, especially the important exchange of vegetable food for fish which takes place between the inland and coastal villagers. In the building of houses, the framework is made by men, and the women help with the thatching. Both sexes share in the carrying of burdens; the men shoulder the heavier ones, while the women make up by carrying more frequently. And, as we have seen, there is a characteristic sexual distinction in the mode of placing the burden.

As regards the minor work of manufacturing small objects, the women have to make the mats and plait the armlets and belts. Of course, they alone fashion their personal dress, just as men have to tailor their own not very extensive but very carefully finished garment, the pubic leaf. Men do the wood carving, even in the case of objects used exclusively by women; they manufacture lime gourds for betel chewing and, in the old days, they used to polish and sharpen all stone implements.

This specialization of work according to sex gives, at certain seasons, a characteristic and picturesque touch to village life. When harvest approaches new skirts of the colored variety have to be made, ready to wear when the crops are brought in and at the subsequent festivities. Quantities of banana and pandanus leaf are brought to the villages, and are there bleached and toughened at the fire. At night the whole village is bright with shining of these fires, at each of which a couple of women sit opposite each other and pass the leaf to and fro in front of the flame. Loud chatter and song enlivens the work, gay with anticipation of the coming entertainments. When the material is ready, it has still to be cut, trimmed, and dyed. Two kinds of roots are brought from the bush for the dyeing, one giving a deep purple, and the other a bright crimson. The dye is mixed in large bowls made of giant clam shells; in these the leaf strips are steeped, and then they are hung up in thick bunches to dry in the central place, enlivening the whole village with their gay color. After a very complex process of piecing together, a resplendent "creation" results; the golden yellow of the pandanus, the soft hay-green or dun of the banana leaf, the crimson and purple of the dyed layers form a really beautiful harmony of color against the smooth, brown skin of the woman.

Some manufactures are carried out by men and women together. Both sexes, for example, take part in the elaborate process which is necessary in preparing certain shell ornaments,[6] while nets and water-vessels may be made by either sex.

It will have been seen, then, that women do not bear the brunt of all the drudgery and hard work. Indeed, the heaviest tasks in the gardens and the most monotonous ones are performed by men. On the other hand, women have their own province in economic activity; it is a conspicuous one, and through it they assert their status and importance.

NOTES

[1] For a full general account of the Northern Massim, of whom the Trobrianders form a section, cf. the classical treatise of Professor C. G. Seligman, *Melanesians of British New Guinea,* Cambridge, 1910, which also shows the relation of the Trobrianders to the other races and cultures on and around New Guinea. A short account of Trobriand culture will also be found in my *Argonauts of the Western Pacific* (E. P. Dutton and Co., 1922).

[2] Cf. my *Crime and Custom in Savage Society* (Harcourt, Brace, 1926).

[3] For further references to this eminent personage and for an account of chieftainship, see C. G. Seligman, *op. cit.,* chapters xlix and li; also my *Argonauts of the Western Pacific,* passim, and "Baloma, Spirits of the Dead," *Journ. R. Anthrop. Inst.,* 1916.

[4] The following account has been already published (in *Crime and Custom*, pp. 101 *sq.*). Since it is an almost exact reproduction of the original entry in my field-notes, I prefer to give it here once more in the same form, with a few verbal alterations only.

[5] Cf. *Argonauts of the Western Pacific*, ch. vi, and passim.

[6] Cf. ch. xv of *Argonauts of the Western Pacific*.

FORMAL SEX RELATIONS IN SAMOA *

By MARGARET MEAD

THE first attitude which a little girl learns towards boys is one of avoidance and antagonism. She learns to observe the brother and sister taboo towards the boys of her relationship group and household, and together with the other small girls of her age group she treats all other small boys as enemies elect. After a little girl is eight or nine years of age she has learned never to approach a group of older boys. This feeling of antagonism towards younger boys and shamed avoidance of older ones continues up to the age of thirteen or fourteen, to the group of girls who are just reaching puberty and the group of boys who have just been circumcised. These children are growing away from the age-group life and the age-group antagonisms. They are not yet actively sex-conscious. And it is at this time that relationships between the sexes are least emotionally charged. Not until she is an old married woman with several children will the Samoan girl again regard the opposite sex so quietly. When these adolescent children gather together there is a good-natured banter, a minimum of embarrassment, a great deal of random teasing which usually takes the form of accusing some little girl of a consuming passion for a decrepit old man of eighty, or some small boy of being the father of a buxom matron's eighth child. Occasionally the banter takes the form of attributing affection between two age-mates and is gayly and indignantly repudiated by both. Children at this age meet at informal *siva* parties, on the outskirts of more formal occasions, at community reef fishings (when many yards of reef have been enclosed to make a great fish trap) and on torch-fishing excursions.

* *Coming of Age in Samoa.* New York: William Morrow & Co.

Good-natured tussling and banter and coöperation in common activities are the keynotes of these occasions. But unfortunately these contacts are neither frequent nor sufficiently prolonged to teach the girls coöperation or to give either boys or girls any real appreciation of personality in members of the opposite sex.

Two or three years later this will all be changed. The fact that little girls no longer belong to age groups makes the individual's affection less noticeable. The boy who begins to take an active interest in girls is also seen less in a gang and spends more time with one close companion. Girls have lost all of their nonchalance. They giggle, blush, bridle, run away. Boys become shy, embarrassed, taciturn, and avoid the society of girls in the daytime and on the brilliant moonlit nights for which they accuse the girls of having an exhibitionistic preference. Friendships fall more strictly within the relationship group. The boy's need for a trusted confidant is stronger than that of the girl, for only the most adroit and hardened Don Juans do their own courting. There are occasions, of course, when two youngsters just past adolescence, fearful of ridicule, even from their nearest friends and relatives, will slip away alone into the bush. More frequently still an older man, a widower or a divorced man will be a girl's first lover. And here there is no need for an ambassador. The older man is neither shy nor frightened, and futhermore there is no one whom he can trust as an intermediary; a younger man would betray him, an older man would not take his amours seriously. But the first spontaneous experiment of adolescent children and the amorous excursions of the older men among the young girls of the village are variants on the edge of the recognized types of relationships; so also is the first experience of a young boy with an older woman. But both of these are exceedingly frequent occurrences, so that the success of an amatory experience is seldom jeopardized by double ignorance. Nevertheless, all of these occasions are outside the recognized forms into which sex relations fall. The little boy and girl are branded by their companions as guilty of *tautala lai titi* (presuming above their ages) as is the boy who loves or aspires to love an older woman, while the idea of an older man pursuing a young girl appeals strongly to their sense of humor; or if the girl is very young and naïve, to their sense of unfitness. "She is too young, too young yet. He is too old," they will say, and the whole weight of vigorous disapproval fell upon a *matai* who was known to be the father of the child of Lotu, the sixteen-year-old feeble-minded girl on Olesega. Discrepancy in age or experience always strikes them as comic or pathetic according to the degree. The theoretical punishment which is meted out to a disobedient and runaway daughter is to marry her to a very old man, and I have heard a nine-year-old giggle contemptuously over her mother's preference for a seventeen-year-old boy. Worst among these unpatterned deviations is that of the man who makes love to some young and dependent woman of his household, his adopted child or his wife's younger sister. The cry of incest is raised against him and sometimes feeling runs so high that he has to leave the group.

Besides formal marriage there are only two types of sex relations which receive any formal recognition from the community—love affairs between unmarried young people (this includes the widowed) who are very nearly of the same age, whether leading to marriage or merely a passing diversion; and adultery.

Between the unmarried there are three forms of relationship: the clandestine encounter, "under the palm trees," the published elopement, *Avaga,* and the ceremonious courtship in which the boy "sits before the girl"; and on the edge of these, the curious form of surreptitious rape, called *moetotolo,* crawling, resorted to by youths who find favor in no maiden's eyes.

In these three relationships, the boy requires a confidant and ambassador whom he calls a *soa.* Where boys are close companions, this relationship may extend over many love affairs, or it may be a temporary one, terminating with the particular love affair. The *soa* follows the pattern of the talking chief who makes material demands upon his chief in return for the immaterial services which he renders him. If marriage results from his ambassadorship, he receives a specially fine present from the bridegroom. The choice of a *soa* presents many difficulties. If the lover chooses a steady, reliable boy, some slightly younger relative devoted to his interests, a boy unambitious in affairs of the heart, very likely the ambassador will bungle the whole affair through inexperience and lack of tact. But if he chooses a handsome and expert wooer who knows just how "to speak softly and walk gently," then as likely as not the girl will prefer the second to the principal. This difficulty is occasionally anticipated by employing two or three *soas* and setting them to spy on each other. But such a lack of trust is likely to inspire a similar attitude in the agents, and as one overcautious and disappointed lover told me ruefully, "I had five *soas,* one was true and four were false."

Among possible *soas* there are two preferences, a brother or a girl. A brother is by definition loyal, while a girl is far more skillful for "a boy can only approach a girl in the evening, or when no one is by, but a girl can go with her all day long, walk with her and lie on the mat by her, eat off the same platter, and whisper between mouthfuls the name of the boy, speaking ever of him, how good he is, how gentle and how true, how worthy of love. Yes, best of all is the *soafafine,* the woman ambassador." But the difficulties of obtaining a *soafafine* are great. A boy may not choose from his own female relatives. The taboo forbids him ever to mention such matters in their presence. It is only by good chance that his brother's sweetheart may be a relative of the girl upon whom he has set his heart; or some other piece of good fortune may throw him into contact with a girl or woman who will act in his interests. The most violent antagonisms in the young people's groups are not between ex-lovers, arise not from the venom of the deserted nor the smarting pride of the jilted, but occur between the boy and the *soa* who has betrayed him, or a lover and the friend of his beloved who has in ar y way blocked his suit.

In the strictly clandestine love affair the lover never presents himself at the house of his beloved. His *soa* may go there in a group or upon some trumped-up errand, or he also may avoid the house and find opportunities to speak to the girl while she is fishing or going to and from the plantation. It is his task to sing his friend's praise, counteract the girl's fears and objections, and finally appoint a rendezvous. These affairs are usually of short duration and both boy and girl may be carrying on several at once. One of the recognized causes of a quarrel is the resentment of the first lover against his successor of the same night, "for the boy who came later will mock him." These clandestine lovers make their rendezvous on the outskirts of the village. "Under the palm trees" is the conventionalized designation of this type of intrigue. Very often three or four couples will have a common rendezvous, when either the boys or the girls are relatives who are friends. Should the girl ever grow faint or dizzy, it is the boy's part to climb the nearest palm and fetch down a fresh cocoanut to pour on her face in lieu of *eau de co. gne*. In native theory, barrenness is the punishment of promiscuity; and, *vice versa,* only persistent monogamy is rewarded by conception. When a pair of clandestine experimenters, whose rank is so low that their marriages are not of any great economic importance, become genuinely attached to each other and maintain the relationship over several months, marriage often follows. And native sophistication distinguishes between the adept lover whose adventures are many and of short duration and the less-skilled man who can find no better proof of his virility than a long affair ending in conception.

Often the girl is afraid to venture out into the night, infested with ghosts and devils, ghosts that strangle one, ghosts from far-away villages who come in canoes to kidnap the girls of the village, ghosts who leap upon the back and may not be shaken off. Or she may feel that it is wiser to remain at home, and if necessary, attest her presence vocally. In this case the lover braves the house; taking off his *lavalava,* he greases his body thoroughly with cocoanut oil so that he can slip through the fingers of pursuers and leave no trace, and stealthily raises the blinds and slips into the house. The prevalence of this practice gives point to the familiar incident in Polynesian folk tales of the ill fortune that falls the luckless hero who "sleeps until morning, until the rising sun reveals his presence to the other inmates of the house." As perhaps a dozen or more people and several dogs are sleeping in the house, a due regard for silence is sufficient precaution. But it is this habit of domestic rendezvous which lends itself to the peculiar abuse of the *moetotolo,* or sleep crawler.

The *moetotolo* is the only sex activity which presents a definitely abnormal picture. Ever since the first contact with white civilization, rape, in the form of violent assault, has occurred occasionally in Samoa. It is far less congenial, however, to the Samoan attitude than *moetotolo,* in which a man stealthily appropriates the favors which are meant for another. The need for guarding against discovery makes conversation impossible, and the sleep crawler relies upon the girl's expecting a lover or the chance that she will indiscriminately accept any comer. If the girl suspects and resents him, she raises a great outcry and the whole household gives chase. Catching a *moetotolo* is counted great sport, and the women, who feel their safety endangered, are even more active in pursuit than the men. One luckless youth in Luma neglected to remove his *lavalava.* The girl discovered him and her sister succeeded in biting a piece out of his *lavalava* before he escaped. This she proudly exhibited the next day. As the boy had been too dull to destroy his *lavalava,* the evidence against him was circumstantial and he was the laughing stock of the village; the children wrote a dance song about it and sang it after him wherever he went. The *moetotolo* problem is complicated by the possibility that a boy

of the household may be the offender and may take refuge
in the hue and cry following the discovery. It also provides
the girl with an excellent alibi, since she has only to call
out *"moetotolo"* in case her lover is discovered. "To the family and the village that may be a *moetotolo,* but it is not so in
the hearts of the girl and the boy."

Two motives are given for this unsavory activity, anger
and failure in love. The Samoan girl who plays the coquette
does so at her peril. "She will say, 'Yes, I will meet you to-
night by that old cocoanut tree just beside the devilfish stone
when the moon goes down.' And the boy will wait and wait
and wait all night long. It will grow very dark; lizards will
drop on his head; the ghost boats will come into the channel.
He will be very much afraid. But he will wait there until
dawn, until his hair is wet with dew and his heart is very
angry and still she does not come. Then in revenge he will
attempt a *moetotolo.* Especially will he do so if he hears
that she has met another that night." The other set explanation is that a particular boy cannot win a sweetheart by any
legitimate means, and there is no form of prostitution, except guest prostitution, in Samoa. As some of the boys who
were notorious *moetotolos* were among the most charming
and good-looking youths of the village, this is a little hard
to understand. Apparently, these youths, frowned upon in
one or two tentative courtships, inflamed by the loudly
proclaimed success of their fellows and the taunts against
their own inexperience, cast established wooing procedure
to the winds and attempt a *moetotolo.* And once caught,
once branded, no girl will ever pay any attention to them
again. They must wait until as older men, with position and
title to offer, they can choose between some weary and
bedraggled wanton or the unwilling young daughter of
ambitious and selfish parents. But years will intervene before this is possible, and shut out from the amours in which
his companions are engaging, a boy makes one attempt after
another, sometimes successfully, sometimes only to be
caught and beaten and mocked by the village, and always

digging the pit deeper under his feet. Often partially satisfactory solutions are relationships with men. There was one
such pair in the village, a notorious *moetotolo,* and a serious-
minded youth who wished to keep his heart free for political
intrigue. The *moetotolo,* therefore, complicates and adds zest
to the surreptitious love-making which is conducted at home,
while the danger of being missed, the undesirability of
chance encounters abroad, rain and the fear of ghosts, complicate "love under the palm trees."

Between these strictly *sub-rosa* affairs and a final offer
of marriage there is an intermediate form of courtship in
which the girl is called upon by the boy. As this is regarded
as a tentative move towards matrimony, both relationship
groups must be more or less favorably inclined towards the
union. With his *soa* at his side and provided with a basket
of fish, an octopus or so, or a chicken, the suitor presents
himself at the girl's home before the late evening meal. If
his gift is accepted, it is a sign that the family of the girl are
willing for him to pay his addresses to her. He is formally
welcomed by the *matai,* sits with reverently bowed head
throughout the evening prayer, and then he and his *soa*
stay for supper. But the suitor does not approach his
beloved. They say: "If you wish to know who is really the
lover, look then not at the boy who sits by her side, looks
boldly into her eyes and twists the flowers in her necklace
around his fingers or steals the hibiscus flower from her
hair that he may wear it behind his ear. Do not think it is
he who whispers softly in her ear, or says to her, 'Sweetheart, wait for me to-night. After the moon has set, I will
come to you,' or who teases her by saying she has many
lovers. Look instead at the boy who sits afar off, who sits
with bent head and takes no part in the joking. And you
will see that his eyes are always turned softly on the girl.
Always he watches her and never does he miss a movement
of her lips. Perhaps she will wink at him, perhaps she will
raise her eyebrows, perhaps she will make a sign with her
hand. He must always be wakeful and watching or he will

miss it." The *soa* meanwhile pays the girl elaborate and osten-
tatious court and in undertones pleads the cause of his
friend. After dinner, the center of the house is accorded the
young people to play cards, sing or merely sit about, exchanging a series of broad pleasantries. This type of courtship
varies from occasional calls to daily attendance. The food
gift need not accompany each visit, but is as essential at the
initial call as is an introduction in the West. The way of
such declared lovers is hard. The girl does not wish to marry,
nor to curtail her amours in deference to a definite betrothal.
Possibly she may also dislike her suitor, while he in turn
may be the victim of family ambition. Now that the whole
village knows him for her suitor, the girl gratifies her vanity
by avoidance, by perverseness. He comes in the evening, she
has gone to another house; he follows her there, she immediately returns home. When such courtship ripens into an
accepted proposal of marriage, the boy often goes to sleep
in the house of his intended bride and often the union is
surreptitiously consummated. Ceremonial marriage is deferred until such time as the boy's family have planted or
collected enough food and other property and the girl's
family have gotten together a suitable dowry of tapa
and mats.

In such manner are conducted the love affairs of the
average young people of the same village, and of the plebeian
young people of neighboring villages. From this free and
easy experimentation, the *taupo* is excepted. Virginity is a
legal requirement for her. At her marriage, in front of
all the people, in a house brilliantly lit, the talking chief
of the bridegroom will take the tokens of her virginity.[1] In
former days should she prove not to be a virgin, her female
relatives fell upon and beat her with stones, disfiguring and
sometimes fatally injuring the girl who had shamed their
house. The public ordeal sometimes prostrated the girl as
much as a week, although ordinarily a girl recovers from
first intercourse in two or three hours, and women seldom
lie abed more than a few hours after childbirth. Although

this virginity-testing ceremony was theoretically observed at wedding of people of all ranks, it was simply ignored if the boy knew that it was an idle form, and "a wise girl who is not a virgin will tell all to the talking chiefs of her husband, so that she be not ashamed before all the people."

The attitude towards virginity is a curious one. Christianity has, of course, introduced a moral premium on chastity. The Samoans regard this attitude with reverent but complete skepticism and the concept of celibacy is absolutely meaningless to them. But virginity definitely adds to a girl's attractiveness, the wooing of a virgin is considered far more of a feat than the conquest of a more experienced heart, and a really successful Don Juan turns most of his attention to their seduction. One youth who at twenty-four married a girl who was still a virgin was the laughing stock of the village over his freely related trepidation which revealed the fact that at twenty-four, although he had had many love affairs, he had never before won the favors of a virgin.

The bridegroom, his relatives and the bride and her relatives all receive prestige, if she proves to be a virgin, so that the girl of rank who might wish to forestall this painful public ceremony is thwarted not only by the anxious chaperonage of the relatives but by the boy's eagerness for prestige. One young Lothario eloped to his father's house with a girl of high rank from another village and refused to live with her because, said he, "I thought maybe I would marry that girl and there would be a big *malaga* and a big ceremony and I would wait and get the credit for marrying a virgin. But the next day her father came and said that she could not marry me, and she cried very much. So I said to her, 'Well, there is no use now to wait any longer. Now we will run away into the bush.'" It is conceivable that the girl would often trade the temporary prestige for an escape from the public ordeal, but in proportion as his ambitions were honorable, the boy would frustrate her efforts.

Just as the clandestine and casual "love under the palm trees" is the pattern irregularity for those of humble birth, so the elopement has its archetype in the love affairs of the *taupo,* and the other chiefs' daughters. These girls of noble birth are carefully guarded; not for them are secret trysts at night or stolen meetings in the daytime. Where parents of lower rank complacently ignore their daughters' experiments, the high chief guards his daughters' virginity as he guards the honor of his name, his precedence in the kava ceremony or any other prerogative of his high degree. Some old woman of the household is told off to be the girl's constant companion and duenna. The *taupo* may not visit in other houses in the village, or leave the house alone at night. When she sleeps, an older woman sleeps by her side. Never may she go to another village unchaperoned. In her own village she goes soberly about her tasks, bathing in the sea, working in the plantation, safe under the jealous guardianship of the women of her own village. She runs little risk from the *moetotolo,* for one who outraged the *taupo* of his village would formerly have been beaten to death, and now would have to flee from the village. The prestige of the village is inextricably bound up with the high repute of the *taupo* and few young men in the village would dare to be her lovers. Marriage to them is out of the question, and their companions would revile them as traitors rather than envy them such doubtful distinction. Occasionally a youth of very high rank in the same village will risk an elopement, but even this is a rare occurrence. For tradition says that the *taupo* must marry outside her village, marry a high chief or a *manaia* of another village. Such a marriage is an occasion for great festivities and solemn ceremony. The chief and all of his talking chiefs must come to propose for her hand, come in person bringing gifts for her talking chiefs. If the talking chiefs of the girl are satisfied that this is a lucrative and desirable match, and the family are satisfied with the rank and appearance of the suitor, the marriage is agreed upon. Little attention is paid to the opinion of the girl. So fixed is the idea that the marriage of the *taupo* is the affair of the talking chiefs that Europeanized natives on the main island refuse to make their daughters *taupos* because the missionaries say a girl should make her own choice, and once she is a *taupo,* they regard the matter as inevitably taken out of their hands. After the betrothal is agreed upon the bridegroom returns to his village to collect food and property for the wedding. His village sets aside a piece of land which is called the "Place of the Lady" and is her property and the property of her children forever, and on this land they build a house for the bride. Meanwhile, the bridegroom has left behind him in the house of the bride, a talking chief, the counterpart of the humbler *soa.* This is one of the talking chief's best opportunities to acquire wealth. He stays as the emissary of his chief, to watch over his future bride. He works for the bride's family and each week the *matai* of the bride must reward him with a handsome present. As an affianced wife of a chief, more and more circumspect conduct is enjoined upon the girl. Did she formerly joke with the boys of the village, she must joke no longer, or the talking chief, on the watch for any lapse from high decorum, will go home to his chief and report that his bride is unworthy of such honor. This custom is particularly susceptible to second thought on the part of either side. Does the bridegroom repent of the bargain, he bribes his talking chief (who is usually a young man, not one of the important talking chiefs who will benefit greatly by the marriage itself) to be oversensitive to the behavior of the bride or the treatment he receives in the bride's family. And this is the time in which the bride will elope, if her affianced husband is too unacceptable. For while no boy of her own village will risk her dangerous favors, a boy from another village will enormously enhance his prestige if he elopes with the *taupo* of a rival community. Once she has eloped, the projected alliance is, of course, broken off, although her angry parents may refuse to sanction her marriage with her lover and marry her for punishment to some old man.

So great is the prestige won by the village, one of whose young men succeeds in eloping with a *taupo,* that often the whole effort of a *malaga* is concentrated upon abducting the *taupo,* whose virginity will be respected in direct relation to the chances of her family and village consenting to ratify the marriage. As the abductor is often of high rank, the village often ruefully accepts the compromise.

This elopement pattern, given meaning by the restrictions under which the *taupo* lives and this intervillage rivalry, is carried down to the lower ranks where indeed it is practically meaningless. Seldom is the chaperonage exercised over the girl of average family severe enough to make elopement the only way of consummating a love affair. But the elopement is spectacular; the boy wishes to increase his reputation as a successful Don Juan, and the girl wishes to proclaim her conquest and also often hopes that the elopement will end in marriage. The eloping pair run away to the parents of the boy or to some of his relatives and wait for the girl's relatives to pursue her. As one boy related the tale of such an adventure: "We ran away in the rain, nine miles to Leone, in the pouring rain, to my father's house. The next day her family came to get her, and my father said to me, 'How is it, do you wish to marry this girl, shall I ask her father to leave her here?' And I said, 'Oh, no. I just eloped with her for public information.'" Elopements are much less frequent than the clandestine love affairs because the girl takes far more risk. She publicly renounces her often nominal claims to virginity; she embroils herself with her family, who in former times, and occasionally even to-day, would beat her soundly and shave off her hair. Nine times out of ten, her lover's only motive is vanity and display, for the boys say, "The girls hate a *moetotolo,* but they all love an *avaga* (eloping) man."

The elopement also occurs as a practical measure when one family is opposed to a marriage upon which a pair of young people have determined. The young people take refuge with the friendly side of the family. But unless the recalcitrant family softens and consents to legalize the marriage by a formal exchange of property, the principals can do nothing to establish their status. A young couple may have had several children and still be classed as "elopers," and if the marriage is finally legalized after long delay, this stigma will always cling to them. It is far more serious a one than a mere accusation of sexual irregularity, for there is a definite feeling that the whole community procedure has been outraged by a pair of young upstarts.

Reciprocal gift-giving relations are maintained between the two families as long as the marriage lasts, and even afterwards if there are children. The birth of each child, the death of a member of either household, a visit of the wife to her family, or if he lives with her people, of the husband to his, is marked by the presentation of gifts.

In premarital relationships, a convention of love-making is strictly adhered to. True, this is a convention of speech, rather than of action. A boy declares that he will die if a girl refuses him her favors but Samoans laugh at stories of romantic love, scoff at fidelity to a long-absent wife or mistress, believe explicitly that one love will quickly cure another. The fidelity which is followed by pregnancy is taken as proof positive of a real attachment, although having many mistresses is never out of harmony with a declaration of affection of each. The composition of ardent love songs, the fashioning of long and flowery love letters, the invocation of the moon, the stars and the sea in verbal courtship, all serve to give Samoan love-making a close superficial resemblance to our own, yet the attitude is far closer to that of Schnitzler's hero in *The Affairs of Anatol*. Romantic love as it occurs in our civilization, inextricably bound up with ideas of monogamy, exclusiveness, jealousy and undeviating fidelity does not occur in Samoa. Our attitude is a compound, the final result of many converging lines of development in Western civilization, of the institution of monogamy, of the ideas of the age of chivalry, of the ethics of Christianity. Even a passionate attachment to one person which lasts for a long period and persists in the face of discouragement but does not bar out other relationships, is rare among the

Samoans. Marriage, on the other hand, is regarded as a social and economic arrangement, in which relative wealth, rank, and skill of husband and wife, all must be taken into consideration. There are many marriages in which both individuals, especially if they are over thirty, are completely faithful. But this must be attributed to the ease of sexual adjustment on the one hand, and to the ascendancy of other interests, social organization for the men, children for the women, over sex interests, rather than to a passionate fixation upon the partner in the marriage. As the Samoans lack the inhibitions and the intricate specialization of sex feeling which makes marriages of convenience unsatisfactory, it is possible to bulwark marital happiness with other props than temporary passionate devotion. Suitability and expediency become the deciding factors.

Adultery does not necessarily mean a broken marriage. A chief's wife who commits adultery is deemed to have dishonored her high position, and is usually discarded, although the chief will openly resent her remarriage to any one of lower rank. If the lover is considered the more culpable, the village will take public vengeance upon him. In less conspicuous cases the amount of fuss which is made over adultery is dependent upon the relative rank of the offender and offended, or the personal jealousy which is only occasionally aroused. If either the injured husband or the injured wife is sufficiently incensed to threaten physical violence, the trespasser may have to resort to a public *ifoga,* the ceremonial humiliation before some one whose pardon is asked. He goes to the house of the man he has injured, accompanied by all the men of his household, each one wrapped in a fine mat, the currency of the country; the suppliants seat themselves outside the house, fine mats spread over their heads, hands folded on their breasts, heads bent in attitude of the deepest dejection and humiliation. "And if the man is very angry he will say no word. All day he will go about his business; he will braid cinet with a quick hand, he will talk loudly to his wife, and call out greetings to those who pass in the roadway, but he will take no notice of those who sit on his own terrace, who dare not raise their eyes or make any movement to go away. In olden days, if his heart was not softened, he might take a club and together with his relatives go out and kill those who sit without. But now he only keeps them waiting, waiting all day long. The sun will beat down upon them, the rain will come and beat on their heads and still he will say no word. Then towards evening he will say at last: 'Come, it is enough. Enter the house and drink the kava. Eat the food which I will set before you and we will cast our trouble into the sea.'" Then the fine mats are accepted as payment for the injury, the *ifoga* becomes a matter of village history and old gossips will say, "Oh, yes, Lua! no, she's not Iona's child. Her father is that chief over in the next village. He *ifod* to Iona before she was born." If the offender is of much lower rank than the injured husband, his chief, or his father (if he is only a young boy) will have to humiliate himself in his place. Where the offender is a woman, she and her female relatives will make similar amends. But they will run far greater danger of being roundly beaten and berated; the peaceful teachings of Christianity—perhaps because they were directed against actual killing, rather than the slightly less fatal encounters of women—have made far less change in the belligerent activities of the women than in those of the men.

If, on the other hand, a wife really tires of her husband, or a husband of his wife, divorce is a simple and informal matter, the non-resident simply going home to his or her family, and the relationship is said to have "passed away." It is a very brittle monogamy, often trespassed and more often broken entirely. But many adulteries occur—between a young, shy bachelor and a married woman, or a temporary widower and some young girl—which hardly threaten the continuity of established relationships. The claim that a woman has on her family's land renders her as independent as her husband, and so there are no marriages of any duration in which either person is actively unhappy. A tiny flare-up and a woman goes home to her own people; if her husband does not care to conciliate her, each seeks another mate.

Within the family, the wife obeys and serves her husband, in theory, though, of course, the hen-pecked husband is a frequent phenomenon. In families of high rank, her personal service to her husband is taken over by the *taupo* and the talking chief but the wife always retains the right to render a high chief sacred personal services, such as cutting his hair. A wife's rank can never exceed her husband's because it is always directly dependent upon it. Her family may be richer and more illustrious than his, and she may actually exercise more influence over the village affairs through her blood relatives than he, but within the life of the household and the village, she is a *tausi,* wife of a talking chief, or a *faletua,* wife of a chief. This sometimes results in conflict, as in the case of Pusa who was the sister of the last holder of the highest title on the island. This title was temporarily extinct. She was also the wife of the highest chief in the village. Should her brother, the heir, resume the higher title, her husband's rank and her rank as his wife would suffer. Helping her brother meant lowering the prestige of her husband. As she was the type of woman who cared a great deal more for wire pulling than for public recognition, she threw her influence in for her brother. Such conflicts are not uncommon, but they present a clear-cut choice, usually reinforced by considerations of residence. If a woman lives in her husband's household, and if, furthermore, that household is in another village, her interest is mainly enlisted in her husband's cause; but if she lives with her own family, in her own village, her allegiance is likely to cling to the blood relatives from whom she receives reflected glory and informal privilege, although no status.

NOTE

[1] This custom is now forbidden by law, but is only gradually dying out.

THE SAVAGE'S DREAD OF INCEST *

By SIGMUND FREUD

PRIMITIVE man is known to us by the stages of development through which he has passed: that is, through the inanimate monuments and implements which he has left behind for us, through our knowledge of his art, his religion and his attitude towards life, which we have received either directly or through the medium of legends, myths and fairy tales; and through the remnants of his ways of thinking that survive in our own manners and customs. Moreover, in a certain sense he is still our contemporary: there are people whom we still consider more closely related to primitive man than to ourselves, in whom we therefore recognize the direct descendants and representatives of earlier man. We can thus judge the so-called savage and semisavage races; their psychic life assumes a peculiar interest for us, for we can recognize in their psychic life a well-preserved, early stage of our own development.

If this assumption is correct, a comparison of the "Psychology of Primitive Races" as taught by folklore, with the psychology of the neurotic as it has become known through psychoanalysis, will reveal numerous points of correspondence and throw new light on subjects that are more or less familiar to us.

For outer as well as for inner reasons, I am choosing for this comparison those tribes which have been described by ethnographists as being most backward and wretched: the aborigines of the youngest continent, namely, Australia, whose fauna has also preserved for us so much that is archaic and no longer to be found elsewhere.

* *Totem and Taboo.* New York: Dodd, Mead & Co.

The aborigines of Australia are looked upon as a peculiar race which shows neither physical nor linguistic relationship with its nearest neighbors, the Melanesian, Polynesian and Malayan races. They do not build houses or permanent huts; they do not cultivate the soil or keep any domestic animals except dogs; and they do not even know the art of pottery. They live exclusively on the flesh of all sorts of animals which they kill in the chase, and on the roots which they dig. Kings or chieftains are unknown among them, and all communal affairs are decided by the elders in assembly. It is quite doubtful whether they evince any traces of religion in the form of worship of higher beings. The tribes living in the interior who have to contend with the greatest vicissitudes of life owing to a scarcity of water, seem in every way more primitive than those who live near the coast.

We surely would not expect that these poor naked cannibals should be moral in their sex life according to our ideas, or that they should have imposed a high degree of restriction upon their sexual impulses. And yet we learn that they have considered it their duty to exercise the most searching care and the most painful rigor in guarding against incestuous sexual relations. In fact, their whole social organization seems to serve this object or to have been brought into relation with its attainment.

Among the Australians the system of *Totemism* takes the place of all religious and social institutions. Australian tribes are divided into smaller *septs* or clans each taking the name of its *totem*. Now what is a totem? As a rule it is an animal, either edible and harmless, or dangerous and feared; more rarely the totem is a plant or a force of nature (rain, water), which stands in a peculiar relation to the whole clan. The totem is first of all the tribal ancestor of the clan, as well as its tutelary spirit and protector; it sends oracles and, though otherwise dangerous, the totem knows and spares its children. The members of a totem are therefore under a sacred obligation not to kill (destroy) their totem, to abstain from eating its meat or from any other enjoyment of it. Any violation of these prohibitions is automatically punished. The character of a totem is inherent not only in a single animal or a single being but in all the members of the species. From time to time festivals are held at which the members of a totem represent or imitate, in ceremonial dances, the movements and characteristics of their totems.

The totem is hereditary either through the maternal or the paternal line (maternal transmission probably always preceded and was only later supplanted by the paternal). The attachment to a totem is the foundation of all the social obligations of an Australian: it extends on the one hand beyond the tribal relationship, and on the other hand it supersedes consanguineous relationship.[1]

The totem is not limited to district or to locality; the members of a totem may live separated from one another and on friendly terms with adherents of other totems.

And now, finally, we must consider that peculiarity of the totemic system which attracts the interest of the psychoanalyst. Almost everywhere the totem prevails there also exists the law that *the members of the same totem are not allowed to enter into sexual relations with each other; that is, that they cannot marry each other.* This represents the *exogamy* which is associated with the totem.

This sternly maintained prohibiton is very remarkable. There is nothing to account for it in anything that we have hitherto learned from the conception of the totem or from any of its attributes; that is, we do not understand how it happened to enter the system of totemism. We are therefore not astonished if some investigators simply assume that at first exogamy—both as to its origin and to its meaning—had nothing to do with totemism, but that it was added to it at some time without any deeper association, when marriage restrictions proved necessary. However that may be, the association of totemism and exogamy exists, and proves to be very strong.

Let us elucidate the meaning of this prohibition through further discussion.

(a) The violation of the prohibition is not left to what is, so to speak, an automatic punishment, as is the case with other violations of the prohibitions of the totem (*e.g.,* not to kill the totem animal), but is most energetically avenged by the whole tribe as if it were a question of warding off a danger that threatens the community as a whole or a guilt that weighs upon all. A few sentences from Frazer's book [2] will show how seriously such trespasses are treated by these savages who, according to our standard, are otherwise very immoral.

"In Australia the regular penalty for sexual intercourse with a person of a forbidden clan is death. It matters not whether the woman is of the same local group or has been captured in war from another tribe; a man of the wrong clan who uses her as his wife is hunted down and killed by his clansmen, and so is the woman; though in some cases, if they succeed in eluding capture for a certain time, the offense may be condoned. In the Ta-Ta-thi tribe, New South Wales, in the rare cases which occur, the man is killed, but the woman is only beaten or speared, or both, till she is nearly dead; the reason given for not actually killing her being that she was probably coerced. Even in casual amours the clan prohibitions are strictly observed; any violations of these prohibitions 'are regarded with the utmost abhorrence and are punished by death'" (Howitt).

(b) As the same severe punishment is also meted out for temporary love affairs which have not resulted in childbirth, the assumption of other motives, perhaps of a practical nature, becomes improbable.

(c) As the totem is hereditary and is not changed by marriage, the results of the prohibiton, for instance in the case of maternal heredity, are easily perceived. If, for example, the man belongs to a clan with the totem of the Kangaroo and marries a woman of the Emu totem, the children, both boys and girls, are all Emu. According to the totem law incestuous relations with his mother and his sister, who are Emu like himself, are therefore made impossible for a son of this marriage.[3]

(d) But we need only a reminder to realize that the exogamy connected with the totem accomplishes more; that is, aims at more than the prevention of incest with the mother or the sisters. It also makes it impossible for the man to have sexual union with all the women of his own group, with a number of females, therefore, who are not consanguineously related to him, by treating all these women like blood relations. The psychological justification for this extraordinary restriction, which far exceeds anything comparable to it among civilized races, is not, at first, evident. All we seem to understand is that the rôle of the totem (the animal) as ancestor is taken very seriously. Everybody descended from the same totem is consanguineous; that is, of one family; and in this family the most distant grades of relationship are recognized as an absolute obstacle to sexual union.

Thus these savages reveal to us an unusually high grade of incest dread or incest sensitiveness, combined with the peculiarity, which we do not very well understand, of substituting the totem relationship for the real blood relationship. But we must not exaggerate this contradiction too much, and let us bear in mind that the totem prohibitions include real incest as a special case.

In what manner the substitution of the totem group for the actual family has come about remains a riddle, the solution of which is perhaps bound up with the explanation of the totem itself. Of course it must be remembered that with a certain freedom of sexual intercourse, extending beyond the limitations of matrimony, the blood relationship, and with it also the prevention of incest, becomes so uncertain that we cannot dispense with some other basis for the prohibition. It is therefore not superfluous to note that the customs of Australians recognize social conditions and festive occasions at which the exclusive conjugal right of a man to a woman is violated.

The linguistic customs of these tribes, as well as of most totem races, reveals a peculiarity which undoubtedly is pertinent in this connection. For the designations of relationship of which they make use do not take into consideration the relationship between two individuals, but between an individual and his group; they belong, according to the expression of L. H. Morgan, to the "classifying" system. That means that a man calls not only his begetter "father" but also every other man who, according to the tribal regulations, might have married his mother and thus become his father; he calls "mother" not only the woman who bore him but also every other woman who might have become his mother without violation of the tribal laws; he calls "brothers" and "sisters" not only the children of his real parents, but also the children of all the persons named who stand in the parental group relation with him, and so on. The kinship names which two Australians give each other do not, therefore, necessarily point to a blood relationship between them, as they would have to according to the custom of our language; they signify much more the social than the physical relations. An approach to this classifying system is perhaps to be found in our nursery, when the child is induced to greet every male and female friend of the parents as "uncle" and "aunt," or it may be found in a transferred sense when we speak of "Brothers in Apollo," or "Sisters in Christ."

The explanation of this linguistic custom, which seems so strange to us, is simple if looked upon as a remnant and indication of those marriage institutions which the Rev. L. Fison has called "group marriage," characterized by a number of men exercising conjugal rights over a number of women. The children of this group marriage would then rightly look upon each other as brothers and sisters although not born of the same mother, and would take all the men of the group for their fathers.

Although a number of authors, as, for instance, E. Wester-marck in his *History of Human Marriage*,[4] oppose the conclusions which others have drawn from the existence of group-relationship names, the best authorities on the Australian savages are agreed that the classificatory relationship names must be considered as survivals from the period of group marriages. And, according to Spencer and Gillen,[5] a certain form of group marriage can be established as still existing to-day among the tribes of the Urabunna and the Dieri. Group marriage therefore preceded individual marriage among these races, and did not disappear without leaving distinct traces in language and custom.

But if we replace individual marriage, we can then grasp the apparent excess of cases of incest-shunning which we have met among these same races. The totem exogamy, or prohibition of sexual intercourse between members of the same clan, seemed the most appropriate means for the prevention of group incest; and this totem exogamy then became fixed and long survived its original motivation.

Although we believe we understand the motives of the marriage restrictions among the Australian savages, we have still to learn that the actual conditions reveal a still more bewildering complication. For there are only a few tribes in Australia which show no other prohibition besides the totem barrier. Most of them are so organized that they fall into two divisions which have been called marriage classes, or phratries. Each of these marriage groups is exogamous and includes a majority of totem groups. Usually each marriage group is again divided into two subclasses (subphratries), and the whole tribe is therefore divided into four classes; the subclasses thus standing between the phratries and the totem groups.

It would hardly serve our purpose to go into the extraordinarily intricate and unsettled discussion concerning the origin and significance of the marriage classes, or to go more deeply into their relation to totemism. It is sufficient for our purposes to point out the great care expended by the Australians as well as by other savage people to prevent incest.[6] We must say that these savages are even more sensitive to incest than we, perhaps because they are more subject to temptations than we are, and hence require more extensive protection against it.

But the incest dread of these races does not content itself with the creation of the institutions described, which, in the main, seem to be directed against group incest. We must add a series of "customs" which watch over the individual behavior to near relatives in our sense, which are maintained with almost religious severity and of whose object there can hardly be any doubt. These customs or custom prohibitions may be called "avoidances." They spread far beyond the Australian totem races. But here again I must ask the reader to be content with a fragmentary excerpt from the abundant material.

Such restrictive prohibitions are directed in Melanesia against the relations of boys with their mothers and sisters. Thus, for instance, on Lepers Island, one of the New Hebrides, the boy leaves his maternal home at a fixed age and moves to the "clubhouse," where he there regularly sleeps and takes his meals. He may still visit his home to ask for food, but if his sister is at home he must go away before he has eaten; if no sister is about he may sit down to eat near the door. If brother and sister meet by chance in the open, she must run away or turn aside and conceal herself. If the boy recognizes certain footprints in the sand as his sister's he is not to follow them, nor is she to follow his. He will not even mention her name and will guard against using any current word if it forms part of her name. This avoidance, which begins with the ceremony of puberty, is strictly observed for life. The reserve between mother and son increases with age and generally is more obligatory on the mother's side. If she brings him something to eat she does not give it to him herself but puts it down before him, nor does she address him in the familiar manner of mother and son, but uses the formal address. Similar customs obtain in New Caledonia. If brother and sister meet, she flees into the bush and he passes by without turning his head toward her.[7]

On the Gazelle Peninsula in New Britain a sister, beginning with her marriage, may no longer speak with her brother, nor does she utter his name but designates him by means of a circumlocution.[8]

In New Mecklenburg some cousins are subject to such restrictions, which also apply to brothers and sisters. They may neither approach each other, shake hands, nor give each other presents, though they may talk to each other at a distance of several paces. The penalty for incest with a sister is death through hanging.[9]

These rules of avoidance are especially servere in the Fiji Islands where they concern not only consanguineous sisters but group sisters as well.

To hear that these savages hold sacred orgies in which persons of just these forbidden degrees of kinship seek sexual union would seem still more peculiar to us, if we did not prefer to make use of this contradiction to explain the prohibition instead of being astonished at it.[10]

Among the Battas of Sumatra these laws of avoidance affect all near relationships. For instance, it would be most offensive for a Battam to accompany his own sister to an evening party. A brother will feel most uncomfortable in the company of his sister even when other persons are also present. If either comes into the house, the other prefers to leave. Nor will a father remain alone in the house with his daughter any more than the mother with her son. The Dutch missionary who reported these customs added that unfortunately he had to consider them well founded. It is assumed without question by these races that a man and a woman left alone together will indulge in the most extreme intimacy, and as they expect all kinds of punishments and evil consequences from consanguineous intercourse they do quite right to avoid all temptations by means of such prohibitions.[11]

Among the Barongos in Delagoa Bay, in Africa, the most rigorous precautions are directed, curiously enough, against the sister-in-law, the wife of the brother of one's own wife. If a man meets this person who is so dangerous to him, he carefully avoids her. He does not dare to eat out of the same dish with her; he speaks only timidly to her, does not dare to enter her hut, and greets her only with a trembling voice.[12]

Among the Akamba (or Wakamba) in British East Africa, a law of avoidance is in force which one would have expected to encounter more frequently. A girl must carefully avoid her own father between the time of her puberty and her marriage. She hides herself if she meets him on the street and never attempts to sit down next to him, behaving in this way right up to her agreement. But after her marriage no further obstacle is put in the way of her social intercourse with her father.[13]

The most widespread and strictest avoidance, which is perhaps the most interesting one for civilized races, is that which restricts the social relations between a man and his mother-in-law. It is quite general in Australia, but it is also in force among the Melanesian, Polynesian and Negro races of Africa as far as the traces of totemism and group relationship reach, and probably further still. Among some of these races similar prohibitions exist against the harmless social intercourse of a wife with her father-in-law, but these are by far not so constant or so serious. In a few cases both parents-in-law become objects of avoidance.

As we are less interested in the ethnographic dissemination than in the substance and the purpose of the mother-in-law avoidance, I will here also limit myself to a few examples.

On the Banks Island these prohibitions are very severe and painfully exact. A man will avoid the proximity of his mother-in-law as she avoids his. If they meet by chance on a path, the woman steps aside and turns her back until he has passed, or he does the same.

In Vanna Lava (Port Patterson), a man will not even walk behind his mother-in-law along the beach until the rising tide has washed away the trace of her footsteps. But they may talk to each other at a certain distance. It is quite out of the question that he should ever pronounce the name of his mother-in-law, or she his.[14]

On the Solomon Islands, beginning with his marriage, a man must neither see nor speak with his mother-in-law. If he meets her he acts as if he did not know her and runs away as fast as he can in order to hide himself.[15]

Among the Zulu Kaffirs custom demands that a man should be ashamed of his mother-in-law and that he should do everything to avoid her company. He does not enter a hut in which she is, and when they meet he or she goes aside, she perhaps hiding behind a bush while he holds his shield before his face. If they cannot avoid each other and the woman has nothing with which to cover herself, she at least binds a bunch of grass around her head in order to satisfy the ceremonial requirements. Communication between them must either be made through a third person or else they may shout at each other a considerable distance if they have some barrier between them as, for instance, the enclosure of a kraal. Neither may utter the other's name.[16]

Among the Basogas, a Negro tribe living in the region of the Nile sources, a man may talk to his mother-in-law only if she is in another room of the house and is not visible to him. Moreover, this race abominates incest to such an extent as not to let it go unpunished even among domestic animals.[17]

Whereas all observers have interpreted the purpose and meaning of the avoidances between near relatives as protective measures against incest, different interpretations have been given for those prohibitions which concern the relationship with the mother-in-law. It was quite incomprehensible why all these races should manifest such great fear of temptation on the part of the man for an elderly woman, old enough to be his mother.[18]

The same objection was also raised against the conception of Fison who called attention to the fact that certain marriage class systems show a gap in that they make marriage between a man and his mother-in-law theoretically not impossible and that a special guarantee was therefore necessary to guard against this possibility.

Sir J. Lubbock, in his book *The Origin of Civilization,* traces back the behavior of the mother-in-law toward the son-in-law to the former "marriage by capture." "As long as the capture of women actually took place, the indignation of the parents was probably serious enough. When nothing but symbols of this form of marriage survived, the indignation of the parents was also symbolized and this custom continued after its origin had been forgotten." Crawley has found it easy to show how little this tentative explanation agrees with the details of actual observation.

E. B. Tylor thinks that the treatment of the son-in-law on the part of the mother-in-law is nothing more than a form of "cutting" on the part of the woman's family. The man counts as a stranger, and this continues until the first child is born. But even if no account is taken of cases in which this last condition does not remove the prohibition, this explanation is subject to the objection that it does not throw any light on the custom dealing with the relation between mother-in-law and son-in-law, thus overlooking the sexual factor, and that it does not take into account the almost sacred loathing which finds expression in the laws of avoidance.[19]

A Zulu woman who was asked about the basis for this prohibition showed great delicacy of feeling in her answer: "It is not right that he should see the breasts which nursed his wife." [20]

The knowledge of hidden psychic feelings which psychoanalytic investigation of individuals has given us, makes it possible to add other motives to the above. Where the psychosexual needs of the woman are to be satisfied in marriage and family life, there is always the danger of dissatisfaction through the premature termination of the conjugal relation, and the monotony in the wife's emotional life. The ageing mother protects herself against this by living through the lives of her children, by identifying herself with them and making their emotional experiences her own. Parents are said to remain young with their children, and this is, in fact, one of the most valuable psychic benefits which parents derive from their children. Childlessness thus eliminates one of the best means to endure the necessary resignation imposed upon the individual through marriage. This emotional identification with the daughter may easily go so far with the mother that she also falls in love with the man her daughter loves, which leads, in extreme cases, to severe forms of neurotic ailments on account of the violent psychic resistance against this emotional predisposition. At all events the tendency to such infatuation is very frequent with the mother-in-law, and either this infatuation itself or the tendency opposed to it joins the conflict of contending forces in the psyche of the mother-in-law. Very often it is just this harsh and sadistic component of the love emotion which is turned against the son-in-law in order better to suppress the forbidden tender feelings.

The relation of the husband to his mother-in-law is complicated through similar feelings which, however, spring from other sources. The path of object selection has normally led him to his love object through the image of his mother and perhaps of his sister; in consequence of the incest barriers his preference for these two beloved persons of his childhood has been deflected and he is then able to find their image in strange objects. He now sees the mother-in-law taking the place of his own mother and of his sister's mother, and there develops a tendency to return to the primitive selection, against which everything in him resists. His incest dread demands that he should not be reminded of the genealogy of his love selection; the actuality of his mother-

in-law, whom he had not known all his life like his mother
so that her picture can be preserved unchanged in his unconscious, facilitates this rejection. An added mixture of
irritability and animosity in his feelings leads us to suspect
that the mother-in-law actually represents an incest temptation for the son-in-law, just as it not infrequently happens
that a man falls in love with his subsequent mother-in-law
before his inclination is transferred to her daughter.

I see no objection to the assumption that it is just this
incestuous factor of the relationship which motivates the
avoidance between son and mother-in-law among savages.
Among the explanations for the "avoidances" which these
primitive races observe so strictly, we would therefore give
preference to the opinion originally expressed by Fison, who
sees nothing in these regulations but a protection against
possible incest. This would also hold good for all the other
avoidances between those related by blood or by marriage.
There is only one difference, namely, in the first case the
incest is direct, so that the purpose of the prevention might
be conscious; in the other case, which includes the mother-
in-law relation, the incest would be a phantasy temptation
brought about by unconscious intermediary links.

We have had little opportunity in this exposition to show
that the facts of folk-psychology can be seen in a new light
through the application of the psychoanalytic point of view,
for the incest dread of savages has long been known as such,
and is in need of no further interpretation. What we can
add to the further appreciation of incest dread is the statement that it is a subtle infantile trait and is in striking
agreement with the psychic life of the neurotic. Psycho-
analysis has taught us that the first object selection of the
boy is of an incestuous nature and that it is directed to the
forbidden objects, the mother and sister; psychoanalysis has
taught us also the methods through which the maturing
individual frees himself from these incestuous attractions.
The neurotic, however, regularly presents to us a piece of
psychic infantilism; he has either not been able to free him-

self from the childlike conditions of psychosexuality, or else he has returned to them (inhibited development and regression). Hence the incestuous fixations of the libido still play or again are playing the main rôle in his unconscious psychic life. We have gone so far as to declare that the relation of the parents instigated by incestuous longings is the central complex of the neurosis. This discovery of the significance of incest for the neurosis naturally meets with the most general incredulity on the part of the grown-up, normal man; a similar rejection will also meet the researches of Otto Rank, which show in even larger scope to what extent the incest theme stands in the center of poetical interest and how it forms the material of poetry in countless variations and distortions. We are forced to believe that such a rejection is above all the product of man's deep aversion to his former incest wishes which have since succumbed to repression. It is, therefore, of importance to us to be able to show that man's incest wishes, which later are destined to become unconscious, are still felt to be dangerous by savage races who consider them worthy of the most severe defensive measures.

NOTES

[1] Frazer, *Totemism and Exogamy*, vol. i, p. 53. "The totem bond is stronger than the bond of blood or family in the modern sense."

[2] Frazer, *loc. cit.*, p. 54.

[3] But the father, who is a Kangaroo, is free—at least under this prohibition—to commit incest with his daughters, who are Emu. In the case of paternal inheritance of the totem the father would be Kangaroo as well as the children; then incest with the daughters would be forbidden to the father and incest with the mother would be left open to the son. These consequences of the totem prohibition seem to indicate that the maternal inheritance is older than the paternal one, for there are grounds for assuming that the totem prohibitions are directed first of all against the incestuous desires of the son.

[4] Second edition, 1902.

[5] *The Native Tribes of Central Australia* (London, 1899).

[6] Storfer has recently drawn special attention to this point in his monograph: *Parricide as a Special Case. Papers on Applied Psychic Investigation*, No. 12 (Vienna, 1911).

[7] R. H. Codrington, *The Melanesians'* also Frazer, *Totemism and Exogamy*, vol. i, p. 77.

[8] Frazer, *loc. cit.*, ii, p. 124, according to Kleintischen: *The Inhabitants of the Coast of the Gazelle Peninsula.*

[9] Frazer, *loc. cit.*, ii, p. 131, according to P. G. Peckel in *Anthropos*, 1908.

[10] Frazer, *loc. cit.*, ii, p. 147, according to the Rev. L. Fison.

[11] Frazer, *loc. cit.*, ii, p. 189.

[12] Frazer, *loc. cit.*, ii, p. 388, according to Junod.

[13] Frazer, *loc. cit.*, ii, p. 424.

[14] Frazer, *loc. cit.*, ii, p. 76.

[15] Frazer, *loc. cit.*, ii, p. 113, according to C. Ribbe: *Two Years Among the Cannibals of the Solomon Islands,* 1905.

[16] Frazer, *loc. cit.*, ii, p. 385.

[17] Frazer, *loc. cit.*, ii, p. 461.

[18] Cf. Crawley: *The Mystic Rose* (London, 1902), p. 405.

[19] Crawley, *loc. cit.*, p. 407.

[20] Crawley, *loc. cit.*, p. 401, according to Leslie: *Among the Zulus and Amatongas,* 1875.

THE INTERMEDIATE TYPE AS PROPHET
OR PRIEST *

By *EDWARD CARPENTER*

A curious and interesting subject is the connection of the Uranian temperament with prophetic gifts and divination. It is a subject which, as far as I know, has not been very seriously considered—though it has been touched upon by Elie Reclus, Westermarck, Bastian, Iwan Bloch, and others. The fact is well known, of course, that in the temples and cults of antiquity and of primitive races it has been a widespread practice to educate and cultivate certain youths in an effeminate manner, and that these youths in general become the priests or medicine-men of the tribe; but this fact has hardly been taken seriously, as indicating any necessary connection between the two functions, or any rela- tion in general between homosexuality and psychic powers. Some such relation or connection, however, I think we must admit as being obviously indicated by the following facts; and the admission leads us on to the further inquiry of what the relation may exactly be, and what its *rationale* and explanation.

Among the tribes, for instance, in the neighborhood of Behring's Straits—the Kamchadales, the Chukchi, the Al- euts, Inoits, Kadiak Islanders, and so forth—homosexuality is common, and its relation to shamanship or priesthood most marked and curious. Westermarck, in his well-known book, *The Origin and Development of the Moral Ideas,*[1] quoting from Dr. Bogoraz, says: "It frequently happens that, under the supernatural influence of one of their sha- mans, or priests, a Chukchi lad at sixteen years of age will

---

* *Intermediate Types Among Primitive Folk*. London: George Allen & Unwin.

suddenly relinquish his sex and imagine himself to be a woman. He adopts a woman's attire, lets his hair grow, and devotes himself altogether to female occupations. Furthermore, this disclaimer of his sex takes a husband into the *yurt* (hut) and does all the work which is usually incumbent on the wife, in most unnatural and voluntary subjection.... These abnormal changes of sex imply the most abject immorality in the community, and appear to be strongly encouraged by the shamans, who interpret such cases as an injunction of their individual deity." Further, Westermarck says, "the change of sex was usually accompanied by future shamanship; indeed nearly all the shamans were former delinquents of their sex." Again he says, "In describing the Koriaks, Krasheninnikoff makes mention of the *Ke'yev,* that is, men occupying the position of concubines, and he compares them with the Kamchadale *Koe'kcuc,* as he calls them, that is, men transformed into women. Every *Koe'kcuc,* he says, 'is regarded as a *magician* and interpreter of dreams.... The *Koe'kcuc* wore women's clothes, did women's work, and were in the position of wives or concubines.'" And (on p. 472): "There is no indication that the North American aborigines attached any opprobrium to men who had intercourse with those members of their own sex who had assumed the dress and habits of women. In Kadiak such a companion was, on the contrary, regarded as a great acquisition; and the effeminate men, far from being despised, were held in repute by the people, most of them being wizards."

The connection with wizardry and religious divination is particularly insisted upon by Elie Reclus, in his *Primitive Folk* (Contemporary Science Series). Speaking of the Inoits (p. 68), he says:—"has a boy with a pretty face also a graceful demeanor? The mother no longer permits him to associate with companions of his own age, but clothes him and brings him up as a girl. Any stranger would be deceived as to his sex, and when he is about fifteen he is sold for a good round sum to a wealthy personage.[2] 'Choupans,' or youths of this kind are highly prized by the Konyagas. On the other hand, there are to be met with here and there among the Esquimaux, or kindred populations, especially in Youkon, *girls* who decline marriage and maternity. Changing their sex, so to speak, they live as boys, adopting masculine manners and customs, they hunt the stag, and in the chase they shrink from no danger; in fishing, from no fatigue."

Reclus then says that the Choupans commonly dedicate themselves to the priesthood; but all are not qualified for this. "To become an *angakok* it is needful to have a very marked vocation, and furthermore a character and temperament which every one has not. The priests in office do not leave the recruiting of their pupils to chance; they make choice at an early age of boys or girls, not limiting themselves to one sex—a mark of greater intelligence than is exhibited by most other priesthoods" (p. 71). The pupil has to go through considerable ordeals:—"Discipline by abstinence and prolonged vigils, by hardship and constraint, he must learn to endure pain stoically and to subdue his bodily desires, to make the body obey unmurmuringly the commands of the spirit. Others may be chatterers; he will be silent, as becomes the prophet and soothsayer. At an early age the novice courts solitude. He wanders throughout the long nights across silent plains filled with the chilly whiteness of the moon; he listens to the wind moaning over the desolate floes;—and then the aurora borealis, that ardently sought occasion for 'drinking in the light,' the *angakok* must absorb all its brilliancies and splendors.... And now the future sorcerer is no longer a child. Many a time he has felt himself in the presence of Sidne, the Esquimaux Demeter, he has divined it by the shiver which ran through his veins, by the tingling of his flesh and the bristling of his hair.... He sees stars unknown to the profane; he asks the secrets of destiny from Sirius, Algol, and Altair; he passes through a series of initiations, knowing well that his spirit will not be loosed from the burden of dense matter and crass ignorance, until the moon has looked him in the face, and

darted a certain ray into his eyes. At last his own Genius,
evoked from the bottomless depths of existence, appears to
him, having scaled the immensity of the heavens, and
climbed across the abysses of the ocean. White, wan, and
solemn, the phantom will say to him: 'Behold me, what
dost thou desire?' Uniting himself with the Double from
beyond the grave, the soul of the *angakok* flies upon the
wings of the wind, and quitting the body at will, sails swift
and light through the universe. It is permitted to probe all
hidden things, to seek the knowledge of all mysteries, in
order that they may be revealed to those who have remained
mortal with spirit unrefined" (p. 73).

Allowing something for poetic and imaginative expression, the above statement of the ordeals and initiations of
the *angakok,* and their connection with the previous career
of the *Choupan* are well based on the observations of many
authorities, as well as on their general agreement with
similar facts all over the world. There is also another passage of Reclus (p. 70) on the duties of the *angakok,* which
seems to throw considerable light on certain passages in
the Bible referring to the *kedeshim* and *kedeshoth* of the
Syrian cults, also on the *kosto* of the Slave Coast and the
early functions of the priesthood in general:—"As soon as
the Choupan has moulted into the *angakok,* the tribe confides to him girls most suitable in bodily grace and disposition; he has to complete their education—he will perfect
them in dancing and other accomplishments, and finally will
initiate them into the pleasures of love. If they display intelligence, they will become seers and medicine-women, priestesses and prophetesses. The summer *kachims* (assemblies)
which are closed to the women of the community, will open
wide before these. It is believed that these girls would be
unwholesome company if they had not been purified by commerce with a man of God."

Catlin, in his *North American Indians* (vol. i, pp. 112-
114), describes how on one occasion he was in a large
tent occupied in painting portraits of some of the chiefs

of the tribe (the Mandans), among whom he was staying, when he noticed at the door of the tent, but not venturing to come in, three or four young men of handsome presence and rather elegantly dressed, but not wearing the eagle's feathers of warriors. He mentally decided to paint the por-trait of one of these also; and on a later day when he had nearly done with the chiefs, he invited one of these others to come in and stand for him. The youth was overjoyed at the compliment, and smiled all over his face. He was clad from head to foot in the skin of the mountain goat, which for softness and whiteness is almost like Chinese crêpe, embroidered with ermine and porcupine quills; and with his pipe and his whip in his hand, made a striking and hand-some figure, which showed, too, a certain grace and gentle-ness as of good breeding. "There was nought about him of the terrible," says Catlin, "and nought to shock the finest, chastest intellect." But to Catlin's surprise, no sooner had he begun to sketch his new subject, than the chiefs rose up, flung their buffalo robes around them, and stalked out of the tent.

Catlin's interpreter afterwards explained to him the posi-tion of these men and the part they played in the tribal life; and how the chiefs were offended at the idea of their being placed on an equality with themselves. But the of-fense, it seemed, was not on any ground of immorality; but —and this is corroborated by the customs of scores of other tribes—arose simply from the fact that the young men were associated with the *women,* and shared their modes of life, and were not worthy therefore to rank among the *warriors.* In their own special way they held a position of some honor.

"Among the Illinois Indians," says Westermarck (vol. ii, p. 473), "the effeminate men assist in (i.e., are present at) all the juggleries and the solemn dance in honor of the calumet, or sacred tobacco-pipe, for which the Indians have such a deference...but they are not permitted either to dance or to sing. They are called into the councils of the

Indians, and nothing can be decided without their advice; for because of their extraordinary manner of living they are looked upon as *manitous,* or supernatural beings, and persons of consequence." "The Sioux, Sacs, and Fox Indians," he continues, "give once a year, or oftener, a feast to the Berdashe, or I-coo-coo-a, who is a man dressed in women's clothes as he has been all his life." And Catlin (*North American Indians,* vol. ii, p. 214) says of this Berdashe: "For extraordinary privileges which he is known to possess, he is driven to the most servile and degrading duties, which he is not allowed to escape; and he being the only one of the tribe submitting to this disgraceful degradation is looked upon as *medicine* and sacred, and a feast is given to him annually; and initiatory to it a dance by those few young men of the tribe who can dance forward and publicly make their boast (without the denial of the *Berdashe*) that" (then follow three or four unintelligible lines of some native dialect; and then) "such and such only are allowed to enter the dance and partake of the feast."

In this connection it may not be out of place to quote Joaquin Miller (who spent his early life as a member of an Indian tribe) on the prophetic powers of these people. He says (*Life Among the Modocs,* p. 360), "If there is a race of men that has the gift of prophecy or prescience I think it is the Indian. It may be a keen instinct sharpened by meditation that makes them foretell many things with such precision, but I have seen some things that looked much like the fulfillment of prophecies. They believe in the gift of prophecy thoroughly, and are never without their seers."

In this connection we may quote the curious remark of Herodotus, who after mentioning (i, 105) that some of the Scythians suffered from a disease of effeminacy ($\theta \acute{\eta} \lambda \epsilon \iota \alpha$ $\nu \acute{o} \acute{o} o \varsigma$), and were called Enarees, says (iv, 67) that "these Enarees, or Androgyni, were endowed by Venus with the power of *divination,*" and were consulted by the King of the Scythians when the latter was ill.

The Jesuit father Lafitau, who published in 1724, at Paris,

an extremely interesting book on the manners and customs of the North American tribes among whom he had been a missionary,[3] after speaking of warlike women and Amazons, says (vol. i, p. 53): "If some women are found possessing virile courage, and glorying in the profession of war, which seems only suitable to men; there exist also men so cowardly as to live like women. Among the Illinois, among the Sioux, in Louisiana, in Florida, and in Yucatan, there are found youths who adopt the garb of women and preserve it all their lives, and who think themselves honored in stooping to all their occupations; they never marry; they take part in all ceremonies in which religion seems to be concerned; and this profession of an extraordinary life causes them to pass for beings of a superior order, and above the common run of mankind. Would not these be the same kind of folk as the Asiatic worshipers of Cybele, or those Easterns of whom Julius Firmicus speaks (*Lib. de Errore prof. Relig.*), who consecrated to the Goddess of Phrygia, or to Venus Urania, certain priests, who dressed as women, who affected an effeminate countenance, who painted their faces and disguised their true sex under garments borrowed from the sex which they wished to counterfeit."

The instance, just quoted, of the Enarees among the Scythians, who by excessive riding were often rendered impotent and effeminate, is very curiously paralleled in quite another part of the world by the so-called *mujerados* (or feminized men) among the Pueblo Indians of Mexico. Dr. W. A. Hammond, who was stationed, in 1850, as military doctor, in New Mexico, reported [4] that in each village one of the strongest men, being chosen, was compelled by unintermitted riding to pass through this kind of metamorphosis. "He then became indispensable for the religious orgies which were celebrated among the Pueblo Indians in the same way as they once were among the old Greeks, Egyptians, and other people.... These Saturnalia take place among the Pueblos in the Spring of every year, and are kept with the greatest secrecy from the observation of non-Indians." [5] And again "To be a *mujerado* is no disgrace to a Pueblo Indian. On the contrary, he enjoys the protection of his tribespeople, and is accorded a certain amount of honor."

Similar customs to those of the American Indians were found among the Pacific Islanders. Captain James Wilson,[3] in visiting the South Sea Islands in 1796-8, found there men who were dressed like women and enjoyed a certain honor; and expresses his surprise at finding that "even their women do not despise these fellows, but form friendships with them." While William Ellis, also a missionary, in his Polynesian Researches [7] (vol. i, p. 340), says that they not only enjoy the sanction of the priests, but even the direct example of one of their divinities. He goes on to say that when he asked the natives why they made away with so many more female than male children, "they generally answered that the *fisheries,* the *service of the temple* and especially *war* were the only purposes for which they thought it desirable to rear children!"

But one of the most interesting examples of the connection we are studying is that of Apollo with the temple at Delphi. Delphi, of course, was one of the chief seats of prophecy and divination in the old world, and Apollo, who presided at this shrine, was a strange blend of masculine and feminine attributes. It will be remembered that he was frequently represented as being very feminine in form—especially in the more archaic statues. He was the patron of song and music. He was also, in some ways, the representative divinity of the Uranian love, for he was the special god of the Dorian Greeks, among whom comradeship became an institution.[8] It was said of him that to expiate his pollution by the blood of the Python (whom he slew), he became the slave and devoted favorite of Admetus; and Muller [9] describes a Dorian religious festival, in which a boy, taking the part of Apollo, "probably imitated the manner in which the god, as herdsman and slave of Alcestis, submitted to the most degrading service." Alcestis, in fact, the wife of Admetus, said of Apollo (in a verse of Sophocles cited by Plutarch): οὑμὸς δἀλέκτωρ αὑτον ἤγε πρὸς "μύλην." When we consider that Apollo, as Sun god, corresponds in some points to the Syrian Baal (masculine), and that in this epithet Karneios, used among the Dorians,[10] he corresponds to the Syrian Ashtaroth *Karnaim* (feminine), we seem to see a possible clue connecting certain passages in the Bible—which refer to the rites of the Syrian tribes and their occasional adoption in the Jewish Temple—with some phases of the Dorian re-ligious ritual.

"The Hebrews entering Syria," says Richard Burton,[11] "found it religionized by Assyria and Babylonia, when the Accadian Ishtar had passed West, and had become Ashto-reth, Ashtaroth, or Ashirah, the Anaitis of Armenia, the Phœnician Astarte, and the Greek Aphrodite, the great Moon-goddess who is queen of Heaven and Love....She was worshiped by men habited as women, and *vice versa;* for which reason, in the Torah (Deut. xxii, 5), the sexes are forbidden to change dress."

In the account of the reforming zeal of King Josiah (2 Kings xxiii) we are told (v. 4) that "the King commanded Hilkiah, the high priest, and the priests of the second order, and the keepers of the door, to bring forth out of the temple of the Lord all the vessels that were made for Baal, and for the grove, and for all the host of heaven; and he burned them without Jerusalem in the fields of Kidron....And he brake down the houses of the sodomites, that were by the house of the Lord, where the women wove hangings for the grove."

The word here translated "sodomites" is the Hebrew word Kedeshim, meaning the "consecrated ones" (males), and it occurs again in 1 Kings xiv, 24; xv, 12; and xxii, 46. And the word translated "grove" is Asherah. There is some doubt, I believe, as to the exact function of these *Kedeshim* in the temple ritual, and some doubt as to whether the translation of the word given in our Authorized Version is justified.[12] It is clear, however, that these men corresponded in some way to the Kedeshoth or sacred women, who were —like the *Devadasis* of the Hindu temples—a kind of courtesan or prostitute dedicated to the god, and strange as it may seem to the modern mind, it is probable that they united some kind of sexual service with prophetic functions. Dr. Frazer, speaking [13] of the sacred slaves or *Kedeshim* in various parts of Syria, concludes that "originally no sharp line of distinction existed between the prophets and the *Kedeshim;* both were 'men of God,' as the prophets were constantly called; in other words they were inspired mediums, men in whom the god manifested himself from time to time by word and deed, in short temporary incarnations of the deity. But while the prophets roved freely about the country, the *Kedeshim* appear to have been regularly attached to a sanctuary, and among the duties which they performed at the shrines there were clearly some which revolted the conscience of men imbued with a purer morality."

As to the Asherah, or sometimes plural Asherim, translated "grove"—for which the women wove hangings—the most generally accepted opinion is that it was a wooden post or tree stripped of its branches and planted in the ground beside an altar, whether of Jehovah or other gods.[14] Several biblical passages, like Jeremiah ii, 27, suggest that it was an emblem of Baal or of the male organ, and others (*e.g.,* Judges ii, 13, and iii, 7) connect it with Ashtoreth, the female partner of Baal; while the weaving of hangings or garments for the "grove" suggests the combination of female with male in one effigy.[15] At any rate we may conclude pretty safely that the thing or things had a strongly sexual signification.

Thus it would seem that in the religious worship of the Canaanites there were male courtesans attached to the temples and inhabiting their precincts, as well as consecrated females, and that the ceremonies connected with these cults were of a markedly sexual character. These ceremonies had probably originated in an ancient worship of sexual acts as being symbolical of, and therefore favorable to, the fertility of Nature and the crops. But though they had penetrated into the Jewish temple they were detested by the more zealous adherents of Jehovah, because—for one reason at any rate—they belonged to the rival cult of the Syrian Baal and Ashtoreth, the *Kedeshim* in fact being "consecrated to the Mother of the Gods, the famous Dea Syria." [16] And they were detestable, too, because they went hand in hand with the cultivation of "familiar spirits" and "wizards"—who of course knew nothing of Jehovah! Thus we see (2 Kings xxi) that Manasseh followed the abominations of the heathen, building up the high places and the "groves" and the altars for Baal. "And he made his son pass through the fire, and observed times, and used enchantments,[17] and dealt with familiar spirits and wizards, and wrought much wickedness ...and he set a graven image of the 'grove' in the house of the Lord." But Josiah, his grandson, reversed all this, and drove the familiar spirits and the wizards out of the land, together with the *Kedeshim.*

So far with regard to Syria and the Bible. But Dr. Frazer points out the curious likeness here to customs existing to-day among the Negroes of the Slave Coast of West Africa. In that region, women, called Kosio, are attached to the temples as wives, priestesses and temple prostitutes of the python-god. But besides these "there are male *Kosio* as well as female *Kosio,* that is there are dedicated men as well as dedicated women, priests as well as priestesses, and the ideas and customs in regard to them seem to be similar." [18] "Indeed," he says, "the points of resemblance between the prophets of Israel and of West Africa are close and curious." [19] It must be said, however, that Dr. Frazer does not in either case insist on the inference of homosexuality. On the contrary, he rather endeavors to avoid it, and of course it would be unreasonable to suppose any *invariable* connection of these "sacred men" with this peculiarity. At the same time the general inference in that direction is strong and difficult to evade.

Throughout China and Japan and much of Malaysia, the so-called Bonzes, or Buddhist priests, have youths or boys attached to the service of the temples. Each priest educates a novice to follow him in the ritual, and it is said that the relations between the two are often physically intimate. Francis Xavier, in his letters from Japan (in 1549), mentions this. He says that the Bonzes themselves allowed that this was so, but maintained that it was no sin. They said that intercourse with woman was for them a deadly sin, or even punishable with death; but that the other relation was, in their eyes, by no means execrable, but harmless and even commendable.[20] And, as it was then, so on the whole it appears to be now, or to have been till very lately. In all the Buddhist sects in Japan (except Shinto) celibacy is imposed on the priests, but homosexual relations are not forbidden.

And to return to the New World, we find Cieza de Leon —who is generally considered a trustworthy authority—describing practices and ceremonials in the temples of New Granada in his time (1550) strangely similar to those referred to in the Hebrew Bible: "Every temple or chief house of worship keeps one or two men, or more, according to the idol—who go about attired like women, even from their childhood, and talk like women, and imitate them in their manner, carriage, and all else." [21] These served in the temples, and were made use of "almost as if by way of sanctity and religion" (casi come por via de santidad y religion); and he concludes that "the Devil had gained such mastery in that land that, not content with causing the people to fall into mortal sin, he had actually persuaded them that the same was a species of holiness and religion, in order that by so doing he might render them all the more subject to him. And this (he says) Fray Domingo told me in his own writing—a man of whom every one knows what a lover of truth he is."

Thus, as Richard Burton remarks,[22] these same usages in connection with religion have spread nearly all over the world and "been adopted by the priestly castes from Mesopotamia to Peru."

It is all very strange and difficult to understand. Indeed, if the facts were not so well-established and so overwhelmingly numerous, it would appear incredible to most of us nowadays that the conception of "sacredness" or "consecration" could be honestly connected, in the mind of any people, with the above things and persons. And yet it is obvious, when one sums up the whole matter, that though in cases Cieza de Leon may have been right in suggesting that religion was only brought in as a cloak and excuse for licentiousness, yet in the main this explanation does not suffice. There must have been considerably more at the back of it all than that: a strange conviction apparently, or superstition, if one likes to call it so, that unusual powers of divination and prophecy were to be found in homosexual folk, and those who adopted the said hybrid kind of life—a conviction, moreover (or superstition), so rooted and persistent that it spread over the greater part of the world.

NOTES

1 2 vols. (Macmillan, 1908), vol. ii, p. 458.

2 See also Bancroft's *Native Races of the Pacific States,* vol. i, p. 82.

3 *Mœurs des Sauvages Amériquains, comparées aux mœurs des premiers temps, par le P. Lafitau.*

4 Wm. A. Hammond in *American Journal of Neurology and Psychiatry,* August, 1882, p. 339.

5 See Dr. Karsch, *Jahrbuch der Sex. Zwisch.,* vol. iii, p. 142.

6 *First Missionary Voyage to the South Sea Islands* (London, 1799), p. 200.

7 2 vols. (London, 1829).

8 See chapters v, vi, and vii in *Intermediate Types Among Primitive Folk* by author.

9 *History and Antiquities of the Doric Race,* vol. i, p. 338.

10 See *infra,* ch. viii, p. 12.

11 *The Thousand Nights and a Night* (1886), vol. x, p. 229.

12 See Frazer's *Adonis, Attis and Osiris* (2nd edition, 1907), pp. 14, 64 note, etc.

13 *Ibid.,* p. 67.

14 See Frazer's *Adonis,* p. 14, note, etc.

15 See a full consideration of this subject in *Ancient Pagan and Modern Christian Symbolism,* by Thomas Inman (2nd edition, 1874), p. 120 *et seq.* Also a long article by A. E. Whatham in *The American Journal of Religious*

Psychology and Education, for July, 1911, on "The Sign of the Mother-goddess."

[16] See Westermarck's *Origin and Development of the Moral Ideas,* vol. ii, p. 488.

[17] All this suggests the practice of some early and primitive science, and much resembles the accusations made in the thirteenth century against our Roger Bacon, pioneer of modern science.

[18] *Adonis,* etc., p. 60.

[19] *Ibid.,* p. 66.

[20] See T. Karsch-Haack, *Forschungen über gleichgeschlechtliche Liebe* (Munich), Die Japaner, p. 77. Also *The Letters of Fr. Xavier,* translated into German by Joseph Burg (3 vols., 1836-40).

[21] See *La Crónica del Peru,* by Cieza de Leon (Antwerp, 1554), ch. 64.

[22] *Op. cit.,* p. 243.

V
RELIGION

ANIMISM *

By SIR EDWARD B. TYLOR

I PROPOSE here, under the name of Animism, to investigate the deep-lying doctrine of Spiritual Beings, which embodies the very essence of Spiritualistic as opposed to Materialistic philosophy. Animism is not a new technical term, though now seldom used. From its special relation to the doctrine of the soul, it will be seen to have a peculiar appropriateness to the view here taken of the mode in which theological ideas have been developed among mankind. The word Spiritualism, though it may be, and sometimes is, used in a general sense, has this obvious defect to us, that it has become the designation of a particular modern sect, who indeed hold extreme spiritualistic views, but cannot be taken as typical representatives of these views in the world at large. The sense of Spiritualism in its wider acceptation, the general belief in spiritual beings, is here given to Animism.

Animism characterizes tribes very low in the scale of humanity, and thence ascends, deeply modified in its transmission, but from first to last preserving an unbroken continuity, into the midst of high modern culture. Doctrines adverse to it, so largely held by individuals or schools, are usually due not to early lowness of civilization, but to later changes in the intellectual course, to divergence from, or rejection of, ancestral faiths; and such newer developments do not affect the present enquiry as to the fundamental religious condition of mankind. Animism is, in fact, the groundwork of the Philosophy of Religion, from

* *Primitive Culture*. London: Murray, 1873.

that of savages up to that of civilized men. And although it may at first sight seem to afford but a bare and meager definition of a minimum of religion, it will be found practically sufficient; for where the root is, the branches will generally be produced. It is habitually found that the theory of Animism divides into two great dogmas, forming parts of one consistent doctrine; first concerning souls of individual creatures, capable of continued existence after the death or destruction of the body; second, concerning other spirits, upward to the rank of powerful deities. Spiritual beings are held to affect or control the events of the material world, and man's life here and hereafter; and it being considered that they hold intercourse with men, and receive pleasure or displeasure from human actions, the belief in their existence leads naturally, and it might almost be said inevitably, sooner or later to active reverence and propitiation. Thus Animism, in its full development, includes the belief in souls and in a future state, in controlling deities and subordinate spirits, these doctrines practically resulting in some kind of active worship. One great element of religion, that moral element which among the higher nations forms its most vital part, is indeed little represented in the religion of the lower races. It is not that these races have no moral sense or no moral standard, for both are strongly marked among them, if not in formal precept, at least in that traditional consensus of society which we call public opinion, according to which certain actions are held to be good or bad, right or wrong. It is that the conjunction of ethics and Animistic philosophy, so intimate and powerful in the higher culture, seems scarcely yet to have begun in the lower. I propose here hardly to touch upon the purely moral aspects of religion, but rather to study the animism of the world so far as it constitutes, as unquestionably it does constitute, an ancient and world-wide philosophy, of which belief is the theory and worship is the practice. Endeavoring to shape the materials for an enquiry hitherto strangely under-

valued and neglected it will now be my task to bring as
clearly as may be into view the fundamental animism of
the lower races, and in some slight and broken outline
to trace its course into higher regions of civilization. Here
let me state once for all two principal conditions under
which the present research is carried on. First, as to the
religious doctrines and practices examined, these are treated
as belonging to theological systems devised by human
reason, without supernatural aid or revelation; in other
words, as being developments of Natural Religion. Second,
as to the connection between similar ideas and rites in
the religions of the savage and the civilized world. While
dwelling at some length on doctrines and ceremonies of
the lower races, and sometimes particularizing for special
reasons the related doctrines and ceremonies of the higher
nations, it has not seemed my proper task to work out
in detail the problems thus suggested among the philoso-
phies and creeds of Christendom. Such applications, extending farthest from the direct scope of a work on primitive culture, are briefly stated in general terms, or touched
in slight allusion, or taken for granted without remark.
Educated readers possess the information required to work
out their general bearing on theology, while more technical
discussion is left to philosophers and theologians specially
occupied with such arguments.

The first branch of the subject to be considered is the
doctrine of human and other souls, an examination of
which will occupy the rest of the present theory of its
development. It seems as though thinking men, as yet at
a low level of culture, were deeply impressed by two groups
of biological problems. In the first place, what is it that
makes the difference between a living body and a dead
one; what causes waking, sleep, trance, disease, death? In
the second place, what are those human shapes which appear in dreams and visions? Looking at these two groups
of phenomena, the ancient savage philosophers probably
made their first step by the obvious inference that every

man has two things belonging to him, namely, a life and a phantom. These two are evidently in close connection with the body, the life as enabling it to feel and think and act, the phantom as being its image or second self; both, also, are perceived to be things separable from the body, the life as able to go away and leave it insensible or dead, the phantom as appearing to people at a distance from it. The second step would seem also easy for savages to make, seeing how extremely difficult civilized men have found it to unmake. It is merely to combine the life and the phantom. As both belong to the body, why should they not also belong to one another, and be manifestations of one and the same soul? Let them then be considered as united, and the result is that well-known conception which may be described as an apparitional-soul, a ghost-soul. This, at any rate, corresponds with the actual conception of the personal soul or spirit among the lower races, which may be defined as follows: It is a thin unsubstantial human image, in its nature a sort of vapor, film, or shadow; the cause of life and thought in the individual it animates; independently possessing the personal consciousness and volition of its corporeal owner, past or present; capable of leaving the body far behind, to flash swiftly from place to place; mostly impalpable and invisible, yet also mani-festing physical power, and especially appearing to men waking or asleep as a phantasm separate from the body of which it bears the likeness; continuing to exist and appear to men after the death of that body; able to enter into, possess, and act in the bodies of other men, of animals, and even of things. Though this definition is by no means of universal application, it has sufficient generality to be taken as a standard, modified by more or less divergence among any particular people. Far from these world-wide opinions being arbitrary or conventional products, it is seldom even justifiable to consider their uniformity among distant races as proving communication of any sort. They are doctrines answering in the most forcible

way to the plain evidence of men's senses, as interpreted
by a fairly consistent and rational primitive philosophy.
So well, indeed, does primitive animism account for the
facts of nature, that it has held its place into the higher
levels of education. Though classic and mediæval philosophy modified it much, and modern philosophy has handled
it yet more unsparingly, it has so far retained the traces
of its original character, that heirlooms of primitive ages
may be claimed in the existing psychology of the civilized
world. Out of the vast mass of evidence, collected among
the most various and distant races of mankind, typical
details may now be selected to display the earlier theory
of the soul, the relation of the parts of this theory, and
the manner in which these parts have been abandoned, modified, or kept up, along the course of culture.

To understand the popular conceptions of the human
soul or spirit, it is instructive to notice the words which
have been found suitable to express it. The ghost or phantasm seen by the dreamer or the visionary is an unsubstantial form, like a shadow, and thus the familiar term
of the *shade* comes in to express the soul. Thus the Tasmanian word for the shadow is also that for the spirit;
the Algonquin Indians describe a man's soul as *otahchuk*,
"his shadow," the Quiché language uses *natub* for "shadow,
soul"; the Arawac *ueja* means "shadow, soul, image"; the
Abipones made the one word *loakal* serve for "shadow,
soul, echo, image." The Zulus not only use the word *tunzi*
for "shadow, spirit, ghost," but they consider that at death
the shadow of a man will in some way depart from the
corpse, to become an ancestral spirit. The Basutos not only
call the spirit remaining after death the *seriti* or "shadow,"
but they think that if a man walks on the river bank, a
crocodile may seize his shadow in the water and draw
him in; while in Old Calabar there is found the same
identification of the spirit with the *ukpon* or "shadow,"
for a man to lose which is fatal. There are thus found
among the lower races not only the types of those familiar

classic terms, the *skia* and *umbra,* but also what seems the fundamental thought of the stories of shadowless men still current in the folklore of Europe, and familiar to modern readers in Chamisso's tale of Peter Schlemihl. Thus the dead in Purgatory knew that Dante was alive when they saw that, unlike theirs, his fingers cast a shadow on the ground. Other   tributes are taken into the notion of soul or spirit, with especial regard to its being the cause of life. Thus the Caribs, connecting the pulses with spiritual beings, and especially considering that in the heart dwells man's chief soul, destined to a future heavenly life, could reasonably use the one word *iouanni* for "soul, life, heart." The Tongans supposed the soul to exist throughout the whole extension of the body, but particularly in the heart. On one occasion, the natives were declaring to a European that a man buried months ago was nevertheless still alive. "And one, endeavoring to make me understand what he meant, took hold of my hand, and squeezing it, said, 'This will die, but the life that is within you will never die'; with his other hand pointing to my heart." So the Basutos say of a dead man that his heart is gone, and of one recovering from sickness that his heart is coming back. This corresponds to the familiar Old World view of the heart as the prime mover in life, thought, and passion. The connection of soul and blood, familiar to the Karens and Papuas, appears prominently in Jewish and Arabic philosophy. To educated moderns the idea of the Macusi Indians of Guiana may seem quaint, that although the body will decay, "the man in our eyes" will not die, but wander about. Yet the association of personal animation with the pupil of the eye is familiar to European folklore, which not unreasonably discerned a sign of bewitchment or approaching death in the disappearance of the image, pupil, or baby, from the dim eyeballs of the sick man.

The act of breathing, so characteristic of the higher animals during life, and coinciding so closely with life in its departure, has been repeatedly and naturally identified with the life or soul itself. Laura Bridgman showed in her instructive way the analogy between the effects of restricted sense and restricted civilization when one day she made the gesture of taking something away from her mouth: "I dreamed," she explained in words, "that God took away my breath to heaven." It is thus that West Australians used one word *waug* for "breath, spirit, soul"; that in the Netela language of California, *piuts* means "life, breath, soul"; that certain Greenlanders reckoned two souls to man, namely, his shadow and his breath; that the Malays say the soul of the dying man escapes through his nostrils, and in Java use the same word *nawa* for "breath, life, soul." How the notions of life, heart, breath, and phantom unite in the one conception of a soul or spirit, and at the same time how loose and vague such ideas are among barbaric races, is well brought into view in the answers to a religious inquest held in 1528 among the natives of Nicaragua. "When they die, there comes out of their mouth something that resembles a person, and is called *julio* (Aztec *yuli, i.e.,* to live). This being goes to the place where the man and woman are. It is like a person, but does not die, and the body remains here." *Question.* "Do those who go up on high keep the same body, the same face, and the same limbs, as here below?" *Answer.* "No; there is only the heart." *Question.* "But since they tear out their hearts (*i.e:,* when a captive was sacrificed), what happens then?" *Answer.* "It is not precisely the heart, but that in them which makes them live, and that quits the body when they die." Or, as stated in another interrogatory, "It is not their heart that goes up above, but what makes them live, that is to say, the breath that issues from their mouth and is called *julio.*" The conception of the soul as breath may be followed up through Semitic and Aryan etymology, and thus into the main streams of the philosophy of the world. Hebrew shows *nephesh,* "breath," passing into all the meanings of "life, soul, mind, animal," while *ruach* and *neshamah* make the like transition from "breath" to "spirit"; and to these the Arabic *nefs* and *ruh* correspond. The same is the history of Sanskrit *atman* and *prana,* of Greek *psyche* and *pneuma,* of Latin *animus, anima, spiritus.* So Slavonic *duch* has developed the meaning of "breath" into that of soul or spirit; and the dialects of the Gypsies have this word *duk* with the meanings of "breath, spirit, ghost," whether these pariahs brought the word from India as part of their inheritance of Aryan speech, or whether they adopted it in their migration across Slavonic lands. German *geist* and English *ghost,* too, may possibly have the same original sense of breath. And if any should think such expressions due to mere metaphor, they may judge the strength of the implied connection between breath and spirit by cases of most unequivocal significance. Among the Seminoles of Florida, when a woman died in childbirth, the infant was held over her face to receive her parting spirit, and thus acquire strength and knowledge for its future use. These Indians could have well understood why at the death-bed of an ancient Roman, the nearest kinsman leant over to inhale the last breath of the departing (*et excipies hanc animam ore pio*). Their state of mind is kept up to this day among Tyrolese peasants, who can still fancy a good man's soul to issue from his mouth at death like a little white cloud.

Among rude races, the original conception of the human soul seems to have been that of ethereality, or vaporous materiality, which has held so large a place in human thought ever since. In fact, the later metaphysical notion of immateriality could scarcely have conveyed any meaning to a savage. It is moreover to be noticed that, as to the whole nature and action of apparitional souls, the lower philosophy escapes various difficulties which down to modern times have perplexed metaphysicians and theologians of the civilized world. Considering the thin ethereal body of the soul to be itself sufficient and suitable for visibility, movement, and speech, the primitive animists had no need of additional hypotheses to account for these manifestations, theological theories such as we may find detailed by Calmet, as that immaterial souls have their own vaporous bodies, or occasionally have such vaporous bodies provided for them by supernatural means to enable them to appear as specters, or that they possess the power of condensing the circumambient air into phantom-like bodies to invest themselves in, or of forming from it vocal instruments. It appears to have been within systematic schools of civilized philosophy that the transcendental definitions of the immaterial soul were obtained, by abstraction from the primitive conception of the ethereal-material soul, so as to reduce it from a physical to a metaphysical entity.

Departing from the body at the time of death, the soul or spirit is considered set free to linger near the tomb, to wander on earth or flit in the air, or to travel to the proper region of spirits—the world beyond the grave. The principal conceptions of the lower psychology as to a Future Life will be considered in the following chapters, but for the present purpose of investigating the theory of souls in general, it will be well to enter here upon one department of the subject. Men do not stop short at the persuasion that death releases the soul to a free and active existence, but they quite logically proceed to assist nature, by slaying men in order to liberate their souls for ghostly uses. Thus there arises one of the most widespread, distinct, and intelligible rites of animistic religion—that of funeral human sacrifice for the service of the dead. When a man of rank dies and his soul departs to its own place, wherever and whatever that place may be, it is a rational inference of early philosophy that the souls of attendants, slaves, and wives, put to death at his funeral, will make the same journey and continue their service in the next life, and the argument is frequently stretched further, to include the souls of new victims sacrificed in order that they may enter upon the same ghostly servitude. It will appear from the ethnography of this rite that it is not strongly marked in the very lowest levels of culture, but that, arising in the higher savagery, it develops itself in the barbaric stage, and thenceforth continues or dwindles in survival.

Of the murderous practices to which this opinion leads, remarkably distinct accounts may be cited from among tribes of the Indian Archipelago. The following account is given of the funerals of great men among the savage Kayans of Borneo: "Slaves are killed in order that they may follow the deceased and attend upon him. Before they are killed the relations who surround them enjoin them to take great care of their master when they join him, to watch and shampoo him when he is indisposed, to be always near him, and to obey all his behests. The female relatives of the deceased then take a spear and slightly wound the victims, after which the males spear them to death." Again, the opinion of the Idaan is "that all whom they kill in this world shall attend them as slaves after death. This notion of future interest in the destruction of the human species is a great impediment to an intercourse with them, as murder goes further than present advantage or resentment. From the same principle they will purchase a slave, guilty of any capital crime, at fourfold his value, that they may be his executioners." With the same idea is connected the ferocious custom of "head-hunting," so prevalent among the Dayaks before Rajah Brooke's time. They considered that the owner of every human head they could procure would serve them in the next world, where, indeed, a man's rank would be according to his number of heads in this. They would continue the mourning for a dead man till a head was brought in, to provide him with a slave to accompany him to the "habitation of souls"; a father who lost his child would go out and kill the first man he met, as a funeral ceremony; a young man might not marry till he had procured a head, and some tribes would bury with a dead man the first head he had taken, together with spears, cloth, rice, and betel. Waylaying and murdering men for their heads became, in fact, the Dayaks' national sport, and they remarked "the white men read books, we hunt heads instead." Of such rites in the Pacific islands, the most hideously purposeful accounts reach us from the Fiji group. Till lately, a main part of the ceremony of a great man's funeral was the strangling of wives, friends, and slaves, for the distinct purpose of attending him into the world of spirits. Ordinarily the first victim was the wife of the deceased, and more than one if he had several, and their corpses, oiled as for a feast, clothed with new fringed girdle, with heads dressed and ornamented, and vermilion and turmeric powder spread on their faces and bosoms, were laid by the side of the dead warrior. Associates and inferior attendants were likewise slain, and these bodies were spoken of as "grass for bedding the grave." When Ra Mbithi, the pride of Somosomo, was lost at sea, seventeen of his wives were killed; and after the news of the massacre of the Namena people, in 1839, eighty women were strangled to accompany the spirits of their murdered husbands. Such sacrifices took place under the same pressure of public opinion which kept up the widow-burning in modern India. The Fijian widow was worked upon by her relatives with all the pressure of persuasion and of menace; she understood well that life to her henceforth would mean a wretched existence of neglect, disgrace, and destitution; and tyrannous custom, as hard to struggle against in the savage as in the civilized world, drove her to the grave. Thus, far from resisting, she became importunate for death and the new life to come, and till public opinion reached a more enlightened state, the missionaries often used their influence in vain to save from the strangling cord some wife whom they could have rescued, but who herself refused to live. So repugnant to the native mind was the idea of a chieftain going unattended into the other world, that the missionaries' prohibition of the cherished custom was one reason of their dislike to Christianity. Many of the nominal Christians, when once a chief of theirs was shot from an ambush, esteemed it most fortunate that a stray shot at the same time killed a young man at a distance from him, and thus provided a companion for the spirit of the slain chief.

In now passing from the consideration of the souls of men to that of the souls of the lower animals, we have first to inform ourselves as to the savage man's idea, which is very different from the civilized man's, of the nature of these lower animals. A remarkable group of observances customary among rude tribes will bring this distinction sharply into view. Savages talk quite seriously to beasts alive or dead as they would to men alive or dead, offer them homage, ask pardon when it is their painful duty to hunt and kill them. A North American Indian will reason with a horse as if rational. Some will spare the rattlesnake, fearing the vengeance of its spirit if slain; others will salute the creature reverently, bid it welcome as a friend from the land of spirits, sprinkle a pinch of tobacco on its head for an offering, catch it by the tail and dispatch it with extreme dexterity, and carry off its skin as a trophy. If an Indian is attacked and torn by a bear, it is that the beast fell upon him intentionally in anger, perhaps to revenge the hurt done to another bear. When a bear is killed, they will beg pardon of him, or even make him condone the offense by smoking the peace-pipe with his murderers, who put the pipe in his mouth and blow down it, begging his spirit not to take revenge. So in Africa, the Kafirs will hunt the elephant, begging him not to tread on them and kill them, and when he is dead they will assure him that they did not kill him on purpose, and they will bury his trunk, for the elephant is a mighty chief, and his trunk is his hand that he may hurt withal. The Congo people will even avenge such a murder by a pretended attack on the hunters who did the deed. Such customs are common among the lower Asiatic tribes. The Stiens of Kambodia ask pardon of the beast they have killed; the Ainos of Yesso kill the bear, offer obeisance and salutation to him, and cut up his carcase. The Koriaks, if they have slain a bear or wolf, will flay him, dress one of their people in the skin, and dance round him, chanting excuses that they did not do it, and especially laying the blame on a Russian. But if it is a fox, they take his skin, wrap his dead body in hay, and sneering tell him to go to his own people and say what famous hospitality he has had, and how they gave him a new coat instead of his old one. The Samoyeds excuse themselves to the slain bear, telling him it was the Russians who did it, and that a Russian knife will cut him up. The Goldi will set up the slain bear, call him "my lord" and do ironical homage to him, or taking him alive will fatten him in a cage, call him "son" and "brother," and kill and eat him as a sacrifice at a solemn festival. In Borneo, the Dayaks, when they have caught an alligator with a baited hook and rope, address him with respect and soothing till they have his legs fast, and then mocking call him "rajah" and "grandfather." Thus when the savage gets over his fears, he still keeps up in ironical merriment the reverence which had its origin in trembling sincerity. Even now the Norse hunter will say with horror of a bear that will attack man, that he can be "no Christian bear."

The sense of an absolute psychical distinction between man and beast, so prevalent in the civilized world, is hardly to be found among the lower races. Men to whom the cries of beasts and birds seem like human language, and their actions guided as it were by human thought, logically enough allow the existence of souls to beasts, birds, and reptiles, as to men. The lower psychology cannot but recognize in beasts the very characteristic which it attributes to the human soul, namely, the phenomena of life and death, will and judgment, and the phantom seen in vision or in dream. As for believers, savage or civilized, in the great doctrine of metempsychosis, these not only consider that an animal may have a soul, but that this soul may have inhabited a human being, and thus the creature may be in fact their own ancestor or once familiar friend. A line of facts, arranged as waymarks along the course of civilization, will serve to indicate the history of opinion from savagery onward, as to the souls of animals during life and after death. North American Indians held every animal to have its spirit, and these spirits their future life; the soul of the Canadian dog went to serve his master in the other world; among the Sioux, the prerogative of having four souls was not confined to man, but belonged also to the bear, the most human of animals. The Greenlanders considered that a sick human soul might be replaced by the sorcerer with a fresh healthy soul of a hare, reindeer, or a young child. Maori tale-tellers have heard of the road by which the spirits of dogs descend to Reinga, the Hades of the departed; the Hovas of Madagascar know that the ghosts of beasts and men, dwelling in a great mountain in the south called Ambondromble, come out occasionally to walk among the tombs or execution-places of criminals. The Kamchadals held that every creature, even the smallest fry, would live again in the under world. The Kukis of Assam think that the ghost of every animal a kuki kills in the chase or for the feast will belong to him in the next life, even as the enemy he slays in the field will then become his slave. The Karens apply the doctrine of the spirit or personal life-phantom, which is apt to wander from the body and thus suffer injury, equally to men and to animals. The Zulus say the cattle they kill come to life again, and become the property of the dwellers in the world beneath. The Siamese butcher, when in defiance of the very principles of his Buddhism he slaughters an ox, before he kills the creature has at least the grace to beseech its spirit to seek a happier abode. In connection with such transmigration, Pythagorean and Platonic philosophy gives to the lower animals undying souls, while other classic opinion may recognize in

beasts only an inferior order of soul, only the "anima"
but not the human "animus" besides. Thus Juvenal:

"Principio indulsit communis conditor illis
    Tantum animas; nobis animum quoque . . ."

Through the middle ages, controversy as to the psychology
of brutes has lasted on into our own times, ranging between two extremes; on the one the theory of Descartes
which reduced animals to mere machines, on the other
what Mr. Alger defines as "the faith that animals have
immaterial and deathless souls." Among modern speculations may be instanced that of Wesley, who thought
that in the next life animals will be raised even above
their bodily and mental state at the creation, "the horrid-
ness of their appearance will be exchanged for their
primeval beauty," and it even may be that they will be
made what men are now, creatures capable of religion.
Adam Clarke's argument for the future life of animals
rests on abstract justice: whereas they did not sin, but
yet are involved in the sufferings of sinful man, and cannot
have in the present state the happiness designed for them,
it is reasonable that they must have it in another. Although,
however, the primitive belief in the souls of animals still
survives to some extent in serious philosophy, it is obvious
that the tendency of educated opinion on the question
whether brutes have soul, as distinguished from life and
mind, has for ages been in a negative and skeptical direction. The doctrine has fallen from its once high estate.
It belonged originally to real, though rude science. It has
now sunk to become a favorite topic in the mild speculative talk which still does duty so largely as intellectual
conversation, and even then its propounders defend it with
a lurking consciousness of its being after all a piece of
sentimental nonsense.

Animals being thus considered in the primitive psychology to have souls like human beings, it follows as the
simplest matter of course that tribes who kill wives and

slaves, to dispatch their souls on errands of duty with their departed lords, may also kill animals in order that their spirits may do such service as is proper to them. The Pawnee warrior's horse is slain on his grave to be ready for him to mount again, and the Comanche's best horses are buried with his favorite weapons and his pipe, all alike to be used in the distant happy hunting-grounds. In South America not only do such rites occur, but they reach a practically disastrous extreme. Patagonian tribes, says D'Orbigny, believe in another life, where they are to enjoy perfect happiness, therefore they bury with the deceased his arms and ornaments, and even kill on his tomb all the animals which belonged to him, that he may find them in the abode of bliss; and this opposes an insurmountable barrier to all civilization, by preventing them from accumulating property and fixing their habitations. Not only do Pope's now hackneyed lines express a real motive with which the Indian's dog is buried with him, but in the North American continent the spirit of the dog has another remarkable office to perform. Certain Esquimaux, as Cranz relates, would lay a dog's head in a child's grave, that the soul of the dog, who ever finds his home, may guide the helpless infant to the land of souls. In accordance with this, Captain Scoresby in Jameson's Land found a dog's skull in a small grave, probably a child's. Again, in the distant region of the Aztecs, one of the principal ceremonies was to slaughter a techichi, or native dog; it was burnt or buried with the corpse, with a cotton thread fastened to its neck, and its office was to convey the deceased across the deep waters of Chiuhnahuapan, on the way to the Land of the Dead. The dead Buraet's favorite horse, led saddled to the grave, killed, and flung in, may serve for a Tartar example. In Tonquin, even wild animals have been customarily drowned at funeral ceremonies of princes, to be at the service of the departed in the next world. Among Semitic tribes, an instance of the custom may be found in the Arab sacrifice of a camel on the grave, for

the dead man's spirit to ride upon. Among the nations
of the Aryan race in Europe, the prevalence of such rites
is deep, wide, and full of purpose. Thus, warriors were
provided in death with horses and housings, with hounds
and falcons. Customs thus described in chronicle and legend,
are vouched for in our own time by the opening of old
barbaric burial-places. How clear a relic of savage meaning lies here may be judged from a Livonian account
as late as the fourteenth century, which relates how men
and women, slaves, sheep, and oxen, with other things,
were burnt with the dead, who, it was believed, would
reach some region of the living, and find there, with the
multitude of cattle and slaves, a country of life and happiness. As usual, these rites may be traced onward in survival. The Mongols, who formerly slaughtered camels and
horses at their owner's burial, have been induced to replace the actual sacrifice by a gift of the cattle to the
Lamas. The Hindus offer a black cow to the Brahmans,
in order to secure their passage across the Vaitarani, the
river of death, and will often die grasping the cow's tail
as if to swim across in herdsman's fashion, holding on to
the cow. It is mentioned as a belief in Northern Europe
that he who has given a cow to the poor will find a cow
to take him over the bridge of the dead, and a custom
of leading a cow in the funeral procession is said to have
been kept up to modern times. All these rites probably
belong together as connected with ancient funeral sacrifice, and the survival of the custom of sacrificing the warrior's horse at his tomb is yet more striking. Saint-Foix
long ago put the French evidence very forcibly. Mentioning the horse led at the funeral of Charles VI, with the four
valets-de-pied in black, and bareheaded, holding the corners
of its caparison, he recalls the horses and servants killed
and buried with pre-Christian kings. And that his readers
may not think this an extraordinary idea, he brings tor-
ward the records of property and horses being presented
at the offertory in Paris, 1329, of Edward III, presenting

horses at King John's funeral in London, and of the funeral service for Bertrand Duguesclin, at St. Denis, in 1389, when horses were offered, the Bishop of Auxerre laid his hand on their heads, and they were afterwards compounded for. Germany retained the actual sacrifice within the memory of living men. A cavalry general named Frederick Kasimir was buried at Treves in 1781 according to the forms of the Teutonic Order; his horse was led in the procession, and the coffin having been lowered into the grave, the horse was killed and thrown in upon it. This was, perhaps, the last occasion when such a sacrifice was consummated in solemn form in Europe. But that pathetic incident of a soldier's funeral, the leading of the saddled and bridled charger in the mournful procession, keeps up to this day a lingering reminiscence of the grim religious rite now passed away.

Plants, partaking with animals the phenomena of life and death, health and sickness, not unnaturally have some kind of soul ascribed to them. In fact, the notion of a vegetable soul, common to plants and to the higher organisms possessing an animal soul in addition, was familiar to mediæval philosophy, and is not yet forgotten by naturalists. But in the lower ranges of culture, at least within one wide district of the world, the souls of plants are much more fully identified with the souls of animals. The Society Islanders seem to have attributed "varua," i.e., surviving soul or spirit, not to men only but to animals and plants. The Dayaks of Borneo not only consider men and animals to have a spirit or living principle, whose departure from the body causes sickness and eventually death, but they also give to the rice its "samangat padi," or "spirit of the paddy," and they hold feasts to retain this soul securely, lest the crop should decay. The Karens say that plants as well as men and animals have their "la" ("kelah"), and the spirit of sickly rice is here also called back like a human spirit considered to have left the body. Their formulas for the purpose have even been written down, and this is part of one: "O come, rice kelah, come. Come to the field. Come to the rice.... Come from the West Come from the East. From the throat of the bird, from the maw of the ape, from the throat of the elephant.... From all granaries, come. O rice kelah, come to the rice." There is reason to think that the doctrine of the spirits of plants lay deep in the intellectual history of South-East Asia, but was in great measure superseded under Buddhist influence. The Buddhist books show that in the early days of their religion it was matter of controversy whether trees had souls, and therefore whether they might lawfully be injured. Orthodox Buddhism decided against the tree-souls, and consequently against the scruple to harm them, declaring trees to have no mind nor sentient principle, though admitting that certain dewas or spirits do reside in the body of trees, and speak from within them. Buddhists also relate that a heterodox sect kept up the early doctrine of the actual animate life of trees, in connection with which may be remembered Marco Polo's somewhat doubtful state-ment as to certain austere Indians objecting to green herbs for such a reason, and some other passages from later writers. Generally speaking, the subject of the spirits of plants is an obscure one, whether from the lower races not having definite opinions, or from our not finding it easy to trace them. The evidence from funeral sacrifices, so valuable as to most departments of early psychology, fails us here, from plants not being thought suitable to send for the service of the dead. Yet, as we shall see more fully elsewhere, there are two topics which bear closely on the matter. On the one hand, the doctrine of trans-migration widely and clearly recognizes the idea of trees or smaller plants being animated by human souls; on the other the belief in tree-spirits and the practice of tree-worship involve notions more or less closely coinciding with that of tree-souls, as when the classic hamadryad dies with her tree, or when the Talein of South-East Asia, considering every tree to have a demon or spirit, offers prayers before he cuts one down.

Thus far the details of the lower animistic philosophy are not very unfamiliar to modern students. The primitive view of the souls of men and beasts as asserted or acted on in the lower and middle levels of culture, so far belongs to current civilized thought, that those who hold the doctrine to be false, and the practices based upon it futile, can nevertheless understand and sympathize with the lower nations to whom they are matters of the most sober and serious conviction. Nor is even the notion of a separable spirit or soul as the cause of life in plants too incongruous with ordinary ideas to be readily appreciable. But the theory of souls in the lower culture stretches beyond this limit, to take in a conception much stranger to modern thought. Certain high savage races distinctly hold, and a large proportion of other savage and barbarian races make a more or less close approach to, a theory of separable and surviving souls or spirits belonging to stocks and stones, weapons, boats, food, clothes, ornaments, and other objects which to us are not merely soulless but lifeless.

Yet, strange as such a notion may seem to us at first if we place ourselves by an effort in the intellectual position of an uncultured tribe, and examine the theory of object souls, from their point of view, we shall hardly pronounce it irrational. In discussing the origin of myth, some account has been already given of the primitive stage of thought in which personality and life are ascribed not to men and beasts only, but to things. It has been shown how what we call inanimate objects—rivers, stones, trees, weapons, and so forth—are treated as living intelligent beings, talked to, propitiated, punished for the harm they do. Hume, whose "Natural History of Religion" is perhaps more than any other work the source of modern opinions as to the development of religion, comments on the influence of this personifying stage of thought. "There is an universal tendency among mankind to conceive all beings like themselves, and to transfer to every object those qualities with which they are familiarly acquainted, and of which they are intimately conscious.... The *unknown causes,* which continually employ their thought, appearing always in the same aspect, are all apprehended to be of the same kind or species. Nor is it long before we ascribe to them thought and reason, and passion, and sometimes even the limbs and figures of men, in order to bring them nearer to a resemblance with ourselves." August Comte has ventured to bring such a state of thought under terms of strict definition in his conception of the primary mental condition of mankind—a state of "pure fetishism, constantly characterized by the free and direct exercise of our primitive tendency to conceive all external bodies soever, natural or artificial, as animated by a life essentially analogous to our own, with mere differences of intensity." Our comprehension of the lower stages of mental culture depends much on the thoroughness with which we can appreciate this primitive, childlike conception, and in this our best guide may be the memory of our own childish days. He who recollects when there was still personality to him in posts and sticks, chairs and toys, may well understand how the infant philosophy of mankind could extend the notion of vitality to what modern science only recognizes as lifeless things; thus one main part of the lower animistic doctrine as to souls of objects is accounted for. The doctrine requires for its full conception of a soul not only life, but also a phantom or apparitional spirit; this development, however, follows without difficulty, for the evidence of dreams and visions applies to the spirits of objects in much the same manner as to human ghosts. Everyone who has seen visions while light-headed in fever, everyone who has ever dreamt a dream, has seen the phantoms of objects as well as of persons. How then can we charge the savage with far-fetched absurdity for taking into his philosophy and religion an opinion which rests on the very evidence of his senses? The notion is implicitly recognized in his accounts of ghosts, which do not come naked, but clothed, and even armed; of course there must be spirits of garments and weapons, seeing that the spirits of men come bearing them. It will indeed place savage philosophy in no unfavorable light, if we compare this extreme animistic development of it with the popular opinion still surviving in civilized countries, as to ghosts and the nature of the human soul as connected with them. When the ghost of Hamlet's father appeared armed cap-a-pie,

> "Such was the very armour he had on,
> When he the ambitious Norway combated."

And thus it is a habitual feature of the ghost-stories of the civilized, as of the savage world, that the ghost comes dressed, and even dressed in well-known clothing worn in life. Hearing as well as sight testifies to the phantoms of objects: the clanking of ghostly chains and the rustling of ghostly dresses are described in the literature of apparitions. Now by the savage theory, according to which the ghost and his clothes are alike imaginary and subjective, the facts of apparitions are rationally met. But the modern vulgar who ignore or repudiate the notion of ghosts of things, while retaining the notion of ghosts of persons, have fallen into a hybrid state of opinion which has neither the logic of the savage nor of the civilized philosopher.

It remains to sum up in a few words the doctrine of souls, in the various phases it has assumed from first to last among mankind. In the attempt to trace its main course through the successive grades of man's intellectual history, the evidence seems to accord best with a theory of its development, somewhat to the following effect. At the lowest levels of culture of which we have clear knowledge, the notion of a ghost-soul animating man while in the body, is found deeply ingrained. There is no reason to think that this belief was learnt by savage tribes from contact with higher races, nor that it is a relic of higher culture from which the savage tribes have degenerated; for what is here treated as the primitive animistic doctrine is thoroughly at home among savages, who appear to hold it on the very evidence of their senses, interpreted on the biological principle which seems to them most reasonable. We may now and then hear the savage doctrines and practices concerning souls claimed as relics of a high religious culture pervading the primeval race of man. They are said to be traces of remote ancestral religion, kept up in scanty and perverted memory by tribes degraded from a nobler state. It is easy to see that such an explanation of some few facts, sundered from their connection with the general array, may seem plausible to certain minds. But a large view of the subject can hardly leave such argument in possession. The animism of savages stands for and by itself; it explains its own origin. The animism of civilized men, while more appropriate to advanced knowledge, is in great measure only explicable as a developed product of the older and ruder system. It is the doctrines and rites of the lower races which are, according to their philosophy, results of point-blank natural evidence and acts of straightforward practical purpose. It is the doctrines and rites of the higher races which show survival of the old in the midst of the new, modification of the old to bring it into conformity with the new, abandonment of the old because it is no longer compatible with the new. Let us see at a glance in what general relation the doctrine of souls among savage tribes stands to the doctrine of souls among barbaric and cultured nations. Among races within the limits of savagery, the general doctrine of souls is found worked out with remarkable breadth and consistency. The souls of animals are recognized by a natural extension from the theory of human souls; the souls of trees and plants follow in some vague partial way; and the souls of inanimate objects expand the general category to its extremest boundary. Thenceforth, as we explore human thought onward from savage into barbarian and civilized life, we find a state of theory more conformed to positive science, but in itself less complete and consistent. Far on into civilization, men still act as though in some half-meant way they believed in souls or ghosts of objects, while nevertheless their knowledge of physical science is beyond so crude a philosophy. As to the doctrine of souls of plants, fragmentary evidence of the history of its breaking down in Asia has reached us. In our own day and country, the notion of souls of beasts is to be seen dying out. Animism, indeed, seems to be drawing in its outposts, and concentrating itself on its first and main position, the doctrine of the human soul. This doctrine has undergone extreme modification in the course of culture. It has outlived the almost total loss of one great argument attached to it— the objective reality of apparitional souls or ghosts seen in dreams and visions. The soul has given up its ethereal substance, and become an immaterial entity, "the shadow of a shade." Its theory is becoming separated from the investigations of biology and mental science, which now discuss the phenomena of life and thought, the sense and the intellect, the emotions and the will, on a groundwork of pure experience. There has arisen an intellectual product whose very existence is of the deepest significance, a "psychology" which has no longer anything to do with "soul." The soul's place in modern thought is in the metaphysics of religion, and its especial office there is that of furnishing an intellectual side to the religious doctrine of the future life. Such are the alterations which have differenced the fundamental animistic belief in its course through successive periods of the world's culture. Yet it is evidence that, notwithstanding all this profound change, the conception of the human soul is, as to its most essential nature, continuous from the philosophy of the savage thinker to that of the modern professor of theology. Its definition has remained from the first that of an animating, separable, surviving entity, the vehicle of individual personal existence. The theory of the soul is one principal part of a system of religious philosophy, which unites, in an unbroken line of mental connection, the savage fetish-worshiper and the civilized Christian. The divisions which have separated the great religions of the world into intolerant and hostile sects are for the most part superficial in comparison with the deepest of all religious schisms, that which divides Animism from Materialism.

THE CONCEPTION OF MANA *

By R. R. MARETT

I⊤ is no part of my present design to determine by an exhaustive analysis of the existing evidence, how the conception of *mana* is understood and applied within its special area of distribution, namely, the Pacific region. Such a task pertains to Descriptive Ethnology; and it is rather a problem of Comparative Ethnology that I would venture to call attention to. I propose to discuss the value, that is to say, the appropriateness and the fruitfulness—of either this conception of *mana* or some nearly equivalent notion, such as the Huron *orenda,* when selected by the science of Comparative Religion to serve as one of its categories, or classificatory terms of the widest extension.

Now any historical science that adopts the comparative methods stands committed to the postulate that human nature is sufficiently homogeneous and uniform to warrant us in classifying its tendencies under formulæ coextensive with the whole broad field of anthropological research. Though the conditions of their occurrence cause our data to appear highly disconnected, we claim, even if we cannot yet wholly make good, the right to bind them together into a single system of reference by means of certain general principles. By duly constructing such theoretical bridges, as Dr. Frazer is fond of calling them, we hope eventually to transform, as it were, a medley of insecure, insignificant sandbanks into one stable and glorious Venice.

So much, then, for our scientific idea. But some skeptical champion of the actual may be inclined to ask: "Are examples as a matter of fact forthcoming, at any rate from

* *The Threshold of Religion.* New York: The Macmillan Co.

within the particular department of Comparative Religion, of categories or general principles that, when tested by use, prove reasonably steadfast?" To this challenge it may be replied that, even when we limit ourselves to the cause of what may be described as "rudimentary" religion—in regard to which our terminology finds itself in the paradoxical position of having to grapple with states of mind themselves hardly subject to fixed terms at all—there are at all events distinguishable degrees of value to be recognized amongst the categories in current employment. Thus most of us will be agreed that, considered as a head of general classification, *"tabu"* works well enough, but "totem" scarcely so well, whilst "fetish" is perhaps altogether unsatisfactory. Besides, there is at least one supreme principle that has for many years stood firm in the midst of these psychological quicksands. Dr. Tylor's conception of "animism" is the crucial instance of a category that successfully applies to rudimentary religion taken at its widest. If our science is to be compared to a Venice held together by bridges, then "animism" must be likened to its Rialto.

At the same time, "lest one good custom should corrupt the world," we need plenty of customs; and the like holds true of categories. In what follows I may seem to be attacking "animism," in so far as I shall attempt to endow *"mana"* with classificatory authority to some extent at the expense of the older notion. Let me, therefore, declare at the outset that I should be the last to wish our time-honored Rialto to be treated as an obsolete or obsolescent structure. If I seek to divert from it some of the traffic it is not naturally suited to bear, I am surely offering it no injury, but a service.

One word more by way of preface. There are those who dislike the introduction of native terms into our scientific nomenclature. The local and general usages, they object, tend to become confused. This may, indeed, be a real danger. On the other hand, are we not more likely to keep in touch with the obscure forces at work in rudimentary religion if we make what use we can of the clues lying ready to hand in the recorded efforts of rudimentary reflection upon religion? The *mana* of the Pacific may be said, I think, without exaggeration to embody rudimentary reflection—to form a piece of subsconscious philosophy. To begin with, the religious eye perceives the presence of *mana* here, there, and everywhere. In the next place, *mana* has worked its way into the very heart of the native languages, where it figures as more than one part of speech, and abounds in secondary meanings of all kinds. Lastly, whatever the word may originally have signified (as far as I know, an unsettled question), it stands in its actual use for something lying more or less beyond the reach of the senses—something verging on what we are wont to describe as the immaterial or unseen. All this, however, hardly amounts to proof that *mana* has acquired in the aboriginal mind the full status of an abstract idea. For instance, whereas a Codrington might decide in comprehensive fashion that all Melanesian religion consists in getting *mana* for oneself,[1] it is at least open to doubt whether a Melanesian sage could have arrived, unassisted, at a generalization so abstract—a "bird's-eye view" so detached from confusing detail. Nevertheless, we may well suspect some such truth as this to have long been more or less inarticulately felt by the Melanesian mind. In fact, I take it, there would have been small difficulty on Bishop Codrington's part in making an intelligent native realize the force of his universal proposition. What is the moral of this? Surely, that the science of Comparative Religion should strive to explicate the meaning inherent in any given phase of the world's religious experience in just those terms that would naturally suggest themselves, suppose the phase in question to be somehow quickened into self-consciousness and self-expression. Such terms I would denominate "sympathetic"; and would, further, hazard the judgment that, in the case of all science of the kind, its use of sympathetic terms is the measure of its sympathetic insight. *Mana,* then, I contend, has, despite its exotic appearance, a perfect right to figure as a scientific category by the side of *tabu*—a term hailing from the same geographical area—so long as a classificatory function of like importance can be found for it. That function let us now proceed, if so may be, to discover.

Codrington defines *mana,* in its Melanesian use, as follows: "a force altogether distinct from physical power, which acts in all kinds of ways for good and evil, and which it is of the greatest advantage to possess or control"; or again he says: "It is a power or influence, not physical, and in a way supernatural; but it shows itself in physical force, or in any kind of power or excellence which a man possesses." It is supernatural just in this way, namely, that it is "what works to effect everything which is beyond the ordinary power of men, outside the common processes of nature." He illustrates his point by examples: "If a man has been successful in fighting, it has not been his natural strength of arm, quickness of eye, or readiness of resource that has won success; he has certainly got the *mana* of a spirit or of some deceased warrior to empower him, conveyed in an amulet of a stone round his neck or a tuft of leaves in his belt, in a tooth hung upon a finger of his bow hand, or in the form of words with which he brings supernatural assistance to his side. If a man's pigs multiply, and his gardens are productive, it is not because he is industrious and looks after his property, but because of the stones full of *mana* for pigs and yams that he possesses. Of course a yam naturally grows when planted, that is well known, but it will not be very large unless *mana* comes into play; a canoe will not be swift unless *mana* be brought to bear upon it, a net will not catch many fish, nor an arrow inflict a mortal wound." [2]

From Polynesia comes much the same story. Tregear in his admirable comparative dictionary of the Polynesian dialects renders the word which may be either noun or adjective, thus: "supernatural power; divine authority; having qualities which ordinary persons or things do not possess." He seems to distinguish, however, what might be called a "secular" sense, in which the term stands generally for "authority," or as an adjective, for "effectual, effective." He cites copious instances from the various dialects to exemplify ᵗhe supernatural mode of *mana*. Thus the word is applied, in Maori, to a wooden sword that has done deeds so wonderful as to possess a sanctity and power of its own; in Samoan, to a parent who brings a curse on a disobedient child; in Hawaiian, to the gods, or to a man who by his death gives efficacy to an idol; in Tongan, to whoever performs miracles, or bewitches; in Mangarevan, to a magic stuff given to a man by his grandfather, or, again, to divination in general; and so forth. In short, its range is as wide as those of divinity and witchcraft taken together. If, on the other hand, we turn to what I have called the secular sense attributed to *mana,* as, for example, when it is used of a chief, a healer of maladies, a successful pleader, or the winner of a race, we perceive at once that the distinction of meaning holds good for the civilized lexicographer rather than for the unsophisticated native. The chief who can impose *tabu,* the caster-out of disease-devils, and, in hardly less a degree, the man who can exercise the magic of persuasion, or who can command the luck which the most skilled athlete does not despise, is for the Polynesian mind not metaphorically "gifted" or "inspired," but literally. Of course, as in Europe, so in Polynesia, the coin of current usage may have become clipped with lapse of time. Thus Plato tells us that both the Spartans and the Athenian ladies of his day used to exclaim of any male person they happened to admire, "what a divine man!" It need not surprise us, therefore, that in Mangarevan you may say of any number over forty *manamanana*—an "awful" lot, in fact. Such an exception, however, can scarcely be allowed to count against the generalization that, throughout the Pacific region, *mana* in its essential meaning connotes what both Codrington and Tregear describe as the supernatural.

Now mark the importance of this in view of the possible use of *mana* as a category of Comparative Religion. Comparative Religion, I would maintain, at all events so long as it is seeking to grapple with rudimentary or protoplasmic types of religious experience, must cast its net somewhat widely. Its interest must embrace the whole of one, and, perhaps, for savagery the more considerable, of the two fundamental aspects under which his experience or his universe (we may express it either way) reveals itself to the rudimentary intelligence of man. What to call this aspect, so as to preserve the flavor of the aboriginal notion, is a difficulty, but a difficulty of detail. The all-important matter is to establish by induction that such an aspect is actually perceived at the level of experience I have called "rudimentary." This, I believe, can be done. I have, for instance, shown elsewhere that even the Pygmy, a person perhaps not overburdened with ideas, possesses in his notion of *oudah* an inkling of the difference that marks off the one province of experience from the other. Of course he cannot deal with *oudah* abstractly; provinces of experience and the like are not for him. But I found that, when confronted with particular cases, or rather types of case, my Pygmy friend could determine with great precision whether *oudah* was there or not. What practical results, if any, would be likely to flow from this effort of discernment my knowledge of Pygmy customs, unfortunately, does not enable me to say; but I take it that the conception is not there for nothing. I shall assume, then, that an inductive study of the ideas and customs of savagery will show, firstly, that an awareness of a fundamental aspect of life and of the world, which aspect I shall provisionally term "supernatural," is so general as to be typical, and, secondly, that such an awareness is no less generally bound up with a specific group of vital reactions.

As to the question of a name for this aspect different views may be held. The term our science needs ought to express the bare minimum of generic being required to constitute matter for the experience which, taken at its highest, though by no means at its widest, we call "religious." "Raw material for good religion and bad religion, as well as for magic white or black"—how are we going to designate that in a phrase? It will not help us here, I am afraid, to cast about amongst native words. Putting aside *oudah* as too insignificant and too little understood to be pressed into this high service, I can find nothing more nearly adapted to the purpose than the Siouan *wakan* or *wakanda;* of which M'Gee writes: "the term may be translated into 'mystery' perhaps more satisfactory than in (*sic*) any other single English word, yet this rendering is at the same time too limited, as *wakanda* vaguely denotes also power, sacred, ancient, grandeur, animate, immortal." But when vagueness reaches this pitch, it is time, I think, to resort to one of our own more clear-cut notions. Amongst such notions that of "the supernatural" stands out, in my opinion, as the least objectionable. Of course it is our term; that must be clearly understood. The savage has no word for "nature." He does not abstractly distinguish between an order of uniform happenings and a higher order of miraculous happenings. He is merely concerned to mark and exploit the difference when presented in the concrete. As Codrington says: "A man comes by chance upon a stone which takes his fancy; its shape is singular, it is like something, it is certainly not a common stone, there must be *mana* in it. So he argues with himself, and he puts it to the proof; he lays it at the root of a tree to the fruit of which it has a certain resemblance, or he buries it in the ground when he plants his garden; an abundant crop on the tree or in the garden shows that he is right, the stone is *mana,* has that power in it." Here, however, we have at all events the germs of our formal antithesis between the natural and the supernatural; which, by the way, is perhaps not so nicely suited to the taste of the advanced theology of our day that it would have much scruple about dedicating the expression to the service of rudimentary religion. I should like to add that in any case the English word "supernatural" seems to suit this context better than the word "sacred." *L'idée du sacre* may be apposite enough in French, since *sacré* can stand either for "holy" or for "damned"; but it is an abuse of the English language to speak of the "sacredness" of some accursed wizard. Hence, if our science were to take over the phrase, it must turn its back on usage in favor of etymology; and then, I think, it would be found that the Latin *sacer* merely amounts to *tabu,* the negative mode of the supernatural—a point to which I now proceed.

Tabu, as I have tried to prove elsewhere, is the negative mode of the supernatural, to which *mana* corresponds as the positive mode. I am not confining my attention to the use of these terms in the Pacific region, but am considering them as transformed, on the strength of their local use, into categories, of worldwide application. Given the supernatural in any form there are always two things to note about it: firstly, that you are to be heedful in regard to it; secondly, that it has power. The first may be called its negative character, the second its positive. Perhaps stronger expressions might seem to be required. *Tabu,* it might be argued, is not so much negative as prohibitive, or even minatory; whilst *mana* is not merely positive but operative and thaumaturgic. The more colorless terms, however, are safer when it is a question of characterizing universal modes of the supernatural. Given this wide sense *tabu* simply implies that you must be heedful in regard to the supernatural, not that you must be on your guard against it. The prohibition to have dealings with it is not absolute; otherwise practical religion would be impossible. The warning is against casual, incautious, profane dealings. "Not to be lightly approached" is Codrington's translation for the corresponding term used in the New Hebrides. Under certain conditions man may draw nigh, but it is well for him to respect those conditions. Thus "prohibitive" and "minatory" are too strong. *Tabu,* as popularly used, may in a given context connote something like absolute prohibition, but in the universal appli-

cation I have given to it can only represent the supernatural
in its negative character—the supernatural, so to speak, on
the defensive.

We come now to *mana*. Here, again, we must shun descriptions that are too specific. *Mana* is often operative and
thaumaturgic, but not always. Like energy, *mana* may be
dormant or potential. *Mana,* let us remember, is an adjective as well as a noun, expressing a possession which is likewise a permanent quality. The stone that looks like a banana
is and has *mana,* whether you set it working by planting it
at the foot of your tree or not. Hence it seems enough to say
that *mana* exhibits the supernatural in its positive capacity
—ready, but not necessarily in act, to strike.

At this point an important consideration calls for notice.
Tabu and *mana* apply to the supernatural solely as viewed
in what I should like to call its first, or existential, dimension. With its second, or moral, dimension they have nothing
to do whatever. They register judgments of fact, as philosophers would say, not judgments of value; they are constitu-
tive categories, not normative. Thus, whatever is supernatural
is indifferently *tabu*—perilous to the unwary; but as such it
may equally well be holy or unclean, set apart for God or
abandoned to devil, sainted or sinful, cloistered or quaran-
tined. There is plenty of linguistic evidence to show that
such distinctions of value are familiar to the savage mind.
Nor is it hard to see how they arise naturally out of the
tabu idea. Thus in Melanesia everything supernatural is at
once *tambu* and *rongo,* words implying that it is fenced
round by sanctions human and divine; but there is a
stronger term *buto,* meaning that the sanctions are specially
dreadful and thereupon becoming equivalent to "abominable," where we seem to pass without a break from degree
of intensity to degree of worth. Passing on to *mana,* we find
exactly the same absence of moral significance. The mystic
potentiality is alike for good and evil. Take, for example,
two Samoan phrases found side by side in Tregear's dictionary: *fa'a-mana,* to show extraordinary power or energy, as

in healing; *fa'a-mana-mana* to attribute an accident or misfortune to supernatural powers. Or again, in Melanesia European medicine is called *pei mana,* but, on the other hand, there is likewise *mana* in the poisoned arrow. Similarly, *orenda* is power to bless or to curse; and the same holds good of a host of similar native expressions, for instance, *wakan, qube, manitu, oki,* not to go outside North America. Meanwhile, in this direction also moral valuations soon make themselves felt. Thus in the Pacific region we have plenty of special words for witchcraft; and in Maori mythology we even hear of a personified witchcraft *Makutu* dwelling with the wicked goddess *Miru,* of whom Tregear writes: "the unclean *tapu* was her power (*mana*)." Or again, in Huron, there is a word *otgon,* denoting specifically the malign and destructive exercise of *orenda;* and Hewitt notes the curious fact that the former term is gradually displacing the latter— as if, he observes, the bad rather than the good manifestations of supernatural power produced a lasting impression on the native mind. Elsewhere I have given Australian examples of a similar distinction drawn between wonder-working power in general, and a specifically noxious variety of the same, such as, for instance, the well-known *arungquiltha* of the Arunta.

I have said enough, I trust, to show that there exists, deep ingrained in the rudimentary thought of the world, a conception of a specific aspect common to all sorts of things and living beings, under which they appear at once as needing insulation and as endowed with an energy of high, since extraordinary, potential—all this without any reference to the bearing of these facts on human welfare. In this connection I would merely add that our stock antithesis between magic and religion becomes applicable only when we pass from this to the second or moral dimension of the supernatural. Presented in its double character of *tabu* and *mana* the supernatural is not moral or immoral, but simply unmoral. It is convenient to describe its sphere as that of the magico-religious; but strictly speaking it is that which is neither magical nor religious, since these terms of valuation have yet to be superinduced. I am aware that the normative function of these expressions is not always manifest, that it is permissible to speak of false religion, white magic, and so on. But, for scientific purposes, at any rate, an evaluatory use ought, I think, to be assigned to this historic disjunction, not merely in view of the usage of civilized society, but as a consequence of that tendency to mark off by discriminative epithets the good and the bad supernaturalisms, the kingdoms of God and of the Devil, which runs right through the hierological language of the world.

The rest of this paper will be concerned with a more perplexing and hence, probably, more controversial, side of the subject. Put in a nutshell the problem is the following: How does "animism" fit into the scheme? Is the supernatural identical with the spiritual, and is *mana* nothing more or less than spiritual power? Or, on the contrary, are *mana* and "soul" or "spirit" categories that belong to relatively distinct systems of ideas—do the two refuse to combine?

As regards this latter question, our minds may quickly be set at rest. Somehow these categories do manage to combine freely, and notably in that very Pacific region where *mana* is at home. The Melanesian evidence collected by Codrington is decisive. Wherever *mana* is found—and that is to say wherever the supernatural reveals itself—this *mana* is referred to one of three originating sources, namely, a living man, a dead man's ghost, or a "spirit"; spirits displaying one of two forms, that of a ghostlike appearance—as a native put it, "something indistinct, with no definite outline, gray like dust, vanishing as soon as looked at"—or that of the ordinary corporeal figure of a man. Other manifestations of the supernatural are explained in terms of these three, or rather the last two, agencies. A sacred animal, or again, a sacred stone, is one which belongs to a ghost or spirit, or in which a ghost or spirit resides. Can we say, then, that "animism" is in complete possession of the field? With a little stretching of the term, I think, we can. Ghosts and spirits of ghostlike form are obviously animistic to the core. Supernatural beings of human and corporeal form may perhaps be reckoned by courtesy as spirits; though really we have here the rudiments of a distinct and alternative development, namely, anthropomorphic theism, a mode of conception that especially appeals to the mythological fancy. Finally, animism can be made without much trouble to cover the case of the living man with *mana*. If a man has *mana*, it resides in his "spiritual part" or "soul," which after his death becomes a ghost. Besides, it appears, no man has this power of himself; you can say that he has *mana* with the use of the substantive, not that he is *mana*, as you can say of a ghost or spirit. This latter "puts the *mana* into the man" (*mana*—a causative verb) or "inspires" him; and an inspired man will even, in speaking of himself, say not "I" but "we two." There seems, however, to be a certain flaw in the native logic, involving what comes perilously near to argument in a circle. Not every man has *mana*, not every ghost; but the soul of man of power becomes as such a ghost of power, though in his capacity of ghost he has it in greater force than when alive. On the ground of this capacity for earning, if not enjoying, during life the right to be *mana*, I have ventured provisionally to class the living man with the ghost and with the spirit as an independent owner of *mana*; but it is clear that, in defiance of logic, animism has contrived to "jump the claim."

Having thus shown in the briefest way that *mana* and "animism" can occur in combination, I proceed to the awkward task of determining how, if treated as categories applicable to rudimentary religion in general, they are to be provided each with a classificatory function of its own. Perhaps the simplest way of meeting, or rather avoiding, the difficulty is to deny that "animism" is a category that belongs intrinsically to our science at all. Certainly it might be said to pertain more properly to some interest wider than the magico-religious, call it rudimentary philosophy or what we will. It makes no difference whether we take animism in the vaguer Spencerian sense of the attribution of life and animation—an attitude of mind to which I prefer to give the distinguishing name of "animatism"—or in the more exact Tylorian sense of the attribution of soul, ghost, or ghost-like spirit. In either case we are carried far beyond the bounds of rudimentary religion, even when magic is made co-partner in the system. There is obviously nothing in the least supernatural in being merely alive. On the other hand, to have soul is, as we have seen, not necessarily to have *mana* here or hereafter. The rudimentary philosophy of Melanesia bounds in nice distinctions of an animistic kind as follows: A yam lives without intelligence, and therefore has no *tarunga* or "soul." A pig has a tarunga and so likewise has a man, but with this difference that when a pig dies he has no *tindalo* or "ghost," but a man's *tarunga* at his death becomes a *tindalo*. Even so, however, only a great man's *tarunga* becomes a *tindalo* with *mana,* a "ghost of worship," as Codrington renders it. Meanwhile, as regards a *vui* or "spirit," its nature is apparently the same as that of a soul, or at any rate a human soul, but it is never without *mana*. Thus only the higher grades of this animistic hierarchy rank as supernatural beings; and you know them for what they are not by their soul-like nature, but by the *mana* that is in them.

It remains to add that *mana* can come very near to meaning "soul" or "spirit," though without the connotation of wraith-like appearance. Tregear supplies abundant evidence from Polynesia. *Mana* from meaning indwelling power naturally passes into the sense of "intelligence," "energy of character," "spirit"; and the kindred term *manawa* (*manava*) expresses "heart," "the interior man" "conscience," "soul"; whilst various other compounds of *mana* between them yield a most complete psychological vocabulary—words for thought, memory, belief, approval, affection, desire and so forth. Meanwhile, *mana* always, I think, falls short of expressing "individuality." Though immaterial it is perfectly transmissible. Thus only last week a correspondent wrote to me from Simbo in the Solomon Islands to say that a native has no objection to imparting to you the words of a *mana* song. The mere knowledge will not enable you to perform miracles. You must pay him money, and then *ipso facto* he will transmit the *mana* to you—as we should say, the "good-will" of the concern. On the other hand, animism lends itself naturally to this purpose. It is true that there is often very little individuality attaching to the nameless spirit (*vui*) that may enter into a man. But the ghost (*tindalo*) that inspires you is apt to retain its full selfhood, so that the possessed one speaks of "we two—So-and-so and I."

I conclude, then, that *mana,* or rather the *tabu-mana* formula, has solid advantages over animism, when the avowed object is to find what Dr. Tylor calls "a minimum definition of religion." *Mana* is coextensive with the supernatural; animism is far too wide. *Mana* is always *mana,* supernatural power, differing in intensity—in voltage, so to speak—but never in essence; animism splits up into more or less irreducible kinds, notably "soul," "spirit," and "ghost." Finally, *mana,* whilst fully adapted to express the immaterial —the unseen force at work behind the seen—yet, conformably with the incoherent state of rudimentary reflection, leaves in solution the distinction between personal and impersonal, and in particular does not allow any notion of a high individuality to be precipitated. Animism, on the other hand, tends to lose touch with the supernatural in its more impersonal forms, and is not well suited to express its transmissibility nor indeed its immateriality; but, by way of compensation, it can, in a specialized form, become a means of representing supernatural agents of high individuality, whenever the social condition of mankind is advanced enough to foster such a conception.

The last consideration paves the way for a concluding observation. Throughout I have been in search of classificatory categories applicable to rudimentary religion as a whole. In other words, I have assumed that the subject is to be treated as if it represented a single level of experience, and, moreover, that the treatment is to limit itself to the work of classifying—that is, arranging the facts under synoptic head-lines. Now such, I think, must be the prime object of our science at its present stage of development. We must not try to move too fast. Some day, however, when our knowl-edge is fuller and better organized, we may hope to be able to deal with the history of religion genetically—to exhibit the successive stages of a continuous process of orthogenic or central evolution, whilst making, at the same time, full allowance for the thousand and one sideshoots of the wide-spreading family tree of human culture. Now when it comes to exhibiting genesis, it may well be, I think, that, along certain lines of growth, and perhaps along the central line itself, *mana* will at a certain point have to give way to one or another type of animistic conception. Where marked in-dividualities tend to be lacking in society, as in Australia, there it will be found that the supernatural tends normally to be apprehended under more or less impersonal forms. This holds true even within the strict *habitat* of the *mana* doctrine. Thus in the New Hebrides, where the culture is relatively backward, the prevailing animistic conception is that of the *vui,* or "spirit," a being often nameless, and, at the best, of vague personality. On the other hand, in the Solomon Islands, where the culture is more advanced, the religious interest centers in the *tindalo mana* or ghost of power—the departed soul of some well-known individual. In effect, hero-worship has, with the evolution of the hero, superinduced itself upon some sort of polydæmonism redo-lent of democracy. But I refrain from further speculations about religious evolution. They are tempting, but, in the present state of our knowledge, hardly edifying. I would merely add, glancing forwards for a moment from rudimen-tary religion to what we call "advanced," that to the end animism never manages to drive the more impersonal con-ceptions of the supernatural clean out of the field. The "ghost," clearly, does not hold its own for long. Anthropomorphic theism, on the other hand, a view that is bred from animatism rather than from animism proper, dominates many of the higher creeds, but not all. Buddhism is a standing example of an advanced type of religion that exalts the impersonal aspect of the divine. It is, again, especially noticeable how a thinker, such as Plato, with all his interest in soul, human personality, and the subjective in general, hesitates between a personal and an impersonal rendering of the idea of God. Thus the ambiguity that lies sleeping in *mana* would seem to persist to some extent even when religious experience is at its most self-conscious. In the meantime all religions, low and high, rudimentary and advanced, can join in saying with the psalmist that "power belongeth unto God."

NOTES

[1] R. H. Codrington, *The Melanesians* (Oxford, 1891), p. 119 *n*.
[2] Codrington, *op. cit.*, pp. 118-120.

ANIMISM AND THE OTHER WORLD *

By GEZA ROHEIM

SYMPATHETIC MAGIC

AMONG the Tharumba and neighboring tribes, if a sorcerer obtains some of the excreta, hair, nails, or other parts of the enemy's body, he takes it to a "squeaking tree" and places it between the touching surfaces of the two branches causing the "squeak." When the wind blows, this fragment is squeezed and ground to atoms, and the owner is believed to suffer in the same way.[1] The Koko-minni blacks of the Palmer River employ an instrument known as Ti or Eti for injuring one another at a distance. It is formed of a piece of human shinbone or a slip of bamboo, the free end being covered with cement, and the whole is enclosed in a bark covering. When the magician has put some of the intended victim's hair, urine, or excrement into the bone or bamboo, he burns it and so makes his victim sick. A cure can be effected by taking the patient's spear and dilly-bag to the waterside. A supernatural serpent, visible only to the medicine man, devours these objects, and the patient is saved. The Proserpine River black makes an enemy sick by sticking a bone pin into the place where he has been defecating or micturating.[2] Among the Kabi and Wakka, to obtain possession of a man's hair or ordure was to ensure his death. He declined as these decayed. It was dangerous to pass under a leaning tree or fence. The reason alleged for caution in this respect was that a woman might have been under the tree or fence and that blood from her might have fallen upon it.

Akin to this dread of passing under an elevated object,

* Animism, Magic and the Divine King. New York: Alfred A. Knopf, Inc.

and due no doubt to the same cause, is that fear of another person's stepping over one's body.[3]

This kind of sorcery is called *ngadhungi* by the Narrinyeri. It is practiced in the following manner: every adult black-fellow is constantly on the lookout for bones of ducks, swans, or other birds, or of the fish called ponde, the flesh of which has been eaten by a human being. Of these he constructs his charms. All the natives, therefore, are careful to burn the bones of the animals which they eat, so as to prevent their enemies from getting hold of them; but in spite of this precaution, such bones are commonly obtained by disease-makers who want them. When a man has obtained a bone—for instance, the leg bone of a duck—he imagines that he possesses the power of life and death over the man, woman, or child who ate its flesh. The bone is prepared by being scraped into something like a skewer; a small round lump is then made by mixing a little fish oil and red ochre into a paste, and enclosing in it the eye of a Murray cod and a small piece of the flesh of a dead human body. This lump is stuck on the top of the bone and a covering tied over it, and it is put in the bosom of a corpse in order that it may derive deadly potency by contact with corruption. After it has remained there for some time it is considered fit for use, and is put away until its assistance is required. Should circumstances arise calculated to excite the resentment of the disease-maker towards the person who ate the flesh of the animal from which the bone was taken, he immediately sticks the bone in the ground near the fire so that the lump aforesaid may melt away gradually, firmly believing that as it dissolves it will produce disease in the person for whom it was designed, however distant he may be. The entire melting and dropping off of the lump is supposed to cause death.[4]

This form of magic is well known to anthropologists, and is usually, but loosely, called sympathetic magic, on account of the sympathy which is still supposed to connect the original owner with the severed part of his body. Sir James

Frazer lays stress on the former connection of the severed part with the whole and speaks therefore of contagious magic.[5] It is remarkable that this well-nigh universal form of magic is conspicuous by its absence in Central Australia. We quote Spencer and Gillen:

"In connection with the question of magic, it may be noticed, in conclusion, that a special form which is widely met with in other Australian tribes is not practiced amongst these. We refer to the attempt to injure an enemy by means of securing and then practicing some form of charm upon some part of his person such as hair or nail clippings." [6]

We can guess the reason of this difference. The Central Australian native dreads something else; the loss of his churinga. If this is the real reason, we should say that the displacement of a phobia has taken place and then there must be an identical meaning underlying these two losses. Be that as it may, at any rate, we find sympathetic magic again among the Kakadu who have only the rudiments of the churinga concept.[7] On account of this magic, called *korno* (excrement), they are very careful to hide from view all excremental matter, so that their camps are more cleanly than those of other tribes. But a medicine man, of course, can find the desired *korno*. They put it in little wax spheres, dig a pit, and when the fire is hot enough the real performance begins. The men bend forward each of them with his hand between his legs, and the women do the same, because the spirit must not, on any account, see their private parts. If it were to do so they would swell enormously.

Now some feathers that have been prepared are knocked into the sphere, one by one, the natives saying: "Keep quiet, keep quiet," the idea being that the birds they represent will thereby be persuaded not to give notice to the victim that any danger such as a snake or crocodile threatens him. Then the men sway about, looking as fierce as they possibly can, while they place the wax spheres in the *peindi*. Away in the distance they can hear the spirit cursing and swearing, saying: *"Mulyarinyu koiyu,"* [8] and using other opprobrious expressions. The men say: *"Nerk, nerk, nerk,"* and beckon it onwards. It is under a spell and comes on cursing more and more loudly. When it is near, the natives crouch down silently, the front man ready for action. On it comes like a whirlwind, rushes along the trench, scraping against the sharp Pandanus leaves. Suddenly, when it reaches the brink of the *peindi,* the front man knocks the stick representing it into the fire on the top of the *korno.* All of them shout: "Ah, Ah, Ah, Ach, Ach, Brng, Brng!" at the top of their voices. Without a moment's pause, stones and earth are piled on the *Yalmuru* (soul), one specially large stone being placed on top, the men pressing down hard with all their might to keep it in. The spirit underneath can be heard sizzling and swearing. It tries to lift the stone, but cannot. At length it is heard to say: "Grr, Grr, u-u." Then it is quiet and all is over. The Pandanus leaves are rubbed on the top stone, while the names of different snakes, Ngabadaua, Yidaburabara, and Numberanerji, are hissed out. One or other of them is supposed to be sure to bite the victim before long. Finally a log of wood that is supposed to represent a crocodile, which it is hoped will seize him some day when he is bathing, is placed on top, and then, when the performers have smeared their bodies over with burnt corkwood and grass, the ceremony is at an end, and they go back to camp. Any one coming across the remains of the trench, and seeing the stones and log piled up above the small mound, knows that evil magic has been performed. It is supposed that, by the capture of the *Yalmuru,* the man is left without his protector. If, for example, he be out in the bush, there will be no spirit to warn him of approaching danger, or guide him to where he can secure his food. [9]

After having thus given a few facts from the Australian continent, we must call the reader's attention to some prominent features of this form of magic. It seems that the fundamental fear of savages is connected with the idea of a *part being separated from the whole.* This part is inserted be-

tween two branches, put into a bamboo, or burnt. From the
case of the Kakadu we gather the idea that the whole ceremony must have something to do with the genital act;
otherwise why do they cover the private parts and why
does the bad language used by the spirit refer to the
mother?

If we make use of explanations arrived at elsewhere our
work will be made easy indeed. We have shown frequent
use of the tree as a mother-symbol in Australia; between the
two branches would therefore mean between the two legs,
in the vagina. The churinga is a penis-symbol, and therefore
the loss of the churinga would be castration. This is curiously confirmed by the fact that Mathew, after describing
sympathetic magic, passes on to the phobia of the aboriginals
with regard to women's blood, a phobia that develops into
a dread of passing under a tree, thus confirming our
view of the symbolic equation woman (mother)＝tree, and
at the same time revealing the real dread as that of passing
under a woman, *i.e.,* into her vagina. The next analogy again
confirms this; they are afraid of somebody stepping over
them. We have already found sufficient reason for explaining "stepping over" as a symbol of *coitus,*[10] and in point of
fact. it is in coitus that a *part is separated from the whole.*
This is what the whole body feels in a hallucinatory fashion,
the penis itself gets nearer to this danger and finally the
seminal fluid really suffers this separation.[11] From the wish-
fulfillment point of view, all this refers to uterine regression,
and it is also from this point of view that we may, following
Ferenczi, call the penis the wish-object or ego-ideal of the
body and the seminal fluid a still more "ideal" representative
of the same tendency. The fundamental dread of primitive
man, therefore, seems to be the dread of castration, or, what
amounts to the same thing from the unconscious point of
view, the dreaded expenditure of the semen.

It is very probable that the peculiar Australian punishment for breaking certain taboos, the abnormal swelling
of the genitalia, is only a cover for the opposite dread

(castration) and that those who are castrating their enemy in the Kakadu ceremony dread the talion punishment of their nefarious wishes.

The Kai, in New Guinea, have this phobia in a very prominent degree. They believe that anything done to their "soul-substance" is done to their whole person. As the "soul-substance" is believed to be present in every particle of his body, and in anything that may come into contact with his body, a member of these tribes is in perpetual danger of being killed by means of any careless deed of his own. Hence the great anxiety in the behavior of these tribes. If a thread of his girdle or a lock of his hair gets entangled in the bush and torn off, he does not pass on before having annihilated every trace of its presence. He does not throw anything away, and the leavings of his meals he carefully hides or throws into the fire. Soul-substance also remains where he sat; therefore, when he rises he makes it disappear by stamping with his leg or poking the place with a stick. Or he may sprinkle water on the place, or use "cool" leaves to cool it down, *i.e.,* to drive the soul-substance away.[12] The black art itself is called *hafe,* *i.e.,* to bind. The first thing is to procure a *ga,* a medium containing the soul-substance of the victim. As the soul-substance is contained in the smallest particle of the body, and in anything that comes into contact with a person, some hair, a drop of perspiration, the excrements, or anything else can be used. But it must be quite fresh, otherwise it is possible that the soul-substance has already evaporated. As the chief thing seems to be not to let it cool down, it is therefore quickly put into a little tube of bamboo and this is hidden under the arm-pit. The object must not come into contact with water or fire. Sharp or pointed objects are also prohibited as they might frighten the soul out of the parcel. Trees from a "ghost-place" must be used for making the parcel. The first bamboo tube is put into a second, and this again into a third of correspondingly larger size. During the preparation they sing:

"Cockatoo, cockatoo, come and tear his body open, and hack his bowels into pieces till he dies." The spirits are expected to come from a mythical cave and take the victim's soul with them into the other world. After various other incantations the magician finishes with the following spell:

> "Fall off and rot like cucumbers.
> X. wind himself in pain.
> His arms and legs shall wind themselves in pain.
> His whole body shall wind itself in pain.
> His head shall wind itself in pain.
> His bowels shall wind themselves in pain.
> His genital organ shall wind itself in pain."

Now comes the application of fire to the parcel. The medicine-man is identified with the man whose soul is in the parcel and he strictly avoids water or anything that has come into contact with water. Water would cool him, and hence cool the soul he has caught. By cooling it, it would stop the "roasting," and hence the burning pain the patient suffers from the fire would be alleviated. The other great taboo of our practitioner in the black arts is woman, presumably for the same reason. Intercourse would certainly cool him, by relieving him of sexual tension, and it seems that his tension is somehow identical with the feverish state of disease. The whole thing comes to an end at a village festival where all the parcels are finally burnt. At the moment when the bark envelope is cut through the little tubes fall to the ground, and the magicians "act" the agony of their victims.[13] At the King William Cape they call this "binding the soul." The chief thing is that the parcel containing the hair or nail-parings should not come into contact with water.[14]

A Bukaua lives in perpetual fear of these devices, and it is therefore very difficult to get the substance needed. But they have their cunning methods. The magician offers some betel-fruit to the intended victim in a friendly manner. Before doing so, however, he pinches a small piece off the fruit and this is sufficient for magic to work on. When they have made the victim ill there are two possibilities. Either "he comes back to himself" (*eng king tau*), that is, gets better, or the reverse takes place. What is meant by coming back to himself? The Bukaua tell us that a slimy excretion proceeds from people who are dangerously ill. This slime is a continuous sticky sort of jelly: it hangs down through the clefts of the floor and sparkles at night. If the victim gets better the slimy mass returns into his body, that is, "he comes to himself." But if the "undefinable mass" is torn off, loses connection with the body, then *"eng king tau tom"* ("he does not come to himself"), and the victim dies.[15]

Among the Mafulu the use of the inedible remnants of recently consumed vegetable food as a medium for causing illness and death is confined to the case of a victim who has passed the stage of very young childhood. A man or woman never carelessly throws aside his own food remnants of this character; and his reason for this is fear of sorcery. He carefully keeps them under his control until he can take them to a river, into which he throws them, after which they are harmless as a medium against him. The fear concerning these remains is that a sorcerer will use them for a ceremony somewhat similar to that described in connection with the death of a chief, but in a hostile way. No such precautions are taken with reference to similar food eaten by very young children.

Secondly, there are the discharged excrements and urine. This, for some reason, only applies to the case of an infant or quite young child. Here again it is not possible to learn the reason for the limitation; but it is confirmed by the fact that grown-up persons take no pains whatever to prevent the passing of these things into the possession of other people, whereas, as regards little children, the mothers or other persons having charge of them always take careful precautions. The mother picks up her little child's excrement and wraps it in a leaf, and then either carefully hides it in a hole in the ground, or throws it into the river, or places it in a little raised-up, nest-like receptacle, which is sometimes erected near the house for this purpose, and where also it is regarded as being safe. As regards the urine, she pours upon it, as it lies on the ground or on the house floor or platform, a little clean water, which she obtains from any handy source, or sometimes from a little store which, when away from other water supply, she often carries about with her for the purpose.[16]

According to Romilly the hair-cutting and the refuse of a man's meals are the chief objects for a sorcerer to work on.[17] The Marindanim call the particle of the body they obtain for a sorcery a *papahi*. Hair, excrement, the remains of food, may all serve as a *papahi,* as they all contain the soul-substance of their owner. If they put this *papahi* into a bamboo and then throw the bamboo into a swamp the person concerned will become ill, and if the *papahi* is burnt the victim will die. The idea is that while the patient is being tortured by the disease, it is really the *papahi-nakari* who are playing with the *papahi* and throwing it about. By *nakari* the Marind mean certain mythical girls who, according to their ideas, are connected with nearly everything in nature.[18]

In reconsidering this small collection of facts from New Guinea, the point we must lay stress on seems first to be that the body particle operated on seems to be identified with the soul. True, this was the case among the most northern of the Australian tribes we took into consideration, the Kakadu, but it was certainly not so prominent in Australia as in New Guinea. What the soul really is seems evident enough if we consider the belief of the Bukaua that a slimy jelly proceeds from the patient and when it falls off, he dies. The jelly is the seminal fluid and its loss in the act of cohabitation seems to be an experience fraught with such anxiety that the idea of death is modeled on it. If this explanation is valid, we can also understand why the spell of the Kai lead up to the pains in the genitalia as to a sort of climax, the other pains serving merely as an introduction to this one. Water being a very frequent symbol of woman, the two taboos of our sorcerer seem to mean the same thing; and as he identifies himself with his victim who is to be castrated, it is both easy to see why woman should be taboo to him and why with the Marind the disease arises from the circumstance that mythical females are trifling with the tiny part that has been segregated from the whole.

In Melanesia the wizards who cure the diseases are very often the same men who cause them, the mana derived from spirits and ghosts being in both cases the agent employed; but it often happens that the darker secrets of the magic art are possessed and practiced only by those whose power lies in doing harm, and who are resorted to when it is desired to bring evil upon an enemy. Their secrets, like others connected with mana, are passed down from one generation to another, and may be bought. The most common working of this malignant witchcraft is that, so common among savages, in which a fragment of food, bit of hair or nail, or anything closely connected with the person to be injured, is the medium through which the power of the ghost or spirit is brought to bear. Some relic such as a bone of the dead person whose ghost is set to work is, if not necessary, very desirable for bringing his power into the charm; and a stone may have its mana for doing mischief. What is needed is the bringing together of the man who is to be injured and the spirit of the ghost that is to injure him; this can be done when something which pertains to the man's person can be used, such as a hair, a nail, a leaf with which he has wiped the perspiration from his face, and with equal effect when a fragment of the food which has passed into the man forms the link of union. Hence in Florida when a scrap from a man's meal could be secreted and thrown into the *vunuha* haunted by the *tindalo* ghost, the man would certainly be ill; and in the New Hebrides, when the male snake carried away a fragment of food into the place sacred to spirits, the man who had eaten of the food would sicken as the fragment decayed. It was for this reason that a constant care was exercised to prevent anything that might be used in witchcraft from falling into the hands of ill-wishers; it was the regular practice to hide hair and nail-parings and to give the remains of food most carefully to the pigs. There is little doubt that the common practice of retiring into the sea or a river has its origin in the belief that water is a bar to the use of excrement in charms. It is remarkable that at Mota where clefts in rocks are used (no doubt also for security) the word used is *tas,* which means sea. In the Banks' Islands the fragment of food, or whatever it may be, by which a man is charmed is called *garata;* this is made up by the wizard with a bit of human bone, and smeared with a magic decoction in which it would rot away. Or the *garata* would be burnt, and while it was burning the wizard sang his charm; as the *garata* was consumed, the wizard burning it by degrees day after day, the man from whom it came sickened, and would die, and the ghost of the man whose bone was burning would take away his life. In Aurora the fragment of food is made up with certain leaves; as these rot and stink the man dies. In Lepers' Island the *garata* is boiled together with certain magical substances in a clam shell with charms which call on Tagaro. It is evident that no one who intends to bring mischief to a man by means of a fragment of his food will partake of that food himself, because by doing so he would bring the mischief on himself also. Hence a native offering even a single banana to a visitor will bite the end of it before he gives it, and a European giving medicine to a sick native gives confidence by himself taking a little first.[19]

It is interesting to note the ambivalency underlying these customs, for, whereas in New Guinea this pinching off is a dark practice of the magician, in fact, castration itself, here it occurs as the indication of a sort of covenant

between the two parties. On the Gazelle Peninsula black
magic will only take effect if the medium contains a particle
of the intended victim; for instance, his hair, a shred of
his clothes, his saliva or footprints.[20] The central tribe of
New Ireland call this method *mumut*. Here the magician
makes two little parcels; one of them he puts near the fire
and the other he dangles over a swamp by means of a rod
and a string. Now he goes to the swamp, and lo there the
poor soul is sitting staring into the water; now to the fire,
there again he sees the soul warming itself.[21]

At Limbo, Vellalavella, and Rubiana all personal refuse
is usually burnt from fear of wizards. Their method here
is to make a parcel of leaves and dig the object into the
earth. Then they tread on it and put three hot stones above
—this kills the victim.[22]

In Fiji if a man desired the death of a rival he procured
something that had belonged to this person—a lock of
hair, the parings of his nails, a scrap of food, or, best of
all, his excreta, for witchcraft produced incurable dysentery
through these. The wizard then prepared the charm by
wrapping the object in certain leaves of magical properties
and burying the parcel in a bamboo case either in the
victim's plantation or in the thatch of his house.[23] A man
will take the remains of the food, clothing or tobacco
left by his enemy. With these he mixes certain leaves and
slugs from the sea. He carries the mixture into the woods,
puts it in empty coconuts, pieces of bamboo, or native
jars. Then he buries the vessel and believes that his enemy
sickens as the mixture ferments.[24]

One mode of operating is to bury a coconut, with the eye
upward, beneath the temple-hearth, on which a fire is kept
constantly burning; and as the life of the nut is destroyed
so the health of the person it represents will fail, till death
ensues. At Matuku there is a grove sacred to the god
Tokalau—the wind. The priest promises the destruction
of any hated person in four days if those who wish his
death bring a portion of his hair, dress, or food which he

has left. This priest keeps a fire burning, and approaches the place on his hands and knees. If the victim bathe before the fourth day, the spell is broken. The most common method, however, is the *Vakadranikau,* or compounding of certain leaves supposed to possess a magical power, and which are wrapped in other leaves, or put into a small bamboo case, and buried in the garden of 'the person to be bewitched, or hidden in the thatch of his house. Processes of this kind are the most dreaded, and the people about Mbua are reputed to prepare the most potent compounds. The native imagination is so absolutely under the control of fear of these charms that persons, hearing that they were the objects of such spells, have lain down on their mats and died through fear.

Those who have reason to suspect others of plotting against them avoid eating in their presence, or are careful to leave no fragment of food behind; they also dispose their garment so that no part can be removed. Most natives, on cutting their hair, hide what is cut off in the thatch of their homes. Some build themselves a small house and surround it with a moat, believing that a little water will neutralize the charms which are directed against them.[25]

We have hitherto found reason to assume that the one great terror in the life of primitive mankind is the same that plays such a fundamental part in individual neurosis: the dread of castration. This complex rooted in the resistance offered by the narcissistic libido of the cell to fission as the fundamental feature of archaic life is never absent in coitus where there is always a reluctance of the male towards the expenditure of semen. The ideas of primitive man on death are modeled by the pleasure principle, being based on the unconscious view of coitus. The soul separated from the body is either the seminal fluid ejaculated in the act, or what amounts to the same thing, the phallus cut off. This interpretation of the soul is fully borne out by experience derived from the study of psychotic and neurotic patients. Dr. Almasy tells me of a case of shell-shock treated by him in a lunatic asylum. The soldier was a Hungarian lad from Transylvania. He declared in the asylum that the shell in question had robbed him of his "double," and added that the "double" was the Székely [26] word for the penis. A patient of mine (character analysis, *ejaculatio præcox* in a moderate degree) has the phantasy that the analyst's easy chairs are transformed at night-fall into stallions and on these stallions the analysts fly through the air and appear as nightmares in the patients' dreams. The couch on which he lies is not a stallion but a hippopotamus (called water-horse in Hungarian), and it goes and wallows in the mud at night. What a fine thing it would be to have a penis as big as a hippopotamus; he could go and knock the policeman down with such a club. At night his penis would leave his body, assume the shape of a hippopotamus and roam about. It is hardly necessary to tell the anthropologist that we here have the explanation of the savage dream-soul leaving the body at night and roaming in search of desirable things. "King Gunthram lay in the wood asleep with his head in his faithful henchman's lap; the servant saw as it were a snake issue from his lord's mouth and run to the brook, but it could not pass, so the servant laid his sword across the water and the creature ran along it and up into a mountain, after a while came back and returned into the mouth of the sleeping king, who waking told him how he went over an iron bridge into a mountain full of gold." [27] King Gunthram's serpent and the penis-hippopotamus of my patient mean one and the same thing.

From the starting-point the work of repression sets in. The first consolation offered to mortal man is the same as the temptation of coitus; the valuable part of his personality is not lost but given into the custody of a being with whom he has successfully identified himself in the sexual act. There is another world for the soul after this one and this other world is simply a posthumous projection of the womb. The passage itself is the passage of the penis or the sperm into the vagina. While at a lower level the castration aspect of this passage is emphasized, the grim features of this last journey gradually become obscured by the brilliant vision of everlasting love-fire. But just as we know full well that the gods, the "Living Ones" of Irish and other mythologies, are really the dead, we can have no doubt of the nature of the wound that lies behind the phantasy of an Isle of Women.

As, moreover, the sexual act is the portal of life, and as the act of giving birth is the female equivalent of the fission that takes place in the male in the act of coitus, death becomes obscured under the guise of birth and appears as the first step into a new life. In this concept, which it is so easy to find in the phantasies and dreams of individual neurotics, the secondary elaboration due to the tendency to obscure the impending danger probably reached its highest pitch. If we return for a moment to the story of Little Dog our attention is attracted by the series formed of three episodes; first Little Dog's whole body in the giant moose and his exit from that animal, then his being in a house inhabited by a woman (magic staff holds the door ajar—finger chopped off) and at last his overcoming the danger of castration by the magic staff in actual coitus. The series represents a gradual retransformation of the myth towards the true situation. In the first episode the danger of fission (castration) is completely overlaid by the aid of another phantasy, this time formed on the basis of the pre-natal situation and of birth itself, by means of the idea of evading coitus by returning not with a part but with the whole body into the maternal womb. Therefore, if the recent experiences of Dr. Ferenczi and other analysts show that the ideas of birth and uterine regression appear in analysis as a consolation to overlay the dread of castration, we can say that in the history of mankind the function of animism offers a distinct parallel to these tendencies. The solace found by the pious in the visions of a happy heaven is of the same type as that sought by the neurotic in the various symptoms that correspond to uterine regression.

King Arthur feels his end drawing near. He first commands his sword Excalibur to be cast back into the lake whence it came. We believe that this sword is fundamentally identical with the sword of the Grail romances, the meaning of which has been described in the language of "Life-Symbolism" by Miss Jessie Weston.[28]

Like the supernatural branch, the silver bough, it belongs to the king as long as he lives and returns to its origin at his death.[29] First this phallic symbol disappears into the lake, then Queen Morgan le Fay appears on the scene with her fairies in a barge to take her beloved hero and brother to her realm. And thus spake Sir Arthur:

> "I am going a long way....
>
> .   .   .   .   .   .
>
> To the island-valley of Avilion
> Where falls not hail, or rain, or any snow,
> Nor ever wind blows loudly; but it lies
> Deep-meadowed, happy, fair with orchard lawns
> And bowery hollows crown'd with summer sea,
> Where I will heal me of my grievous wound." [30]

However fair the fairy queen may be, mortal man can scarce forget the wound.

NOTES

[1] R. H. Mathews, *Ethnological Notes on the Aboriginal Tribes of New South Wales and Victoria*, 1905.

[2] W. E. Roth, "Superstition, Magic, and Medicine," *North Queensland Ethnography*, Bull. 5, 1920, pp. 31, 32.

[3] J. Mathews, *Eaglehawk and Crow*, 1899, p. 144. *Idem.*, *Two Representative Tribes of Queensland*, 1910, p. 177.

[4] Taplin, *The Narrinyeri Tribe*, 1879, p. 24.

[5] Frazer, *The Magic Art*, 1911, 1, § 3.

[6] Spencer and Gillen, *Native Tribes*, p. 553.

[7] Cf. Róheim, *Australian Totemism*, 1925, pp. 313, 184.

[8] Curse directed against the mother.

[9] B. Spencer, *Native Tribes of the Northern Territory of Australia*, 1914, pp. 259, 260.

[10] Cf. Róheim, "The Significance of Stepping Over," *International Jour-*

nal of Psychoanalysis, iii, p. 370. See also on the churinga, *Australian Totemism,* 1925, p. 183.

[11] Ferenczi, *Genitaltheorie,* 1923.

[12] Ch. Keysser, *Aus dem Leben der Kaileute,* Neuhauss, *Deutsch Neu Guinea,* iii, p. 117.

[13] Keysser, *loc. cit.,* pp. 135-138.

[14] Stolz, *Die Umgebung von Kap König Wilhelm,* p. 248.

[15] St. Lehner, *Bukaua.* Neuhauss, *loc. cit.,* iii, p. 464.

[16] Williamson, *The Mafulu, Mountain People of British New Guinea,* 1912, pp. 280-281.

[17] H. H. Romilly, *From My Verandah in New Guinea,* 1889, p. 83.

[18] P. Wirz, *Die Marind-anim von Holländisch-Süd-Neu-Guinea* (Hamburgische Universität, 1925, pp. 72-73.

[19] R. H. Codrington, *The Melanesians,* 1891, pp. 202-204.

[20] Parkinson, *Dreissig Jahre in der Südsee,* 1907, p. 118.

[21] Parkinson, *loc. cit.,* p. 192.

[22] R. Thurnwald, *Forschungen auf den Salomo Inseln und dem Bismarck Archipel,* i, pp. 443-444.

[23] B. Thomson, *The Fijians,* 1908, p. 164.

[24] W. Deane, *Fijian Society,* 1921, p. 162.

[25] B. C. A. I. van Dinter, "Eenige geographische en ethnographische aantee keningen betreffende het eiland Siaoe," *Tijdschrift voor Indische Taal, Land- en Volkenkunde,* xli, 1899, p. 381. Frazer, *Totem and Taboo,* p. 228.

[26] Hungarian dialect in Transylvania.

[27] E. B. Tylor, *Primitive Culture,* i, p. 442, quoting Grimm, *D.M.* 1036.

[28] J. L. Weston, *The Quest of the Holy Grail,* 1913. *Idem., From Ritual to Romance,* 1920.

[29] A. B. Cook, "The European Sky God," *Folk-Lore,* xvii, 1906, p. 152.

[30] Tennyson, *Morte d'Arthur.* Malory, *Le Morte d'Arthur,* bk. xxi, ch. v

MAGIC AND RELIGION *

By SIR JAMES FRAZER

WHEREVER sympathetic magic occurs in its pure unadulterated form, it assumes that in nature one ever follows another necessarily and invariably without the intervention of any spiritual or personal agency. Thus its fundamental conception is identical with that of modern science; underlying the whole system is a faith, implicit but real and firm, in the order and uniformity of nature. The magician does not doubt that the same causes will always produce the same effects, that the performance of the proper ceremony, accompanied by the appropriate spell, will inevitably be attended by the desired results, unless indeed, his incantations should chance to be thwarted and foiled by the more potent charms of another sorcerer. He supplicates no higher power; he sues the favor of no fickle and wayward being; he abases himself before no lawful deity. Yet his power, great as he believes it to be, is by no means arbitrary and unlimited. He can wield it only so long as he strictly conforms to the rules of his art, or to what may be called the laws of nature as conceived by him. To neglect these rules, to break these laws in the smallest particular is to incur failure, and may even expose the unskillful practitioner himself to the utmost peril. If he claims a sovereignty over nature, it is a constitutional sovereignty rigorously limited in its scope and exercised in exact conformity with ancient usage. Thus the analogy between the magical and the scientific conceptions of the world is close. In both of them the succession of events is perfectly regular and certain, being determined by immutable laws, the operation of which can be foreseen and calculated precisely;

* *The Golden Bough.* New York: The Macmillan Co.

693

the elements of caprice, of chance, and of accident are banished from the course of nature. Both of them open up a seemingly boundless vista of possibilities to him who knows the causes of things and can touch the secret springs that set in motion the vast and intricate mechanism of the world. Hence the strong attraction which magic and science alike have exercised on the human mind; hence the powerful stimulus that both have given to the pursuit of knowledge. They lure the weary inquirer, the footsore seeker, on through the wilderness of disappointment in the present by their endless promises of the future; they take him up to the top of an exceeding high mountain and show him, beyond the dark clouds and rolling mists at his feet, a vision of the celestial city, far off, it may be, but radiant, with unearthly splendor, bathed in the light of dreams.

The fatal flaw of magic lies not in its general assumption of a succession of events determined by law, but in its total misconception of the nature of the particular laws which govern that succession. If we analyze the various cases of sympathetic magic which have been passed in review in the preceding pages, and which may be taken as fair samples of the bulk, we shall find them to be all mistaken applications of one or other of two great fundamental laws of thought, namely, the association of ideas by similarity and the association of ideas by contiguity in space or time. A mistaken association of similar ideas produces imitative or mimetic magic; a mistaken association of contiguous ideas produces sympathetic magic in the narrower sense of the word. The principles of association are excellent in themselves, and indeed absolutely essential to the working of the human mind. Legitimately applied they yield science; illegitimately applied they yield magic, the bastard sister of science. It is therefore a truism, almost a tautology, to say that all magic is necessarily false and barren; for were it ever to become true and fruitful, it would no longer be magic but science. From the earliest times man has been engaged in a search for general rules whereby to turn the order of natural phenomena to his own advantage, and in the long search he has scraped together a great hoard of such maxims, some of them golden and some of them mere dross. The true or golden rules constitute the body of applied science which we call the arts; the false are magic.

If magic is thus next of kin to science, we have still to inquire how it stands related to religion. But the view we take of that relation will necessarily be colored by the idea which we have formed of the nature of religion itself; hence a writer may reasonably be expected to define his conception of religion before he proceeds to investigate its relation to magic. There is probably no subject in the world about which opinions differ so much as the nature of religion, and to frame a definition of it which would satisfy every one must obviously be impossible. All that a writer can do is, first, to say clearly what he means by religion, and afterwards to employ the word consistently in that sense throughout his work. By religion, then, I understand a propitiation or conciliation of powers superior to man which are believed to direct and control the course of nature and of human life. In this sense it will readily be perceived that religion is opposed in principle both to magic and to science. For all conciliation implies that the being conciliated is a conscious or personal agent, that his conduct is in some measure uncertain, and that he can be prevailed upon to vary it in the desired direction by a judicious appeal to his interests, his appetites, or his emotions. Conciliation is never employed towards things which are regarded as inanimate, nor towards persons whose behavior in the particular circumstances is known to be determined with absolute certainty. Thus in so far as religion assumes the world to be directed by conscious agents who may be turned from their purpose by persuasion, it stands in fundamental antagonism to magic as well as to science, both of which take for granted that the course of nature is determined, not by the passions or caprice of personal beings, but by the operation of immutable laws acting mechanically. In magic, indeed, the assumption is only implicit, but in science it is explicit. It is true that magic often deals with spirits, which are personal agents of the kind assumed by religion; but whenever it does so in its proper form, it treats them exactly in the same fashion as it treats inanimate agents— that is, it constrains or coerces instead of conciliating or propitiating them as religion would do. In ancient Egypt, for example, the magicians claimed the power of compelling even the highest gods to do their bidding, and actually threatened them with destruction in case of disobedience. Similarly in India at the present day the great Hindoo trinity itself of Brahma, Vishnu, and Siva is subject to the sorcerers, who, by means of their spells, exercise such an ascendency over the mightiest deities, that these are bound submissively to execute on earth below, or in heaven above, whatever commands their masters the magicians may please to issue. This radical conflict of principle between magic and religion sufficiently explains the relentless hostility with which in history the priest has often pursued the magician. The haughty self-sufficiency of the magician, his arrogant demeanor towards the higher powers, and his unabashed claim to exercise a sway like theirs could not but revolt the priest, to whom, with his awful sense of the divine majesty, and his humble prostration in presence of it, such claims and such a demeanor must have appeared an impious and blasphemous usurpation of prerogatives that belong to God alone. And sometimes, we may suspect, lower motives concurred to whet the edge of the priest's hostility. He professed to be the proper medium, the true intercessor between God and man, and no doubt his interests as well as his feelings were often injured by a rival practitioner, who preached a surer and smoother road to fortune than the rugged and slippery path of divine favor.

Yet this antagonism, familiar as it is to us, seems to have made its appearance comparatively late in the history of religion. At an earlier stage the functions of priest and sorcerer were often combined or, to speak perhaps more correctly, were not yet differentiated from each other. To serve his purpose man wooed the good-will of gods or spirits by prayer and sacrifice, while at the same time he had recourse to ceremonies and forms of words which he hoped would of themselves bring about the desired result without the help of god or devil. In short, he performed religious and magical rites simultaneously; he uttered prayers and incantations almost in the same breath, knowing or reckoning little of the theoretical inconsistency of his behavior, so long as by hook or crook he contrived to get what he wanted. Instances of this fusion or confusion of magic with religion have already met us in the practices of Melanesians and of some East Indian islanders. So far as the Melanesians are concerned, the general confusion cannot be better described than in the words of Dr. R. H. Codrington: "That invisible power which is believed by the natives to cause all such effects as transcend their conception of the regular course of nature, and to reside in spiritual beings, whether in the spiritual part of living men or in the ghosts of the dead, being imparted by them to their names and to various things that belong to them, such as stones, snakes, and indeed objects of all sorts, is that generally known as *mana*. Without some understanding of this it is impossible to understand the religious beliefs and practices of the Melanesians; and this again is the active force in all they do and believe to be done in magic, white or black. By means of this men are able to control or direct the forces of nature, to make rain or sunshine, wind or calm, to cause sickness or remove it, to know what is far off in time and space, to bring good luck and prosperity, or to blast and curse." "By whatever name it is called, it is the belief in this supernatural power, and in the efficacy of the various means by which spirits

and ghosts can be induced to exercise it for the benefit of
men, that is the foundation of the rites and practices which
can be called religious; and it is from the same belief
that everything which may be called Magic and Witchcraft draws its origin. Wizards, doctors, weather-mongers,
prophets, diviners, dreamers, all alike, everywhere in the
islands, work by this power. There are many of these who
may be said to exercise their art as a profession; they
get their property and influence in this way. Every considerable village or settlement is sure to have some one
who can control the weather and the waves, some one
who knows how to treat sickness, some one who can work
mischief with various charms. There may be one whose
skill extends to all these branches; but generally one man
knows how to do one thing, and one another. This various
knowledge is handed down from father to son, from
uncle to sister's son, in the same way as is the knowledge
of the rites and methods of sacrifice and prayer; and very
often the same man who knows the sacrifice knows also
the making of the weather, and of charms for many purposes besides. But as there is no order of priests, there
is also no order of magicians or medicine-men. Almost
every man of consideration knows how to approach some
ghost or spirit, and has some secret of occult practices."

The same confusion of magic and religion has survived
among peoples that have risen to higher levels of culture. It
was rife in ancient India and ancient Egypt; it is by no
means extinct among European peasantry at the present
day. With regard to ancient India we are told by an eminent
Sanscrit scholar that "the sacrificial ritual at the earliest
period of which we have detailed information is pervaded
with practices that breathe the spirit of the most primitive
magic." Again, the same writer observes that "the ritual of
the very sacrifice for which the metrical prayers were composed is described in the other Vedic texts as saturated from
beginning to end with magical practices which were to be
carried out by the sacrificial priests." In particular he tells

us that the rites celebrated on special occasions, such as marriage, initiation, and the anointment of a king, "are complete models of magic of every kind, and in every case the forms of magic employed bear the stamp of the highest antiquity." Speaking of the importance of magic in the East, and especially in Egypt, Professor Maspero remarks that "we ought not to attach to the word magic the degrading idea which it almost inevitably calls up in the mind of a modern. Ancient magic was the very foundation of religion. The faithful who desired to obtain some favor from a god had no chance of succeeding except by laying hands on the deity, and this arrest could only be effected by means of a certain number of rites, sacrifices, prayers, and chants, which the god himself had revealed, and which obliged him to do what was demanded of him." According to another distinguished Egyptologist "the belief that there are words and actions by which man can influence all the powers of nature and all living things, from animals up to gods, was inextricably interwoven with everything the Egyptians did and everything they left undone. Above all, the whole system of burial and of the worship of the dead is completely dominated by it. The wooden puppets which relieved the dead man from toil, the figures of the maid-servants who baked bread for him, the sacrificial formulas by the recitation of which food was procured for him, what are these and all the similar practices but magic? And as men cannot help themselves without magic, so neither can the gods; the gods also wear amulets to protect themselves, and use magic spells to constrain each other." But though we can perceive the union of discrepant elements in the faith and practice of the ancient Egyptians, it would be rash to assume that the people themselves did so. "Egyptian religion," says Professor Widemann, "was not one and homogeneous; it was compounded of the most heterogeneous elements, which seemed to the Egyptian to be all equally justified. He did not care whether a doctrine or a myth belonged to what, in modern scholastic phraseology,

we should call faith or superstition; it was indifferent to him
whether we should rank it as religion or magic, as worship
or sorcery. All such classifications were foreign to the
Egyptian. To him no one doctrine seemed more or less justified than another. Nay, he went so far as to allow the most
flagrant contradictions to stand peaceably side by side."

Among the ignorant classes of modern Europe the same
confusion of ideas, the same mixture of religion and magic,
crops up in various forms. Thus we are told that in France
"the majority of the peasants still believe that the priest possesses a secret and irresistible power over the elements. By
reciting certain prayers which he alone knows and has the
right to utter, yet for the utterance of which he must afterwards demand absolution, he can, on an occasion of pressing
danger, arrest or reverse for a moment the action of the
eternal laws of the physical world. The winds, the storms,
the hail, and the rain are at his command and obey his will.
The fire also is subject to him, and the flames of a conflagra-
tion are extinguished at his word." For example, French
peasants used to be, perhaps are still, persuaded that the
priests could celebrate, with certain special rites, a "Mass
of the Holy Spirit," of which the efficacy was so miraculous
that it never met with any opposition from the divine will;
God was forced to grant whatever was asked of Him in this
form, however rash and importunate might be the petition.
No idea of impiety or irreverence attached to the rite in
the minds of those who, in some of the great extremities
of life, sought by this singular means to take the kingdom
of heaven by storm. The secular priests generally refused to
say the "Mass of the Holy Spirit"; but the monks, especially
the Capuchin friars, had the reputation of yielding with less
scruple to the entreaties of the anxious and distressed. In the
constraint thus supposed by Catholic peasantry to be laid
by the priest upon the deity we seem to have an exact
counterpart of the power which, as we saw, the ancient
Egyptians ascribed to their magicians. Again, to take another example, in many villages of Provence the priest is

still reputed to possess the faculty of averting storms. It is not every priest who enjoys this reputation; and in some villages when a change of pastors takes place, the parishioners are eager to learn whether the new incumbent has the power (*pouder*), as they call it. At the first sign of a heavy storm they put him to the proof by inviting him to exorcise the threatening clouds; and if the result answers to their hopes, the new shepherd is assured of the sympathy and respect of his flock. In some parishes, where the reputation of the curate in this respect stood higher than that of his rector, the relations between the two have been so strained in consequence, that the bishop has had to translate the rector to another benefice. Again, Gascon peasants believe that to revenge themselves on their enemies bad men will sometimes induce a priest to say a mass called the Mass of Saint Sécaire. Very few priests know this mass, and three-fourths of those who do know it would not say it for love or money. None but wicked priests dare to perform the gruesome ceremony, and you may be quite sure that they will have a very heavy account to render for it at the last day. No curate or bishop, not even the archbishop of Auch, can pardon them; that right belongs to the pope of Rome alone. The Mass of Saint Sécaire may be said only in a ruined or deserted church, where owls mope and hoot, where bats flit in the gloaming, where gypsies lodge of nights, and where toads squat under the desecrated altar. Thither the bad priest comes by night with his light o' love, and at the first stroke of eleven he begins to mumble the mass backwards, and ends just as the clocks are knelling the midnight hour. His leman acts as clerk. The host he blesses is black and has three points; he consecrates no wine, but instead he drinks the water of a well into which the body of an unbaptized infant has been flung. He makes the sign of the cross, but it is on the ground and with his left foot. And many other things he does which no good Christian could look upon without being struck blind and deaf and dumb for the rest of his life. But the man for whom the mass is said withers away little by little, and nobody can say what is the matter with him; even the doctors can make nothing of it. They do not know that he is slowly dying of the Mass of Saint Sécaire.

Yet though magic is thus found to fuse and amalgamate with religion in many ages and in many lands, there are some grounds for thinking that this fusion is not primitive, and that there was a time when man trusted to magic alone for the satisfaction of such wants as transcended his immediate animal cravings. In the first place a consideration of the fundamental notions of magic and religion may incline us to surmise that magic is older than religion in the history of humanity. We have seen that on the one hand magic is nothing but a mistaken application of the very simplest and most elementary processes of the mind, namely, the association of ideas by virtue of resemblance or contiguity; and on the other hand that religion assumes the operation of conscious or personal agents, superior to man, behind the visible screen of nature. Obviously the conception of personal agents is more complex than a simple recognition of the similarity or contiguity of ideas; and a theory which assumes that the course of nature is determined by conscious agents is more abstruse and recondite, and requires for its apprehension a far higher degree of intelligence and reflection than the view that things succeed each other simply by reason of their contiguity or resemblance. The very beasts associate the ideas of things that are like each other or that have been found together in their experience; and they could hardly survive for a day if they ceased to do so. But who attributes to the animals a belief that the phenomena of nature are worked by a multitude of invisible animals or by one enormous and prodigiously strong animal behind the scenes? It is probably no injustice to the brutes to assume that the honor of devising a theory of this latter sort must be reserved for human reason. Thus, if magic be deduced immediately from elementary processes of reasoning, and be, in fact, an error into which the mind falls almost spontaneously, while religion rests on conceptions which the merely animal intelligence can hardly be supposed to have yet attained to, it becomes probable that magic arose before religion in the evolution of our race, and that man essayed to bend nature to his wishes by the sheer force of spells and enchantments before he strove to coax and mollify a coy, capricious, or irascible deity by the soft insinuation of prayer and sacrifice.

The conclusion which we have thus reached deductively from a consideration of the fundamental ideas of religion and magic is confirmed inductively by what we know of the lowest existing race of mankind. To the student who investigates the development of vegetable and animal life on our globe, Australia serves as a sort of museum of the past, a region in which strange species of plants and animals, representing types that have long been extinct elsewhere, may still be seen living and thriving, as if on purpose to satisfy the curiosity of these later ages as to the fauna and flora of the antique world. This singularity Australia owes to the comparative smallness of its area, the waterless and desert character of a large part of its surface, and its remote situation, severed by wide oceans from the other and greater continents. For these causes, by concurring to restrict the number of competitors in the struggle itself; and thus many a quaint old-fashioned creature, many an antediluvian oddity, which would long ago have been rudely elbowed and hustled out of existence in more progressive countries, has been suffered to jog quietly along in this preserve of Nature's own, this peaceful garden, where the hand on the dial of time seems to move more slowly than in the noisy bustling world outside. And the same causes which have favored the survival of antiquated types of plants and animals in Australia, have conserved the aboriginal race at a lower level of mental and social development than is now occupied by any other set of human beings spread over an equal area elsewhere. Without metals, without houses, without agriculture, the Australian savages represent the stage of material culture which was reached by our remote ancestors in the Stone Age; and the rudimentary state of the arts of life among them reflects faithfully the stunted condition of their minds. Now in regard to the question of the respective priority of magic or religion in the evolution of thought, it is very important to observe that among these rude savages, while magic is universally practiced, religion in the sense of a propitiation or conciliation of the higher powers seems to be nearly unknown. Roughly speaking, all men in Australia are magicians, but not one is a priest; everybody fancies he can influence his fellows or the course of nature by sympathetic magic, but nobody dreams of propitiating gods or spirits by prayer and sacrifice. "It may be truly affirmed," says a recent writer on the Australians, "that there was not a solitary native who did not believe as firmly in the power of sorcery as in his own existence; and while anybody could practice it to a limited extent, there were in every community a few men who excelled in pretension to skill in the community; by unanimous consent the whites have called them 'doctors,' and they correspond to the medicine men and rain-makers of other barbarous nations. The power of the doctor is only circumscribed by the range of his fancy. He communes with spirits, takes aerial flights at pleasure, kills or cures, is invulnerable and invisible at will, and controls the elements."

But if in the most primitive state of human society now open to observation on the globe we find magic thus conspicuously present and religion conspicuously absent, may we not reasonably conjecture that the civilized races of the world have also at some period of their history passed through a similar intellectual phase, that they attempted to force the great powers of nature to do their pleasure before they thought of courting their favor by offering and prayer —in short that, just as on the material side of human culture there has everywhere been an Age of Stone, so on the intellectual side there has everywhere been an Age of Magic? There are reasons for answering this question in the affirmative. When we survey the existing races of mankind from Greenland to Tierra del Fuego, or from Scotland to Singapore, we observe that they are distinguished one from the other by a great variety of religions, and that these distinctions are not, so to speak, merely coterminous with the broad distinctions of race, but descend into the minuter subdivisions of states and commonwealth, nay, that they honeycomb the town, the village, and even the family, so that the surface of society all over the world is cracked and seamed, wormed and sapped with rents and fissures and yawning crevasses opened up by the disintegrating influence of religious dissension. Yet when we have penetrated through these differences, which affect mainly the intelligent and thoughtful part of the community, we shall find underlying them all a solid stratum of intellectual agreement among the dull, the weak, the ignorant, and the superstitious, who constitute, unfortunately, the vast majority of mankind. One of the great achievements of the century which is now nearing its end is to have run shafts down into this low mental stratum in many parts of the world, and thus to have discovered its substantial identity everywhere. It is beneath our feet—and not very far beneath them—here in Europe at the present day, and it crops up on the surface in the heart of the Australian wilderness and wherever the advent of a higher civilization has not crushed it underground. This universal faith, this truly Catholic creed, is a belief in the efficacy of magic. While religious systems differ not only in different countries, but in the same country in different ages, the system of sympathetic magic remains everywhere and at all times substantially alike in its principles and practice. Among the ignorant and superstitious classes of modern Europe it is very much what it was thousands of years ago in Egypt and India, and what it now is among the lowest savages surviving in the remotest corners of the world. If the test of truth lay in a show of hands or a counting of heads, the system of magic might appeal, with far more reason than the Catholic Church, to the proud motto,

"Quod semper, quod ubique, quod ab omnibus," as the sure and certain credential of its own infallibility.

It is not our business here to consider what bearing the permanent existence of such a solid layer of savagery beneath the surface of society, and unaffected by the superficial changes of religion and culture, has upon the future of humanity. The dispassionate observer, whose studies have led him to plumb its depths, can hardly regard it otherwise than as a standing menace to civilization. We seem to move on a thin crust which may at any moment be rent by the subterranean forces slumbering below. From time to time a hollow murmur underground or a sudden spit of flame into the air tells of what is going on beneath our feet. Now and then the polite world is startled by a paragraph in a newspaper which tells how in Scotland an image has been found stuck full of pins for the purpose of killing an obnoxious laird or minister, how a woman has been slowly roasted to death as a witch in Ireland, or how a girl has been murdered and chopped up in Russia to make those candles of human tallow by whose light thieves hope to pursue their midnight trade unseen. But whether the influences that make for further progress, or those that threaten to undo what has already been accomplished, will ultimately prevail; whether the kinetic energy of the minority or the dead weight of the majority of mankind will prove the stronger force to carry us up to higher heights or to sink us into lower depths, are questions rather for the sage, the moralist, and the statesman, whose eagle vision scans the future, than for the humble student of the present and the past. Here we are only concerned to ask how far the uniformity, the universality, and the permanence of a belief in magic, compared with the endless variety and the shifting character of religious creeds, raises a presumption that the former represents a ruder and earlier phase of the human mind, through which all the races of mankind have passed or are passing on their way to religion and science.

If an Age of Religion has thus everywhere, as I venture

to surmise, been preceded by an Age of Magic, it is natural that we should inquire what causes have led mankind, or rather a portion of them, to abandon magic as a principle of faith and practice and to betake themselves to religion instead. When we reflect upon the multitude, the variety, and the complexity of the facts to be explained, and the scantiness of our information regarding them, we shall be ready to acknowledge that a full and satisfactory solution of so profound a problem is hardly to be hoped for, and that the most we can do in the present state of our knowledge is to hazard a more or less plausible conjecture. With all due diffidence, then, I would suggest that a tardy recognition of the inherent falsehood and barrenness of magic set the more thoughtful part of mankind to cast about for a truer theory of nature and a more fruitful method of turning her resources to account. The shrewder intelligences must in time have come to perceive that magical ceremonies and incantations did not really effect the results which they were designed to produce, and which the majority of their simpler fellows still believed that they did actually produce. This great discovery of the inefficacy of magic must have wrought a radical though probably slow revolution in the minds of those who had the sagacity to make it. The discovery amounted to this, that men for the first time recognized their inability to manipulate at pleasure certain natural forces which hitherto they had believed to be completely within their control. It was a confession of human ignorance and weakness. Man saw that he had taken for causes what were no causes, and that all his efforts to work by means of these imaginary causes had been vain. His painful toil had been wasted, his curious ingenuity had been squandered to no purpose. He had been pulling at strings to which nothing was attached; he had been marching, as he thought, straight to his goal, while in reality he had only been treading in a narrow circle. Not that the effects which he had striven so hard to produce did not continue to manifest themselves. They were still produced, but not by him. The rain still fell on the thirsty ground; the sun still pursued his daily, and the moon her nightly journey across the sky; the silent procession of the seasons still moved in light and shadow, in cloud and sunshine across the earth; men were still born to labor and sorrow, and still after a brief sojourn here, were gathered to their fathers in the long home hereafter. All things indeed went on as before, yet all seemed different to him from whose eyes the old scales had fallen. For he could no longer cherish the pleasing illusion that it was he who guided the earth and the heaven in their courses, and that they would cease to perform their great revolutions were he to take his feeble hand from the wheel. In the death of his enemies and his friends he no longer saw a proof of the resistless potency of his own or of hostile enchantments; he now knew that friends and foes alike had succumbed to a force stronger than any that he could wield, and in obedience to a destiny which he was powerless to control.

Thus cut adrift from his ancient moorings and left to toss on a troubled sea of doubt and uncertainty, his old happy confidence in himself and his powers rudely shaken, our primitive philosopher must have been sadly perplexed and agitated till he came to rest, as in a quiet haven after a tempestuous voyage, in a new system of faith and practice, which seemed to offer a solution of his harassing doubts and a substitute, however precarious, for that sovereignty over nature which he had reluctantly abdicated. If the great world went on its way without the help of him or his fellows, it must surely be because there were other beings, like himself but far stronger, who, unseen themselves, directed its course and brought about all the varied series of events which he had hitherto believed to be dependent on his own magic. It was they, as he now believed, and not he himself, who made the stormy wind to blow, the lightning to flash, and the thunder to roll; who had laid the foundations of the solid earth and set bounds to the restless sea that it might not pass; who caused all the glorious lights of heaven to shine; who gave the fowls of the air their meat and the wild beasts of the desert their prey; who bade the fruitful land to bring forth in abundance, the high hills to be clothed with forests, the bubbling springs to rise under the rocks in the valleys, and the green pastures to grow by still waters; who breathed into man's nostrils and made him live, or turned him to destruction by famine and pestilence and war. To these mighty beings, whose handiwork he traced in all the gorgeous and varied pageantry of nature, man now addressed himself, humbly confessing his dependence on their invisible power, and beseeching them of their mercy to furnish him with all good things, to defend him from the perils and dangers by which our mortal life is compassed about on every hand, and finally to bring his immortal spirit, freed from the burden of the body, to some happier world beyond the reach of pain and sorrow, where he might rest with them and with the spirits of good men in joy and felicity forever.

In this, or some such way as this, the deeper minds may be conceived to have made the great transition from magic to religion. But even in them the change can hardly ever have been sudden; probably it proceeded very slowly, and required long ages for its more or less perfect accomplishment. For the recognition of man's powerlessness to influence the course of nature on a grand scale must have been gradual; he cannot have been shorn of the whole of his fancied dominion at a blow. Step by step he must have been driven back from his proud position; foot by foot he must have yielded, with a sigh, the ground which he had once viewed as his own. Now it would be the wind, now the rain, now the sunshine, now the thunder, that he confessed himself unable to wield at will; and as province after province of nature thus fell from his grasp, till what had once seemed a kingdom threatened to shrink into a prison, man must have been more and more profoundly impressed with a sense of his own helplessness and the might of the invisible beings by whom he believed himself to be surrounded. Thus religion, beginning as a slight and partial acknowledgment of powers superior to man, tends with the growth of knowledge to deepen into a confession of man's entire and absolute dependence on the divine; his old free bearing is exchanged for an attitude of lowliest prostration before the mysterious powers of the unseen. But this deepening sense of religion, this more perfect submission to the divine will in all things, affects only those higher intelligences who have breadth of view enough to comprehend the vastness of the universe and the littleness of men. Small minds cannot grasp great ideas; to their narrow comprehension, their purblind vision, nothing seems really great and important but themselves. Such minds hardly rise into religion at all. They are, indeed, drilled by their betters into an outward conformity with its precepts and a verbal profession of its tenets; but at heart they cling to their old magical superstitions, which may be discountenanced and forbidden, but cannot be eradicated by religion, so long as they have their roots deep down in the mental framework and constitution of the great majority of mankind.

The reader may well be tempted to ask, How was it that intelligent men did not sooner detect the fallacy of magic? How could they continue to cherish expectations that were invariably doomed to disappointment? With what heart persist in playing venerable antics that led to nothing, and mumbling solemn balderdash that remained without effect? Why cling to beliefs which were so flatly contradicted by experience? How dare to repeat experiments that had failed so often? The answer seems to be that the fallacy was far from easy to detect, the failure by no means obvious, since in many, perhaps in most cases, the desired event did actually follow, at a longer or shorter interval, the performance of the rite which was designed to bring it about; and a mind of more than common acuteness was needed to perceive that, even in these cases, the rite was not necessarily the cause of the event. A ceremony intended to make the wind blow or the rain fall, or to work the death of an enemy, will always be followed, sooner or later, by the occurrence it is meant to bring to pass; and primitive man may be excused for regarding the occurrence as a direct result of the ceremony and the best possible proof of its efficacy. Similarly, rites observed in the morning to help the sun to rise, and in spring to wake the dreaming earth from her winter sleep, will invariably appear to be crowned with success, at least within the temperate zones; for in these regions the sun lights his golden fire in the east every morning, and year by year the vernal earth decks herself afresh with a rich mantle of green. Hence the practical savage, with his conservative instincts, might well turn a deaf ear to the subtleties of the theoretical doubter, the philosophic radical, who presumed to hint that sunrise and spring might not, after all, be direct consequences of the punctual performance of certain daily or yearly devotions, and that the sun might perhaps continue to rise and trees to blossom though the devotions were occasionally intermitted, or even discontinued altogether. These skeptical doubts would naturally be repelled by the other with scorn and indignation as airy reveries subversive of the faith, and manifestly contradicted by experience. "Can anything be plainer," he might say, "than that I light my two-penny candle on earth and that the sun then kindles his great fire in heaven? I should be glad to know whether, when I have put on my green robe in spring, the trees do not afterwards do the same? These are facts patent to everybody, and on them I take my stand. I am a plain practical man, not one of your theorists and splitters of hairs and choppers of logic. Theories and speculation and all that may be very well in their way, and I have not the least objection to your indulging in them, provided, of course, you do not put them in practice. But give me leave to stick to facts; then I know where I am." The fallacy of this reasoning is obvious to us, because it happens to deal with facts about which we have long made up our minds. But let an argument of precisely the same caliber be applied to matters which are still under debate, and it may be questioned whether a British audience would not applaud it as sound, and esteem the speaker who used it a safe man—not brilliant or showy, perhaps, but thoroughly sensible and hard-headed. If such reasonings could pass muster among ourselves, need we wonder that they long escaped detection by the savage?

The patient reader may remember—and the impatient reader who has quite forgotten is respectfully reminded—that we were led to plunge into the labyrinth of magic, in which we have wandered for so many pages, by a consideration of two different types of man-god. This is the clue which has guided our devious steps through the maze, and brought us out at last on higher ground, whence, resting a little by the way, we can look back over the path we have already traversed and forward to the longer and steeper road we have still to climb.

As a result of the foregoing discussion, the two types of human gods may conveniently be distinguished as the religious and the magical man-god respectively. In the former, a being of an order different from and superior to man is supposed to become incarnate, for a longer or a shorter time, in a human body, manifesting his superhuman power and knowledge by miracles wrought and prophecies uttered through the medium of the fleshly tabernacle in which he has deigned to take up his abode. This may also appropriately be called the inspired or incarnate type of man-god. In it the human body is merely a frail earthly vessel filled with a divine and immortal spirit. On the other hand, a man-god of the magical sort is nothing but a man who possesses in an unusually high degree powers which most of his fellows arrogate to themselves on a smaller scale; for in rude society there is hardly a person who does not dabble in magic. Thus, whereas a man-god of the former or insipid type derives his divinity from a deity who has stooped to hide his heavenly radiance behind a dull mask of earthly mold, a man-god of the latter type draws his extraordinary power from a certain physical sympathy with nature. He is not merely the receptacle of a divine spirit. His whole being, body and soul, is so delicately attuned to the harmony of the world that a touch of his hand or a turn of his head may send a thrill vibrating through the universal framework of things; and conversely his divine organism is acutely sensitive to such slight changes of environment as would leave ordinary mortals wholly unaffected. But the line between these two types of man-god, however sharply we may draw it in theory, is seldom to be traced with precision in practice, and in what follows I shall not insist on it.

To readers long familiarized with the conception of natural law, the belief of primitive man that he can rule the elements must be so foreign that it may be well to illustrate it by examples. When we have seen that in early society men who make no pretense at all of being gods, do nevertheless commonly believe themselves to be invested with powers which to us would seem supernatural, we shall have the less difficulty in comprehending the extraordinary range of powers ascribed to persons who are actually regarded as divine.

Of all natural phenomena there are, perhaps, none which civilized man feels himself more powerless to influence than the rain, the sun, and the wind; yet all these are commonly supposed by savages to be in some degree under their control.

THE GROWTH OF A PRIMITIVE
RELIGION *

By A. L. KROEBER

REGIONAL VARIATION OF CULTURE

As one first becomes acquainted with a totally strange
people spread over a large area, such as the Indians of
North America, they are likely to seem rather uniform.
The distinctions between individual and individual, and
even the greater distinctions between one group and another, become buried under the overwhelming mass-effect
of their difference from ourselves. Growing familiarity,
however, renders individual, local, and tribal peculiarities
plainer. The specialist, finally, comes to concern himself
with particular traits until the peculiarities occupy more
of his attention than the uniformities. His danger always
is to let himself get into the habit of taking sweeping similarities so much for granted that he ends by underempha-
sizing or forgetting them. At the same time his business
is to add something new to human understanding—facts
at any rate, interpretation if possible. Generalities are likely
to be pretty widely known, and progress, new formulations,
therefore depend ultimately on mastery of detail. This
means that if a scientist is to contribute anything to the
world's comprehension, is to add a new mental tool to its
chest, he must devote himself to specific traits, to discrimina-
tions of fine detail. It is only by finding new trees that he
helps to make the woods larger.

If then we approach a race like the American Indians
with the scientist's or student's purpose of discovering
something more than we already know, we quickly find
that institutions, customs, and utensils, in other words, the

* *Anthropology.* New York: Harcourt, Brace & Co.

714

cultures, vary from tribe to tribe. When one compares
tribes living so far apart as to be no longer united in
intercourse, nor even by communication with common
intermediaries, there is scarcely a trait in which their cultures are wholly identical. Within a limited district a fair
degree of uniformity is found to prevail. Yet when the
boundaries of such an area are crossed, a new type of
culture begins to be encountered, which again holds with
local variations until a third district is entered.

PLAINS, SOUTHWEST, NORTHWEST AREAS

For instance, the Indians of the Plains between the
Rocky mountains and the Mississippi river form a comparative unit. They are all warlike, the great aim in life
of every man in these tribes being attainment of military
glory. All the Plains tribes subsisted to a large extent on
buffalo, lived in tipis—tents made of buffalo skins—and
boiled their food with hot stones in buffalo rawhide. Nearly
all of them performed a four days' religious ceremony
known as the Sun Dance, of which one of the outstanding
acts was fasting and sometimes self-torture inflicted with
skewers drawn through the skin and torn out. These customs were common to the Sioux, Cheyenne, Arapaho, Crow,
Blackfeet, Assiniboine, Omaha, Kiowa, Comanche, and
other tribes.

As one passes from this region to the mountainous
plateau which constitutes the present New Mexico and
Arizona—the Southwest of the United States—one encounters a series of tribes often inhabiting stone houses,
subsisting by agriculture, cooking in earthenware pots,
little given to fighting, according authority to priests rather
than warriors, erecting altars, and performing masked
dances representing divinities. This Southwestern culture,
its internal relations, and the tribes participating in it, have
already been discussed in another connection.

If, however, on leaving the Plains one turns northwest
to the shores of British Columbia and southern Alaska,

a third distinctive type of native civilization appears. Among these Northwestern or North Pacific Coast tribes, such as the Tlingit, Haida, Tsimshian, Kwakiutl, Nutka, and Salish, the priest as well as the warrior bowed before the rich man, an elaborate set of rules and honors separating the wealthy high-born from the poor and lowly. Aristocracy, commoners, and slaves made up distinct strata of society in this region. Public rituals were occasions for the ostentation of wealth. Houses were carpentered of wood. Cooking was done in boxes. The prevalent food was fish.

The significant thing is that these are not three tribes, but three groups each consisting of a number of politically independent tribes spread over a considerable territory and evincing a fairly fundamental similarity of customs and institutions. We are confronting three kinds of culture, each supertribal in range and attached to a certain area. These areas have sometimes been called "ethnographic provinces"; they are generally known as "culture-areas." Of such areas ten are generally recognized on the North American continent. These are the Plains, Southwest, North Pacific Coast, Mackenzie-Yukon, Arctic, Plateau, California, Northeast, Southeast, and Mexico.

Obviously we have here a classification comparable to that which the naturalist makes of animals. As the zoölogist divides the vertebrate animals into mammals, birds, reptiles, amphibians, and fishes, so the anthropologist divides the generic North American Indian culture into the cultures of these ten areas. The naturalist however cannot stop with a group as inclusive as the mammals, and goes on to subdivide them into orders, such as the rodents, carnivores, ungulates, and the like. Each of these again he goes on splitting into families, genera, and finally species. The species correspond to the smallest groups in human society, namely, the tribes or nations. Parallel to the family or order which the naturalist finds between a particular species and the great class of mammals, one may therefore expect to discover groups intermediate between particular tribes and the large culture-areas. Such intermediate groups would consist of clusters of tribes constituting fractions of a culture-area: clearly pertaining to this area, but yet somewhat set off from other clusters within the same area—like the Pueblos and Navaho within the Southwest, as already described. We may call such clusters or fractions sub-culture-areas, and must concern ourselves with them if we desire to deepen our understanding of aboriginal American civilization.

For the sake of simplicity, it will be well to select a limited portion of North America, instead of wrestling with the intricacies of the continent as a whole, in an endeavor to see how its culture-areas and sub-culture-areas reveal themselves in detail and help to throw a light on native history. California will serve as a type example.

CALIFORNIA AND ITS SUB-AREAS

Modern state boundaries frequently do not coincide with either ethnic lines of division or with natural physiographic areas, especially when political units are created by legislative enactment, as has been the case with most of the United States. This partial discrepancy holds for California. The native culture most distinctive of California covered only the middle two-thirds of the present state, but took in Nevada and much of the Great Basin.

Northernmost California, especially along the ocean, was inhabited by Indians that affiliated with the tribes of the North Pacific coast. One after another their customs and arts prove on examination to be related to the customs and arts of the coast of British Columbia, and to differ more or less from the corresponding practices of the Central California Indians. Here then we have a second cultural type, that of northwestern California, which constitutes a subdivision of the North Pacific Coast culture-area.

The southern California Indians link with the Indians of the adjoining states of Arizona and New Mexico. In short, this part of California forms part of the Southwest culture-area. The southern California tribes are however not wholly uniform among themselves, but constitute two groups: those of the islands, coast, and mountains, and those of the Colorado River. These are distinguished primarily by the fact that only the river tribes practiced agriculture. We may designate these two divisions as "Southern California" proper and "Lower Colorado River."

THE SHAPING OF A PROBLEM

So far we have been discriminating, that is, looking for characteristic differences. On the other hand, there has always existed a consensus of impression, among experienced as well as hasty observers, that a certain likeness runs through the culture of most of the tribes of California, northern, central, and southern. With scarcely an exception they were unwarlike; nearly all of them made excellent baskets, but were deficient in wood-working. Obviously it is necessary to reconcile these uniformities with the peculiarities that distinguish the four regional types or sub-culture-areas, as well as to account for the peculiarities.

Let us simplify the problem by considering only one aspect of the four native cultures instead of the whole cultures. In this way there will be more likelihood of making a substantial beginning; any results obtained from the example can be subsequently checked from other aspects of the cultures to see if the findings are broadly representative. Further, let us arrange the items of information that are available on this one aspect of culture, not haphazardly, nor mechanically as under an alphabetic classification, nor in the sequence in which authors have published their observations, but naturally, or according to some principle that is likely to work out into an interpretation. Since part of the problem is the relation of the uniform features to the peculiar ones, a promising order will be to put at one end of the line or series of data the most universal features and at the other the most particular or localized ones.

Let us select religion as that part of native culture to be examined, and limit this still farther by eliminating from consideration, for the time being, all forms of religion except public rituals, which among Indians are frequently accompanied or signalized by sacred dances. We may forget, for the moment, private rites, individual sacrifices, superstitions and taboos, medicine men, myths, and the like, and direct attention to dances made by groups of people, or the obvious equivalents of such dances, and ritual acts definitely associated with the dances or the common weal.

Choice of this phase of native culture is not quite random; ritual ordinarily is rather freer from the complications caused by natural environment than most other institutions and customs. Had industrial arts, for instance, been selected as the point of attack, it might be imagined that certain tribes made pottery, and others did not, because of the presence or absence of suitable clay in their respective habitats; or perhaps that a particular weave of basketry occurred universally because this weave followed more or less directly from the physical properties of some plant material that abounded everywhere in the state. On the other hand, when tribes do or do not make dances in honor of their divinities, or when they do or do not practice an elaborate mourning for their dead, these are customs into which the influence of natural environment can scarcely enter, since all peoples believe in spirits and suffer the loss of relatives.

GIRLS' ADOLESCENCE RITE

When, then, we review the religious dances of the California tribes en masse, we find that there are only two which come near to being universal. One of these is the Victory Dance held over the head or scalp of a slain enemy; the other is an Adolescence Rite performed for girls at puberty. The latter is the more profitable to consider. It is the more widely spread, having been performed in every district of California, and by almost every tribe. The Victory Dance was not made by the Indians of northern California, who substituted for it a war incitement dance of different character. Further, a tribe having the tradition of the Victory Dance might often be at peace and go for a generation or two without the celebration. But a ceremony which it was thought necessary to make for each girl at puberty was obviously due to be performed every few years even among a small group.

There are many local variations in the Californian Adolescence Rite, but certain of its features emerge with constancy. These traits are based on the belief that the girl who is at this moment passing from childhood to maturity must be undergoing a critical transition. The occasion was considered critical not only for her but for the community, and, since the Indians' outlook was limited, for the whole of their little world. A girl who at this period did not show fortitude to hardship would be forever weak and complaining: therefore she fasted. If she carried wood and water industriously, she would remain a good worker all her life, whereas if she defaulted, she would grow up a lazy woman. So crucial, in fact, was this moment, that she was thought extremely potent upon her surroundings, as constituting a latent danger. If she looked abroad upon the world, oak trees might become barren and next year's crop of acorns fail, or the salmon refuse to ascend the river: Among many tribes, therefore, the maturing girl was covered with a blanket, set under a large basket, or made to wear a visor of feathers over her eyes. Others had her throw her hair forward and keep her head bowed. She was given the benefit of having ancient religious songs sung over her, and dances revolved around her, night after night. Certain additional developments of the ceremony were locally restricted. Thus it was only in the south that the girl was put into a pit and baked in hot sand. But a number of specific features occur from the north to the south end of the state. Among these are the following rules. The girl must not eat meal, fat, or salt. She must not scratch her head with her fingers, but use a stick or bone implement made for the purpose. She must not look at people; and she should be sung over.

It should be added that most of these traits of the Girls' Rite recur among the tribes of a much larger area than California, including those of Nevada and the Great Basin and Pacific coast for a long distance north. This institution, then, is remarkably widespread and has preserved nearly the same fundamental features wherever it is found.

THE FIRST PERIOD

What can be inferred from this uniformity and broad diffusion? It seems fair to try the presumptive conclusion of antiquity. A continent is likely to be older than an island. A family of animals has probably existed longer than a single species. A world-wide custom normally is more ancient than one that is confined to a narrow locality. If it spread from one people to another, this diffusion over the whole earth would usually require a long time. If on the other hand such a custom had originated separately among each people, its very universality would indicate it as the response to a deep and primary need, and such a need would presumably manifest itself early in the history of the race.

It is true that one may not place too positive a reliance on evidence of this sort. The history of civilization furnishes some contrary examples. Thus the Persian fire-worshiping religion is older than Christianity, yet is now confined to the Parsees of Bombay and to one or two small groups in Persia. The use of tobacco has spread over the eastern hemisphere in four centuries. Still, such cases are exceptional; and in the absence of specific contrary considerations, heavy weight must be given to wideness of occurrence in rating antiquity.

If the Girls' Rite were identical among all the tribes that

practice it, there might be warrant for the conclusion that it had originated only a few centuries ago but had for some reason been carried from one tribe to another with such unusual rapidity as not to have been subjected to the alterations of time. Yet the fact that the essential uniformity of the rite is overlaid by so much local diversity— as for instance the baking custom restricted to southern California—indicated the unlikelihood of such a rapid and late diffusion. The ceremony is much in the status of Christianity, which, in the course of its long history, has also become broken into national varieties or sects, all of which however remain Christian.

The facts then warrant this tentative conclusion: that the Girls' Rite is representative of the oldest stratum of religion that can be traced among the Indians of California —their "First Period." The Victory Dance would presumably be of nearly but not quite the same antiquity.

THE SECOND PERIOD: MOURNING ANNIVERSARY AND FIRST-SALMON RITE

Pursuing the same method farther, let us look for rituals that are less widely spread than these but yet not confined to small districts. The outstanding one in this class is the Mourning Anniversary. This is a custom of bewailing each year, or at intervals of a few years, those members of the tribe who have died since the last performance, and the burning of large quantities of wealth—shell money, baskets, and the like—in their memory. Each family offers for its own dead, but people of special consideration are honored by having images made of them and consumed with property. Until the anniversary has been performed, the relatives of the dead remain mourners. After it, they are free to resume normal enjoyment of life; and the name of the deceased, which until then has been strictly taboo, may now be bestowed on a baby in the family.

The Mourning Anniversary as here outlined is practiced with little variation, less than the Girls' Rite shows, throughout southern California and a great part of central California, especially the Sierra Nevada district. Its distribution thus covers more than half of the state. But it has not spread elsewhere except to a small area in southern Nevada and western Arizona.

In northern California the Mourning Anniversary is lacking. It is not that the Indians here fail to mourn their dead. In fact, they frequently bewail them for a longer time than most civilized peoples think necessary. They may bury or burn some property with the corpse. But they do not practice the regular public commemoration of the southerly tribes. They do not assiduously accumulate wealth for months or years in order to throw it into a communal fire at the end. And they do not make images of their dead. In fact, they would be shocked at the idea as indelicate, if not impious. Is there anything in this northern part of California that takes the place of the anniversary?

Not as a psychological equivalent; but as regards distribution, there is. This is the custom, established in northern California and parts of Oregon, for a leading shaman or medicine-man to conduct a ceremony at the beginning of each year's salmon run. Until he had done this, no one fished for salmon or ate them. If any got caught, they were carefully returned to the river. When the medicine-man had gone through his secret rites, he caught and ate the first fish of the year. After this, the season was open. To eat salmon no longer brought illness and disaster as it was thought that it would a few days earlier. Moreover, the prayers or formulas recited by the shaman propitiated the salmon and caused them to run abundantly, so that every one had plenty. There is clearly a communal motive in the rite, even though its performance was entrusted to an individual.

The one specific element common to the Mourning Anniversary and this First-salmon Rite is their connection with the natural year, the cycle of the seasons, a trait necessarily lacking in the Girls' Rite with its intimately personal char-

acter. Because of this common feature; because, also, neither
of these two rituals is as widespread as the Girls' Rite and
yet between them they cover the whole of California with
substantially mutual exclusiveness, it seems fair to assume
that they both originated at a later time than the Girls'
Rite, but still in fairly remote antiquity. They may therefore be provisionally assigned to a Second Period of the
prehistory of California.

ERA OF REGIONAL DIFFERENTIATION

It is now necessary to return to the four regional divisions
or sub-culture-areas of the modern tribes of California. Since
the Northwestern one affiliated with extensive North Pacific
culture, and those of Southern California and the Colorado River with the great culture of the Southwest, many
of their customs must have originated in those parts of
these two culture-areas which lie outside of California. Even
if the northern and southern Californians "lent" as well
as "borrowed" inventions and institutions, they must on the
whole have received or learned or imitated more in the
interchange than they imparted. This is clear from the fact
that the Indians of British Columbia are more advanced
in their manufacturing ability, richer in variety of tools and
utensils, and more elaborate in their organization of society,
than those of Northwestern California; and a similar relation of superiority and priority exists between the Pueblos
of New Mexico and Arizona and the Southern California
tribes. In other words, a stream of civilizational influences
has evidently run from southern Alaska and British Columbia southward along the coast as far as Northwestern
California, and another from the town-dwelling Pueblos
to the village-inhabiting tribes of Southern California, in
much the same way that civilization flowed from ancient
Babylonia into Palestine, from Egypt into Crete, from
Greece to Rome, from Rome to Gaul and Britain, from
western Europe to the Americas after their discovery, and
from the Christian to the non-Christian nations of to-day.

Somewhere in the unraveling of the prehistory of California the first indications of these streams from the outside should be encountered.

They are not manifest in the two periods which have so far been established. The distribution of the Girls' Rite of the First Period and of the Mourning Anniversary and First-salmon Rite of the Second, does not coincide with the major culture-areas of the continent. The Southwest, for instance, from which the modern southern Californians have received so much, does not possess any of these ceremonies. The Southwest culture therefore evidently originated, or began to take on its recent aspect, or at least to influence Southern California, chiefly after the two periods had passed by in which these ceremonies became established in California. The Girls' Rite, to be sure, extends up the Pacific coast into Alaska. Yet this is more widespread than the North Pacific Coast culture, since this has its southerly limit in Northwestern California, whereas the ceremony is universal as far as to the southern end of the state, besides occurring inland throughout the Great Basin and Plateau regions. Being more widely spread than the Coast culture, the Girls' Rite is presumptively more ancient.

The beginnings of the four modern types of California native culture must thus evidently be looked for at about the point now reached in our reconstruction. At first there was a single very widespread ceremony; then two less widely diffused ones; the next logical step in development would have been the growth of a still larger number of ceremonies or ritual systems. These, on account of their greater recency, and perhaps on account of conflicting with one another, would have spread only over comparatively small areas. Let us therefore assume that to this Third Period belonged the beginnings of the Wealth-display dances of the Northwestern Indians which are coupled with the idea of world renovation; the so-called Kuksu dances made among the Central Californians by members of a secret society; and the series of long singings that the Colorado River tribes are addicted to and believe they have miraculously dreamed.

Of course, the idea could scarcely be entertained that these four local systems sprang into existence full-fledged. They are complicated sets of rituals, quite different from the simple Girls' Rite and Mourning Anniversary. They must have grown up gradually from more meager beginnings and have been a considerable time reaching their present elaboration. It would thus seem justifiable to add not only one but two further periods of religious growth, in the earlier of which—the Third—these ceremonial systems of the historic Indians began their development, whereas in the later or Fourth they achieved it.

THIRD AND FOURTH PERIODS IN CENTRAL CALIFORNIA
KUKSU AND HESI

For instance, in the Central California sub-culture-area a series of tribes possess a society to which young men are admitted only after a double initiation with formal teaching by their elders, the first initiation coming in boyhood, the second soon after puberty. The society holds great four-day dances in large earth-covered houses. Time is beaten to the dance and song with rattles of split sticks, and stamped with the feet on a great log drum. The dancers wear showy feather costumes which disguise them to the uninitiated women, children, and strangers, who take them to be spirits of old who have come to exhibit themselves for the good of the people. There may be as many as twelve divinities represented in this way, each with his distinctive name and dress. One of the most prominent of these is the god or "first-man" Kuksu, the founder of the sacred rites, after whom the entire system has been named the "Kuksu Cult."

The tribes participating in the Kuksu Cult are the Patwin, nearer Maidu, Pomo, Yuki, Miwok, and several others. They occupy an area which may be described as the heart of California; namely, the districts adjoining the lower Sacramento and San Joaquin rivers and the Bay of San Francisco into which the two streams pour the drainage of the great interior valley.

Beyond the Kuksu-dancing tribes there are others, like the farther Maidu, the Wailaki, and some of the Yokuts, among whom the medicine-men are wont to gather for public demonstration of their magical prowess. Thus, they assemble for a competition of "throwing" sickness into one another, or to charm the rattlesnakes so that they can be handled and that no one in the tribe may be bitten during the ensuing year. In these gatherings there is the idea of an association of people endowed with particular powers and operating more or less jointly for the benefit of the community. In short, this fringe of Central tribes beyond the border of the Kuksu Cult evince some of the psychology and motives of the Cult, but without the definite organization of the latter, and also without some of its specific practices, such as god-impersonation. These gatherings of the medicine men thus look as if they might have been the simple and generalized substratum out of which the Kuksu Cult grew by a process of gradual formalization and ritualistic elaboration. This conclusion is corroborated by the distribution. It is the tribes at the ends of the great interior valley, or in the hills above it, whose rites are of this loose type, while in the center are the true Kuksu-dancing groups. There is a periphery of low organization and a core of high organization. According to our previous rule, recency in acquisition but antiquity of stage pertain to the marginal as the more widely distributed; the geographically more compact nucleus representing an earlier beginning but a later stage of present development. That is, it is reasonable to believe that the Kuksu Cult grew out of semi-formal gatherings of medicine-men such as still survive in the outlying districts—the "backwoods" of the Central area.

Evidently if a still later religious movement developed as an elaboration or addition of the Kuksu Cult, it should be less widely diffused than this system, forming a sort of nucleus within the core. Actually there is such a later growth. This is the Hesi Dance, confined to the Patwin and Maidu of the lower Sacramento Valley, and regarded by them as the most sacred portion of the Kuksu system. It is the one of all their rituals into which the largest number of differently garbed performers enter, and is made twice a year as the spectacular beginning and finale of the series of lesser Kuksu dances.

The history of native ritual in Central California thus is fairly plain. Early in the Third Period, perhaps already during the Second, the specialists in religion, the medicine-men, had acquired the habit of giving public demonstrations. This resulted in a bond of fellowship among themselves and a sense of exclusiveness toward the community as a whole. Out of this sense there was elaborated during the Third Period, somewhere about the lower Sacramento Valley, the idea of an organized secret society with initiated members. The performances became more and more elaborate, and the production of proof of supernatural power gradually crystallized into impersonations of deities. By the beginning of the Fourth Period, the Kuksu Cult had been established. During this period, it was carried from the center of origin to its farthest limits, whereas at the center the Hesi Dance was evolved as a characteristic addition. If native development had been able to proceed undisturbed, if, for instance, the coming of the white race had been deferred a few centuries longer, the Hesi might have followed the diffusion of the earlier Kuksu Cult; and while this new spread was in progress, the Patwin who form the central nucleus of the whole Kuksu-Hesi movement might have been devising a still newer increment to the system.

THIRD AND FOURTH PERIODS IN SOUTHERN CALIFORNIA
JIMSONWEED AND CHUNGICHNISH

The Southern California Jimsonweed Rites are quite distinct from the Kuksu Cult in their regalia, dances, and teachings, but are also based on initiation. It may there-

fore be concluded, first, that they grew up contemporane-
ously in the Third Period; and next, that they sprang out
of the same soil, a growing tendency of the medicine-men
toward professional association. The selection of the jimsonweed as the distinctive element in the South seems to
have been due to influences from Mexico and the Southwest. The tribes of Arizona and New Mexico use the
plant in religion, the Aztecs ascribed supernatural powers
to it, and the modern Tepecano of Mexico pray to it like
a god. The Spanish-American name for the plant, toloache,
is an Aztec word. Because Mexican civilization was so
much the more advanced, it seems likely that the use of
jimsonweed originated in Mexico, was carried into the
Southwest, and from there spread into Southern California
—perhaps at the receptive moment when the medicine-
men's associations were drawing more closely together and
feeling the need of some powerful emotional element to
lend an impetus to their cults.

While the Jimsonweed religion was followed by Californian tribes from the Yokuts on the north to the Diegueno
on the south, its most elaborate forms occur among groups
near the center of Southern California, especially the Gabrielino of Los Angeles and Catalina Island. This group associates the greatest number of rituals and dances with the
Jimsonweed Society, and is therefore likely to have had
the leading share in the working out of the religion.

By the opening of the Fourth Period the Gabrielino must
have had the Jimsonweed Rites pretty fully developed, while
the peripheral tribes like the Yokuts and Diegueno were
perhaps only learning the religious use of the drug. The
Gabrielino however did not stand still during this Fourth
Period, and while the original rather simple Jimsonweed
Rites spread north and south, they were adding a new
element. This is the Chungichnish Cult, based on belief
in a great, wise, powerful god of this name, to whom are
due the final ordaining of the world and the institution of
the Jimsonweed Rites and their correct performance. Asso-

ciated with this belief is the use of the "ground painting." This is a large picture, usually of the world, drawn in colored earths, sands, seeds, or paints, on the floor of the sacred enclosure in which the Jimsonweed rituals were practiced. This ground painting served both as an altar for the rites and as a means of instructing the initiates. The custom of this sacred painting became firmly established among the Gabrielino, and is known to have spread from them to other tribes, such as the Luiseno. From these it has been carried, in part during the last century, after the white man was in the land, to still more remote tribes like the Diegueno, who recognize the Gabrielino island of Catalina as the source of the Chungichnish Cult and sing its songs to Gabrielino words.

THIRD AND FOURTH PERIODS ON THE LOWER COLORADO
DREAM SINGING

In Southeastern California, among the tribes of the Lower Colorado River, the Third and Fourth Periods are less easily distinguished. The reason for this seems to be the fact that religion developed among these tribes less through the invention or establishment of new elements, than by the lopping away of older ones, with the result of a rather narrow specialization on the few elements that were retained. Tribes like the Yuma and Mohave scarcely danced for religious purposes. The special costumes, showy feather headdresses, disguises, musical instruments, sand-paintings, altars, and ritualistic processions that mark the Kuksu and Jimsonweed cults, were lacking among them. They did adhere to the widespread and ancient idea that dreams are a source of evidence of supernatural power. In short, their religion turned inward, not outward. Instead of their medicine-men forming a society based on initiation, the Colorado River tribes came to feel that every one might be a medicine-man according to his dreams. They put emphasis on these internal experiences. The result has been that they believe that a legend can be true and sacred only if it has been dreamed, and that a man's songs should be acquired in the same way. Religion, therefore, is an intensely individualistic affair among them. Since no two men can dream quite alike, no two Yumas or Mohaves tell their myths or sing their song cycles identically. This cast to their religion is so strong that it looks to be fairly ancient. The beginnings of this local type of religion may therefore be set in the Third Period. As for the Fourth Period, it may be inferred that this chiefly accentuated the tendencies developed in the Third, the dream basis augmenting as ceremonialism dropped away.

NORTHWESTERN CALIFORNIA: WORLD-RENEWAL AND WEALTH-DISPLAY

The Third and Fourth Periods are also not readily distinguishable in Northwestern California. Yet here the rooting of these two eras in the Second is clearer. We have seen that all through northern California there exists the First-salmon Rite conducted by a prominent medicine-man of each locality; and we have referred the probable origin of this rite to the Second Period. The modern Indians of Northwestern California consider their great dances of ten or twelve days' duration as being essentially the showy public accompaniment of an extremely sacred and secret act performed by a single priest who recites a magical formula. His purpose in some instances is to open the salmon season, in others to inaugurate the corn crop, in still others to make new fire for the community. But whatever the particular object, it is always believed that he renews something important to the world. He "makes the world," as the Indians call it, for another year. These New-year or World-renewing functions of the rites of the modern Indians of Northwestern California thus appear to lead back by a natural transition to the First-salmon Rite which is so widely spread in Northern California. Evidently this specific rite that originated in the Second Period was developed in the Northwest during the Third and Fourth eras by being broadened in its objective and having attached to it certain characteristic dances.

These dances are the Deerskin and Jumping Dances. They differ from those of the Central and Southern tribes in that every one may participate in them. There is no idea of a society with membership, and hence no exclusion of the uninitiated. In fact, the dances are primarily occasions for displays of wealth, which are regarded as successful in proportion to the size of the audience. The albino deerskins, ornaments of woodpecker scalps, furs, and great blades of flint and obsidian which are carried in these dances, constitute the treasures of these tribes. The dances are the best opportunity of the rich men to produce their heirlooms before the public and in that way signalize the honor of ownership—which is one of the things dearest in life to the Northwest Californian.

Another feature of these Northwestern dances which marks them off from the Central and Southern ones is the fact that they can only be held in certain spots. A Kuksu dance is rightly made indoors, but any properly built dance house will answer for its performance. A Yurok or Hupa however would consider it fundamentally wrong to make a Deerskin Dance other than on the accepted spot where his great-grandfather had always seen it. The reason for this attachment to the spot seems to be his conviction that the most essential part of the dance is a secret, magical rite enacted only in the specified place because the formula recited as its nucleus mentions that spot.

In the Northwest we again seem to be able to recognize, as in the Central and Southern regions, an increasing contraction of area for each successively developed ritual. Whereas the First-salmon Rite of the Second Period covers the whole northern third of California and parts of Oregon, the Wealth-display dances and World-renewing rites of the Third and Fourth Periods occur only in Northwestern California. The Jumping Dance was performed at a dozen or more villages, the slightly more splendid Deerskin Dance only in eight. This suggests that the Jumping Dance is the earlier, possibly going back to the Third Period, whereas the Deerskin Dance more probably originated during the Fourth.

The history of religious cults among the Indians of California seems thus to be reconstructible, with some probability of correctness in its essential outlines, as a progressive differentiation during four fairly distinct periods. During these four eras, the most typical cults gradually changed from a personal to a communal aim, ceremonies grew more numerous as well as more elaborate, influences from the outside affected the tribes within California, and local differences increased until the original rather close uniformity had been replaced by four quite distinct systems of cults, separated in most cases by transitional areas in which the less specialized developments of the earlier stages have been preserved.

A natural question arises here. Does this reconstructed history apply only to ritual cults, or can a parallel development be traced for other elements of religion, for industries, inventions, and economic relations, for social institutions, for knowledge and art? The findings are that this history holds for all phases of native culture. Material and social development progressed much as did religion. Each succeeding stage brought in new implements and customs, these became on the whole more specialized as well as more numerous, and differed more and more locally in the four sub-culture-areas. Thus the plain or self bow belongs demonstrably to an earlier stratum than the sinew-backed one, basketry precedes pottery, twined basketry is earlier than coiled, the stone mortar antedates the slab with basketry mortar as the oval metate does the squared one, earth-covered sweat houses are older than plank roofed ones, and totemism may have become established before the division of society into exogamic moieties. It would be a long story to adduce the evidence for each of these determinations and all others that could be made. It will perhaps suffice to say that the principles by which they are arrived at are the same as those which have guided us in the inquiry into religion.

OUTLINE OF THE CULTURE HISTORY OF CALIFORNIA

In general terms, the net results of our inquiry can be stated thus.

First Period: a simple, meager culture, nearly uniform throughout California, similar to the cultures of adjacent regions, and only slightly influenced by these.

Second Period: definite influences from the North Pacific Coast and the Southwest, affecting respectively the northern third and southern two-thirds of California, and thus leading to a first differentiation of consequence.

Third Period: more specific influences from outside, resulting in the formation of four local types: the Northwestern, under North Pacific influences; the Southern and Lower Colorado under stimulus of the Southwest; and the Central, farthest remote from both and thus developing most slowly but also most independently.

Fourth Period: consummation of the four local types. Influences from outside continue operative, but in the main the lines of local development entered upon in the previous era are followed out, reaching their highest specialization in limited tracts central to each area.

This summary not only outlines the course of culture history in native California: it also explains why there are both widely uniform and narrowly localized culture elements in the region. It thus answers the question why from one aspect the tribes of the state seem so much alike and from another angle they appear endlessly different. They are alike largely in so far as they have retained certain old common traits. They are different to the degree that they have severally added traits of later and localized development.

THE QUESTION OF DATING

A natural question is how long these periods lasted. As regards accurate dating, there is only one possible answer: we do not know nearly enough. Moreover modern historians, who possess infinitely fuller records on chronology than anthropologists can ever hope to have on primitive peoples, tend more and more to lay little weight on specific dates. They may set 476 A.D., the so-called fall of Rome, as the point of demarcation between ancient and medieval history because it is sometimes useful, especially in elementary presentation, to speak definitely. But no historian believes that any profound change took place between 475 and 477 A.D. That is an impression beginners may get from the way history is sometimes taught. Yet it is well recognized that certain slow, progressive changes were going on uninterruptedly for centuries before and after; and that if the date 476 A.D. is arbitrarily inserted into the middle of this development, it is because to do so is conventionally convenient and with full understanding that the event marked was dramatic or symbolic rather than intrinsically significant. In fact, the value of a historian's work lies precisely in his ability to show that the forces which shaped medieval history were already at work during the period of ancient times and that the causes which had molded the Roman empire continued to operate in some degree for many centuries after the fall of Rome.

Nevertheless, there is no doubt that occasional dates have the virtue of impressing the mind with the vividness which specific statements alone possess. Also, if the results of anthropological studies are to be connected with the written records of history proper, at least tentative dates must be formulated, though of course in a case like this of the periods of native culture in California it is understood that all chronology is subject to a wide margin of error.

History provides a start toward a computation, although its aid is a short one. California began to be settled about 1770. The last tribes were not brought into contact with the white man until 1850. As early, however, as 1540 Alarcon rowed and towed up the lower Colorado and wrote an account of the tribes he encountered there. Two years later, Cabrillo visited the coast and island tribes of southern California, and wintered among them. In 1579 Drake spent some weeks on shore among the central Californians and a member of his crew has left a brief but spirited description of them. In all three instances these old accounts of native customs tally with remarkable fidelity witn all that has been ascertained in regard to the recent tribes of the same regions. That is, native culture has evidently changed very little since the sixteenth century. The local sub-cultures already showed substantially their present form; which means that the Fourth Period must have been well established three to four centuries ago. We might then assign to this period about double the time which has elapsed since the explorers visited California; say, seven hundred years. This seems a conservative figure, which would put the commencement of the Fourth Period somewhere about 1200 A.D.

All the remainder must be reconstructed by projection. In most parts of the world for which there are continuous records, it is found that civilization usually changes more rapidly as time goes on. While this is not a rigorous law, it is a prevailing tendency. However, let us apply this principle with reserve, and assume that the Third Period was no longer than the Fourth. Another seven hundred years would carry back to 500 A.D.

Now, however, it seems reasonable to begin to lengthen our periods somewhat. For the Second, a thousand years does not appear excessive; approximately from 500 B.C. to 500 A.D. By the same logic the First Period should be allowed from a thousand to fifteen hundred years. It might be wisest to set no beginning, at all, since our "First" period is only the first of those which are determinable with present knowledge. Actually, it may have been preceded by a still more primitive era on which as yet no specific evidence is available. It can however be suggested that by 2000 or 1500 B.C. the beginnings of native Californian culture as we know it had already been made.

THE EVIDENCE OF ARCHÆOLOGY

There is left as a final check on the problem of age a means of attack which under favorable circumstances is sometimes the most fruitful: archæological excavation, espe-cially when it leads to stratigraphic determination, that is, the finding of different but superimposed layers. Unfor-tunately archæology affords only limited aid in California— much less, for instance, than in the Southwest. Nothing markedly stratigraphical has been discovered. Pottery, which has usually proved the most serviceable of all classes of prehistoric remains for working out sequences of culture and chronologies, is unrepresented in the greater part of California, and is sparse and rather recent in those southern parts in which it does occur.

Still, archæological excavation has brought to light some-thing. It has shown that the ancient implements found in shellmounds and village sites in Southern California, those from the shores of San Francisco Bay in Central California, and those along the coast of Northwestern California, are distinct. Certain peculiar types of artifacts are found in each of these regions, are found only there, and agree closely with objects used by the modern tribes of the same districts. For instance, prehistoric village and burial sites in North-western California contain long blades of flaked obsidian like those used until a few years ago by the Yurok and Hupa. Sites in Southern California have brought to light soapstone bowls or "ollas" such as the Spaniards a century ago found the Gabrielino and Luiseno employing in cook-ing and in Jimsonweed administration. Both these classes of objects are wanting from the San Francisco Bay shell mounds and among the recent Central Californian tribes.

It may thus be inferred (1) that none of the four local cultures was ever spread much more widely than at present; (2) that each of them originated mainly on the spot; and (3) that because many of the prehistoric finds lie at some depth, the local cultures are of respectable antiquity—evidently at least a thousand years old, probably more. This fairly confirms the estimate that the differentiation of the local cultures of the Third Period commenced not later than about 500 A.D.

AGE OF THE SHELLMOUNDS

Archæology also yields certain indications as to the total lapse of time during the four periods. The deposits themselves contribute the evidence. Some of the shellmounds that line the ramifying shores of San Francisco Bay to the number of over four hundred have been carefully examined. These mounds are refuse accumulations. They were not built up with design, but grew gradually as people lived on them year after year, because much of the food of their inhabitants was molluscs—chiefly clams, oysters, and mussels—whose shells were thrown outdoors or trodden under foot. Some of the sites were camped on only transiently, and the layers of refuse never grew more than a few inches in thickness. Other spots were evidently inhabited for many centuries, since the masses of shell now run more than thirty feet deep and hundreds of feet long. The higher such a mound grew, the better it drained off. One side of it would afford shelter from the prevailing winds. The more regularly it came to be lived on, the more often would the inhabitants bring their daily catch home, and, without knowing it, thus help to raise and improve the site still further.

Some of these shellmounds are now situated high and dry, at some distance above tide water. Others lie on the very edge of the bay, and several of these, when shafts were sunk into them, proved to extend some distance below mean sea level. The base of a large deposit known as the Ellis Landing mound, near Richmond, is eighteen feet below high tide level; of one on Brooks Island near by, seventeen feet. The conclusion is that the sites have sunk at least seventeen or eighteen feet since they began to be inhabited. The only alternative explanation, that the first settlers put their houses on piles over the water, is opposed by several facts. The shells and ashes and soil of the Ellis Landing mound are stratified as they would be deposited on land, not as they would arrange in water. There are no layers of mud, remains of inedible marine animals, or ripple marks. There is no record of any recent Californian tribe living in pile dwellings; the shore from which the mound rises is unfavorably situated for such structures, being open and exposed to storms. Suitable timber for piles grows only at some distance. One is therefore perforce driven to the conclusion that this mound accumulated on a sinking shore, but that the growth of the deposit was more rapid than the rise of the sea, so that the site always remained habitable.

How long a time would be required for a coast to subside eighteen feet is a question for geologists, but their reply remains indefinite. A single earthquake might cause a sudden subsidence of several feet, or again the change might progress at the rate of a foot or only an inch a century. All that geologists are willing to state is that the probability is high of the subsidence having been a rather long time taking place.

The archæologists have tried to compute the age of Ellis Landing mound in another way. When it was first examined there were near its top about fifteen shallow depressions. These appear to be the remains of the pits over which the Indians were wont to build their dwellings. A native household averages about 7 inmates. One may thus estimate a population of about 100 souls. Numerous quadruped bones in the mound prove that these people hunted; net sinkers, that they fished; mortars and pestles, that they consumed acorns and other seeds. Accordingly, only part of their subsistence, and probably the minor part, was derived from molluscs. Fifty mussels a day for man, woman, and child seem a fair estimate of what their shellfish food is likely to have aggregated. This would mean that the shells of 5,000 mussels would accumulate on the site daily. Laboratory experiments prove that 5,000 such shells, with the addition of the same percentage of ash and soil as occurs in the mound, all crushed down to the same consistency of compactness as the body of the mound exhibits, occupy a volume of a cubic foot. This being the daily increment, the growth of the mound would be in the neighborhood of 365 feet per year. Now the deposit contains roughly a million and a quarter cubic feet. Dividing this figure by 365, one obtains about 3,500 as the presumable number of years required to accumulate the mound.

This result may not be accepted too literally. It is the result of a calculation with several factors, each of which is only tentative. Had the population been 200 instead of 100, the deposit would, with the other terms of the computation remaining the same, have built up twice as fast, and the 3,500 years would have to be cut in half. On the other hand, it has been assumed that occupation of the site was continuous through the year. Yet all that is known of the habits of the Indians makes it probable that the mound inhabitants were accustomed to go up into the hills and camp about half the time. Allowance for this factor would double the 3,500 years. All that is maintained for the computed age is that it represents a conscientious and conservative endeavor to draw a conclusion from all available sources of knowledge, and that it seems to hit as near the truth as a calculation of this sort can.

One verification has been attempted. Samples of mound material, taken randomly from different parts, indicate that 14 per cent of its weight, or about 7,000 tons, are ashes. If the mound is 3,500 years old, the ashes were deposited at the rate of two tons a year, or about eleven pounds daily.

Experiments with the woods growing in the neighborhood have shown that they yield less than one per cent of ash. The eleven daily pounds must therefore have come from 1,200 pounds of wood. On the assumption, as before, that the population averaged fifteen families, the one-fifteenth share of each household would be eighty pounds daily. This is a pretty good load of firewood for a woman to carry on her back, and with the Indians' habit of nursing their fires economically, especially along a timberless shore, eighty pounds seems a liberal allowance to satisfy all their requirements for heating and cooking. If they managed to get along on less than eighty pounds per hut, the mound age would be correspondingly greater.

This check calculation thus verifies the former estimate rather reasonably. It does not seem rash to set down three to four thousand years as the indicated age of the mound.

This double archæological conclusion tallies as closely as one could wish with the results derived from the ethnological method of estimating antiquity from the degree and putative rapidity of cultural change. Both methods carry the First traceable period back to about 1500 or 2000 B.C. After all, exactness is of little importance in matters such as these, except as an indication of certitude. If it could be proved that the first mussel was eaten by a human being on the site of Ellis Landing in 1724 B.C., this piece of knowledge would carry interest chiefly in proving that an exact method of chronology had been developed, and would possess value mainly in that the date found might ultimately be connectible with the dates of other events in history and so lead to broader formulations.

GENERAL SERVICEABILITY OF THE METHOD

The anthropological facts which have been analyzed and then recombined in the foregoing pages are not presented with the idea that the history of the lowly and fading Californians is of particular intrinsic moment. They have been discussed chiefly as an illustration of method, as one example out of many that might have been chosen. That it was the California Indians who were selected, is partly an accident of the writer's familiarity with them. The choice seems fair because the problem here undertaken is rather more difficult than many. The Californian cultures were simple. They decayed quickly on contact with civilization. The bulk of historical records go back bareiy a century and a half. Archæological exploration has been imperfect and yields comparatively meager results. Then, too, the whole Californian culture is only a fragment of American Indian culture, so that the essentially local Californian problems would have been further illuminated by being brought into relation with the facts available from North America as a whole—an aid which has been foregone in favor of compact presentation. In short, the problem was made difficult by its limitations, and yet results have been obtained. Obviously, the same method applied under more favorable circumstances to regions whose culture is richer and more diversified, where documented history projects farther back into the past, where excavation yields nobler monuments and provides them in stratigraphic arrangement, and especially when wider areas are brought into comparison, can result in determinations that are correspondingly more exact, full, and positive.

It is thus clear that cultural anthropology possesses a technique of operation which needs only vigorous, sane, and patient application to be successful. This technique is newer and as yet less refined than those of the mechanical sciences. It is also under the disadvantage of having to accept its materials as they are given in nature; it is impossible to carry cultural facts into the laboratory and conduct experiments on them. Still, it is a method; and its results differ from those of the so-called exact sciences in degree of sharpness rather than in other quality.

It will be noted that throughout this analysis there has been no mention of laws; that, at most, principles of method have been recognized—such as the assumption that widely spread culture elements are normally more ancient than locally distributed ones. In this respect cultural anthropology is in a class with political and economic history, and with all the essentially historical sciences such as natural history and geology. The historian rarely enunciates laws, or if he does, he usually means only tendencies. The "laws" of historical zoölogy are essentially laws of physiology; those of geology, laws of physics and chemistry. Even the "laws" of astronomy, when they are not mere formulations of particular occurrences which our narrow outlook on time causes to seem universal, are not really astronomical laws but mechanical and mathematical ones. In other words, anthropology belongs in the group of the historical sciences; those branches of knowledge concerned with things as and how and when they happen, with events as they appear in experience; whereas the group of sciences that formulates laws devotes itself to the inherent and immutable properties of things, irrespective of their place or sequence or occurrence in nature.

Of course, there must be laws underlying culture phenomena. There is no possibility of denying them unless one is ready to remove culture out of the realm of science and set it into the domain of the supernatural. Where can one seek these laws that inhere in culture? Obviously in that which underlies culture itself, namely, the human mind. The laws of anthropological data, like those of history, are then laws of psychology. As regards ultimate explanations for the facts which it discovers, classifies, analyzes, and recombines into orderly reconstructions and significant syntheses, cultural anthropology must look to psychology. The one is concerned with "what" and "how"; the other with "why"; each depends on the other and supplements it.

WOMAN AND RELIGION *

By ROBERT H. LOWIE

IF we were asked whether women or men are the more religious, most of us should unhesitatingly answer in favor of women and should presumably cite their proverbially greater emotionalism as an explanation. On the Continent— say, in Spain—it is a familiar enough thing to have women go to mass while their free-thinking brothers and husbands never enter a church, and in Anglo-Saxon countries pietism or any obtrusively religious or ethical reform movement is more definitely associated with the feminine psyche,—and this irrespective of the fact that in most denominations women are barred from the positions of priest or minister. But when we survey the corresponding phenomena of ruder cultures, the significant fact appears that in various regions women are not only ineligible for office but seem to be shut out from all religious activity. In most Australian tribes it would be death for a woman to witness the initiation procedures; corresponding conditions have been described for New Guinea and Melanesia and have a sporadic distribution elsewhere. Does this mean that women in such areas are really debarred from religious manifestations? And if not, how do they display the relevant sentiments? To what extent are their disabilities founded in some innate peculiarity, how far are they due to a specific cultural environment? And how do woman's subjective reactions differ from man's?

At the present stage of our knowledge some of these questions are more easily asked than answered. If in spite of our ignorance a special chapter is devoted to the topic, it is in order to direct attention to an interesting but neg-

* *Primitive Religion.* New York: Horace Liveright, Inc.

744

lected field of inquiry. On the last-mentioned problem in particular I have ransacked the literature in vain for even a shred of enlightening material. One turns naturally to those regions in which women are least hampered by social conventions. Thus, among the Northwestern Californians the part of shaman is most commonly played by the female sex, and Professor Kroeber has secured the confessions of one of these medicine-women. Yet when one analyzes her statements, the personal factor seems wholly submerged in the characteristic tribal (Yurok) trait of greed for money: she is obsessed with the desire of acquiring wealth through her practice, precisely as her fellows, male or female, are in the ordinary business of life: "So whatever I did I spoke of money constantly. . . . I said to myself: 'When people are sick, I shall cure them if they pay me enough.'" From such stereotyped longings of avarice it is impossible to distill the faintest flavor of distinctively feminine character.

Among the Crow there are relatively few restrictions because of sex. Women, as well as men, have the right to seek visions and if they avail themselves more rarely of the privilege it is because in so intensely martial a culture the craving for success in war is the most usual impetus to a vision-quest. In the important ceremonial society concerned with the sacred Tobacco there are no offices for which members are ineligible because of sex, and the part played by women in the dances is a conspicuous one. Of the women I knew, Muskrat was probably the most positive personality that figured in religious activities. She was very well informed and intelligent, but inordinately vain, and her attempts at self-aggrandizement were sometimes ridiculed by her fellow-tribesmen—in her absence. She had been Mixer in the Weasel chapter of the Tobacco society, and to the resentment of some old people she continued to exercise the duties of the office after having sold the prerogative. She herself explained that she had only sold part of it and at all events remained a dominant figure in the organization. I repeatedly interviewed her and obtained much interesting information but nothing that would suggest a positive sex difference. Thus, she had a revelation of a particular tobacco-mixing recipe such as any man might have secured; on another occasion a weasel entered her body, a not uncommon experience of either sex; precisely like any other member of the Tobacco organization she adopted new members; and again like other Crow Indians with corresponding revelations she exercised specific functions, such as charming an unfaithful husband or doctoring broken bones. Her taboos also wholly resemble those of other visionaries in principle.[1]

It is of course conceivable—though hardly a priori probable—that no sex differences exist. On the other hand, it is possible that our field methods have hitherto been too gross to sense such elusive differences as may occur; and at all events a resolute attempt in that direction—if possible, by a woman anthropologist—would be eminently worth while.

If very little can be said on the subjective side, I think we can definitely dispose of a plausible misconception based on objective observations. It does not follow that women are excluded from the religious life of the community because their social status is inferior or because certain spectacular features are tabooed to them. In the striking Ekoi case we found that women were indeed prohibited from touching a strong *njomm* or seeing a bull-roarer or a stilt-walking exhibition and from ever intruding into an Egbo meeting; but by way of compensation they exclude men from the Nimm sorority and through that cult play no mean part in tribal ritual. Elsewhere in Africa the legal subordination of women in no wise interferes with very important religious offices. Among the Zulu, women no less than men detect sorcerers, and the same is reported for the Thonga, where Mholombo, whom M. Junod not unnaturally describes as "an extraordinarily acute woman," would confound evil magicians, work such miracles as walking on the water, and interpret the divining-bones through the agency of a spirit possessing her. Other women have been known to become diviners, though not so often as men, and to be possessed by ancestral ghosts; and though normally the eldest brother acts as priest in ancestral worship the duty may also devolve on the eldest sister.[2]

The condition characteristic of these African tribes is of very wide distribution: that is to say, women may not participate so frequently or so fully as men, yet their rôle is far from negligible in the religious life. For instance, the highest reaches of Chukchi shamanism—those connected with the practice of ventriloquism—are inaccessible to the female sex, yet lesser forms of inspiration are more commonly bestowed on women than otherwise. In the Andaman Islands women do not join in ordinary dances, though they attend to form the chorus; but they have a mourning dance of their own and act as shamans, though less frequently than men. In Polynesia, again, all kinds of taboos hedged in the life of the women: in Hawaii they were obliged to eat food apart from the men and were not even allowed to enter a man's eating-house prior to the abolition of the old rule by a decree of Kamehameha II in 1819; they were not admitted to the sacred college of the Maori of New Zealand and might not travel by boat in the Marquesas. But in spite of Malo's statement that in Hawaii the majority of them "had no deity and just worshiped nothing," his own description tells of their worship of female deities; and in Tonga inspirational dreams of consequence were not denied to women.[3]

It is, however, particularly noteworthy that even in regions where some rigid penalty seems wholly to eliminate women from ceremonial participation closer scrutiny reveals a very different state of affairs. Oceania and Australia furnish stock examples of the former, but the less obtrusive assertion of women in religious life has not been adequately recognized. Thus, among the Tami of New Guinea we have seen that while the female sex was excluded from the initiation ceremony and terrorized by its performers, women normally call

the spirits of recently deceased tribesmen. An equally striking illustration is provided by Australia. Among the Euah-
layi of New South Wales the inner mysteries of the
initiation ritual also remain a sealed book to women, nay,
even the usual name, Byamee, of its divine inaugurator is
concealed from them. But this does not prevent them from
praying to him under another designation, as did that remarkable old shaman, Bootha, whose portrait has been so
vividly painted by Mrs. Parker. When probably well over
sixty, she absented herself from camp in order to grieve
over the loss of a favorite granddaughter. After a long
seclusion in more or less demented condition she returned
a full-fledged medicine-woman. Henceforth she was able
to summon and interrogate the guardian spirits acquired;
with their aid she performed miraculous cures and produced rain at will, evidently exerting a considerable influence on the aborigines in the vicinity and apparently in no
way inferior to her male colleagues.[4]

An American instance may be added for good measure.
The Northern Athabaskans generally are hardly conspicuous for their chivalrous attitude toward women, and the
Anvik, who inhabit an Alaskan village some hundred and
twenty-five miles inland, form no exception. Even from
infancy a girl is carefully watched lest she step on anything lying on the floor that might affect the welfare of
her family. "The spirit of the boy is stronger than the
spirit of the girl, so a boy may step where he pleases." As
the child grows older, restrictions multiply, especially from
puberty on, nor has the girl a will of her own in the
choice of a mate. Again, there is discrimination in the
ceremonial use of masks: men may wear female masks, but
no woman is allowed to put on a man's mask. Yet, all these
taboos to the contrary notwithstanding, the weaker sex is
by no means wholly debarred from participation in the
religious activities of the community. Some women own
sacred songs and chant them at the tribal festivals. There
are female shamans who treat sick members of their sex,

and the wives of shamans are favored to the extent of being allowed to sing at the more important dances and to inherit something of their deceased husbands' supernatural gifts. Individual cases are known of women who gained great influence.

Cries-for-salmon's mother is a woman with power. She has many strong songs. Her father had been a great hunter, with wolverene and bear songs. She is always consulted in the village, she knows her power, and there is no one to check her or to talk about her.[5]

This notable trio of instances establishes a sort of a fortiori conclusion. Evidently even marked sexual disabilities do not exclude women from exercising religious functions of social significance, and there is not the slightest indication that their limitations are the consequence of innate incapacity or that a lack of emotional interest in religion has been engendered by compulsory disuse. As a matter of fact, as soon as outward pressure is somewhat relaxed the sexes share quite equitably in ceremonial duties. This is clear even from the African cases cited above, and the case for North America could be easily strengthened by additional instances. Among the Plains Indians the custody of sacred objects, such as shields, was regularly entrusted to a favorite wife; membership in secret organizations was often open to women on equal terms with men; nay, they were even at times eligible to the highest ceremonial offices. To turn to another area, nothing could be fairer than the allotment of ritualistic privileges among the Bagobo of Mindanao, and indeed other natives of the Philippines. Old men offer sacred food, recount their exploits while holding the ceremonial bamboo poles they have cut, prepare for human sacrifices, perform magical rites, while old women conduct altar rites at the harvest, make offerings at shrines, and recite the accompanying prayers. If the men direct the ceremonial as a whole, it is virtually a feminine prerogative (as in New Guinea) to summon the spirits at a séance.

Indeed, the women "direct many ceremonial details and are often called into consultation with the old men; they exercise a general supervision over the religious behavior of the young people." [6]

Where pronounced religious disabilities occur, I am inclined to impute them predominantly to the savage man's horror of menstruation. Lest this seem a fanciful suggestion, I offer by way of substantiation a part of the abundant evidence.

Among the Ila, a Bantu tribe of Rhodesia, a woman during her periodic illness is dangerous "and must be separated as far as possible from contact with her fellows." A man eating with her would lose his virility, and sick people would be most injuriously affected by her. She may not use the common fire or handle other people's pots or drink from their cups or cook or draw water for others. In Central Australia a menstruating woman is carefully avoided, while in Queensland she is secluded and must not even walk in a man's tracks. In the Torres Straits Islands investigators have found an "intense fear of the deleterious and infective powers of the menstrual fluid," and various taboos are imposed on the menstruant, who must live in seclusion, shun the daylight, and abstain from sea-food. Her Marshall Island sister dwells in a special menstrual hut, is limited to a prescribed diet, and is believed to exert an inauspicious influence. [7]

However, for no other region is the evidence so convincing as for America. One of the most illuminating reports is that of an eighteenth century observer among the Choctaw of Louisiana. Here the women at once left the house, hid from the sight of men, were not permitted to use the family fire lest the household be polluted, and under no condition were supposed to cook for other people. The French narrator, having once stumbled upon a menstruant, prevailed upon her to make him "some porridge of little grain," and after the arrival of the husband invited him to partake of the meal. At first the Choctaw unwittingly fell to eating, but suddenly grew suspicious and inquired for the cook.

. . . When I replied that it was his wife who had been my cook, he was at once seized with sickness and went to the door to vomit. Then, reëntering and looking into the dish, he noticed some red things in the porridge, which were nothing else than the skin of the corn, some grains of which are red. He said to me: "How have you the courage to eat of this stew? Do you not see the blood in it?" Then he began vomiting again and continued until he had vomited up all that he had eaten; and his imagination was so strongly affected that he was sick on account of it for some days afterward.

In intensity of reaction the Menomini of Wisconsin rival the Choctaw. A woman must use her own culinary utensils during her illness, and she must not touch a tree, a dog, or a child lest it die. She is not supposed to scratch herself with her fingers but with a special stick. As Mr. Skinner reports:

To this day many pagan Menomini positively refuse to eat in Christian houses for fear of losing their powers through partaking of food prepared by a woman undergoing her monthly terms.

The Winnebago go so far as to assert that sacred objects lose their power through contact with a menstruating woman.

If the Winnebago can be said to be afraid of any one thing it may be said it is this—the menstrual flow of women—for even the spirits die of its effects.[8]

In the Far West the same psychological attitude appears practically unchanged. A Blackfoot menstruant must keep away from sacred articles and from sick people: something would strike the patient "like a bullet and make him worse." What is particularly noteworthy is the diffusion of corresponding beliefs throughout the area of rudest culture.

As late as 1906 I myself was able to observe the seclusion of Shoshoni women in Idaho, where abstention from meat was likewise imperative during the period. The same food taboo was observed by their kinsmen, the Paviotso of Nevada, who gave as a justification that if the women ate antelope flesh the game impounded in a drive would break through the enclosure. In north-central California the Shasta impose a special hut, the scratching-stick, strict food taboos, and the rule that the woman must not look at people or the sun or the moon. Should a woman be taken unexpectedly ill while at home,

all men leave at once, taking with them their bows, spears and nets, lest they become contaminated and thus all luck desert them.

Among the Chinook of the lower Columbia the adolescent girl is under rigorous restrictions.

She must not warm herself. She must never look at the people. She must not look at the sky, she must not pick berries. It is forbidden. When she looks at the sky it becomes bad weather. When she picks berries it will rain. She hangs up her towel of cedar bark on a certain spruce tree. The tree dries up at once. After one hundred days she may eat fresh food, she may pick berries and warm herself.

In subsequent catamenial periods she must not be seen by a sick person, nor must berries picked by her be eaten by the sick. Finally (though the list could be greatly enlarged), there are the Northern Athabaskans. According to Father Morice, "hardly any other being was the object of so much dread as a menstruating woman," who ate only dried fish, drank water through a tube, and was not allowed to live with her male kin nor to touch anything belonging to men or related to the chase "lest she would thereby pollute the same, and condemn the hunters to failure, owing to the anger of the game thus slighted." More than a century ago Samuel Hearne made corresponding observations among the related Chipewyan: women in question lived apart in a hovel and were not permitted to walk near a net or to eat the head of an animal or cross the track where a deer head had lately been carried,—and all this to ward off bad hunting luck. Quite similar notions prevail among their fellow-Athabaskans, the Anvik, of Alaska.[9]

It is not so easy to trace the distribution of such a trait in the southern half of the New World, yet, thanks mainly to Father Schmidt's indefatigable industry, we are in a position to state positively that in one form or another the usage extends all the way to Tierra del Fuego, being found in southern Central America, Colombia, Guiana, Peru, Brazil, Patagonia, and around Cape Horn. The descriptions are not always so circumstantial as for North America. Thus, from a Fuegian report I glean merely the imposition of a puberty fast on girls. The Mundrucu added exposure to smoke, the Paravilhana corporal punishment. Among the Siusi the girl was under dietary restrictions, her hair was cut, and her back was daubed with paint. The Arawak of Guiana present the typical complex of seclusion, fire and food taboos.[10] To what extent fuller knowledge of all these tribes would bring ampler accounts, remains obscure. We should like to know especially whether later menstruation is likewise linked with definite regulations. But even in our present state of ignorance it is proper to advance the hypothesis that some sort of menstrual taboo is a deep-rooted, an archaic element of American culture.

Let us now survey the remainder of the world. I have already pointed out that the sentiment underlying menstrual prohibitions exists in Oceania, Australia, and Africa. In the rudest tribes for which I can get evidence it likewise occurs, but not in the extreme form typical of, say, the Choctaw. The Andamanese do not insist on departure from the camp, but proscribe certain kinds of food for their alleged evil effects *on the woman*. Bushman practice, at least at the time of adolescence, conforms more closely to type: the adolescent is segregated in a tiny hut with a door closed upon her by her mother; she must not walk about

freely nor look at the springbok lest they become wild;
and when going out she must look down at the ground.
On rules of subsequent periods I cannot find any data. Of
the Paleo-Siberians, the Maritime Chukchi do not allow
a menstruating woman to approach her husband; even her
breath is impure and might contaminate him, destroying
his luck as sea-hunter, nay, causing him to be drowned.
Under similar circumstances, her Koryak sister must not
tamper with her husband's hunting and fishing apparatus
or sit on his sledge, while among the Yukaghir she is
forbidden to touch the sacred drum.[11]

From the occurrence of the custom among the rudest
peoples of the Old World—the Paleo-Siberians, Andamanese, Bushmen—and the rudest peoples of America, and
its wide distribution on somewhat higher levels, we can
draw the conclusion that menstrual restrictions are of great
antiquity in the history of human culture, though probably not in the extreme form distinctive of many Indian
tribes of Canada and the United States. Reverting now to
my hypothesis that disabilities are correlated with the awe
inspired by menstruation, I should like to cite several facts
by way of corroboration. Where the relevant taboos exist
in mild form or are lacking, sex discrimination seems to be
likewise moderate. The Bagobo let women share in ceremonial life on a footing of virtual equality and I cannot
find evidence of menstrual restrictions. In the Andamans
women do not ordinarily join in the dancing but attend,
forming the chorus; and quite similarly the Bushman
women beat the drum and clap their hands for the male
dancers.[12] Still more interesting, where the discrimination
is intense, it is relaxed in old age; *old* women enjoy privileges in Australia and New Guinea that are denied to their
younger sisters. The reason is not difficult to divine and is
explicitly stated by a Winnebago informant:

> At a feast . . . the old women, who have passed their cli-
> macteric, sit right next to the men, because they are considered
> the same as men as they have no menstrual flow any more.

That is to say, before the menopause women are weird creatures, after the menopause they become ordinary human beings, though in many cases, no doubt, their former uncanniness still in some measure clings to them. A fact otherwise obscure can be explained from this angle. Why do the Chukchi, who close the highest grade of shamanism to women, fail to bar male inverts who in every way dress and act as women? Obviously because in their case the sentiments produced by the thought of menstruation are eliminated.

In closing the discussion of this topic I am painfully conscious of having contributed very little to a highly important subject. But I hope the attempt to treat it as a distinct set of problems will lead to more systematic research,—especially in the field.

This is perhaps as good a place as any to express what little I have to say about a theory broached rather vociferously in some quarters, to wit, the view that religion is at bottom nothing but misunderstood erotic emotion. It must be obvious that two phenomena that exert so profound an influence on so many phases of human conduct must have certain points of contact. The simplest kind of interrelationship occurs where the gratification of erotic desire is merely one of the life-values, which accordingly like other life-values can be secured by an appropriate intercourse with the extraordinary. Following the traditional technique of his tribe, a Crow will seek a vision, where a Bukaua mutters a spell and uses some magical charm. But these procedures, employed for a hundred other purposes, can obviously not be derived from a single, arbitrarily selected motive for their application.

There are, however, a group of other facts adduced by the adherents of the theory to prove the dependence of religious feeling on the sex instinct. I will follow the convenient summary provided by Mr. Thouless. It is asserted that adolescence is preëminently the period of religious conversion, hence religious experience is functionally related with the instinct that comes to maturity at this period. Secondly, religion employs the language characteristic of the expression of erotic passion. Finally, the theory assumes a special concern of religion with the suppression of normal sexual activity, and a compensatory reaction against such asceticism.

Viewing the question primarily from the ethnological angle, I find myself in substantial agreement with James and Thouless in rejecting the evidence as ludicrously inconclusive for the attempted demonstration.[13] Mystic experiences are indeed commonly sought and secured at the age of puberty but by no means exclusively so. Indeed, as Dr. R. F. Benedict has proved, several of the Plains Indian tribes regularly permitted the obtaining of a revelation in mature middle age, sometimes to the exclusion of the puberty fast.[14] On the other hand, among the tribes of the Great Lakes the experience considerably antedated what could by the wildest stretch of the imagination be called adolescence. Here, as everywhere, the psychological problem is complicated by the influence of cultural environment. It is evidently a matter of social tradition whether the religious thrill is looked for and obtained at seven, at fifteen, or at forty. Hence, it might be argued that these conventions artificially defer or accelerate the advent of religious emotion that "naturally" comes with the approach of adolescence. But this would be an arbitrary assertion pending empirical confirmation.

The argument from religious phraseology seems weaker still. It is true that a Crow visionary is greeted by his patron with the words "I adopt you as my son," and the associated ideas are undoubtedly those of the aid and protection the "son" is henceforth to receive from his "father." But I am quite unable to see in this any adumbration of an occult "father-complex." As James wisely remarks, religious sentiment simply utilizes "such poor symbols as our life affords," and he amply proves that digestive and respiratory concepts serve the same purpose of

vivid representation as directly or indirectly amatory
ones. If we attach undue importance to the words used
by man in his groping for an adequate expression of his
thoughts and feelings, we may be driven to reduce the sex
instinct to that of nutrition when a lover "hungers" for the
sight of his sweetheart and charge him with a latent cannibalistic inclination which is at least improbable.

As for the repression and compensatory overindulgence
of the sex appetite, neither can be said to be characteristic
of primitive religion. Special phenomena, appearing in
restricted points of space and time, are here confounded
with the universal essence of religion. The same applies to
the orgies that are sometimes spectacular accompaniments
of ceremonialism; interesting specimens of the ideas that
may become associated with religious phenomena, they do
not as a rule touch the core of religion. *That* must be sought
where James looked for it, in "the immediate content of
the religious consciousness," and I quite agree that "few
conceptions are less instructive than this reinterpretation
of religion as perverted sexuality."

NOTES

[1] Lowie, 1919; p. 119 *sq.; ibid.,* 1922, p. 339 *sq.*

[2] Talbot, pp. 21, 23, 25, 95, 225, 284. Shooter, pp. 174-183. Junod, ii,
pp. 377, 438, 444, 456, 466.

[3] Bogoras, p. 415. Brown, pp. 129, 131, 176. Malo, pp. 50-53, 112.
Mariner, p. 262.

[4] Parker, pp. 6, 8, 42-49, 59.

[5] Parsons, 1922, p. 337 *sq.*

[6] L. W. Benedict, pp. 10, 76 *sq.,* 193 *sq.*

[7] Smith and Dale, ii, p. 26 *f.* Spencer and Gillen, 1904, p. 601. Roth,
1897, p. 184. *Reports of the Cambridge Expedition,* v, pp. 196, 201 *sq.*
Erdland, p. 135.

[8] Swanton, 1918, p. 59. Skinner, 1913, p. 52. Radin, 1923, p. 136 *f.*

[9] Wissler, 1911, p. 29. Dixon, 1907, p. 457 *sq.* Boas, 1894, p. 246. Morice,
p. 218. Hearne, p. 313 *sq.* Parsons, 1922, p. 344.

[10] Schmidt, 1913. Martius, i, pp. 390, 631. Koch-Grünberg, p. 181. Roth,
1915, p. 312 *f.* Buschan, pp. 217, 360.

[11] Brown, p. 94. Bleek and Lloyd, p. 76 *f.* Bogoras, p. 492. Jochelson,
1905-1908, p. 54; *idem.,* 1910, p. 104.

[12] Brown, p. 131. Bleek and Lloyd, p. 355.

[13] James, p. 11. Thouless, p. 130 *sq.*

[14] R. F. Benedict, p. 49 *sq.*

VI
EVOLUTION OF ATTITUDES

EVOLUTION OF HUMAN SPECIES *

By ROBERT BRIFFAULT

IN the days when the theory of organic evolution was
a struggling heresy, the chief weight of prejudice against
which it had to contend had reference to the origin of the
human species. Darwin, in his first great exposition of the
theory, cautiously abstained from discussing its manifest
corollary. The co-discoverer of the principle of natural selection, Wallace, refused to apply it to the origin of the human
mind. Many who, in those days, yielded to the weight of
evidence as regards the continuity of living organization and
the gradual modification of structure, and were even ready
to admit its bearing on the origin of man's bodily structure,
thought they saw an unsurmountable obstacle in accounting
by the same process for the development of the mind of
man. Those doubts are now no longer a subject of dispute
among those whose judgment in the matter is of account.
Many psychologists would, at the present day, claim that
the principle of evolution has shed no less light over the
field of psychology than over that of biology, and that a
scientific psychology has, in truth, only become possible
since the fact has been apprehended that the human mind
is built upon a foundation of primal impulses common to
all forms of life, of instincts similar to those which shape
animal behavior.

In the complete and comparatively rapid triumph of
evolutionary science, the fact of the origin of the human
from the animal mind has, indeed, tended in general to be
taken somewhat too much for granted, and the manner in
which that momentous development has taken place has not
perhaps been the object of as much consideration and dis-

* *Scientia*, June, 1927.

cussion as it deserves. Darwin's later work, in which he showed that there are in the mental constitution of man scarcely any aspects which have not their germ or analogues in animal mentality, is still perhaps the most exhaustive discussion of the subject. Beyond various suggestions as to what may have been the most important factors in bringing about the development of the human brain, such as the adoption of the erect attitude, the adaptation of the hand, the change from a frugivorous to a flesh diet, with the consequent growth of ingenuity in the devising of weapons and in social coördination, little has been added by way of elucidating the most remarkable step in organic evolution.

Without in any way suggesting a doubt as to its reality, it must be admitted to a greater extent than is generally done, that there is considerable weight in the objections which were at one time urged against it. Between the mental constitution of the rudest savages and that of any animal, including the anthropoids, there is a wide gap, and that gap consists of more than a difference in degree; it amounts to a difference in kind. Primarily that difference depends upon the conceptual character of human mentality. Of conceptual thought and all that it implies, there is, in spite of the collections of anecdotes of "animal intelligence," no scrap of evidence among animals. So competent and sympathetic an authority as Professor Lloyd Morgan concluded that animals are without any perception of relations, that their memory is entirely of the desultory type, and that "the evidence now before us is not sufficient to justify the hypothesis that any animals have reached that stage of mental evolution at which they are even incipiently rational." Quite recently Dr. Köhler, working with chimpanzees in a semiwild condition at Tenerife, has made what is probably the most exhaustive and scientific study of the behavior and mentality of anthropoids. His results give a high idea of the intelligence of the chimpanzee, but they, at the same time, bring out the entire absence of any indication of conceptual mentality.

'The apes show ingenuity in solving practical problems, but they "must have the factors for the solution of the problem within visual range, for they seem to have a very limited capacity of working with mental images." Upon that capacity of working by means of mental images, that is, upon conceptual thought, depends human mentality and the difference between it and the psychism of animals. Once acquired it has rendered the difference an abysmal one. It has not merely furnished more efficient means of solving practical problems; it has transplanted mental life from the sensory, and subconscious psychism of animals to a medium of symbols, ideas, values, to a world which is not the creation of the individual, or inherited by him through physiological processes, but is the transmitted legacy of a social tradition. That mentality is dependent upon the permanent and undying social group, not upon the transitory individual. Let the means of its transmission be abolished, as in the uneducated deaf-mute, and the human individual is not mentally distinguished from the animal; not only does he lack the human instrument of intellect, but human emotions, social sentiments and affections also. Evolutionary development has, in the human species, been transferred from organic elements physiologically inherited to social *tradition*. It may be doubted whether the modern civilized individual differs greatly as regards inherited capacities from his ancestors of the Stone Age; the difference between savagedom and civilization is not organic, but cultural. The increase in our knowledge of ancient types of man has, in some respects, accentuated rather than attenuated the abruptness of the transition from animality to humanity; the oldest human remains and the tools associated with them indicate a brain-capacity which is not markedly, if at all, inferior to that of existing races.

The problem has, for the most part, been considered in a false light; it has been regarded from the point of view of the individual organism, whereas the human mind is from the first essentially a social product. It is not so much the result of structural and physiological characters, as of the characters of social groups, of their constitution, of the relations between their component individuals.

Conceptual thought, the feature of human mentality towards which the bridge from animal psychism must of necessity lead, depends in turn upon language; it is the creation of the word. And language cannot, even in fully evolved humanity, develop in the isolated individual; it is the product of social relations, of particularly close and extensive social relations. As Professor Carveth Read remarks, the development of language would not be possible in a group consisting of a few individuals only, such as the primordial "family" has been conceived.

The association of individuals is not a common feature in the animal world. As in all else, the human interpreter reads in his observations of animal life the condition of his own. A great deal has been said concerning animal societies, animal families, "gregariousness." But apart from the communities of insects, which are elaborately differentiated reproductive groups and lie quite outside the line of evolution of the higher vertebrates, there is in the animal world very little that is even analogous to social relations. Gregariousness, the local aggregation of life, is not necessarily association. Herding animals are of all the higher animals the most devoid of social instincts; maternal care is with them poorly developed, they are lacking in affection and sympathy, they are the most stupid of quadrupeds, and are in every respect greatly inferior to the solitary carnivores. There is nowhere any evidence of concerted action and social coördination. The romantic stories which were once current concerning the constitution of communities of beavers, of prairie-dogs, are known to be fables devoid of all foundation. The nearest apparent approach to concerted action is to be found in some packs of the dog-tribe. But it is apparent only; there is no subordination of individual to social aims. The animals are essentially solitary, pack-formation being much more rare and temporary than is commonly supposed; and, as Dr. W. T. Hornaday remarks, "they are the meanest brutes on earth." The only rudiments of social groups in the animal kingdom are, without exception, sexual and reproductive groups. Among all mammals sexual association is, notwithstanding much sentimental inaccuracy to the contrary, for the most part very slight and transient, and commonly altogether absent. Separation and avoidance between the sexes, except during brief pairing seasons, is much more conspicuous than association. Among the apes social relations differ profoundly from the anthropomorphic conceptions of them that have been current. The orang-utan have no sexual association at all; males and females do not cohabit. The only association is that of mother and offspring during the period of the latter's immaturity. The gorilla lives in bands, often of considerable size, in which, according to the latest and most detailed observations, those of Prince William of Sweden, sexual segregation seems to obtain, females and young forming one group, the males keeping apart. The abundance of solitary males would seem to indicate that the male population is a shifting one, and its aggregation with the females, as with the orang, transient and variable. There is no more coöperation among the primates than there is among herding animals or rodents. Each individual fends for himself. With one exception: the young are dependent upon their mother, who devotes herself to providing for them and defending them with an instinct into which the reckless passion of the reproductive instinct is transfused.

There is one known factor which establishes a profound distinction between the constitution of the most rudimentary human group and all other animal groups; and it has reference precisely to that association of mother and offspring which is the sole form of true social solidarity among animals. Throughout the class of mammals there is a continuous increase in the duration of that association, which is the consequence of the prolongation of the period of infantile dependence, and is correlated with a concomitant protraction of gestation and the advance in intelligence and social instincts. Among the unintelligent herbivora the duration of gestation, which is always proportional to the average weight of the animal, and must for purposes of comparison be reduced to a common denominator in this respect, is relatively brief. Infancy is equally curtailed; the young can follow their mother a few hours after birth, and are independent in a few weeks. Among carnivora the duration of both gestation and dependent infancy is greatly prolonged. That prolongation is greater still in the anthropoids, and reaches its maximum in the human species. A young orang-utan goes through the same process of development, in a month, which a lion cub accomplishes in a week, and which takes the human infant a year. The lion cub is potentially independent when eighteen months old, the anthropoid at about five years. At that age many savage babies are still being suckled by their mother, and puberty ceremonies generally take place towards the age of twelve or thirteen. The association of mother and offspring is among all animals, including the apes, a temporary one, coming to an end when the young reach sexual maturity. In the human group by the time that one generation has become sexually mature, new generations have been added to the group. The association between the younger generations, pronounced in all primates, is greatly increased as regards solidarity in the human group. From being a transitory association, it tends to become a permanent one. The only analogue in the animal world of the social relation, the association of mother and offspring during the latter's infancy, becomes, owing to the great prolongation of that infancy in the human group, a lasting feature. The human individual is permanently a member of a solitary social group.

Correlated with that circumstance is another equally momentous, and deriving from the same cause. Retarded development, prolonged immaturity imply the completion of growth under the influence not of physiological heredity alone, but of experience derived from the environment, natural and social. Hence the superior intelligence, the "educability" of infantile carnivora as compared with precocious herbivora, of the yet more infantile apes as compared with other mammals. Infantile immaturity is not manifested in the higher animals by any gross deficiency in organic structure. The new-born carnivore, ape, human infant are not, like the young of some lower vertebrates, larval forms; they are anatomically and functionally, except in a few minor details, perfect according to the pattern of their parents. Their various systems of organs are complete as in the adult, with only two exceptions: the reproductive and the central nervous system. Reproductive development is deferred till puberty. The structural development which takes place during the period of infancy has, in a preponderant degree, reference to one organ only, the brain. The precocity of the young of herbivores is the result of the complete development of their central nervous system; the infantility of carnivores, of apes, of the human infant is proportionately correlated with the gradual development of the elements of that system. "I have found," observes Dr. Below, "that among animals that bring forth their young in a condition of helplessness, such as man, the dog, the cat, rat, mouse, rabbit, the development of ganglion-cells is incomplete at the time of birth and even soon after; whereas the horse, calf, sheep, guinea-pig show completely developed ganglion-cells in every part of the brain almost always in the earlier periods of fœtal life, invariably before birth." That incompleteness of development is much more pronounced in the human infant than in any other mammalian young. The processes of the pyramidal cells in the frontal cerebral cortex have, in the sixth month of intrauterine life, only one-fourth of their full development; at birth only one-half. The growth of the brain does not consist, as does that of other tissues and organs, in the multiplication of its cells; these cease to multiply before any other in the body, and their number is never added to. The increase in the brain is exclusively the result of the growth of processes and arborizations which are thrown out by its developing cells, establishing various connections. Although the brain is, relatively to the rest of the body, larger and heavier at birth than in the adult, it grows after birth more rapidly than any other organ. In the first three months the body as a whole adds 20 per cent to its weight; the brain adds nearly 90 per cent. In less than nine months the weight of the brain is doubled, in three years it is trebled. That growth is not, as in other tissues, nutritional and due to cell-reproduction; it is entirely functional. It takes place under the direct influence of experience, of education; if the sense-organs, eyes, ears, be destroyed or functionless, the corresponding brain-development does not take place. If an infant be born prematurely the growth is accelerated.

Brain-development and intelligence are, then, dependent upon retarded growth, the protraction of infantile immaturity. These, far more than the erect attitude or any other specialized organic function, are the fundamental conditions and determining factors of the development of human brain-power. The question is sometimes mooted whether young gorillas or chimpanzees might not, by careful training, be taught to speak. The difficulty in the way of such an educational feat is that there is not sufficient time; the brain of the young anthropoid grows too fast; it is formed, it has lost its malleability before the time required for such an education even in the human infant. In the human species itself, the lower races are precocious as compared with the higher, their development is completed and arrested earlier. The superiority of the white races is associated with their slow individual development, their prolonged infantilism.

Those conditions of the functional development of the brain are in turn correlated with, and inseparable from, the increased permanency of the maternal group. With this goes an increased strength of the ties of instinct that bind it, the maternal instinct, the filial instincts of dependence, the social instincts which unite the members of the group. It is under the influence of those instincts that the human brain has developed. It is highly improbable that language, upon which conceptual intelligence depends, has developed in the first instance to express concepts, as a device for the purpose of communicating ideas, of naming objects. There can be little doubt that long before it was put to such uses, language had already arisen as an expression of emotions and sentiments. Its germ lies not in concepts, which are impossible without it, and are its products, not its cause, but in emotional sounds. The precocious herbivores are mute even under the influence of pain; carnivorous cubs yell, even when their belly is full, if left alone; the anthropoid apes have a varied range of emotional sounds. Language has its root in social sentiments; the favoring conditions for its development are the same as those which confirm those sentiments and the solidarity of the group, and depend upon the educational protraction of human development.

The transition from animality to humanity has, thus, not solely consisted in structural changes, in the evolution of an animal with a large brain. A merely large brain is not necessarily a human brain. The differentiation of the human species has been the evolution of a social group rendered permanent by the prolonged infantile development of its members under the protection of the maternal and social instincts. It has from the first been a social rather than a biological process. It has been rendered possible by the gradual accentuation of given characters, by the slow accumulation of favoring predispositions; it has been, in short, an evolution. But, like many steps in organic evolution, it has been the crossing of a definite boundary-line. Once beyond it, the course of the evolutionary process was turned into a new channel; the very method of its operation was changed. Its products became the products of a new entity, the social group; and a new heredity, the heredity of transmitted tradition, came to overshadow organic heredity. The gulf between humanity and animality was established as soon as the boundary-line was crossed. It is not established by culture, but by the conditions of culture, by the permanency of the social group and its tradition. In many parts of Europe evidence is found of primitive populations as low in culture as any known race, or lower. With scarcely any fashioned tools, they lived, as do animals, by gathering available food, roots, shell-fish. The Romans knew of such populations of naked European savages. Some of these, coming into contact with Syrian travelers, with Roman empire-builders, acquired in a generation or two a higher culture, which became merged in that of barbaric Europe; they are the not very remote ancestors of civilized Europeans of the present day. Given the nexus of the permanent social group, whose members feel themselves bound together by unseverable ties, intercommunicate by vocal signs, inherit a group-tradition, it matters not that they are naked, toolless, deviceless, brutal. They are essentially capable of inheriting the elements of any human tradition, and stand in that respect separated by an abysmal gulf from the anthropoid, who is, maybe, only just on the other side of the boundary-line. The conceptual tradition which every individual acquires and which makes him human is a social product; the essential conditions of the emergence of the human species from animality have likewsie been, not purely organic, but social.

COLLECTIVE REPRESENTATION IN PRIMITIVES' PERCEPTIONS AND THE MYSTICAL CHARACTER OF SUCH *

By LUCIEN LEVY-BRUHL

BEFORE undertaking an investigation of the most general laws governing collective representations among undeveloped peoples, it may be as well to determine what the essential characteristics of these representations are, and thus avoid an ambiguity which is otherwise almost inevitable. The terminology used in the analysis of mental functions is suited to functions, such as the philosophers, psychologists, and logicians of our civilization have formulated and defined. If we admit these functions to be identical in all human aggregates, there is no difficulty in the matter; the same terminology can be employed throughout, with the mental reservation that "savages" have minds more like those of children than of adults. But if we abandon this position—and we have the strongest reasons for considering it untenable—then the terms, divisions, classifications we make use of in analyzing our own mental functions are not suitable for those which differ from them; on the contrary, they prove a source of confusion and error. In studying primitive mentality, which is a new subject, we shall probably require a fresh terminology. At any rate it will be necessary to specify the new meaning which some expressions already in use should assume when applied to an object differing from that they have hitherto betokened.

This is the case, for instance, with the term "collective representations."

In the current parlance of psychology which classifies

* How Natives Think. London: George Allen & Unwin.

phenomena as emotional, motor, or intellectual, "representation" is placed in the last category. We understand by it
a matter of cognizance, inasmuch as the mind simply has
the image or idea of an object. We do not deny that in the
actual mental life every representation affects the inclinations
more or less, and tends to produce or inhibit some movement. But, by an abstraction which in a great many cases
is nothing out of the ordinary, we disregard these elements
of the representation, retaining only its essential relation to
the object which it makes known to us. The representation is,
par excellence, an intellectual or cognitive phenomenon.

It is not in this way, however, that we must understand
the collective representations of primitives. Their mental
activity is too little differentiated for it to be possible to
consider ideas or images of objects by themselves apart from
the emotions and passions which evoke these ideas or are
evoked by them. Just because our mental activity is more
differentiated, and we are more accustomed to analyzing
its functions, it is difficult for us to realize by any effort of
imagination, more complex states in which emotional or
motor elements are *integral* parts of the representation. It
seems to us that these are not really representations, and in
fact if we are to retain the term we must modify its meaning
in some way. By this state of mental activity in primitives
we must understand something which is not a purely or
almost purely intellectual or cognitive phenomenon, but a
more complex one, in which what is really "representation"
to us is found blended with other elements of an emotional
or motor character, colored and imbued by them, and therefore implying a different attitude with regard to the objects
represented.

Moreover, these collective representations are very often
acquired by the individual in circumstances likely to make
the most profound impression upon his sensibility. This is
particularly true of those transmitted at the moment when
he becomes a man, a conscious member of the social group,
the moment when the initiation ceremonies cause him to

undergo new birth,[1] when the secrets upon which the very life of the group depends are revealed to him, sometimes amid tortures which subject his nerves to the most severe tests. It would be difficult to exaggerate the intense emotional force of such representations. The object is not merely discerned by the mind in the form of an idea or image; according to the circumstances of the case, fear, hope, religious awe, the need and the ardent desire to be merged in one common essence, the passionate appeal to a protecting power—these are the soul of these representations, and make them at once cherished, formidable, and really *sacred* to the initiated. We must add, too, that the ceremonies in which these representations are translated into action, so to speak, take place periodically; consider the conscious effect of the emotional excitement of witnessing the movements which express them, the nervous exaltation engendered by excessive fatigue, the dances, the phenomena of ecstasy and of possession —in fact everything which tends to revive and enhance the emotional nature of these collective representations. At any time during the intervals between the occurrences of these ceremonies, whenever the object of one of these representations once more arises in the consciousness of the "primitive," even should he be alone and in a calm frame of mind at the moment, it can never appear to him as a colorless and indifferent image. A wave of emotion will immediately surge over him, undoubtedly less intense than it was during the ceremonies, but yet strong enough for its cognitive aspect to be almost lost sight of in the emotions which surround it. Though in a lesser degree, the same character pertains to other collective representations—such, for instance, as those transmitted from generation to generation by means of myths and legends, and those which govern manners and customs which apparently are quite unimportant; for if these customs are respected and enforced, it is because the collective representations relating to them are imperative and something quite different from purely intellectual phenomena.

The collective representations of primitives, therefore, differ very profoundly from our ideas or concepts, nor are they their equivalent either. On the one hand, as we shall presently discover, they have not their logical character. On the other hand, not being genuine representations, in the strict sense of the term, they express, or rather imply, not only that the primitive actually has an image of the object in his mind, and thinks it real, but also that he has some hope or fear connected with it, that some definite influence emanates from it, or is exercised upon it. This influence is a virtue, an occult power which varies with objects and circumstances, but is always real to the primitive and forms an integral part of his representation. If I were to express in one word the general peculiarity of the collective representations which play so important a part in the mental activity of undeveloped peoples, I should say that this mental activity was a *mystic* one. In default of a better, I shall make use of this term—not referring thereby to the religious mysticism of our communities, which is something entirely different, but employing the word in the strictly defined sense in which "mystic" implies belief in forces and influences and actions which, though imperceptible to sense, are nevertheless real.

In other words, the reality surrounding the primitives is itself mystical. Not a single being or object or natural phenomenon in their collective representations is what it appears to be to our minds. Almost everything that we perceive therein either escapes their attention or is a matter of indifference to them. On the other hand, they see many things there of which we are unconscious. For instance, to the primitive who belongs to a totemic community, every animal, every plant, indeed every object, such as the sun, moon, and stars, forms part of a totem, and has its own class and subclass. Consequently, each individual has his special affinities, and possesses powers over the members of his totem, class and sub-class; he has obligations towards them, mystic relations with other totems, and so forth. Even in communities where this form does not exist, the group idea of certain animals (possibly of all, if our records were complete) is mystic in character. Thus, among the Huichols, "the birds that soar highest ... are thought to see and hear everything, and to possess mystic powers, which are inherent in their wing and tail feathers." These feathers, carried by the shaman, "enable him to see and hear everything both above and below the earth ... to cure the sick, transform the dead, call down the sun, etc." [2] The Cherokees believe that fishes live in companies like human beings, that they have their villages, their regular paths through the waters, and that they conduct themselves like beings endowed with reason.[3] They think, too, that illness—rheumatic affections in particular—proceed from a mystic influence exercised by animals which are angry with the hunters, and their medical practices testify to this belief.

In Malaya and in South Africa the crocodile, and in other places the tiger, leopard, elephant, snake, are the object of similar beliefs and practices, and if we recall the myths of which animals are the heroes, in both hemispheres, there is no mammal or bird or fish or even insect to which the most extraordinary mystic properties have not been attributed. Moreover, the magic practices and ceremonies which, among nearly all primitive peoples, are the necessary accompaniment of hunting and fishing, and the sacrificial rites to be observed when the quarry has been killed, are sufficiently clear testimony to the mystic properties and powers which enter into the collective representation relating to the animal world.

It is the same with plant life. It will doubtless suffice to mention the *intichiuma* ceremonies described by Spencer and Gillen, designed to secure, in mystic fashion, the normal reproduction of plants—the development of agrarian rites, corresponding with the hunting and fishing ceremonial, in all places where primitive peoples depend wholly or partly on the cultivation of the soil for their subsistence—and lastly, the highly unusual mystic properties ascribed to sacred plants, as, for instance, the soma in Vedic India, and the *hikuli* among the Huichols.

Again, if we consider the human body, we shall find that each organ of it has its own mystic significance, as the widespread practice of cannibalism and the rites connected with human sacrifices (in Mexico, for instance) prove. The heart, liver, kidney, the eyes, the fat, marrow and so on, are reputed to procure such and such an attribute for those who feed on them. The orifices of the body, the excreta of all kinds, the hair and nail-parings, the placenta and umbilical cord, the blood, and the various fluids of the body, can all exercise magic influences.[4] Collective representations attribute mystic power to all these things, and many widespread beliefs and practices relate to this power. So, too, certain parts of plants and animals possess peculiar virtues. "*Badi* is the name given to the evil principle which ... attends (like an evil angel) everything in his life.... Von de Wall describes it as the 'enchanting or destroying influence which issues from anything; for example, from a tiger which one sees, from a poisonous tree which one passes under, from the saliva of a mad dog, from an action which one has performed.' " [5]

Since everything that exists possesses mystic properties, and these properties, from their very nature, are much more important than the attributes of which our senses inform us, the difference between animate and inanimate things is not of the same interest to primitive mentality as it is to our own. As a matter of fact, the primitive's mind frequently disregards it altogether. Thus rocks, the form or position of which strike the primitive's imagination, readily assume a sacred character in virtue of their supposed mystic power. Similar power is ascribed to the rivers, clouds, winds. Districts in space, direction (the points of the compass), have mystic significance. When the Australian aborigines assemble in large numbers, each tribe, and each totem of a tribe, has its own place, a place assigned to it by virtue of its mystic affinity with a particular spatial region. Facts of a similar nature have been noted in North America. I shall not lay any stress on the rain, lightning, or thunder, the symbols of which play so important a part in the religious ceremonies of the Zuñi, the Australian aborigines, and all aggregates where a prolonged drought is a serious menace to the very existence of the group. Finally, in Loango, the soil "is something more to the Bafioti than the scene upon which their lives are played out. There is in the ground, and there issues from it, a vital influence which permeates everything, which unites the present and the past.... All things that live owe their powers to the soil.... The people regard their land as a fief from their god ... the ground is sacred." [6] The same belief obtains among the North American Indians, who consider it sacrilege to till the ground, for by so doing they would run a risk of offending the mystic power and drawing down dire calamities upon themselves.

Even things made, and constantly used, by man have their mystic properties and can become beneficent or terrifying according to circumstances. Cushing, who had lived among the Zuñis, had made them adopt him, and whose unusual versatility of mind led him finally to think like them, says that they, "no less than primitive peoples generally, conceive of everything made ... whether structure or utensil or weapon, ... as living ... a still sort of life, but as potent and aware nevertheless and as capable as functioning not only obdurately and resistingly, but also actively and powerfully in occult ways, either for good or for evil. As for living things, they observe, every animal is formed, and acts or functions according to its form—the feathered and winged bird flying, because of its feathered form, the furry four-footed animal running and leaping, and the scaly and finny fish swimming.... So the things made or born in their special forms by the hands of man also have life and functions variously according to their various forms." Even the differences in the claws of beasts, for example, are supposed to make the difference between the hugging of the bear and the clutching of the panther. "The forms of these things not only give their power, but also restrict their power, so that if properly made, that is made and shaped strictly as other things of their kind have been made and shaped, they will perform only such safe uses as their prototypes have been found to serve." It is therefore of the utmost importance that they shall be faithfully reproduced, so that one may not have to fear the unknown "powers" which a fresh form might possess.[7]

In this way, according to Cushing, we can account for the extraordinary persistence of the same forms among primitive peoples, including even the most minute details of the ornamentation with which they decorate the products of their industries and arts. The Indians of British Guiana, for instance, "show extraordinary skill in many of the things they manufacture but they never improve upon them. They make them exactly as their fathers did before them."[8] This is not, as we have been told, merely the result of habit, and of a spirit of conservatism peculiar to these peoples. It is the direct result of active belief in the mystic properties of the things, properties connected with their shape, and which can be controlled through this, but which would be beyond the power of man to regulate, if there were the slightest change of form. The most apparently trifling innovation may lead to danger, liberate hostile forces, and finally bring about the ruin of its instigator and all dependent upon him.

In the same way, any change effected by manual labor in the state of the soil, building, digging, mining, the making of a pavement or the demolition of a building, or even a slight modification in its shape by the addition of a wing, may be the cause of the greatest misfortunes.

"Should any one fall suddenly ill and die," says De Groot, "his kindred are immediately ready to impute the cause to somebody who has ventured to make a change in the established order of things, or who has made an improvement in his own property.... Instances are by no means rare of their having stormed his house, demolished his furniture, assailed his person.... No wonder Chinamen do not repair their houses until they are ready to fall and become uninhabitable." [9] The steeple to be placed on the Catholic church in Pekin raised such a storm of protestation that the erection of it had to be abandoned. This mystic belief is ultimately associated with that which the Chinese call the *fungshui*. But we find similar instances in other places. Thus, in the Nicobar Isles, "some of the chief men of Mus, Lapati, and Kenmai came and requested me to postpone fixing the beacon until the arrival of their people from Chowra, for they said that in consequence of this new work, and of a tree that had been felled down by Mr. Dobie in their graveyard, near the object, the sea was annoyed and had caused high wind and big surf, until they supposed that their friends would be drowned at sea." [10]

In Loango, "the stranger who goes away must not demolish his buildings or lay waste his plantations, but leave them just as they are. That is the reason why the natives protest when Europeans take down whole houses which they had built, to transport them elsewhere. The cornerstones and pillars at least should not be taken out of the ground.... It is even forbidden to carry away the trunks of trees, to make excavations for mines, and so forth. A contractor exposes himself to serious trouble if, consulting his own wishes, he is so presuming as to make a new path, even if much shorter and more convenient than the one in use," [11] This is not mere misoneism, the dislike of any change which breaks established custom. With the old road, they know how matters stand, but they are ignorant of the unforeseen consequences, possibly calamitous, which might ensue upon the abandonment of it and the opening up of a fresh one. A road, like everything else, has its own peculiar mystic properties. The natives of Loango say of an abandoned path that it is "dead." To them, as to us, such an expression is metaphorical, but in their case it is fraught with meaning. For the path, "in active existence," has its secret powers, like houses, weapons, stones, clouds, plants,

animals, and men—in short, like everything of which the
primitive has a group idea. "All things have an invisible existence as well as a visible one," say the Igorots of the
Philippine Islands.[12]

From these facts and many similar ones which we might
quote, we can draw one conclusion: primitives perceive
nothing in the same way as we do. The social *milieu,* which
surrounds them, differs from ours, and precisely because
it is different, the external world they perceive differs from
that which we apprehend. Undoubtedly they have the same
senses as ours—rather more acute than ours in a general
way, in spite of our persuasion to the contrary—and their
cerebral structure is like our own. But we have to bear in
mind that which their collective representations instill into
all their perceptions. Whatever the object presented to their
minds, it implies mystic properties which are inextricably
bound up with it, and the primitive, in perceiving it, never
separates these from it.

To him there is no phenomenon which is, strictly speaking, a physical one, in the sense in which we use the term.
The rippling water, the whistling wind, the falling rain,
any natural phenomenon whatever, a sound, a color—these
things are never perceived by him as they are by us, that is,
as more or less compound movements bearing a definite
relation to preceding and to subsequent movements. His perceptive organs have indeed grasped the displacement of a
mass of material as ours do; familiar objects are readily
recognized according to previous experience; in short, all
the physiological and psychological processes of perception
have actually taken place in him as in ourselves. Its result,
however, is immediately enveloped in a state of complex
consciousness, dominated by collective representations.
Primitives see with eyes like ours, but they do not perceive
with the same minds. We might almost say that their perceptions are made up of a nucleus surrounded by a layer
of varying density of representations which are social in
their origin. And yet such a simile seems somewat clumsy

and inexact, for the primitive has not the least feeling of such a nucleus and surrounding layer; it is we who separate them; we, who by virtue of our mental habits cannot help distinguishing them. To the primitive the complex representation is still undifferentiated.

The profound difference which exists between primitive mentality and our own is shown even in the ordinary perception or mere apprehension of the very simplest things. Primitive perception is fundamentally mystic on account of the mystic nature of the collective representations which form an integral part of every perception. Ours has ceased to be so, at any rate with regard to most of the objects which surround us. Nothing appears alike to them and to us. For people like ourselves, speaking the language familiar to us, there is insurmountable difficulty in entering into their way of thinking. The longer we live among them, the more we approximate to their mental attitude, the more do we realize how impossible it is to yield to it entirely.

It is not correct to maintain, as is frequently done, that primitives associate occult powers, magic properties, a kind of soul or vital principle with all the objects which affect their senses or strike their imagination, and that their perceptions are surcharged with animistic beliefs. It is not a question of *association*. The mystic properties with which things and beings are imbued form an integral part of the idea to the primitive, who views it as a synthetic whole. It is at a later stage of social evolution that what we call a natural phenomenon tends to become the sole content of perception to the exclusion of the other elements, which then assume the aspect of beliefs, and finally appear superstitions. But as long as this "dissociation" does not take place, perception remains an undifferentiated whole. We might call it "polysynthetic," like words in the languages spoken by certain primitive peoples.

In the same way, we shall find ourselves in a blind alley, whenever we propound a question in such terms as: How would the primitive's mind explain this or that natural phenomenon? The very enunciation of the problem implies a false hypothesis. We are supposing that his mind apprehends these phenomena like our own. We imagine that he simply perceives such facts as sleep, dreaming, illness, death, the rise and decline of the heavenly bodies, rain, thunder, etc., and then, stimulated by the principle of causality, tries to account for them. But to the mentality of undeveloped peoples, there are no natural phenomena such as we understand by the term. Their mentality has no need to seek an explanation of them; for the explanation is implied in the mystic elements of the collective representations of them. Therefore problems of this nature must be inverted. What we must seek is not the logical process which might have resulted in the interpretation of phenomena, for this mentality never perceives the phenomenon as distinct from the interpretation; we must find out how the phenomenon became by degrees detached from the complex in which it first found itself enveloped, so that it might be apprehended separately, and how what originally was an integral part of it should later on have become an "explanation."

II

The very considerable part played by collective representations in the primitive's perceptions does not result alone in impressing a mystic character upon them. The same cause leads to another consequence, and these perceptions are accordingly *oriented* differently from our own. In that which our perceptions retain, as well as in that which is disregarded, the chief determining factor is the amount of reliance that we can place upon the unvarying reappearance of phenomena in the same given conditions. They conduce to effect the maximum "objective" validity, and, as a result, to eliminate everything prejudicial or merely unnecessary to this objectivity. From this standpoint, too, primitives do not perceive as we do. In certain cases where direct practical interests are at stake, we undoubtedly find that they pay great attention to, and are often very skillful in detecting differences in, impressions which are very similar, and in recognizing external signs of objects or phenomena, upon which their subsistence, and possibly even their lives, depend. (The shrewdness of the Australian aborigines in finding and profiting by the dew which has fallen during the night,[13] and other similar facts, are an example of this.) But, even setting aside that which these fine perceptions owe to training and memory, we still find that in most cases primitives' perceptive powers, instead of tending to reject whatever would lessen objectivity, lay special stress upon the mystic properties, the occult forces of beings and phenomena, and are thus oriented upon factors which, to us, appear subjective, although to primitives they are at least as real as the others. This characteristic of their perceptions enables them to account for certain phenomena, the "explanation" of which, when based solely upon mental or logical processes in the individual, does not appear adequate.

It is a well-known fact that primitives, even members of communities which are already somewhat advanced, regard artificial likenesses, whether painted, carved, or sculptured, as real, as well as the individual they depict. "To the Chinese," says De Groot, "associations of images with beings actually becomes identification, both materially and psychically. An image, especially if pictorial or sculptured, and thus approaching close to the reality, is an *alter ego* of the living reality, an abode of the soul, nay it is that reality itself. ... Such intense association is, in fact, the very backbone of China's inveterate idolatry and fetish-worship." [14] In support of this statement, De Groot gives a long series of tales which seem wholly incredible, but which Chinese authors find perfectly natural. A young widow has a child by a clay statue of her husband; portraits are endued with life; a wooden dog starts running; paper animals, horses, for instance, act exactly like living animals; an artist, meeting a horse of a certain color in the street, recognizes it as a work of his.... From these the transition to customs which are very general in China is an easy one.... Such customs as placing upon the tombs of the dead miniature figures of animals, burning paper money there, for instance.

In North America, the Mandans believe that the portraits taken by Catlin are alive like their subjects, and that they rob these of part of their vitality. It is true that Catlin is inclined to draw a long bow, and his stories must be taken with a grain of salt. In this respect, however, the beliefs and sentiments he attributes to the Mandans are exactly what we find noted elsewhere in similar circumstances. "I know," says one man, "that this man put *many of our buffaloes in his book,* for I was with him, and we have had no buffaloes since to eat, it is true." [15]

"They pronounced me the greatest medicine-man in the world," writes Catlin, "for they said I had made *living being*s —they said they could see their chiefs alive in two places— those that I had made were a *little* alive—they could see their eyes move—could see them smile and laugh, and that if they could laugh, they could certainly speak, if they should try, and they must therefore have some life in them." [16] Therefore, most Indians refused him permission to take their likenesses. It would be parting with a portion of their own substance, and placing them at the mercy of any one who might wish to possess the picture. They are afraid, too, of finding themselves faced by a portrait which, as a living thing, may exercise a harmful influence.

"We had placed," say the Jesuit missionaries, "images of St. Ignatius and St. Xavier upon our altar. They regarded them with amazement; they believed them to be living persons, and asked whether they were *ondaqui* (plural form of *wakan,* supernatural beings), in short, that which they recognize as superior to humanity. They inquired whether the tabernacle were their dwelling, and whether these *on-daqui* used the adornments which they saw around the altar." [17]

In Central Africa, too, "I have known natives refuse to enter a room where portraits were hanging on the walls, because of the *masoka* souls which were in them." [18] The same author tells the story of a chief who allowed himself to be photographed, and who, several months later, fell ill. In accordance with his request, the negative had been sent to England, and "his illness was attributed to some accident having befallen the photographic plate."

Thus the similitude can take the place of the model, and possess the same properties. In Loango, the followers of a certain eminent wonder-worker used to make a wooden image of their master, imbued it with "powers," and gave it the name of the original. Possibly even they would ask their master to make his own substitute, so that after his death, as well as during his life, they could use it in performing their miracles.[19] On the Slave Coast, if one of twins happens to die, the mother ". . . to give the spirit of the deceased child something to enter without disturbing the survivor, carries about, with the latter, a little wooden figure, about seven or eight inches long, roughly fashioned in human shape, and of the sex of the dead child. Such figures are nude, as an infant would be, with beads around the waist." [20] With reference to the Bororo of Brazil we read "they begged Wilhelm most earnestly not to let the women see the drawings he had made of the bull-roarers; for the sight of the drawings would kill them as the real things would." [21] Many similar instances had already been collected by Tylor.[22]

Are these to be explained from a purely psychological point of view, as is so frequently the case, by the association of ideas? Must we say, with De Groot, that it is impossible for them to distinguish a mere resemblance from identity, and admit that primitives suffer from the same illusions as the child who believes her doll to be alive? First of all, however, it is difficult to decide whether the child herself is quite sure of it. Perhaps her belief is part of the game and at the same time sincere, like the emotions of grown-up people at the theater, shedding real tears about misfortunes which they nevertheless know to be but feigned. On the contrary, it is impossible to doubt that the primitives' beliefs which I have just mentioned *are* serious; their actions prove it. How then can a portrait be "materially and psychically" identified with its original? To my mind, it is not on account of a childish trust in analogy, nor from mental weakness and confusion; it is not due to a naïve generalization of the animist theory, either. It is because, in perceiving the similitude, as in looking at the original, traditional collective representations imbue it with the same mystic elements.

If primitives view the pictured resemblance differently from ourselves, it is because they view the original otherwise also. In the latter we note its objective and actual characteristics, and those only: the shape, size, and proportions of the body; the color of the eyes; the facial expression, and so forth; we find these reproduced in the picture, and there too, we find these alone. But to the primitive, with his perceptions differently oriented, these objective features, if he apprehends them as we do, are neither the only ones nor the most important; most frequently, they are but the symbols or instruments of occult forces and mystic powers such as every being, especially a living being, can display. As a natural consequence, therefore, the image of such a being would also present the mingling of characteristics which we term objective and of mystic powers. It will live and prove beneficial or malevolent like the being it reproduces; it will be its surrogate. Accordingly we find that the image of an unknown—and consequently dreaded—object often inspires extraordinary dread. "I had," says Father Hennepin, "a pot about three feet high shaped like a lion, which we used for cooking our food in during the voyage.... The savages never ventured to touch it with their hands unless they had previously covered them with beaver skins. They imparted such terror of it to their wives that the latter had it fastened to the branches of a tree, for otherwise they would not have dared to sleep or even enter the hut if it were inside. We wished to make a present of it to some of the chiefs, but they would neither accept it nor make use of it, because they feared that it concealed some evil spirit which might have killed them." [23] We know that these Indians in the valley of the Mississippi had never before seen a white man, or a lion, or a cooking utensil. The likeness of an animal they did not know awakened in them the same mystic fears that its appearance among them would have done.

This identification which appears so strange to us must therefore occur naturally. It does not arise out of gross mental hallucination or childish confusion of ideas. As soon as we realize *how* primitives view entities, we see that they view reproductions of them in exactly the same way. If their perceptions of the originals ceased to be mystic, their images would also lose their mystic properties. They would no longer appear to be alive, but would be what they are to our minds—merely material reproductions.

In the second place, primitives regard their names as something concrete and real, and frequently sacred. Here are a few of the many proofs of it.

"The Indian regards his name, not as a mere label, but as a distinct part of his personality, just as much as are his eyes or his teeth, and believes that injury will result as surely from the malicious handling of his name as from a wound inflicted on any part of his physical organism. This belief was found among the various tribes from the Atlantic to the Pacific." [24] On the East African coast, "there is a real and material connection between a man and his name, and ... by means of the name injury may be done to the man. ... In consequence of this belief the name of the king ... is always kept secret. ... It appears strange that the birth-name only, and not alias, should be believed capable of carrying some of the personality of the bearer elsewhere ... but the native view seems to be that the alias does not really belong to the man." [25]

Accordingly all kinds of precautions become necessary. A man will avoid uttering his own name [26] and the names of others, while the names of the dead, above all, will never be pronounced; very frequently, too, even ordinary words in which the name of a dead person is implied will fall into desuetude. Alluding to a name is the same thing as laying hands on the very person or being that bears the name. It is making an attack upon him, outraging his individuality, or again, it is invoking his presence and forcing him to appear, a proceeding which may be fraught with very great danger. There are excellent reasons, therefore, for avoiding such a practice. "When they (the Santals) are hunting and see a leopard or a tiger they will always call the attention of their companions to the fact by calling out 'a cat,' or some similar name." [27] With the Cherokees, too, "it is never said that a person has been bitten by a snake, but that he has been 'scratched by a brier.' In the same way, when an eagle has been shot for a ceremonial dance, it is announced that 'a snow-bird has been killed,' the purpose being to deceive the rattlesnake or eagle spirits which might be listening." [28] The Warramunga, instead of mentioning the snake *Wollunqua* by its name when speaking of it, call it *Urkulu nappaurima,* "because," say they, "if they were to call it too often by its right name, they would lose their control over it, and it would come out and eat them all up." [29]

At the beginning of a fresh epoch in his life—at his initiation, for instance—an individual receives a new name, and it is the same when he is admitted to a secret society. A town changes its name to indicate that it is commencing a new era; Yedo becomes Tokyo. [30] A name is never a matter of indifference; it implies a whole series of relationships between the man who bears it and the source whence it is derived. "A name implies relationship, and consequently protection; favor and influence are claimed from the source of the name, whether this be the gens or the vision. A name, therefore, shows the affiliation of the individual; it grades him, so to speak." [31] In British Columbia, "names, apart from the staz or nickname, are never used as mere appellations to distinguish one person from another, as among ourselves, nor do they seem to have been used ordinarily as terms of address. They are primarily terms of relation or affiliation, with historic and mystic reference. They were reserved for special and ceremonial occasions. The ordinary terms of address among the Salish tribes, as among other primitive peoples, were those expressive of age." [32] With the Kwakiutl, "each clan has a certain limited number of names. Each individual has only one name at a time. The bearers of these names form the nobility of the tribe. When a man receives the totem of his father-in-law, he at the same time receives his name, while the father-in-law gives up the name, and takes what is called 'an old man's name,' which does not belong to the names constituting the nobility of the tribe." [33] Finally De Groot notes that "the Chinese have a tendency to identify names with the persons who bear them, a tendency which may be classed on a level with their inability, already illustrated by numerous instances, of clearly discriminating between semblances or symbols and the realities which these call to mind." [34]

This last comparison seems perfectly correct, to my mind, and I think, as De Groot does, that the same cause may account for both tendencies. This cause is not to be found in a childish association of ideas, however. It is in the collective representations which form an integral part of their perception of the likeness and the name which betokens them. The reality of the similitude is of the same kind as that of the original—that is, essentially mystic, and it is the same with the reality of the name. The two cases are alike except in one point—that which appeals to the sight in the first case, appeals to the hearing in the second, but otherwise the process is identical. The mystic properties in the name are not separated from those in the being they connote. To us the name of a person, an animal, a family, a town, has the purely external significance of a label which allows us to discern without any possibility of confusion who the person is, to what species the animal belongs, which family and which town it is. To the primitive, however, the designation of the being or object, which seems to us the sole function of the name, appears a mere accessory and of secondary importance; many observers expressly state that that is not the real function of the name. To make up for this, there are very important functions of which our names are deprived. The name expresses and makes real the relationship of the individual with his totemic group; with the ancestor of whom he is frequently a reincarnation; with the particular totem or guardian angel who has been revealed to him in a dream; with the invisible powers who protect the secret societies to which he belongs, etc. How does this arise? Evidently because beings and objects do not present themselves to the primitive's mind apart from the mystic properties which these relations involve. As a natural consequence, names derive their characteristic from the characteristics of these same beings and objects. The name is mystic, as the reproduction is mystic, because the perception of things, oriented differently from our own, through the collective representations, is mystic.

We can therefore extend also to names Cushing's acute reflections, already quoted, with regard to the forms of objects. Names condition and define the occult powers of the beings who participate in them. Hence are derived the feelings and fears they awaken, and the precautions to which these fears lead. The problem is not to discover how the simple term "is associated" with mystic elements which are never separable from it in the minds of primitives. What is given is the ensemble of collective representations of a mystic nature expressed by the name. The actual problem is to ascertain how these collective representations become gradually impaired and dissociated, how they have assumed the form of "beliefs" less and less closely "attached" to the name, until the moment arrives when, as with us, it serves but as a distinctive designation.

The primitive is, as we know, no less careful about his

shadow than he is about his name or his counterfeit present-ment. If he were to lose it he would consider himself hopelessly endangered. Should it come into the power of another, he has everything to dread. Folklore of all coun-tries has made us familiar with facts of this kind; we shall cite but a few of them only. In the Fiji Islands, as in many places inhabited by people of a similar stage of development, it is a mortal insult to walk upon anybody else's shadow. In East Africa, murders are sometimes com-mitted by means of a knife or nail thrust through the shadow of a man; if the guilty person is caught in the act he is executed forthwith. Miss Kingsley, in reporting this fact, shows clearly to what extent the West African negroes dread the loss of their shadow. "It strikes one as strange," she writes, "to see men who have been walking, say, through forest or grass land, on a blazing hot morning quite happily, on arrival at a piece of clear ground of a village square, most carefully go round it, not across, and you will soon notice that they only do this at noon-time, and learn that they fear losing their shadow. I asked some Bakwiri I once came across who were particularly careful in this matter, why they were not anxious about losing their shadows when night came down and they disappeared in the surrounding darkness, and was told that was all right, because at night all shadows lay down in the shadow of the Great God, and so got stronger. Had I not seen how strong and how long a shadow, be it of man or tree or of the great mountain itself, was in the early morning time?" [35]

De Groot notes similar precautions in China. "When the lid is about to be placed on the coffin, most of the bystanders, not belonging to the nearest kindred, retire a few steps, or even make off for the side apartments, as it is dangerous to health and detrimental to good luck to have one's shadow enclosed in a coffin." [36] What then *is* the shadow? It is not the exact equivalent of what we call the soul; but it is of the nature of the soul, and where the soul is represented as multiple, the shadow (according to Miss Kingsley) is sometimes one of the souls. On his side, De Groot says: "We find nothing in the books of China which points positively to identification of shadows and souls." [37] But, on the other hand, ghosts have no shadows. And De Groot concludes by saying that "the shadow is a part of the personality which has an immense influence on his destiny," a characteristic which applies equally, as we have seen, to a person's picture or his name.

I shall therefore refer it to the same theory. If we ask ourselves: how has the primitive come to associate with the idea of his shadow beliefs which we find to be almost universal? we might reply by an ingenious explanation, and one which would be psychologically probable, but it would be unsound, because the problem cannot be propounded in such terms as these. To enunciate it thus would be to imply that the idea of his shadow to the primitive is the same as to us, and the rest is superimposed. Now it really is nothing like that. The perception of the shadow, as of the body itself, like that of the image or the name, is a mystic perception, in which that which we properly call the shadow—the design upon the ground of a figure which recalls the form of a being or object lighted from the opposite side—is only one element among many. We have not to discover how the perception of the shadow has been placed in juxtaposition or united with such and such a representation: these indeed form an integral part of the perception, so far as we can trace it in past observations. For this reason I should be prepared to take up a counterposition to that of De Groot. "The Chinese," he says, "are even to these days without ideas of the physical causation of shadows. . . . They must needs see in a shadow something more than a negation of light." [38] I, on the contrary, should say: the Chinese, having a mystic perception of the shadow, as participating in the life and all the properties of the tangible body, cannot represent it as a mere "negation of light." To be able to see a purely physical phenomenon in the production of the shadow, it would be necessary to have an idea of such a phenomenon, and we know that such an idea is lacking to the primitive. In undeveloped communities, there is no perception unaccompanied by mystic qualities and occult properties, and why should the shadow be any exception?

Finally, the same considerations apply equally to another class of phenomena—dreams—which occupy an important place in the primitive mind. To primitives the dream is not, as it is to us, simply a manifestation of mental activity which occurs during sleep, a more or less orderly series of representations to which, when awake, the dreamer would give no credence, because they lack the conditions essential to objective validity. This last characteristic, though it does not escape the primitives, seems to interest them but slightly. On the other hand, the dream, to them, is of far greater significance than to us. It is first a percept as real as those of the waking state, but above all, it is a prevision of the future, a communication and intercourse with spirits, souls, divinities, a means of establishing a relation with their own special guardian angel, and even of discovering who this may be. Their confidence in the reality of that which the dream makes known to them is very profound. Tylor, Frazer, and the representatives of the English school of anthropology have brought together a vast number of facts which bear witness to this, collected by investigators of primitive peoples of the most diverse types. Shall I, too, quote some? In Australia "sometimes a man dreams that some one has got some of his hair or a piece of his food, or of his possum rug, or indeed anything almost that he has used. If he dreams this several times he feels sure of it and calls his friends together, and tells them of his dreaming too much about 'that man,' who must have something belonging to him. . . . Sometimes natives only know about having their fat taken out by remembering something of it as in a dream." [39]

That which to us is perception is to him mainly the

communication with spirits, souls, invisible and intangible mysterious powers encompassing him on all sides, upon which his fate depends, and which loom larger in his consciousness than the fixed and tangible and visible elements of his representations. He has therefore no reason to depreciate the dream, and consider it as a subjective and dubious representation, in which he must place no trust. The dream is not a form of inferior and illusory perception. On the contrary, it is a highly favored form, one in which, since its material and tangible elements are at a minimum, the communication with invisible spirits and forces is most direct and most complete.

This accounts for the confidence which the primitive has in his dreams, a confidence which is at least as great as that he accords his ordinary perceptions. It accounts also for his seeking after means of procuring dreams which shall be revelatory and, among the North American Indians, for instance, for the whole technique of securing the sincerity and validity of dreams. Thus the young man, arrived at the age of initiation, who is going to try and see in a dream the animal which will be his guardian angel, his personal totem, has to prepare himself for this purpose by carrying out a series of observances. "He first purifies himself by the *impi* or steam bath, and by fasting for a term of three days. During the whole of this time, he avoids women and society, is secluded in his habits and endeavors in every way to be pure enough to receive a revelation from the deity whom he invokes" ... then he subjects himself to various tortures "until the deities have vouchsafed him a vision or revelation." [40]

This, too, accounts for the deference and respect shown to dreamers, seers, prophets, sometimes even to lunatics. A special power of communicating with invisible reality, that is, a peculiarly privileged perception, is attributed to them. All these well-known facts naturally result from the orientation of the collective representations which obtains in primitive peoples, and which endows with mysticism both the real world in which the "savage" dwells, and his perception of it.

Further differences between the primitives' perception and our own arise out of this mystic character. To us one of the essential signs by which we recognize the objective validity of a perception is that the being or phenomenon perceived appears to all alike under the same conditions. If, for instance, one person alone among a number present hears a certain sound repeatedly, or sees an object close by, we say that he or she is subject to delusions, or has a hallucination. Leibniz, Taine, and many others have insisted upon the agreement between the subjects who are perceiving as a means of distinguishing between real "and imaginary phenomena." Current opinion on this· point, too, is wholly on the side of the philosophers. With the primitives, on the contrary, it constantly happens that beings or things manifest themselves to certain persons to the exclusion of others who may be present. No one is astonished at this, for all regard it as perfectly natural. Howitt writes, for instance: "Of course, the Ngarang was invisible to all but the *wirarap* (medicine-man)." [41] A young medicine-man in training, who is telling of his initiation, remarks: "After that I used to see things that my mother could not see. When out with her I would say, 'Mother, what is that out there yonder?' She used to say, 'Child, there is nothing.' These were the *jir* (or ghosts) which I began to see." [42] The aborigines observed by Spencer and Gillen think that during the night the sun visits the place where it arises in the morning, "and that it might actually be seen at night times by... clever medicine-men, and the fact that it cannot be seen by ordinary persons only means that they are not gifted with sufficient power, and not that it is not there." [43] In their case, as with many other aggregates of the same stage of development, the medicine-man extracts from the body of the sufferer a small object

only visible to the operator. "After much mysterious searching he finds and cuts the string which is invisible to every
one except himself. There is not a doubt amongst the
onlookers as to its having been there." [44] In the form of
witchcraft which the Australian aborigines called "pointing the death bone," a complicated series of operations
would be carried on without any one's perceiving them.
"The blood of the victim, in some fashion which is unper-
ceived, flows from him to the medicine-man, and thence
to the receptacle where it is collected; at the same time, by
a corresponding movement a bone, a magic stone proceeds
from the body of the sorcerer to the body of his victim—
still invisibly—and, entering there, induces a fatal malady." [45]

We find the same beliefs in Eastern Siberia. "In the
Alarsk department of the Government of Irkutsk ... if any
one's child becomes dangerously ill, the Buryats ... believe
that the crown of his head is being sucked by Onokhoi, a
small beast in the form of a mole or cat.... No one except
the shaman can see this beast." [46]

In North America, among the Klamaths of Oregon, the
kiuks (medicine-man) who is called to treat a case of disease must consult the spirits of certain animals. "Such
persons only as have been trained during five years for
the profession of conjurers can see these spirits, but by them
they are seen as clearly as we see the objects around us." [47]
"Dwarfs can be seen only by those initiated into the mysteries of witchcraft." [48] Among the Tarahumares "large
serpents, which only the shaman can see, are thought to
live in the rivers. They have horns and very big eyes." [49]
"The great Hikuli" (a sacred plant personified) "eats with
the shaman, who alone is able to see him and his companions." [50] In one of the Huichol ceremonies, the heads
of the does are placed with the heads of the bucks, because
they, too, have horns, "though only the shaman sees
them." [51]

All such phenomena are to be expected if it be true that
the perception of primitives is oriented differently from

our own, and not preëminently concerned, as ours is, with the characteristics of the beings and manifestations which we call objective. To them the most important properties of the beings and objects they perceive, are their occult powers, their mystic qualities. Now one of these powers is that of appearing or not appearing in given circumstances. Either the power is inherent in the subject who perceives, who has been prepared for it by initiation, or else holds it by virtue of his participation in some superior being, and so on. In short, mystic relations may be established between certain persons and certain beings, on account of which these persons are exclusively privileged to perceive these beings. Such cases are analogous to the dream. The primitive, far from regarding the mystic perception in which he has no part, as suspect, sees in it, as in the dream, a more precious, and consequently more significant communication with invisible spirits and forces.

IV

Conversely, when collective representations imply the presence of certain qualities in objects, nothing will persuade the primitives that they do not exist. To us, the fact that we do not perceive them there is decisive. It does not prove to them that they are not there, for possibly it is their nature not to reveal themselves to perception, or to manifest themselves in certain conditions only. Consequently, that which we call experience, and which decides, as far as we are concerned, what may be admitted or not admitted as real, has no effect upon collective representations. Primitives have no need of this experience to vouch for the mystic properties of beings and objects: and for the same reason they are quite indifferent to the disappoinr· ments it may afford. Since experience is limited to what is stable, tangible, visible, and approachable, in physical reality, it allows the most important of all, the occult powers, to escape. Hence we can find no example of the non-success of a magic practice discouraging those who believe in it.

Livingstone gives an account of a prolonged discussion which he had with the rain-makers, and ends by saying: "I have never been able to convince a single one of them that their arguments are unsound. Their belief in these 'charms' of theirs is unbounded." [52] In the Nicobar Islands, "the people in all the villages have now performed the ceremony called *tanangla*, signifying either 'support' or 'prevention.' Its object is to prevent illness caused by the north east monsoon. Poor Nicobarese! They do the same thing year after year, but to no effect." [53]

Experience is peculiarly unavailing against the belief in the virtues of "fetishes" which secure invulnerability: a method of interpreting what happens in a sense which favors the belief is never lacking. In one case an Ashanti, having procured a fetish of this kind, hastened to put it to the proof, and received a gunshot wound which broke his arm. The "fetish man" explained the matter to the satisfaction of all, saying that the incensed fetish had that moment revealed the reason to him. It was because the young man had had sexual relations with his wife on a forbidden day. The wounded man confessed that this was true, and the Ashantis retained their convictions.[54] Du Chaillu tells us that when a native wears an iron chain round his neck he is proof against bullets. If the charm. is not effectual, his faith in its remains unshaken, for then he believes that some maleficent wonder-worker has produced a powerful "counter-spell," to which he falls a victim.[55] Elsewhere he says: "As I came from seeing the king, I shot at a bird sitting upon a tree, and missed it. I had been taking quinine, and was nervous. But the negroes standing around at once proclaimed that this was a fetish-bird, and therefore I *could* not shoot it. I fired again, and missed again. Hereupon they grew triumphant in their declarations, while I . . . loaded again, took careful aim, and to my own satisfaction and their dismay, brought my bird down. Immediately they explained that I was a white man, and not entirely amenable to fetish laws; so that I do not suppose my shot proved anything to them after all." [56]

It is the same in Loango. "I had been presented," writes Pechuel-Loesche, "with a very fine collar, made of hair from the tail of an elephant...and adorned with teeth from a sea-fish and a crocodile. These teeth were to preserve me from any danger connected with water.... It frequently happened that my boat was upset when I was crossing the bar, and one day I had great difficulty in reaching the shore. I was told quite seriously that it was the teeth alone that had saved me, for without them my swimming powers would not have sufficed to help me clear the heavy breakers. *I was not wearing the collar,* but its efficacy was in no manner of doubt from that fact." [57] The fetish and the medicine-man always have the last word.

Primitive man, therefore, lives and acts in an environment of beings and objects, all of which, in addition to the properties that we recognize them to possess, are endued with mystic attributes. He perceives their objective reality mingled with another reality. He feels himself surrounded by an infinity of imperceptible entities, nearly always invisible to sight, and always redoubtable: ofttimes the souls of the dead are about him and always he is encompassed by myriads of spirits of more or less defined personality. It is thus at least that the matter is explained by a large number of observers and anthropologists, and they make use of animistic terms to express this. Frazer has collected many instances which tend to show that this phenomenon obtains everywhere among undeveloped peoples. [58] Is it necessary to quote some of them? "The Oraon's imagination tremblingly wanders in a world of ghosts. Every rock, road, river, and grove is haunted."...Sometimes, too, there are "malignant spirits." [59] Like the Santals, Mundas, and the Oraons of the Chota-Nagpur, "the Kadars believe themselves to be compassed about by a host of invisible powers, some of whom are thought to be the spirits of departed ancestors, while others seem to embody nothing more definite than the vague sense of the mysterious and uncanny with which hills, streams, and lonely forests inspire the savage imagination.... Their names are legion, and their attributes barely known." [60] In Korea, "spirits occupy every quarter of heaven and every foot of earth. They lie in wait for a man along the wayside, in the trees, on the rocks, in the mountains, valleys, and streams. They keep him under a constant espionage day and night.... They are all about him, they dance in front of him, follow him, fly over his head and cry out against him from the earth. He has no refuge from them even in his own house, for there they are plastered into or pinned on the walls or tied to the beams.... Their ubiquity is an ugly travesty of the omnipresence of God." [61] In China, according to the ancient doctrine, "the universe is filled up in all its parts with legions of *shen* and *kwei*.... Every being and every thing that exists is animated either by a *shen,* or by a *kwei,* or by a *shen* and a *kwei* together." [62] With the Fang of East Africa "spirits are everywhere; in rocks, trees, forests, and streams; in fact, for the Fang, this life is one continual fight against spirits corporal and spiritual." [63] "In every action of his daily life," writes Miss Kingsley, "the African negro shows you how he lives with a great, powerful spirit world around him. You will see him before starting out to hunt or fight rubbing medicine into his weapons to strengthen the spirits within them, talking to them the while; telling them what care he has taken of them, reminding them of the gifts he has given them, though these gifts were hard for him to give, and begging them in the hour of his dire necessity not to fail him. You will see him bending over the face of a river talking to its spirit with proper incantations, asking it when it meets a man who is an enemy of his to upset his canoe, or drown him, or asking it to carry down with it some curse to the village below which has angered him." [64]

Miss Kingsley lays great stress upon the homogeneity of the African native's representations of everything. "The

African mind naturally approaches all things from a spiritual point of view ... things happen because of the action of spirits upon spirit." [65] When the doctor applies a remedy "the spirit of the medicine works upon the spirit of the disease." The purely physical effect is beyond the power of conception unless it be allied with the mystic influence. Or rather, we may say that there is no really physical influence, there are only mystic ones. Accordingly it is almost impossible to get these primitives to differentiate, especially when it is a case of an accusation of murder through the practice of witchcraft, for instance. Here is a typical case. "I explain to my native questioner," says Nassau, "that if what the accused has done in fetish rite with intent to kill, had any efficiency in taking away life, I allow that he shall be put to death; if he made only fetishes, even if they were intended to kill, he is not guilty of this death, for a mere fetish cannot kill. But if he used poison, with or without fetish, he is guilty.

"But even so," adds Nassau, "the distinction between a fetish and a poison is vague in the thought of many natives. What I call a 'poison' is to them only another material form of a fetish power, both poison and fetish being supposed to be made efficient by the presence of an adjuvant spirit." [66] This means that to their minds the mere fetish kills as certainly as the poison does. More certainly even; for the poison kills only by virtue of a mystic power of which, in certain circumstances, it may be deprived. The idea of its physical properties, which is so clear to the European mind, does not exist for the African.

We thus have good authority for saying that this mentality differs from our own to a far greater extent than the language used by those who are partisans of animism would lead us to think. When they are describing to us a world peopled by ghosts and spirits and phantoms for primitives, we at once realize that beliefs of this kind have not wholly disappeared even in civilized countries. Without referring to spiritualism, we recall the ghost stories which are so numerous in our folklore, and we are tempted to think that the difference is one of degree only. Doubtless such beliefs may be regarded in our communities as a survival which testifies to an older mental condition, formerly much more general. But we must be careful not to see in them a faithful, though faintly outlined, reflection of the mentality of primitives. Even the most uneducated members of our societies regard stories of ghosts and spirits as belonging to the realm of the supernatural: between such apparitions and magical influences and the data furnished by ordinary perception and the experience of the broad light of day, the line of demarcation is clearly defined. Such a line, however, does not exist for the primitive. The one kind of perception and influence is quite as natural as the other, or rather, we may say that to him there are not two kinds. The superstitious man, and frequently also the religious man, among us, believes in a twofold order of reality, the one visible, palpable, and subordinate to the essential laws of motion; the other invisible, intangible, "spiritual," forming a mystic sphere which encompasses the first. But the primitive's mentality does not recognize two distinct worlds in contact with each other, and more or less interpenetrating. To him there is but one. Every reality, like every influence, is mystic, and consequently every perception is also mystic.

NOTES

[1] *Vide* ch. viii, pp. 352-353, *How Natives Think,* by author.
[2] C. Lumholtz, *Unknown Mexico,* ii, pp. 7-8.
[3] J. Mooney, "The Sacred Formulas of the Cherokee," *E. B. Rept.,* vii, p. 375.
[4] K. Th. Preuss, "Der Ursprung der Religion und Kunst," *Globus,* lxxxvi, p. 20; lxxxvii, p. 19.
[5] W. W. Skeat, *Malay Magic,* p. 427.
[6] Dr. Pechuel-Loesche, *Die Loango-Expedition,* iii, 2, pp. 194 *et seq.*
[7] P. H. Cushing, "Zuñi Creation Myths," *E. B. Rept.,* xiii, pp. 361-363.
[8] Bernau, *Missionary Labours in British Guiana,* p. 46 (1847).
[9] *The Religious System of China,* i, p. 1041.
[10] Solomon, "Diaries Kept in Cap Nicobar," *J. A. I.,* xxxii, p. 230.
[11] Dr. Pechuel-Loesche, *Die Loango-Expedition,* iii, 2, pp. 209-212.
[12] Jenks, *The Bontoc Igorot,* p. 196 (Manila, 1905).

13 Eyre, *Journals of Expeditions of Discovery into Central Australia*, ii, p. 247.

14 J. J. M. de Groot, *The Religious System of China*, ii, pp. 340-355.

15 Catlin, *The North American Indians*, i, pp. 122-123 (Edinburgh, 1903).

16 *Ibid.*

17 Ed. Thwaites, *Relations des Jesuits*, v, p. 256 (1633).

18 Hetherwick, "Some Animistic Beliefs of the Yaos," *J. A. I.*, xxxii, pp. 89-90.

19 Dr. Pechuel-Loesche, *Die Loango-Expedition*, iii, 2, pp. 378-379 (1907).

20 A. B. Ellis, *The Yoruba-Speaking Peoples*, p. 80.

21 K. von den Steinen, *Unter den Naturvölkern Zentral-Brasiliens*, p. 386.

22 *Primitive Culture*, ii, pp. 169 *et seq.*

23 L. Hennepin, *Nouveau Voyage de l'Amerique Septentrionale*, pp. 366-367.

24 J. Mooney, "The Sacred Formulas of the Cherokees," *E. B. Rept.*, vii, p. 343.

25 A. B. Ellis, *The Ewe-Speaking Peoples*, pp. 98-99.

26 Rivers, *The Todas*, p. 627.

27 Bodding, "On Taboo Customs Amongst the Santals," *Journal of the Asiatic Society of Bengal*, iii, p. 20 (1898).

28 J. Mooney, *The Sacred Formulas of the Cherokees*, p. 352.

29 Spencer and Gillen, *The Northern Tribes of Central Australia*, p. 227.

30 Chamberlain, *Things Japanese*, p. 344 (1902).

31 Dorsey, "Siouan Cults," *E. B. Rept.*, xi, p. 368.

32 Hill Tout, "Ethnology of the Statlum H of British Columbia," *J. A. I.*, xxxv, p. 152.

33 F. Boas, "The Northwestern Tribes of Canada," *Reports of the British Association*, p. 675 (1898).

34 *The Religious System of China*, i, p. 212.

35 Mary Kingsley, *West African Studies*, p. 176.

36 J. J. M. de Groot, *The Religious System of China*, i, pp. 94, 210.

37 *Ibid.*, ii, p. 83.

38 *Ibid.*, ii, p. 83.

39 Howitt, "On Australian Medicine-Men," *J. A. I.*, xvi, i, pp. 29-30.

40 Dorsey, "Siouan Cults," *E. B. Rept.*, xi, pp. 436-437.

41 Howitt, "On Some Australian Medicine-Men," *J. A. I.*, xvi. i, p. 42.

42 *Ibid.*, p. 50.

43 *The Native Tribes of Central Australia*, pp. 561-562.

44 *Ibid.*, p. 532.

45 W. E. Roth, *Ethnological Studies Among the N. W. Central Queensland Aborigines*, No. 264.

46 V. Mikhailovski, *Shamanism in Siberia and European Russia*, analyzed in *J. A. I.*, xxiv, p. 99; cf. p. 133.

47 A. Gatschet, *The Klamath Language*, p. xcviii.

48 *Ibid.*, p. xcix.

49 C. Lumholtz, *Unknown Mexico*, i, p. 340.

50 *Ibid.*, p. 372.

51 *Idem.*, *Symbolism of the Huichol Indians*, p. 68.

[52] *Missionary Travels*, pp. 24-25 (1857).

[53] Solomon, "Diaries Kept in Cap Nicobar," *J. A. I.*, xxxii, p. 213.

[54] Bowditch, *Mission to Ashanti*, p. 439.

[55] *Explorations and Adventures in Equatorial Africa*, p. 338.

[56] *Ibid.*, p. 179.

[57] *Die Loango-Expedition*, iii, 2, p. 352.

[58] *The Golden Bough* (2nd edit.), iii, pp. 41 *et seq.*

[59] Risley, *Tribes and Castes of Bengal*, ii, pp. 143-145.

[60] *Ibid.*, i, p. 369.

[61] G. H. Jones, "The Spirit Worship in Korea," *Transactions of the Korea Branch of the Royal Asiatic Society*, ii, i, p. 58.

[62] J. J. M. De Groot, *The Religious System of China*, iv, p. 51.

[33] Bennett, "Ethnographical Notes on the Fang," *J. A. I.*, xxix, p. 87.

[54] *West African Studies*, p. 110.

[65] *Ibid.*, p. 330.

[66] *Fetichism in West Africa*, p. 263.

THE SCIENCE OF CUSTOM *

THE BEARING OF ANTHROPOLOGY ON CONTEMPORARY THOUGHT

By RUTH BENEDICT

ANTHROPOLOGY is the study of primitive peoples—a statement which helps us to understand its bearing on contemporary thought as little as if, in the time of Copernicus, we had defined astronomy as the study of the stars, or biology, in the time of Darwin, as the science of bugs. It was not facts about stars that made astronomy suddenly of first-class importance, but that—quite casually, as it were—the Copernican scheme placed the earth, this planetary scene of human life, in a perspective of such infinitesimal insignificance. In much the same way the significance of anthropology to modern thought does not lie in any secrets that the primitive has saved for us from a simpler world, with which to solve the perplexities of this existence. Anthropology is not a search for the philosopher's stone in a vanished and golden age. What anthropologists find in the study of primitive people is a natural and well-nigh inexhaustible laboratory of custom, a great workshop in which to explore the major rôle it has played in the life-history of the world.

Now custom has not been commonly regarded as a subject of any great moment. It is not like the inner workings of our own brains, which we feel to be uniquely worthy of investigation. Custom, we have a way of thinking, is behavior at its most commonplace. As a matter of fact, it is the other way around. Traditional custom, taken the world over, is a mass of detailed behavior more astonishing than any one person can ever evolve in personal acts no

* This article was published in *The Century Magazine,* April, 1929.

matter how aberrant. Yet that is a rather trivial aspect of
the matter. The fact of first-rate importance is the predominant rôle that custom plays in experience and in belief. No
man ever looks at the world with pristine eyes. He sees it
edited by a definite set of customs and institutions and ways
of thinking. Even in his philosophical probings he cannot
go behind these stereotypes; his very concepts of the true
and the false will still have reference to the structure of his
particular traditional customs. John Dewey has said in all
seriousness that the part played by custom in shaping the
behavior of the individual as over against any way in which
he can affect traditional custom, is as the proportion of the
total vocabulary of his mother tongue over against those
words of his own baby talk that are taken up into the
vernacular of his family. There is no social problem it is
more incumbent upon us to understand than that of the
rôle of custom in our total life. Until we are intelligent as
to the laws and the varieties of customs, the main complicat-
ing facts of human life will remain to us an unintelligible
book.

The first concern of the anthropologist is always for an
understanding of this affair of custom: how each society
comes to be possessed of whole systems of it, how it is stabilized, cross-fertilized, how it is inculcated into all the members of the group among whom it flourishes. In other words,
the business of the anthropologist is with the great idea-
tional systems of language, social organization and religion
of which every people on earth finds itself possessed, and
which are passed on to every child as it is born into the
group, but of which no child born in any other territory
could ever achieve the thousandth part.

This matter of culture, to give it its anthropological term
—that complex whole which includes all the habits acquired
by man as a member of society—has been late in claiming
scientific attention. There are excellent reasons for this.
Any scientific study requires first of all that there be no
preferential weighting of one or another of the items in

the series it selects for its consideration. Anthropology was therefore by definition impossible as long as those old distinctions between ourselves and the barbarian, ourselves and the pagan, held sway over people's minds. It was necessary first to arrive at that degree of sophistication where one no longer set his belief over against his neighbor's superstition, and it is worth considering that it is barely one hundred years ago that any one took his superstitious neighbors seriously enough to include them in any general purview of serious belief.

In the second place, custom did not challenge the attention of social theorists, because it was the very stuff of their own thinking. We do not see the lens through which we look. Precisely in proportion as it was fundamental, it was automatic, and had its existence outside the field of conscious attention. The custom of greeting a guest by an array of weeping women who sit in his lap and embrace him, may not need more or less psychological elucidation than the handshake, but it communicates the necessary shock, and the subject of the handshake will remain unexplored long after we have mustered our efforts toward the understanding of the tears-greeting. We have only to admit alien customs to the same rank in regulating human nature that ours have for us, and we are perpetually galvanized into attention.

It is not fair to lay our blindness to custom wholly to the fact that it is closer to us than breathing. Primitive people are sometimes far more conscious of the rôle of cultural traits than we are, and for good reason. They have had intimate experience of different cultures, and we have not. White civilization has standardized itself over most of the globe. We have never seen an outsider unless he is already Europeanized. The uniformity of custom, of outlook, seems convincing enough, and conceals from us the fact that it is after all an historical accident. All our observation reinforces the testimony of our easy assent to the familiar, and we accept without any ado the equivalence of human nature and of our own cultural standards. But many primitives have a different experience. They have seen their religion go down before the white man's, their economic system, their marriage prohibitions. They have laid down the one and taken up the other, and are quite clear and sophisticated about variant arrangements of human life. If they talk about human nature, they do it in plurals, not in the absolute singular, and they will derive dominant characteristics of the white man from his commercial institutions, or from his conventions of warfare, very much after the fashion of the anthropologist. If civilized Europeans have been especially dense to the scientific implications of custom, it has been not only because their own customs were too familiar to be discernible, and because they resisted the implication that their culture belonged to a series that included the customs of lesser people, but also because the standardization of their own culture over the globe has given an illusion of a world-wide uniform human behavior.

What is it that anthropologists have to say about this matter of custom? In the first place, it is man's distinguishing mark in the animal kingdom. Man is the culture-making animal. It is not that insects, for instance, do not have complex cultural traits like the domestication of plants and animals, political organization, division of labor. But the mechanism of transmission makes them contrast sharply with man's particular contribution of traditionally *learned* behavior. Insect society takes no chances; the pattern of the entire social structure is carried in the cell structure of each individual ant, so that one isolated individual can automatically reproduce the entire social order of its own colony just as it reproduces the shape of antennæ or of abdomen. For better or worse, man's solution has been at the opposite pole. Not one item of his tribal social organization, of language, of his local religion, is carried in his germ-cell. His whole centuries-evolved civilization is at the mercy of any accident of time and space. If he is taken at birth to another continent, it will be the entire set of cultural traits of the adoptive society that he will learn, and the set that' was his by heredity will play no part. More than this, whole peoples in one generation have shaken off their patterns, retaining hardly a residual vestige, and have put on the customs of an alien group.

What is lost in nature's guarantee of safety, is made up in the advantage of greater plasticity. The human animal does not, like the bear, have to wait to grow himself a polar coat before he can adapt himself to the arctic; he learns to sew himself a coat and put up a snow house. It is a direct corollary of this difference in the mechanism of human culture that, as Professor W. M. Wheeler tells us, ant societies have been stable for sixty-five million years, and human societies are never to-morrow what they are to-day.

Anthropology has no encouragement to offer to those who would trust our spiritual achievements to the automatic perpetuation of any selected hereditary germ-plasms. Culture, it insists, is not carried in that fashion for the human race. We cannot trust any program of racial purity. It is a significant fact that no anthropologist has ever taught, along with so many popular theorists, that high civilization is bound up with the biological homogeneity of its carriers. Race is a classification based on bodily form, and the particular cultural behavior of any group is strikingly independent of its racial affiliations. We must accept all the implications of our human inheritance, one of the most important of which is the small scope of biologically transmitted behavior, and the enormous rôle of the cultural process of the transmission of tradition.

There is another analogy with the animal world which has to be laid aside in the study of culture: no less than the idea of evolution. The modern anthropologist at this point is only throwing in his lot with the psychologist and the historian, emphasizing the fact that the order of events in which they all deal in common is best studied without the complications of any attempted evolutionary arrangement. The psychologist is not able to demonstrate any evolutionary series in the sensory or emotional reactions of the individuals he studies, and the historian is not helped in the reconstruction of Plantagenet England by any concept of the evolution of government; just as superfluous for him also, the anthropologist insists, is any scheme of cultures arranged according to an ascending scale of evolution.

Since the science of anthropology took shape in the years when the "Origin of Species" was still new, it was inevitable that there should have been this attempt to arrange human societies from this point of view. It was simplicity itself. At the summit of the ascent was placed our own culture, to give meaning and plan to all that had preceded; to the lowest rungs was relegated by hypothesis all that was most different from this consummation; and the intermediate steps were arranged as these two fixed points suggested. It is important to insist that there was never any argument from actual chronology; even in cases where it could have been ascertained, it was not considered of such importance that it could compete with the *a priori* hypothesis. In this way the development of art, religion and marriage institutions was classically charted. It is a monument to the force of a theory that asked no proof other than its own conviction.

Now if there is no positive correlation between culture and an evolutionary scheme, is there any order and arrangement of any kind in the diversity of human customs? To answer this question it is necessary to go back to fundamentals, to man's equipment of basic responses to environment. These responses, as anthropologists see them, are mere rough sketches, a list of bare facts; but they are hints that may be illimitably fertile. They are focal centers which any peoples may ignore, or which they may make the starting point of their most elaborated concepts. Let us take, for instance, the example of adolescence. Adolescence is a necessary biological fact for man and for his animal forebears, but man has used it as a spring-board. It may be made the occasion for the major part of the ritual the group practices; it may be ignored as completely as Margaret Mead has recently shown that it is in Samoa. It may be seen, as among the African Masai, as one item of an elaborate crisis ceremonialism that institutionalizes not only adolescence but provides, for instance, a ceremony for putting the father on the shelf after his son has attained young manhood. It may be, on the other hand, a magic occasion that will, in after life, give back as from a mirror every technique that is practiced at this time. So a girl will pick each needle carefully from a pine-tree that she may be industrious, or a boy will race a stone down the mountain that he may be swift of foot. The rites may be limited to the young girls, or, it may be, to the boys; the period may be marked with horror and with torture, it may be a consecration to the gods. It is obvious that the physical fact of adolescence is only the touch to the ball of custom, which then follows grooves of thought not implied in the original impetus.

What these grooves are we can sometimes account for out of the cultural history of a people; more often we can only record the facts. We know that traits that have once found themselves in company are likely to maintain that association quite apart from any intrinsic fitness in their nature. So bone head-scratchers and the pursuit of a supernatural vision may go hand in hand over a continent, and the absence of foot-gear may coincide with carved door-posts.

What we do know is that there is no one of the bare reactions of the human animal that may not be selected by some people for a position in the very forefront of its attention and be elaborated past belief. It may be that the economic facts of life, as for instance the buffalo herds of the Todas of India, may be singled out, and the whole life of the people may turn on the ritual, of perpetuating and renewing the sacred *pep,* the soured milk saved by the

Todas from day to day as the continuum of their culture, and used to hasten the next day's souring. The dairymen are the priests, anointed and sacrosanct, the holy of holies is the sacred cow bell. Most of the taboos of the people have to do with the infinite sacredness of the milk.

Or a culture may, instead, elaborate an item of the social organization. All people over the earth recognize some forbidden degrees within which marriage may not take place. These are alike only in the common idea of incest; the degrees themselves differ entirely. In a large part of the world you may marry only one variety of own cousin, say your mother's brother's daughter, and it is incest to marry the other variety, say your father's sister's daughter. But however unreasonable the distinctions may seem from our point of view, some concept of forbidden degrees all men have, and animals, it seems, have not. Now this idea has been taken up by the aborigines of Australia and made the basis of a social system that knows no restraint in the elaboration of its favorite pattern. Not satisfied with stipulating one cousin group within which, and no other, one must find a mate, certain of these tribes have heaped the incest taboos on lineages, on local groups, on all who participate with them in certain ceremonies, until even in the specified cousin group there is no one who is not touched by some one of the taboos. Quite in keeping with the violence of their obsession with this detail of social organization, they are accustomed to visit death upon any one who transgresses the fantastic rules. Do they pull themselves together before they have reached the point of tribal suicide and reject their overgrown anti-social rulings? No, they get by with a subterfuge. Young men and women may escape together to an island which is regarded as asylum. If they succeed in remaining in seclusion until the birth of a child, they may return with no more than a formalized drubbing. So the tribe is enabled to maintain its ethics without acknowledged revision, and still avoid extinction.

But it need not be incest that has run away with itself

in the culture of a group; it may be some trick of ritualism, or love of display, or passion of acquisitiveness. It may be fish-hooks. In a certain island of Oceania fish-hooks are currency, and to have large fish-hooks came gradually to be the outward sign of the possession of great wealth. Fish-hooks therefore are made very nearly as large as a man. They will no longer catch fish, of course. In proportion as they have lost their usefulness they are supremely coveted.

After a long experience of such cultural facts anthropologists have made up their minds on two points. In the first place, it is usually beside the point to argue, from its important place in behavior, the social usefulness of a custom. Man can get by with a mammoth load of useless lumber, and he has a passion for extremes. Once his attention is engaged upon one trait of behavior, he will juggle his customs till they perforce accommodate themselves to the outward manifestations of his obsession. After all, man has a fairly wide margin of safety, and he will not be forced to the wall even with a pitiful handicap. Our own civilization carries its burden of warfare, of the dissatisfaction and frustration of wage-earners, of the overdevelopment of acquisitiveness. It will continue to bear them. The point is that it is more in line with the evidence to regard them as our equivalents of the fish-hooks or of the Australian marriage rules, and to give over the effort to prove their natural social utility.

For every people will always justify their own folkways. Warfare, as long as we have it, will be for our moralists the essential school in which justice and valor are to be learned: the desire for possession similarly will be the one motive power to which it is safe to trust the progress of the world. In the same way, China relied upon reverence for one's ancestors. There are too many of these folkways. They cannot all be the *sine qua non* of existence, and we shall do better to concentrate our attention upon an objective appreciation of different schemes, and to give our enthusiasms to those special values we can always discern in the most diverse civilizations.

The second point on which anthropologists have made up their minds in this connection—and this holds true for all customs whether or not they have been carried to extremes—is that in any study of behavior it is these cultural patternings that turn out to be compulsive, not any original instincts with which we are born equipped. Even the basic emotions of fear and love and rage by the time they have been shaped over the different cultural lasts are well-nigh unrecognizable. Is there a jealousy of the mate innate in our sexual organization? Perhaps, but it will not dictate behavior except according to a cultural permit. Over a large part of the world, the woman is aggrieved if her husband does not take other wives—it may be to aid her in the duties of the household, or to relieve her of child-bearing, or to make plain her husband's social importance. And in other parts of the world, the male's virtues of generosity and of dignity are chiefly summed up in his practice of sharing his wife, and his calm acceptance of her desertion. Is there a maternal instinct? It will always be operative according to the conventions of the group. If there is great emphasis upon rank, women may voluntarily kill their children to raise their own status, as among the Natchez, or the Polynesian Tonga. If there is a pattern of seemingly meaningless adoption, most families will place their infants in other households, sometimes assigning them before birth. And how often have different apologists tried to give reasons for infanticide, when all the reasons they list are just as operative outside as within the region where this cultural compulsion rests upon the women.

Man evolves always elaborate traditional ways of doing things, great superstructures of the most varying design, and without very striking correlations with the underpinnings on which they must each and all eventually rest. It is only in a fundamental and non-spectacular sense that these superstructures are conditioned by their foundation in man's original endowment. And it is the superstructure in which man lives, not the foundation. The compulsion of folkways in a well-knit culture is just as strong as the compulsion of a style in architecture, Gothic, or Renaissance, or Egyptian. It fashions as it will the instincts of the people who live within it, remaking them in conformity with its own requirements. So it is that the cultural patterns are themselves creative; they take the raw material of experience and mold it into fifty different shapes among fifty different peoples. The traditional patterns of behavior set the mold and human nature flows into it.

It follows that man's established folkways are also his morals. Judgments of right and wrong and of the glory of God grow up within the field of group behavior and attach themselves to those traits that have become automatic in the group. Interference with automatic behavior is always unpleasant, and it is rationalized as evil. No people have any truly empirical ethics; they uphold what they find themselves practicing. Even our own literature of ethics is far from being a detached survey of different possible solutions; it is a system of apologetics for the well-known scheme of our own culture. It is not that the anthropologist would subtract a jot or tittle from this preference for one's own customs; there are values in any way of living that can be plumbed only by those who have been born and bred in them, and in an ideal world every man would love best his own culture. What the anthropologist would have us add to our understanding is that all cultures have alike grown up blindly, the useful and cumbersome together, and not one of them is so good that it needs no revision, and not one is so bad that it cannot serve, just as ours can, the ideal ends of society and of the individual.

And how is it with regard to religion? All peoples have been religious; it is only what constituted religion that has varied. There is no item of experience, from the orientation of a house, to sleight of hand or foretelling the future, that has not been somewhere, it seems, the distinguishing matter of religion. Surely it is not this heterogeneous content of religion that is its essence. The rôle of religion is its slow and halting exploration of the spiritual life. Often it has wedged itself into blind alleys and wasted generations of experiment. It made a mistake and included within its scope not only its proper field, but also all that area of existence that is better handled in secular fashion. Its special field of the spiritual life is still in the process of delimitation. In that field it shares with art and with abstract thought and with all enthusiastic dedications of the self, the spiritual rewards of life. What the future holds we do not know, but it is not too much to hope that it will include a reinstating and reshaping of the spiritual values of existence that will balance the present immense unfolding of the material values.

What is the upshot of this analysis of custom for our contemporary thinking? Is it subversive? Certainly not, except in the sense in which Copernicus's demonstration of the stellar series to which this earth belonged, was subversive. The culture we are born into, according to anthropology, is also—as the earth is in the solar scheme—one of a series of similar phenomena all driven by the same compulsions. What we give up, in accepting this view, is a dogged attachment to absolutes; what we gain is a sense of the intriguing variety of possible forms of behavior, and of the social function that is served by these communal patternings. We become culture-conscious.

We perceive with new force the ties that bind us to those who share our culture. Ways of thinking, ways of acting, goals of effort, that we tend so easily to accept as the order of the universe, become rather the precious and special symbols we share together. Institutions that were massive Juggernauts demanding their toll become instead a world of the imagination to which all those of common culture have common access. For the social function of custom is that it makes our acts intelligible to our neighbors. It binds us together with a common symbolism, a common religion, a common set of values to pursue. In the past these groups have been geographical, and there has been little individual difference of choice among the members of a group. In the future there will be less geographical differentiation, more differentiation perhaps of voluntary groups. But though it will change the picture of civilization, it will not change the necessity in every sort of complicated human behavior of the cultural symbol, the framework within which alone our acts have meaning. The most individualistic rebel of us all would play a foolish rôle stripped of the conventions of his culture. Why should he make wholesale attack upon its institutions? They are the epic of his own people, written not in rime but in stone and currency and merchant marines and city colleges. They are the massive creation of the imaginations of generations, given a local habitation and a name.

We do not stand to lose by this tolerant and objective view of man's institutions and morals and ways of thought. On the one hand, we shall value the bold imagination that is written in all great systems of behavior; on the other, we shall not fear for the future of the world because some item in that system is undergoing contemporary change. We know all culture changes. It is one of its claims upon our interest. We hope, a little, that whereas change has hitherto been blind, at the mercy of unconscious patternings, it will be possible gradually, in so far as we become genuinely culture-conscious, that it shall be guided by intelligence.

For what is the meaning of life except that by the discipline of thought and emotion, by living life to its fullest, we shall make of it always a more flexible instrument, accepting new relativities, divesting ourselves of traditional absolutes? To this end we need for our scientific equipment something of the anthropologist's way of looking at human behavior, something of respect for the epic of our own culture, something of fine tolerance for the values that have been elaborated in other cultures than our own.

CONCEPT OF RIGHT AND WRONG *

By PAUL RADIN

ON no subject connected with primitive people does so much confusion exist in the mind of the general public and have so many ill-considered statements been made as on the nature of their behavior to one another. The prevalent view to-day among laymen is that they are at all times the plaything of their passions, and that self-control and poise are utterly alien to their character, if not, indeed, quite beyond their reach. Quite apart from the manifest absurdity involved in the belief that any parent in a primitive group would wreak his rage at his lack of success in hunting, in this murderous fashion upon the first object that came within his reach, even if it be his innocent and beloved child, there are a hundred and one reasons that would have deterred him, even had he been the uncontrolled animal the illustration assumes him to have been. However, let that pass. The illustration has its uses, for it permits the contrast between the generally accepted belief and the true nature of the facts to emerge all the more definitely. Actually the situation is quite different.

Briefly stated, the underlying idea of conduct among most primitive tribes is self-discipline, self-control and a resolute endeavor to observe a proper measure of proportion in all things. I am well aware that in some tribes this is more definitely expressed than in others and that not infrequently certain excrescences in their ceremonial life seem to contradict this assertion. Yet I think most field ethnologists would agree with me. Since in the face of so formidable a body of opinion apparently to the contrary, incontrovertible evidences will be demanded of me to substantiate so broad

* *Primitive Man as Philosopher.* New York: D. Appleton & Co.

and explicit a statement, I shall confine myself in my presentation of the facts to a tribe which I know personally and where the material which I use can be definitely controlled. The data upon which I rely come from the Winnebago Indians of Wisconsin and Nebraska and are to be found in two monographs published by me. Only statements made by the Winnebago themselves in accounts either actually written by themselves or contained in verbatim descriptions of the rituals obtained in the original Winnebago are used in order to obviate all inaccuracy.

I can think of no better method of introducing the subject than by quoting appropriate passages from the Winnebago texts secured and then discussing them in the light of the knowledge they throw upon the system of ethics enunciated and, more specifically, upon the type of self-control implied. For facility of reference I shall number these passages:

1. It is always good to be good.
2. What does life consist of but love?
3. Of what value is it to kill?
4. You ought to be of some help to your fellow men.
5. Do not abuse your wife; women are sacred.
6. If you cast off your dress for many people, they will be benefited by your deed.
7. For the good you do every one will love you.
8. Never do any wrong to children.
9. It is not good to gamble.
10. If you see a helpless old man, help him if you have anything at all.
11. If you have a home of your own, see to it that whoever enters it obtains something to eat. Such food will be a source of death to you if withheld.
12. When you are recounting your war deeds on behalf of the departed soul, do not try to add to your honor by claiming more for yourself than you have actually accomplished. If you tell a falsehood then and exaggerate your achievements you will die beforehand. The telling of truth

is sacred. Tell less than you did. The old men say it is wiser.

13. Be on friendly terms with every one and then every one will love you.

14. Marry only one person at a time.

15. Do not be haughty with your husband. Kindness will be returned to you and he will treat you in the same way in which you treat him.

16. Do not imagine that you are taking your children's part if you just speak about loving them. Let them see it for themselves.

17. Do not show your love for other people so that people notice it. Love them but let your love be different from that for your own.

18. As you travel along life's road, never harm any one or cause any one to feel sad. On the contrary, if at any time you can make a person feel happy, do so. If at any time you meet a woman away from your village and you are both alone and no one can see you, do not frighten her or harm her.

19. If you meet any one on the road, even if it is only a child, speak a cheering word before you pass on.

20. If your husband's people ever ask their own children for something when you are present, assume that they had asked it of you. If there is anything to be done, do not wait till you are asked to do it but do it immediately.

21. Never think a home is yours until you have made one for yourself.

22. If you have put people in charge of your household, do not nevertheless act as though the home were still yours.

23. When visiting your husband's people, do not act as if you were far above them.[1]

Obviously we are here in the presence of a fairly well elaborated system of conduct. To those who consistently deny to primitive man any true capacity for abstract thinking or objective formulation of an ethical code—and their number is very large both among scholars and laymen—the injunctions given above would probably be interpreted as having a definitely concrete significance. That is, they are not to be regarded as attempts at generalization in any true sense of the word but merely as inherently wise saws and precepts of a practical and personal application. Now there is sufficient justification for such a view to warrant our discussing it before we proceed any further.

A number of the precepts given avowedly allow a concrete practical and personal application. In 5, for example, we are told, "If you abuse your wife you will die in a short time. Our grandmother Earth is a woman and in abusing your wife you will be abusing her. Since it is she who takes care of us, by your actions you will be practically killing yourself." To precept 10 is added the following: "If you happen to possess a home, take him (the old man) there and feed him for he may suddenly make uncomplimentary remarks about you. You will be strengthened thereby."

We thus do indeed seem to obtain the impression that a Winnebago in being good to a helpless old man is guided by motives secondary to those implied in the precept as quoted. And what follows would seem to strip our apparently generous precept of whatever further altruistic value still attaches to it, for there it is stated that perhaps the old man is carrying under his arm a box of medicines that he cherishes very much and which he will offer to you. Similarly in precept 11 we find, "If you are stingy about giving food some one may kill you." Indeed, I think we shall have to admit that in the majority of cases none of the Winnebago virtues or actions are extolled for their own sake, and that in every instance they have reference to and derive their validity from whatever relation they possess to the preponderatingly practical needs of human intercourse. "Don't be a fool," precept 5 seems to imply, "and don't treat your wife badly, because if you do, you'll run the risk of having the woman's protecting deity, the Earth, punish you." I should not even be surprised if, in concrete instances, the moral was further emphasized by giving examples of how men were punished who had abused their wives. We are fairly obviously told to be guided by the practical side of the question, i.e., take no risks and get the most out of every good action you perform.

Now all this sounds extremely cynical and practical. But we must be fair and not too hasty in drawing our inferences. First of all it should be asked if the Winnebago in actual practice give the impression of always being guided by ego-tistical and ulterior motives, and second it should be borne in mind that if we can really prove that the ideal of human conduct is on a high plane, we need not concern ourselves needlessly with the apparent nature of the motives prompt-ing individual acts. As a matter of fact primitive people are much less guided by consciously selfish and ulterior motives than we are, not because of any innate superiority over ourselves in this regard but because of the conditions under which they live. But, quite apart from this considera-tion, ought we in fact to lay undue stress on illustrations following what is clearly a general principle? Are we not after all, in our illustrations, merely dealing with a state-ment of what happens when some general principle of the ethical code is transgressed, and not primarily with an ex-planation of the principle? I do not feel, therefore, that even those instances which seem superficially to corroborate the prevalent assumption of primitive man's inability to formu-late an abstract ethical creed, actually bear out, when more carefully examined, the contention of its advocates.

Now the question of the capacity of the Winnebago to formulate an ethical code in a fairly abstract fashion is of fundamental importance for the thesis of this chapter and that is why I am laying so much stress on it; for if it were not true our precepts would have to be regarded in the nature of mere proverbs and practical folk wisdom, as nothing higher indeed than crystallized maxims of conduct.

There are, however, in our list certain precepts where the abstract formulation is undeniable, where, in fact, reference to the particular context in which the precepts occur not only shows no secondary concrete significance, but, on the

contrary, a reinforcement of their abstract and general connotation. In precept 1 the full statement is this: "If you
hear of a person traveling through your country and you
want to see him, prepare your table and send for him. In
this manner you will do good and it is always good to do
good, it is said." Similarly in precept 2. Here it is in the
course of a speech delivered at a ceremony that the phrase
occurs: "what does life consist of but love?" "All the
members of the clan have given me counsel," the speaker
says, "and all the women and children have pleaded in my
behalf with the spirits. What love that was! And of what
does life consist but of love?"

Here we have no concrete practical implications. The
statements are meant to be taken as general propositions.
They are very remarkable enunciations and we may legitimately draw from their existence the inference that even in
so-called "primitive" tribes, certain individuals have apparently felt within themselves the same moral truths that
are regarded as the glory of our great moralists, and that
they have formulated these truths in general terms.

So much for the actual formulation. What, however, does
this Winnebago creed tell us about the idea of conduct
itself? Does it teach us that love and forbearance are to
be practiced for their own sake and is the love of which
they speak identical with or even comparable to our idea
of love?

When a Western European speaks of love, forbearance,
remorse, sorrow, etc., he generally understands by these
terms some quality belonging to an individual and for the
possession of which he is to be honored and praised. We do
not ask whether the love or the virtue in question is of an
intelligent nature, whether it does harm or good, or whether
we have any right to it. Who among us would speak of
an individual not being entitled to his remorse or sorrow?
We assume that the mere expression of remorse and sorrow
is somehow ethically praiseworthy. If we see a man of
manifestly weak character but of a loving disposition, even

if his actions are inconsistent with a true love for his fellow men, insist that he loves them, while we may condemn him, we are inclined to overlook much in recognition of his enunciation of the principle that love of mankind is the highest ideal of life. In much the same way do we look upon any manifestation of sincere remorse or sorrow. We simply regard love, remorse, sorrow, etc., as inalienable rights of man, quite independent of any right, as it were, he may possess to express them. In other words, the Western European ethics is frankly egocentric and concerned primarily with self-expression. The object toward which love, remorse, repentance, sorrow, is directed is secondary. Christian theology has elevated them all to the rank of virtues as such, and enjoins their observance upon us because they are manifestations of God's if not of man's way.

Among primitive people this is emphatically not true. Ethics there is based upon behavior. No mere enunciation of an ideal of love, no matter how often and sincerely repeated, would gain an individual either admiration, sympathy, or respect. Every ethical precept must be submitted to the touchstone of conduct. The Winnebago moralist would insist that we have no right to preach an ideal of love or to claim that we love, unless we have lived up to its practical implications. That is the fundamental basis of all primitive education and is unusually well expressed among the Winnebago. "When you are bringing up children," runs the injunction to a young mother, "do not imagine that you are taking their part if you merely speak of loving them. Let them see it for themselves; let them know what love is by seeing you give away things to the poor. Then they will see your good deeds and then they will know whether you have been telling the truth or not." An exactly similar attitude is taken toward remorse. "If you have always loved a person, then when he dies you will have the right to feel sorrow." No amount of money spent upon the funeral of a person with whom you had been quarreling will make amends.

But it is not merely love, remorse, etc., to which you have no right as such. You have equally no right to the glory attendant upon joining a war party unless it is done in the right spirit. In the document from which most of our statements have been taken—the autobiography of a Winnebago Indian—a man is represented as being about to embark on a war party because his wife has run away from him. "Such a man," the author insists, "is simply throwing away his life. If you want to go on the warpath, do not go because your wife has been taken away from you but because you feel courageous enough to go."

In consonance with such an attitude is the differentiation in the degree of love insisted upon. Love everybody, it is demanded, but do not love them all equally. Above all do not love your neighbor as you love those of your own blood. "Only if you are wicked," the injunction says, "will you love other people's children more than your own." The injunction certainly says that we must love everybody, but this must be humanly understood, and humanly understood you cannot, of course, love every one alike. The Winnebago would contend that such a statement would be untrue and that any attempt to put it into practice must manifestly lead to insincerity. It would, moreover, be definitely unjust in that it might make for the neglect of those whom primarily you ought to love most. Here the difference between the attitude of primitive man and that of Western Europe is most clearly brought out. According to primitive standards you deserve neither credit nor discredit, neither praise nor condemnation, for giving expression to a normal human emotion. It is the manner in which, in your relations to the other members of the tribe, you *distribute* this emotion and the degree to which it is felt by others to be sincere, that calls forth respect and admiration. It is wicked to love other people's children as much as your own; it is wicked to love your wife to the detriment of your family and yourself; it is wicked to love your enemy while he is your enemy. An excellent illustration of this conviction—

that it is fundamentally wicked and unintelligent to make the expression of even a socially commendable emotion like love an end in itself—is contained in the following passage taken from the autobiography quoted above:

When you get married do not make an idol of the woman you marry; do not worship her. If you worship a woman she will insist upon greater and greater worship as time goes on. It may be that when you get married you will listen to the voice of your wife and you will refuse to go on the warpath. Why should you thus run the risk of being ridiculed? After a while you will not be allowed to go to a feast. In time even your sisters will not think anything of you. (You will become jealous) and after your jealousy has developed to its highest pitch your wife will run away. You have let her know by your actions that you worship a woman and one alone. As a result she will run away from you. If you think that a woman (your wife) is the only person you ought to love, you have humbled yourself. You have made the woman suffer and have made her feel unhappy. You will be known as a bad man and no one will want to marry you again. (Perhaps afterwards) when people go on the warpath you will join them because you feel unhappy at your wife's desertion. You will then, however, simply be throwing away your life.

A complete insight is afforded by this example into every phase of Winnebago ethics. You are to love your wife, for instance, but it is to be kept within personally and socially justifiable limits. If not, the whole adjustment of an individual to his environment is disturbed and injustice is eventually done to every one concerned—to his family, to his wife, and to himself. Marked exaggeration and disproportion would, from a practical point of view, be unthinkable in a primitive community. The result, in the hypothetical case we discussed above, is clear; loss of life and suicide, and possibly even the dragging of innocent people into your calamity—those, for instance, who are going on a warpath properly prepared spiritually.

The psychology expressed here is unimpeachable. To have

analyzed the situation so completely and so profoundly and to have made this analysis the basis of social behavior is not a slight achievement, and this achievement is to be evaluated all the more highly because the Winnebago was predominantly a warrior culture. The objectivity displayed is altogether unusual, the husband's, the wife's, the tribal viewpoints, all are presented fairly and clearly.

NOTE

[1] All these passages, with the exception of 3, 18, 19, and 20, come from *Crashing Thunder: The Autobiography of an American Indian,* edited by Paul Radin; 3 comes from the myth given on page 79 of *Primitive Man as Philosopher,* and the others from the 37th *Report of the Bureau of American Ethnology.*

CLASS RELATIONS *

By L. T. HOBHOUSE

MORALITY at its outset is bound up with the structure of the social group. Between members of any one community the obligations recognized may be many and stringent, while in relation to outsiders no obligations are recognized at all. The typical primitive community is, as it were, a little island of friends amid a sea of strangers and enemies. The consequences of the group principle we have traced in the history of warfare. We have seen it applied in its extreme form in the treatment of conquered enemies as men destitute of any title to consideration; we have seen that as moral development proceeds, it is moderated and softened, but that, except in the highest ethical thought, it does not wholly disappear. Throughout history we have the standing contrast of the comparative peace, order and coöperation within each organized society, and the disunion constantly tending to hostility found in the relations of different societies to one another. We have now to trace the operation of the same principle upon the structure of society itself.

The primitive community is, as a rule, small, but compact and homogeneous. There is always the distinction between its own members and outsiders; there is also a greater or less distinction in the rights enjoyed by the two sexes. In other respects the obligations constituting its ethical life are fairly uniform. But as society grows and its industrial life develops, as primitive barbarism gives way to some degree of culture, this simplicity of the early social organizations breaks up, and now the group principle obtains a fresh development. Distinct groups arise within each society, within the limits of a simple community, under one king

* *Morals in Evolution.* London: Chapman and Hall.

or one governing body. Besides the group of free men—to use that term provisionally—who constitute the members of the community in the fullest sense of the word, there arise inferior classes, slaves or serfs or low-caste men who are in the community and yet not of it, who are subject to its laws and customs, but not possessed of all the civil rights which membership confers. These inferior groups within the community occupy a position which is morally and legally analogous to that of strangers and enemies. In extreme cases they are wholly devoid of rights, in other cases their inferiority is marked by a more or less serious lack of the civil rights enjoyed by their superiors. Historically, in the case of slaves, their position is, in point of fact, very largely that of incorporated enemies, and whether this corresponds to the historical fact or not, ethically speaking, the denial of personal rights from which they suffer is a consequence of that same group-morality which from the first contrasts friend and neighbor with stranger and enemy, and denies to the one the elementary rights of a human being, which are readily accorded to the other.

Not merely political privileges, but civil rights, the right of holding property, the right of personal freedom, the right of marriage, even the right of protection of life or limb, are wholly or in part denied to classes excluded from full membership of the community. Such distinctions of personal status are found in one form or another in the great mass of societies, civilized or uncivilized, which stand above the lowest stages of culture. They persist well into the modern period, and are but slowly modified, and partially abrogated in proportion as the whole principle of group-morality yields to ethical criticism. Of these distinctions the commonest is, of course, the distinction between slave and free, but slavery is in many cases replaced by serfdom and in others by caste. What is common to all three institutions is the derogation from full rights which they imply. In detail, they are distinct, though the line of demarcation is not always easy to draw. We may say that the slave, properly regarded, is a man whom law and custom regard as the property of another. In extreme cases he is wholly without rights, a pure chattel; in other cases he may be protected in certain respects, but so may an ox or an ass. As long as he is for all ordinary purposes completely at his master's disposal, rendering to his master the fruits of his work, performing his work under orders, rewarded at his master's discretion, and liable to punishment on his master's judgment, he may, though protected in other relations, fairly be called a slave. If, on the other hand, he acquires a certain position of his own, obtains property from which he cannot be dislodged except for some default, enjoys the right of marriage and protection for life and limb, he becomes, though still liable to labor under his master's direction, still subject, perhaps, to punishment and still in an inferior legal position, no longer a slave, strictly so called, but a serf. Serf and slave alike belong as a rule to private masters. A servile caste, on the other hand, is not necessarily in the ownership of any man or body of men. It is distinguished by a greater or less lack of personal rights, by social inferiority, and probably by a taboo cutting it off from intercourse with others. And as there may be servile castes falling below the normal level of free men, so there may be privileged castes of nobles possessing, as it were, an excess of rights, and these privileges may indirectly depress the position of the ordinary member of society and impair his freedom by withholding protection from him in relation to one of the nobility. Finally, the whole community may suffer a similar depression in relation to the king, who, in the extreme development of the despotic principle, becomes, as we have seen, eminent owner of all property and lord of the persons of his subjects. In such cases, though there may still be distinct grades in society, yet all subjects alike are in principle destitute of rights.

Now all these methods of the gradation of rights, if the phrase be allowed, rest ultimately on the principle of group-morality—the principle that rights and duties do not attach to the human being as such, but are determined by extraneous considerations, social, political, or religious. The development which this principle attains varies very greatly in different societies, and depends upon economic and social, as well as on ethical and religious conditions; but its operation in one form or another persists throughout history, and is one of the dominant facts, if not *the* dominant fact, ethically considered, in the evolution of human society. In tracing its varied development, we shall for the most part follow the history of slavery and serfdom as the main line along which it runs. We shall, however, deal with other forms which the principle assumes, as occasion requires.

2. In the primitive group, as has been said, we find, as a rule, no distinction of slave and free, no serfdom no caste, and little, if any, distinction between chief and follower. Taking this statement alone, one might infer that the primitive savage realizes the ideal of the philosopher of a community of free men and equals; but the savage enjoys freedom and equality, not because he has realized the value of those conceptions, but because neither he nor his fellow is strong enough to put himself above his neighbor. Two conditions suffice to ensure the growth of slavery or of a servile caste in the savage world. The first condition is a certain development of industrialism. In a hunter tribe, which lives from hand to mouth, there is little occasion for the services of a slave. The harder and less interesting work can be put upon the women, and the chief occupation of the men is to fight. This brings us at once to the second condition, which is a measure of warlike prowess, giving to a tribe the means of supplying slaves from its captives. But not only must a tribe that is to obtain captive slaves, conquer; it must also refrain from putting its captives to death. The difficulty of exercising such restraint militates against the rise of slavery in savage society, and in consequence, though the idea of slavery is widely diffused in the uncivilized world, the institution grows more important step by step with the development of civilization. We find

many civilized people, where slavery has attained a luxuriant
growth, retaining a tradition of a time at which there were
no slaves, and these traditions may well preserve an historical truth. But the enslavement of the vanquished is not
the only alternative open to a conquering people. Instead
of apportioning the captives to individuals as their booty,
they may reduce the conquered tribe collectively to a servile
position. In that case we get from the first a system of
public serfdom. In other cases, again, possibly as a development of this practice, the distinction of conqueror and conquered hardens into a distinction of caste sanctioned by
religion. Finally, the development of military organization,
and the consequent rise of the power of the chief, are
responsible for that form of "rightlessness" in which all
members of the tribe become slaves of the king.[1]

In one or other of these different forms we find the
conception of a class of men, wholly or partly destitute of
rights, widely diffused throughout the uncivilized world.
The special home of slavery is, of course, Negro Africa,
where the exceptions in which the institution is not found
are quite inconsiderable.[2] In Oceania there is more variety.
In some of the islands, as has been seen, war is but little
known, and in these cases slavery is also absent; [3] but there
are other causes militating against its development. In
Melanesia cannibalism is frequent, and, in some cases, for
example, in Fiji, slaves are kept for cannibal purposes.[4] In
Micronesia, again, a strongly marked caste division partially replaces slavery, though there may be slaves in the
proper sense in addition to the servile caste. Throughout
Polynesia caste is more prominent than slavery.[5] It is a
Polynesian saying, that "a chief cannot steal," and in Tahiti,
if a chief asks, "Whose is that tree, etc.," the owner answers,
"Yours and mine." The killing of one of the lower by a
member of the higher class is regarded as merely a peccadillo.[6] In Micronesia the original principle of the constitution seems to have been a division into two castes, the one
god-like, immortal, and possessing all the power; the other

having no souls, no property, no wives, and doing all the hard labor; but below these again were the enslaved prisoners.[7] In the Malay region slavery is widely diffused, especially in the towns,[8] though, as we shall see later, its forms differ, and in some cases, particularly under Mohammedan influence, the slave is by no means rightless. Among the rude Indian hill tribes the institution is naturally less developed. In some cases, as among the Bodos and Dhimals, there are apparently no slaves, and the same is said to be true of some of the Naga tribes. Other Nagas, however, make slaves of captives[9] and among many other hill tribes slaves are held.[10] The nomad tribes of Central Asia do not generally spare their captives, and still practice human sacrifice, but the richer tribes are slave-holders.[11] Among the North American Indians slavery is but little developed east of the Rockies, though there were a few tribes which occasionally practiced[12] it as an alternative to the torture or adoption of prisoners. In the west and north, however, it was widely diffused[13] though here also, in some cases, the indiscriminate massacre of prisoners was the common alternative. In the tribes of tropical South America slavery appears to be confined to war captives, but prisoners may also be put to death or adopted as members of the tribe.[14]

Thus while avoiding undue generalization we may fairly say (1) that in the rudest tribes there are no class distinctions, the harder and more menial work falling often (though not always) upon the women; (2) as a tribe grows in culture, and especially in military strength, the first result is, as a rule, that the conquered enemies are sacrificed, eaten, tortured, or in any case put to death. But (3) with a certain softening of manners, or at any rate with a cooler perception of permanent advantage, prisoners are spared and enslaved. This grace is first reserved for women and children, but is afterwards extended to male captives. A class is thus formed who are within the jurisdiction of the conquering tribe, but from the point of view of law and morals remain outside it. Either in the form of a class of slaves or of a degraded quasi-servile lower caste, the presence of such an element in the population is a general feature in societies which have emerged from the lower savagery and the rawest militarism. On the strict principle of group-morality this class is destitute of rights, and only too often the principle is consistently carried out. The typical slave can neither marry nor hold property except on sufferance. His very life is in his master's hands. He may be flogged, maimed, sold, pawned, given away, exchanged, or put to death.

3. In many slave systems, however, this "rightlessness" is qualified in various ways. How this qualification arises we shall best understand if we take a more complete view of the actual sources from which slaves are recruited. Hitherto we have spoken only of captives in war. But this, though probably the original method by which a servile class is formed, is not the only method by which it is recruited. Of other methods the first and greatest is inheritance —for normally a slave's child is also a slave. Secondly, in most barbaric and semi-civilized societies the numbers of the slave class are swollen by other causes, principally by debt, crime, and the slave trade. In some cases slavery is the prescribed penalty for crime. More often the man who cannot pay the prescribed composition either falls into slavery himself as a debt-slave in order, as it were, to work out his debt, or sells, particularly under the sway of the fully developed *patria potestas,* his wife or child for that purpose. "What! shall I starve as long as my sister has children whom she can sell?" was the remark of an African negro to Burton—a remark which comprises a whole chapter upon primitive ethics in a few words.

The formation of debtor-slaves, and even the increase of hereditary slaves, has, however, a certain softening influence upon the institution of slavery itself, for while the captive slave remains as enemy in the sight of law and morals and is therefore rightless, the debtor or the criminal was originally a member of the community, and in relation to him there is apt to arise some limitation of the power of the master. The family of the debtor-slave will not see him treated with unlimited cruelty; they retain some right of protection over the purchased wife, however illogically. In fact, the slave is no longer a mere stranger or enemy. He is partially incorporated in the community and has some recognized rights, though by no means those of a free man. The improvement tends to extend itself to the hereditary slave who also was born in the community, though within the slave class. Thus there comes to be a distinction between the domestic slave and the slave who is captured or bought from abroad. The one remains a chattel-slave, the other is becoming a serf. There are thus many gradations of "rightlessness" in the servile status, and these must very briefly be passed in review.

Customs protecting the slave from undue tyranny are found in the barbaric and semi-civilized world, though in many cases they are not derived from barbaric ideas, but are traceable to the influence of Mohammedanism. In these customs the distinction between the domestic and the foreign slave is generally well marked. Illustrations of almost every degree in "rightlessness" may be drawn from African slavery. Thus, among the Foulah, house slaves are treated as members of the family, and are sold only in necessity or for a punishment, while war captives and purchased foreign slaves are wholly without rights. In Bambara captives are pure chattels, but house slaves have a good position and in some cases are treated as members of the family. Among the Timmanees, the Bulloms, and the Beni-amer, no one is sold as a slave who was not bought as such. Among the Mandingoes native slaves are protected, while others are at the mercy of the master to sell or kill. On the Congo the captive slave may be sold, but house slaves only after a palaver, that is, with the consent of the community. Among the Barea and Kunama the master has no right of life and death over native slaves. At Timbuctoo no native can be enslaved at all. Among the West Equatorial tribes the slave may be killed by his master, but not sold abroad except for some transgression. At Nuffi a master may strike, but not mutilate or kill his slave. In Sokoto and among the Yolofs the captive slave may be sold at will, the born slave only after repeated chastisement. In Bihé pawn-slaves are protected, while bought ones can be arbitrarily punished, and only in the case of their death is a small fine due from the owner to the king. Among the Mpongwe the house slave can only be sold for some offense, and here slaves call their master "father" and are well treated. The Fantis recognize the distinction between the slaves of their own tribe and those of other tribes, and among the Ibu, on the Niger, slaves can hold property, build houses and marry.[15] They then rank as free, owing only a yearly tax, and the relation, in fact, passes into a kind of light serfdom. Similarly at Sokoto the slave is at about the age of twenty given a wife and set up in a hut in the country. At Boussa they farm the land on the matayer principle, and though in law the masters could sell them and take their wives, children and goods, in practice they enjoy much liberty and property.[16] Various forms of serfdom, existing often side by side with slavery, are common in Africa, the serf cultivating the land and owing labor service or payment in kind, and sometimes holding property of his own.[17]

A right frequent in Mohammedan countries, found also in one or two instances of non-Mohammedan tribes, is that of changing the master. This a slave can effect by the legal process of *noxæ datio,* by which, on inflicting some injury on some man other than his own master, he, *ipso facto,* becomes that man's slave. Among the Barea and Kunama a native slave can simply leave for another village and so become free. In Zanzibar slaves obtain this right as the result of deliberate ill-treatment, and the same custom is found on the Congo, among the Apingi, and other West Equatorial tribes. In Ashanti slaves can commend themselves to a new master by giving him the right of life and death over them, and in Timbuctoo, if ill-treated, a slave may appeal to the court in order to be sold. Among the Beni-amer the distinction between the born slave and the foreign slave is well marked in the case of homicide. For the bought slave only the "wer" can be demanded, but the born slave can be avenged by blood. The marriage of slaves depends generally upon the will of the master. In relation to property their rights vary greatly and here again the distinction of origin of slaves makes itself felt, *e.g.*, among the Bogos and Marea a slave who is the son of a free-born man has the right to buy his freedom, a right which is denied to the slave by birth.[18]

Of the various tribes mentioned, those in which protection is carried furthest are for the most part either partially Mohammedanized or partially Christianized,[19] and while some distinction between domestic and foreign slaves may be attributed to Negroland generally, such further amelioration of the slave's position as is to be found in barbarous or semi-civilized Africa is probably to be attributed to the higher ethics of a civilized religion.[20] The same influence is found at work among the Malays, where the distinction of native and foreign slaves also reappears. Speaking generally, the captive slaves are destitute of rights, and the capture and sale of slaves is a chief line of business among all Malays who trade in ships of their own. But crime and debt are also rich sources of slavery,[21] and in some parts at least the slave has a measure of protection. In the Malacca Peninsula, where the influence of Islam is strong, the slave if struck may bring his master into court, and the slave woman who bears a child to her master goes free.[22] The Battaks also, head-hunters though they are, put a limit on the master's right of punishment.[23]

Thus in the barbaric world we already find degrees of rightlessness, and a measure of legal or customary protection, at least for certain classes of slaves. This alleviation is often but not always[24] traceable to the influence of one of the higher religions. The free man who has become a slave is not wholly cut off from membership of the community, but retains certain recognized rights, though by no means those which full membership confers. We have now to see how the idea of slavery, and of rightlessness generally, fare in the main forms of civilization.

4. Slavery, like polygamy and divorce, was an institution which Mohammed found fully established among his fellow-countrymen, which he disliked and set himself to mitigate, but could not attempt to abolish. A difference, however, is made between Moslem and non-Moslem captives. In a war with Moslems prisoners were not enslaved. If the prisoner on the battlefield became a Moslem he might not be killed, but according to the traditions he ought even to be set free, though if he became a Moslem subsequently he remained a slave.[25] The holding of Moslem slaves was not, as such, prohibited, but their emancipation was regarded as an act of special merit. According to the tradition: "Whosoever frees a slave who is a Moslem, God will redeem every member of his body limb for limb from hell fire." [26] Mohammed sought mitigation of the slave's lot by ethical rather than legal means. The slave has no civil liberty, and can only possess property by the owner's permission. The master's power is unlimited, and he is not slain for the murder of his slave. He has unlimited power over his female slaves; as a matter of law he may prostitute them; he may give a slave in marriage to whom he will, though he may not annul the marriage when once completed.[27] On the other hand, the Prophet enjoins upon Moslems to exercise kindness to slaves, forbids the prostitution of slave-girls as a religious offense, and enjoins emancipation whenever a slave is able to redeem himself. "When a slave of yours has money to redeem his bond, then you must not allow him to come into your presence afterwards." "Behaving well to slaves is a means of prosperity, and behaving ill to them is a cause of loss." "Whenever any one of you is about to beat a slave and the slave asks pardon in the name of God, then withhold yourself from beating him. Feed your slaves with food of that which you eat and

clothe them with such clothing as you wear, and command them not to do that which they are unable." Wrongful punishment, which, in some institutions, as we have seen, is a legal ground of manumission, was held by Mohammed to be a moral ground. "He who beats his slave without fault or slaps him on the face, his atonement for this is freeing him." As an illustration of the spirit in which this behest was conceived, we may quote the story of the Caliph Othman, who, having twisted his memlook's ear, bade the slave twist his own.[28] A further humane provision forbade the separation of mother and child: "Whoever is the cause of separation between mother and child by selling and giving, God will separate him from his friends on the day of resurrection."[29]

Conversely, the Prophet had certain promises for the dutiful slave: "It is well for a slave who regularly worships God and discharges his master's work properly"; and again: "When a slave wishes well to his master and worships God well, for him are double rewards." On the whole, the authorities tell us that the Prophet's rules of good treatment are observed. Masters are bound to maintain their slaves or emancipate them. To sell a slave of long standing is considered disgraceful, and female slaves are seldom emancipated without being provided for. The Egyptian slaves in Lane's time were numerous but well cared for, and ranked socially above free servants. With all these mitigations it must be admitted that the recognition of the slave traffic by Mohammedanism has been, and is to this day, a curse to Africa and a source of disturbance to the world's politics.

5. *Greece.*—Like the Chinese, the Greeks had a tradition of a prehistoric epoch in which there were no slaves.[30] But in the Homeric epoch we find slavery in full swing, and the regular issue of the capture of a town is that the men should be slain and the women enslaved. Hector knows— and no thought is so bitter to him—that when Troy is taken and he himself is slain, it will be Andromache's fate to be

a bondwoman to one of her conquerors. Her family had already suffered the same fate. The swift-footed, godlike Achilles had destroyed her father and her seven brothers, and had carried off her mother "with the rest of the spoil," though he afterwards set her free for an immense ransom. Now, Hector was all these to her, but the day would come when the Argives would sack the sacred town of Ilium and Hector in his turn be taken from her, and it would be her lot to fall into slavery.[31] Apart from legitimate warfare, piracy—which for that matter was in the Homeric view hardly less legitimate—was a frequent source of slavery. Many children suffered the fate of Eumæus the swineherd, and were carried off by the pirate and sold across the wine-dark sea. Slavery was hereditary, and the slave might be sold or put to death, as the faithless female slaves were hanged by Telemachus.[32] On the other hand, slaves might own houses and property of their own and live in the practical freedom in which we find the goodly Eumæus. Lastly, it should be noted that the slaves were not the only rightless class, for the stranger is also outside the protection of the law, though, even if a beggar and a fugitive, he is under the shelter of Zeus so long as he is a guest and claims the right of hospitality.

In the rural districts of Greece slavery remained rare. Pericles lays stress on the fact that the Peloponnesians are *autourgoi*—cultivators of their own lands.[33] It is even said that slave-holding was forbidden in Phocis and Lokris down to the fourth century.[34] But in the more developed states the growth of wealth meant, as always in the ancient world, increase in the number of slaves and—what was most fatal—the belief that work was not compatible with the dignity of a free man. Slavery remained a recognized fate for prisoners of war as an alternative to massacre, and even Plato could only hope that Greeks would abandon the practice of enslaving fellow-Greeks, restricting themselves to the barbarian, who, as Aristotle held, was the only natural slave. But through the institution of debt slavery the poorer classes in each state were frequently menaced with falling into enslavement. Before Solon's time the land was tilled by poor cultivators for the rich, and on their failure to pay five-sixths of their produce to the landlord, they fell into the position of serfs along with their wives and children. The prohibition of debt slavery and the pledging of the person by Solon was thus the salvation of civil freedom for Athens; and with the progress of Athenian democracy, although it was a democracy of free men only, the position of the slaves was indirectly improved. The master had the right of corporal punishment and of branding, but could not put a slave to death without a judicial decision.[35] A right of action for ὕβρις protected the slave from ill-treatment by strangers, and if maltreated by his master he could take refuge in the Theseum or some other asylum and demand to be sold—a demand which was investigated either by the priests or by a judicial process. On the other hand, the slave was not directly recognized as a personality by the law; he could only be represented by his master, who could sue for damages on his account. Except in murder cases he could only give evidence under torture, to which he might be given up at the will of his master, the belief being that this was the only way to get truth from him. He could only give evidence against his master upon a charge of treason. At the same time he was often allowed to hold property and found a family, while he might buy his freedom by entrusting his earnings to a priest.

The development in the Dorian states was somewhat different. Here serfdom was more prominent than slavery, though the two institutions existed sometimes side by side. The Dorian conquerors divided part of the land among themselves, leaving it to be tilled by the conquered people as public serfs, while part was left to its original possessors, who were personally free but had no political rights. Hence the two classes of Helots and Periocci. The conquered population were bound to the soil, but could not be sold or set free except by the State, though the landlord, for whom they cultivated the land at a fixed rate, was their immediate master. The Helots of Sparta, as is well known, were seditious, and were ill-treated and frequently put to death in fear, or at least in anticipation, of some rising. The Penestæ of Thessaly, who were otherwise in a closely analogous position to the Helots, were better off in this respect, as they could only be put to death by judicial process. In Crete there were two classes of serfs, those on the public land and those belonging to private owners, who might contract a legal marriage and hold and inherit property, and, according to Aristotle, were treated by masters on terms of social equality. Besides these two classes of serfs there were slaves who might be bought and sold.

It should be added that the distinction between the citizen and the non-citizen is strongly marked throughout Greek history. Aliens were forbidden at Sparta altogether, and at Athens, where their numbers became great, they were as such destitute of rights, but in practice they•were required to inscribe themselves on the list of resident aliens. They then came under special State protection, for which, and for the right to exercise a trade, they paid a certain tribute. They still required a representative in a law court, and had neither the right of marriage with citizens unless by treaty with their own State, nor the right of holding land.[36]

The organization of the City State, in fact, led naturally to a deeply-marked distinction between the full citizen and all others, whether Greek or Barbarian, whether free or unfree. And we may take it as a mark of the ethical superiority of the Greeks that the logical consequences were so far mitigated, as we have seen them to have been in the legislation for the protection of slaves.

6. *Rome.*—At Rome the strict limitation of civil rights to full citizens, combined with the peculiar development of the powers of the paterfamilias, had a depressing effect upon the position of slaves. Not only captured enemies, but, even down to the time of Justinian, any unprotected foreigner was liable to enslavement. A free Roman could not become

a slave within Rome itself, but deserters, and all those who were omitted from the census, could be sold abroad by the magistrate, children by their parents, debtors by their creditors, the thief by the injured party.

In practice the slave of the earlier period was, as a rule, fairly well treated, and there was probably no great social distinction between him and his master; but he was in law a chattel. He had no family of his own; his union (*contubernium*) was no legal marriage. He had no status in a court of justice, but if he wished to sue for an injury, could only do so through his master. Even if abandoned by his master he did not become free, but was the lawful property of the first comer. Not that cruel treatment passed without condemnation. Cruelty, even to animals, was subject to religious and even legal penalties.[37] Gross cases might involve the intervention of the censor. Though the slave could legally hold no property, custom secured him his own *peculium,* and he might even come to purchase his freedom.

Such was the position of the slave in early Rome. The growth of the Roman dominion, the rise of the great estates, submerging the old freeholder with his small plot of ground, and the facility of obtaining slaves from the numbers thrown into the market by capture in war and by traffic with pirates, combined to give Roman slavery towards the close of the Republic a new and dark character. The land was cultivated in many districts by slave-gangs, working in chains and confined by night in prison workhouses under conditions described by Mommsen as such that by comparison with their sufferings it is probable that all that was endured by negro slaves was but a drop. But some relief came from the humaner ideas of advancing civilization, fostered by contact with Greek culture. In particular, the Stoic philosophy was the champion of the slaves. Seneca vigorously pleads their cause, and in particular reprobates the cruelty of the gladiatorial games. The jurists of the next century went further, and distinctly laid down that by natural law all men are equal and that slavery is a human institution contrary to

nature. "Quod ad jus naturale attinet, omnes homines
æquales sunt," writes Ulpian;[38] and more distinctly Floren-
tinus: "Servitus est constitutio juris gentium, qua quis
dominio alieno contra naturam subjicitur."[39] The Stoical
teaching had its effect on legislation. The practice of the
exposure and sale of children and of pledging them for debt
was forbidden, while an edict of Diocletian forbade a free
man to sell himself. Man-stealers were punished with death.
The insolvent debtor was no longer made a slave. The right
of bequest was granted to slaves. Some approach was made
to a recognition of their marriage, not only after emancipation, but even [40] while in slavery, with a view to hindering
the separation of families. Some legal security had already
been given to their personal property, the *peculium,* by the
prætorian edicts. The *Lex Petronia* (perhaps of A.D. 19) forbade throwing a slave to the wild beasts without a judicial
decision.[41] Under Hadrian the power of life and death was
taken from the master, and under Antoninus Pius the master who killed his own slave *sine causa* was punished as a
homicide. An edict of Claudius had meanwhile enfranchised
the old or sick slave who was abandoned by his master.[42]
Under Nero the slave had been given the right to complain
of ill-treatment to the magistrate. Under Pius the slave who
was cruelly treated could claim to be sold, and by a special
refinement it was held cruelty to employ an educated slave
on degrading or manual work. Constantine deprived masters who abandoned new-born slaves, of their rights over
them.[43] Emancipation, though restricted by Augustus, was
again made easier, and though the use of torture at judicial
investigation remained, it was in some respects limited.[44]

While the legal position of the slave was being thus improved by the imperial legislation, a new form of serfdom
was growing up under the name of the Colonate. Some of
the Coloni were probably foreign captives and immigrants
settled upon the soil, while others were originally free
tenants, who lapsed into a semi-servile condition through
the insecurity of the times and largely through self-commen-

dation. The status of the Coloni was regulated in the fourth century for fiscal purposes. Under Constantine, in 332, the Colonus could not quit his holding nor could he marry off the property of his lord. On the other hand, he could not be disturbed or be subjected arbitrarily to increased charges, and as the status was hereditary, we have here a fully-developed predial serfdom with fixed but limited rights for the serf.[45] The master might inflict moderate chastisement, but the Colonus had a legal remedy for injury or excessive demands.[46] While the Colonate was partly recruited from the previously free peasantry, a compensating process was going on whereby rural slaves obtained a settlement upon the land as quasi-Coloni or Casati. They were assimilated to the Coloni by the law of Valentinian I in 377, could not be sold apart from the land, and by the end of the seventh century were merged in the Colonate.[47]

We have now reached a point in the history of slavery at which two fresh influences have to be considered. The first of these is the barbarian conquests; the second that of the mediæval Church. The German tribes, generally speaking, recognized chattel slavery, and slaves were recruited from the sources ordinarily recognized among barbarisms—war, unprotected strangers, voluntary commendation, and in certain cases debt (*i.e.* in cases of incapacity to pay the wergild. This was the only form of debt slavery known).[48] Even in Merovingian times the slave was a true chattel, whose life had indeed a price, but a price payable, like that of the Babylonian slave, to his lord, and not a fixed wer like a free man, but a sum proportionate to his value.[49] But besides the slaves, who were not numerous, the Germans recognized a class of imperfectly free men, the Liti, who had land of their own, without which a German could not be a citizen, but were in a dependent position. Their status varied very much from tribe to tribe, and from one period to another. At first tributary to the people, we find them at a later stage in subjection to an individual master. They took no part in the meetings of the people, and while originally they could plead before a court, their wergild was ordinarily half that of a free man. Their marriage with free people was a *mesalliance,* wherein the children followed the rank of the mother. As we approach the "Frankish" period we find their position more distinctly assimilated to that of serfs.[50]

7. Thus the Middle Ages begin with two fairly distinct classes of the unfree; on the one hand, the slaves proper, whose position has been ameliorated in Roman law, but remains that of pure chattels by the law of the conquerors; on the other hand, a class of serfs in various degrees of freedom, which had already grown up in the later ages of the Empire and was reinforced by the corresponding class of Liti among the conquerors.

The history of the decline of serfdom in the later Middle Ages, both in France and England, is not very clear. The lawyers who had been unfavorable to freedom down to the thirteenth century changed their attitude during that period under the influence of the new ideas of the State as a whole, no longer broken up into half-independent feudal territories, but, as a single authority, having equal claim upon all its subjects alike.[51] That these more enlightened ideas accompanied the improvement of social organization was an extremely fortunate circumstance for the English serf. In England, as on the Continent, freedom might be acquired by escaping from the lord's jurisdiction, and the courts now favored liberty. Feudal barbarism admitted this rough and ready method of emancipation largely because it lacked the means of securing the person of the runaway. With the growth of the kingly power and the better settlement of society, this primitive check upon oppression would naturally disappear, and thus where the ethical conception of freedom was wanting, the growth of civilization meant the prolongation of the bondage and even, as in Russia and Germany, deterioration in its character. In England and France, upon the other hand, there was something of the nature of an ethical resistance to any tightening of the bonds, and thus the development of order had a beneficial effect on the slave rather than the reverse, for it tended to encourage the system of money payments as a substitute for labor service, and though in theory the serf remained the lord's man, yet in practice, in proportion as labor services were commuted for a money rent his position became scarcely distinguishable from that of a tenant farmer. From whatever causes, servile tenure was in fact rapidly becoming obsolete during the fourteenth century. One of the latest records we have of the existence of bondmen in England is in a document in which Elizabeth enfranchises some remaining serfs of the Crown in 1574,[52] but there were Scottish miners who remained serfs down to 1799 and were not particularly desirous of having their condition changed.

Yet elements of servility remain in the position of the laborer. The Statute of Laborers in 1348 was passed in the intention of preventing workmen from taking advantage of the rise in wages due to the depopulation of the country by the Black Death, and was the beginning of a series of labor laws which brought the laborer into a position which as described in Blackstone stood as follows: (1) The law first of all compels all persons with no visible effects to work; (2) defines their hours in summer and winter; (3) punishes those who desert their work; (4) empowers justices to fix the rate of wage for agricultural labor and punishes those who give or exact more than the wages so settled.[53] We know that these laws were largely a dead letter. Nevertheless they illustrate the attitude of the governing classes. What was in practice more important was the Statute of Apprentices (Fifth of Elizabeth), which restricted the right to carry on a trade to those who had served an apprenticeship, while the operation of the Poor Law, especially of the Act of Settlement, tended in practice to restrict the motions of the English laborer almost as much as regular serfdom would do.[54] Indeed had this statute been rigidly and universally carried out, it would have had the effect of fixing the laborer in his parish like a predial serf without the right upon the land which redeems the serf's position. To describe its practical operation in these terms might savor of exaggeration, yet the historian of the Poor Law declares that with this Act the "iron of slavery entered into the soul of the English laborer," and those who know the midland or south country laborer of the present day can see the scar still there. Again, Blackstone writes:

A master may by law correct his apprentice or servant for negligence or other misbehavior, so it be done with moderation; though if the master's wife beats him, it is good cause of departure. But if any servant, workman or laborer assaults his master or dame he shall suffer one year's imprisonment and other open corporal punishment not extending to life or limb.

Further, in Blackstone's time a servant through whose negligence a fire happens forfeits £100, and in default of payment might be committed to a workhouse with hard labor for eighteen months. It is not difficult to recognize in these distinctions between the rights of master and servant an echo of the law as to lord and serf.

Nor was the English law altogether free from caste distinctions in the earlier part of the modern period. The benefit of clergy, which had originally been an immunity claimed by ecclesiastics from the secular courts, had been gradually transformed into a mere class privilege, whereby educated persons could escape punishment for secondary offenses. Thus in the eighteenth century the question whether a man would be hanged for larceny or not depended on whether he could read, unless indeed he had forfeited the benefit of clergy by contracting a second marriage or by marrying a widow. In 1705 the necessity for reading was abolished, and benefit of clergy could thereafter be claimed by all persons alike for a first offense in the case of secondary crimes. But important distinctions were still made. The offender, unless he was a peer or a clerk in orders, was, until 1779, branded in the hand and liable to seven years' transportation. Clerks in orders, on the other hand, might plead their clergy for any number of offenses, and peers had received the same privileges as clerks by the statute of 1547. On the other hand, during the eighteenth century benefit of clergy was gradually withdrawn from an increasing number of offenses, but it was not until 1827 that it was finally abolished, and even then it was doubtful whether the privilege of peers fell with it. This question was not settled until 1841, when the statute of Edward VI was repealed, and peers accused of felony became liable to the same punishments as other persons.

When it is remembered, further, that the whole administration of petty justice and of the preliminary process in graver crimes was in the hands of the landed gentry, upon whose estates the laboring classes, rendered landless by economic changes, were fixed, as has been shown, by the Act of Settlement, when it is further borne in mind that the same justices had the power of fixing wages, and that the whole of the working classes in the country were always upon or over the verge of pauperism and dependent upon the support of the poor law, the control of which was substantially in the same hands, it will be recognized that the nominal freedom of the English laborer down to the beginning of the reform period was a blessing very much disguised, and that the reality compared unfavorably with the lighter forms of serfdom. The first stages in the progress of the factory system made matters even worse. The new demand for child labor introduced for a period what was in essence if not in name a form of child slavery, pauper children being regularly imported in the manufacturing districts as apprentices and set to work under conditions as to hours and also as to housing which would have been onerous even at less tender years. But these abuses, when fully realized by the public, were met within a period of time which, in comparison with the normal slowness of reform, may almost be called brief, by a series of legislative measures, overriding the so-called freedom of contracts, and protecting the children from their legal guardians. The factory system, in short, reproduced

the economic conditions under which, in other circumstances, a form of slavery would have arisen. And from this
result England and the other industrial nations with it have
been saved by a distinctively ethical movement.

Upon the Continent the direct manumission of serfs was
perhaps more frequent than in England. Enfranchisements
en bloc were common. We even hear of such things being
done by abbeys. St. Benedict of Aniane in the ninth century
emancipates serfs on the land which he receives.[55] Charters
were sometimes given upon payment to whole villages and
by kings to whole counties. In 1315 Louis X invited all the
serfs on the Crown lands to purchase their liberty, but the
price asked was too high. A general abolition of personal
serfdom was demanded by the Third Estate at Blois in 1576,
and again in Paris in 1614. This was not granted, but the
institution was quite unknown in many provinces in the
seventeenth century. It remained in Franche-Comté, Bour-
goyne, Alsace-Lorraine, Trois Evêchés, Champagne, Bour-
bonnais, La Marche, Nivernois, Berry: but the burden was
relatively light, and when the Duke of Lorraine proposed
a money commutation for their services in 1711, the serfs
who were to benefit by it themselves raised objections. The
question was raised by Voltaire, and by an edict of 1779
Louis XVI enfranchised the serfs of the royal domain and
encouraged general abolition. Serfdom was finally abolished
in France without compensation on the night of August 4,
1789, along with the other incidents of feudal tenure. At the
same time fell the whole system of privileges which had
made the nobles and the clergy castes set apart from the
mass of the people.

In the German Empire the progress, which we have seen
going forward until the thirteenth century, was arrested in
the fifteenth, and a reaction took place, leading to the peasant war at the time of the Reformation. Serfdom lingered
on, but in 1719-20 it was abolished on the Crown lands of
East Prussia by Frederick William I. Frederick the Great
attempted to forbid corporal punishment and aimed at a

general emancipation, but achieved little except in Prussian Poland. The liberation of the German serf was to come indirectly from the French Revolution. Napoleon carried out emancipation in the conquered territory, and as part of the general preparation for resistance to France, the Prussian statesmen issued an edict in 1807 by which the whole population of Prussia was made free by a stroke of the pen.[56] Serfdom admitting arbitrary exactions and corporal punishment remained, notwithstanding the efforts of Maria Theresa and her successors, in a great part of the Austrian Empire down to 1848. It was abolished in Russia in 1861. The emancipation of the Russian serf may be taken as the final termination of the enslavement by law, whether complete or partial, of white men. The later stages of the process in the more backward countries were thus clearly deliberate acts of government, based upon general conceptions either of human rights or of the conditions of social well-being. And on the whole the continental serf gained something through the delay. Emancipated in England more by economic causes than on ethical principles, he tended to become a landless laborer, more abject in some relations than a serf with defined rights. On the Continent in most countries he retained his land, subject to servile restrictions, and when the ethical movement struck off his chains, it left him a free peasant cultivator. In England his practical freedom was to be won at a later date and at the cost of a depletion of the rural districts, which is raising the agrarian problem in a form elsewhere unknown. So much depends on the nature of the causes determining a change like that from servitude to freedom, however great the inherent importance of the change itself.

8. The abolition of slavery and serfdom in the modern world may, from one point of view, be described as a process whereby the obligations of group-morality were extended so as to cover all Christians, or at any rate all white Christians. Unfortunately, this result is not the same thing as a strictly universalistic morality. As long as the Christian

communities lived in isolation, and did not come into touch with weaker races as their conquerors, the matter was not one of any very practical moment, but when, with the discovery of a new world and the circumnavigation of Africa, a fresh economic position arose, making slave labor industrially advantageous, while at the same time a vast black population was put at the disposal of the far stronger white man, slavery grew up again in a new and, in some respects, a more debased form. It is worth noting, as illustrating the ethical principle involved, that the old Roman slavery had never entirely disappeared. In the eleventh century we find Gregory VII exacting from Demetrius of Dalmatia a promise not to sell men. There was a slave trade with Mussulmans in Venice and in Sicily right through the medieval period. In the twelfth century slaves were sold at fairs in Champagne, and Saracen slaves were found in the south of France in possession of a bishop at that period.[57] Though the French law in the sixteenth century recognized that no slave could exist on French soil, the maxim, as formulated by Loisel, is applied to those who enter France only upon their being baptized. But these smoldering embers of slavery were now destined to burst out into flame. The Portuguese began importing negro slaves in 1442, and obtained a bull sanctioning the practice from Pope Nicholas V in 1454. The reason was characteristic. A great number of the captives had been converted to the Catholic faith, "and it is hoped that by the favor of the divine clemency, if this process is continued, the nations themselves may be converted to the faith, or at any rate the souls of many from among them may be made of profit to Christ." [58] In fact, the hope— probably the quite sincere hope—of saving souls, paralyzed, to say the least, the protest which would otherwise have been made against what was in essence a revival of one of the worst features of barbarism. It was quite a logical exception made by Pope Calixtus III in 1456, when he prohibited the enslavement of Christians in the East, and by Pius II in 1462, when he severely blamed Christians who enslaved negro neophytes. When Columbus shipped 500 enslaved Indian prisoners to Spain to sell as slaves, the law of the case was investigated by Isabella, and, theologians differing in their view, she finally ordered the Indians to be sent back to their homes.[59] Meanwhile, in the New World the Spaniards were making slaves freely of Indians and treating them with great cruelty. Las Casas, impressed with the horrors which he saw, was struck with the idea that negroes would endure that bondage without sinking under it, and with the most benevolent intentions gave the most unfortunate advice that residents in Hispaniola should be allowed to import negro slaves.[60] Regular black traffic accordingly began, notwithstanding successive efforts made by the Popes, when they grasped the situation, to suppress it.[61] All the great trade nations of Western Europe joined in the traffic, and must share the blame alike. Europe itself was not preserved whole from this scourge. In England, indeed, it was held in the case of the negro Somerset (1772) that English soil emancipated, but this doctrine, which had been good law in France in 1571, was suspended in 1716 and again in 1738. Slaves became common, and were even sold at Paris down to 1762. From the sixteenth to the eighteenth century the Popes themselves had Turkish galley-slaves, and Louis XIV, besides these, had Jewish slaves and Russian captives.[62]

This second slavery was put down by a distinctly ethical movement. It began with the Quakers in the seventeenth century. George Fox had already desired the Friends in America to treat their negroes well, and "that after certain years of servitude they should set them free." In 1727 the Society declared that slavery was not an allowed practice. In 1761 they excluded from membership all concerned in it, and in 1783 formed an association for liberating negroes and discouraging the traffic. The Pennsylvanian Quakers had condemned it from 1696 onwards. Many leading names in English thought are quoted in Dr. Ingram's History as opponents of the slave trade from the end of the seventeenth century to that of the eighteenth. Among them are Baxter,

Steele, Pope, Cowper, Day, Hutcheson, Wesley, Whitefield, Adam Smith, Johnson and Paley. An English Committee for the abolition of the slave trade was formed in 1787, and the motion for the abolition, which was defeated in the House of Lords in 1794, was carried under Fox's premiership in 1807.[63] The French Revolution had gone further. In 1791 the old principle that the French soil emancipates was reasserted by the Convention, and in 1794 slavery in the French colonies was abolished by decree. But the moment was ill-chosen, as Hayti was in revolt, and Napoleon restored slavery in 1802. At the Congress of Vienna, British influence was active in obtaining the consent of other nations for the suppression of the slave trade, and France acquiesced, in the treaties of 1814 and 1815. The British and Foreign Anti-Slavery Society was founded in 1823, and secured Abolition ten years later. Slavery was abolished by France in 1848, by Portugal in 1858, by the Dutch in 1863, and by Brazil in 1888. The founders of the United States had been opposed to slavery and attempted to exclude it by the Constitution, but were defeated by the opposition of South Carolina and Georgia. An Abolition Society was formed in 1774 and reconstructed by Franklin in 1787. The Northern States adopted measures for abolition between 1777 and 1804, and importation was prohibited by the United States in 1807. An Anti-Slavery Society was founded in 1833, and at the cost of civil war emancipation was proclaimed in 1863.[64] Unfortunately, the legacy of slavery remains in the Southern States, taking, on the one hand, the form of the most horrible personal cruelties which disgrace any nation claiming to be civilized, and on the other hand, the efforts to reintroduce slavery by a side wind through the corrupt use of the criminal law.

9. Slavery is no longer admittedly[65] practiced by any white nation. On the other hand, the problem of dealing with colored labor has not been yet satisfactorily solved. Here and there "forced labor" has been allowed, and forms of contract labor are common, which, to say the least, are

difficult to keep free from every servile taint. The questions raised by the various forms of contract allowed by the British and other civilized governments since the abolition of slavery belong, however, rather to the controversies of the moment than to the historical study which is the object of the present work, and I do not propose to discuss them here. It may, however, be allowable to say that the modern tendency to the concentration of wealth, or at least of the forces directing labor in a few hands, taken in conjunction with the vast reserves of cheap labor to which access has been given by the opening up of China and the African continent reproduce in very essential features the conditions out of which great slave systems have arisen in the past, and the temptation to utilize the cheap and relatively docile labor of a weaker and perhaps a subjugated race against the well-organized battalions of the white artisans, is one by which leaders of industry, being human, cannot fail to be attracted, and therefore raises possibilities which no statesman can ignore.

The result of this brief review is to show that the principle of the equality of all classes before the law can hardly be said to have been accepted by the Western world as a whole before the revolutionary period. The whole structure of medieval society has been based upon the principle of subordination and was molded in the spirit of caste. Confronted at all times with the doctrine of Christian Brotherhood, and, later on, with the principle of natural equality, this structure was also undermined by the growth of industry and the complex forces, ethical, political, and economic, which transformed the feudal kingdom into the organized state. Under these influences slavery proper disappeared as we have seen in the course of the twelfth century; and in the most advanced nations serfdom followed it in the period between the thirteenth century and the sixteenth. But for the completion of the work fully two more centuries were required. In the less advanced countries serfdom itself lingered on into the nineteenth century. In France, though caste privileges grew more and more out of harmony with the spirit of the time, they could only be destroyed by a revolution. In England, where they were rather a practical consequence of political superiority than the express subject of legal enactment, they yielded later but more peacefully to the influences of the Reform period. So modern is the change whereby law and public institutions have turned towards equality rather than subordination as their ideal. An ideal such equality must perhaps always be. Wealth and influence will always have their weight, not only in social life, but in the business of government and even in the administration of justice. Yet the true spirit of caste is gradually being reduced to a shadow of its former self. Expelled by slow degrees from the sphere of law and government, it has been left to amuse itself with a mock kingdom in the region of ceremonial and social intercourse, in which the ghosts of bygone realities keep up a mock state for the amusement of the philosopher.

As long as class, racial, and national antagonism play a part in life we cannot say that group-morality has been altogether overcome. Nevertheless, the evolution sketched in the present and preceding chapter is of no small significance for ethics. At the outset men are organized in small groups bound to mutual aid and forbearance, while they are indifferent or hostile to outsiders. There is no organic bond uniting humanity as a whole. Hence the captive enemy and, in principle, unless there are special reasons to the contrary, the peaceful stranger are "rightless." But by degrees a wider conception of obligation arises. Fellow-Greeks, co-religionists, fellow-white men, ultimately fellow-men, enter the circle to which obligations apply, and even the violence of conquest is limited by the rights attaching to the conquered as human beings. The "group" is thus widened till it includes all humanity, at which point group-morality disappears, merged in universalism. But the rights first recognized are those of the person. To take into account the rights of the organized community is a further step, following logically from the first, no doubt, but following slowly. Here too we recognize a slow advance in the civilized world, an advance which, if unimpeded, would finally overcome the "group-morality" of nations in favor of a true internationalism of morals and law.

Turning next to the internal composition of the community, we saw that the primitive group was relatively small and homogeneous. But as society grows divisions come, and a new form of group-morality arises—distinctions, of high caste and low caste, bond and free, and the like. In engendering, accentuating and maintaining these distinctions, military conquest, economic inequalities, religious differences, race and color antipathies, have all played their part, and up to the middle civilization social divisions probably tend to increase rather than diminish. Combated by the teaching of the higher ethical and religious systems, they have been mitigated and in large measure overcome in the modern world. Most tenaciously maintained where the "color line" is the outward and too visible symbol of deep-seated differences of race, culture, character, and traditions, they are countered even here by the fundamental doctrine of the modern state that equal protection and equal opportunity are the birthright of its subjects. Thus though the color line is the last ditch of group-morality, here too in the modern period, taken as a whole, Universalism has made great inroads. With the improvement of communication and the growth of commerce, Humanity is rapidly becoming, physically speaking, a single society—single in the sense that what affects one part tends to affect the whole. This unification intensifies the difficulties of ethics because it brings into closer juxtaposition races and classes who are not prepared by their previous history to live harmoniously together. Hence it is not surprising that law and morals do not show a regular, parallel advance. Nevertheless the upshot of the evidence here reviewed is that, ethically as well as physically, humanity is becoming one—one, not by the suppression of differences of the mechanical arrangement of lifeless parts, but by a widened consciousness of obligation, a more sensitive response to the claims of justice, a greater forbearance towards differences of type, a more enlightened conception of human purposes.

NOTES

[1] Post, *Afrik. Jurisp.*, vol. i, p. 115, *seq.*, gives a number of African peoples in which the king has absolute powers of life and death over his people, and a number in which all subjects are regarded as his slaves. Among the Kaffirs the king could take any man's cattle to replace his own.

[2] According to Waitz, vol. ii, p. 398, slavery was for the most part unknown among Kaffirs, and the case of a sale of children recorded by Moffat is regarded as exceptional. A less favorable view of Kaffir warfare is taken by Letourneau (*Esclavage*, p. 53), who says that they took girl prisoners as concubines and youths as slaves, though their manners were too savage for regular slavery. Letourneau also draws attention (pp. 54, 55) to a servile class, called balala, among the Bechuanas, who had no possessions, had to perform manual labor in return for food, might be slain for disobedience, and supplied victims for human sacrifice upon occasion. We have here something more nearly approaching a caste distinction than ordinary slavery.

The Hottentots, according to Letourneau (*ibid.*, pp. 49-51), gave no quarter and held no slaves, but, according to authorities cited by Kohler (*Z. f. V. R.*, 1902, p. 340), slavery, though it has now disappeared, existed formerly, and the slaves were at the masters' mercy and often ill-treated.

[3] For example, in the little island of Rotuma slavery proper did not exist and casual strangers were usually married and adopted into a clan. Some Fijians and Melanesians, however, have been treated as inferiors, not being adopted (J. S. Gardiner in *J. A. I.*, xxvii, p. 486). In parts of New Guinea there is no slavery (Letourneau, p. 39): it is the exception among the Papuas (*ibid.*, p. 35, and Kohler, *Z. f. V. R.*, 1900, p. 364).

[4] Letourneau, *op. cit.*, p. 41. Broadly, Letourneau concludes Melanesian slavery originated for the sake of cannibalism.

[5] Thus in the Marquesas Islands there were no slaves, but a despised lower class who furnishea victims for human sacrifice (Letourneau, p. 183).

[3] *Ibid.*, p. 188.

[7] Waitz, vol. ii, p. 125. In the Carolinas not only was intermarriage forbidden, but the lower caste had to avoid contact with the higher on pain of death. Fishery and seafaring were forbidden occupations to the lower caste.

[8] See Waitz, *Anthropologie*, vol. i, p. 154, *seq.;* Ratzel, *History of Mankind*, i, p. 446.

[9] Slavery is said to be universal among the Aos (Godden, *J. A. I.*, xxvi, p. 184), but the Luhupas and one or two other tribes are said to have no slaves and to be opposed to the institution. All the Nagas are head hunters (Godden, *J. A. I.*, xxvii, p. 12).

[10] E. Q. Jukis, *Garos, Gonds, and Khonds,* who use slaves for sacrifices. The Lakka Kols have serfs instead of slaves (Letourneau, pp. 305-306).

[11] Ratzel, vol. iii, p. 346. According to Letourneau (p. 223), a form of serf cultivation is more strongly developed than personal slavery.

[12] *E.g.,* according to Waitz, vol. iii, p. 158, the tribes of North Carolina the Navajos, Iroquois and Hurons.

[13] Thus among the Oregons prisoners were enslaved "from time immemorial" and sometimes sacrificed at the death of a master (Alvord, in *School-craft,* v, p. 654). Slavery is said to have extended over the whole northwest coast (Waitz, iii, p. 329). At Nootka Sound prisoners when spared were enslaved. The Chinooks made slave razzias and held the slave as a chattel and object of trade (*ibid.,* pp. 334, 338). The Apaches killed the male captives, but sometimes held the women as slaves (Reclus, p. 128).

[14] Schmidt, *Z. f. V. R.,* 1898, p. 294. According to Letourneau (p. 123) the Nomads of the Pampas rarely give quarter to males, but sometimes take women as slave concubines and bring up children to be adopted into the conquering tribe.

[15] See Post, *Afrik. Jurisprudenz,* i, pp. 88, 92, 96; Waitz, ii, 213-214.

[16] Letourneau, p. 103. Yet at Sokoto captive slaves, besides being frequently sold, are treated as beasts of burden and chained for trivial offenses (Post, *A. J.,* i, p. 96; Letourneau, *L'Esclavage,* p. 102).

[17] For instance see Post, *Afrik. Jurisp.,* pp. 98, 101, 106. In case of failure to make due payments the serf is often reduced to the position of a slave, *e.g.* among the Takue, Marea, and Bogos. Among the Beni-amer the penalty of failure is death (Post, *A. J.,* i, p. 101).

[18] Instances are found at Khartoum, among the Usagara, the Futatoro, and among the Kimbunda (Post, *A. J.,* pp. 103, 105, 112).

[19] Letourneau, p. 88.

[20] *Ibid.,* p. 72, *seq.*

[21] Waitz, vol. i, pp. 143, 153.

[22] *Ibid.,* pp. 153-155.

[23] According to Letourneau (p. 200), the master may punish, but not put the slaves to death. According to Waitz, *op. cit.,* p. 188, punishment must be inflicted by a magistrate. The slave becomes a concubine by prolonged cohabitation, and sometimes a legitimate wife (Letourneau, *loc. cit.*). Among the more savage Battaks slaves are used for human sacrifices (Letourneau, p. 203).

[24] Apart from some of the instances already given, in ancient Mexico, where captive slaves were taken principally for food, domestic slaves were protected. They might not be sold without their consent, nor chastised without previous warning. If ill-treated they might take refuge with the king, and to kill them was a capital offense. They could hold property and marry, and their children were free (Letourneau, pp. 157, 158; cf. also Payne, vol. ii, p. 485, note 3).

[25] But according to Hidayah, the conversion to Islam on the battlefield did not necessarily save a man from slavery (Hughes, *Dictionary of Islam,* p. 597).

[26] *Ibid.,* p. 597.

[27] If a slave-girl has a child by her master she becomes free at his death, while if the child be acknowledged by the master, she becomes free thereupon (*ibid.,* pp. 597, 598).

28 Hughes, *Dictionary of Islam*, p. 599.

29 Though this saying is attributed to Mohammed, it is said by Tabir that "we used to sell the mothers of children in the time of the Prophets and of Abu Bekr, but Umar forbade it in his time" (Hughes, p. 599).

30 Herod., vi, p. 137; Busolt, *Handbuch*, p. 11.

31 *Iliad*, vi, pp. 414-495.

32 *Odyssey*, xxii., trsl. Butcher and Lang, p. 374.

33 *Thucyd.*, i, p. 141.

34 Busolt, p. 12.

35 This held in other states as well. See Isocrates, *Panath.*, 181, in Busolt, p. 12. In the *Laws*, ix, p. 865, the slayer of his own slave is to undergo a legal purification corresponding to that imposed on the unintentional homicide of a free man, and incur no further penalty. For a case in which the killing of a slave might be treated as murder, cf. *ibid.*, p. 872.

36 Busolt, pp. 12-14, 15, 68, 119.

37 Girard, *Manuel*, pp. 89, 91.

38 See Girard, p. 92.

39 *Ibid.*, p. 88, Note 1.

40 *Assez timidement*, Girard, p. 94.

41 Girard, p. 94.

42 *Ibid.*, p. 94.

43 *Ibid.*, p. 95.

44 Ingram, *History of Slavery*, pp. 60-64, etc.

45 *Ibid.*, pp. 78, 79, etc.

46 The Colonus could also contract a valid marriage, but he had to marry within the domain unless he purchased a dispensation. The right of punishment was conceded to the master for certain specified faults (Letourneau, *L'Esclavage*, pp. 422, 423).

47 Ingram, *History of Slavery*, p. 80; cf. Viollet, *Histoire du Detroit Civil Français*, p. 312. Valentinian prohibited their sale apart from the land.

48 Schröder, *Lehrbuch*, p. 46.

49 *Ibid.*, p. 346. The price was, however, becoming a fixed tariff, and so gradually approximating to a true wergild (*ibid.*, p. 218).

50 *Ibid.*, pp. 50, 51, 221-223. In the latter period their position still varied very greatly as between different peoples.

51 Vinogradoff, *Villeinage in England*, p. 131.

52 This is sometimes spoken of as the latest record, but Prof. Vinogradoff informs me that this is not absolutely correct.

53 I., p. 414.

54 In the effort to deal with vagabondage the law has at different times come perilously near to reintroducing slavery. A statute of Edward VI ordained that all idle vagabonds should be made slaves, fed on bread and water and refuse meat, wear iron rings, and be compelled by beating, chains, etc., to do the work assigned to them. This was repealed in two years. It is now laid down that slaves acquire freedom by landing in England, but this does not affect the right a master may have acquired to a man's perpetual service, and "the infamous and unchristian practice of withholding baptism from negro servants, lest they should thereby gain their liberty, was totally without foundation." The Law of England will not dissolve a civil obligation between master and servant on account of the

alteration of faith in either of the parties, "but the slave is entitled to the same liberty in England before as after baptism; and, whatever service the heathen negro owed to his English master, the same is bound to render when a Christian" (Blackstone, i, pp. 412, 413).

[55] Ingram, *op. cit.*, p. 93.

[56] *Ibid.*, pp. 119-129.

[57] So at Narbonne and in Provence in the thirteenth century, and in Roussillon down to its annexation by France. A Saracen was publicly sold in 1296 (Viollet, pp. 329, 330).

[58] Viollet, p. 330.

[59] Ingram, pp. 142, 143.

[60] "Which advice," says Las Casas himself, "after he had apprehended the nature of the thing, he would not have given for all he had in the world" (Ingram, p. 144).

[61] *E.g.* The Bull of Urban VIII, 1537, and of Benedict XIV, 1741 (Viollet, p. 331).

[62] Viollet, p. 332. The position of slaves in France and her colonies was minutely regulated by the Code Noir of Louis XIV, 1685.

[63] The trade had been abolished by Denmark in 1792.

[64] Ingram, pp. 154-182.

[65] Not even by the Congo State.

BIOGRAPHIES

BIOGRAPHIES

Johann Jakob Bachofen, 1815-1887, was professor of Roman Law at Basel. He was one of the earliest European writers on anthropological subjects. *Das Mutterrecht,* 1861, is his best work, and it is to be regretted that there exists no English translation. Other publications, also untranslated, are *Versuch über die Gräbersymbolik der Alten,* 1859, and *Antiquarische Briefe,* 1881-1886.

Ruth Benedict was born in 1887. She is the author of many monographs on Folklore and has done field work among several Indian tribes, in particular the Pueblos and the Pimas. She has been the editor of the *Journal of American Folklore* and at the present time is associated with the Anthropology Department of Columbia University.

Franz Boas, founder of the American school of anthropology, was born in Westphalia, 1858. He studied at Heidelberg, Bonn, and Kiel. He was one of the first anthropologists to realize the necessity for direct study of primitive people. His investigations have carried him into all parts of North America and Mexico and his monographs on phases of Indian life are of inestimable value. Besides these, and contributions to various scientific journals, his published works are, *The Growth of Children, Changes in Form of Body of Descendants of Immigrants, The Mind of Primitive Man, Primitive Art,* and *Anthropology and Modern Life.*

Pierre Marcelin Boule, French scientist, was born in 1861 and was educated at Toulouse. His interests are geology and palæontology. He has been president of the French Geological Society and of the French Archæological Institute, and director of the Institute of Human Palæontology. His best known works are *Les grottes de Grimaldi* and *Les hommes fossiles.*

Robert Briffault, philosopher and scientist, was born in London in 1876 and graduated in medicine from the University of London. He has studied in New Zealand and at universities in Italy and Germany, and has done field work in Melanesia. He is the author of *The Making of Humanity, Psyche's Lamp,* and his remarkable contribution to anthropology, *The Mothers.* His most recent book deals with modern morality, and will appear in the spring of 1931.

Huntington Cairns was born in Baltimore in 1904. He is a member of the Baltimore bar and practices law, in addition to contributing articles on jurisprudence to various journals. He is at work at present on a life of Henry Adams.

Edward Carpenter, poet and socialist, was born in Brighton, 1844. After relinquishing orders and fellowship at Cambridge he lectured on science and music until in 1883 he settled on a small farm where he engaged in literary work and gardening. In 1884 he came to the United States to meet Walt Whitman, later recording his experiences in *Days with Walt Whitman.* His most popular books are: *Towards Democracy, Civilisation, Its Cause and Cure, Love's Coming of Age, The Intermediate Sex,* and *Pagan and Christian Creeds.* He died June 28, 1929.

Joseph Déchelette, born in Roanne, France, 1862, was by profession a capitalist. His interest in archæology gradually absorbed him, and from an amateur, he became the leading authority in his field. His *Manuel d'archéologie, préhistorique, celtique et gallo-romaine,* 1908-1914, is the standard work of French archæology. He was killed in the early days of the war, October 4, 1914.

Sir James G. Frazer was born in Glasgow, 1854. His education was received at Cambridge. He is the recipient of honorary degrees from the Universities of Cambridge, Durham, Manchester, Paris, and Strasbourg. His literary and anthropological works are numerous and well-known. Most significant perhaps are *The Golden Bough, Totemism and Exogamy, Folk-Lore in the Old Testament,* and *The Worship of Nature.*

Sigmund Freud was born in Moravia, 1856. He was educated in Vienna and Paris. Since 1902 he has been professor of neurology at Vienna University. As founder of the school of psycho-analysis, he is universally known. He is director of the *International Journal of Psycho-Analysis.* His most widely-read works are *The History of Psycho-Analysis,*

1910; *Totem and Taboo*, 1903; *General Introduction to Psycho-Analysis*, 1920; *The Problem of Lay-Analyses*, 1927; *Psychopathology of Everyday Life*, 1914; *The Interpretation of Dreams*. His latest book is *Civilization and its Discontents*, 1930.

Alexander Goldenweiser is a native of Russia, where he was born in 1880. His education was received at the Kiev Gymnasium, Harvard University, and at Columbia University. From 1910 to 1919 he lectured at Columbia; from 1919 to 1926 he was associated with the New School for Social Research, and is now Professor of Thought and Culture at the University of Oregon. He is the author of *Totemism, an Analytical Study, Early Civilization,* and has contributed widely to scientific and popular journals on social theory, psycho-analysis, education and modern social problems.

Robert Fritz Graebner, Ph.D., was born in 1877 in Berlin. He is Director of the Rautenstrauch-Joest Museum at Cologne, and Privat-Dozent in Ethnology at the University of Bonn. He is the author of *Neu-Mecklenburg; Die Küste von Urnudda bis Kap St. Georg,* 1907; and has been a contributor to *Globus; Zeitschrift für Ethnologie; Anthropos; Petermann's Mittheilungen.*

Edwin Sidney Hartland was born in England in 1848. He was editor of *Folklore* and author of several books on folk tales. He is best known for the following: *The Science of Fairy Tales,* 1890; *English Fairy and Other Folk-Tales,* 1890; *The Legend of Perseus,* 1894-1896; and *Primitive Paternity.*

Leonard Trelawney Hobhouse, professor of sociology at University of London since 1907, was born in 1864. He was on the editorial staff of the *Manchester Guardian,* 1897-1902 and of the *Tribune,* 1906-1907. His published works are: *The Labour Movement,* 1893; *The Theory of Knowledge,* 1896; *Mind in Evolution,* 1901; *Democracy and Reaction,* 1904; *Morals in Evolution,* 1906; *Development and Purpose,* 1913.

Alfred L. Kroeber was born in Hoboken, N. J., 1876. His education was received at Columbia University. Since 1900 he has engaged in frequent anthropological expeditions to South America, Mexico, and California, the results of which

THE MAKING OF MAN

are recorded in his studies: *The Youths Language, Zuñi Kin and Clan, The Arapaho,* and *Handbook of the Indians of California.* His *Anthropology* is one of the finest expositions of this comparatively recent science. At present, he is Professor of Anthropology at the University of California.

Lucien Lévy-Bruhl, philosopher and ethnologist, was born in Paris in 1857. Since 1899 he has been professor of philosophy at the Sorbonne. He is best known to American audiences for his work on primitive mentality. His chief works are *Les Fonctions mentales dans les sociétés inférieures,* 1910; *La mentalité primitive,* 1922; and *L'Ame primitive,* 1927.

Robert Heinrich Lowie was born in Vienna, 1883. At the age of eight, he was brought to America, where he studied later at the College of the City of New York and at Columbia University. He was Associate Curator of Anthropology at the American Museum of Natural History, but since 1921 has been associated with the University of California. He has done extensive field work among the American Indians. His most important publications are: *Culture and Ethnology,* 1917; *Myths and Traditions of the Crow Indians,* 1918; *Primitive Society,* 1920; *Primitive Religion,* 1924; *The Origin of the State,* and *Are We Civilized?*

Bronislaw Malinowski, professor of anthropology in the University of London, is the son of Polish parents. He was educated at the Polish University of Cracow. The results of his field work in New Guinea and Melanesia are recorded in his contributions to numerous scientific publications and notably in his works: *The Family Among the Australian Aborigines,* 1913; *Argonauts of the Western Pacific,* 1922; *Crime and Custom in Savage Society,* 1926; *The Father in Primitive Psychology,* 1927; *Sex and Repression in Savage Society,* 1927, and *The Sexual Life of Savages,* 1929.

Robert Ranulph Marett was born in the island of Jersey in 1866. Since 1891 he has been lecturer in philosophy at Oxford. Besides various papers in philosophic and scientific periodicals, he is the author of several books. His best known works are: *The Threshold of Religion,* 1909; *Anthropology,* 1912; and *Psychology and Folklore,* 1930.

James Howard McGregor was born in Bellaire, Ohio, in 1872. A graduate of Columbia, he has been connected with the zoölogical staff at Columbia since 1897. He has contributed numerous papers on zoölogical topics to the scientific magazines. Reptilian and primate paleontology have been his specialties. He has also done a great deal of study on the fossil races of man.

Margaret Mead was born in Philadelphia in 1901. She studied anthropology at Columbia University and has done field work in Samoa and in the Admiralty Islands. Her *Coming of Age in Samoa* is a study of the adolescent girl in the primitive community. Miss Mead is at present on the staff of the American Museum of Natural History. Her latest book is *Growing Up in New Guinea.*

Lewis Henry Morgan, "father of American anthropology," was born in Aurora, New York, 1818. He was a lawyer by profession and his interest in anthropology was at first only a hobby. Later, in order to further his researches among American Indians, he lived among them, recording his discoveries in pamphlets issued by the Smithsonian Institution. His books, *Systems of Consanguinity and Affinity of the Human Family,* 1869, and *Ancient Society,* 1877, were of revolutionary importance to nineteenth century thought. Morgan died in 1881.

William James Perry has been reader in Cultural Anthropology at the University of London, and lecturer in the History of Religions at Oxford and at the University of Manchester. His chief works are: *The Children of the Sun,* 1923; *Megalithic Culture of Indonesia,* 1918; *The Origin of Magic and Religion,* 1923; and *The Growth of Civilization,* 1924.

Paul Radin, born in Poland in 1883, was brought to America in infancy. He was educated at the College of the City of New York, at Columbia University and at the universities of Berlin and Munich. His interest is absorbed by the American Indian. Besides various articles in scientific magazines, he is the author of numerous studies of the American Indian. Chief among these are: *Literary Aspects of North*

American Mythology, 1915; *Primitive Man as Philosopher,* 1921; and *The Story of the American Indian,* 1927.

William Halse Rivers, one of England's most distinguished anthropologists, was born in 1864. He was educated at Tonbridge and at St. Bartholomew's Hospital. At one time he was lecturer at the Royal College of Physicians. His best known work is his *History of Melanesian Society.* His other publications are: *Kinship and Social Organization, The Todas, Influence of Alcohol and other Drugs on Fatigue,* and *Instinct and the Unconscious.* During his later years he was strongly influenced by the theories of Freud. He died in 1922.

Geza Róheim is the author of a number of books and papers on anthropology, ethnology, and psycho-analysis—some of these have originally appeared in Hungarian, although most of them originally appeared in German. He is the first psycho-analyst to do field work in anthropology. He is the author of *Social Anthropology,* 1926; and *Animism, Magic, and the Divine King,* 1930. His papers have appeared in numerous psycho-analytical and anthropological journals.

Edward Sapir was born in Pomerania, 1884, but was brought to America when five years old. His education was received at Columbia University. He has taught at the University of California, the University of Pennsylvania, and is now professor of anthropology and general linguistics at the University of Chicago. Besides his studies of American Indians, and his remarkable monographic studies in linguistics, American and comparative, he is the author of *Language, an Introduction to the Study of Speech,* 1921.

G. Elliot Smith is a native of New South Wales, where he was born in 1871. He was educated at the University of Sydney and at Cambridge. For several years he was professor of anatomy at the University of Manchester. He was the President of the Anatomical Society of Great Britain and Ireland, and in 1912 was elected President of the Anthropological Section of the British Association. He has lectured on scientific subjects in the universities of England and Scotland, and was one time Herter Lecturer at New York University. In 1924 he published the *Evolution of Man.*

His chief contribution to the study of anthropology is concerned with the history of Egypt and early history of civilization. He is the chief exponent of modern "diffusionism."

William Johnson Sollas was born in Birmingham, England, in 1849. His education was acquired at the Royal School of Mines, London, and at St. John's College, Cambridge. He has written extensively on geological subjects. His best known works are: *The Age of the Earth,* 1905, and *Ancient Hunters,* 1911. He is at present associated with Oxford University.

Sir Walter Baldwin Spencer was born in Lancashire in 1860. After finishing his education at Oxford, he went to Australia where he became professor of biology at the University of Melbourne. He is now Emeritus Professor. His greatest contributions to knowledge are his scientific studies of primitive people, notably *The Native Tribes of Central Australia* and the *Northern Tribes of Central Australia.* Both these works were written in collaboration with F. J. Gillen.

William Graham Sumner was born in Paterson, New Jersey, 1840. After graduation from Yale, he studied in Geneva and at the University at Göttingen. From 1872 to 1909 he was professor of political and social science at Yale. His well-known *Folkways* is a classic. His death occurred in 1910.

Richard Thurnwald was born in Vienna in 1869. He was professor of ethnology and sociology at the University of Berlin. He traveled in the South Seas and New Guinea. During the war he was in Berkeley, California. From 1919 to 1923 he was instructor in ethnology and psychology of races at Halle. He has written extensively about the peoples of the South Seas, and is also the author of *Psychology of Primitive Peoples* and *Psychology of Totemism,* in addition to many ethnological monographs.

Sir Edward Burnett Tylor was born in London, 1832. He traveled in the United States and Mexico, and wrote about Mexico in his first work, *Anahuac; or Mexico and the Mexicans, Ancient and Modern.* In 1865 his reputation as a scientist was made on the publication of *Researches into the Early History of Mankind.* A few years later his *Primitive Culture* appeared. It was for years the standard treatise on anthropology. Tylor was lecturer in anthropology at Oxford and at Aberdeen University. In 1896, he became the first professor of anthropology at Oxford. He died in 1917.

Wilson Dallam Wallis was born in Maryland in 1886. After graduation from Dickinson College, he studied as a Rhodes Scholar at Oxford. He has been instructor in anthropology at the University of Pennsylvania and at the University of California, and is now Professor of Anthropology at the University of Minnesota. He is author of *An Introduction to Anthropology.*

Edward Alexander Westermarck was born in Helsingfors, 1862. He was graduated from the University of Helsingfors, where his dissertation was his well-known *Origin of Human Marriage,* 1889. *The History of Human Marriage* appeared in 1891, and the *Origin and Development of the Moral Ideas* in 1906. He is the author of numerous anthropological studies, dealing particularly with Morocco, where he has engaged in field work. Since 1907 he has been professor of sociology at the University of London.

Clark Wissler was born in Indiana, 1870. He studied at the University of Indiana and at Columbia University. He is Curator of Anthropology in the American Museum of Natural History and consulting anthropologist of the Bishop Museum in Honolulu. Since 1924, he has been professor of anthropology at Yale. His published works are: *North American Indians of the Plains,* 1912; *The American Indian,* 1917; *Man and Culture,* 1922, and other anthropological monographs.

BIBLIOGRAPHY

BIBLIOGRAPHY

ALLEN, Grant, *The Evolution of the Idea of God*, 1897.
ALLIER, Raoul, *The Mind of the Savage*.
ARMITAGE, F. P., *Diet and Race*, 1922.
ASTLEY, H. J. D., *Biblical Anthropology*, 1929.
AULT, Harman, *Life in Ancient Britain*, 1920.
AVEBURY, John Lubbock, Lord, *The Origin of Civilization and the Primitive Condition of Man; Mental and Social Condition of Savages*, 1870.

BACHOFEN, J. J., *Das Mutterrecht*.
BALFOUR, Henry, *The Evolution of Decorative Art*, 1893.
BASTIAN, Adolph, *Der Mensch in der Geschichte*, 1860.
BAUDIN, P., *Fetishism*, 1850.
BOAS, Franz, *Anthropology and Modern Life*, 1928; *Primitive Art*, 1927; *Handbook of American Indian Languages*, 1910.
BOULE, Marcelin, *Fossil Men, Elements of Human Palæontology*, 1923; *Les Grottes de Grimaldi*.
BOYLE, Mary E., *Man Before History*, 1924.
BRIFFAULT, Robert, *The Mothers*, 1927; *The Making of Humanity*, 1919; *Psyche's Lamp*, 1921.
BURKITT, M. C., *Our Early Ancestors*, 1926; *Prehistory*, 1921.
BUXTON, L. H. Dudley, *Primitive Labour*, 1924.

CALVERTON, V. F., *The Bankruptcy of Marriage*, 1927.
CARRIER, Lyman, *The Beginnings of Art Culture in America*, 1923.
CHAPIN, F. Stuart, *Social Evolution*, 1919.
CLELAND, Herdman Fitzgerald, *Our Prehistoric Ancestors*, 1928.
CODRINGTON, Robert H., *The Melanesians*, 1891.
CRAWLEY, Alfred E., *The Idea of the Soul*, 1909; *The Mystic Rose*, 1902.
CUNOW, H., *Die Verwandtschafts-Organizationen der Australneger*, Stuttgart, 1894.

DÉCHELETTE, Joseph, *Manuel d'archéologie préhistorique*, 4 vols., 1907.

876 THE MAKING OF MAN

DE GUBERNATIS, *Zoölogical Mythology*, 1872.

DEMORGAN, Jacques, *Prehistoric Man, A General Outline of Prehistory*, 1925.

DENISON, J. H., *Emotion as the Basis of Civilization*, 1928.

DIXON, Roland B., *The Racial History of Mankind*, 1922; *The Building of Cultures*, 1928.

DUCKWORTH, W. H., *Prehistoric Man*, 1912; *Morphology and Anthropology*, 2 vols., 1915.

DURKHEIM, Emile, *The Elementary Forms of the Religious Life.*

ELLIOT, G. F. Scott, *Prehistoric Man and History*, 1925.

ENGELS, F., *The Evolution of the Family.*

FEATHERMAN, A., *Social History of the Races of Mankind*, 7 vols., 1881-91.

FEBVRE, Lucien, *A Geographical Introduction to History*, 1925.

FERRI, Enrico, *Criminal Sociology*, 1895.

FINOT, J., *Race Prejudice*, 1906.

FLEURE, Herbert J., *The Peoples of Europe*, 1922.

FRAZER, James G., *Folklore in the Old Testament*, 1919; *Psyche's Task, The Golden Bough*, 1900; *Myth of the Origin of Fire*, 1930.

FREUD, Sigmund, *Totem and Taboo, The Future of an Illusion.*

FRICHE, V., *Art and Social Life*, Moscow, 1929.

FROBENIUS, Leo, *Der Ursprung der Afrikanischen Kulturen, Das Zeitalter des Sonnengottes, Naturwissenschaftliche Kulturlehre.*

GINSBURG, M., *The Psychology of Society*, 1922.

GOMME, George Laurence, *Mythology as a Historical Science*, 1908.

GRAEBNER, F., *Methods of Ethnology.*

GROSSE, Ernst, *The Beginnings of Art*, 1897.

HADDON, Alfred C., *Evolution in Art*, 1897; *The Races of Man*, 1925; *The Wanderings of People*, 1912.

HALL, S. S., *Adolescence; its Psychology and its Relation to Physiology, Anthropology, Sociology, Sex, Crime, Religion, and Education*, 2 vols, 1904.

HARTLAND, E. Sidney, *The Evolution of Kingship, An African Study*, 1922; *Primitive Society*, 1921; *Mythology and Folktales*.

HARTLEY, C. Gascoigne, *The Age of Mother Power*, 1914.

HEARD, Gerald, *The Ascent of Humanity*, 1929.

HENDERSON, Keith, *Prehistoric Man*, 1927.

HERSKOVITZ, M., *The American Negro*, 1928.

HOBHOUSE, Leonard T., WHEELER, and GINSBURG, *The Material Culture and Social Institutions of Primitive Peoples*, 1914.

HOBHOUSE, L. T., *Morals in Evolution*, 2 vols., 1906.

HRDLICKA, Alex F., *Skeletal Remains of Man*, 1912.

HUNTINGTON, Ellsworth, *Civilization and Climate*, 1915; *The Pulse of Asia*, 1907.

JUDD, Charles H., *Psychology of Social Institutions*, 1926.

KAUTSKY, Karl, *Are the Jews a Race?* 1926.

KEANE, August H., *Ethnology*, 1909.

KEITH, Arthur, *Man: A History of the Human Body*, 1913; *Ancient Types of Man*, 1911; *Antiquity of Man*, 1925.

KLAATSCH, Hermann, *Evolution and Progress of Mankind*, 1923.

KROEBER, A. L., *Anthropology*, 1923.

KROPOTKIN, P. (Prince), *Ethics, Origin and Development*, 1924; *Mutual Aid*, 1902.

LANG, Andrew, *Magic and Religion*, 1901; *The Making of Religion*, 1898; *Social Origins*, 1903.

LECKY, W. E. H., *History of European Morals*, 1911.

LETOURNEAU, Ch., *L'évolution religieuse dans les diverses races humaines*, 1892; *The Evolution of Marriage and of the Family*, 1895.

LEUBA, James H., *The Psychological Origin and the Nature of Religion*, 1909.

LÉVY-BRUHL, Lucien, *The Soul of the Primitive*, 1928; *How Natives Think*.

LOWIE, Robert H., *The Origin of the State*, 1927; *Culture and Ethnology*, 1917; *Primitive Religion*, 1924.

LUQUET, G. H., *The Art and Religion of Fossil Man*, 1930.

MACCURDY, George Grant, *Human Origins*, 1924.

MALINOWSKI, Bronislaw, *The Father in Primitive Psychology*, 1927; *Myth in Primitive Psychology*, 1926; *Crime and Cus-*

tom in Savage Society, 1926; The Sexual Life of Savages, 1929.

MARETT, R. R., The Threshold of Religion, 1909; Psychology and Folklore, 1919.

McDOUGALL, W., The Group Mind; a Sketch of the Principles of Collective Psychology, 1920.

MILLER, N., The Child in Primitive Society, 1928.

MYRES, John L., Position of Woman in Primitive Society, 1926.

NASSAU, Robert H., Fetishism in West Africa, 1907.

OGBURN, W. F., Social Change, with Respect to Culture and Original Nature, 1923.

PARKYN, Ernest A., Paleolithic Art, 1915.

PARSONS, Elsie, Fear and Conventionality, 1914; The Old-Fashioned Woman, 1913; Religious Chastity, 1913; Social Rule, 1916.

PERRIER, Edmond, The Earth Before History, 1925.

PERRY, W. J., The Growth of Civilization, 1923; The Children of the Sun, 1923.

PITTARD, Eugene, Race and History, 1926.

PLECHANOV, George, Materialism and Art.

QUENNELL, M., and C. H. B., Everyday Life in the New Stone, Bronze, Early Iron Age, 1923.

RADIN, Paul; Crashing Thunder: the Autobiography of a Winnebago Indian, 1926.

RATZEL, F., History of Mankind, 1896.

READE, W. Winwood, Savage Africa, 1863.

RIPLEY, W. Z., The Races of Europe, 1899.

RIVERS, Wm. H. R., The Todas, 1906; Medicine, Magic and Religion, 1924; Kinship and Social Organization, 1914; Psychology and Ethnology, 1926.

ROHEIM, Geza, Animism, Magic and the Divine King.

SAPIR, Edward, Language.

SCHMIDT, Max, The Primitive Races of Mankind, 1926.

SCHMIDT, Pater W., L'Origine de l'idée de Dieu.

SCHMUCKER, Samuel C., Man's Life On Earth, 1925.

SEMPLE, Ellen Churchill, *The Influence of Geographical Environment*, 1911.

SMITH, G. Elliot, *The Evolution of Man*, 1924; *Human History*, 1929.

SOLLAS, W. J., *Ancient Hunters, and their Modern Representatives*, 1924.

SONNTAG, Charles F., *The Morphology and Evolution of the Apes and Man*, 1924.

SPENCER, Herbert, *The Principles of Sociology*, 3 vols, 1879-96.

SPENCER and GILLEN, *Northern Tribes of Central Australia*, 1904.

STARCKE, C. N., *The Primitive Famility in Its Origin and Development*, 1889.

STONE, *Story of Phallacism*, 1927.

STORCK, John, *Man and Civilization*, 1926.

SUMNER, W. G., *Folkways*.

TEGGART, Frederick J., *The Processes of History*, 1918.

TOZZER, Alfred M., *Social Origins and Social Continuities*, 1925; *A Comparative Study of the Mayas and the Lacandones*, 1907.

TYLOR, E. B., *Anthropology*, 1895; *Primitive Culture*, 2 vols., 1903; *Researches into the Early History of Mankind*, 1878.

WAKE, Staniland, *The Evolution of Morality*, 1888.

WALLIS, W. D., *An Introduction to Anthropology; Culture and Progress*.

WEBSTER, Hutton, *Primitive Secret Societies*, 1908.

WESTERMARCK, Edward, *Origin and Development of the Moral Ideas*, 2 vols., 1908; *History of Human Marriage*.

WHEELER, W. M., *Social Life Among the Insects*, 1923.

WIDERSHEIM, Dr. R., *Structure of Man*, 1895.

WILDER, Harris H., *Man's Prehistoric Past*, 1923; *Pedigree of the Human Race*, 1926.

WISSLER, Clark, *Man and Culture; The American Indian; Introduction to Social Anthropology*.

WUNDT, Wm., *Elements of Folk Psychology*, 1916.